COLLECTOR'S EDITION

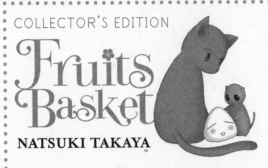

Fruits Basket

NATSUKI TAKAYA

Translation: Sheldon Drzka • Lettering: Lys Blakeslee

This book is a work of fiction. Names, characters, places, and incidents are the product of the author's imagination or are used fictitiously. Any resemblance to actual events, locales, or persons, living or dead, is coincidental.

Fruits Basket Collector's Edition, Vol. 1 by Natsuki Takaya

First published in Japan in 2015 by HAKUSENSHA, INC., Tokyo.
English language translation rights in U.S.A., Canada and U.K. arranged with HAKUSENSHA, INC., Tokyo through Tuttle-Mori Agency, Inc., Tokyo.

Yen Press
Hachette Book Group
1290 Avenue of the Americas
New York, NY 10104

www.HachetteBookGroup.com • www.YenPress.com

Yen Press is an imprint of Hachette Book Group, Inc.
The Yen Press name and logo are trademarks of Hachette Book Group, Inc.

The publisher is not responsible for websites (or their content) that are not owned by the publisher.

Library of Congress Control Number: 2016932692

First Yen Press Edition: June 2016

ISBN: 978-0-316-36016-6

10 9 8 7 6 5 4 3 2 1

BVG

Printed in the United States of America

Page 181

Rice ball: *Onigiri* in Japanese, this food consists of white rice formed into a triangular shape, often wrapped in seaweed (*nori*). Traditionally, *onigiri* have a sour or salty filling for flavor and as a natural preservative. One common ingredient is the incredibly sour and salty pickled plum (*umeboshi*).

Page 292

What do mice eat?: In Japanese, Hatori is asking "What is 1+1?" The answer, 2 (*ni*), achieves the same effect as "Cheese!" when taking photos. It is also the Japanese onomatopoeia for smiling.

Page 331

Kotatsu: A *kotatsu* is a low living room table with a futon under the table top and a heating unit attached to the underside. Central heating is rare in Japan, so sitting under the *kotatsu* is a common way to warm up in the winter. It's also common to nap under the *kotatsu* (legs under the table, head on a cushion on the floor or just on the table).

Page 347

Choking on mochi: Though Kyo says this to express just how careless Tohru is, this traditional New Year's food has proven fatal in the past. Young children and the elderly are especially at high risk.

Page 351

Japan Record Awards: Japan's major music awards show, akin to the Grammy Awards, is held annually on December 30th.

Page 351

Song festival: *NHK Kohaku Uta Gassen* ("Red and White Song Contest"), officially translated as "Year-End Song Festival," is held annually on December 31st and remains Japan's most-watched musical TV program of the year.

Page 358

New Year's Eve soba: Soba noodles are traditonally eaten the night of New Year's Eve. Their length symbolizes long life.

Page 361

Sensei: Not only used for teachers and mentors, "sensei" is also used for respected writers, creators, and even politicians.

Page 374

Sea horse: This is a pun in Japanese, with the original term—*tatsu no otoshiko*—meaning both "sea horse" and "illegitimate son of the dragon."

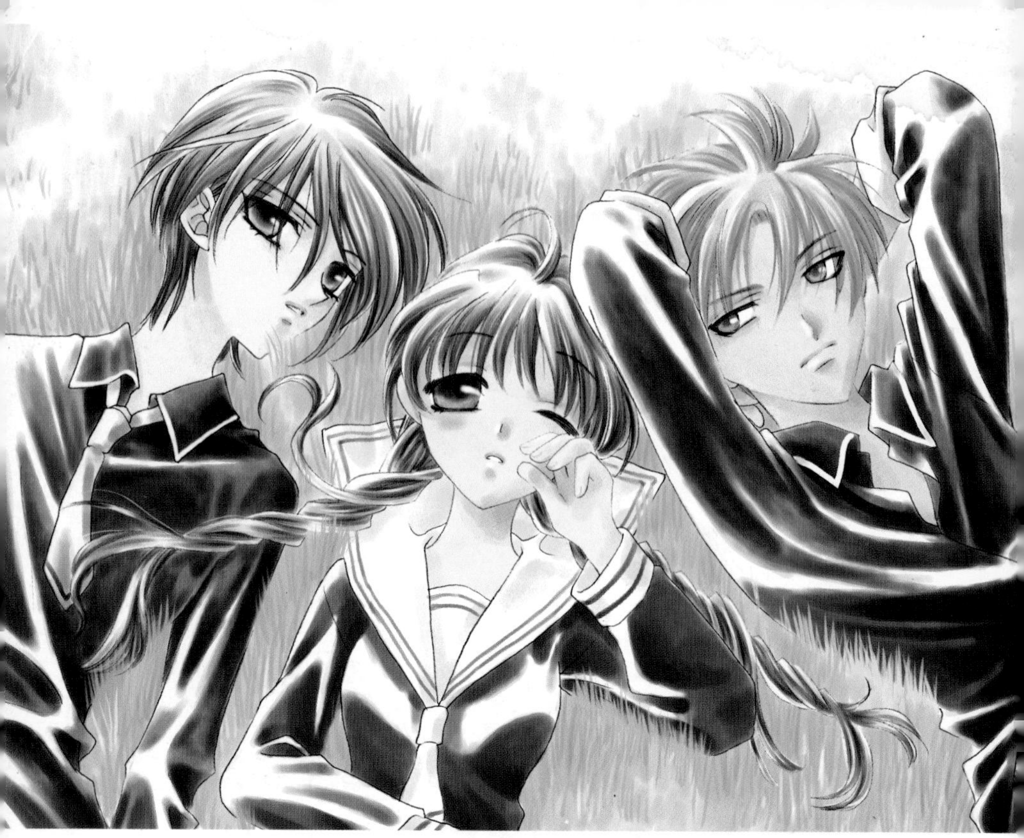

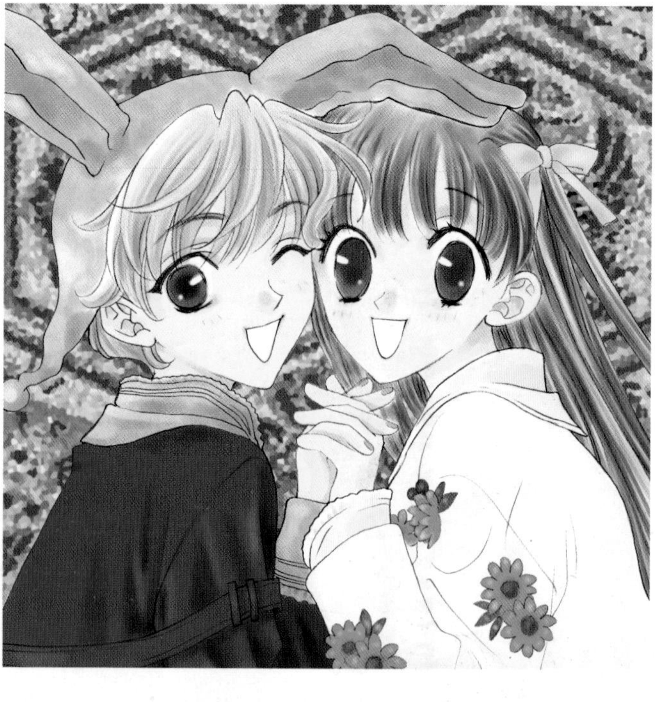

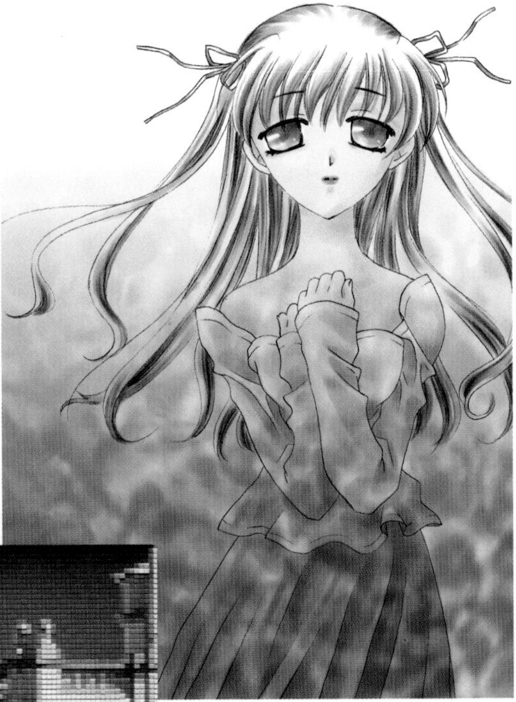
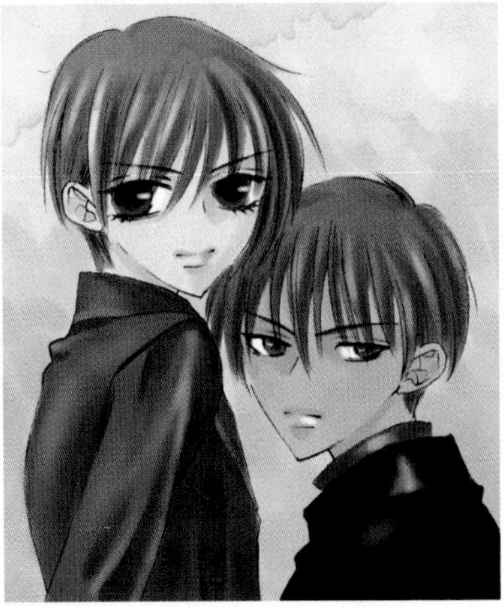
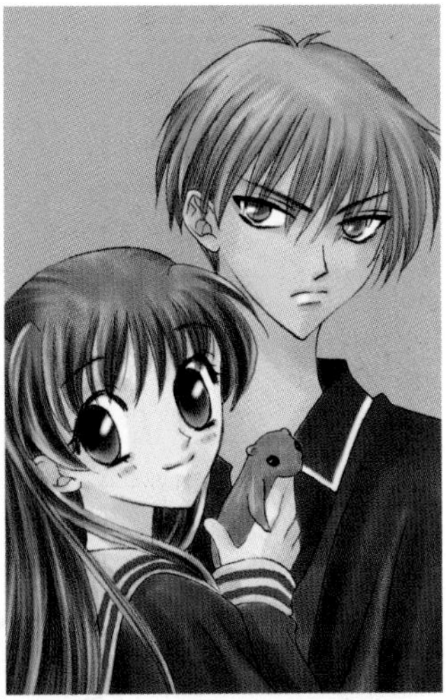
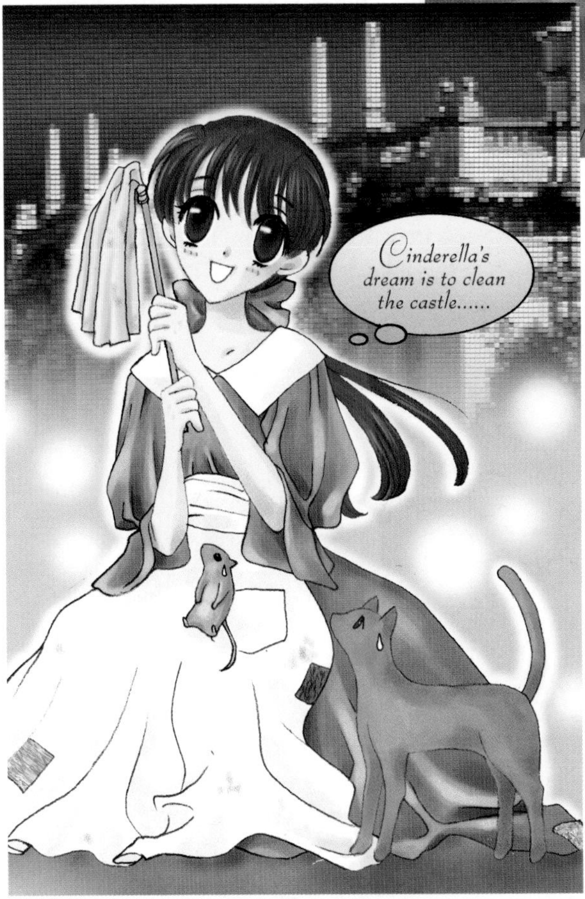
Cinderella's dream is to clean the castle......

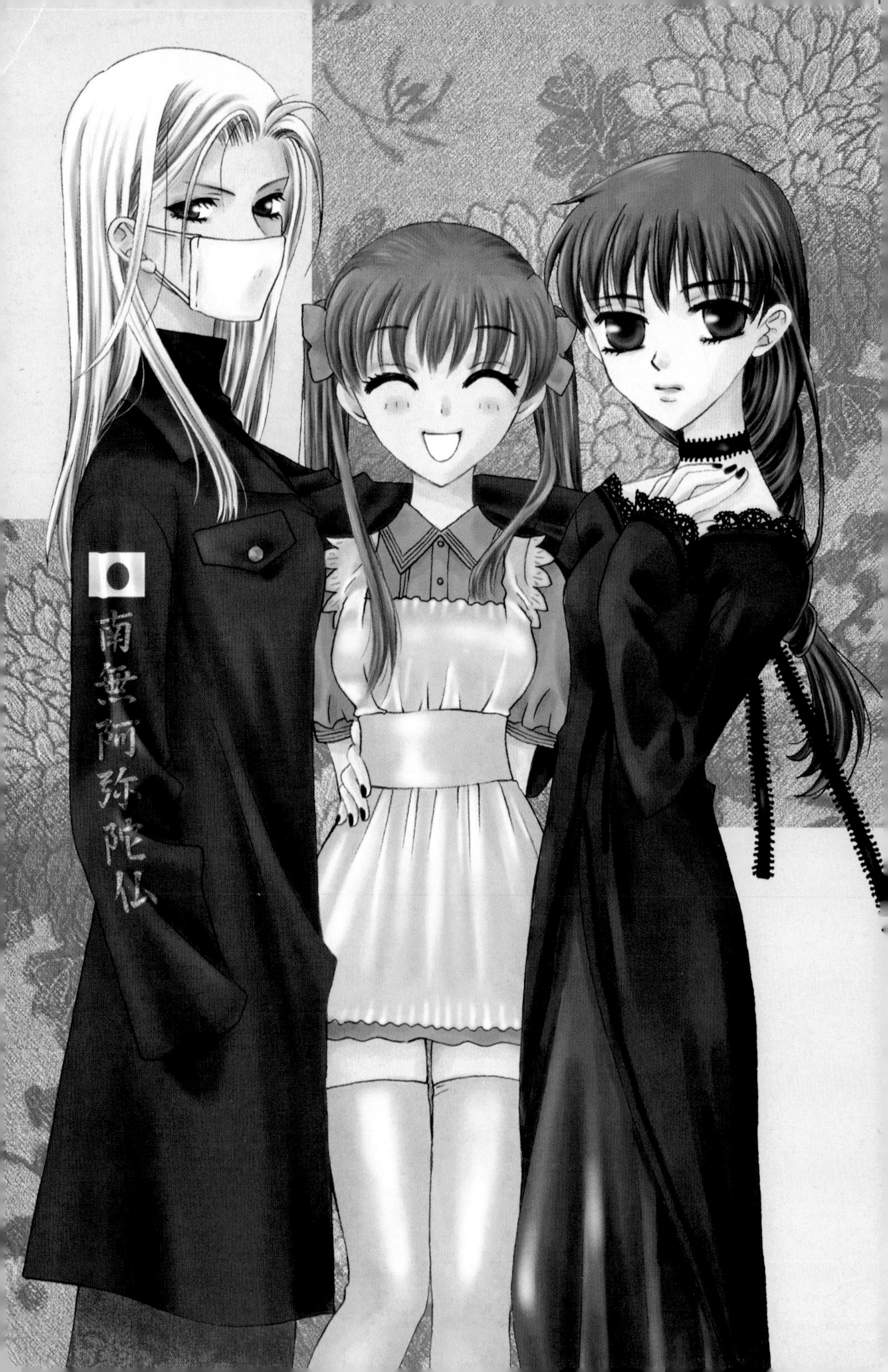
南無阿弥陀仏

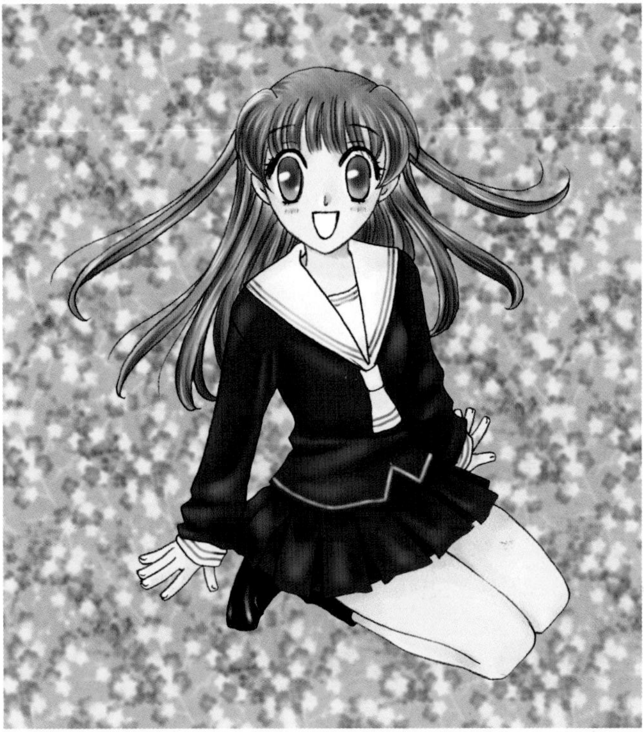
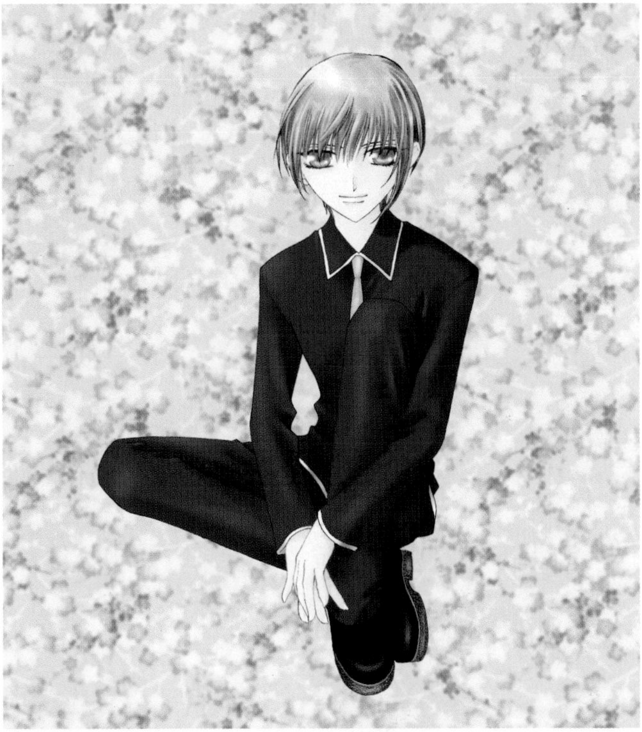

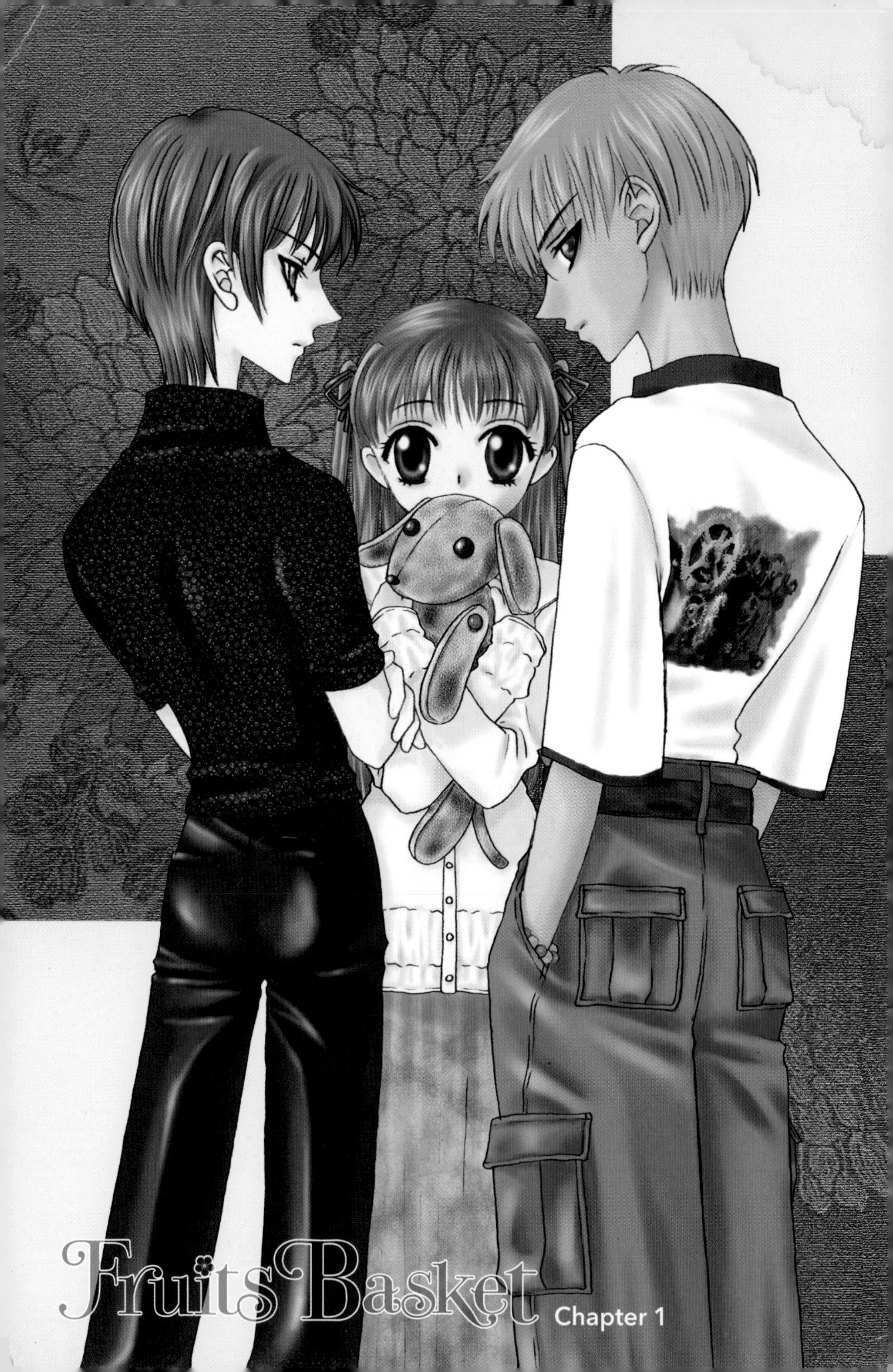
Fruits Basket
Chapter 1

TABLE OF CONTENTS
COLLECTOR'S EDITION

Chapter 1 7
Chapter 2 55
Chapter 3 85
Chapter 4 115
Chapter 5 145
Chapter 6 177
Chapter 7 209
Chapter 8 243
Chapter 9 273
Chapter 10 303
Chapter 11 334
Chapter 12 367
Special Thanks
.... 397

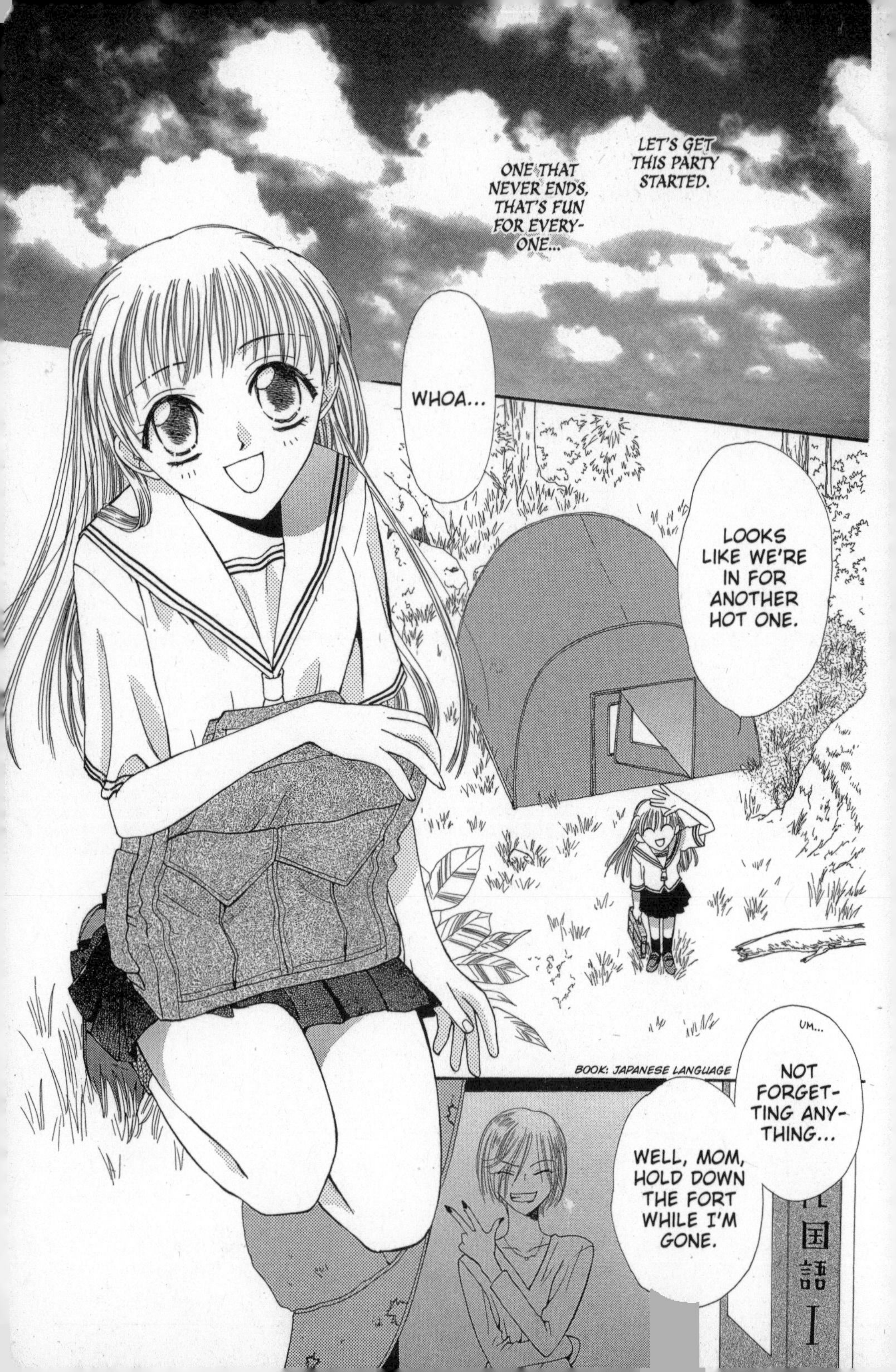
LET'S GET THIS PARTY STARTED.
ONE THAT NEVER ENDS, THAT'S FUN FOR EVERY-ONE...
WHOA...
LOOKS LIKE WE'RE IN FOR ANOTHER HOT ONE.
UM...
NOT FORGET-TING ANY-THING...
WELL, MOM, HOLD DOWN THE FORT WHILE I'M GONE.
BOOK: JAPANESE LANGUAGE
国語I

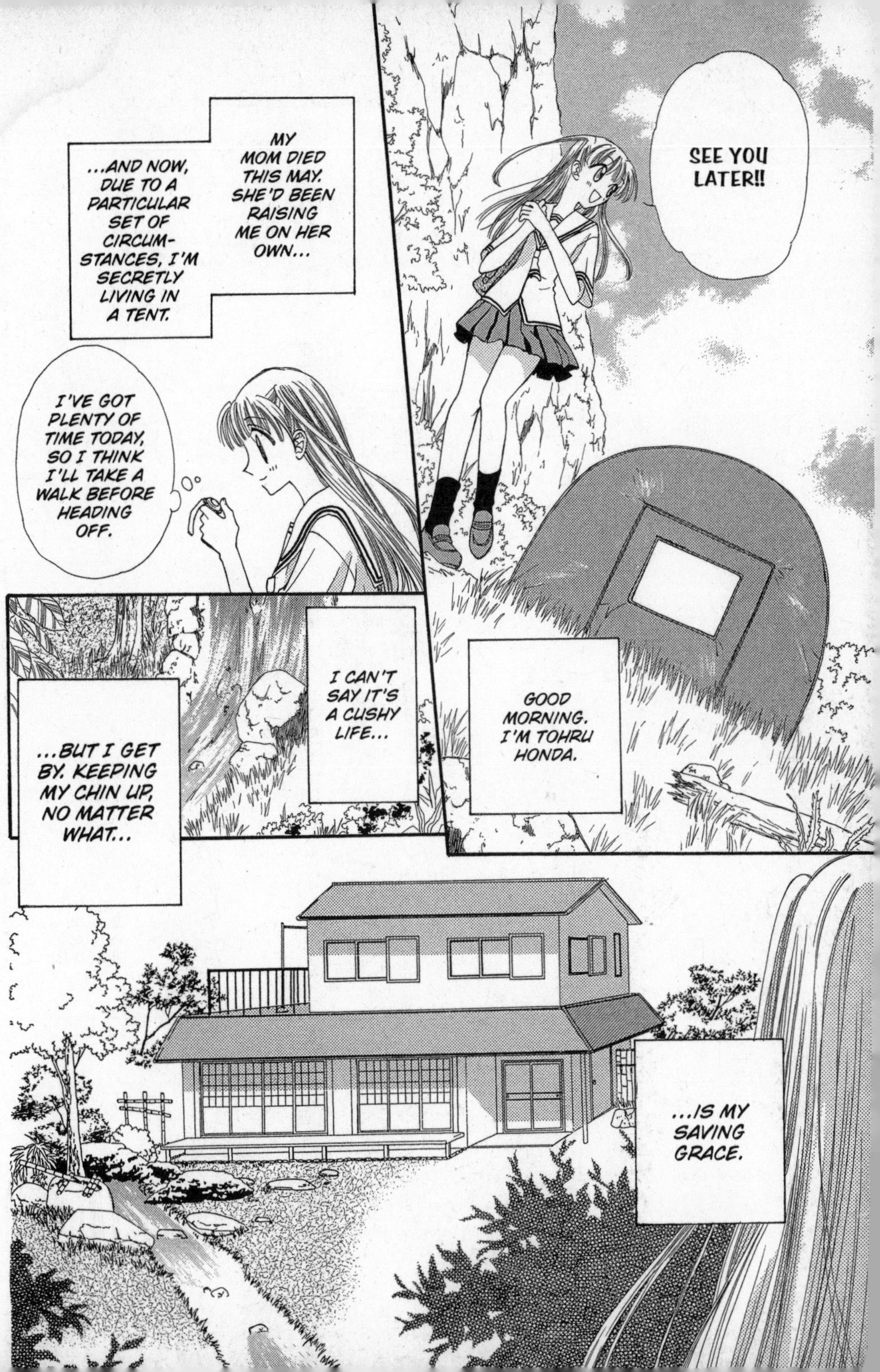
SEE YOU LATER!!
GOOD MORNING. I'M TOHRU HONDA.
MY MOM DIED THIS MAY. SHE'D BEEN RAISING ME ON HER OWN...
...AND NOW, DUE TO A PARTICULAR SET OF CIRCUM-STANCES, I'M SECRETLY LIVING IN A TENT.
I'VE GOT PLENTY OF TIME TODAY, SO I THINK I'LL TAKE A WALK BEFORE HEADING OFF.
I CAN'T SAY IT'S A CUSHY LIFE...
...BUT I GET BY. KEEPING MY CHIN UP, NO MATTER WHAT...
...IS MY SAVING GRACE.

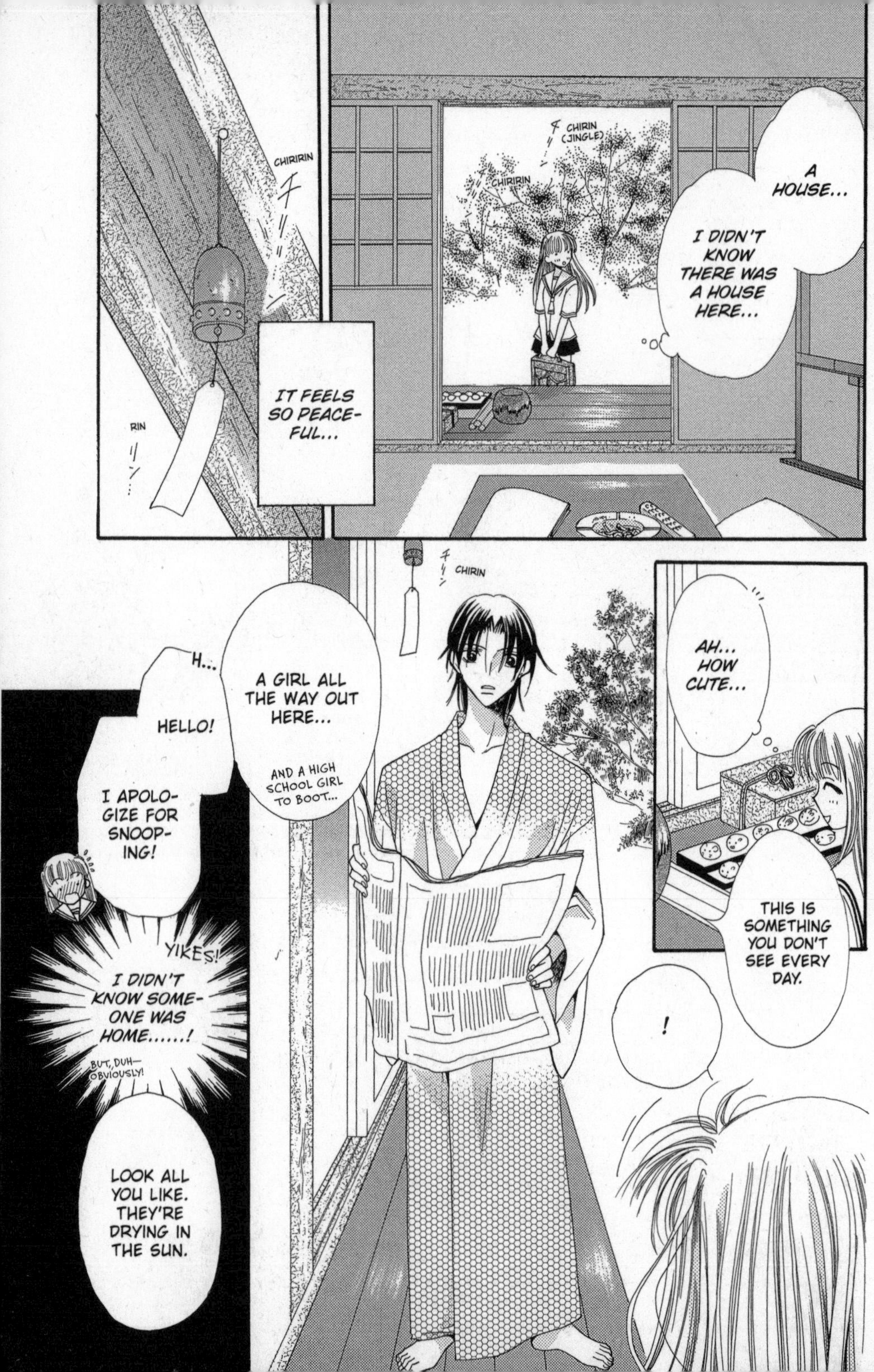
CHIRIN (JINGLE)
CHIRIRIN
A HOUSE...
I DIDN'T KNOW THERE WAS A HOUSE HERE...
IT FEELS SO PEACE-FUL...
CHIRIRIN
RIN
AH... HOW CUTE...
THIS IS SOMETHING YOU DON'T SEE EVERY DAY.
!
CHIRIN
A GIRL ALL THE WAY OUT HERE...
AND A HIGH SCHOOL GIRL TO BOOT...
H...
HELLO!
I APOLO-GIZE FOR SNOOP-ING!
YIKES!
I DIDN'T KNOW SOME-ONE WAS HOME......!
BUT, DUH—OBVIOUSLY!
LOOK ALL YOU LIKE. THEY'RE DRYING IN THE SUN.

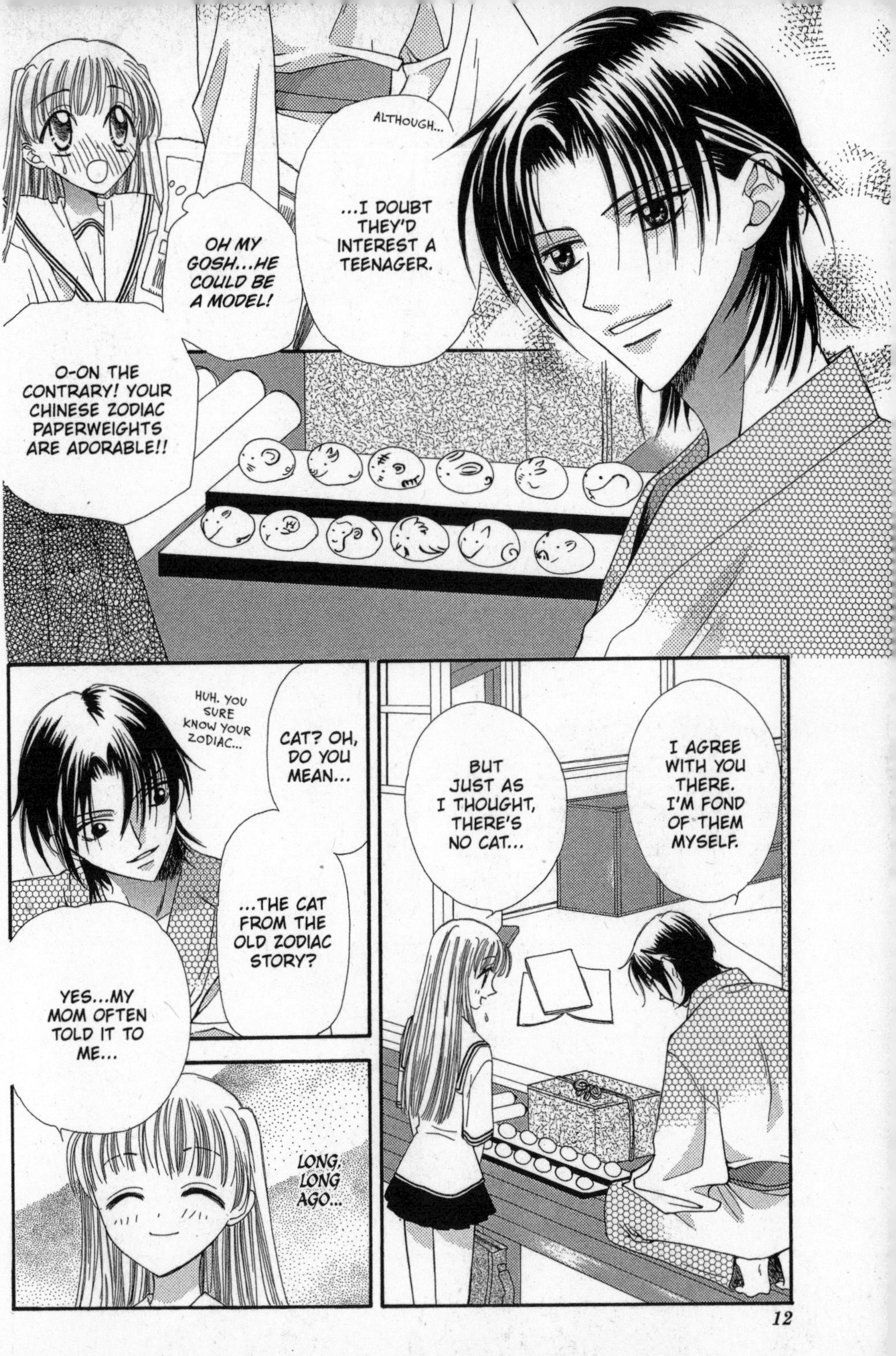
ALTHOUGH...
...I DOUBT THEY'D INTEREST A TEENAGER.
OH MY GOSH...HE COULD BE A MODEL!
O-ON THE CONTRARY! YOUR CHINESE ZODIAC PAPERWEIGHTS ARE ADORABLE!!
I AGREE WITH YOU THERE. I'M FOND OF THEM MYSELF.
BUT JUST AS I THOUGHT, THERE'S NO CAT...
CAT? OH, DO YOU MEAN...
...THE CAT FROM THE OLD ZODIAC STORY?
HUH. YOU SURE KNOW YOUR ZODIAC...
YES...MY MOM OFTEN TOLD IT TO ME...
LONG, LONG AGO...

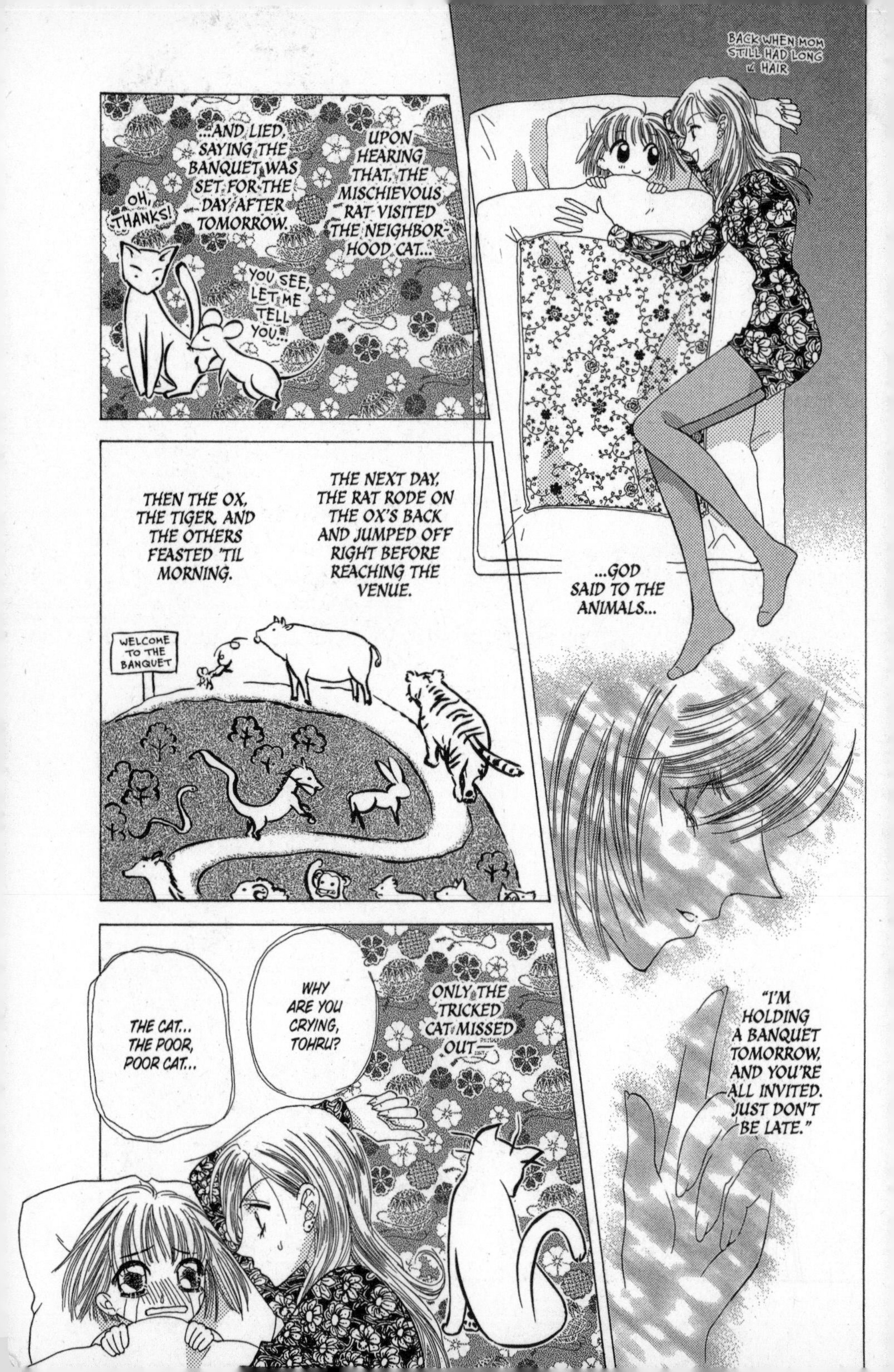
BACK WHEN MOM STILL HAD LONG HAIR
...GOD SAID TO THE ANIMALS...
"I'M HOLDING A BANQUET TOMORROW, AND YOU'RE ALL INVITED. JUST DON'T BE LATE."
UPON HEARING THAT, THE MISCHIEVOUS RAT VISITED THE NEIGHBORHOOD CAT...
...AND LIED, SAYING THE BANQUET WAS SET FOR THE DAY AFTER TOMORROW.
YOU SEE, LET ME TELL YOU...
OH, THANKS!
THE NEXT DAY, THE RAT RODE ON THE OX'S BACK AND JUMPED OFF RIGHT BEFORE REACHING THE VENUE.
THEN THE OX, THE TIGER, AND THE OTHERS FEASTED 'TIL MORNING.
WELCOME TO THE BANQUET
ONLY THE TRICKED CAT MISSED OUT.
WHY ARE YOU CRYING, TOHRU?
THE CAT... THE POOR, POOR CAT...

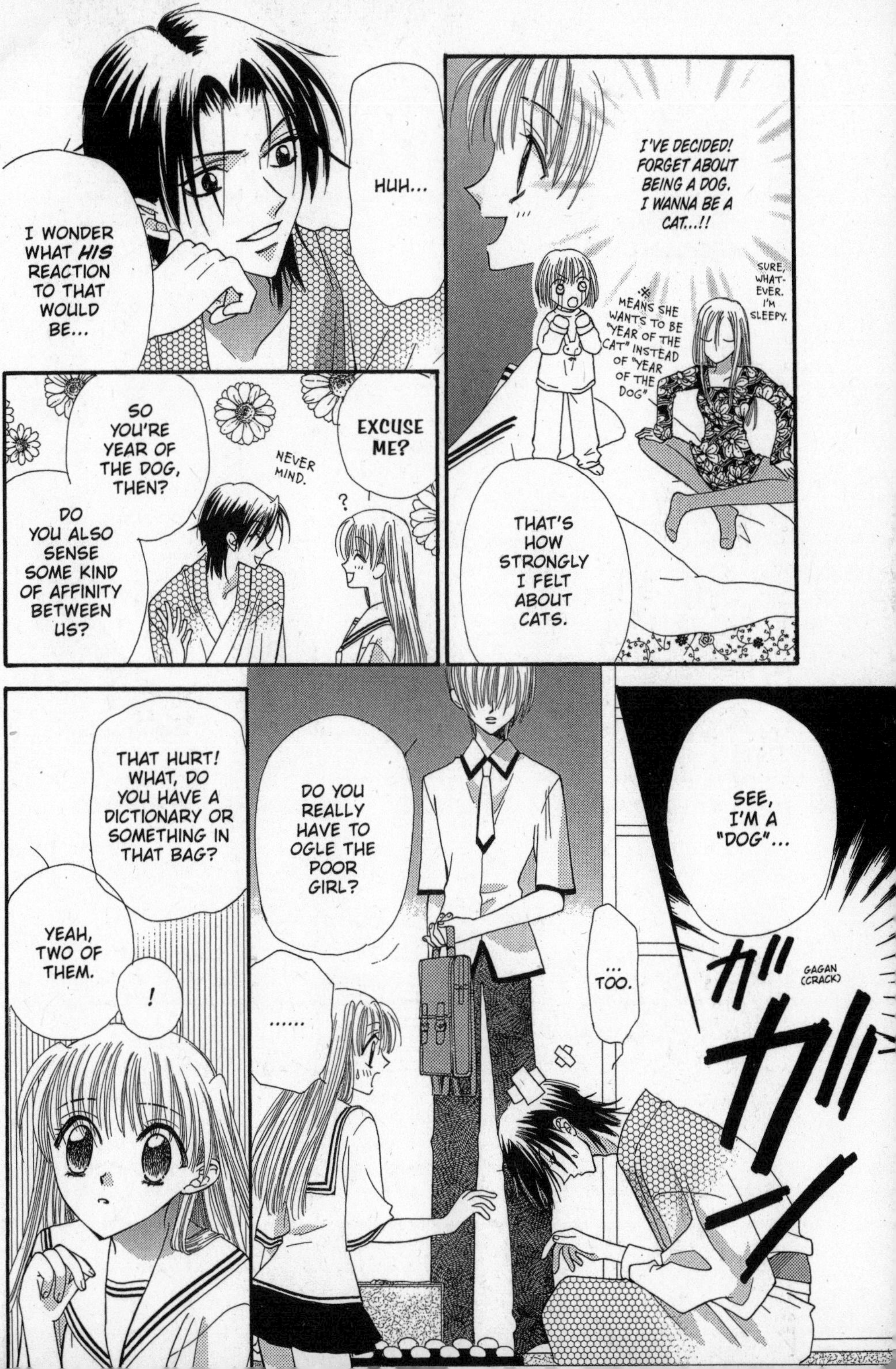
I'VE DECIDED! FORGET ABOUT BEING A DOG. I WANNA BE A CAT...!!
SURE, WHATEVER. I'M SLEEPY.
※MEANS SHE WANTS TO BE "YEAR OF THE CAT" INSTEAD OF "YEAR OF THE DOG"
THAT'S HOW STRONGLY I FELT ABOUT CATS.
HUH...
I WONDER WHAT ***HIS*** REACTION TO THAT WOULD BE...
EXCUSE ME?
NEVER MIND.
?
SO YOU'RE YEAR OF THE DOG, THEN?
DO YOU ALSO SENSE SOME KIND OF AFFINITY BETWEEN US?
SEE, I'M A "DOG"...
... TOO.
GAGAN (CRACK)
DO YOU REALLY HAVE TO OGLE THE POOR GIRL?
......
THAT HURT! WHAT, DO YOU HAVE A DICTIONARY OR SOMETHING IN THAT BAG?
YEAH, TWO OF THEM.
!

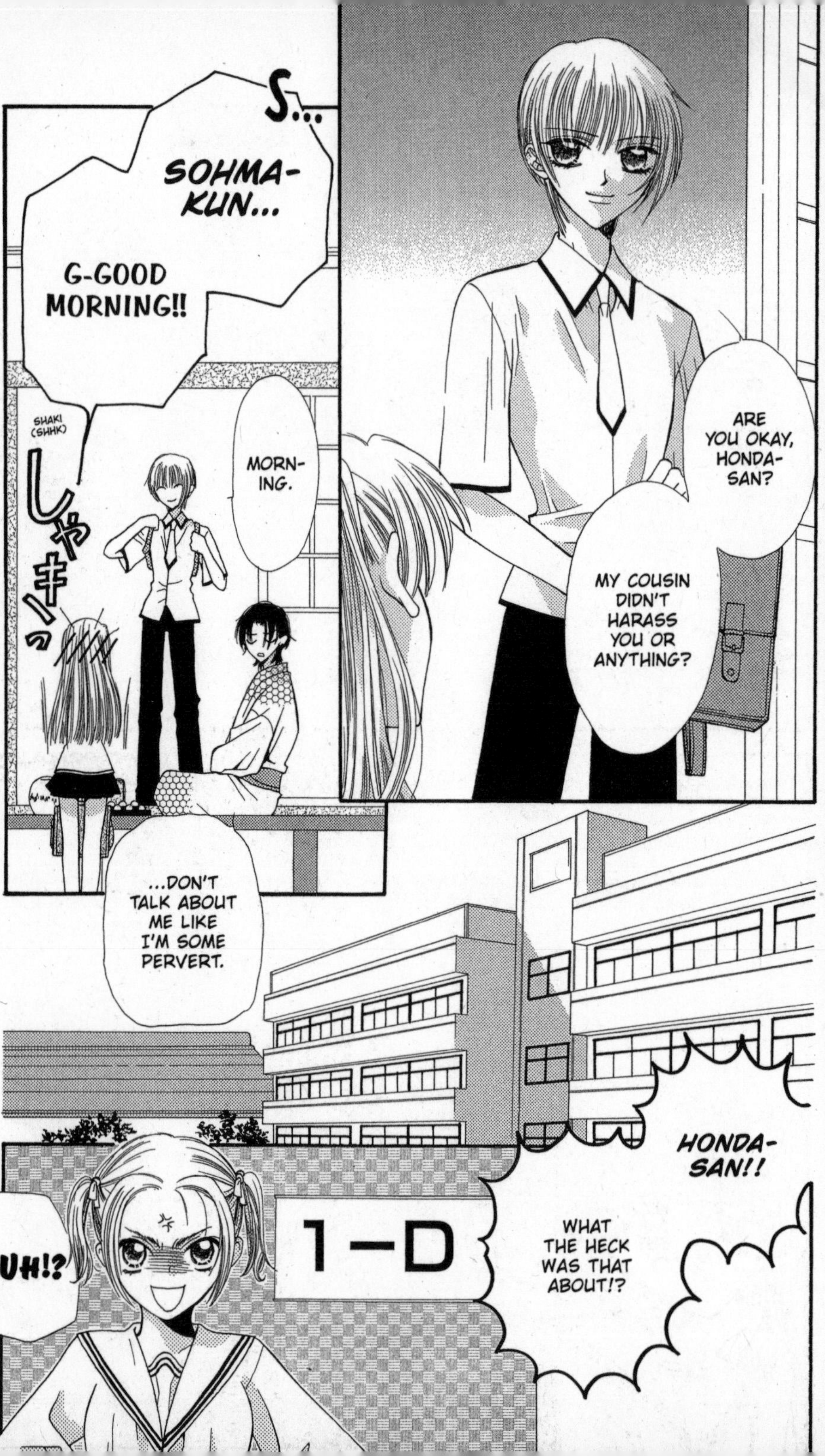
ARE YOU OKAY, HONDA-SAN?
MY COUSIN DIDN'T HARASS YOU OR ANYTHING?
S...
SOHMA-KUN...
G-GOOD MORNING!!
MORNING.
SHAKI (SHHK)
...DON'T TALK ABOUT ME LIKE I'M SOME PERVERT.
HONDA-SAN!!
WHAT THE HECK WAS THAT ABOUT!?
1-D
HUH!?

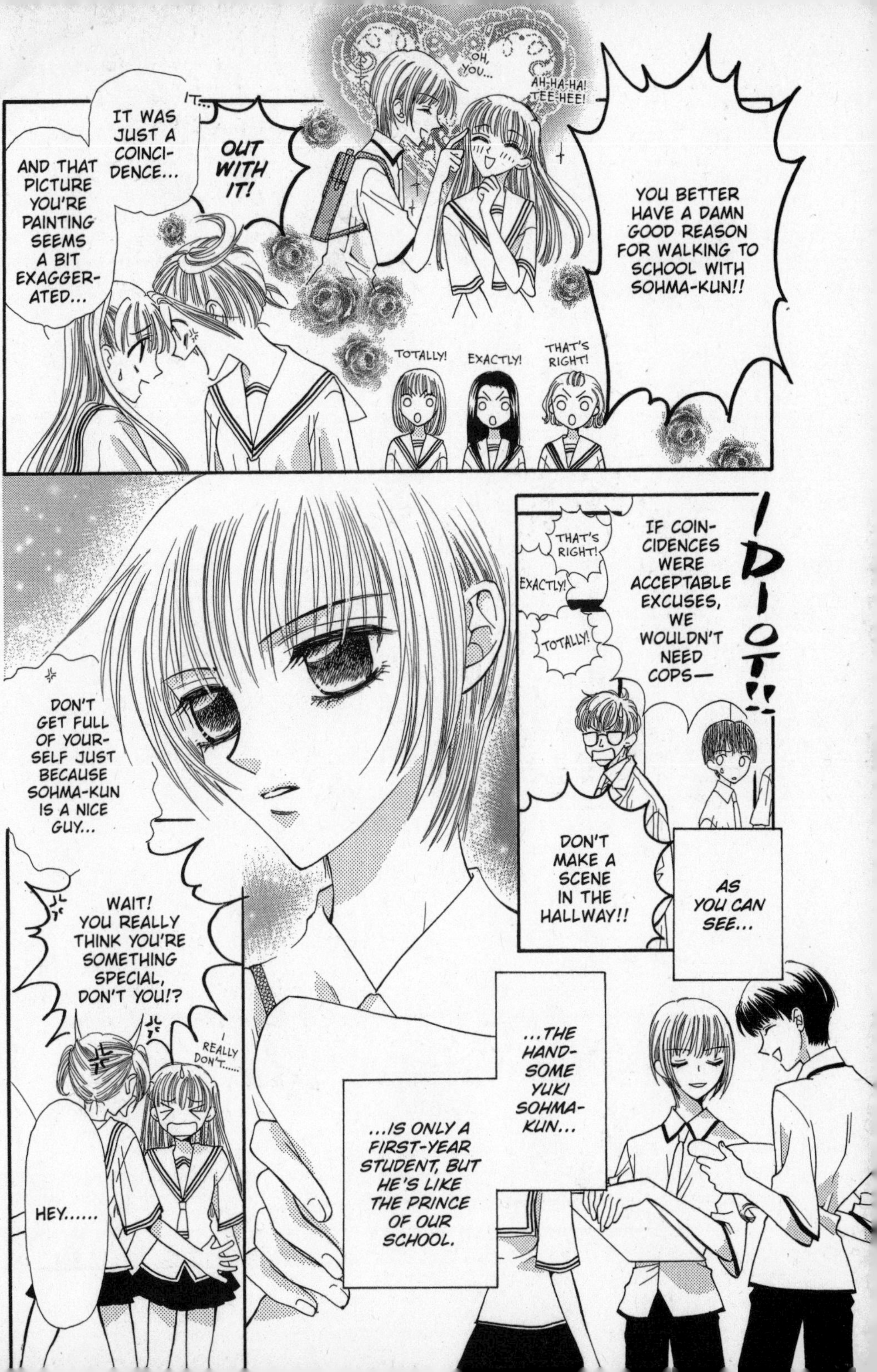
YOU BETTER HAVE A DAMN GOOD REASON FOR WALKING TO SCHOOL WITH SOHMA-KUN!!
OH, YOU...
AH-HA-HA! TEE-HEE!
THAT'S RIGHT!
EXACTLY!
TOTALLY!
OUT WITH IT!
IT...
IT WAS JUST A COINCIDENCE...
AND THAT PICTURE YOU'RE PAINTING SEEMS A BIT EXAGGERATED...
IDIOT!!
IF COINCIDENCES WERE ACCEPTABLE EXCUSES, WE WOULDN'T NEED COPS—
THAT'S RIGHT!
EXACTLY!
TOTALLY!
DON'T MAKE A SCENE IN THE HALLWAY!!
AS YOU CAN SEE...
...THE HANDSOME YUKI SOHMA-KUN...
...IS ONLY A FIRST-YEAR STUDENT, BUT HE'S LIKE THE PRINCE OF OUR SCHOOL.
DON'T GET FULL OF YOURSELF JUST BECAUSE SOHMA-KUN IS A NICE GUY...
WAIT! YOU REALLY THINK YOU'RE SOMETHING SPECIAL, DON'T YOU!?
I REALLY DON'T.....
HEY......

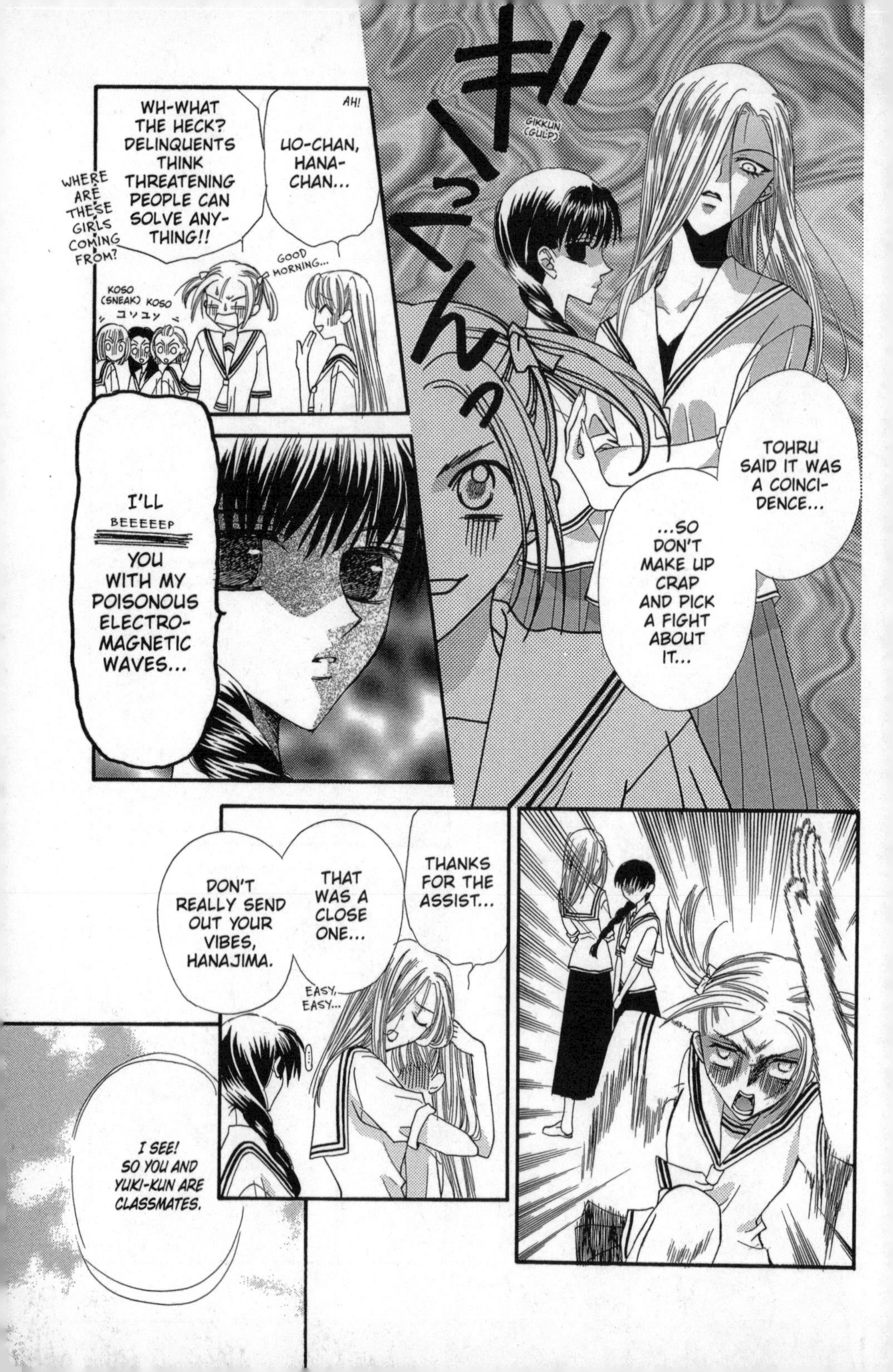
GIKKUN (GULP)
TOHRU SAID IT WAS A COINCI-DENCE...
...SO DON'T MAKE UP CRAP AND PICK A FIGHT ABOUT IT...
AH!
UO-CHAN, HANA-CHAN...
GOOD MORNING...
WH-WHAT THE HECK? DELINQUENTS THINK THREATENING PEOPLE CAN SOLVE ANY-THING!!
WHERE ARE THESE GIRLS COMING FROM?
KOSO (SNEAK) KOSO
コソコソ
I'LL BEEEEEP YOU WITH MY POISONOUS ELECTRO-MAGNETIC WAVES...
THANKS FOR THE ASSIST...
THAT WAS A CLOSE ONE...
DON'T REALLY SEND OUT YOUR VIBES, HANAJIMA.
EASY, EASY...
I SEE! SO YOU AND YUKI-KUN ARE CLASSMATES.

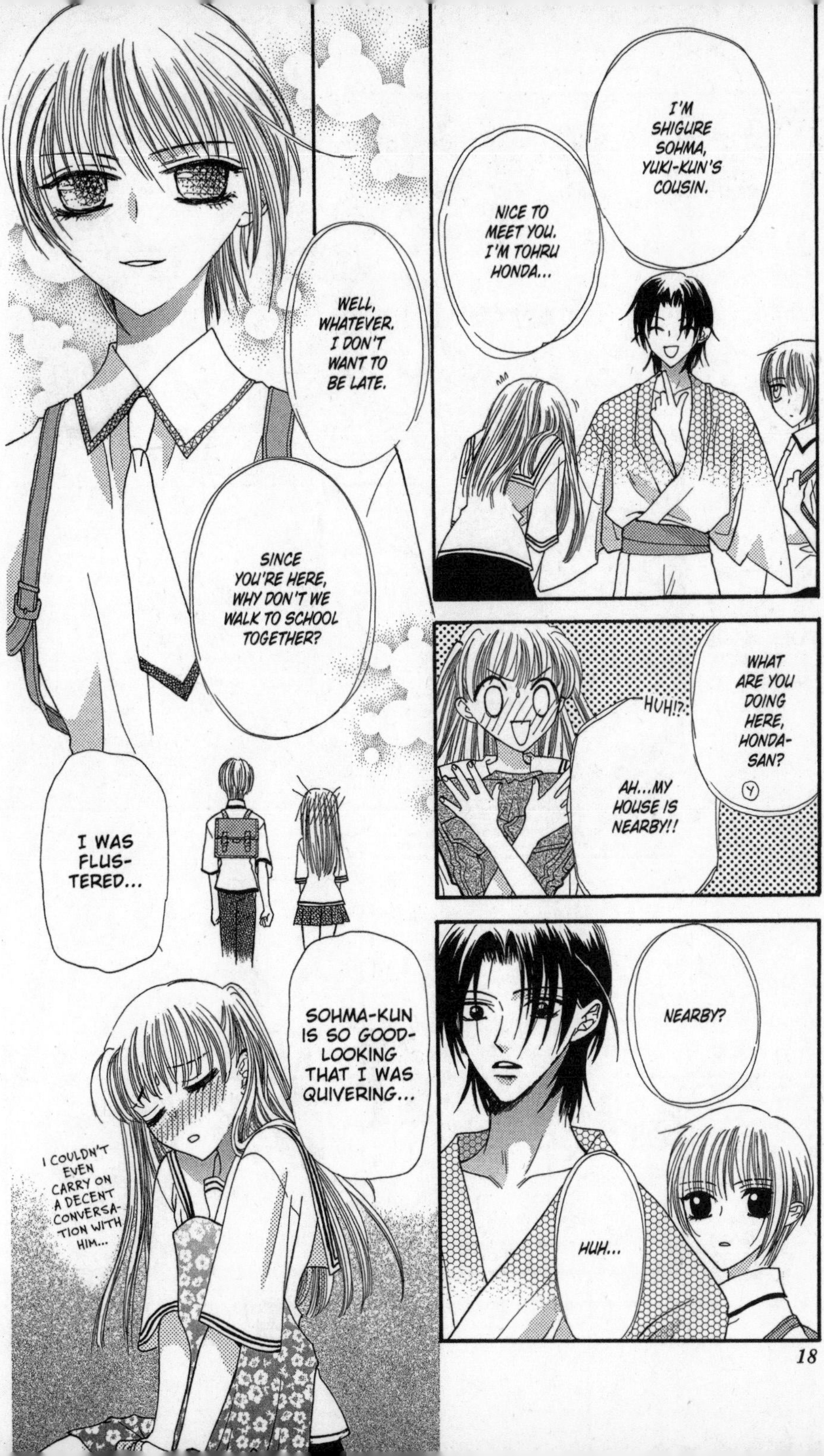
I'M SHIGURE SOHMA, YUKI-KUN'S COUSIN.
NICE TO MEET YOU. I'M TOHRU HONDA...
WHAT ARE YOU DOING HERE, HONDA-SAN?
HUH!?
AH...MY HOUSE IS NEARBY!!
NEARBY?
HUH...
WELL, WHATEVER. I DON'T WANT TO BE LATE.
SINCE YOU'RE HERE, WHY DON'T WE WALK TO SCHOOL TOGETHER?
I WAS FLUSTERED...
SOHMA-KUN IS SO GOOD-LOOKING THAT I WAS QUIVERING...
I COULDN'T EVEN CARRY ON A DECENT CONVERSATION WITH HIM...

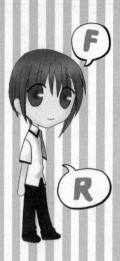

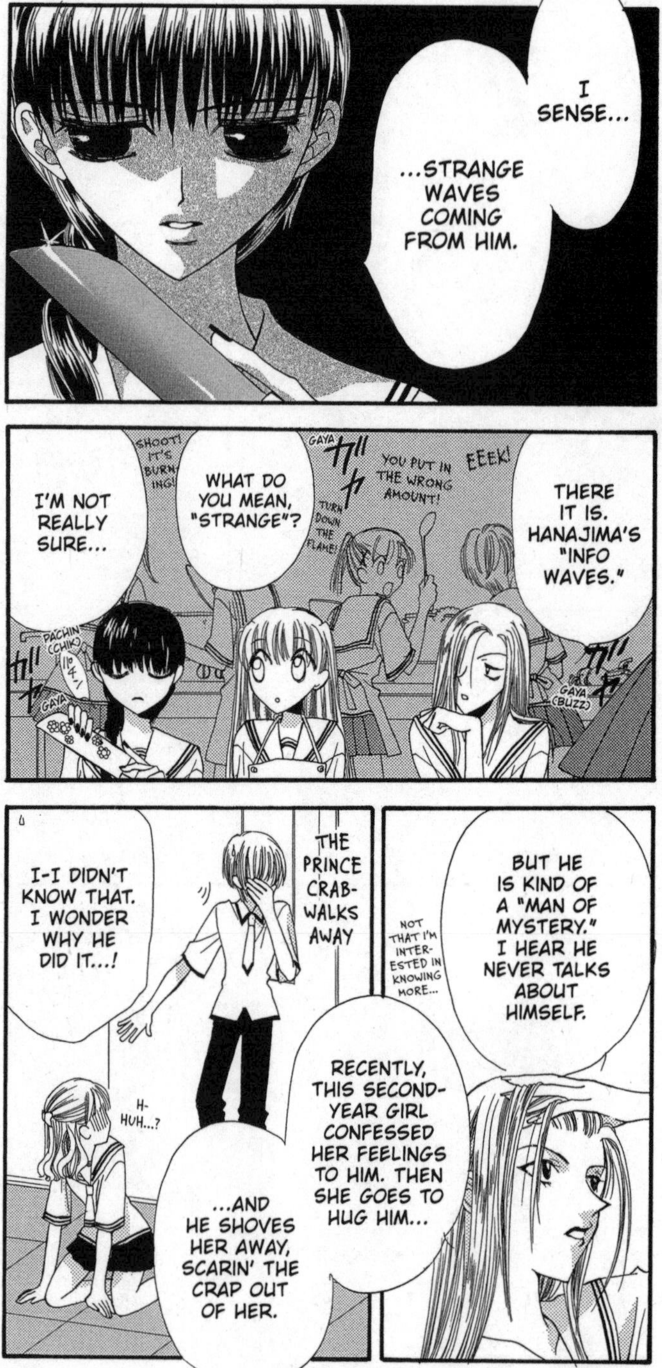
I SENSE...
...STRANGE WAVES COMING FROM HIM.
THERE IT IS. HANAJIMA'S "INFO WAVES."
EEEK!
YOU PUT IN THE WRONG AMOUNT!
TURN DOWN THE FLAME!
GAYA
WHAT DO YOU MEAN, "STRANGE"?
SHOOT! IT'S BURNING!
I'M NOT REALLY SURE...
GAYA (BUZZ)
PACHIN (CHIK)
GAYA
BUT HE IS KIND OF A "MAN OF MYSTERY." I HEAR HE NEVER TALKS ABOUT HIMSELF.
NOT THAT I'M INTERESTED IN KNOWING MORE...
RECENTLY, THIS SECOND-YEAR GIRL CONFESSED HER FEELINGS TO HIM. THEN SHE GOES TO HUG HIM...
THE PRINCE CRAB-WALKS AWAY
I-I DIDN'T KNOW THAT. I WONDER WHY HE DID IT...!
H-HUH...?
...AND HE SHOVES HER AWAY, SCARIN' THE CRAP OUT OF HER.

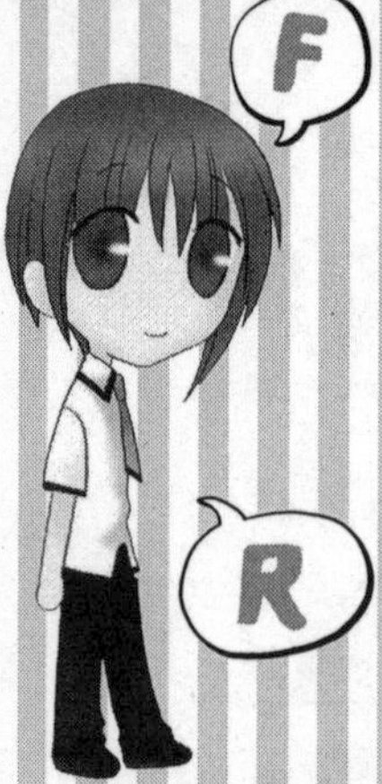
F
R

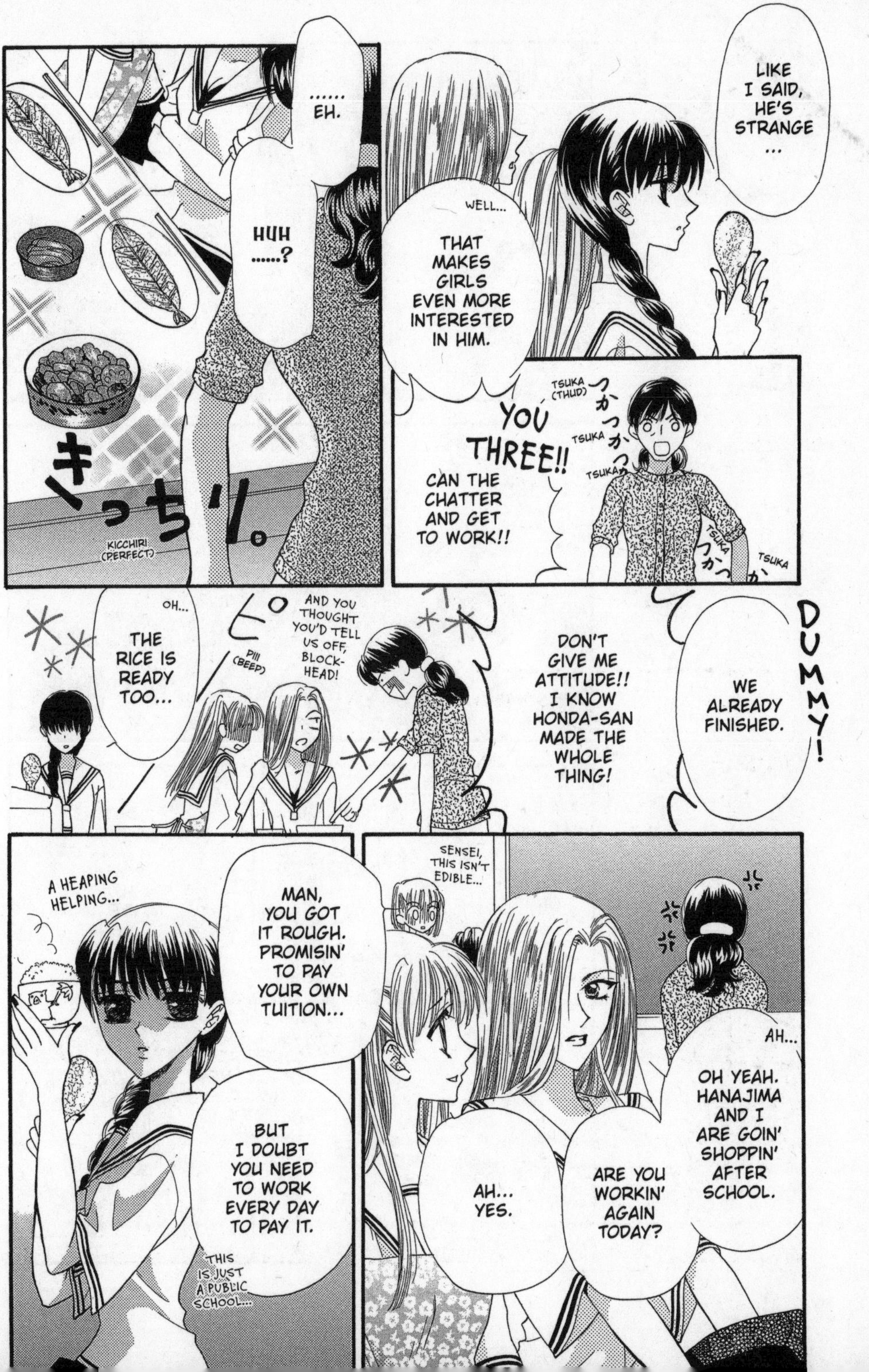
LIKE I SAID, HE'S STRANGE ...
WELL...
THAT MAKES GIRLS EVEN MORE INTERESTED IN HIM.
つかつかつか
TSUKA (THUD)
TSUKA
TSUKA
YOU THREE!!
CAN THE CHATTER AND GET TO WORK!!
つかつか
TSUKA
TSUKA
......EH.
HUH ......?
きっちり。
KICCHIRI (PERFECT)
DUMMY!
WE ALREADY FINISHED.
DON'T GIVE ME ATTITUDE!! I KNOW HONDA-SAN MADE THE WHOLE THING!
AND YOU THOUGHT YOU'D TELL US OFF, BLOCK-HEAD!
ピー
PIII (BEEP)
OH...
THE RICE IS READY TOO...
SENSEI, THIS ISN'T EDIBLE...
AH...
OH YEAH. HANAJIMA AND I ARE GOIN' SHOPPIN' AFTER SCHOOL.
ARE YOU WORKIN' AGAIN TODAY?
AH... YES.
A HEAPING HELPING...
MAN, YOU GOT IT ROUGH. PROMISIN' TO PAY YOUR OWN TUITION...
BUT I DOUBT YOU NEED TO WORK EVERY DAY TO PAY IT.
THIS IS JUST A PUBLIC SCHOOL...

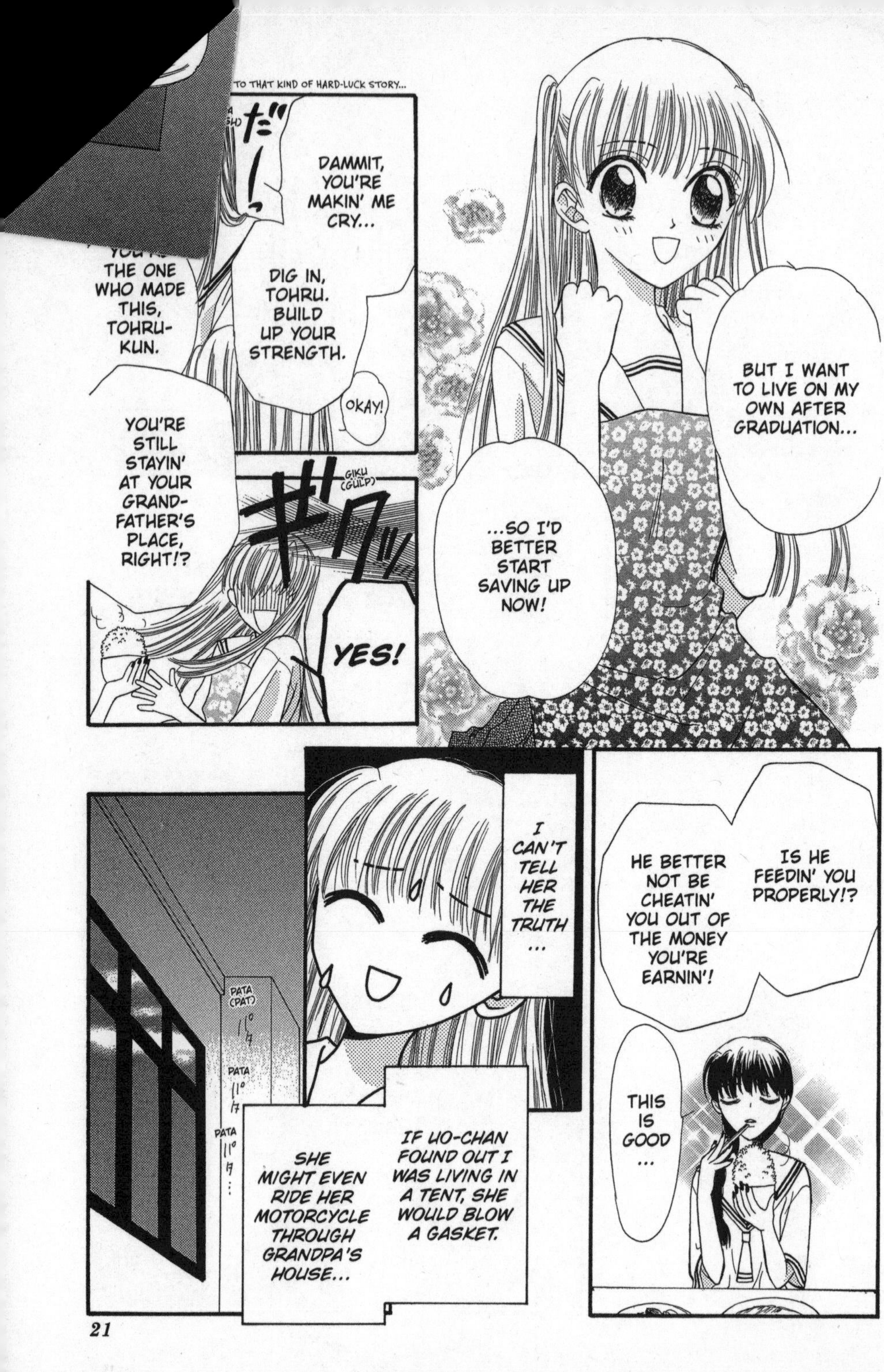
BUT I WANT TO LIVE ON MY OWN AFTER GRADUATION...
...SO I'D BETTER START SAVING UP NOW!
TO THAT KIND OF HARD-LUCK STORY...
DAMMIT, YOU'RE MAKIN' ME CRY...
DIG IN, TOHRU. BUILD UP YOUR STRENGTH.
THE ONE WHO MADE THIS, TOHRU-KUN.
OKAY!
YOU'RE STILL STAYIN' AT YOUR GRAND-FATHER'S PLACE, RIGHT!?
GIKU (GULP)
YES!
IS HE FEEDIN' YOU PROPERLY!?
HE BETTER NOT BE CHEATIN' YOU OUT OF THE MONEY YOU'RE EARNIN'!
THIS IS GOOD...
I CAN'T TELL HER THE TRUTH...
IF UO-CHAN FOUND OUT I WAS LIVING IN A TENT, SHE WOULD BLOW A GASKET.
SHE MIGHT EVEN RIDE HER MOTORCYCLE THROUGH GRANDPA'S HOUSE...
PATA (PAT)
PATA
PATA

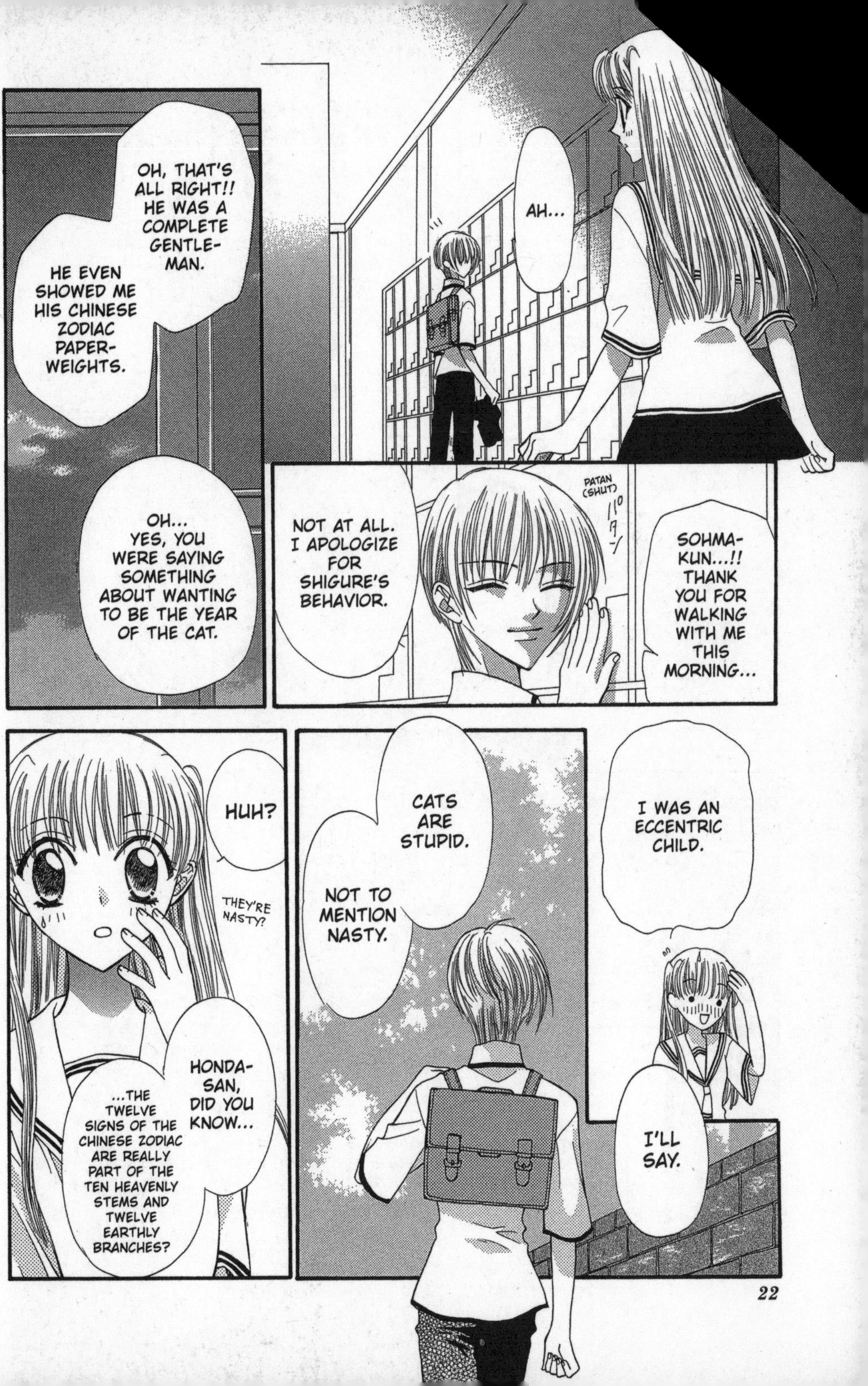
AH...
SOHMA-KUN...!! THANK YOU FOR WALKING WITH ME THIS MORNING...
PATAN (SHUT)
NOT AT ALL. I APOLOGIZE FOR SHIGURE'S BEHAVIOR.
OH, THAT'S ALL RIGHT!! HE WAS A COMPLETE GENTLE-MAN.
HE EVEN SHOWED ME HIS CHINESE ZODIAC PAPER-WEIGHTS.
OH... YES, YOU WERE SAYING SOMETHING ABOUT WANTING TO BE THE YEAR OF THE CAT.
I WAS AN ECCENTRIC CHILD.
I'LL SAY.
CATS ARE STUPID.
NOT TO MENTION NASTY.
HUH?
THEY'RE NASTY?
HONDA-SAN, DID YOU KNOW...
...THE TWELVE SIGNS OF THE CHINESE ZODIAC ARE REALLY PART OF THE TEN HEAVENLY STEMS AND TWELVE EARTHLY BRANCHES?

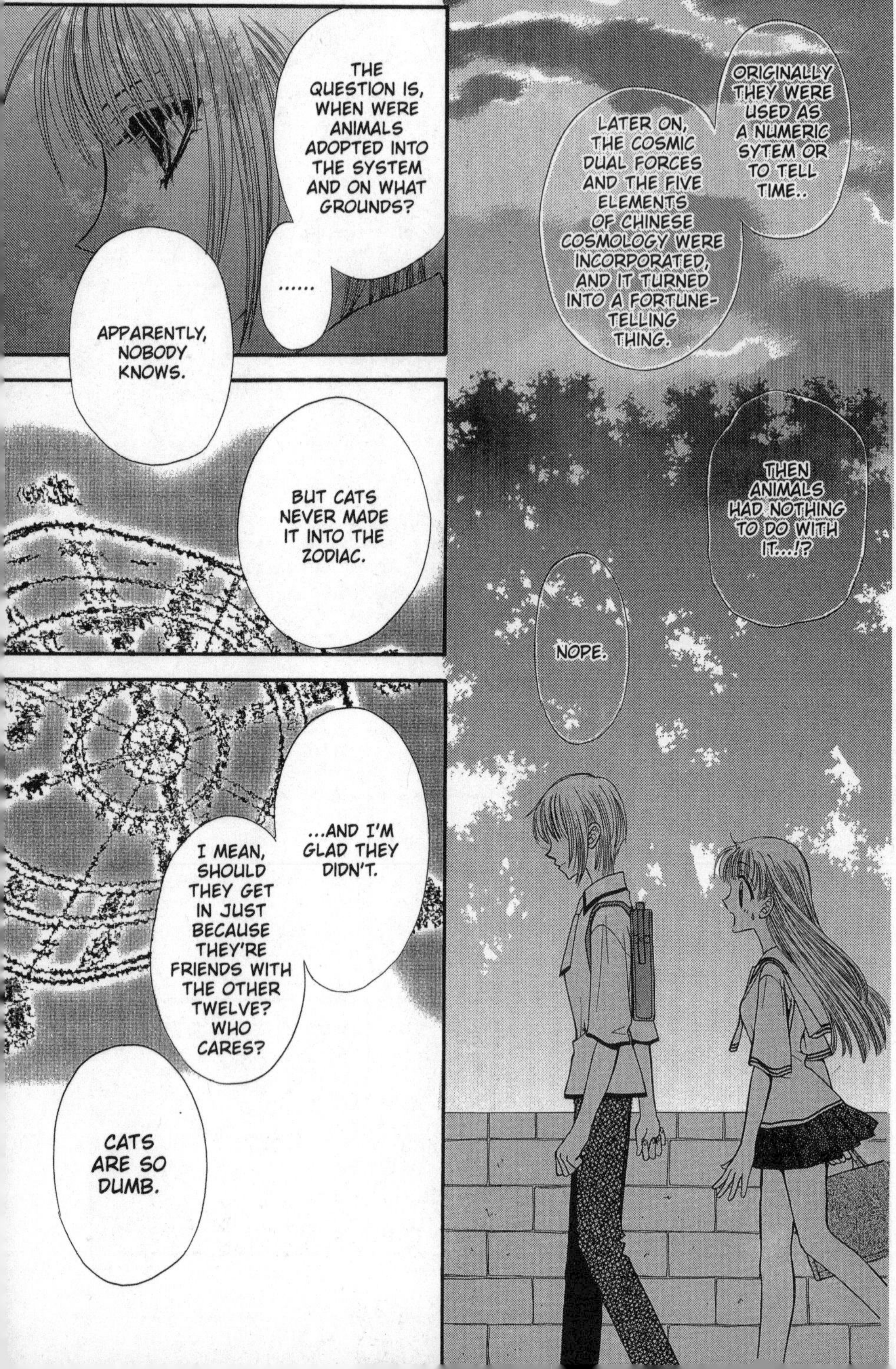
ORIGINALLY THEY WERE USED AS A NUMERIC SYTEM OR TO TELL TIME..
LATER ON, THE COSMIC DUAL FORCES AND THE FIVE ELEMENTS OF CHINESE COSMOLOGY WERE INCORPORATED, AND IT TURNED INTO A FORTUNE-TELLING THING.
THEN ANIMALS HAD NOTHING TO DO WITH IT...!?
NOPE.
THE QUESTION IS, WHEN WERE ANIMALS ADOPTED INTO THE SYSTEM AND ON WHAT GROUNDS?
......
APPARENTLY, NOBODY KNOWS.
BUT CATS NEVER MADE IT INTO THE ZODIAC.
...AND I'M GLAD THEY DIDN'T.
I MEAN, SHOULD THEY GET IN JUST BECAUSE THEY'RE FRIENDS WITH THE OTHER TWELVE? WHO CARES?
CATS ARE SO DUMB.

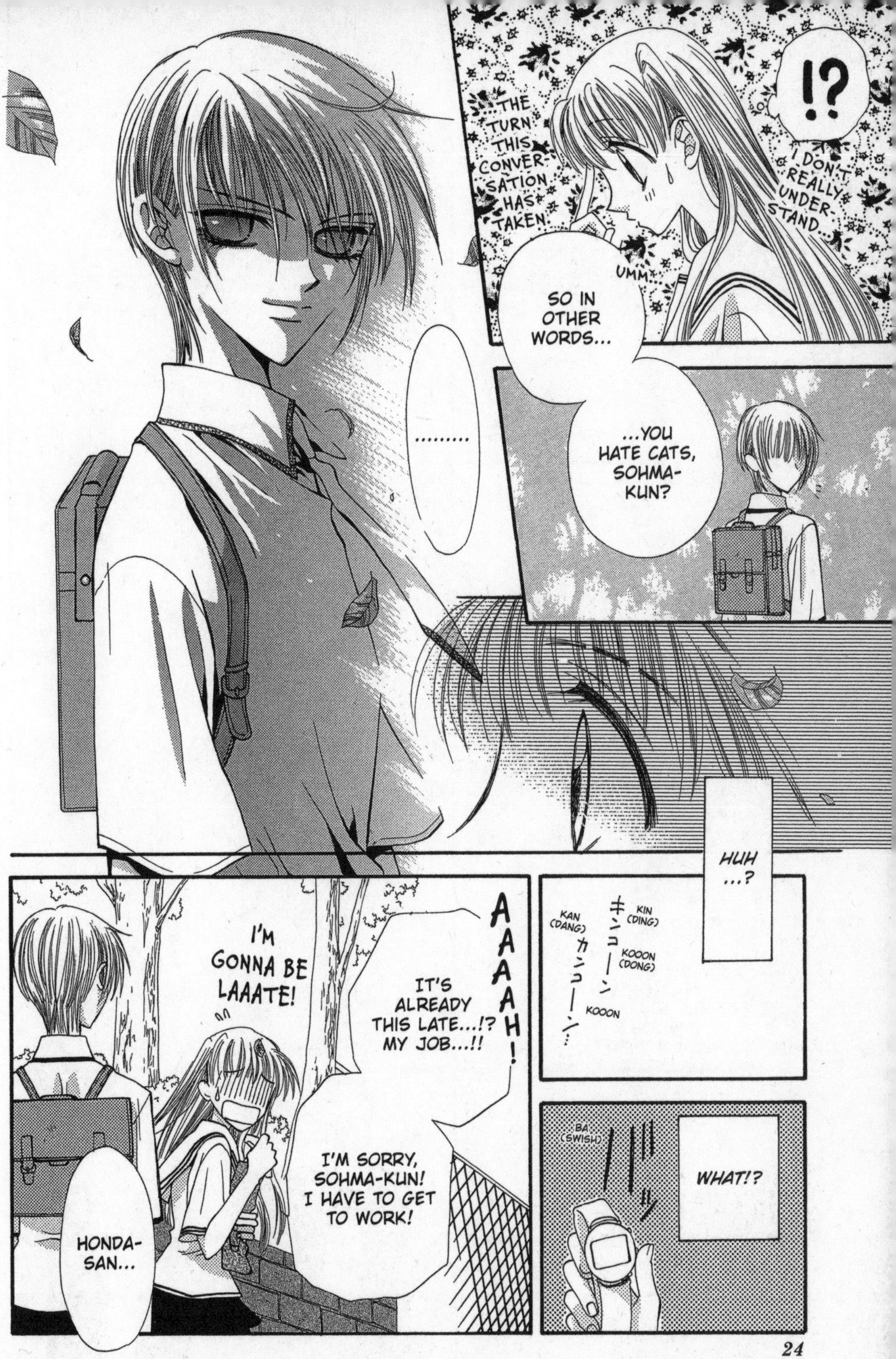
!?
I DON'T REALLY UNDER-STAND...
THE TURN THIS CONVER-SATION HAS TAKEN.
UMM...
SO IN OTHER WORDS...
...YOU HATE CATS, SOHMA-KUN?
HUH ...?
....
キンコーン KIN (DING) KOOON (DONG)
カンコーン KAN (DANG) KOOON
BA (SWISH)
WHAT!?
AAAAAH!
IT'S ALREADY THIS LATE...!? MY JOB...!!
I'M GONNA BE LAAATE!
I'M SORRY, SOHMA-KUN! I HAVE TO GET TO WORK!
HONDA-SAN...

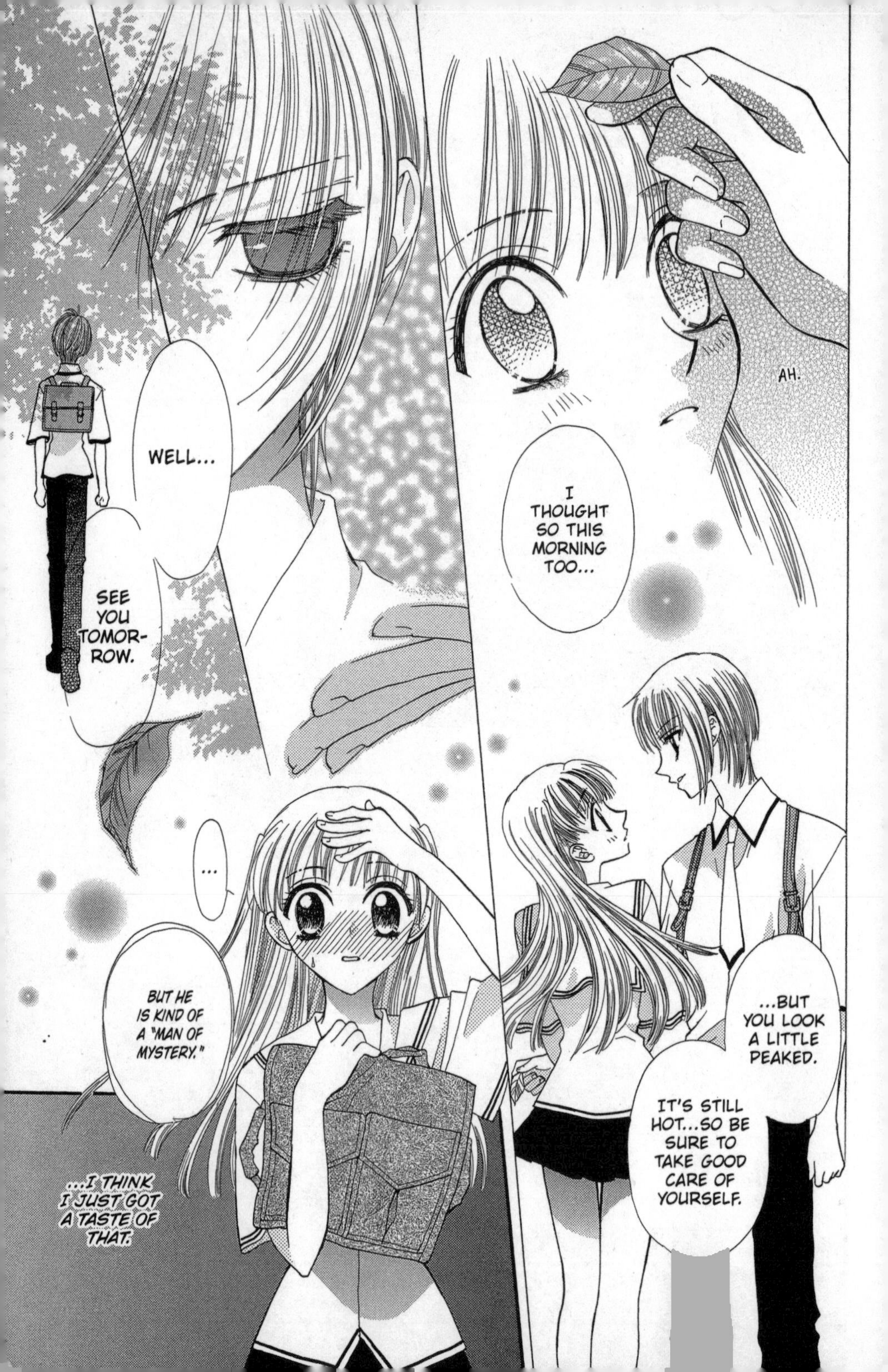
AH.
I THOUGHT SO THIS MORNING TOO...
WELL...
SEE YOU TOMOR-ROW.
...BUT YOU LOOK A LITTLE PEAKED.
IT'S STILL HOT...SO BE SURE TO TAKE GOOD CARE OF YOURSELF.
...
BUT HE IS KIND OF A "MAN OF MYSTERY."
...I THINK I JUST GOT A TASTE OF THAT.

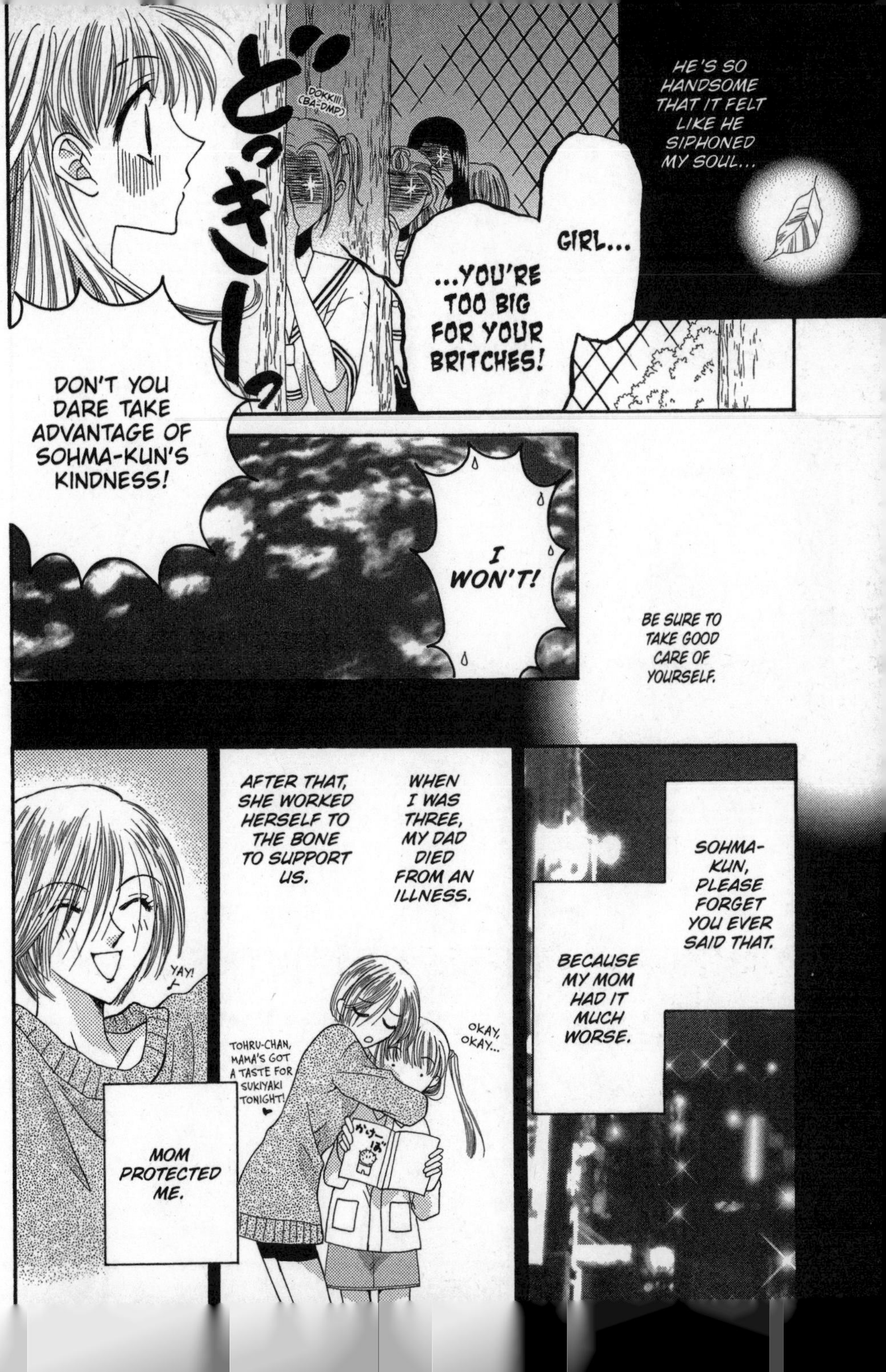
HE'S SO HANDSOME THAT IT FELT LIKE HE SIPHONED MY SOUL...
GIRL...
...YOU'RE TOO BIG FOR YOUR BRITCHES!
DOKKI!! (BA-DMP)
DON'T YOU DARE TAKE ADVANTAGE OF SOHMA-KUN'S KINDNESS!
BE SURE TO TAKE GOOD CARE OF YOURSELF.
I WON'T!
SOHMA-KUN, PLEASE FORGET YOU EVER SAID THAT.
BECAUSE MY MOM HAD IT MUCH WORSE.
WHEN I WAS THREE, MY DAD DIED FROM AN ILLNESS.
AFTER THAT, SHE WORKED HERSELF TO THE BONE TO SUPPORT US.
YAY!
OKAY, OKAY...
TOHRU-CHAN, MAMA'S GOT A TASTE FOR SUKIYAKI TONIGHT!
MOM PROTECTED ME.

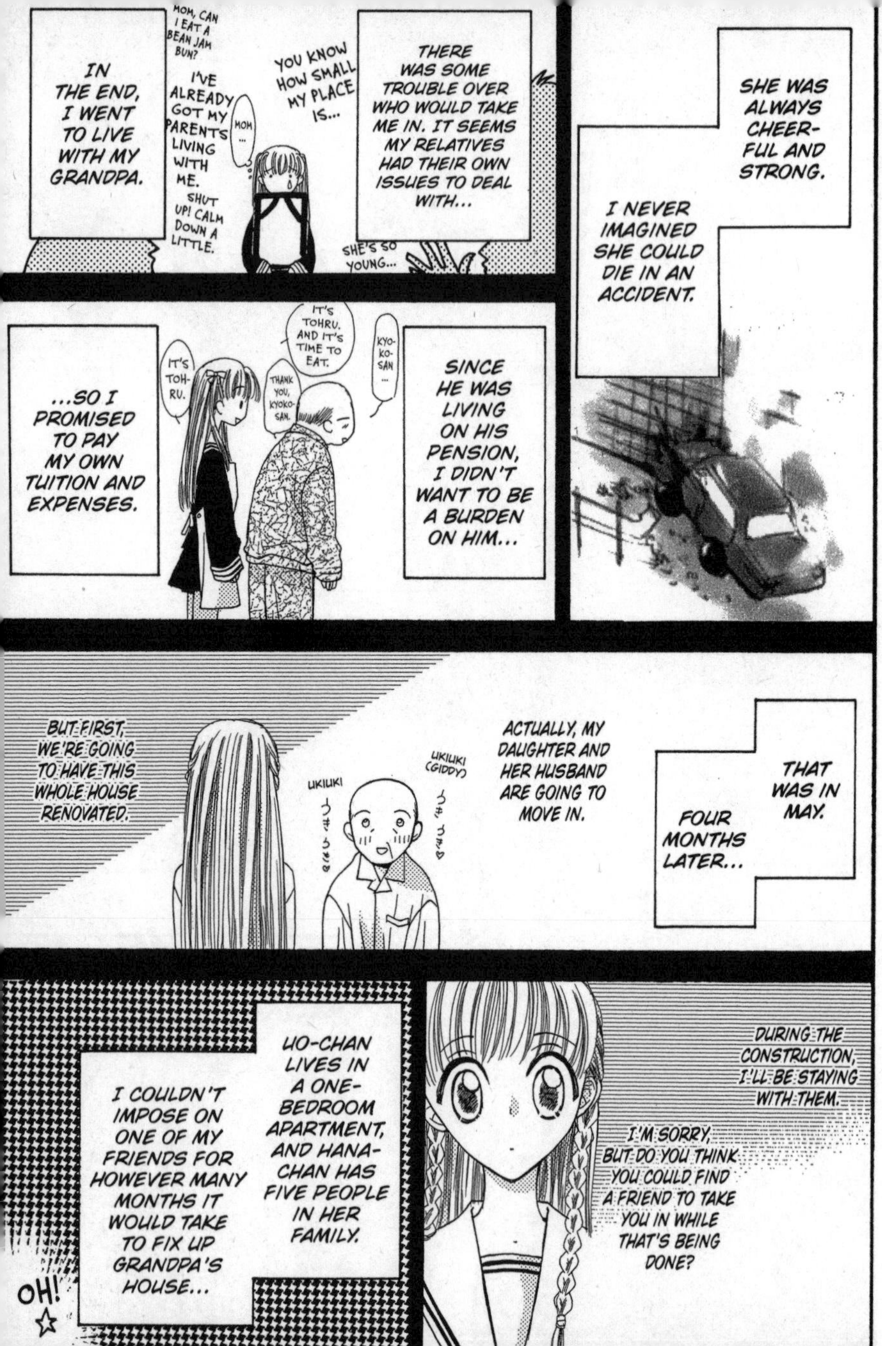
SHE WAS ALWAYS CHEERFUL AND STRONG.
I NEVER IMAGINED SHE COULD DIE IN AN ACCIDENT.
THERE WAS SOME TROUBLE OVER WHO WOULD TAKE ME IN. IT SEEMS MY RELATIVES HAD THEIR OWN ISSUES TO DEAL WITH...
YOU KNOW HOW SMALL MY PLACE IS...
MOM, CAN I EAT A BEAN JAM BUN?
I'VE ALREADY GOT MY PARENTS LIVING WITH ME.
MOM...
SHUT UP! CALM DOWN A LITTLE.
SHE'S SO YOUNG...
IN THE END, I WENT TO LIVE WITH MY GRANDPA.
SINCE HE WAS LIVING ON HIS PENSION, I DIDN'T WANT TO BE A BURDEN ON HIM...
KYO-KO-SAN...
IT'S TOHRU. AND IT'S TIME TO EAT.
THANK YOU, KYOKO-SAN.
IT'S TOH-RU.
...SO I PROMISED TO PAY MY OWN TUITION AND EXPENSES.
THAT WAS IN MAY.
FOUR MONTHS LATER...
ACTUALLY, MY DAUGHTER AND HER HUSBAND ARE GOING TO MOVE IN.
UKIUKI (GIDDY)
UKIUKI
BUT FIRST, WE'RE GOING TO HAVE THIS WHOLE HOUSE RENOVATED.
DURING THE CONSTRUCTION, I'LL BE STAYING WITH THEM.
I'M SORRY, BUT DO YOU THINK YOU COULD FIND A FRIEND TO TAKE YOU IN WHILE THAT'S BEING DONE?
UO-CHAN LIVES IN A ONE-BEDROOM APARTMENT, AND HANA-CHAN HAS FIVE PEOPLE IN HER FAMILY.
I COULDN'T IMPOSE ON ONE OF MY FRIENDS FOR HOWEVER MANY MONTHS IT WOULD TAKE TO FIX UP GRANDPA'S HOUSE...
OH!

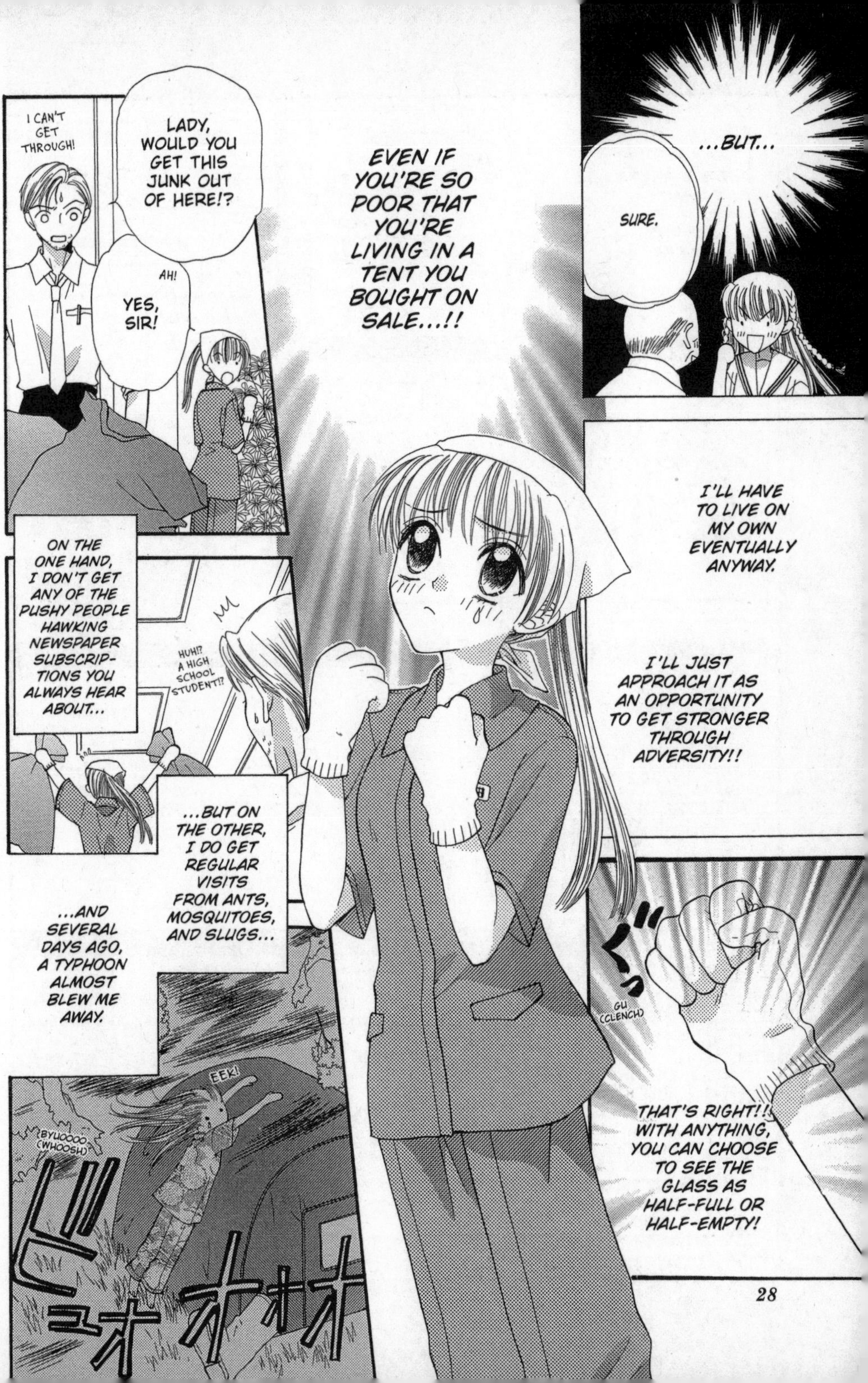
...BUT...
SURE.
EVEN IF YOU'RE SO POOR THAT YOU'RE LIVING IN A TENT YOU BOUGHT ON SALE...!!
LADY, WOULD YOU GET THIS JUNK OUT OF HERE!?
I CAN'T GET THROUGH!
AH!
YES, SIR!
I'LL HAVE TO LIVE ON MY OWN EVENTUALLY ANYWAY.
I'LL JUST APPROACH IT AS AN OPPORTUNITY TO GET STRONGER THROUGH ADVERSITY!!
GU (CLENCH)
THAT'S RIGHT!! WITH ANYTHING, YOU CAN CHOOSE TO SEE THE GLASS AS HALF-FULL OR HALF-EMPTY!
ON THE ONE HAND, I DON'T GET ANY OF THE PUSHY PEOPLE HAWKING NEWSPAPER SUBSCRIP-TIONS YOU ALWAYS HEAR ABOUT...
HUH!? A HIGH SCHOOL STUDENT!?
...BUT ON THE OTHER, I DO GET REGULAR VISITS FROM ANTS, MOSQUITOES, AND SLUGS...
...AND SEVERAL DAYS AGO, A TYPHOON ALMOST BLEW ME AWAY.
EEK!
BYUOOOO (WHOOSH)

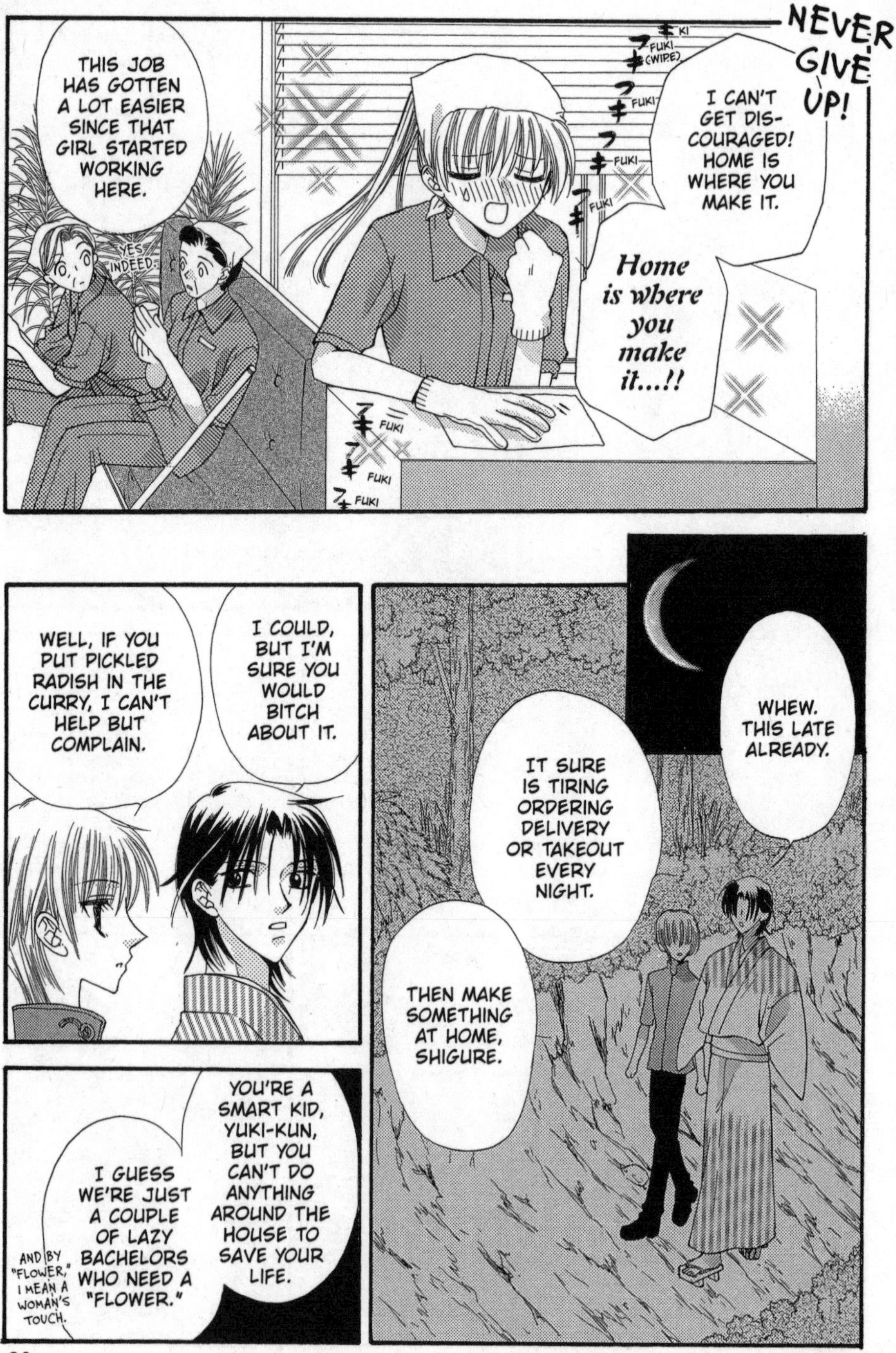
NEVER GIVE UP!
I CAN'T GET DISCOURAGED! HOME IS WHERE YOU MAKE IT.
KI
FUKI (WIPE)
FUKI
FUKI
FUKI
Home is where you make it...!!
THIS JOB HAS GOTTEN A LOT EASIER SINCE THAT GIRL STARTED WORKING HERE.
YES INDEED.
FUKI
FUKI
FUKI
WHEW. THIS LATE ALREADY.
IT SURE IS TIRING ORDERING DELIVERY OR TAKEOUT EVERY NIGHT.
THEN MAKE SOMETHING AT HOME, SHIGURE.
I COULD, BUT I'M SURE YOU WOULD BITCH ABOUT IT.
WELL, IF YOU PUT PICKLED RADISH IN THE CURRY, I CAN'T HELP BUT COMPLAIN.
YOU'RE A SMART KID, YUKI-KUN, BUT YOU CAN'T DO ANYTHING AROUND THE HOUSE TO SAVE YOUR LIFE.
I GUESS WE'RE JUST A COUPLE OF LAZY BACHELORS WHO NEED A "FLOWER."
AND BY "FLOWER," I MEAN A WOMAN'S TOUCH.

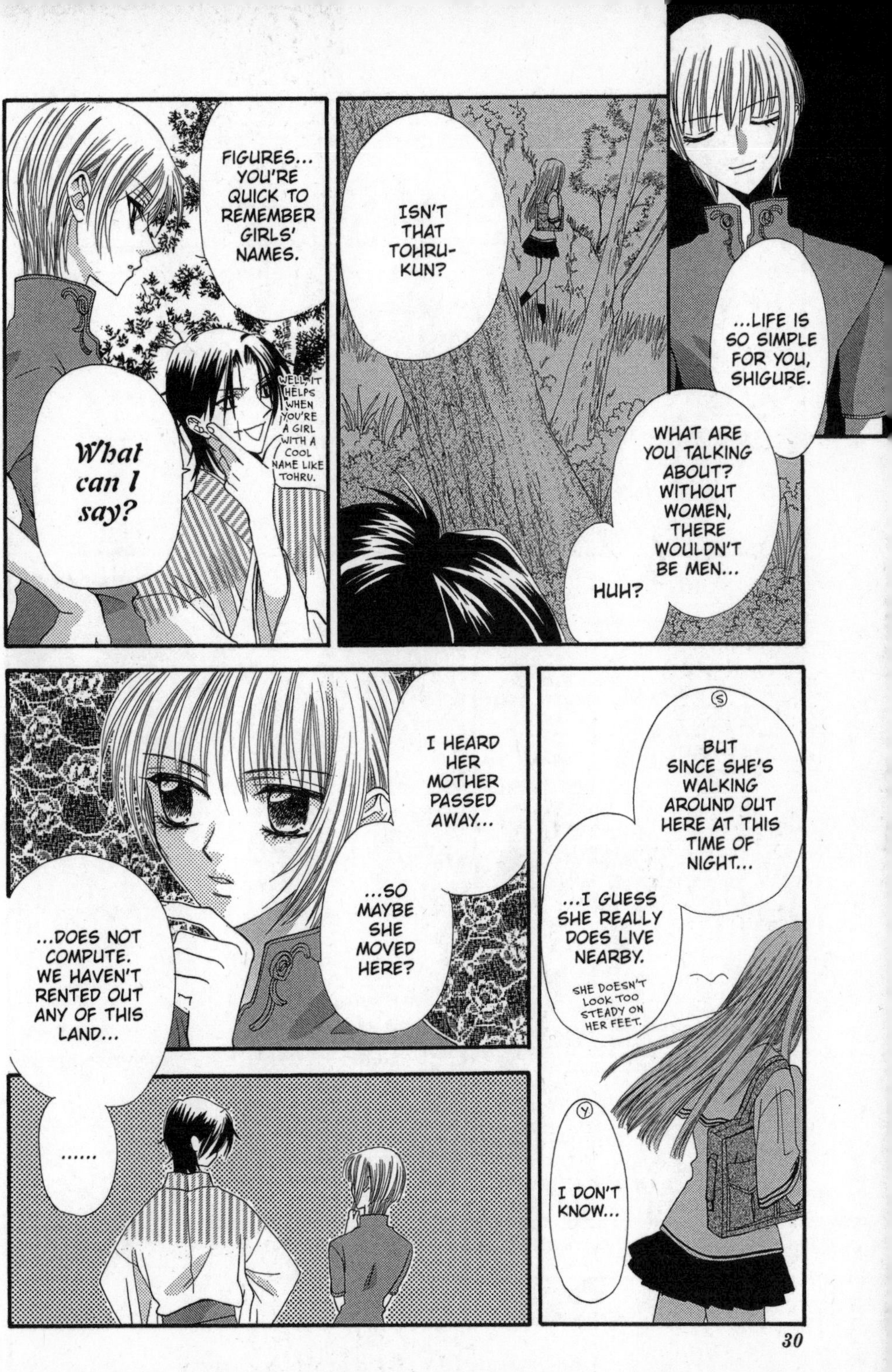

...LIFE IS SO SIMPLE FOR YOU, SHIGURE.
WHAT ARE YOU TALKING ABOUT? WITHOUT WOMEN, THERE WOULDN'T BE MEN...
ISN'T THAT TOHRU-KUN?
HUH?
FIGURES... YOU'RE QUICK TO REMEMBER GIRLS' NAMES.
What can I say?
WELL, IT HELPS WHEN YOU'RE A GIRL WITH A COOL NAME LIKE TOHRU.
BUT SINCE SHE'S WALKING AROUND OUT HERE AT THIS TIME OF NIGHT...
...I GUESS SHE REALLY DOES LIVE NEARBY.
SHE DOESN'T LOOK TOO STEADY ON HER FEET.
I DON'T KNOW...
I HEARD HER MOTHER PASSED AWAY...
...SO MAYBE SHE MOVED HERE?
...DOES NOT COMPUTE. WE HAVEN'T RENTED OUT ANY OF THIS LAND...
......

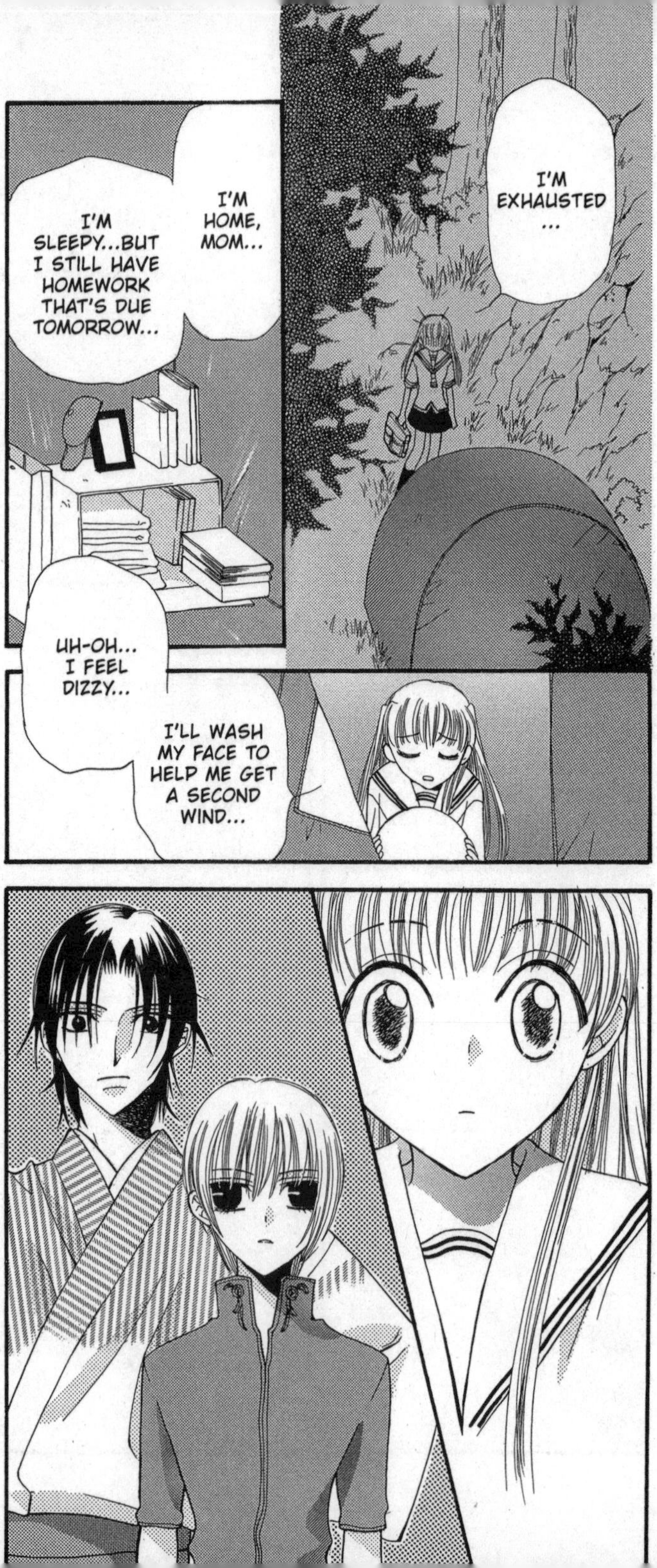
I'M EXHAUSTED ...
I'M HOME, MOM...
I'M SLEEPY...BUT I STILL HAVE HOMEWORK THAT'S DUE TOMORROW...
UH-OH... I FEEL DIZZY...
I'LL WASH MY FACE TO HELP ME GET A SECOND WIND...
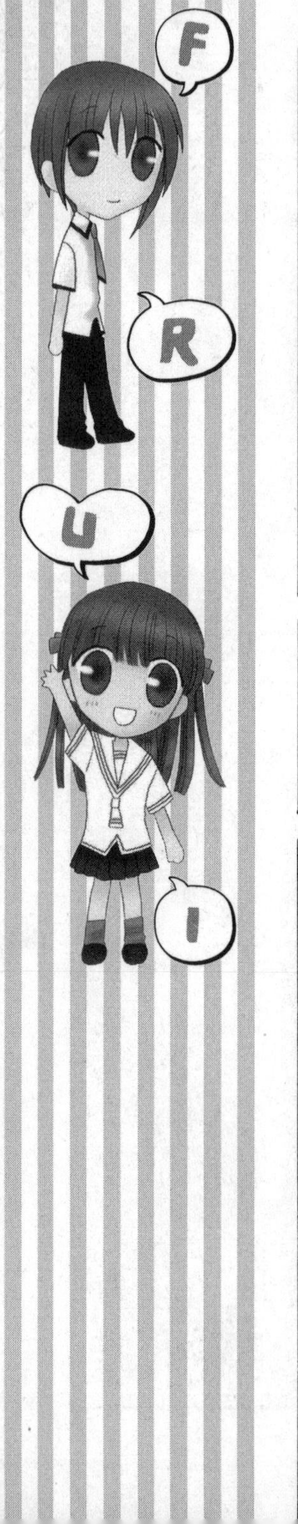
F
R
U
I

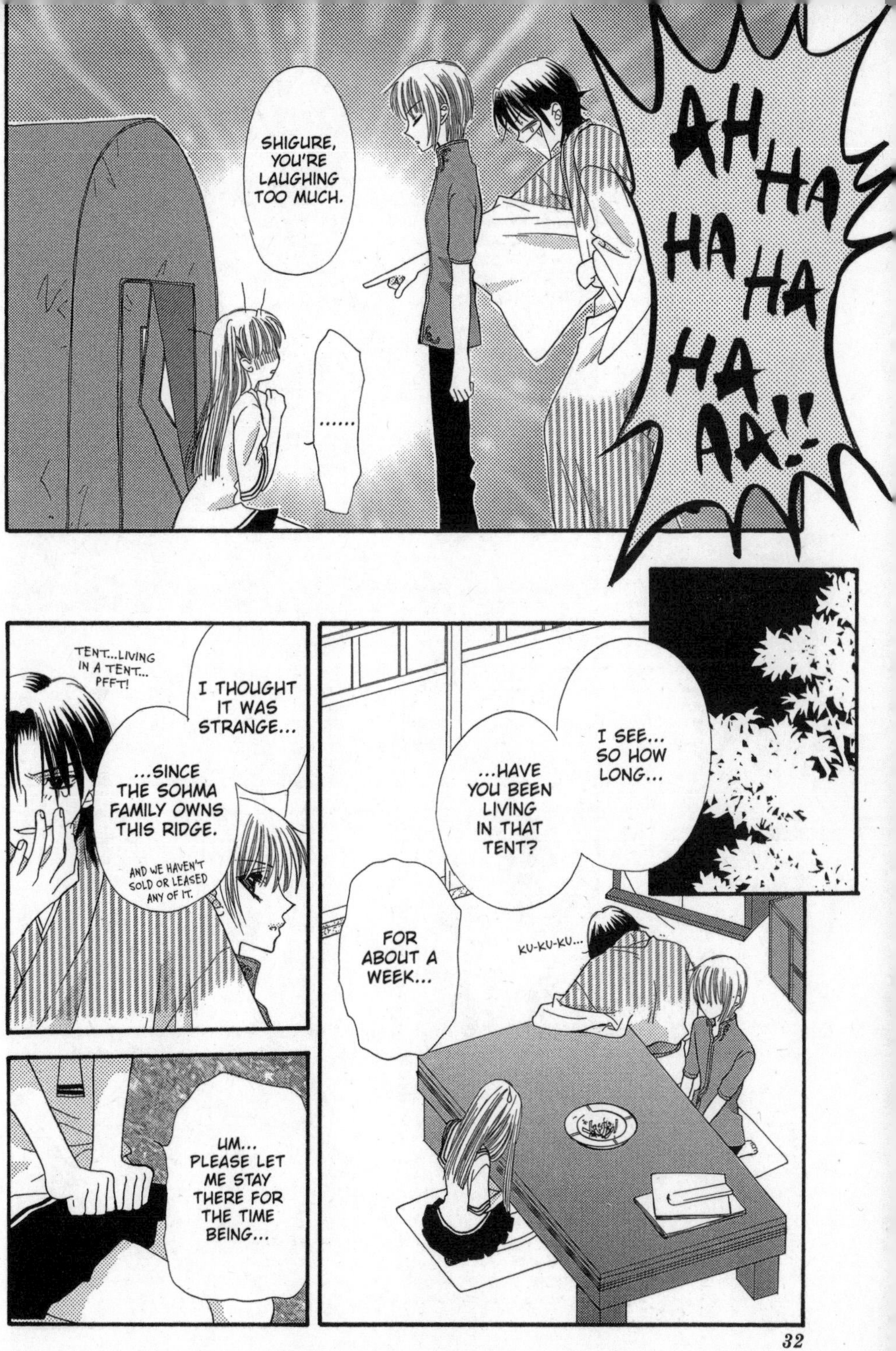
AH HA HA HA HA HA AA!!
SHIGURE, YOU'RE LAUGHING TOO MUCH.
......
I SEE... SO HOW LONG...
...HAVE YOU BEEN LIVING IN THAT TENT?
KU-KU-KU...
FOR ABOUT A WEEK...
TENT...LIVING IN A TENT... PFFT!
I THOUGHT IT WAS STRANGE...
...SINCE THE SOHMA FAMILY OWNS THIS RIDGE.
AND WE HAVEN'T SOLD OR LEASED ANY OF IT.
UM... PLEASE LET ME STAY THERE FOR THE TIME BEING...

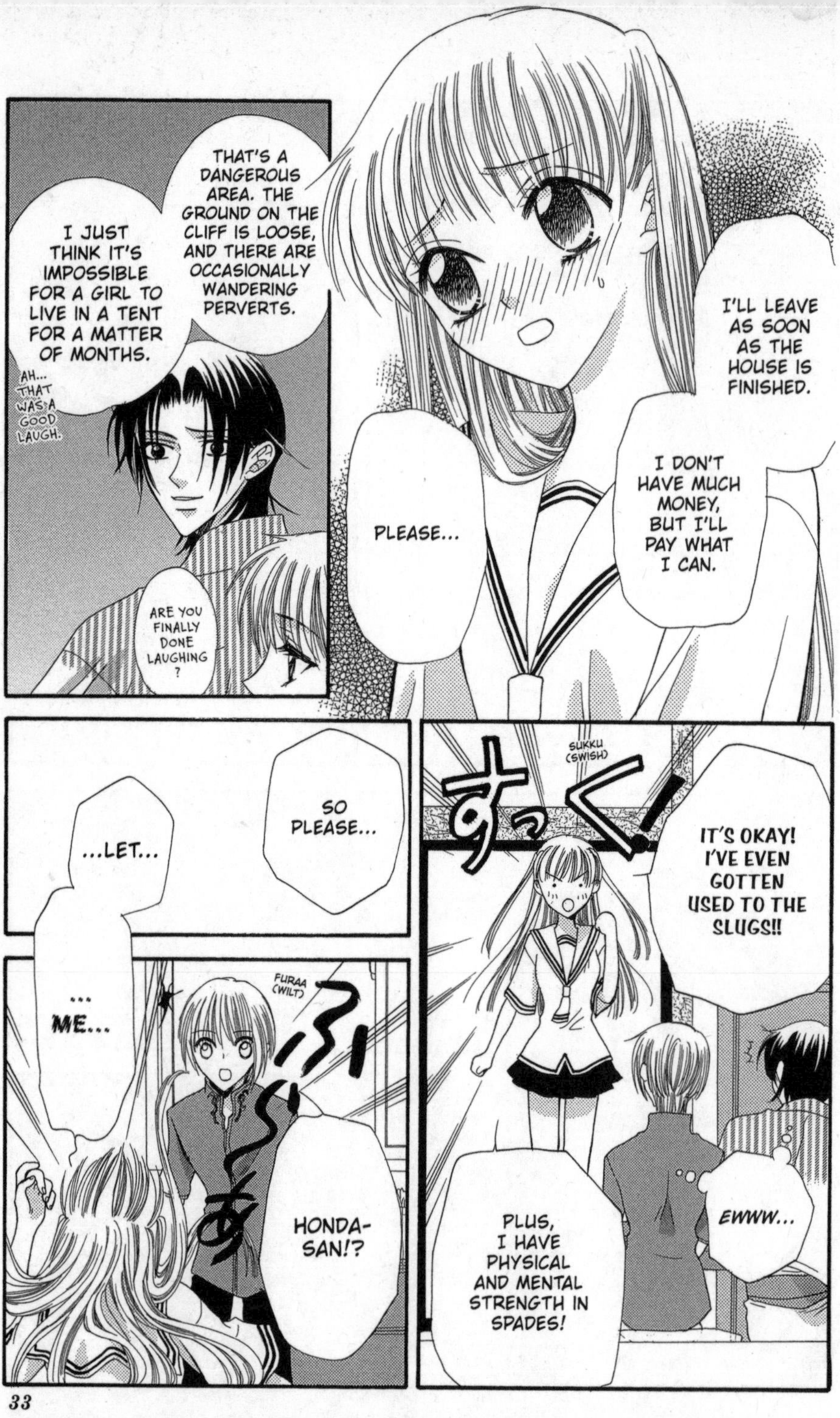
I'LL LEAVE AS SOON AS THE HOUSE IS FINISHED.
I DON'T HAVE MUCH MONEY, BUT I'LL PAY WHAT I CAN.
PLEASE...
THAT'S A DANGEROUS AREA. THE GROUND ON THE CLIFF IS LOOSE, AND THERE ARE OCCASIONALLY WANDERING PERVERTS.
I JUST THINK IT'S IMPOSSIBLE FOR A GIRL TO LIVE IN A TENT FOR A MATTER OF MONTHS.
AH... THAT WAS A GOOD LAUGH.
ARE YOU FINALLY DONE LAUGHING?
SUKKU (SWISH)
IT'S OKAY! I'VE EVEN GOTTEN USED TO THE SLUGS!!
EWWW...
PLUS, I HAVE PHYSICAL AND MENTAL STRENGTH IN SPADES!
SO PLEASE...
...LET...
...ME...
FURAA (WILT)
HONDA-SAN!?

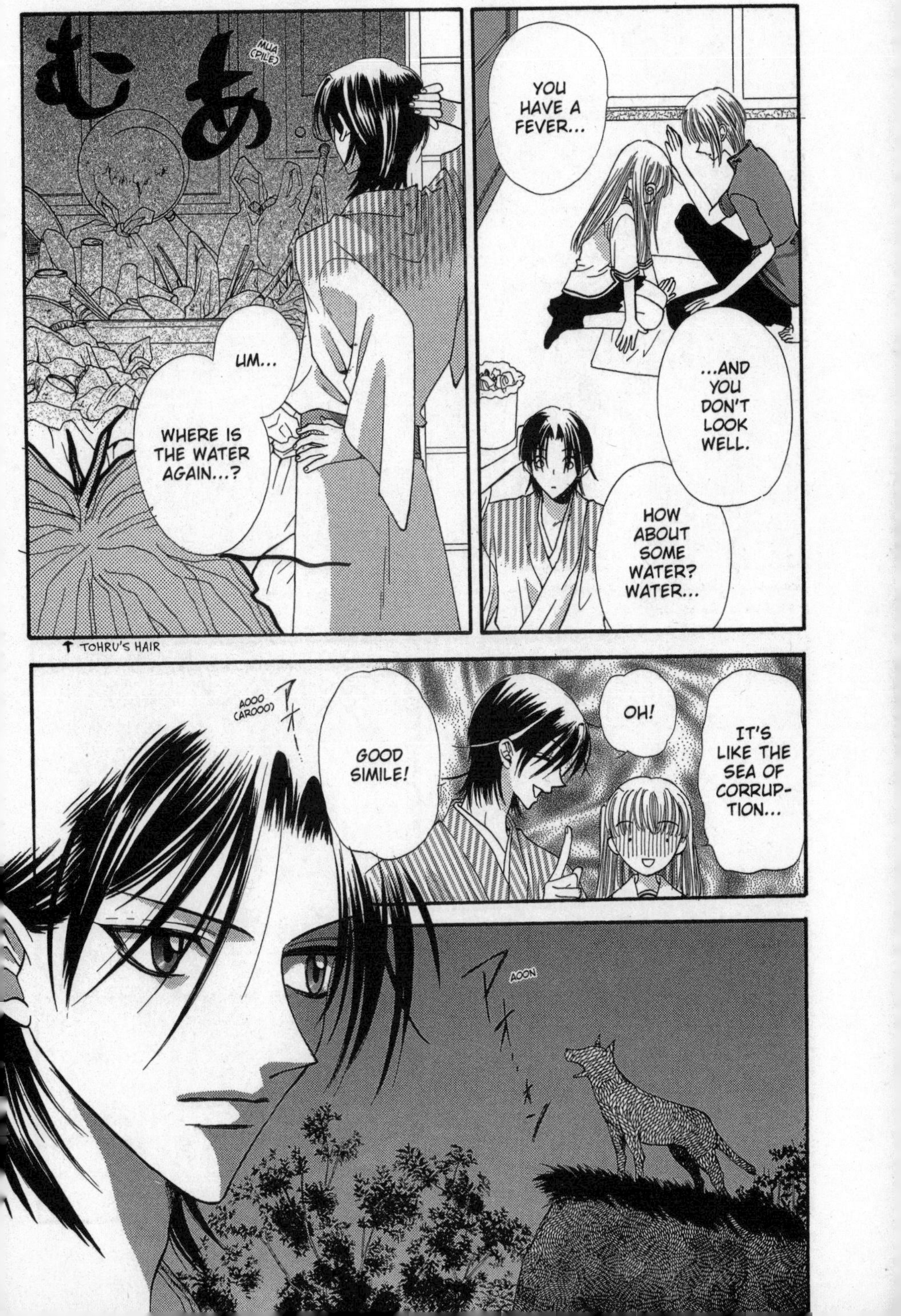
YOU HAVE A FEVER...
...AND YOU DON'T LOOK WELL.
HOW ABOUT SOME WATER? WATER...
MUA (PILE)
UM...
WHERE IS THE WATER AGAIN...?
TOHRU'S HAIR
IT'S LIKE THE SEA OF CORRUP-TION...
OH!
GOOD SIMILE!
AOOO (AROOO)
AOON

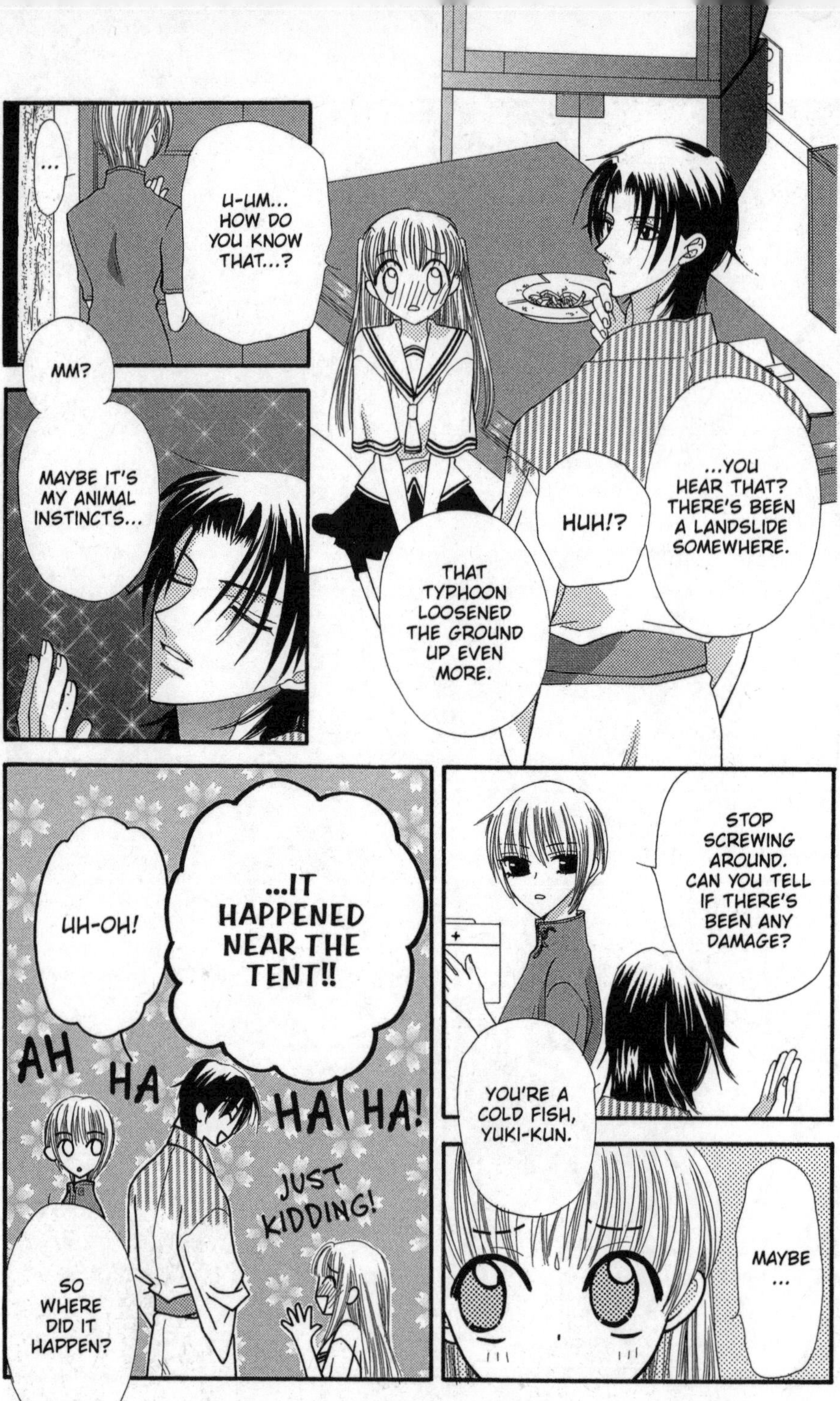
...YOU HEAR THAT? THERE'S BEEN A LANDSLIDE SOMEWHERE.
HUH!?
THAT TYPHOON LOOSENED THE GROUND UP EVEN MORE.
U-UM... HOW DO YOU KNOW THAT...?
...
MM?
MAYBE IT'S MY ANIMAL INSTINCTS...
STOP SCREWING AROUND. CAN YOU TELL IF THERE'S BEEN ANY DAMAGE?
YOU'RE A COLD FISH, YUKI-KUN.
MAYBE...
...IT HAPPENED NEAR THE TENT!!
UH-OH!
AH HA HA HA!
JUST KIDDING!
SO WHERE DID IT HAPPEN?

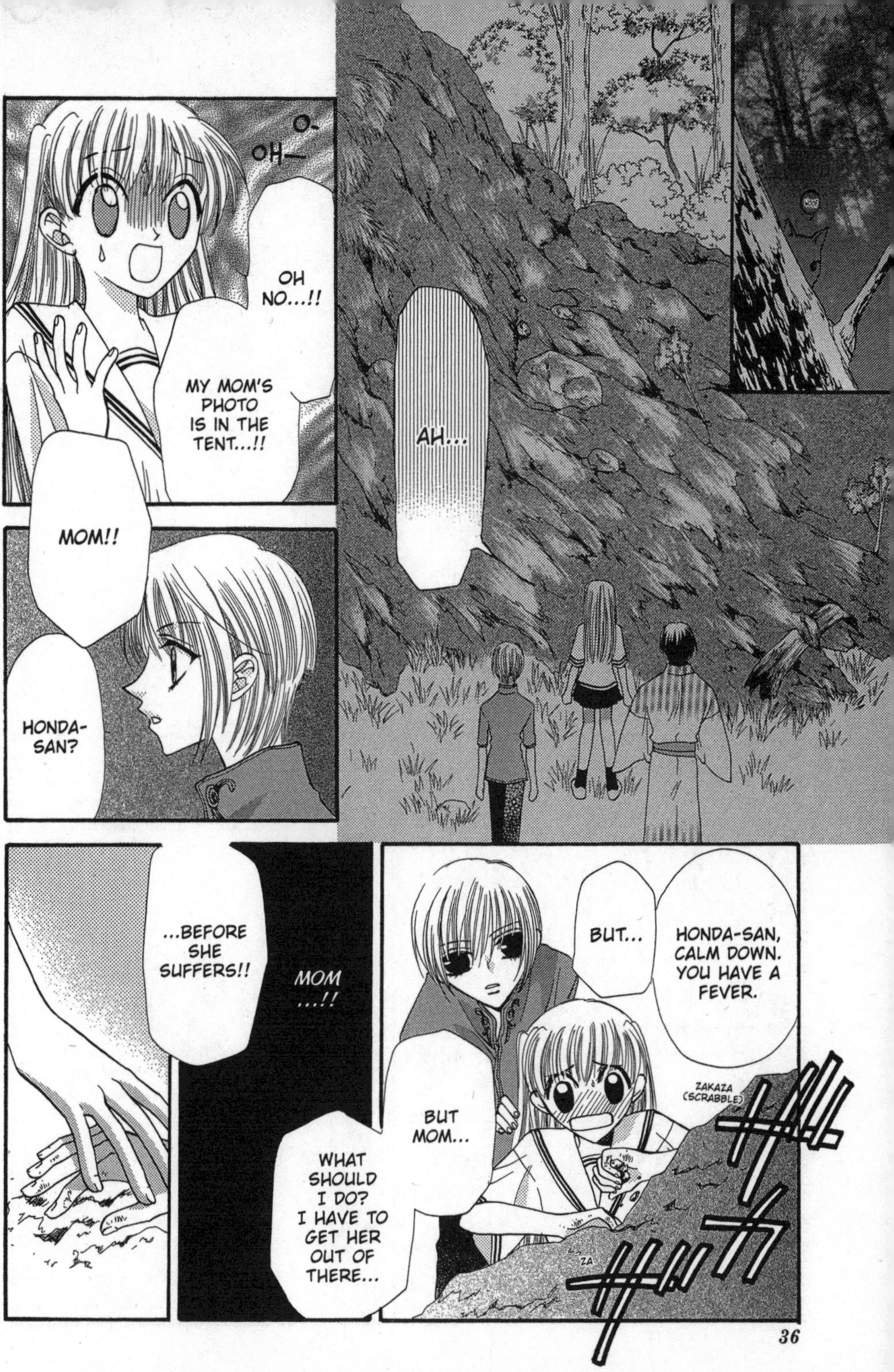
AH...
O-
OH—
OH NO...!!
MY MOM'S PHOTO IS IN THE TENT...!!
MOM!!
HONDA-SAN?
HONDA-SAN, CALM DOWN. YOU HAVE A FEVER.
BUT...
ZAKAZA (SCRABBLE)
BUT MOM...
WHAT SHOULD I DO? I HAVE TO GET HER OUT OF THERE...
ZA
MOM ...!!
...BEFORE SHE SUFFERS!!

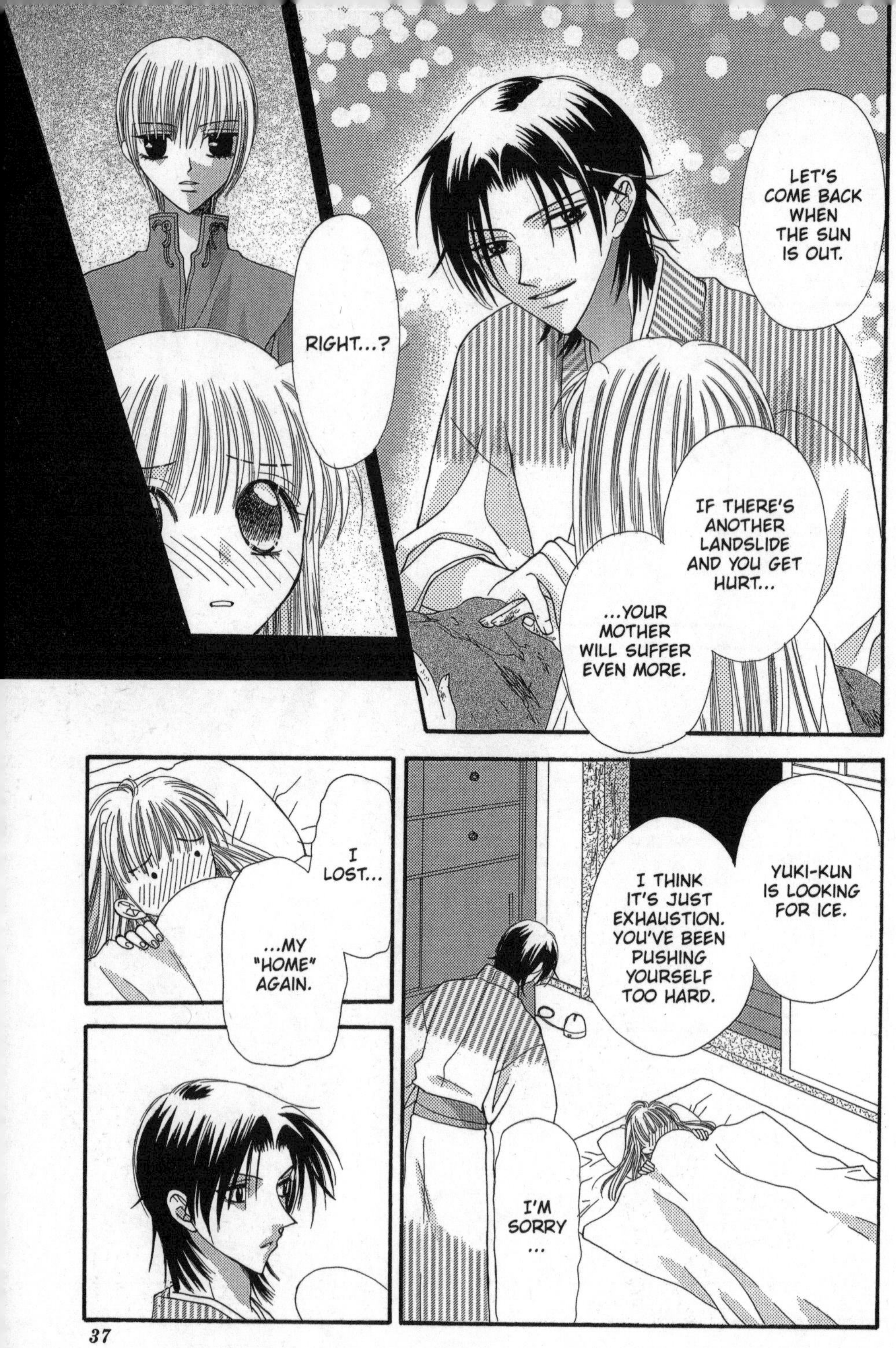
LET'S COME BACK WHEN THE SUN IS OUT.
IF THERE'S ANOTHER LANDSLIDE AND YOU GET HURT...
...YOUR MOTHER WILL SUFFER EVEN MORE.
RIGHT...?
YUKI-KUN IS LOOKING FOR ICE.
I THINK IT'S JUST EXHAUSTION. YOU'VE BEEN PUSHING YOURSELF TOO HARD.
I'M SORRY...
I LOST...
...MY "HOME" AGAIN.

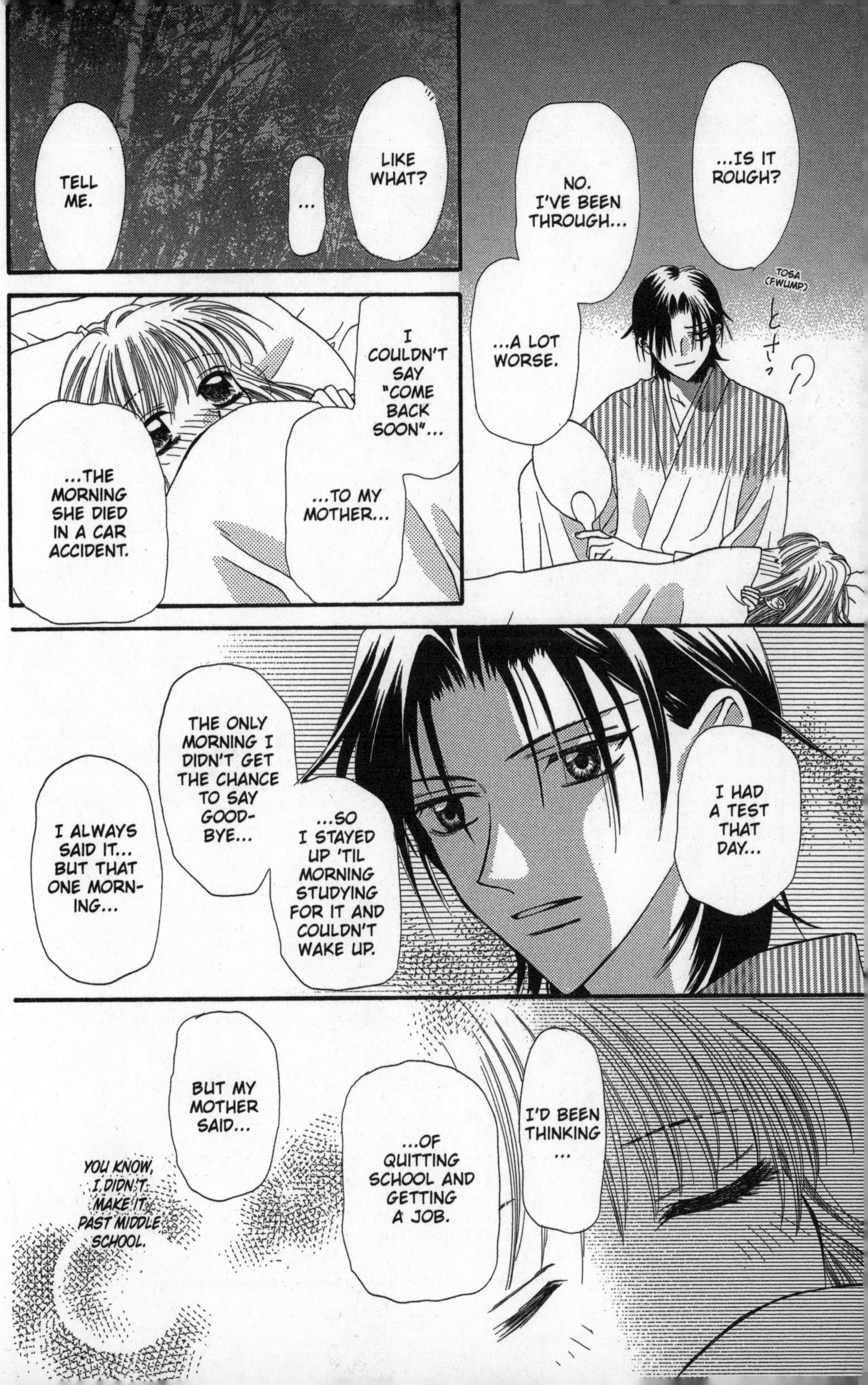
...IS IT ROUGH?
TOSA (F'WUMP)
とさっ
NO. I'VE BEEN THROUGH...
...A LOT WORSE.
LIKE WHAT?
...
TELL ME.
I COULDN'T SAY "COME BACK SOON"...
...TO MY MOTHER...
...THE MORNING SHE DIED IN A CAR ACCIDENT.
I HAD A TEST THAT DAY...
...SO I STAYED UP 'TIL MORNING STUDYING FOR IT AND COULDN'T WAKE UP.
I ALWAYS SAID IT... BUT THAT ONE MORN-ING...
THE ONLY MORNING I DIDN'T GET THE CHANCE TO SAY GOOD-BYE...
I'D BEEN THINKING...
...OF QUITTING SCHOOL AND GETTING A JOB.
BUT MY MOTHER SAID...
YOU KNOW, I DIDN'T MAKE IT PAST MIDDLE SCHOOL.

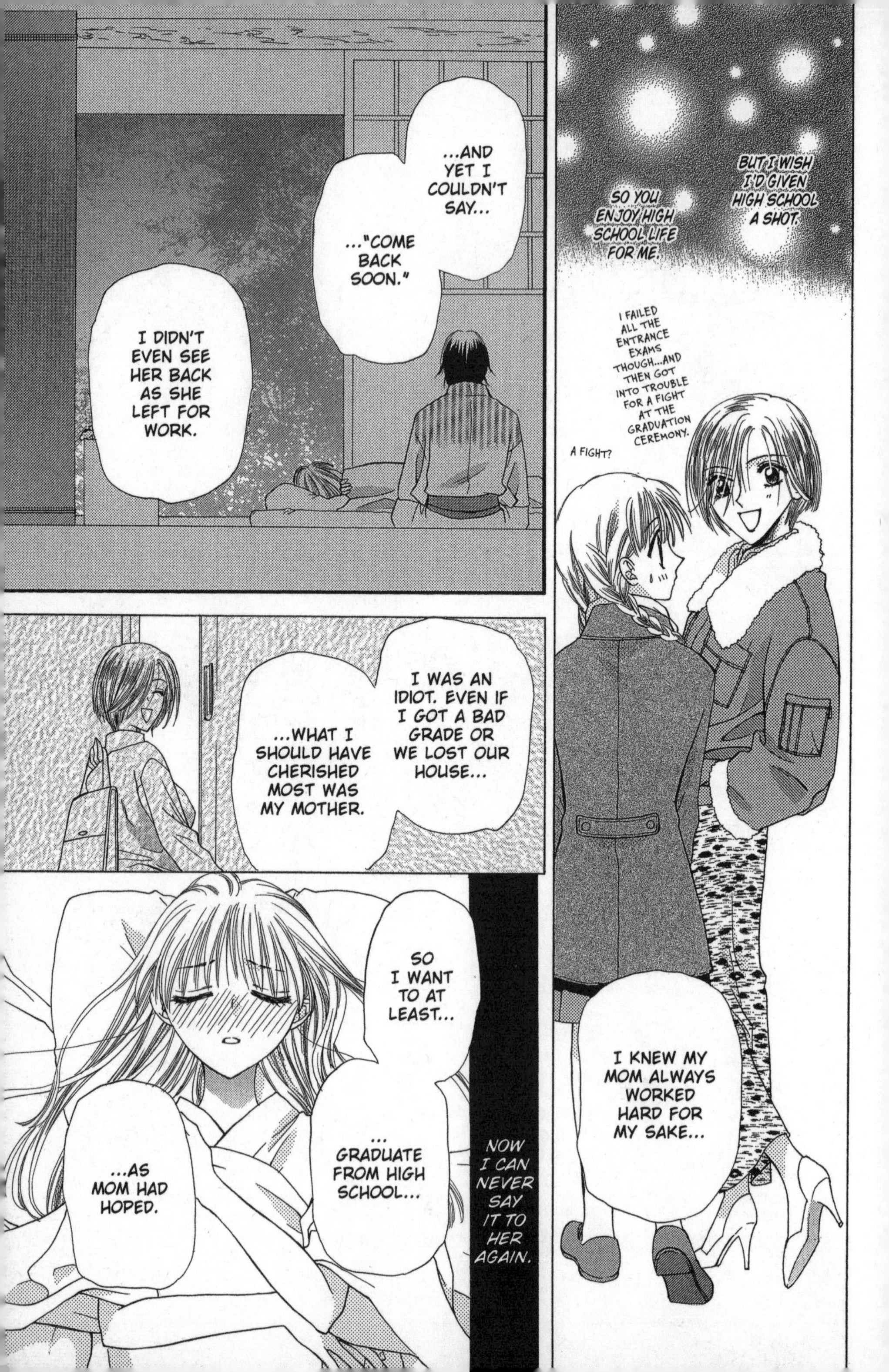
BUT I WISH I'D GIVEN HIGH SCHOOL A SHOT.
SO YOU ENJOY HIGH SCHOOL LIFE FOR ME.
I FAILED ALL THE ENTRANCE EXAMS THOUGH...AND THEN GOT INTO TROUBLE FOR A FIGHT AT THE GRADUATION CEREMONY.
A FIGHT?
I KNEW MY MOM ALWAYS WORKED HARD FOR MY SAKE...
...AND YET I COULDN'T SAY...
..."COME BACK SOON."
I DIDN'T EVEN SEE HER BACK AS SHE LEFT FOR WORK.
I WAS AN IDIOT. EVEN IF I GOT A BAD GRADE OR WE LOST OUR HOUSE...
...WHAT I SHOULD HAVE CHERISHED MOST WAS MY MOTHER.
NOW I CAN NEVER SAY IT TO HER AGAIN.
SO I WANT TO AT LEAST...
...GRADUATE FROM HIGH SCHOOL...
...AS MOM HAD HOPED.

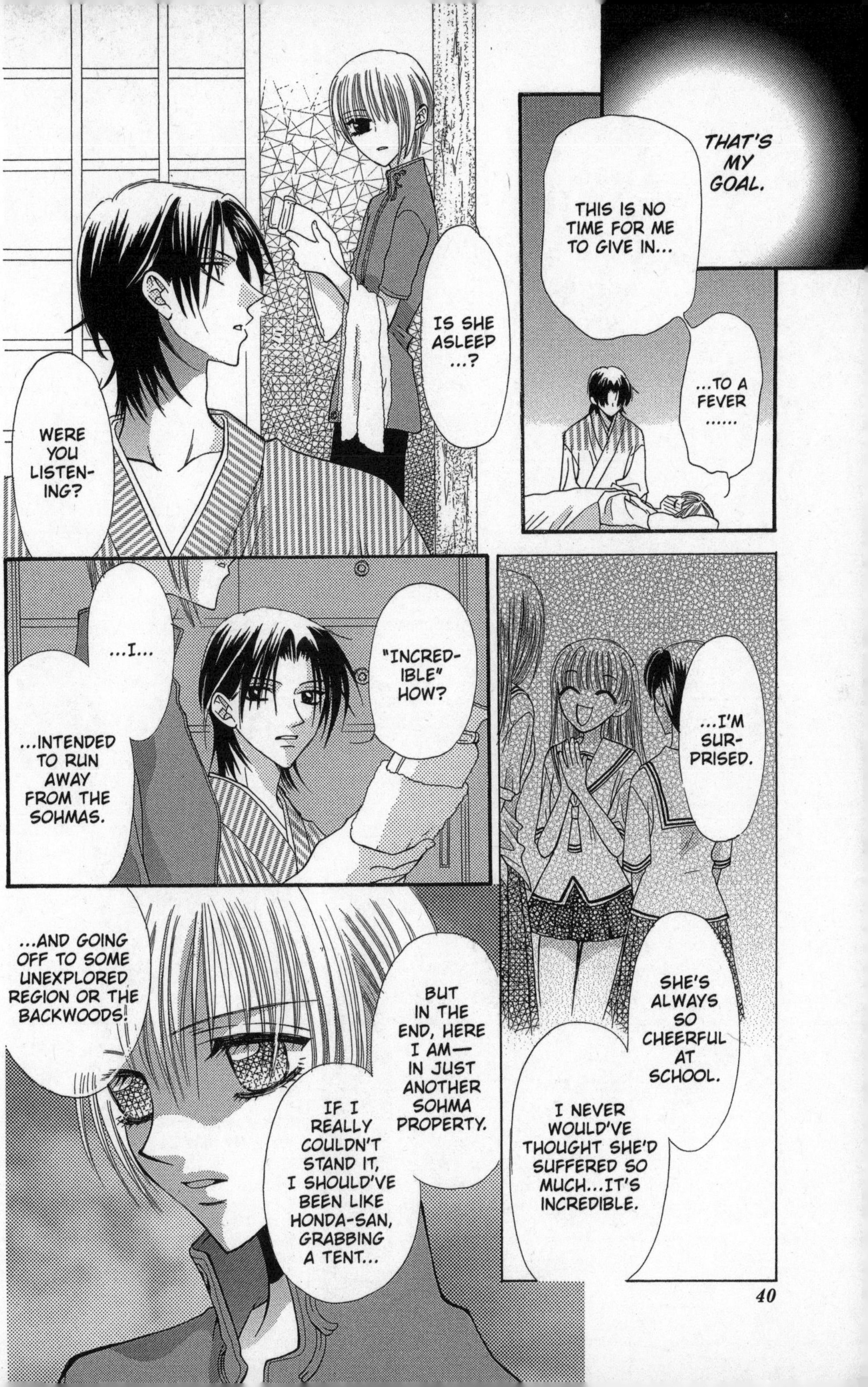
THAT'S MY GOAL.
THIS IS NO TIME FOR ME TO GIVE IN...
...TO A FEVER......
IS SHE ASLEEP ...?
WERE YOU LISTENING?
...I'M SURPRISED.
SHE'S ALWAYS SO CHEERFUL AT SCHOOL.
I NEVER WOULD'VE THOUGHT SHE'D SUFFERED SO MUCH...IT'S INCREDIBLE.
"INCREDIBLE" HOW?
...I...
...INTENDED TO RUN AWAY FROM THE SOHMAS.
BUT IN THE END, HERE I AM— IN JUST ANOTHER SOHMA PROPERTY.
IF I REALLY COULDN'T STAND IT, I SHOULD'VE BEEN LIKE HONDA-SAN, GRABBING A TENT...
...AND GOING OFF TO SOME UNEXPLORED REGION OR THE BACKWOODS!

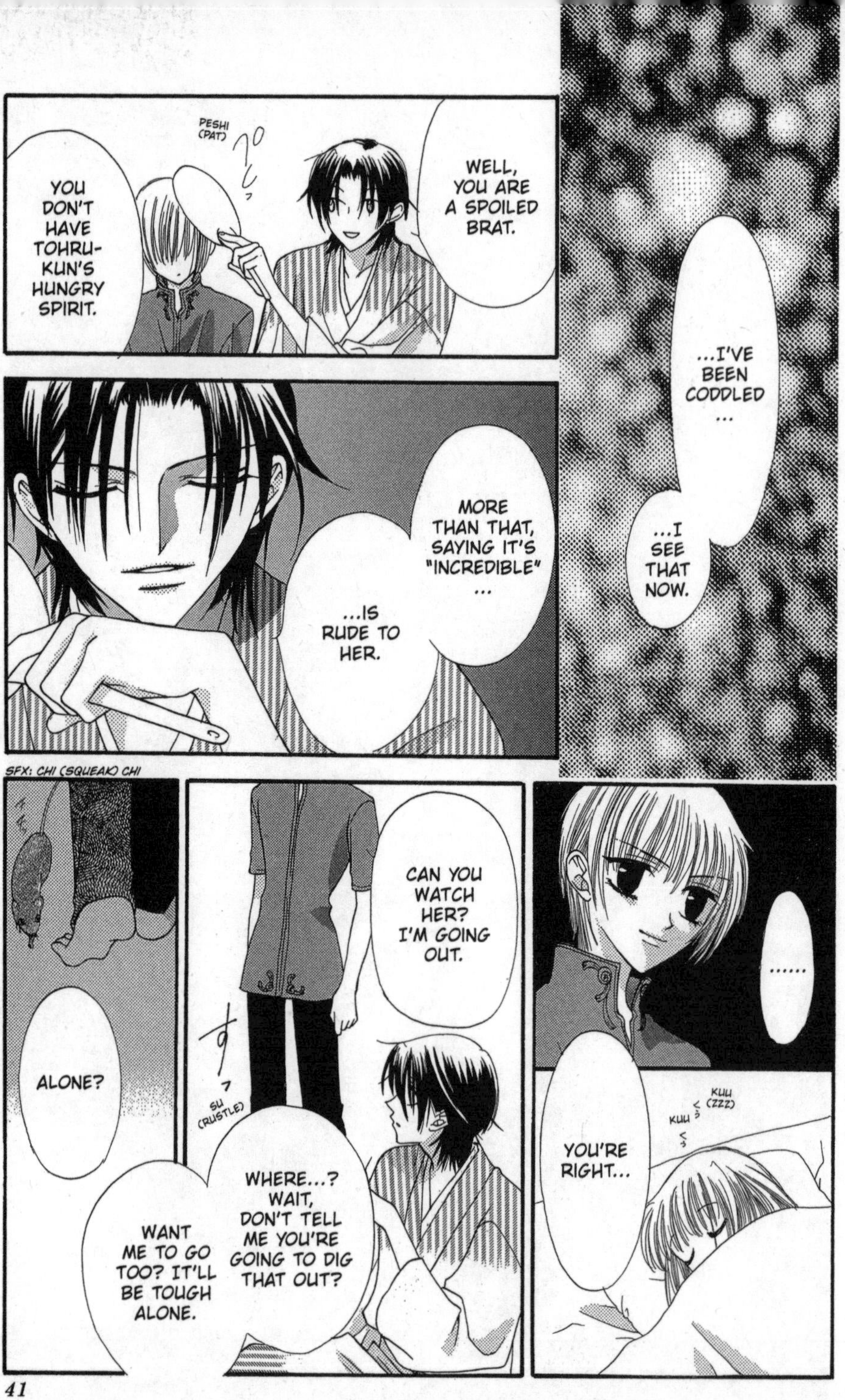
...I'VE BEEN CODDLED ...
...I SEE THAT NOW.
WELL, YOU ARE A SPOILED BRAT.
PESHI (PAT)
YOU DON'T HAVE TOHRU-KUN'S HUNGRY SPIRIT.
MORE THAN THAT, SAYING IT'S "INCREDIBLE" ...
...IS RUDE TO HER.
......
KUU (ZZZ) KUU
YOU'RE RIGHT...
CAN YOU WATCH HER? I'M GOING OUT.
SU (RUSTLE)
WHERE...? WAIT, DON'T TELL ME YOU'RE GOING TO DIG THAT OUT?
WANT ME TO GO TOO? IT'LL BE TOUGH ALONE.
SFX: CHI (SQUEAK) CHI
ALONE?

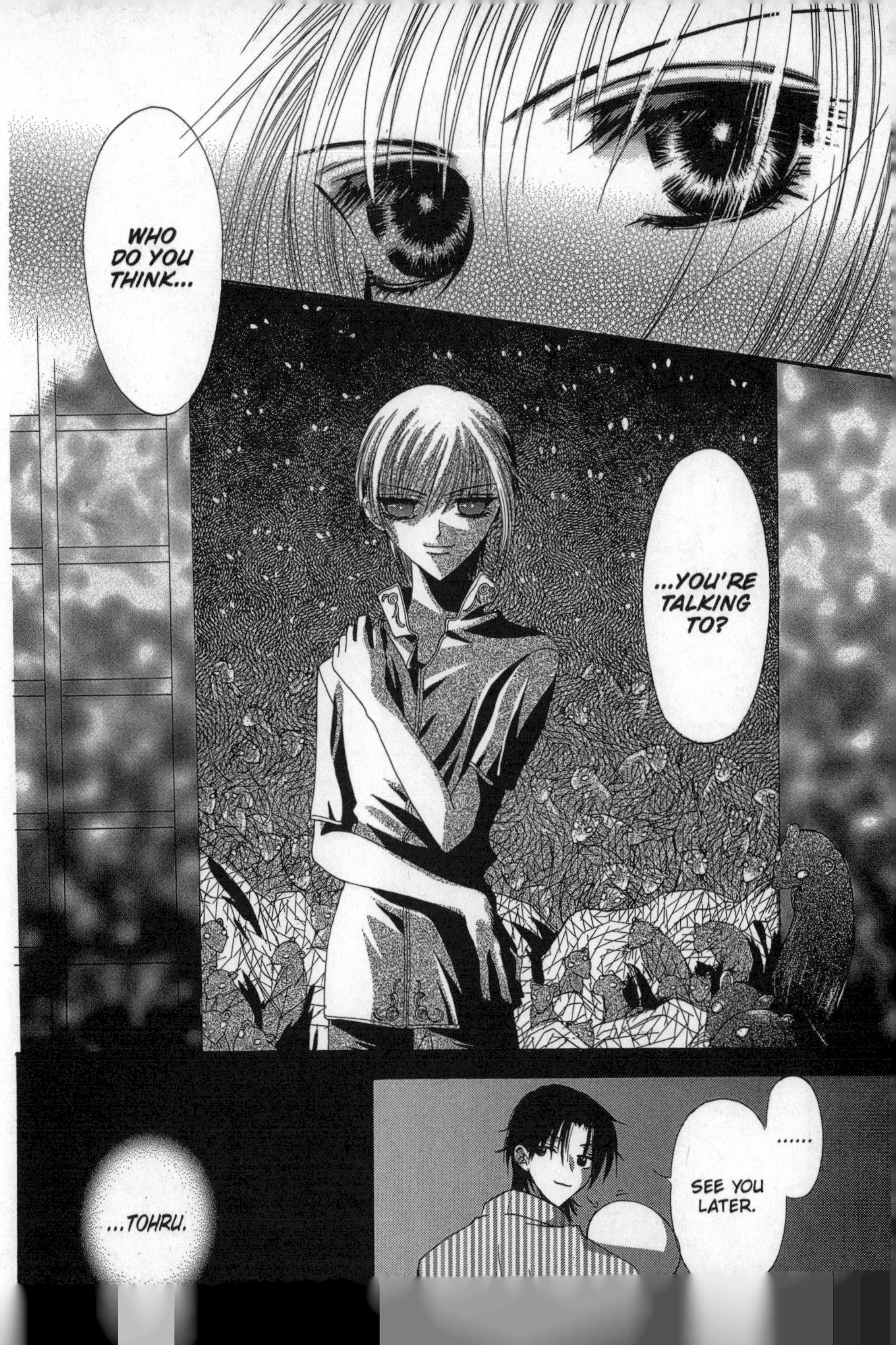
WHO DO YOU THINK...
...YOU'RE TALKING TO?
......
SEE YOU LATER.
...TOHRU.

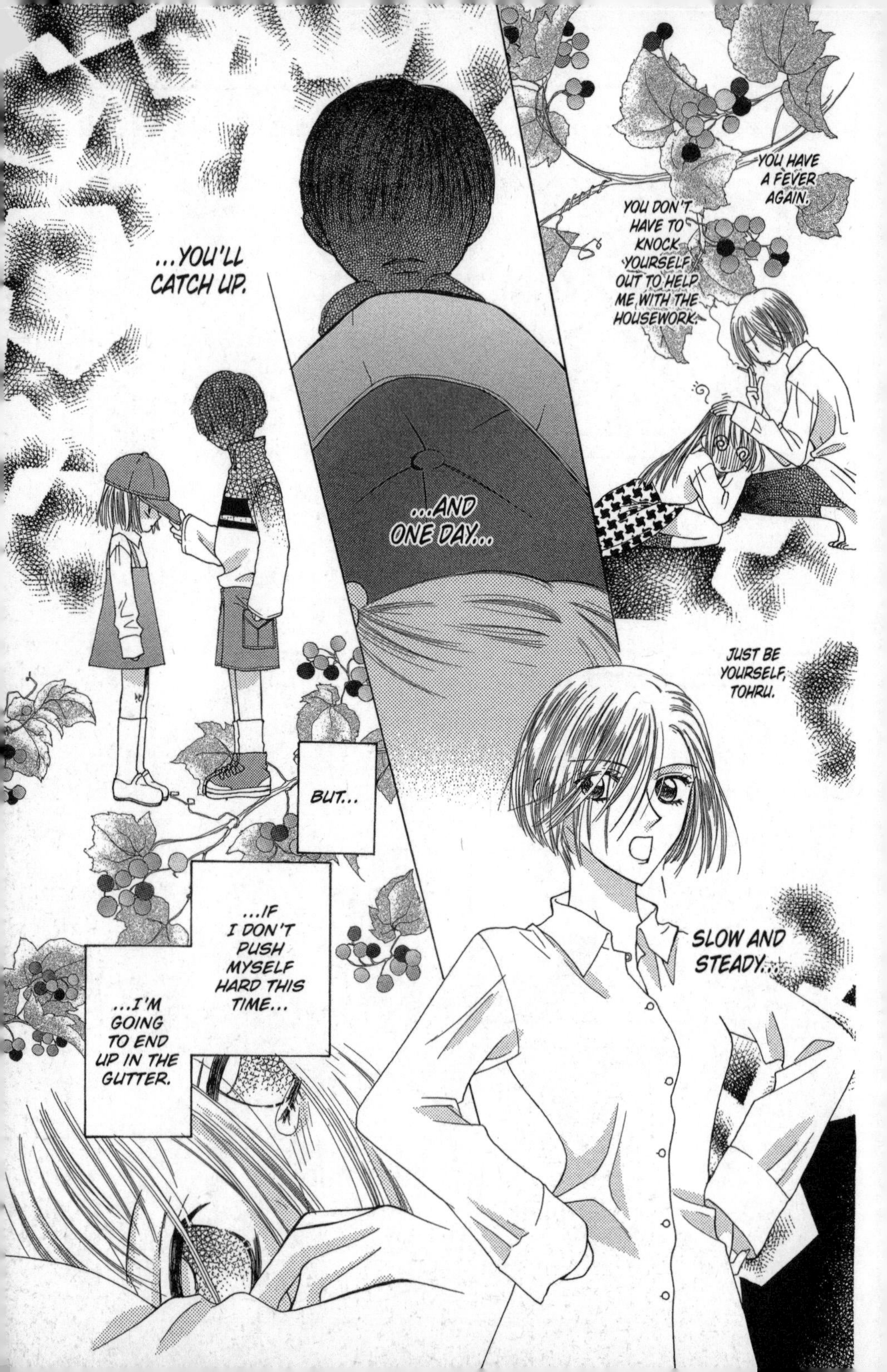
YOU HAVE A FEVER AGAIN.
YOU DON'T HAVE TO KNOCK YOURSELF OUT TO HELP ME WITH THE HOUSEWORK.
JUST BE YOURSELF, TOHRU.
SLOW AND STEADY...
...AND ONE DAY...
...YOU'LL CATCH UP.
BUT...
...IF I DON'T PUSH MYSELF HARD THIS TIME...
...I'M GOING TO END UP IN THE GUTTER.

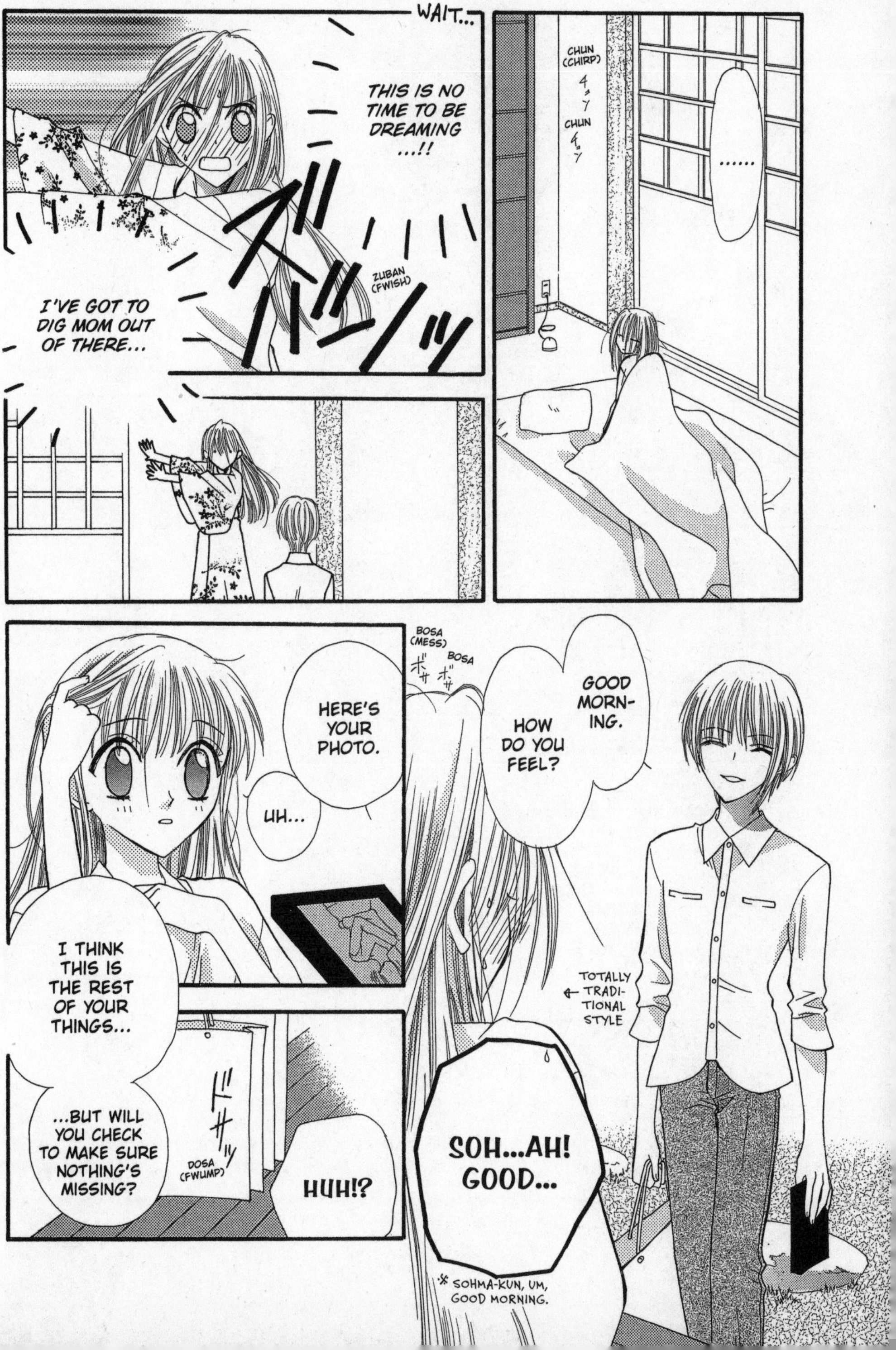

CHUN (CHIRP)
CHUN
......
WAIT...
THIS IS NO TIME TO BE DREAMING ...!!
ZUBAN (FWISH)
I'VE GOT TO DIG MOM OUT OF THERE...
BOSA (MESS) BOSA
GOOD MORNING.
HOW DO YOU FEEL?
TOTALLY TRADITIONAL STYLE
SOH...AH! GOOD...
*SOHMA-KUN, UM, GOOD MORNING.
HERE'S YOUR PHOTO.
UH...
I THINK THIS IS THE REST OF YOUR THINGS...
...BUT WILL YOU CHECK TO MAKE SURE NOTHING'S MISSING?
DOSA (FWUMP)
HUH!?

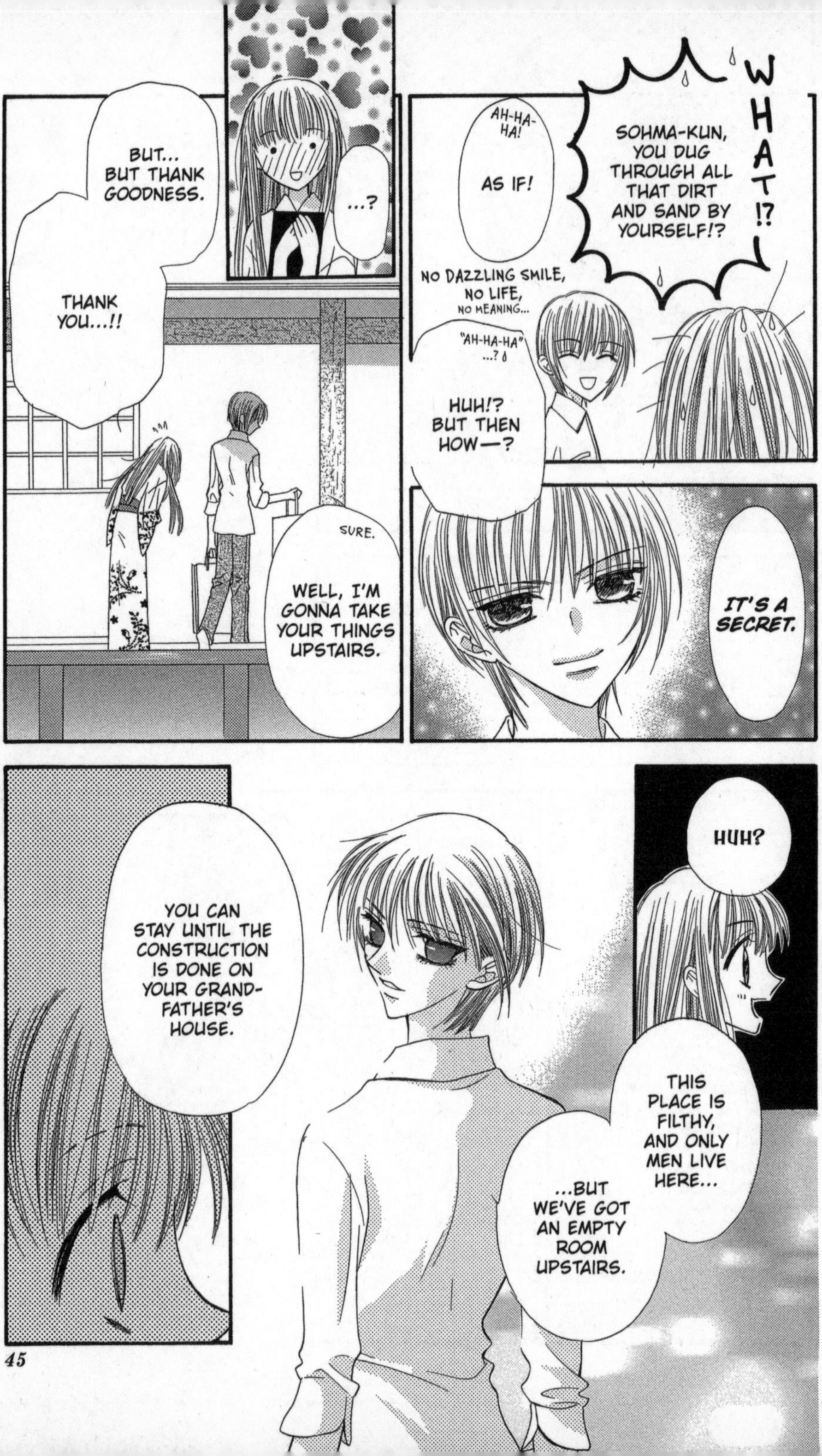
WHAT!?
SOHMA-KUN, YOU DUG THROUGH ALL THAT DIRT AND SAND BY YOURSELF!?
AH-HA-HA! AS IF!
NO DAZZLING SMILE, NO LIFE, NO MEANING...
"AH-HA-HA" ...?
HUH!? BUT THEN HOW—?
IT'S A SECRET.
...?
BUT... BUT THANK GOODNESS.
THANK YOU...!!
SURE.
WELL, I'M GONNA TAKE YOUR THINGS UPSTAIRS.
HUH?
THIS PLACE IS FILTHY, AND ONLY MEN LIVE HERE...
...BUT WE'VE GOT AN EMPTY ROOM UPSTAIRS.
YOU CAN STAY UNTIL THE CONSTRUCTION IS DONE ON YOUR GRAND-FATHER'S HOUSE.

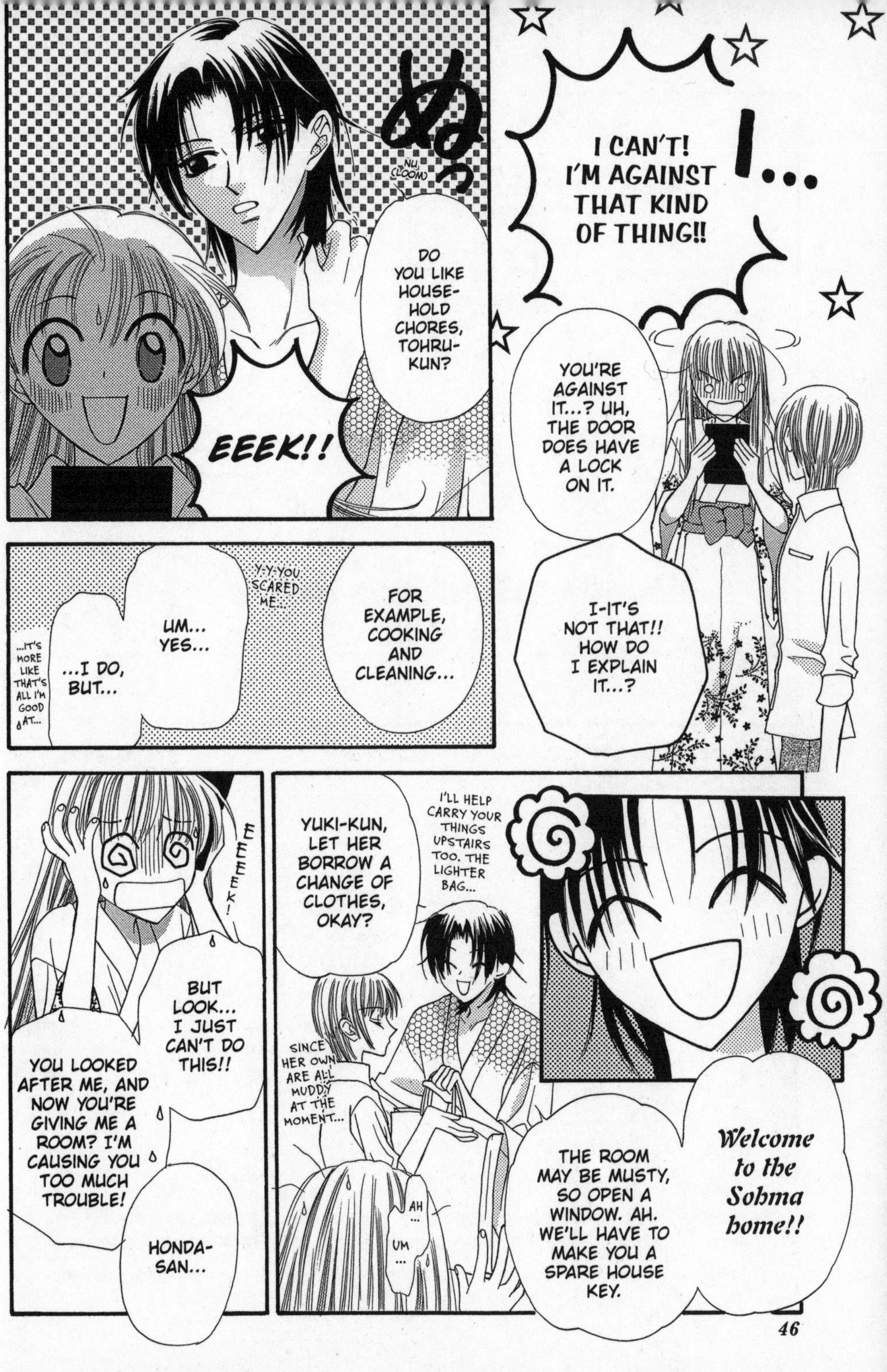
I...
I CAN'T! I'M AGAINST THAT KIND OF THING!!
YOU'RE AGAINST IT...? UH, THE DOOR DOES HAVE A LOCK ON IT.
I-IT'S NOT THAT!! HOW DO I EXPLAIN IT...?
ぬっ
NU (LOOM)
DO YOU LIKE HOUSE-HOLD CHORES, TOHRU-KUN?
EEEK!!
FOR EXAMPLE, COOKING AND CLEANING...
Y-Y-YOU SCARED ME...
UM... YES...
...I DO, BUT...
...IT'S MORE LIKE THAT'S ALL I'M GOOD AT...
Welcome to the Sohma home!!
THE ROOM MAY BE MUSTY, SO OPEN A WINDOW. AH. WE'LL HAVE TO MAKE YOU A SPARE HOUSE KEY.
YUKI-KUN, LET HER BORROW A CHANGE OF CLOTHES, OKAY?
I'LL HELP CARRY YOUR THINGS UPSTAIRS TOO. THE LIGHTER BAG...
SINCE HER OWN ARE ALL MUDDY AT THE MOMENT...
AH...
UM...
EEEEK!
BUT LOOK... I JUST CAN'T DO THIS!!
YOU LOOKED AFTER ME, AND NOW YOU'RE GIVING ME A ROOM? I'M CAUSING YOU TOO MUCH TROUBLE!
HONDA-SAN...

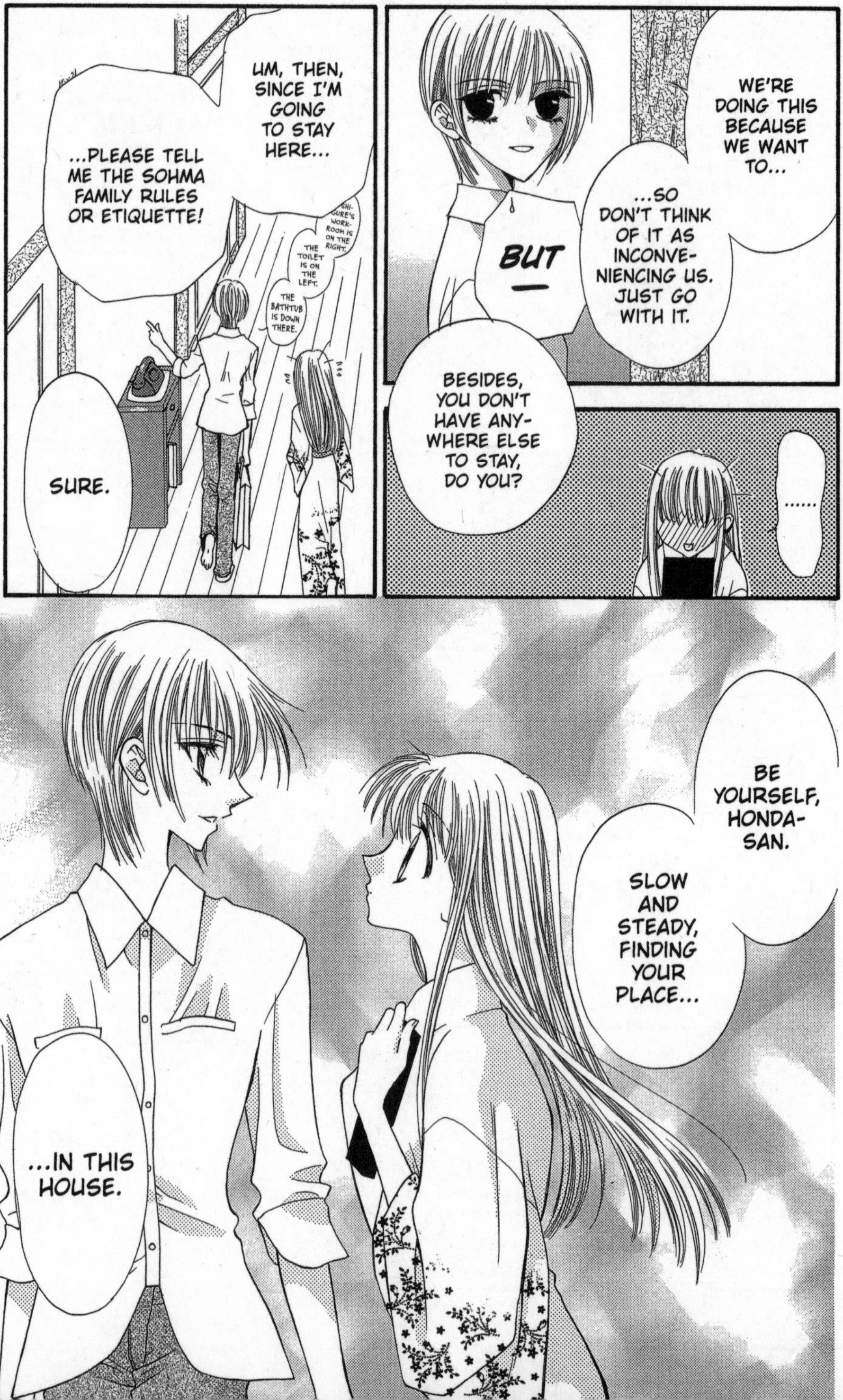
WE'RE DOING THIS BECAUSE WE WANT TO...
...SO DON'T THINK OF IT AS INCONVENIENCING US. JUST GO WITH IT.
BUT —
BESIDES, YOU DON'T HAVE ANYWHERE ELSE TO STAY, DO YOU?
......
UM, THEN, SINCE I'M GOING TO STAY HERE...
...PLEASE TELL ME THE SOHMA FAMILY RULES OR ETIQUETTE!
SHIGURE'S WORKROOM IS ON THE RIGHT.
THE TOILET IS ON THE LEFT.
THE BATHTUB IS DOWN THERE.
SURE.
BE YOURSELF, HONDA-SAN.
SLOW AND STEADY, FINDING YOUR PLACE...
...IN THIS HOUSE.

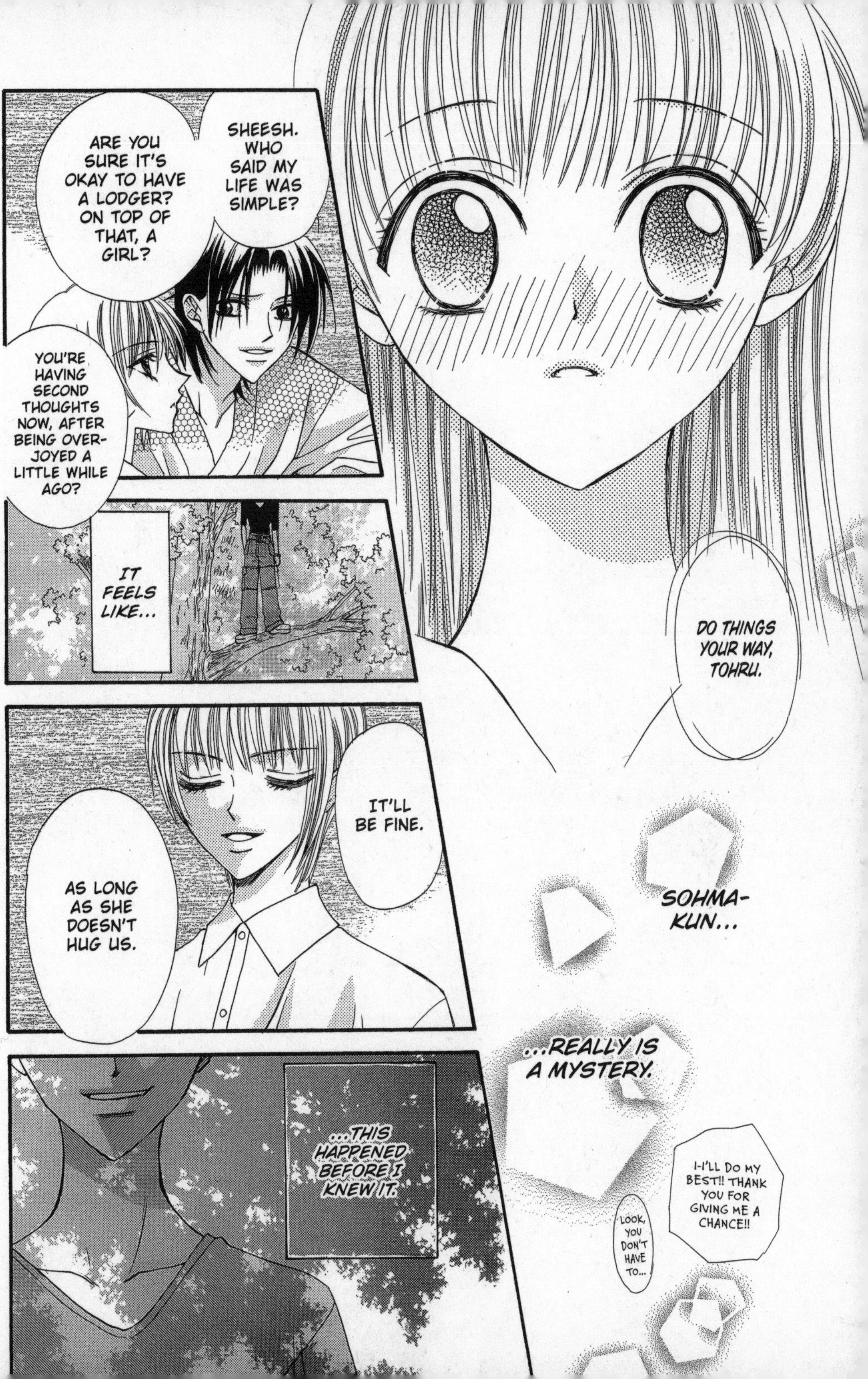
DO THINGS YOUR WAY, TOHRU.
SOHMA-KUN...
...REALLY IS A MYSTERY.
I-I'LL DO MY BEST!! THANK YOU FOR GIVING ME A CHANCE!!
LOOK, YOU DON'T HAVE TO...
SHEESH. WHO SAID MY LIFE WAS SIMPLE?
ARE YOU SURE IT'S OKAY TO HAVE A LODGER? ON TOP OF THAT, A GIRL?
YOU'RE HAVING SECOND THOUGHTS NOW, AFTER BEING OVER-JOYED A LITTLE WHILE AGO?
IT FEELS LIKE...
IT'LL BE FINE.
AS LONG AS SHE DOESN'T HUG US.
...THIS HAPPENED BEFORE I KNEW IT.

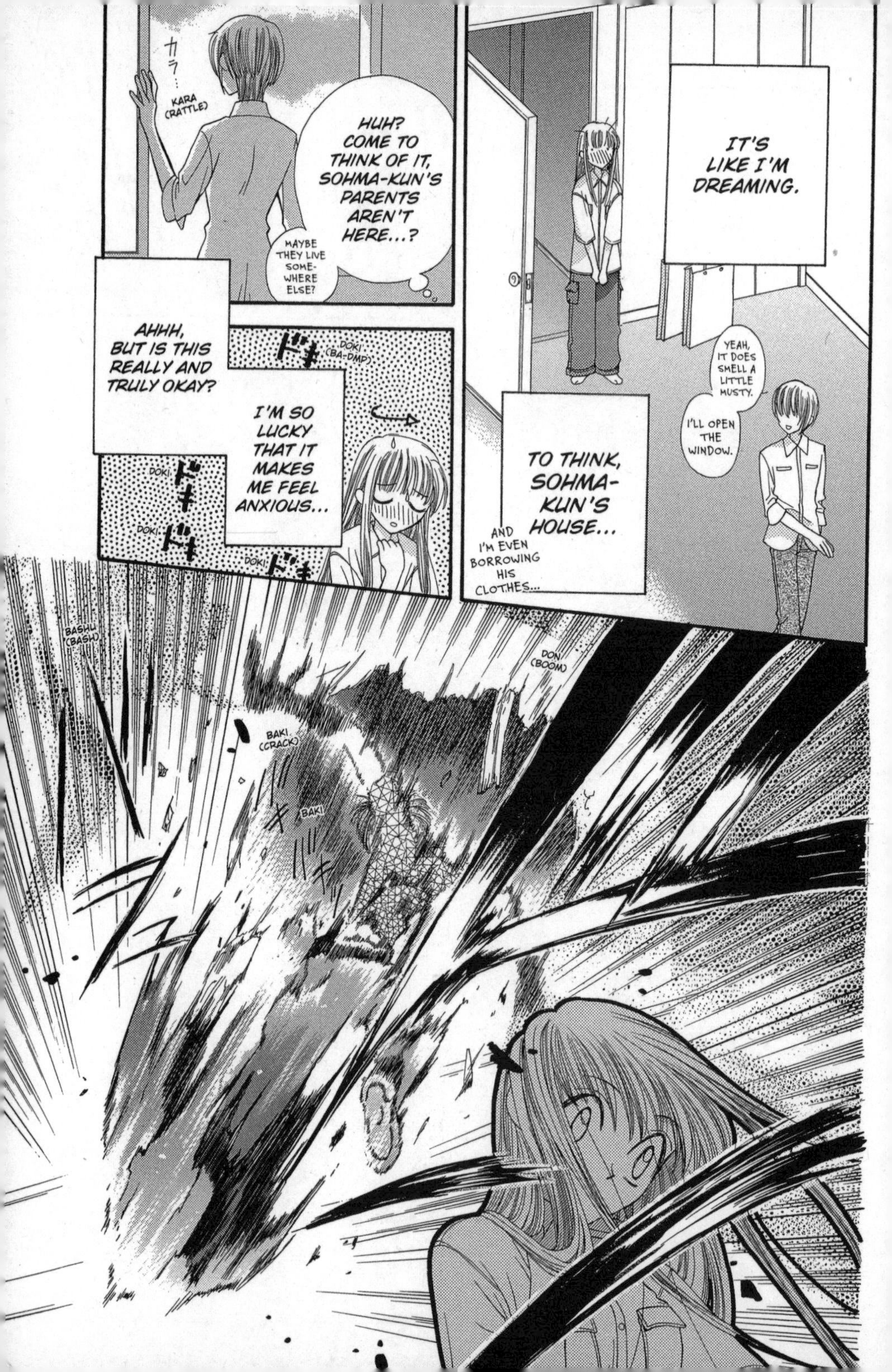
IT'S LIKE I'M DREAMING.
TO THINK, SOHMA-KUN'S HOUSE...
YEAH, IT DOES SMELL A LITTLE MUSTY.
I'LL OPEN THE WINDOW.
AND I'M EVEN BORROWING HIS CLOTHES...
KARA (RATTLE)
HUH? COME TO THINK OF IT, SOHMA-KUN'S PARENTS AREN'T HERE...?
MAYBE THEY LIVE SOMEWHERE ELSE?
AHHH, BUT IS THIS REALLY AND TRULY OKAY?
DOKI (BA-DMP)
I'M SO LUCKY THAT IT MAKES ME FEEL ANXIOUS...
DOKI
DOKI
DOKI
DON (BOOM)
BAKI (CRACK)
BAKI
BASHU (BASH)

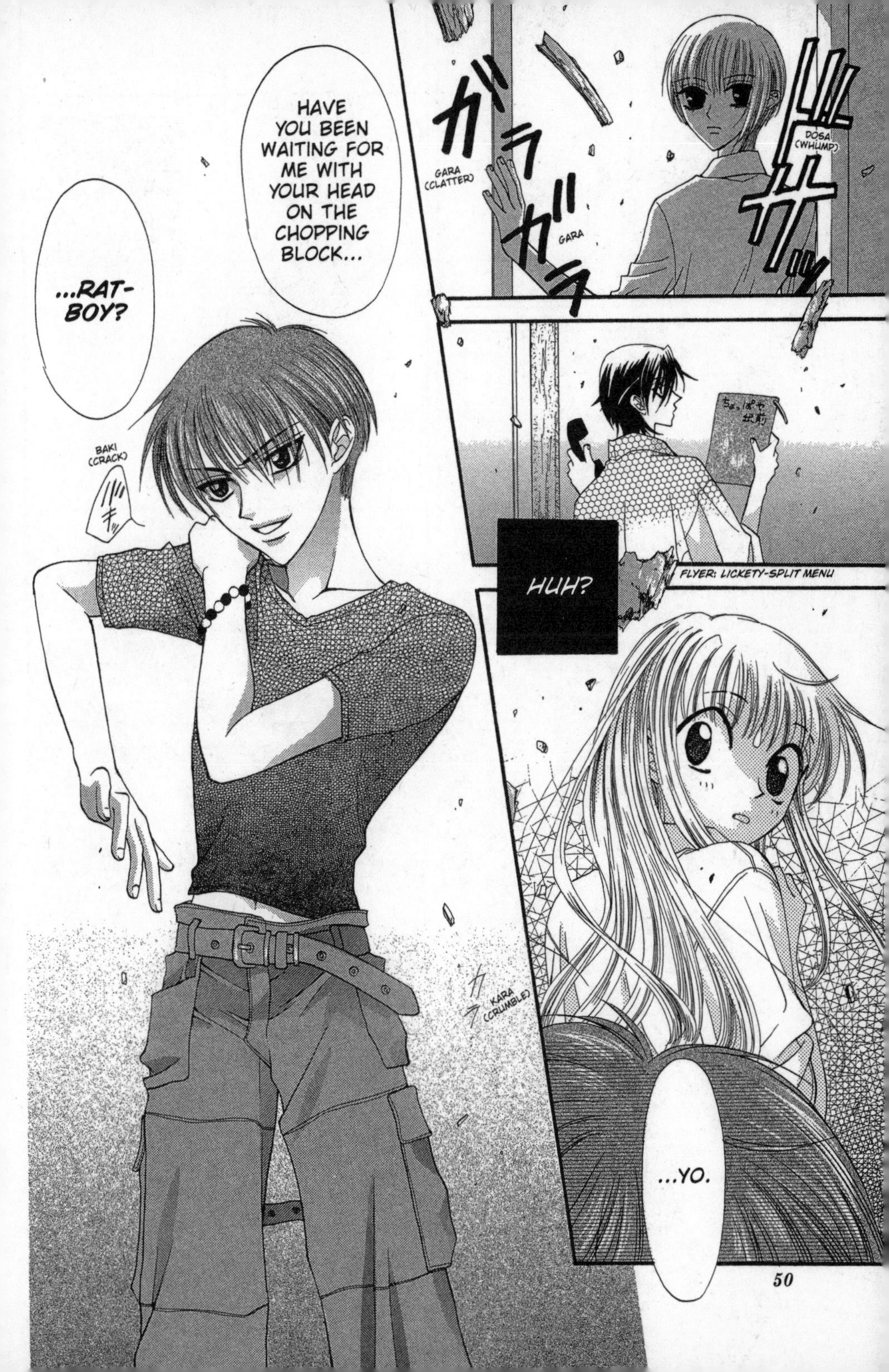

GARA (CLATTER)
GARA
DOSA (WHUMP)
FLYER: LICKETY-SPLIT MENU
HUH?
...YO.
HAVE YOU BEEN WAITING FOR ME WITH YOUR HEAD ON THE CHOPPING BLOCK...
...RAT-BOY?
BAKI (CRACK)
KARA (CRUMBLE)

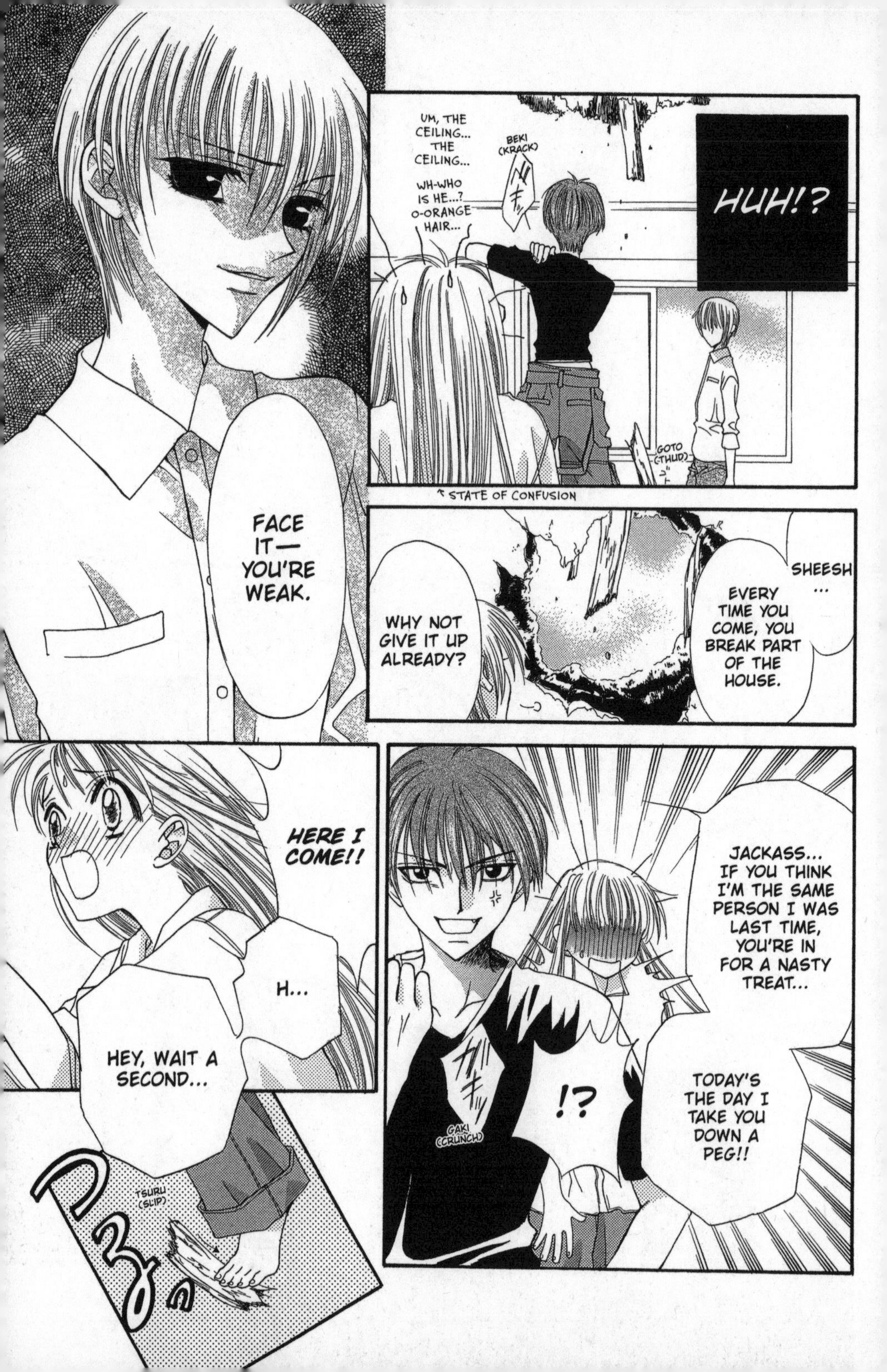
HUH!?
BEKI (KRACK)
UM, THE CEILING... THE CEILING...
WH-WHO IS HE...? O-ORANGE HAIR...
GOTO (THUD)
STATE OF CONFUSION
SHEESH...
EVERY TIME YOU COME, YOU BREAK PART OF THE HOUSE.
WHY NOT GIVE IT UP ALREADY?
FACE IT— YOU'RE WEAK.
JACKASS... IF YOU THINK I'M THE SAME PERSON I WAS LAST TIME, YOU'RE IN FOR A NASTY TREAT...
TODAY'S THE DAY I TAKE YOU DOWN A PEG!!
!?
GAKI (CRUNCH)
HERE I COME!!
H...
HEY, WAIT A SECOND...
TSURU (SLIP)

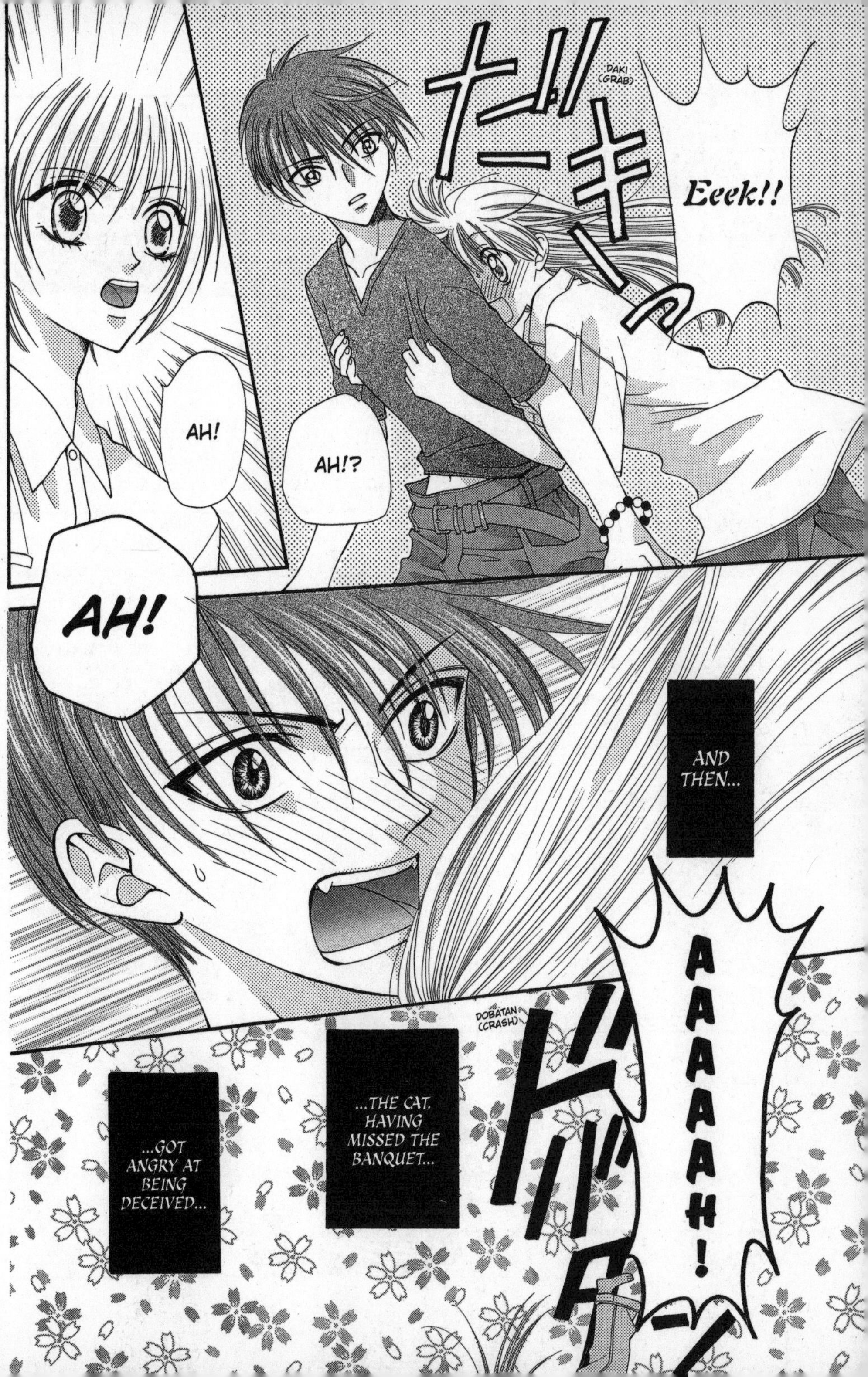
DAKI (GRAB)
Eeck!!
AH!?
AH!
AH!
AND THEN...
AAAAAH!
DOBATAN (CRASH)
...THE CAT, HAVING MISSED THE BANQUET...
...GOT ANGRY AT BEING DECEIVED...

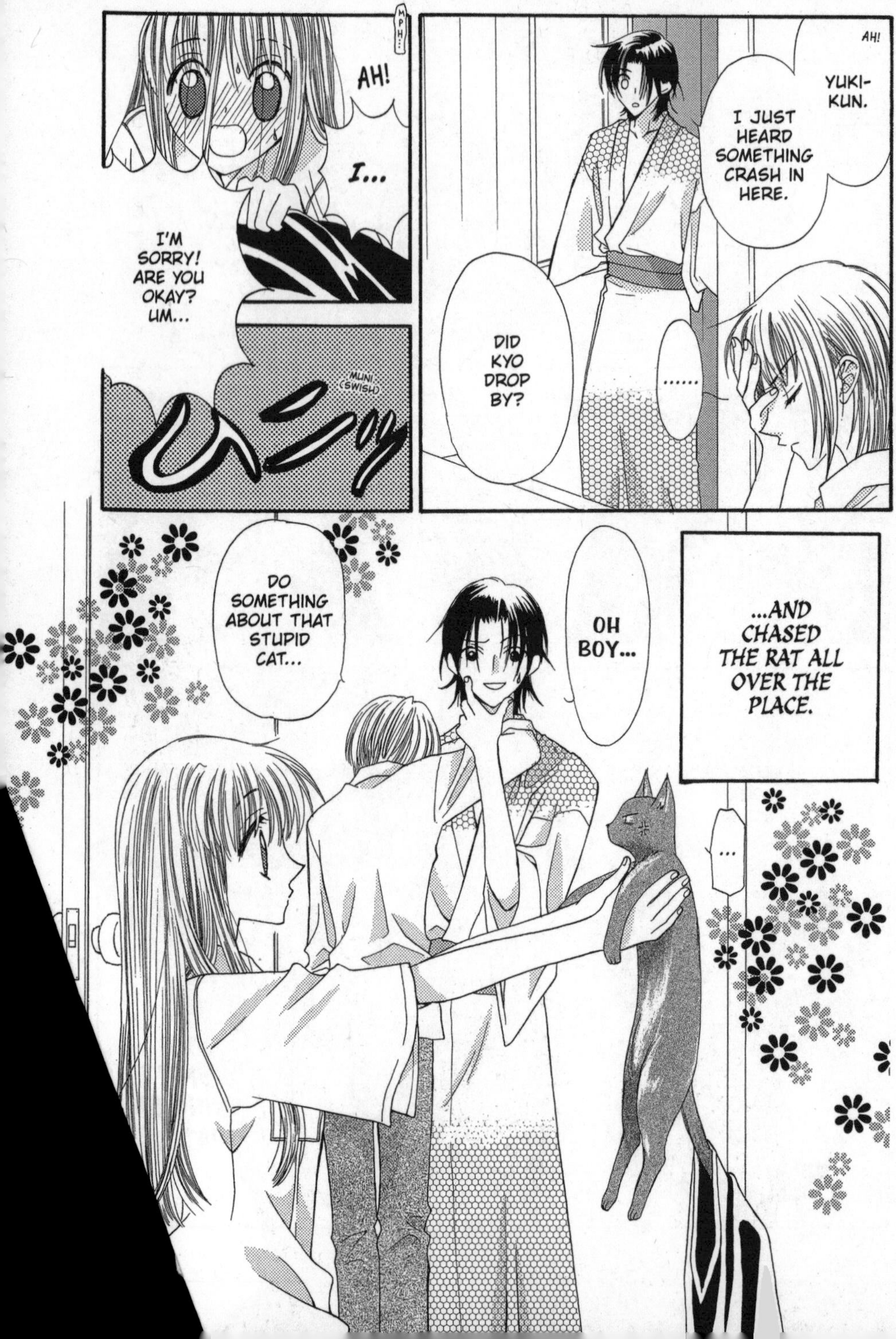
AH!
YUKI-KUN.
I JUST HEARD SOMETHING CRASH IN HERE.
......
DID KYO DROP BY?
MPH...
AH!
I...
I'M SORRY! ARE YOU OKAY? UM...
MUNI (SWISH)
...AND CHASED THE RAT ALL OVER THE PLACE.
OH BOY...
DO SOMETHING ABOUT THAT STUPID CAT...
...

BUT THAT'S PART OF YOUR CHARM (MAYBE).

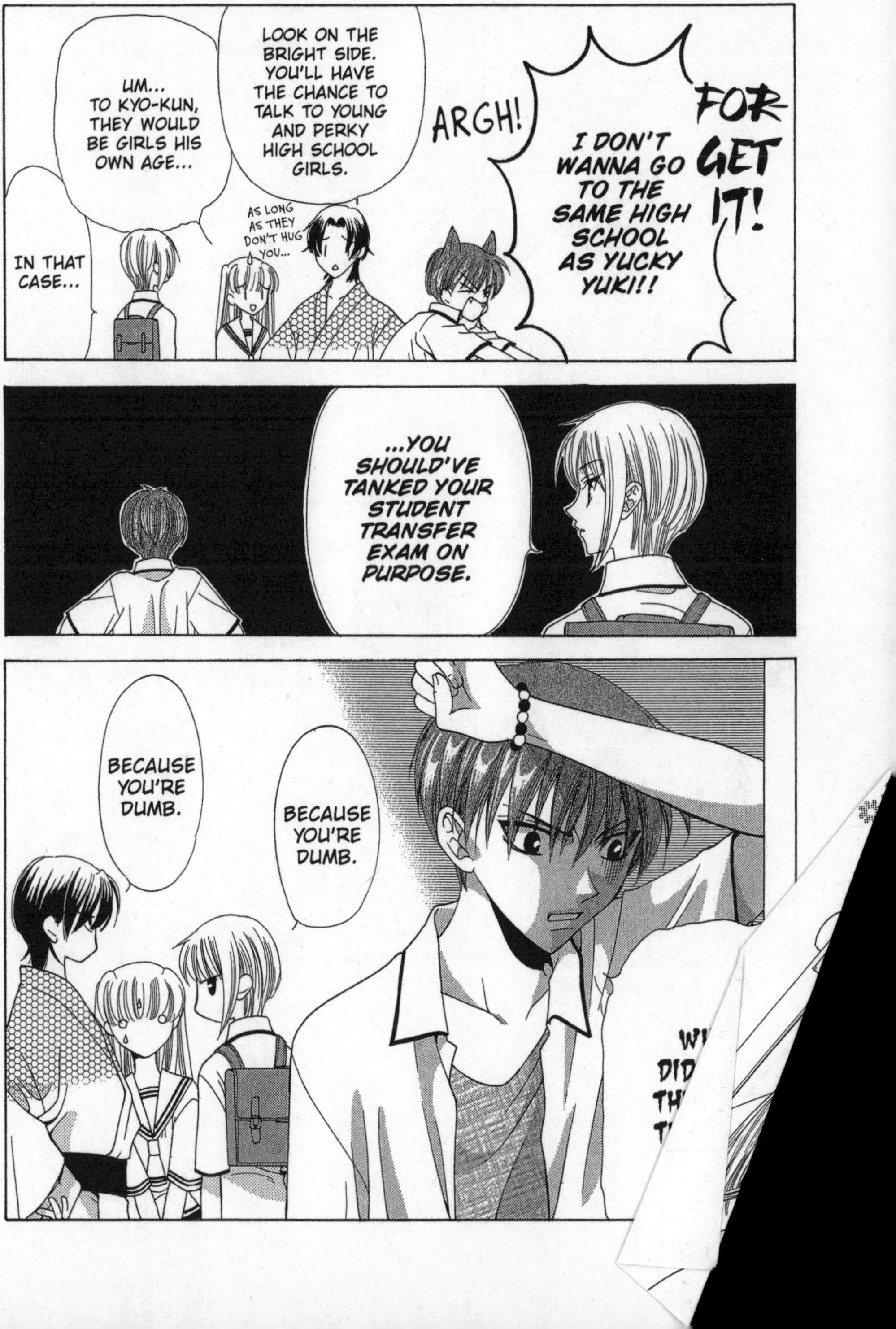

FOR GET IT!
I DON'T WANNA GO TO THE SAME HIGH SCHOOL AS YUCKY YUKI!!
ARGH!
LOOK ON THE BRIGHT SIDE. YOU'LL HAVE THE CHANCE TO TALK TO YOUNG AND PERKY HIGH SCHOOL GIRLS.
AS LONG AS THEY DON'T HUG YOU...
UM... TO KYO-KUN, THEY WOULD BE GIRLS HIS OWN AGE...
IN THAT CASE...
...YOU SHOULD'VE TANKED YOUR STUDENT TRANSFER EXAM ON PURPOSE.
BECAUSE YOU'RE DUMB.
BECAUSE YOU'RE DUMB.

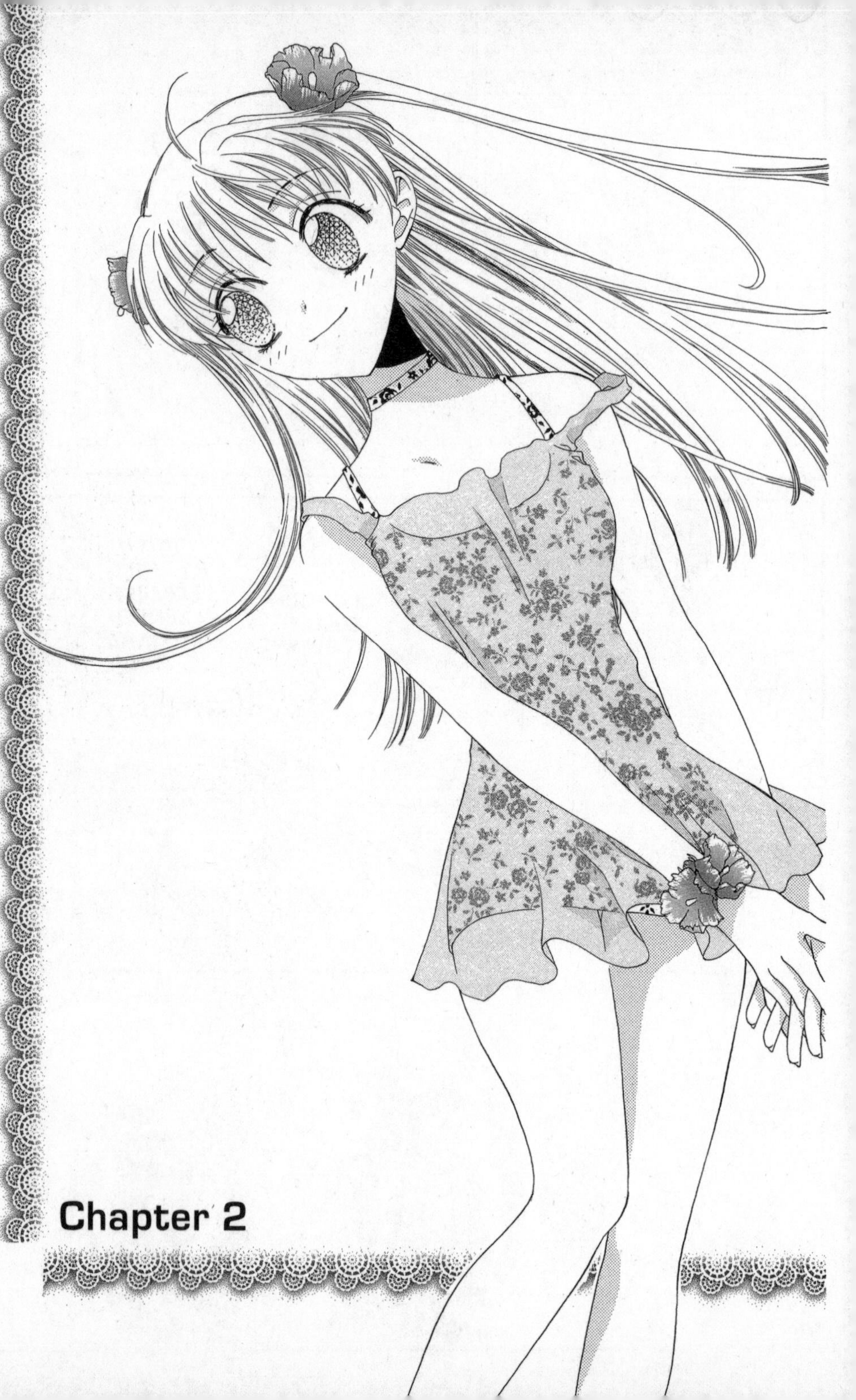

Chapter 2

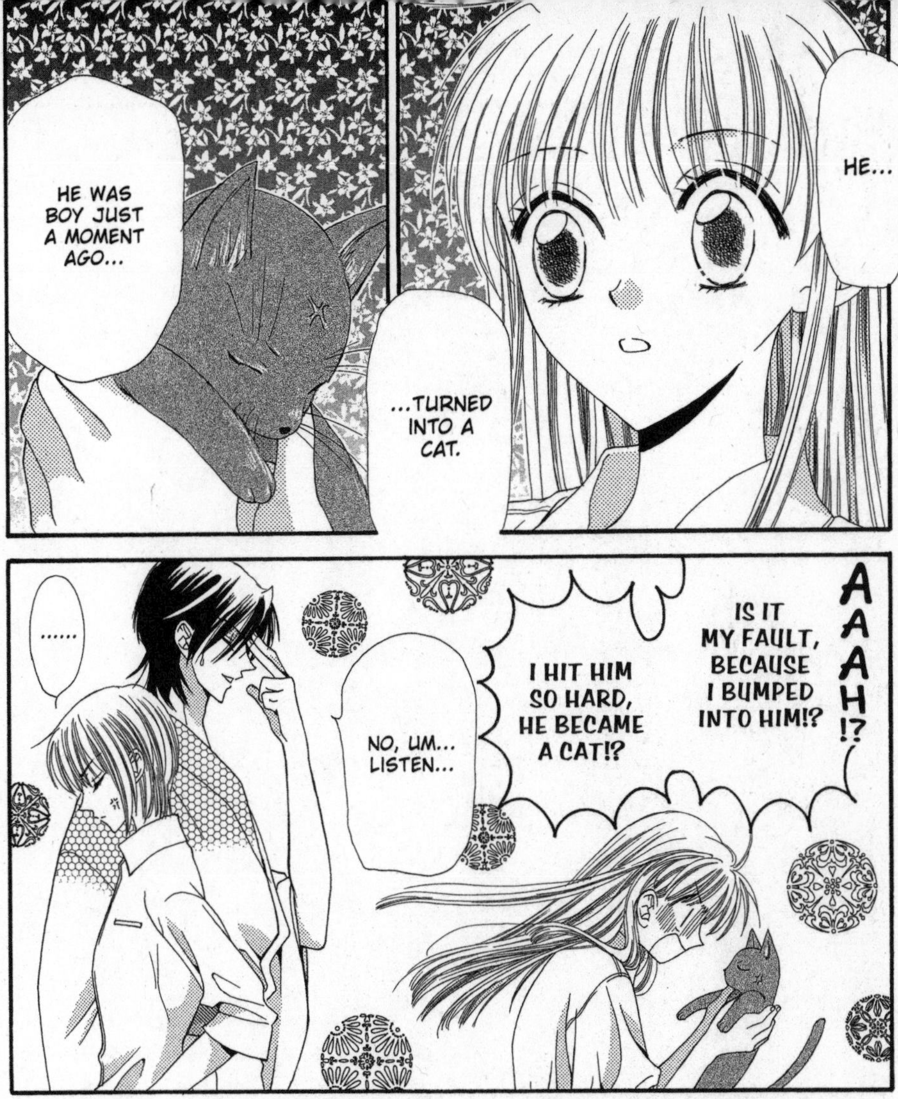
HE...
...TURNED INTO A CAT.
HE WAS BOY JUST A MOMENT AGO...
AAAAH!?
IS IT MY FAULT, BECAUSE I BUMPED INTO HIM!?
I HIT HIM SO HARD, HE BECAME A CAT!?
NO, UM... LISTEN...
......

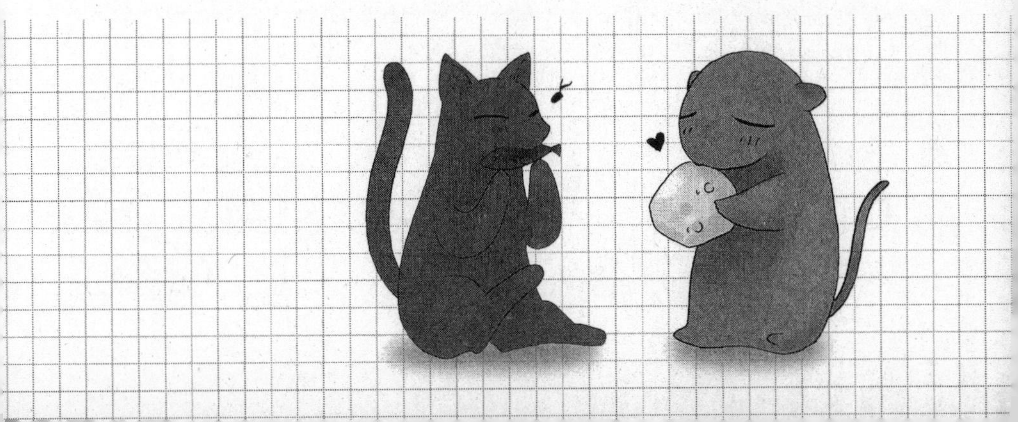

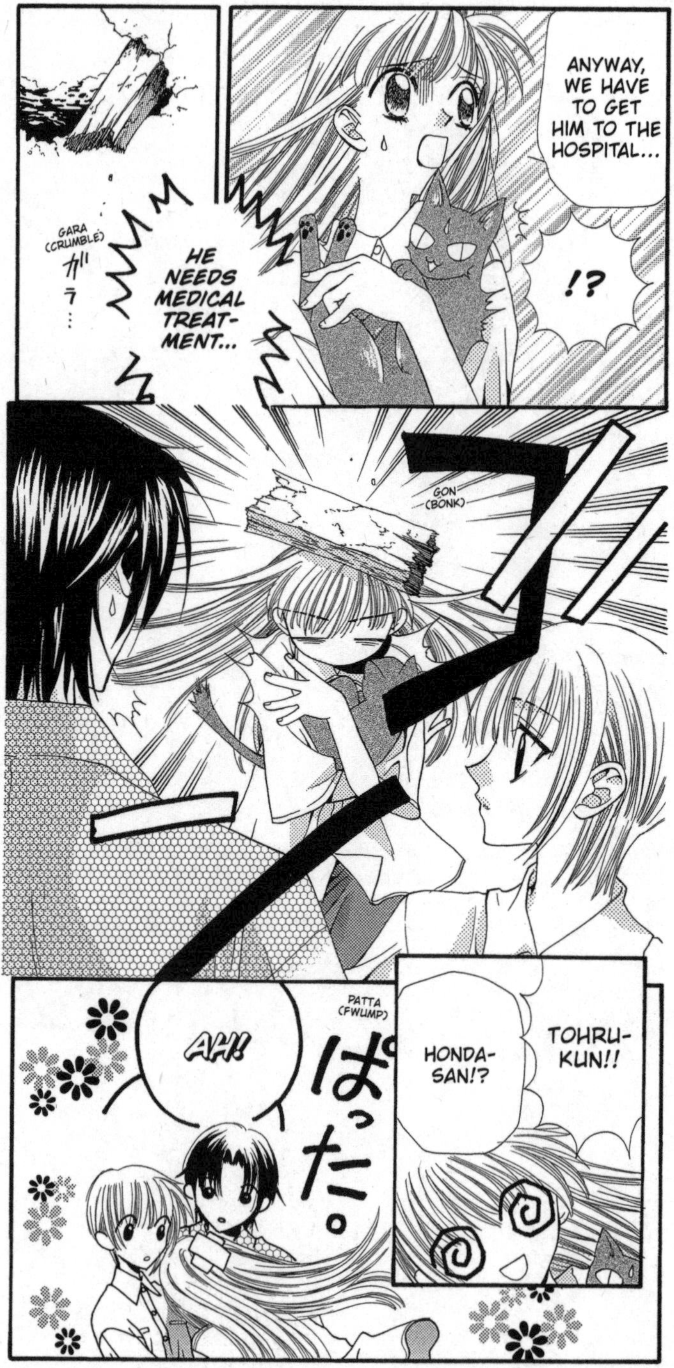
ANYWAY, WE HAVE TO GET HIM TO THE HOSPITAL...
HE NEEDS MEDICAL TREATMENT...
!?
GARA (CRUMBLE)
ガラ…
GON (BONK)
TOHRU-KUN!!
HONDA-SAN!?
AH!
PATTA (FWUMP)
ぱった。

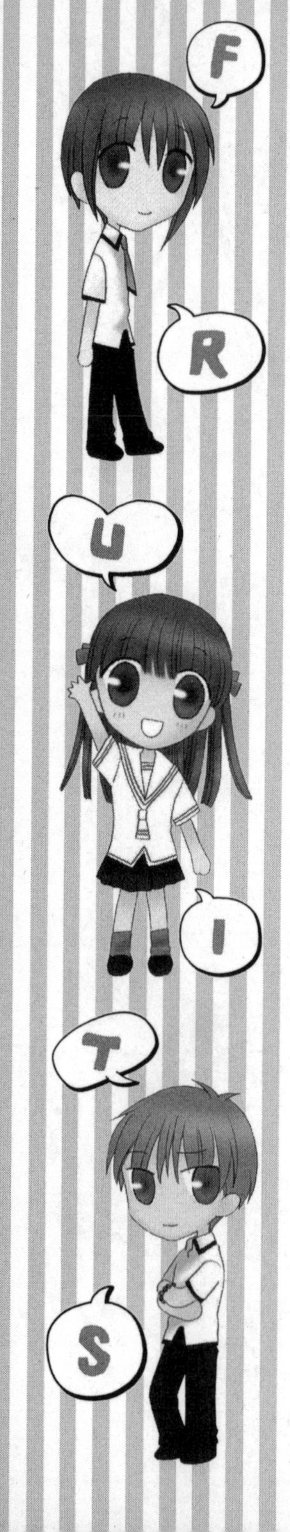
F
R
U
I
T
S

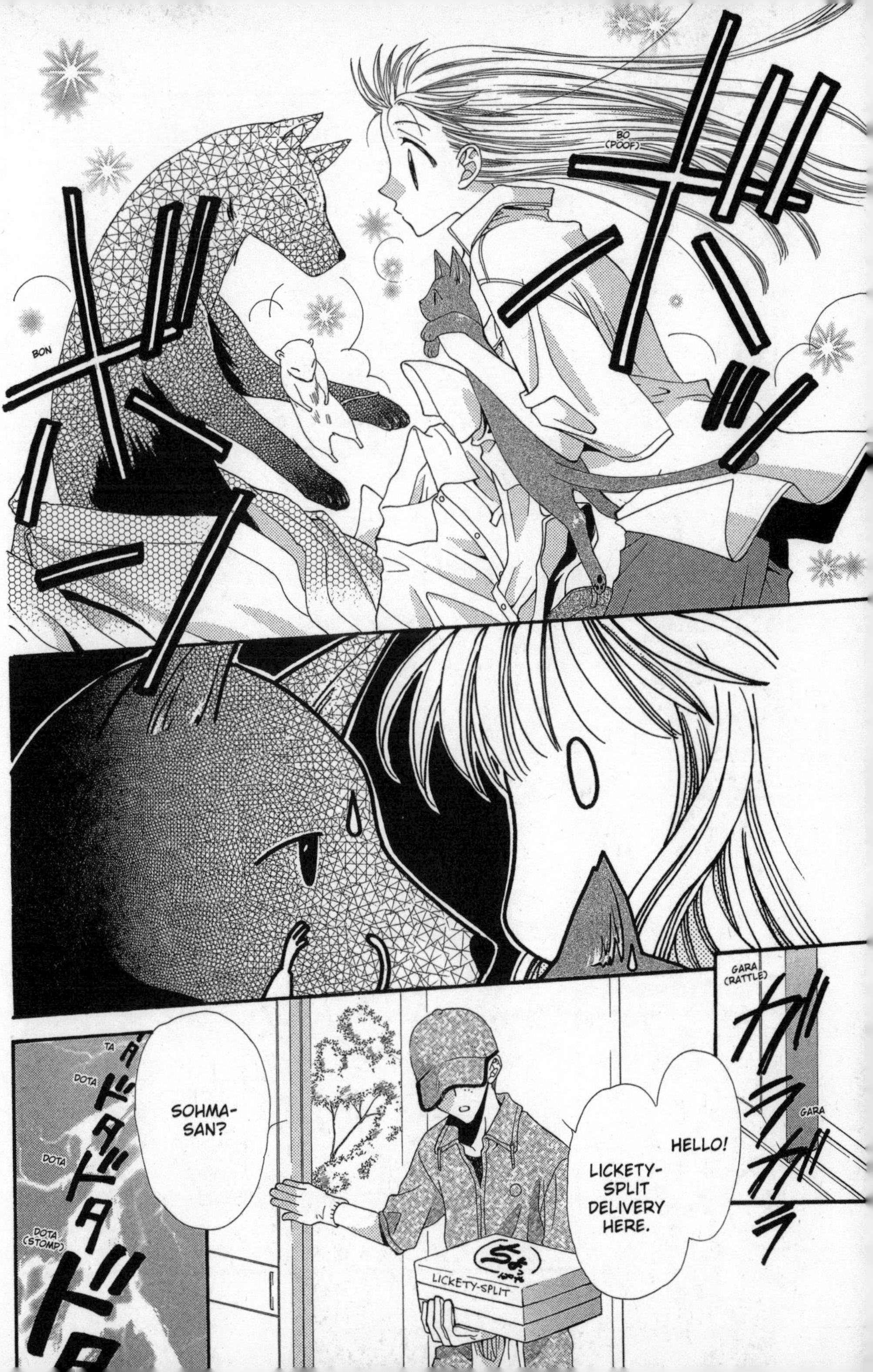
BO (POOF)
BON
GARA (RATTLE)
GARA
HELLO!
LICKETY-SPLIT DELIVERY HERE.
LICKETY-SPLIT
SOHMA-SAN?
TA
DOTA
DOTA
DOTA (STOMP)

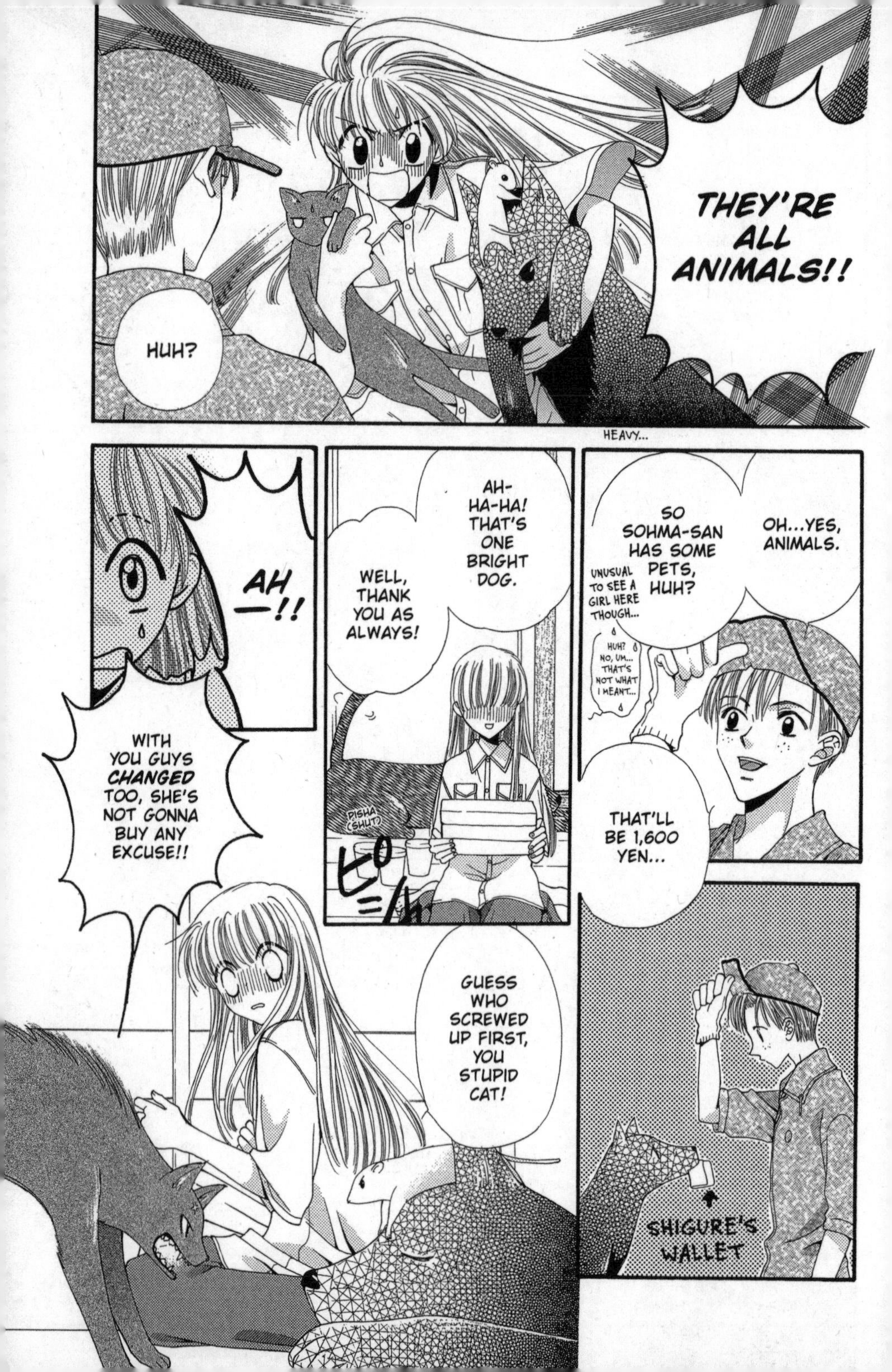
THEY'RE ALL ANIMALS!!
HUH?
HEAVY...
OH...YES, ANIMALS.
SO SOHMA-SAN HAS SOME PETS, HUH?
UNUSUAL TO SEE A GIRL HERE THOUGH...
HUH? NO, UM... THAT'S NOT WHAT I MEANT...
THAT'LL BE 1,600 YEN...
AH-HA-HA! THAT'S ONE BRIGHT DOG.
WELL, THANK YOU AS ALWAYS!
PISHA (SHUT)
AH—!!
SHIGURE'S WALLET
GUESS WHO SCREWED UP FIRST, YOU STUPID CAT!
WITH YOU GUYS CHANGED TOO, SHE'S NOT GONNA BUY ANY EXCUSE!!

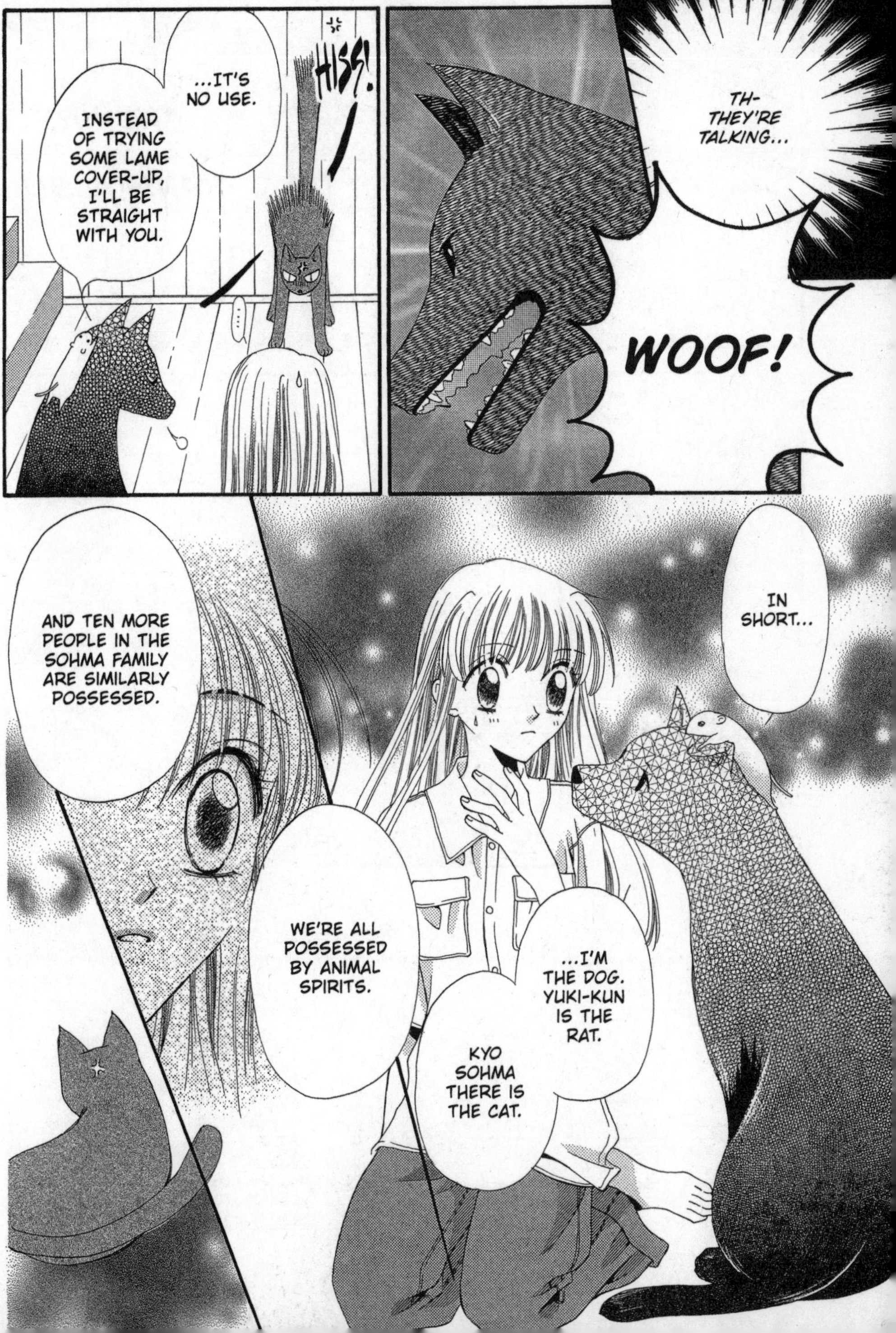
TH- THEY'RE TALKING...
WOOF!
HISS!
...IT'S NO USE.
INSTEAD OF TRYING SOME LAME COVER-UP, I'LL BE STRAIGHT WITH YOU.
...
IN SHORT...
...I'M THE DOG. YUKI-KUN IS THE RAT.
KYO SOHMA THERE IS THE CAT.
WE'RE ALL POSSESSED BY ANIMAL SPIRITS.
AND TEN MORE PEOPLE IN THE SOHMA FAMILY ARE SIMILARLY POSSESSED.

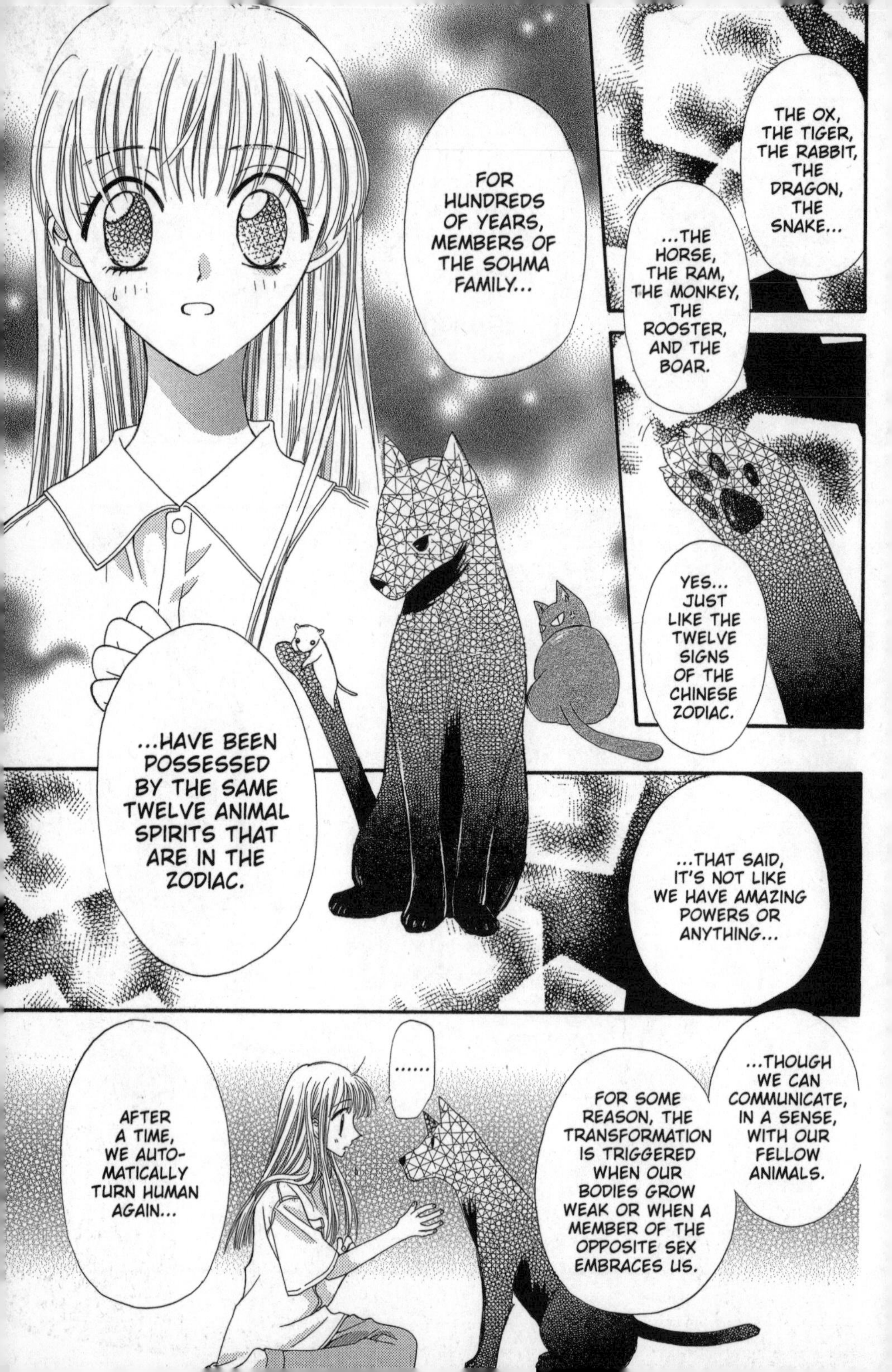
THE OX, THE TIGER, THE RABBIT, THE DRAGON, THE SNAKE...
...THE HORSE, THE RAM, THE MONKEY, THE ROOSTER, AND THE BOAR.
YES... JUST LIKE THE TWELVE SIGNS OF THE CHINESE ZODIAC.
FOR HUNDREDS OF YEARS, MEMBERS OF THE SOHMA FAMILY...
...HAVE BEEN POSSESSED BY THE SAME TWELVE ANIMAL SPIRITS THAT ARE IN THE ZODIAC.
...THAT SAID, IT'S NOT LIKE WE HAVE AMAZING POWERS OR ANYTHING...
...THOUGH WE CAN COMMUNICATE, IN A SENSE, WITH OUR FELLOW ANIMALS.
FOR SOME REASON, THE TRANSFORMATION IS TRIGGERED WHEN OUR BODIES GROW WEAK OR WHEN A MEMBER OF THE OPPOSITE SEX EMBRACES US.
......
AFTER A TIME, WE AUTO-MATICALLY TURN HUMAN AGAIN...

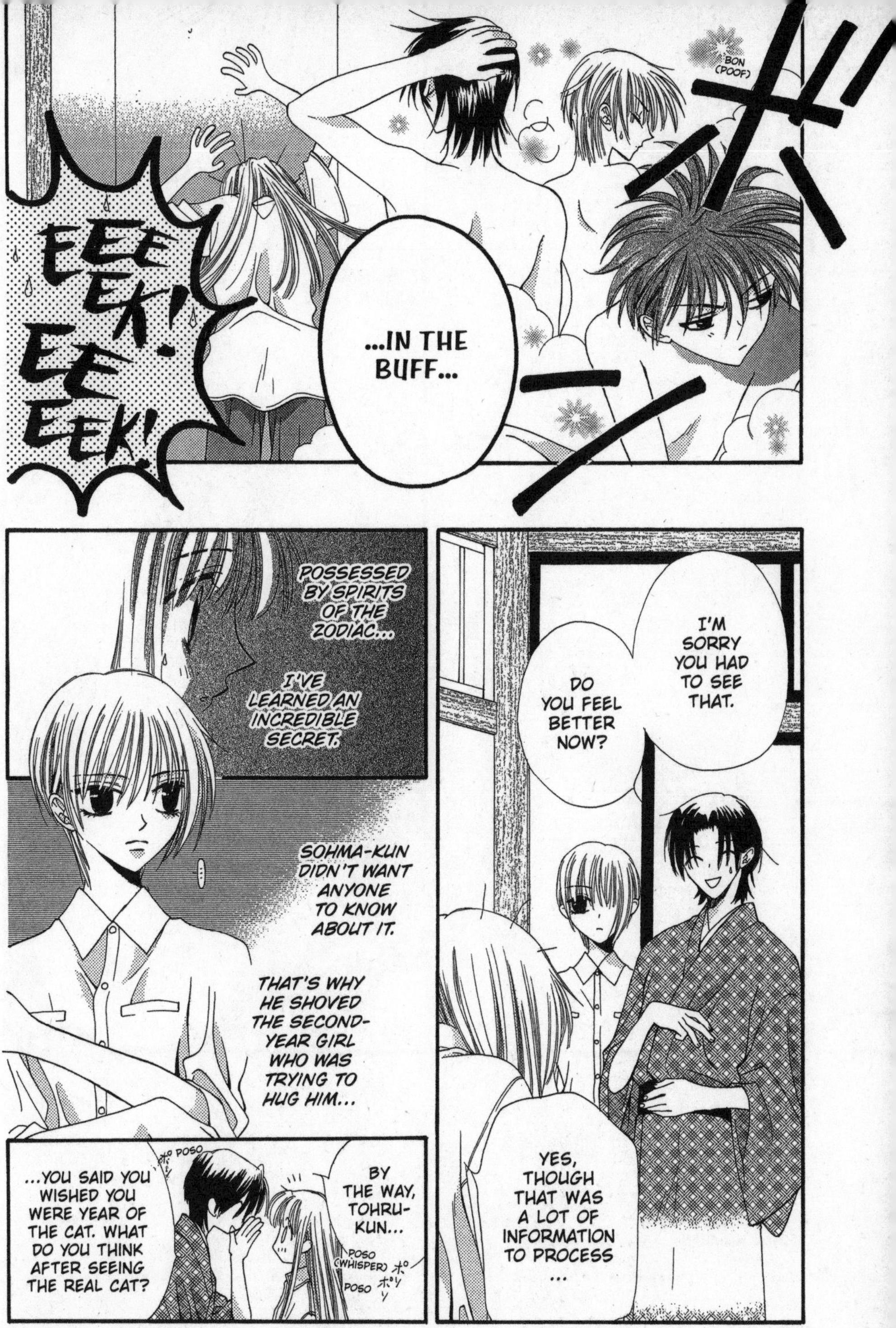
BON (POOF)
...IN THE BUFF...
EEEEK! EEEEK!
I'M SORRY YOU HAD TO SEE THAT.
DO YOU FEEL BETTER NOW?
YES, THOUGH THAT WAS A LOT OF INFORMATION TO PROCESS...
POSSESSED BY SPIRITS OF THE ZODIAC...
I'VE LEARNED AN INCREDIBLE SECRET.
SOHMA-KUN DIDN'T WANT ANYONE TO KNOW ABOUT IT.
THAT'S WHY HE SHOVED THE SECOND-YEAR GIRL WHO WAS TRYING TO HUG HIM...
BY THE WAY, TOHRU-KUN...
POSO (WHISPER) POSO
...YOU SAID YOU WISHED YOU WERE YEAR OF THE CAT. WHAT DO YOU THINK AFTER SEEING THE REAL CAT?

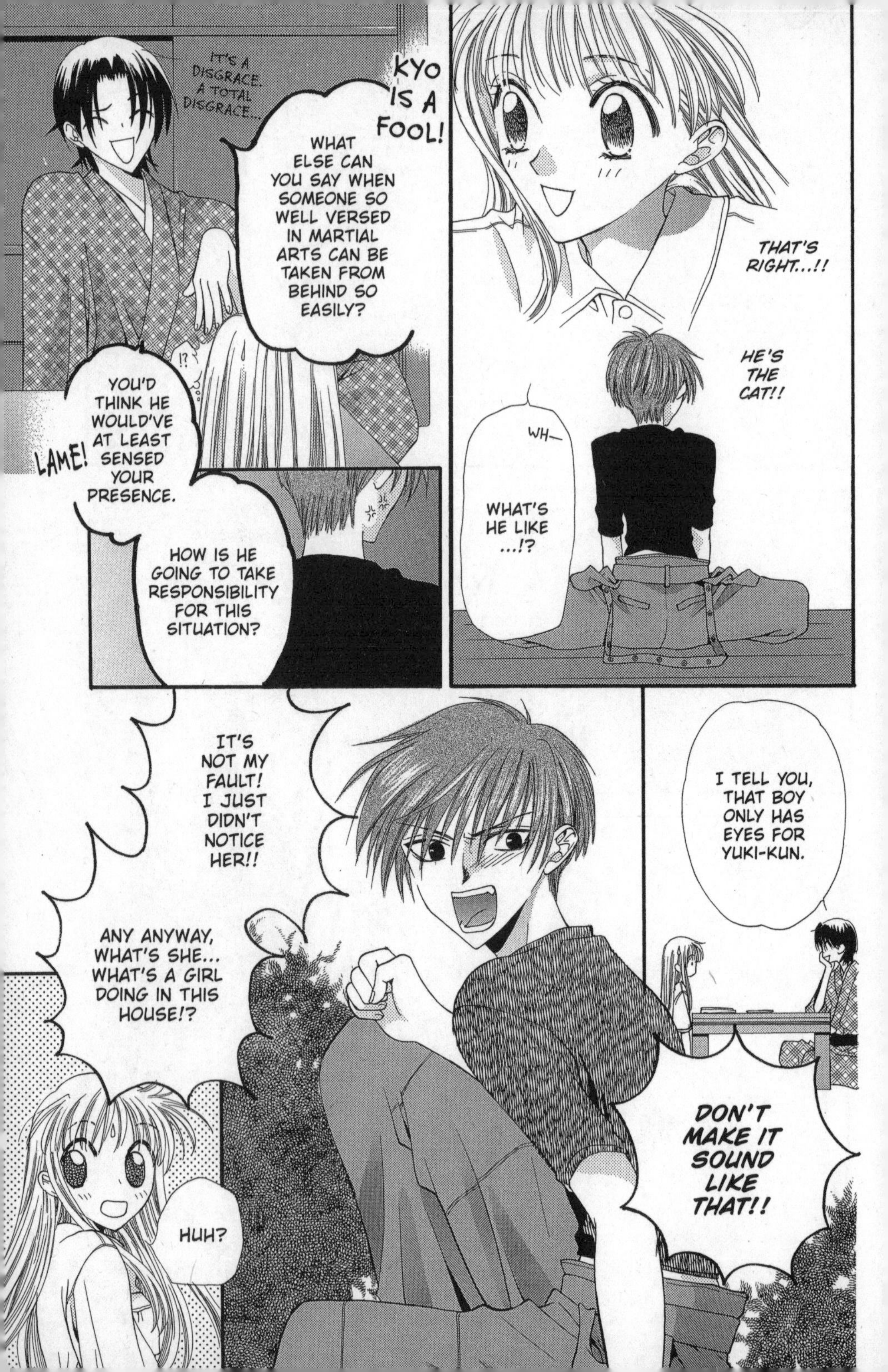
THAT'S RIGHT...!!
HE'S THE CAT!!
WH—
WHAT'S HE LIKE ...!?
IT'S A DISGRACE. A TOTAL DISGRACE...
KYO IS A FOOL!
WHAT ELSE CAN YOU SAY WHEN SOMEONE SO WELL VERSED IN MARTIAL ARTS CAN BE TAKEN FROM BEHIND SO EASILY?
!?
YOU'D THINK HE WOULD'VE AT LEAST SENSED YOUR PRESENCE.
LAME!
HOW IS HE GOING TO TAKE RESPONSIBILITY FOR THIS SITUATION?
I TELL YOU, THAT BOY ONLY HAS EYES FOR YUKI-KUN.
DON'T MAKE IT SOUND LIKE THAT!!
IT'S NOT MY FAULT! I JUST DIDN'T NOTICE HER!!
ANY ANYWAY, WHAT'S SHE... WHAT'S A GIRL DOING IN THIS HOUSE!?
HUH?

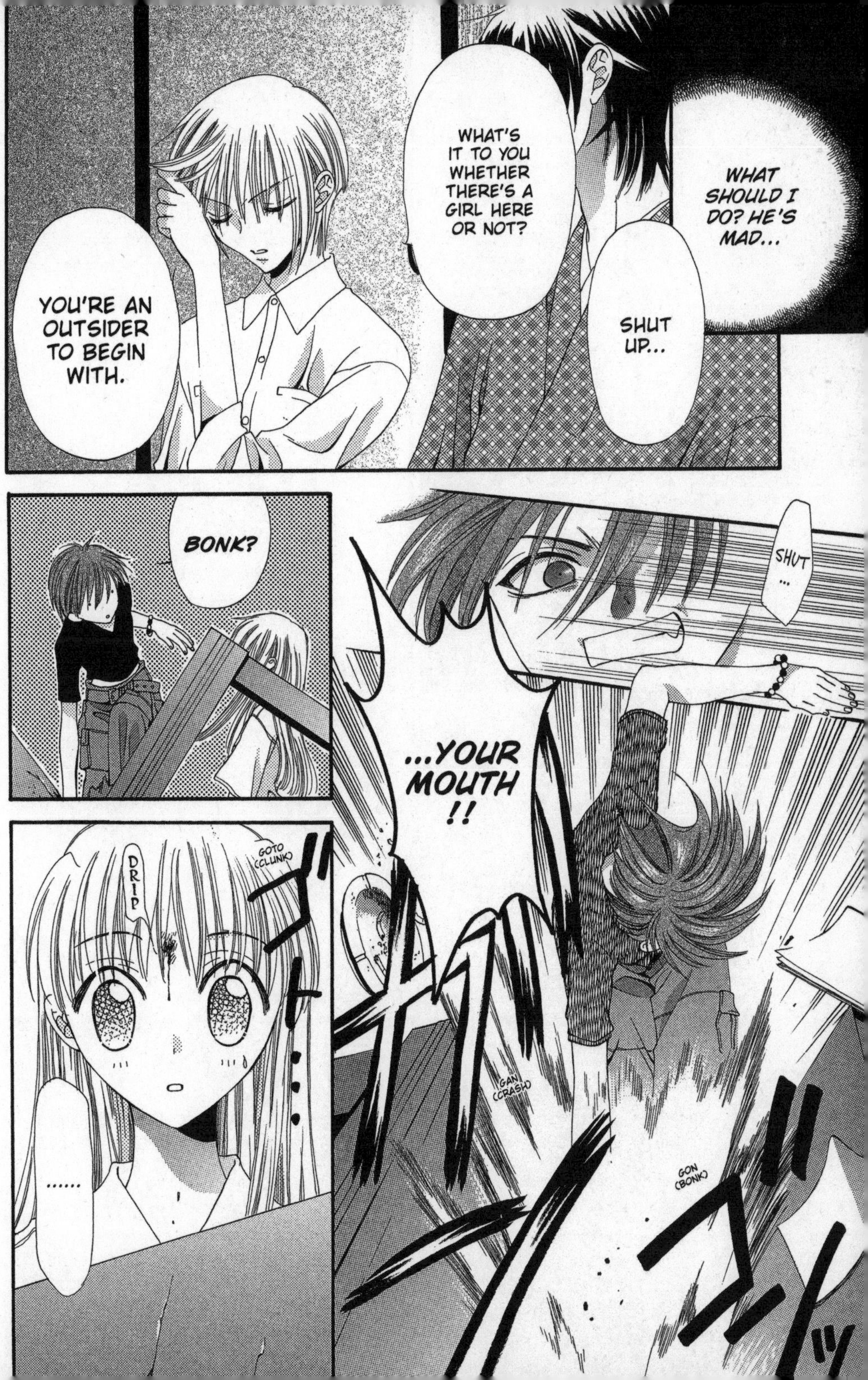
WHAT SHOULD I DO? HE'S MAD...
WHAT'S IT TO YOU WHETHER THERE'S A GIRL HERE OR NOT?
SHUT UP...
YOU'RE AN OUTSIDER TO BEGIN WITH.
SHUT ...
...YOUR MOUTH !!
GAN (CRASH)
GON (BONK)
BONK?
GOTO (CLUNK)
DRIP
......

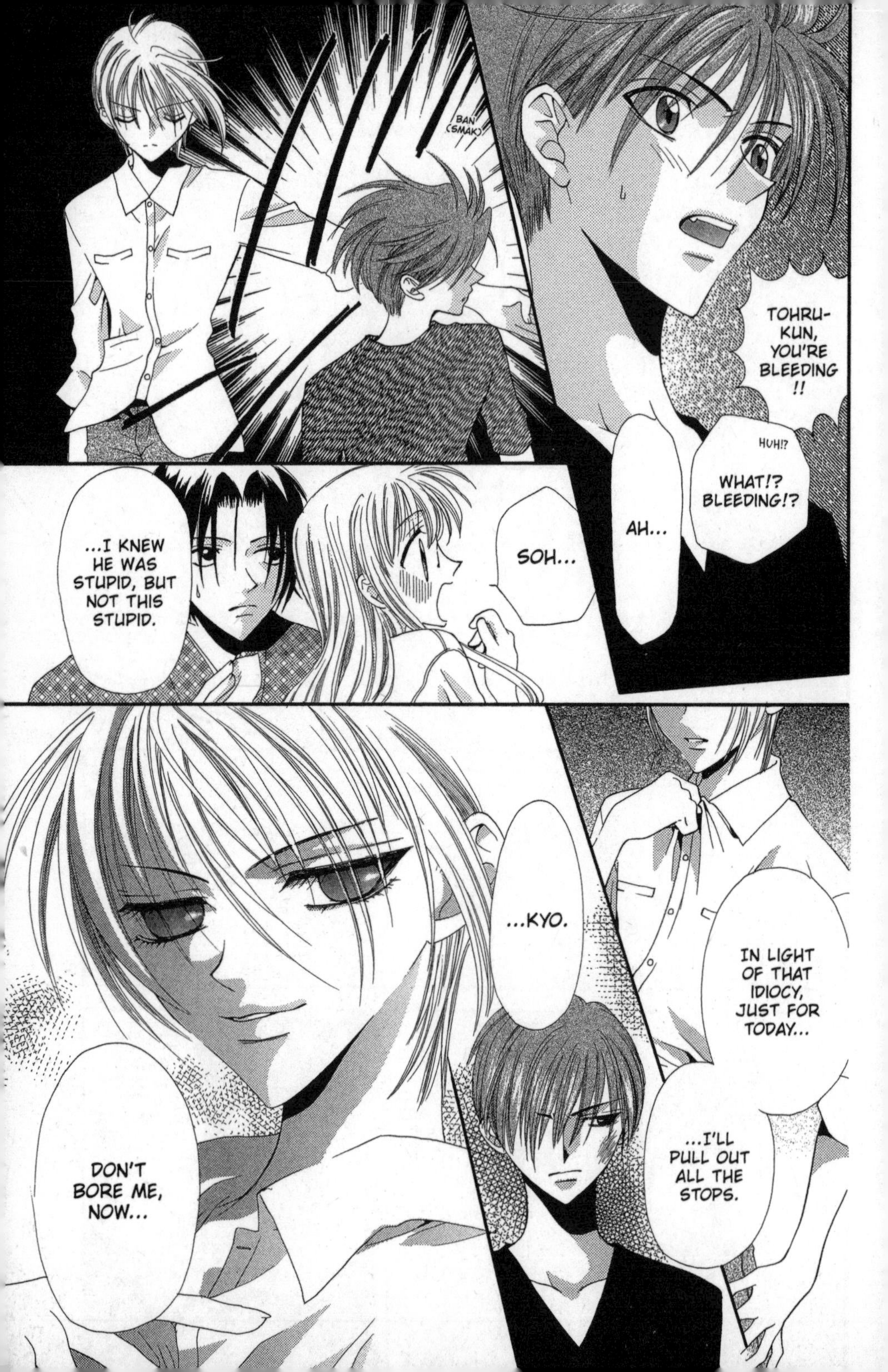

TOHRU-KUN, YOU'RE BLEEDING !!
HUH!?
WHAT!? BLEEDING!?
AH...
BAN (SMAK)
SOH...
...I KNEW HE WAS STUPID, BUT NOT THIS STUPID.
IN LIGHT OF THAT IDIOCY, JUST FOR TODAY...
...I'LL PULL OUT ALL THE STOPS.
...KYO.
DON'T BORE ME, NOW...

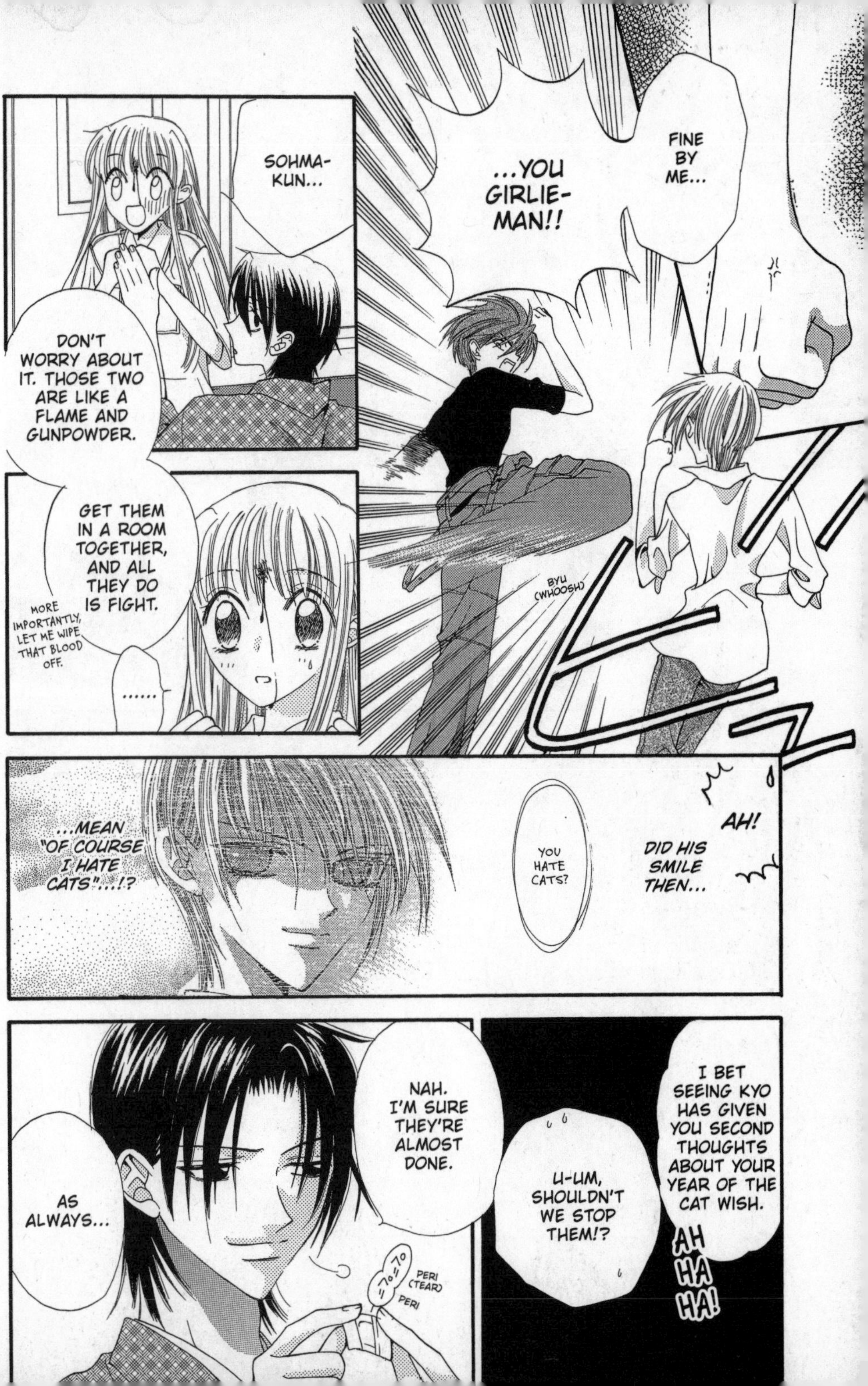

FINE BY ME...
...YOU GIRLIE-MAN!!
BYU (WHOOSH)
SOHMA-KUN...
DON'T WORRY ABOUT IT. THOSE TWO ARE LIKE A FLAME AND GUNPOWDER.
GET THEM IN A ROOM TOGETHER, AND ALL THEY DO IS FIGHT.
MORE IMPORTANTLY, LET ME WIPE THAT BLOOD OFF.
......
AH!
DID HIS SMILE THEN...
YOU HATE CATS?
...MEAN "OF COURSE I HATE CATS"...!?
I BET SEEING KYO HAS GIVEN YOU SECOND THOUGHTS ABOUT YOUR YEAR OF THE CAT WISH.
AH HA HA!
U-UM, SHOULDN'T WE STOP THEM!?
NAH. I'M SURE THEY'RE ALMOST DONE.
PERI (TEAR)
PERI
AS ALWAYS...

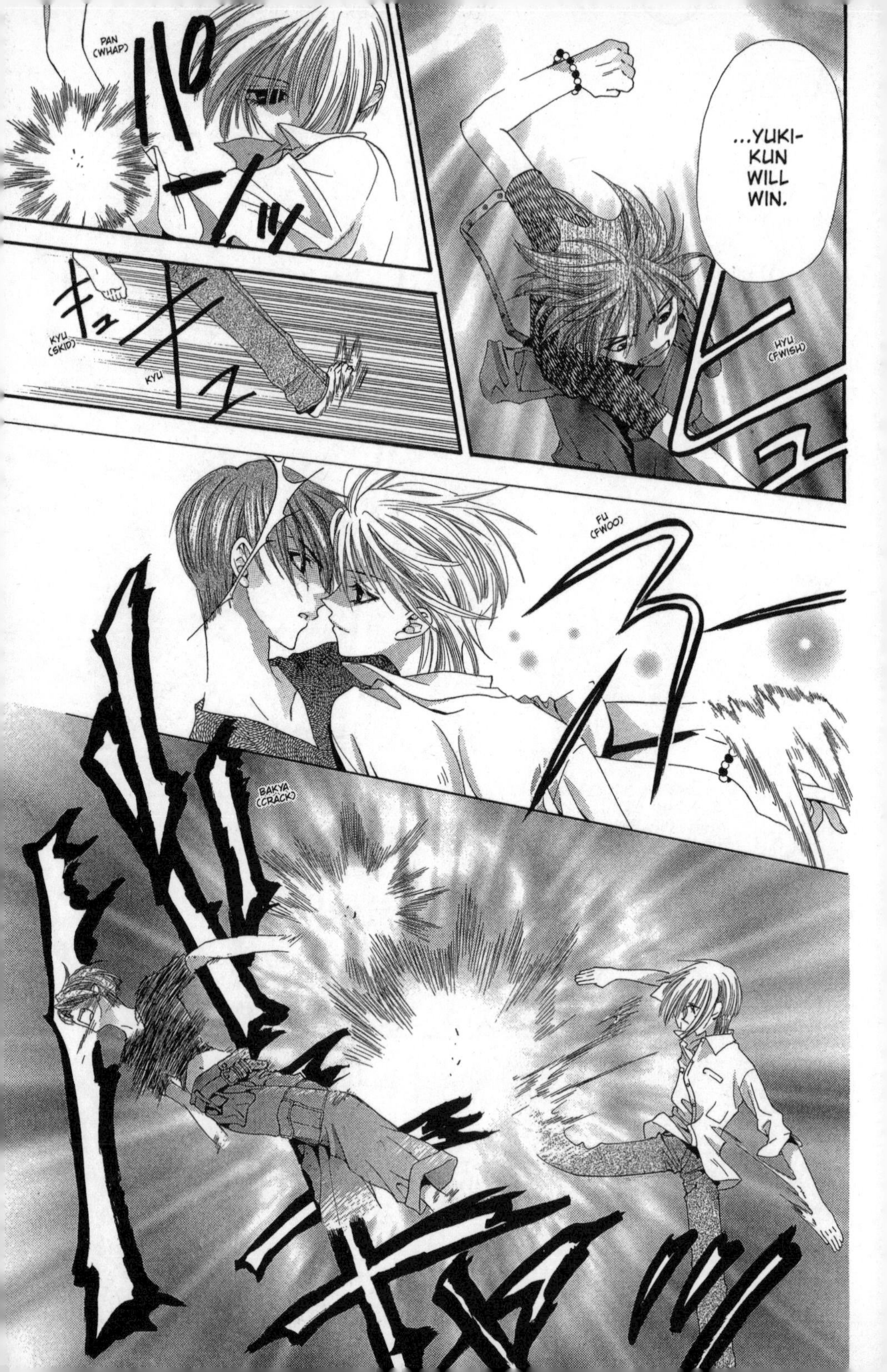
...YUKI-KUN WILL WIN.
HYU (FWISH)
PAN (WHAP)
KYU (SKID)
KYU
FU (FWOO)
BAKYA (CRACK)

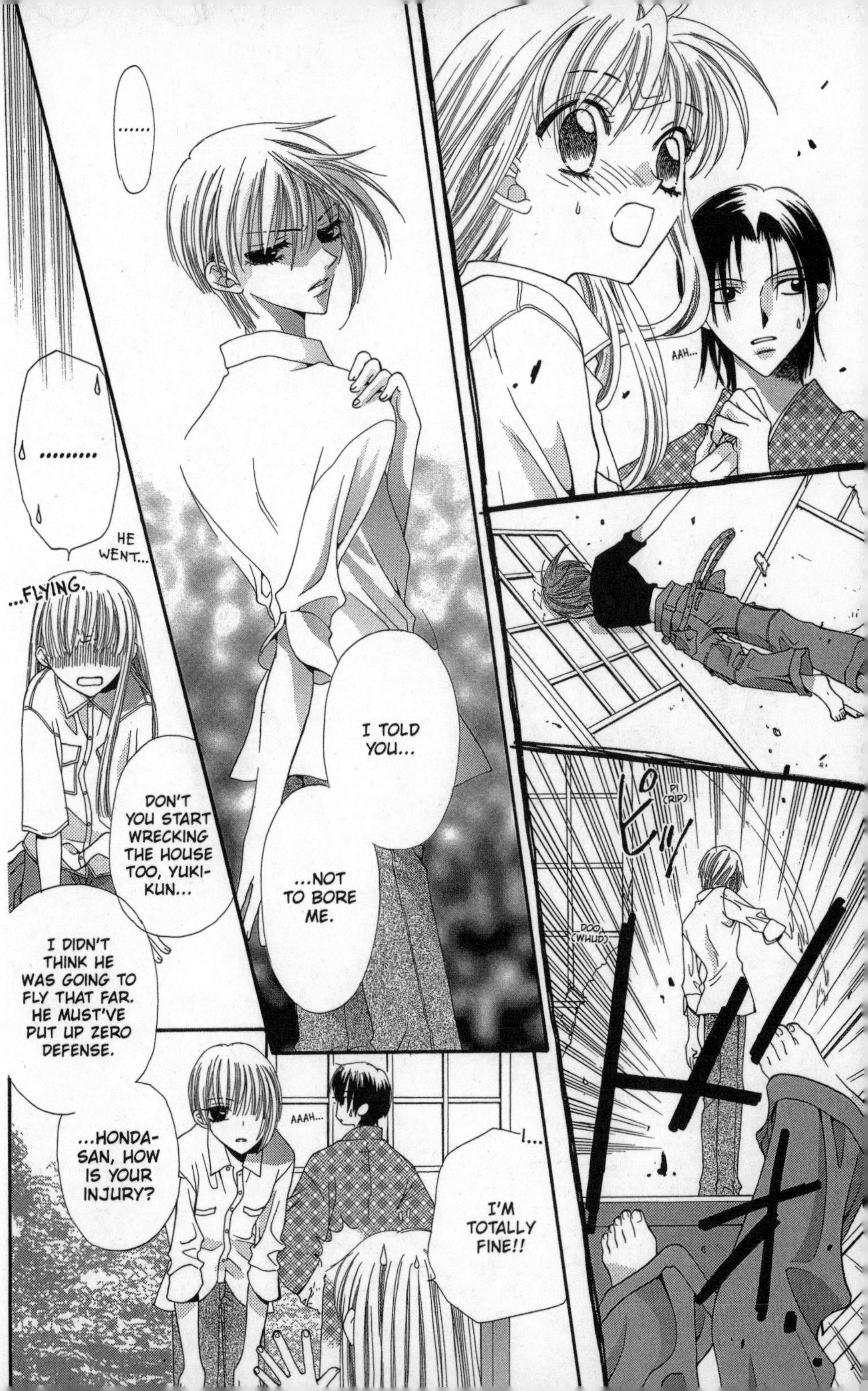
AAH...
PI (RIP)
DOO (WHUD)
......
I TOLD YOU...
...NOT TO BORE ME.
....
HE WENT...
...FLYING.
DON'T YOU START WRECKING THE HOUSE TOO, YUKI-KUN...
I DIDN'T THINK HE WAS GOING TO FLY THAT FAR. HE MUST'VE PUT UP ZERO DEFENSE.
AAAH...
...HONDA-SAN, HOW IS YOUR INJURY?
I...
I'M TOTALLY FINE!!

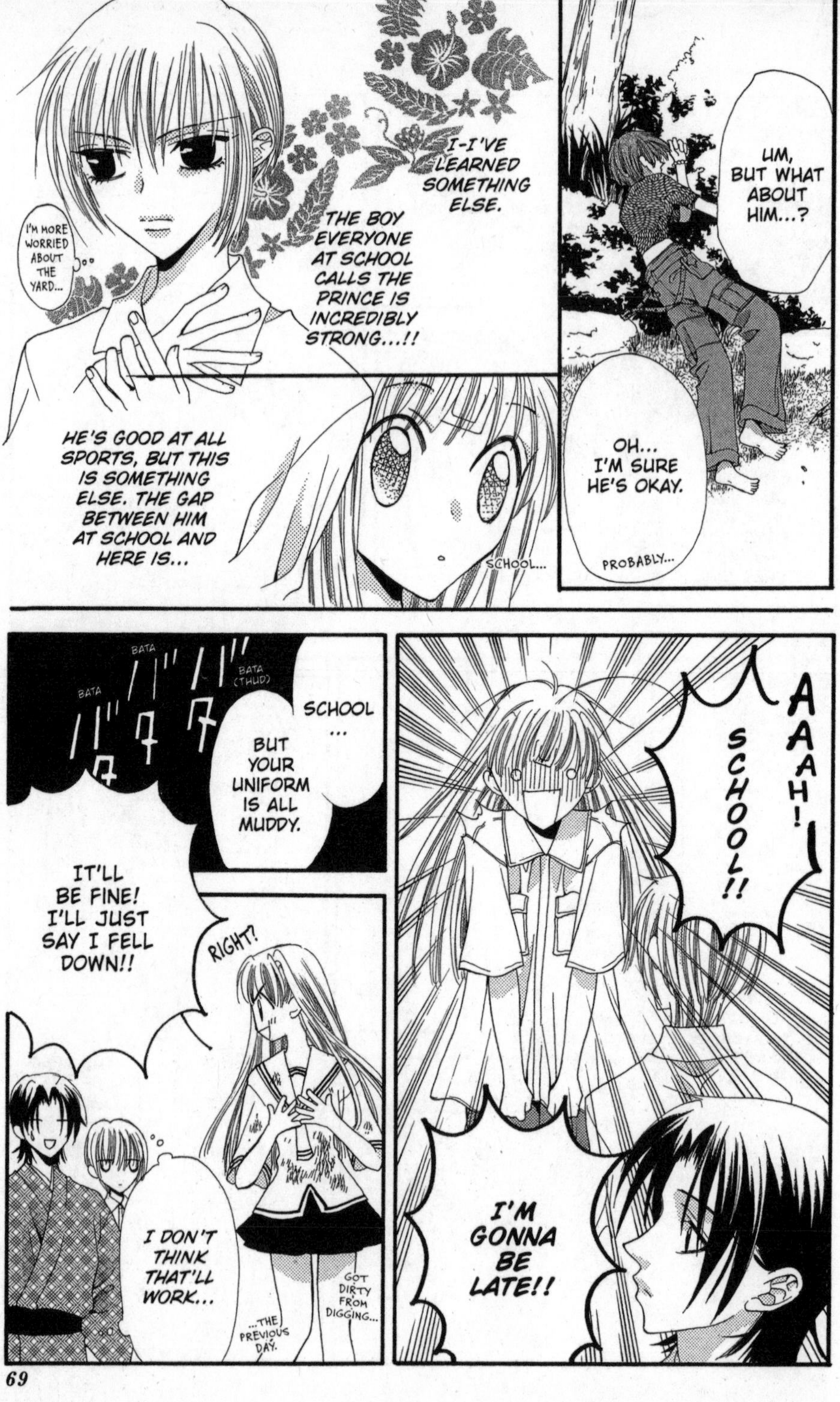
UM, BUT WHAT ABOUT HIM...?
OH... I'M SURE HE'S OKAY.
PROBABLY...
I-I'VE LEARNED SOMETHING ELSE.
THE BOY EVERYONE AT SCHOOL CALLS THE PRINCE IS INCREDIBLY STRONG...!!
I'M MORE WORRIED ABOUT THE YARD...
HE'S GOOD AT ALL SPORTS, BUT THIS IS SOMETHING ELSE. THE GAP BETWEEN HIM AT SCHOOL AND HERE IS...
SCHOOL...
AAAH! SCHOOL!!
I'M GONNA BE LATE!!
BATA
BATA
BATA (THUD)
SCHOOL ...
BUT YOUR UNIFORM IS ALL MUDDY.
IT'LL BE FINE! I'LL JUST SAY I FELL DOWN!!
RIGHT?
I DON'T THINK THAT'LL WORK...
GOT DIRTY FROM DIGGING...
...THE PREVIOUS DAY.

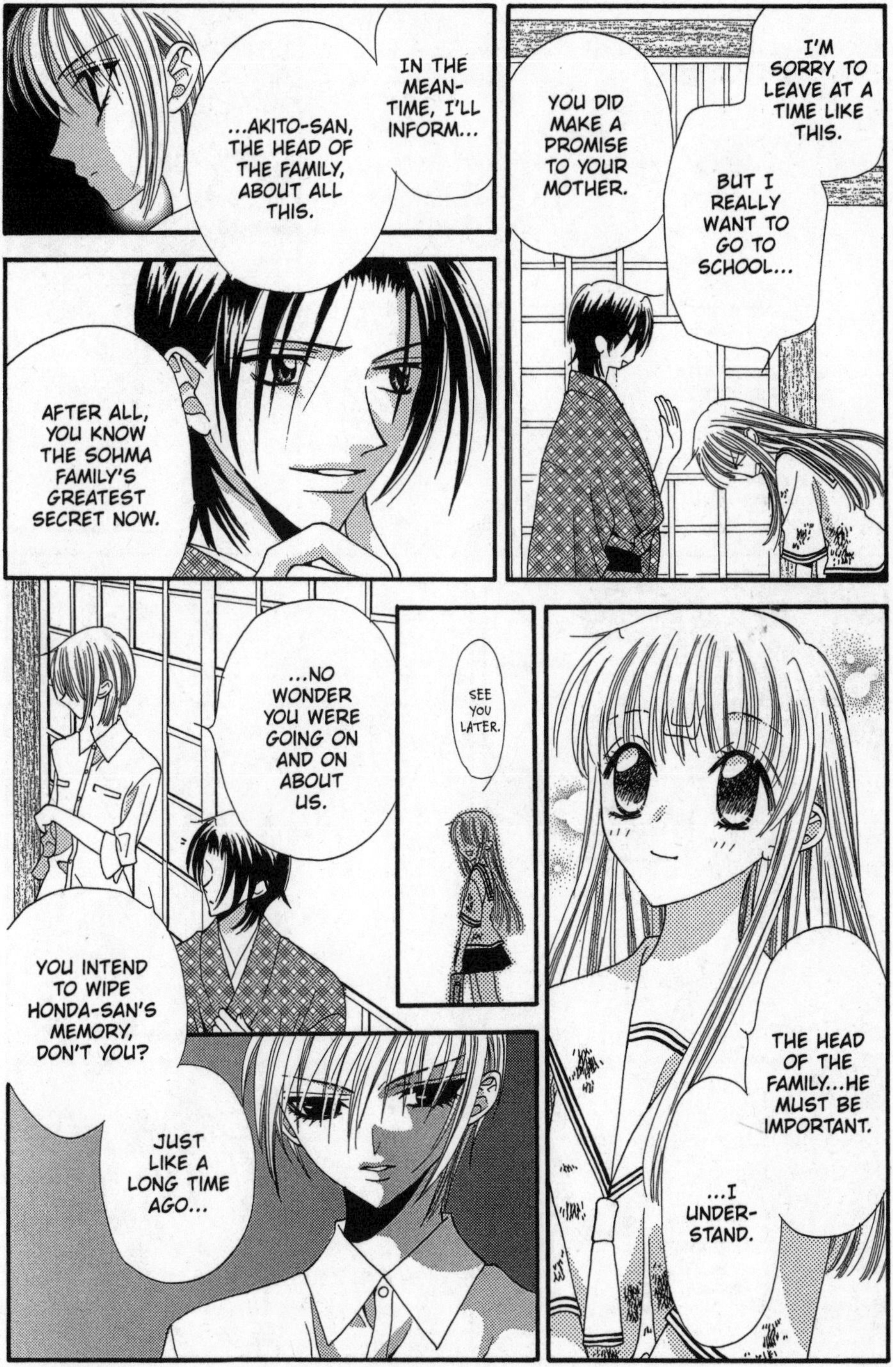
I'M SORRY TO LEAVE AT A TIME LIKE THIS.
BUT I REALLY WANT TO GO TO SCHOOL...
YOU DID MAKE A PROMISE TO YOUR MOTHER.
IN THE MEAN-TIME, I'LL INFORM...
...AKITO-SAN, THE HEAD OF THE FAMILY, ABOUT ALL THIS.
AFTER ALL, YOU KNOW THE SOHMA FAMILY'S GREATEST SECRET NOW.
THE HEAD OF THE FAMILY...HE MUST BE IMPORTANT.
...I UNDER-STAND.
SEE YOU LATER.
...NO WONDER YOU WERE GOING ON AND ON ABOUT US.
YOU INTEND TO WIPE HONDA-SAN'S MEMORY, DON'T YOU?
JUST LIKE A LONG TIME AGO...

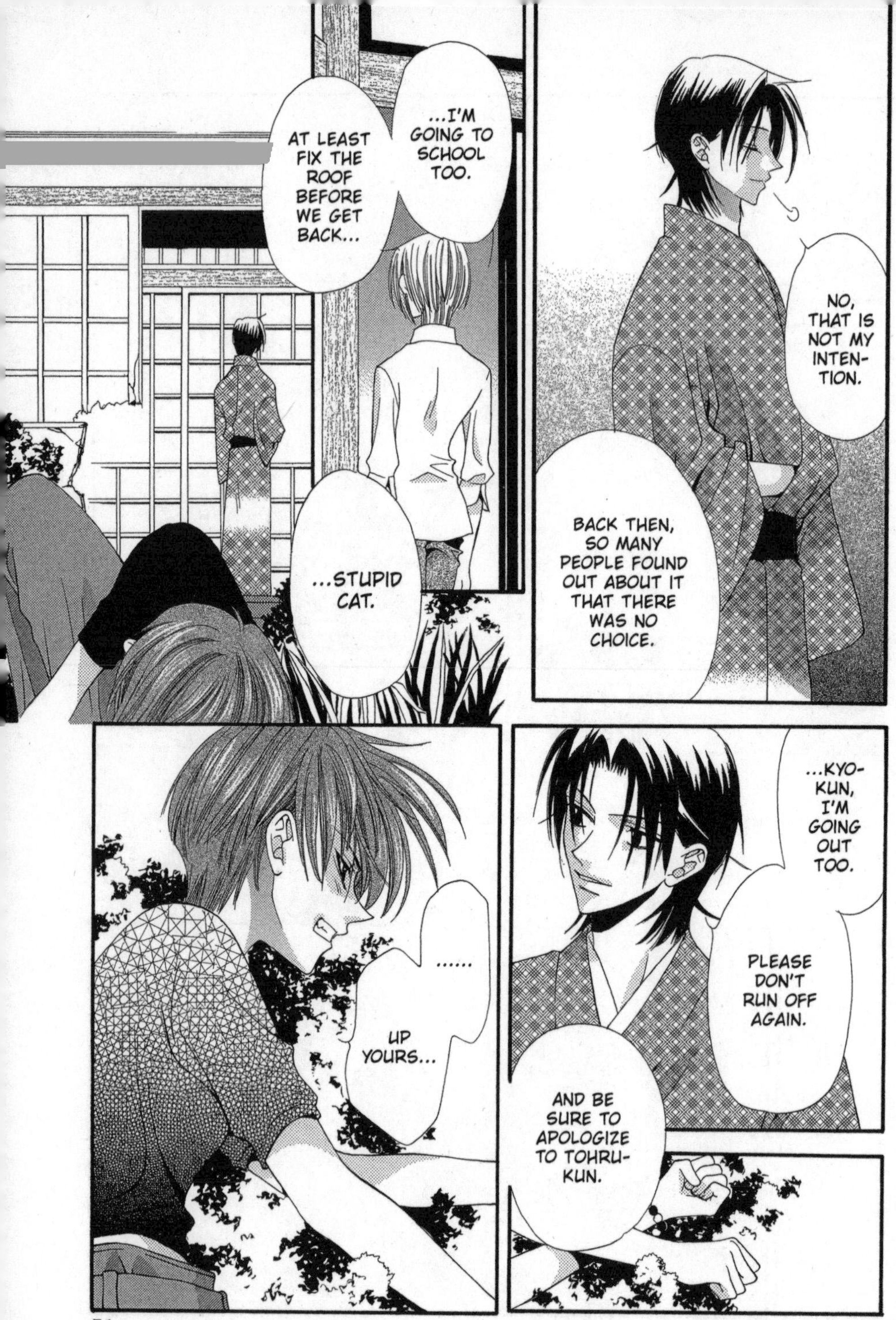
NO, THAT IS NOT MY INTENTION.
BACK THEN, SO MANY PEOPLE FOUND OUT ABOUT IT THAT THERE WAS NO CHOICE.
...I'M GOING TO SCHOOL TOO.
AT LEAST FIX THE ROOF BEFORE WE GET BACK...
...STUPID CAT.
...KYO-KUN, I'M GOING OUT TOO.
PLEASE DON'T RUN OFF AGAIN.
AND BE SURE TO APOLOGIZE TO TOHRU-KUN.
......
UP YOURS...

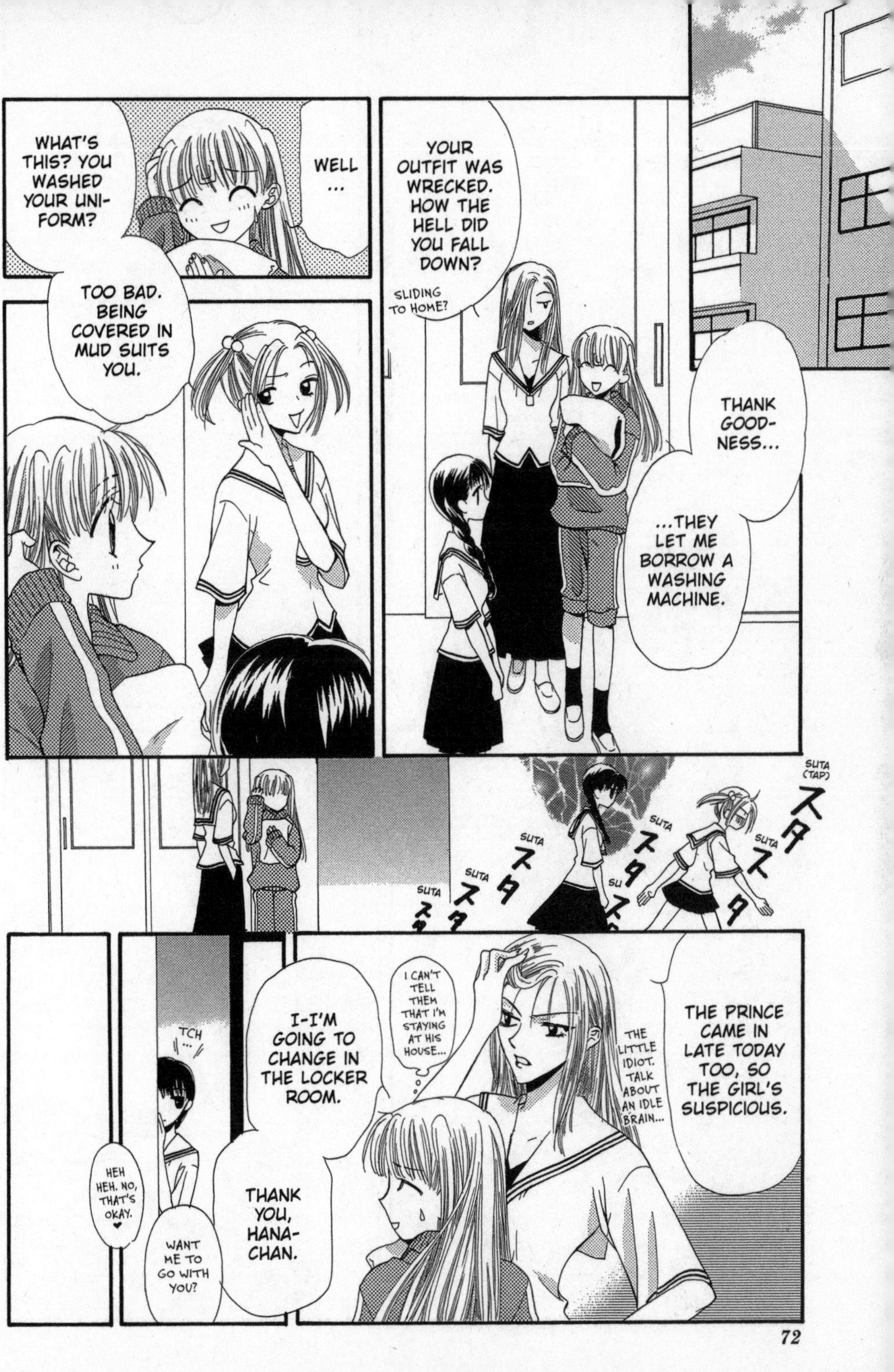
YOUR OUTFIT WAS WRECKED. HOW THE HELL DID YOU FALL DOWN?
SLIDING TO HOME?
THANK GOODNESS...
...THEY LET ME BORROW A WASHING MACHINE.
WHAT'S THIS? YOU WASHED YOUR UNIFORM?
WELL ...
TOO BAD. BEING COVERED IN MUD SUITS YOU.
SUTA (TAP)
スタ
SUTA
スタ
SUTA
スタ
SU
ス
SUTA
スタ
SUTA
スタ
THE PRINCE CAME IN LATE TODAY TOO, SO THE GIRL'S SUSPICIOUS.
THE LITTLE IDIOT. TALK ABOUT AN IDLE BRAIN...
I CAN'T TELL THEM THAT I'M STAYING AT HIS HOUSE...
I-I'M GOING TO CHANGE IN THE LOCKER ROOM.
THANK YOU, HANA-CHAN.
TCH ...
WANT ME TO GO WITH YOU?
HEH HEH. NO, THAT'S OKAY. ♥

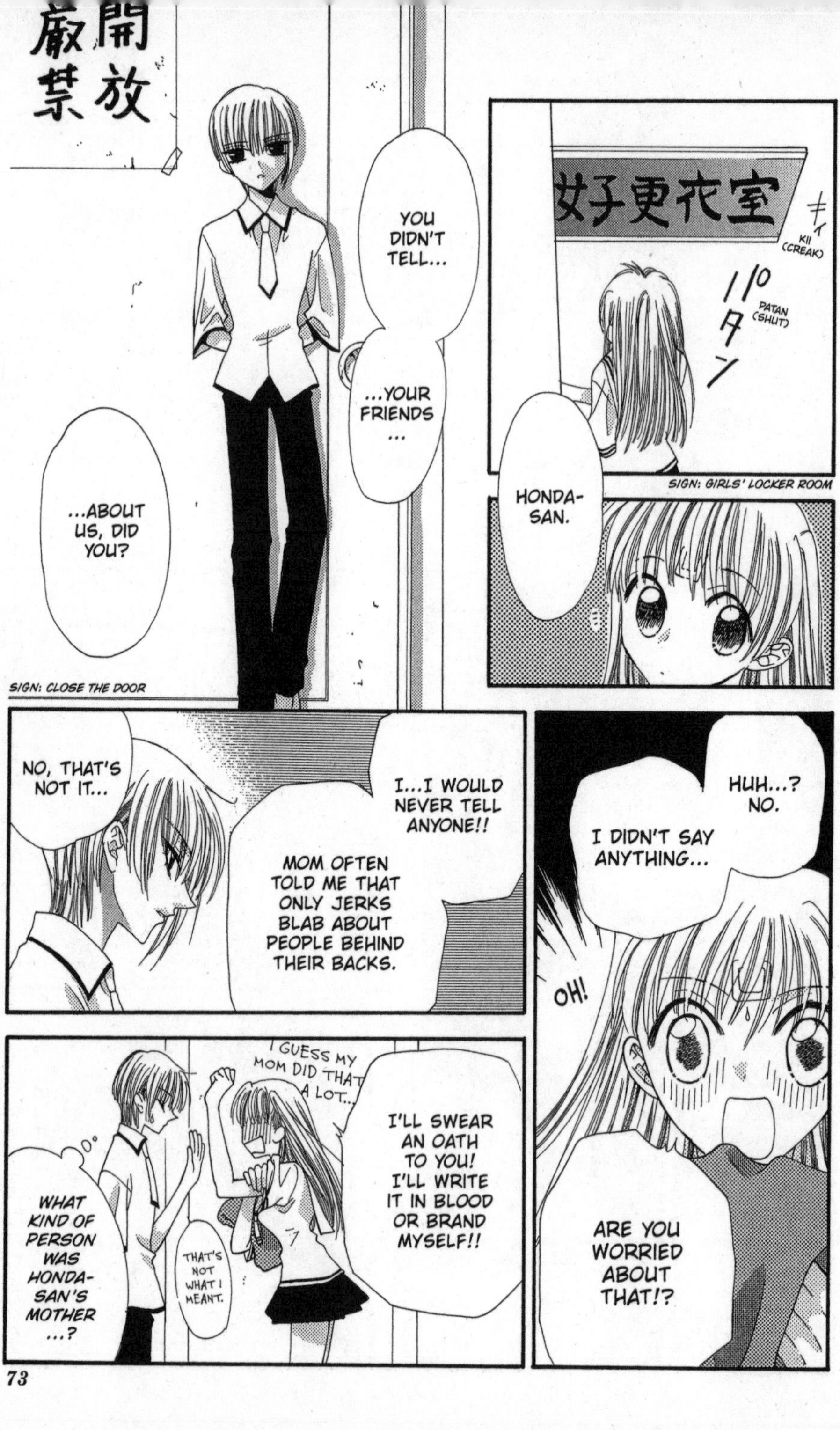
女子更衣室
キイ
KII (CREAK)
パタン
PATAN (SHUT)
SIGN: GIRLS' LOCKER ROOM
HONDA-SAN.
開放厳禁
YOU DIDN'T TELL...
...YOUR FRIENDS ...
...ABOUT US, DID YOU?
SIGN: CLOSE THE DOOR
HUH...? NO.
I DIDN'T SAY ANYTHING...
OH!
ARE YOU WORRIED ABOUT THAT!?
I...I WOULD NEVER TELL ANYONE!!
MOM OFTEN TOLD ME THAT ONLY JERKS BLAB ABOUT PEOPLE BEHIND THEIR BACKS.
NO, THAT'S NOT IT...
I'LL SWEAR AN OATH TO YOU! I'LL WRITE IT IN BLOOD OR BRAND MYSELF!!
I GUESS MY MOM DID THAT A LOT...
THAT'S NOT WHAT I MEANT.
WHAT KIND OF PERSON WAS HONDA-SAN'S MOTHER ...?

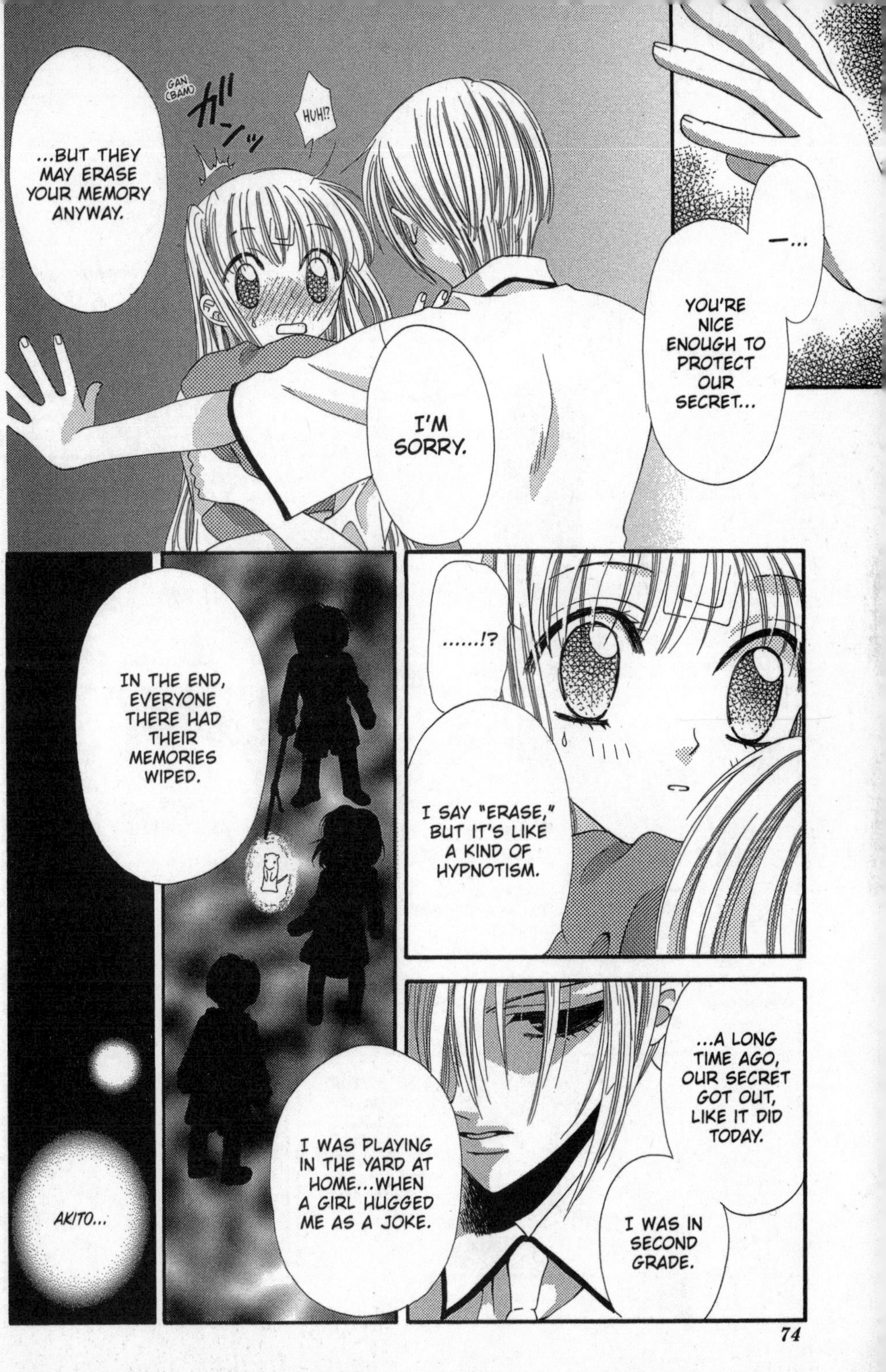
—...
YOU'RE NICE ENOUGH TO PROTECT OUR SECRET...
I'M SORRY.
HUH!?
GAN (BAM)
...BUT THEY MAY ERASE YOUR MEMORY ANYWAY.
......!?
I SAY "ERASE," BUT IT'S LIKE A KIND OF HYPNOTISM.
...A LONG TIME AGO, OUR SECRET GOT OUT, LIKE IT DID TODAY.
I WAS IN SECOND GRADE.
I WAS PLAYING IN THE YARD AT HOME...WHEN A GIRL HUGGED ME AS A JOKE.
IN THE END, EVERYONE THERE HAD THEIR MEMORIES WIPED.
AKITO...

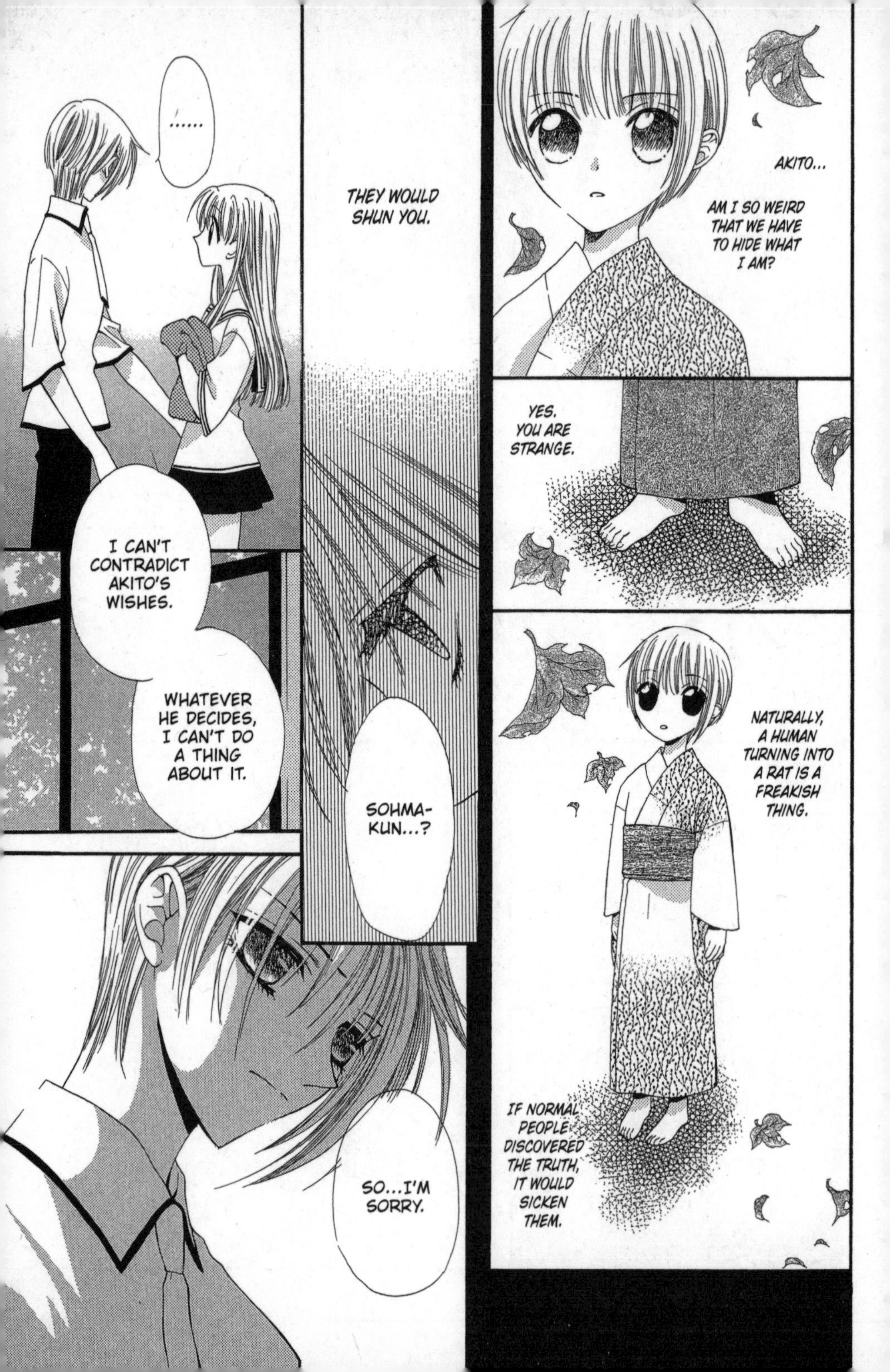

AKITO...
AM I SO WEIRD THAT WE HAVE TO HIDE WHAT I AM?
YES. YOU ARE STRANGE.
NATURALLY, A HUMAN TURNING INTO A RAT IS A FREAKISH THING.
IF NORMAL PEOPLE DISCOVERED THE TRUTH, IT WOULD SICKEN THEM.
THEY WOULD SHUN YOU.
SOHMA-KUN...?
......
I CAN'T CONTRADICT AKITO'S WISHES.
WHATEVER HE DECIDES, I CAN'T DO A THING ABOUT IT.
SO...I'M SORRY.

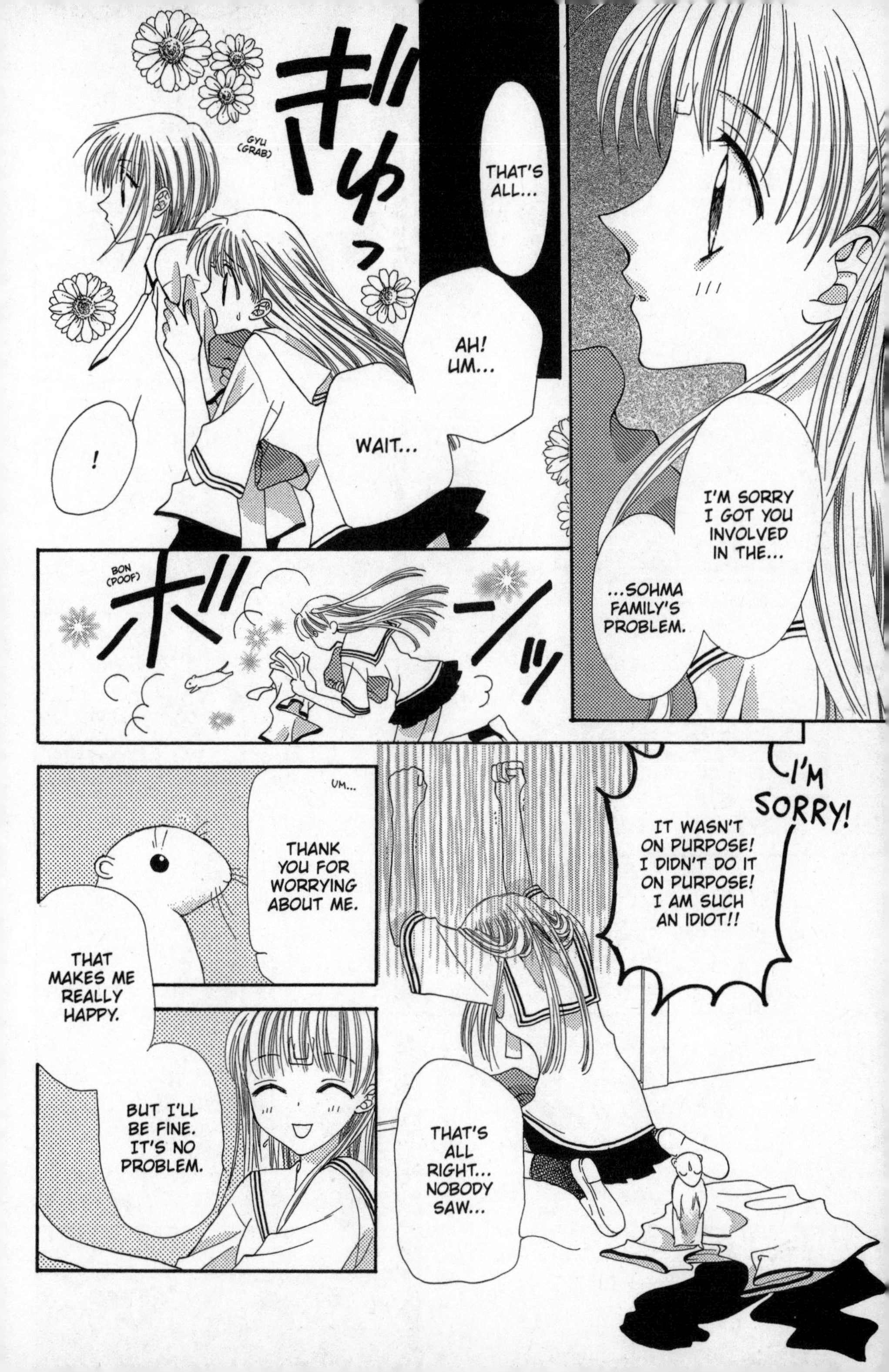
I'M SORRY I GOT YOU INVOLVED IN THE...
...SOHMA FAMILY'S PROBLEM.
THAT'S ALL...
AH! UM...
WAIT...
GYU (GRAB)
!
BON (POOF)
I'M SORRY!
IT WASN'T ON PURPOSE! I DIDN'T DO IT ON PURPOSE! I AM SUCH AN IDIOT!!
THAT'S ALL RIGHT... NOBODY SAW...
UM...
THANK YOU FOR WORRYING ABOUT ME.
THAT MAKES ME REALLY HAPPY.
BUT I'LL BE FINE. IT'S NO PROBLEM.

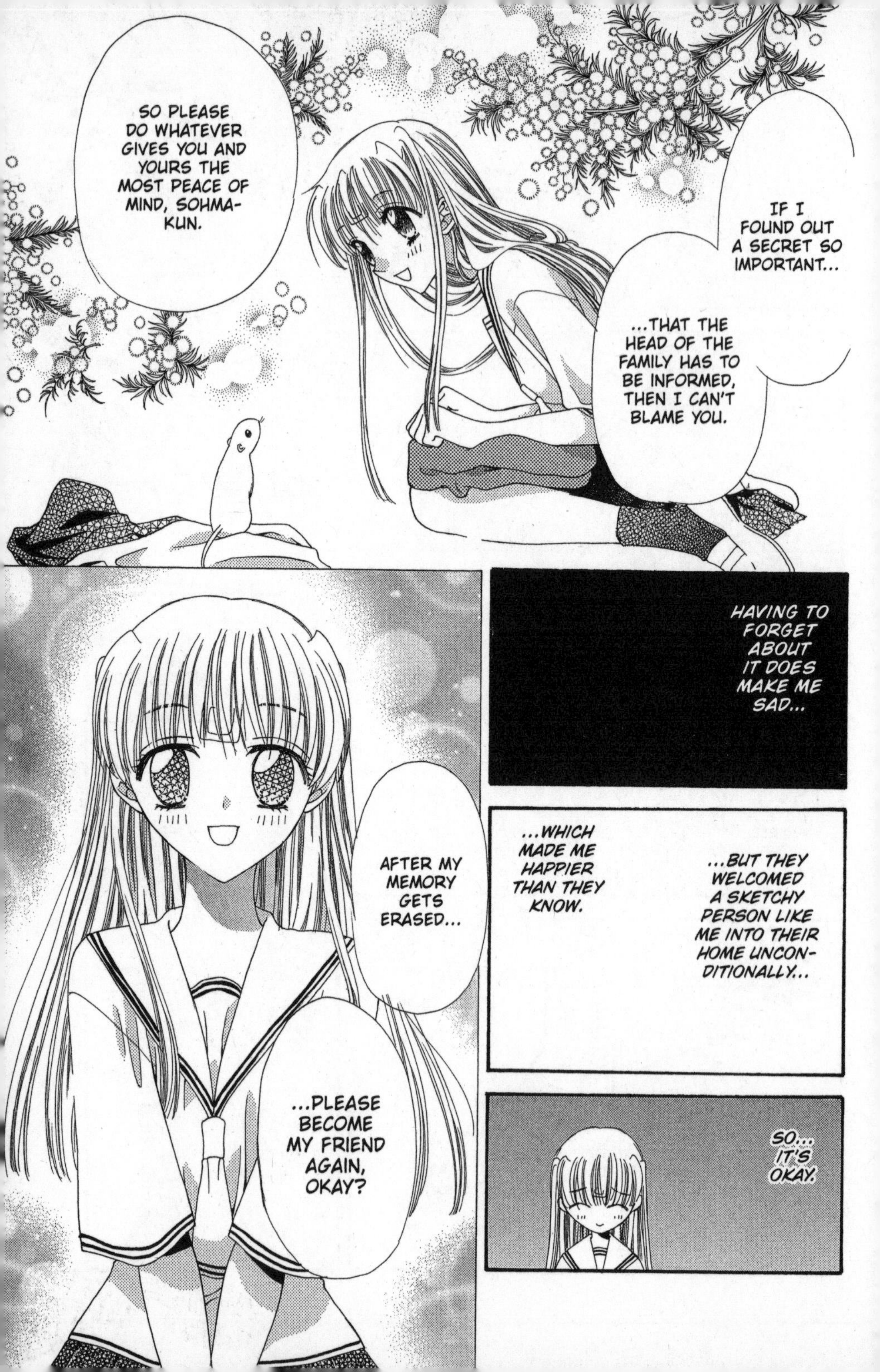
IF I FOUND OUT A SECRET SO IMPORTANT...
...THAT THE HEAD OF THE FAMILY HAS TO BE INFORMED, THEN I CAN'T BLAME YOU.
SO PLEASE DO WHATEVER GIVES YOU AND YOURS THE MOST PEACE OF MIND, SOHMA-KUN.
HAVING TO FORGET ABOUT IT DOES MAKE ME SAD...
...BUT THEY WELCOMED A SKETCHY PERSON LIKE ME INTO THEIR HOME UNCONDITIONALLY...
...WHICH MADE ME HAPPIER THAN THEY KNOW.
SO... IT'S OKAY.
AFTER MY MEMORY GETS ERASED...
...PLEASE BECOME MY FRIEND AGAIN, OKAY?

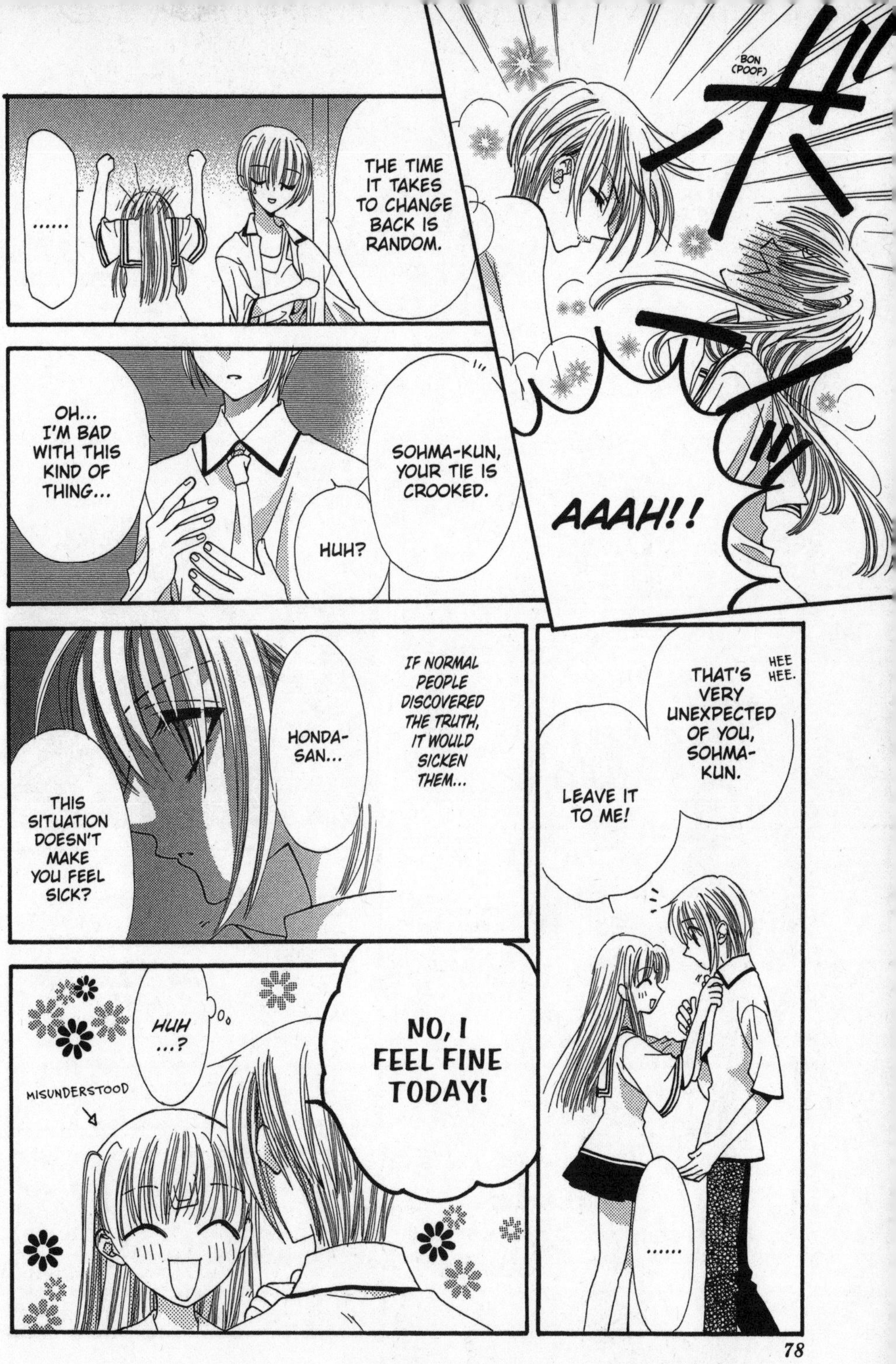
BON (POOF)
AAAH!!
THE TIME IT TAKES TO CHANGE BACK IS RANDOM.
......
SOHMA-KUN, YOUR TIE IS CROOKED.
HUH?
OH... I'M BAD WITH THIS KIND OF THING...
HEE HEE.
THAT'S VERY UNEXPECTED OF YOU, SOHMA-KUN.
LEAVE IT TO ME!
......
IF NORMAL PEOPLE DISCOVERED THE TRUTH, IT WOULD SICKEN THEM...
HONDA-SAN...
THIS SITUATION DOESN'T MAKE YOU FEEL SICK?
NO, I FEEL FINE TODAY!
HUH ...?
MISUNDERSTOOD

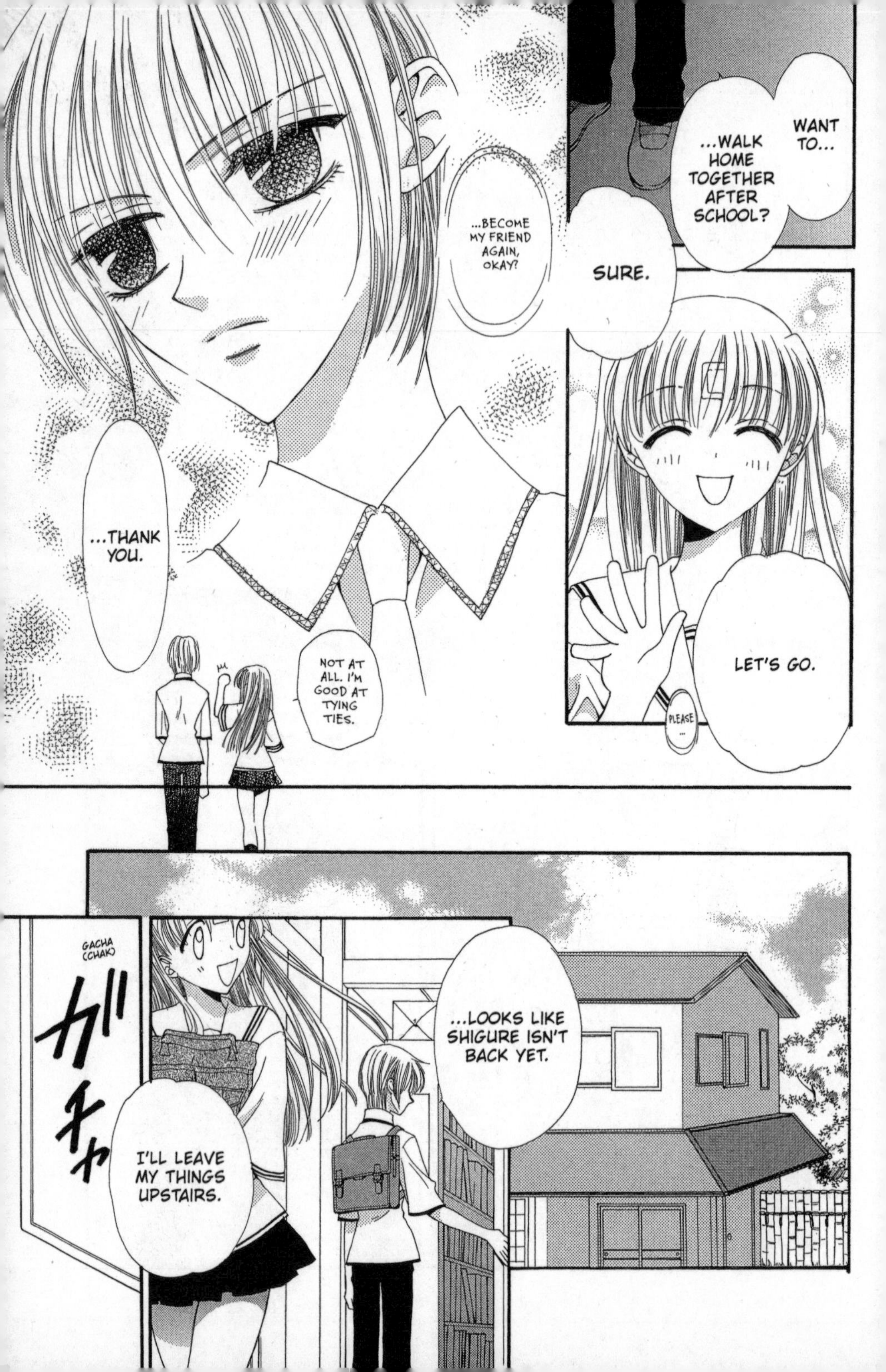
...BECOME MY FRIEND AGAIN, OKAY?
SURE.
WANT TO...
...WALK HOME TOGETHER AFTER SCHOOL?
LET'S GO.
PLEASE...
...THANK YOU.
NOT AT ALL. I'M GOOD AT TYING TIES.
...LOOKS LIKE SHIGURE ISN'T BACK YET.
GACHA (CHAK)
ガチャ
I'LL LEAVE MY THINGS UPSTAIRS.

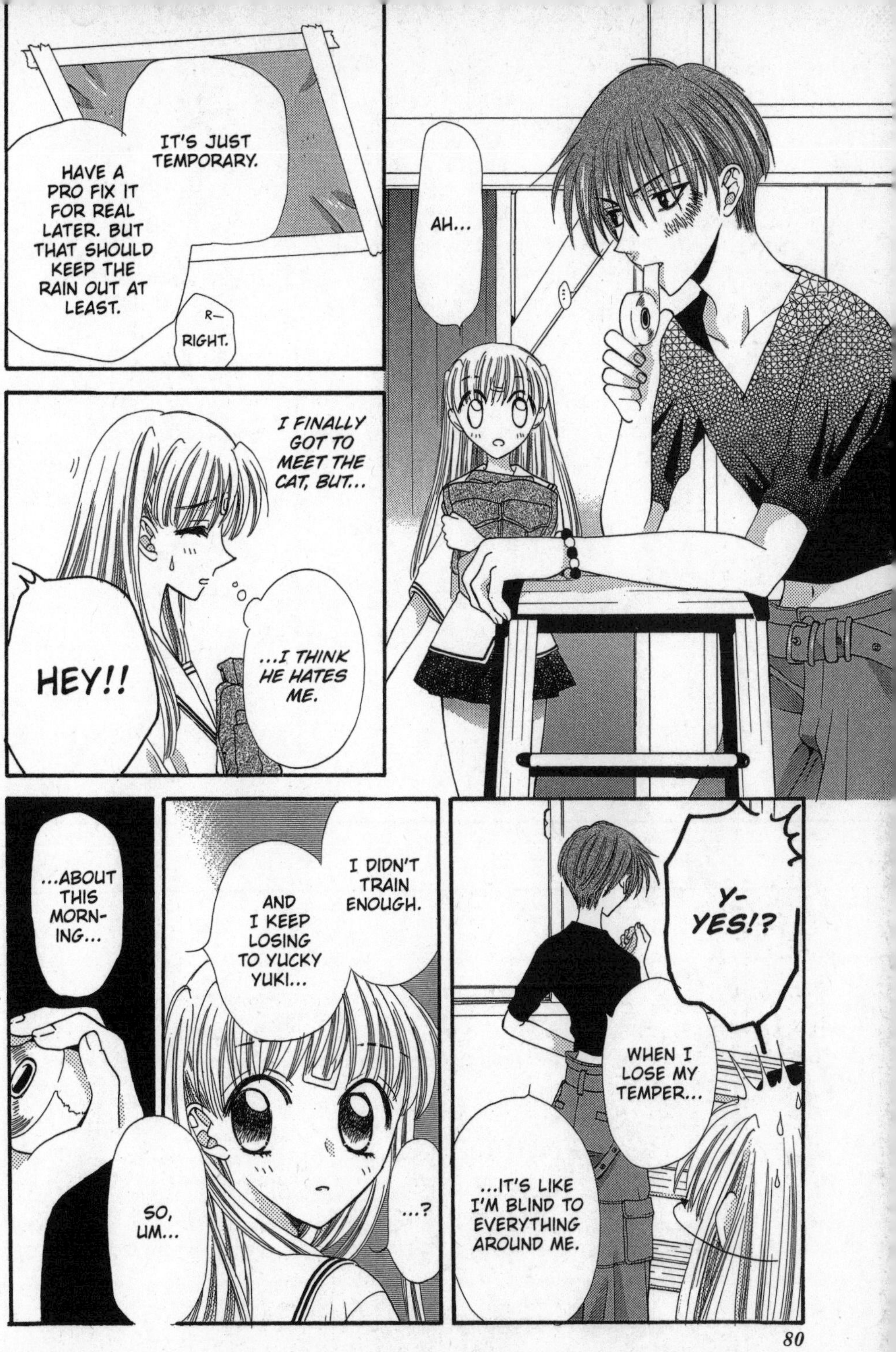
AH...
IT'S JUST TEMPORARY.
HAVE A PRO FIX IT FOR REAL LATER. BUT THAT SHOULD KEEP THE RAIN OUT AT LEAST.
R— RIGHT.
I FINALLY GOT TO MEET THE CAT, BUT...
...I THINK HE HATES ME.
HEY!!
Y- YES!?
WHEN I LOSE MY TEMPER...
...IT'S LIKE I'M BLIND TO EVERYTHING AROUND ME.
I DIDN'T TRAIN ENOUGH.
AND I KEEP LOSING TO YUCKY YUKI...
...?
...ABOUT THIS MORNING...
SO, UM...

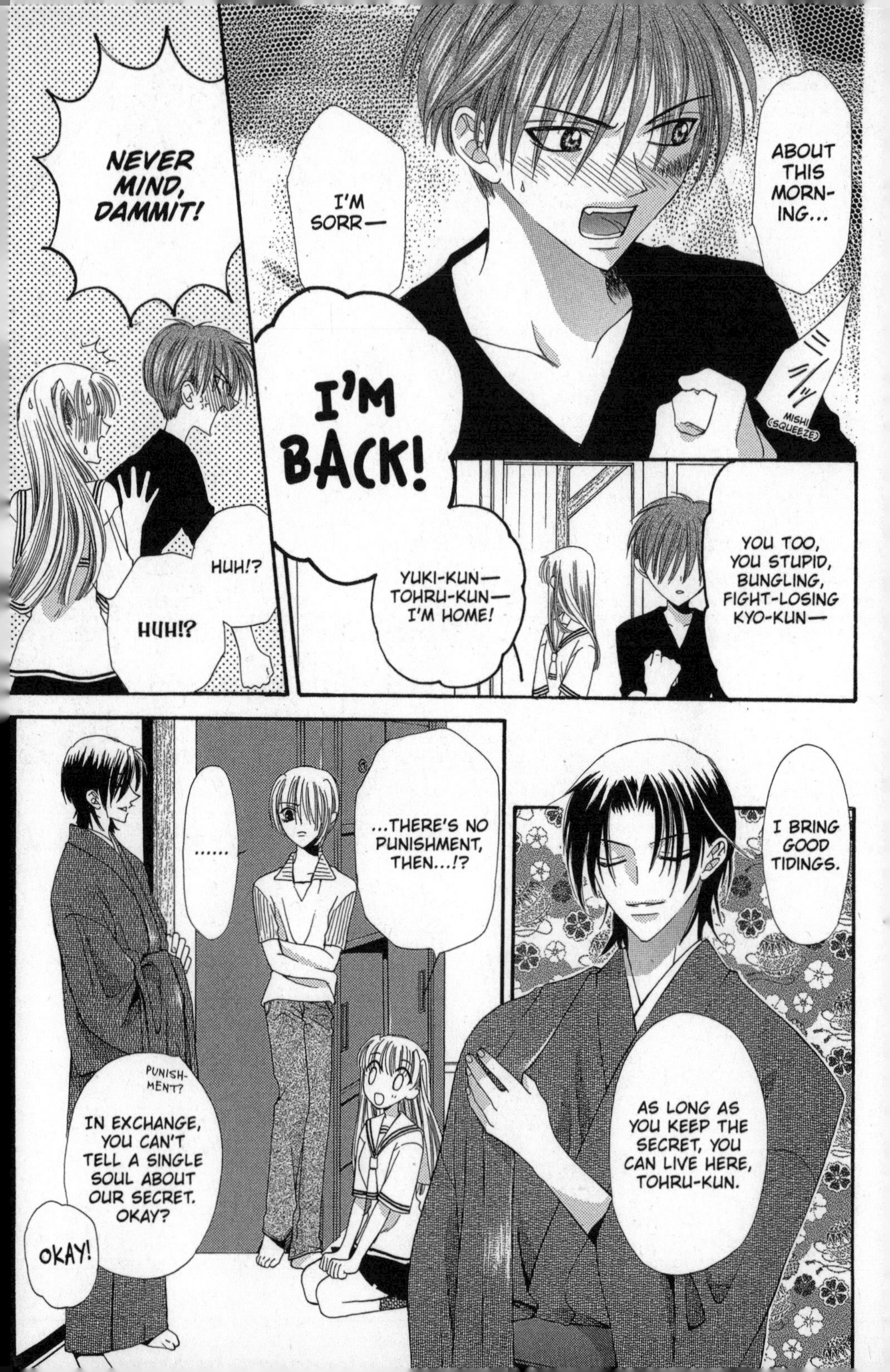

ABOUT THIS MORNING...
I'M SORR—
MISHI (SQUEEZE)
I'M BACK!
YUKI-KUN— TOHRU-KUN— I'M HOME!
YOU TOO, YOU STUPID, BUNGLING, FIGHT-LOSING KYO-KUN—
HUH!?
HUH!?
NEVER MIND, DAMMIT!
I BRING GOOD TIDINGS.
AS LONG AS YOU KEEP THE SECRET, YOU CAN LIVE HERE, TOHRU-KUN.
...THERE'S NO PUNISHMENT, THEN...!?
......
PUNISHMENT?
IN EXCHANGE, YOU CAN'T TELL A SINGLE SOUL ABOUT OUR SECRET. OKAY?
OKAY!

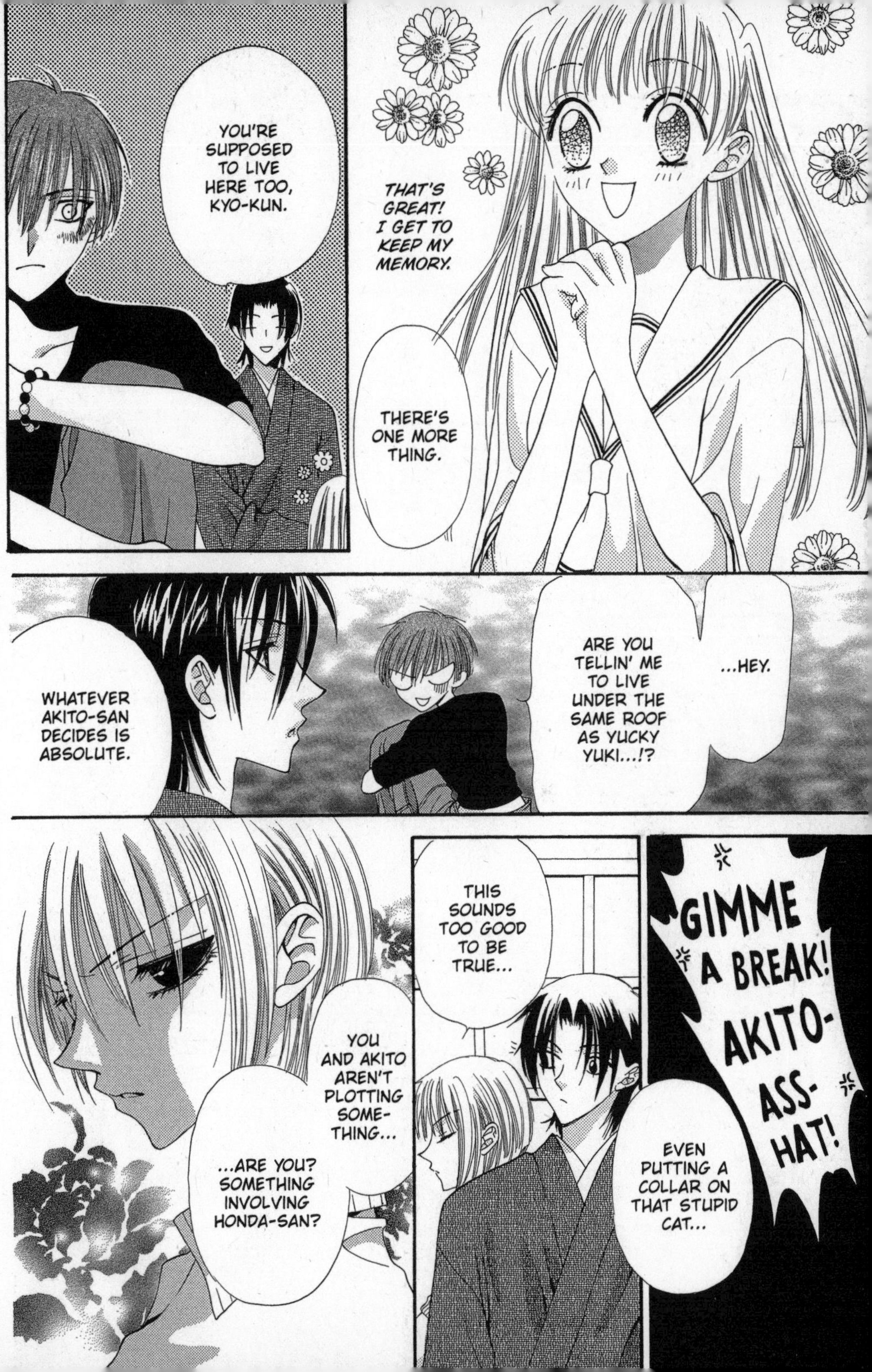
THAT'S GREAT! I GET TO KEEP MY MEMORY.
THERE'S ONE MORE THING.
YOU'RE SUPPOSED TO LIVE HERE TOO, KYO-KUN.
...HEY.
ARE YOU TELLIN' ME TO LIVE UNDER THE SAME ROOF AS YUCKY YUKI...!?
WHATEVER AKITO-SAN DECIDES IS ABSOLUTE.
GIMME A BREAK! AKITO-ASS-HAT!
THIS SOUNDS TOO GOOD TO BE TRUE...
EVEN PUTTING A COLLAR ON THAT STUPID CAT...
YOU AND AKITO AREN'T PLOTTING SOME-THING...
...ARE YOU? SOMETHING INVOLVING HONDA-SAN?

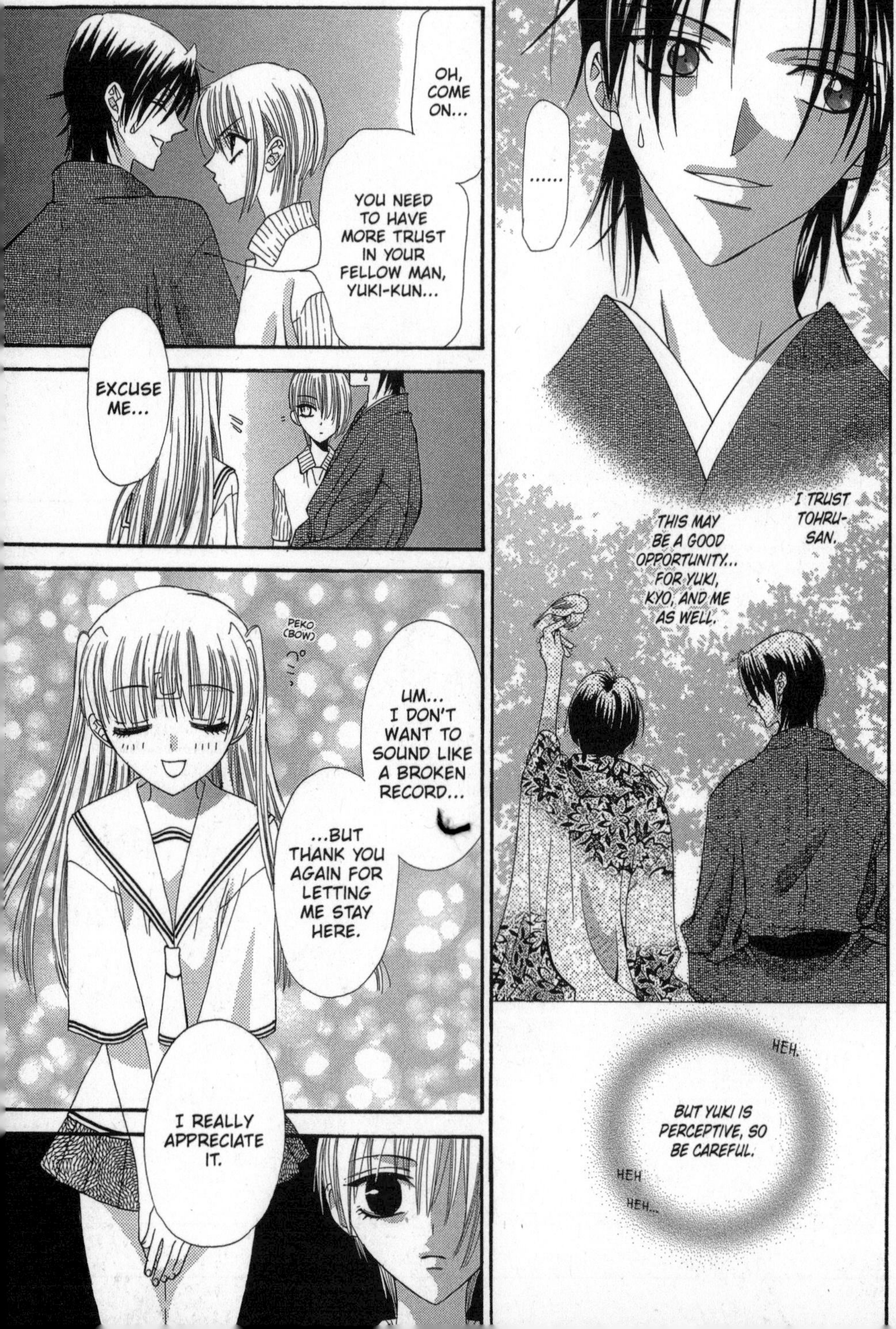
......
I TRUST TOHRU-SAN.
THIS MAY BE A GOOD OPPORTUNITY... FOR YUKI, KYO, AND ME AS WELL.
HEH.
BUT YUKI IS PERCEPTIVE, SO BE CAREFUL.
HEH
HEH...
OH, COME ON...
YOU NEED TO HAVE MORE TRUST IN YOUR FELLOW MAN, YUKI-KUN...
EXCUSE ME...
PEKO (BOW)
UM... I DON'T WANT TO SOUND LIKE A BROKEN RECORD...
...BUT THANK YOU AGAIN FOR LETTING ME STAY HERE.
I REALLY APPRECIATE IT.

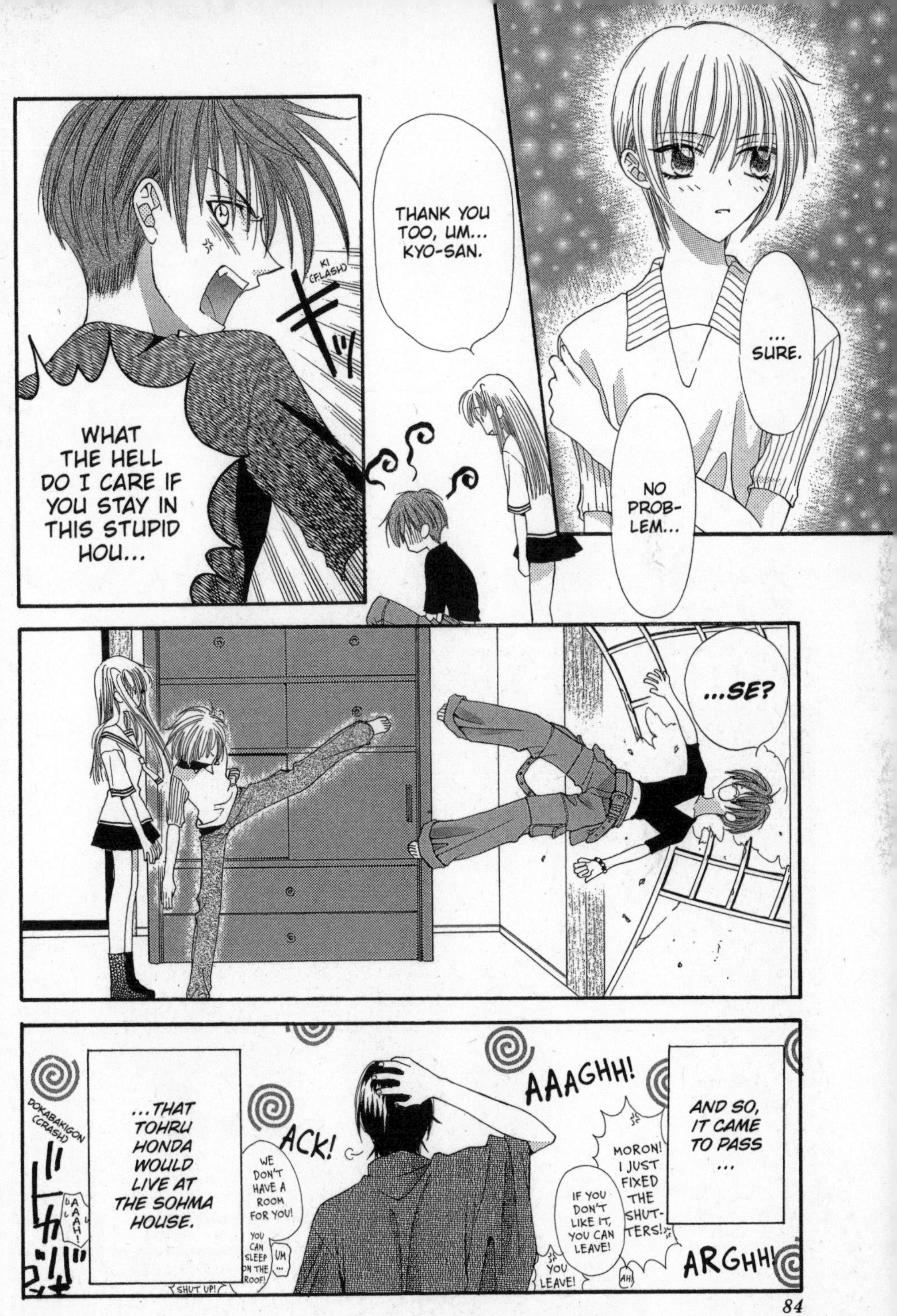
... SURE.
NO PROBLEM...
THANK YOU TOO, UM... KYO-SAN.
KI (FLASH)
WHAT THE HELL DO I CARE IF YOU STAY IN THIS STUPID HOU...
...SE?
AND SO, IT CAME TO PASS ...
ARGHH!
MORON! I JUST FIXED THE SHUTTERS!
AAAGHH!
AH!
IF YOU DON'T LIKE IT, YOU CAN LEAVE!
YOU LEAVE!
ACK!
WE DON'T HAVE A ROOM FOR YOU!
UM ...
YOU CAN SLEEP ON THE ROOF!
SHUT UP!
AAAH!
DOKABAKIGON (CRASH)
...THAT TOHRU HONDA WOULD LIVE AT THE SOHMA HOUSE.

Chapter 3

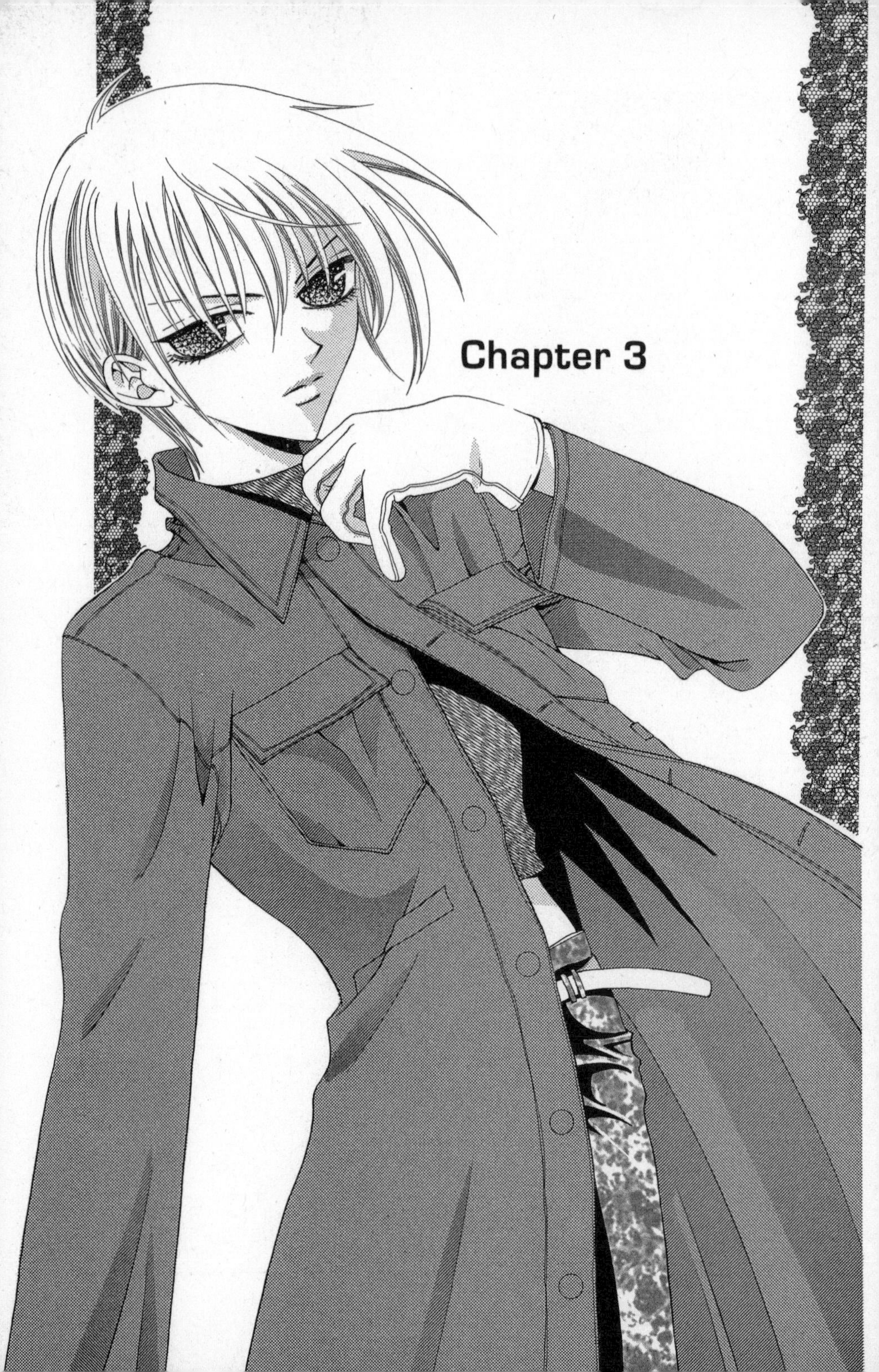

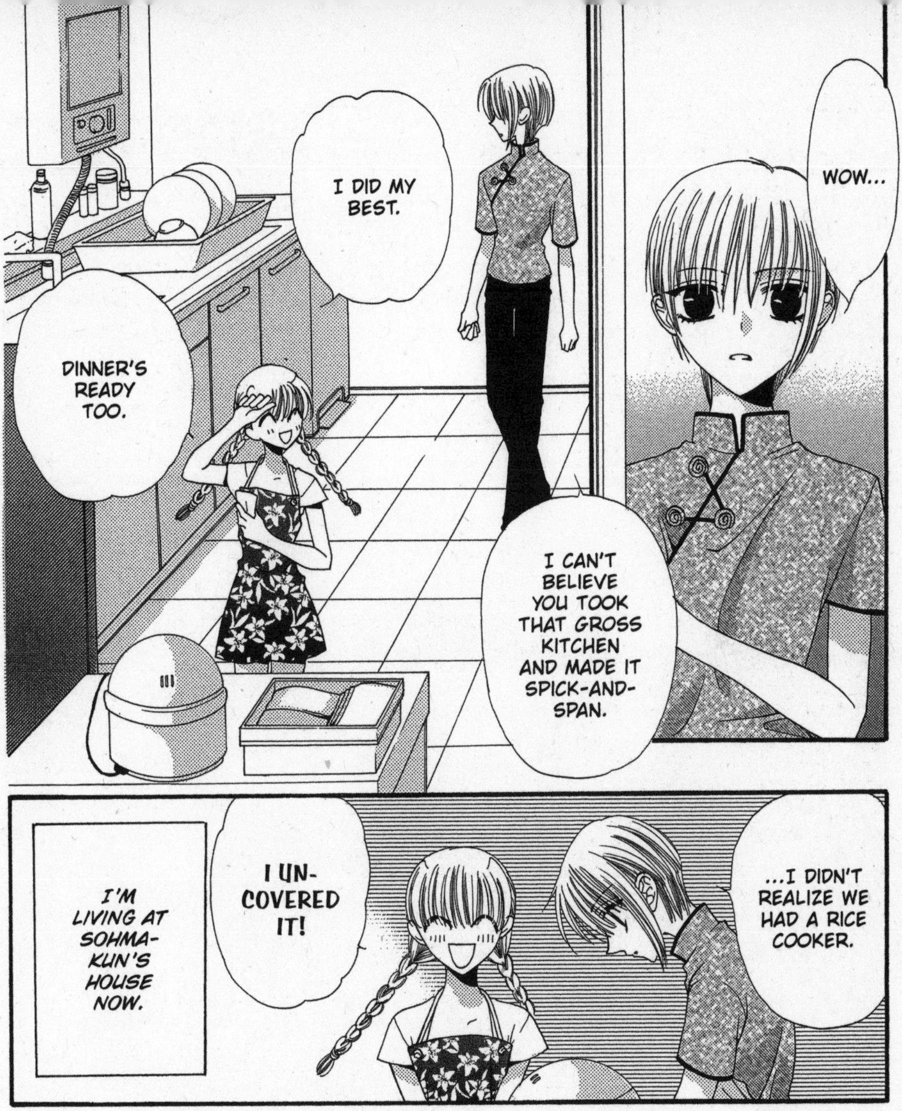
WOW...
I CAN'T BELIEVE YOU TOOK THAT GROSS KITCHEN AND MADE IT SPICK-AND-SPAN.
I DID MY BEST.
DINNER'S READY TOO.
...I DIDN'T REALIZE WE HAD A RICE COOKER.
I UN-COVERED IT!
I'M LIVING AT SOHMA-KUN'S HOUSE NOW.
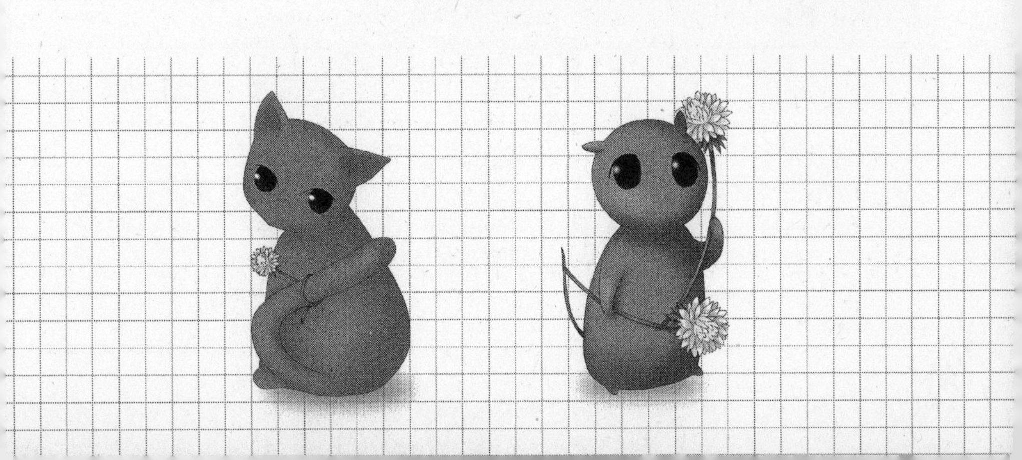

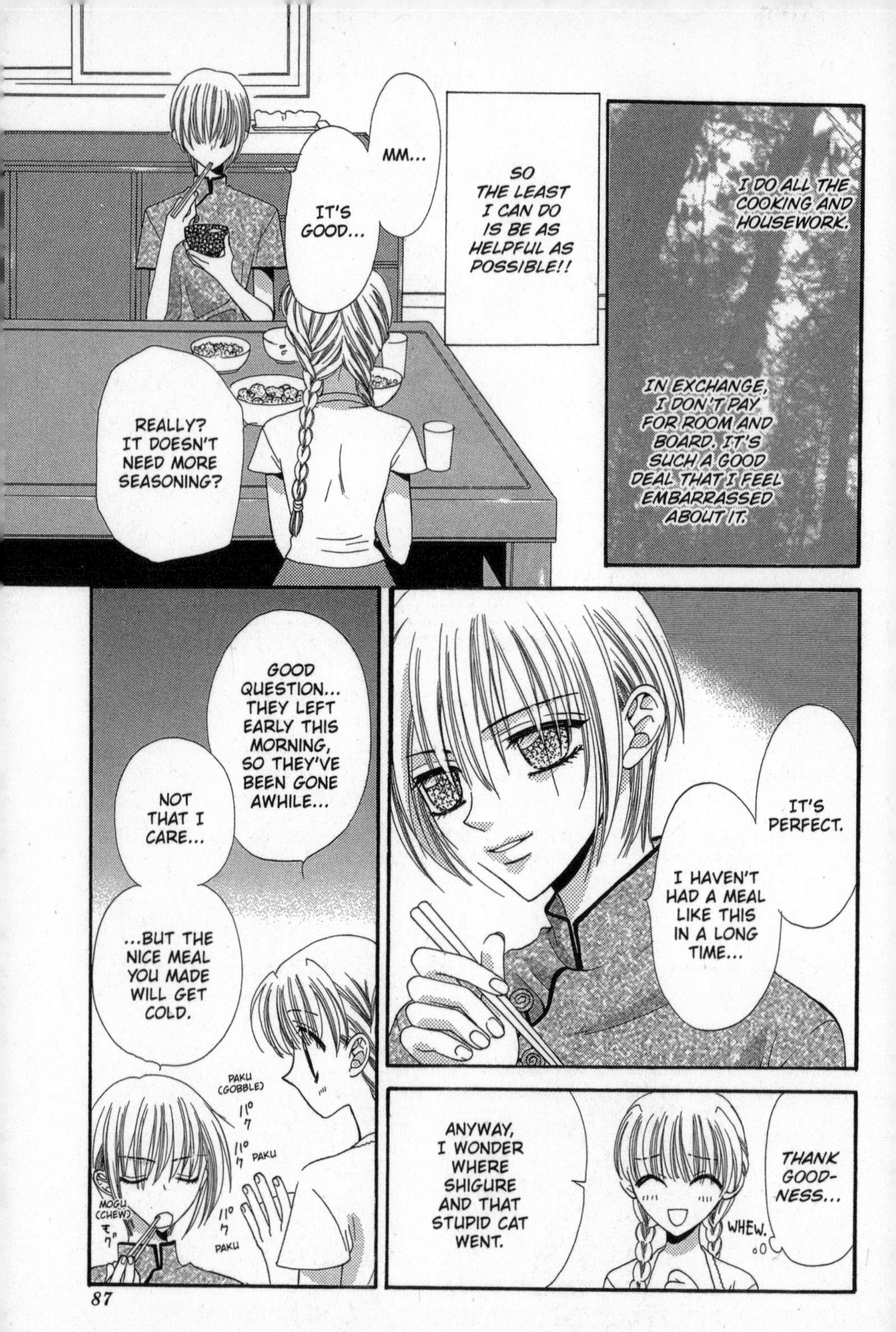
I DO ALL THE COOKING AND HOUSEWORK.
IN EXCHANGE, I DON'T PAY FOR ROOM AND BOARD. IT'S SUCH A GOOD DEAL THAT I FEEL EMBARRASSED ABOUT IT.
SO THE LEAST I CAN DO IS BE AS HELPFUL AS POSSIBLE!!
MM...
IT'S GOOD...
REALLY? IT DOESN'T NEED MORE SEASONING?
IT'S PERFECT.
I HAVEN'T HAD A MEAL LIKE THIS IN A LONG TIME...
THANK GOODNESS...
WHEW.
ANYWAY, I WONDER WHERE SHIGURE AND THAT STUPID CAT WENT.
GOOD QUESTION... THEY LEFT EARLY THIS MORNING, SO THEY'VE BEEN GONE AWHILE...
NOT THAT I CARE...
...BUT THE NICE MEAL YOU MADE WILL GET COLD.
PAKU (GOBBLE)
パク
パク PAKU
MOGU (CHEW)
モグ
パク
PAKU

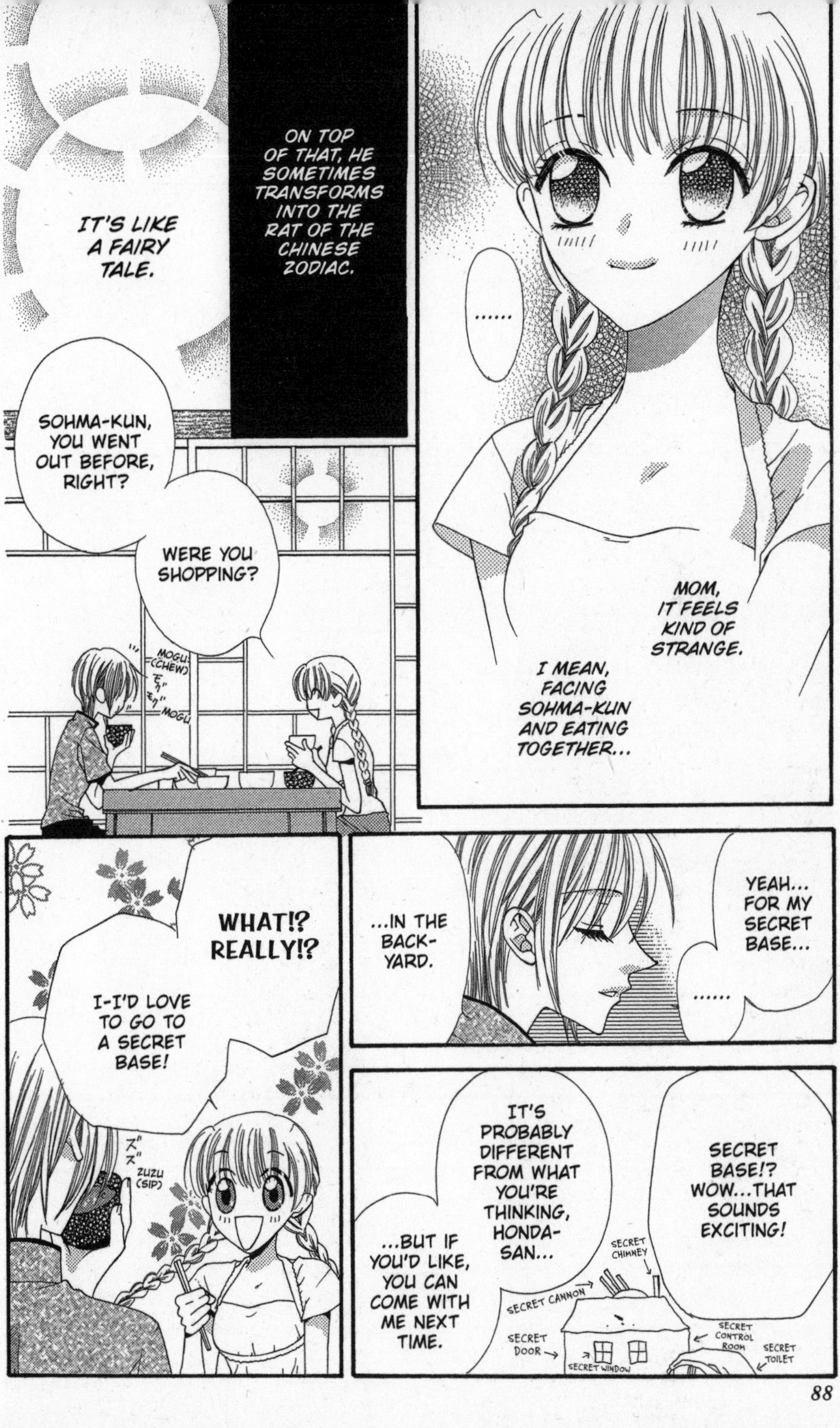
......
MOM, IT FEELS KIND OF STRANGE.
I MEAN, FACING SOHMA-KUN AND EATING TOGETHER...
ON TOP OF THAT, HE SOMETIMES TRANSFORMS INTO THE RAT OF THE CHINESE ZODIAC.
IT'S LIKE A FAIRY TALE.
SOHMA-KUN, YOU WENT OUT BEFORE, RIGHT?
WERE YOU SHOPPING?
MOGU (CHEW)
MOGU
YEAH... FOR MY SECRET BASE...
......
...IN THE BACK-YARD.
SECRET BASE!? WOW...THAT SOUNDS EXCITING!
IT'S PROBABLY DIFFERENT FROM WHAT YOU'RE THINKING, HONDA-SAN...
...BUT IF YOU'D LIKE, YOU CAN COME WITH ME NEXT TIME.
SECRET CHIMNEY
SECRET CANNON
SECRET DOOR
SECRET WINDOW
SECRET CONTROL ROOM
SECRET TOILET
WHAT!? REALLY!?
I-I'D LOVE TO GO TO A SECRET BASE!
ZUZU (SIP)

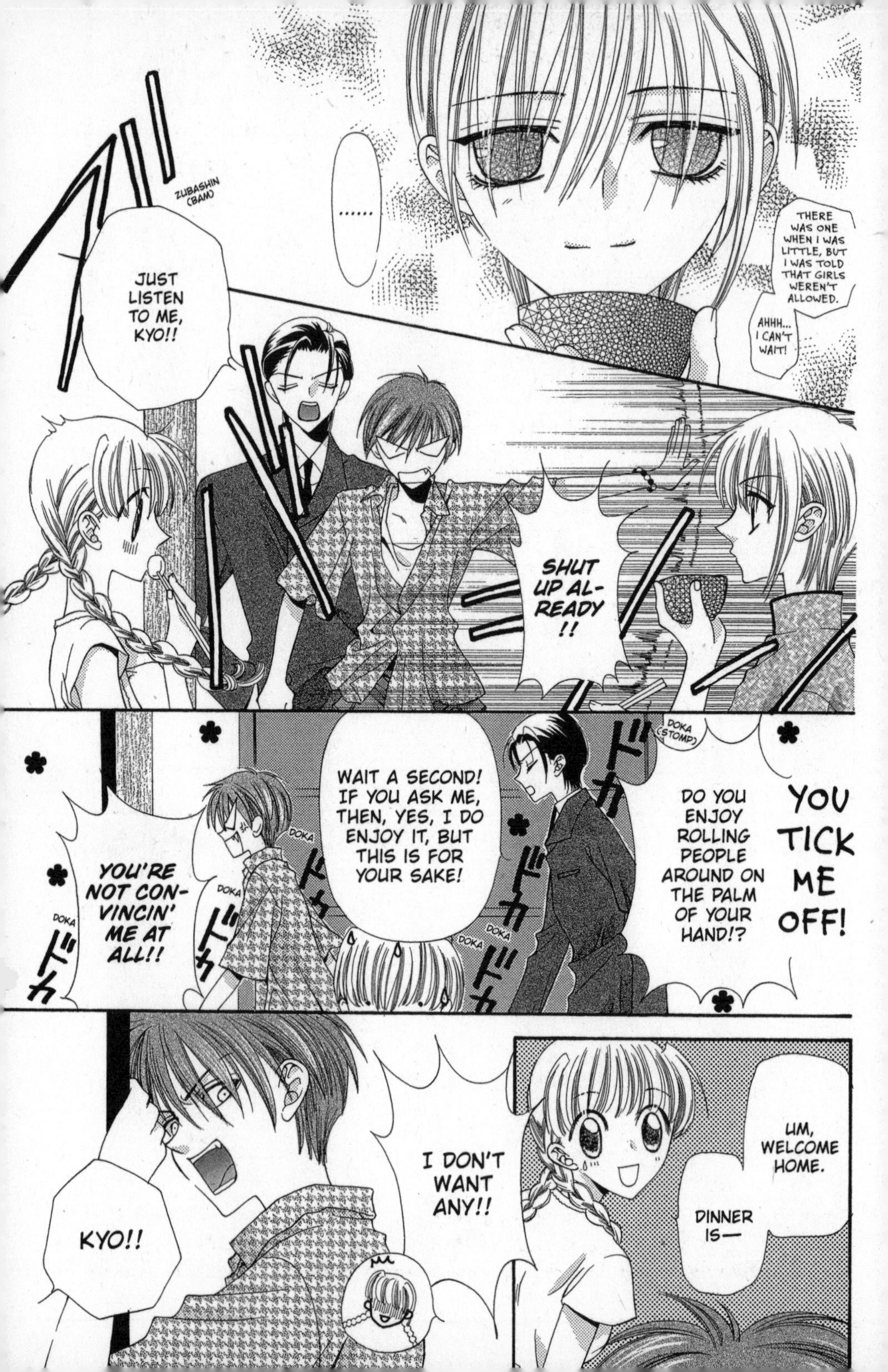

THERE WAS ONE WHEN I WAS LITTLE, BUT I WAS TOLD THAT GIRLS WEREN'T ALLOWED.
AHHH... I CAN'T WAIT!
......
SHUT UP AL-READY!!
ZUBASHIN (BAM)
JUST LISTEN TO ME, KYO!!
YOU TICK ME OFF!
DO YOU ENJOY ROLLING PEOPLE AROUND ON THE PALM OF YOUR HAND!?
DOKA (STOMP)
WAIT A SECOND! IF YOU ASK ME, THEN, YES, I DO ENJOY IT, BUT THIS IS FOR YOUR SAKE!
DOKA
DOKA
DOKA
DOKA
YOU'RE NOT CON-VINCIN' ME AT ALL!!
DOKA
UM, WELCOME HOME.
DINNER IS—
I DON'T WANT ANY!!
KYO!!

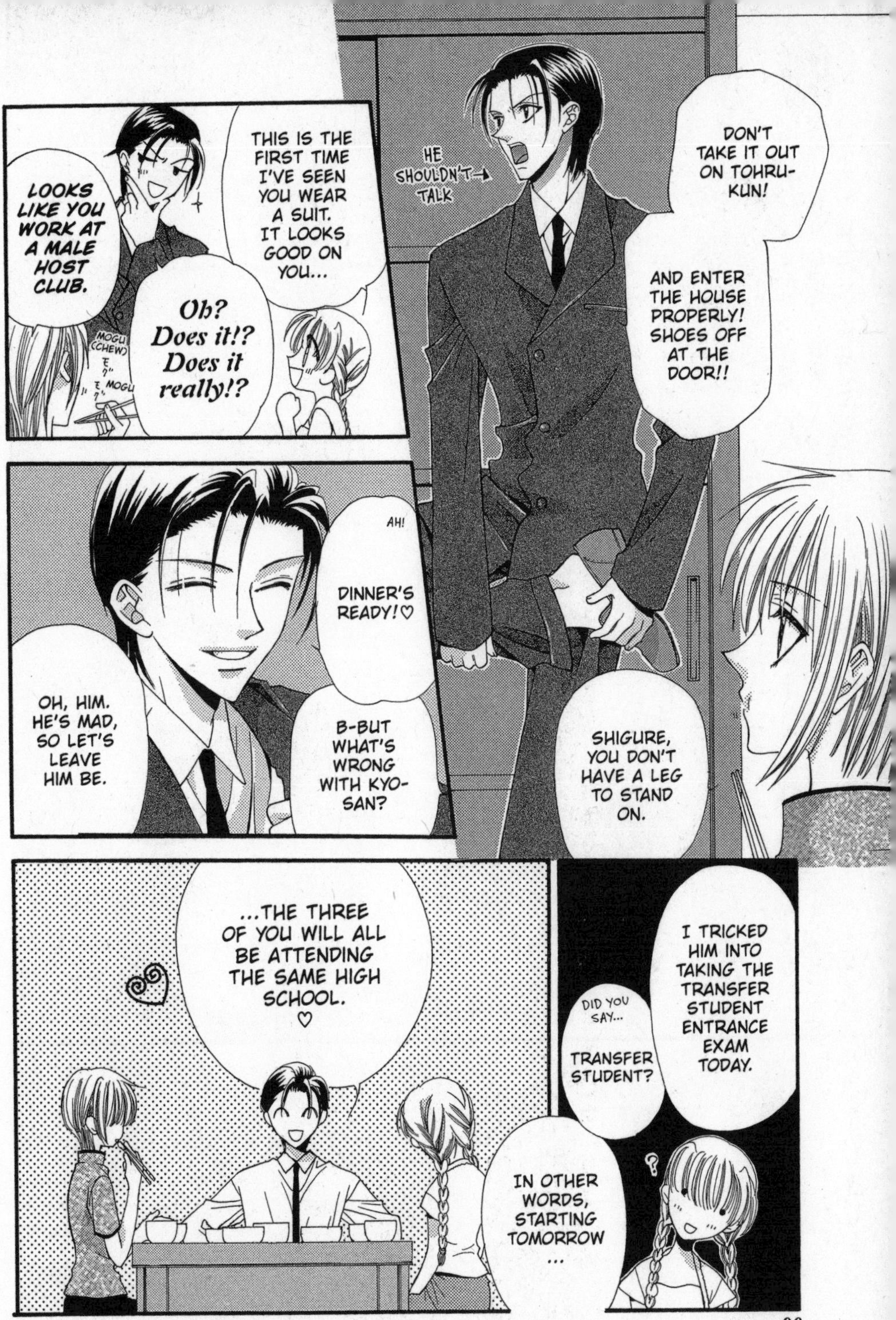
DON'T TAKE IT OUT ON TOHRU-KUN!
AND ENTER THE HOUSE PROPERLY! SHOES OFF AT THE DOOR!!
HE SHOULDN'T TALK
SHIGURE, YOU DON'T HAVE A LEG TO STAND ON.
THIS IS THE FIRST TIME I'VE SEEN YOU WEAR A SUIT. IT LOOKS GOOD ON YOU...
LOOKS LIKE YOU WORK AT A MALE HOST CLUB.
Oh? Does it!? Does it really!?
MOGU (CHEW)
MOGU
AH!
DINNER'S READY!♡
B-BUT WHAT'S WRONG WITH KYO-SAN?
OH, HIM. HE'S MAD, SO LET'S LEAVE HIM BE.
I TRICKED HIM INTO TAKING THE TRANSFER STUDENT ENTRANCE EXAM TODAY.
DID YOU SAY...
TRANSFER STUDENT?
IN OTHER WORDS, STARTING TOMORROW ...
...THE THREE OF YOU WILL ALL BE ATTENDING THE SAME HIGH SCHOOL. ♡

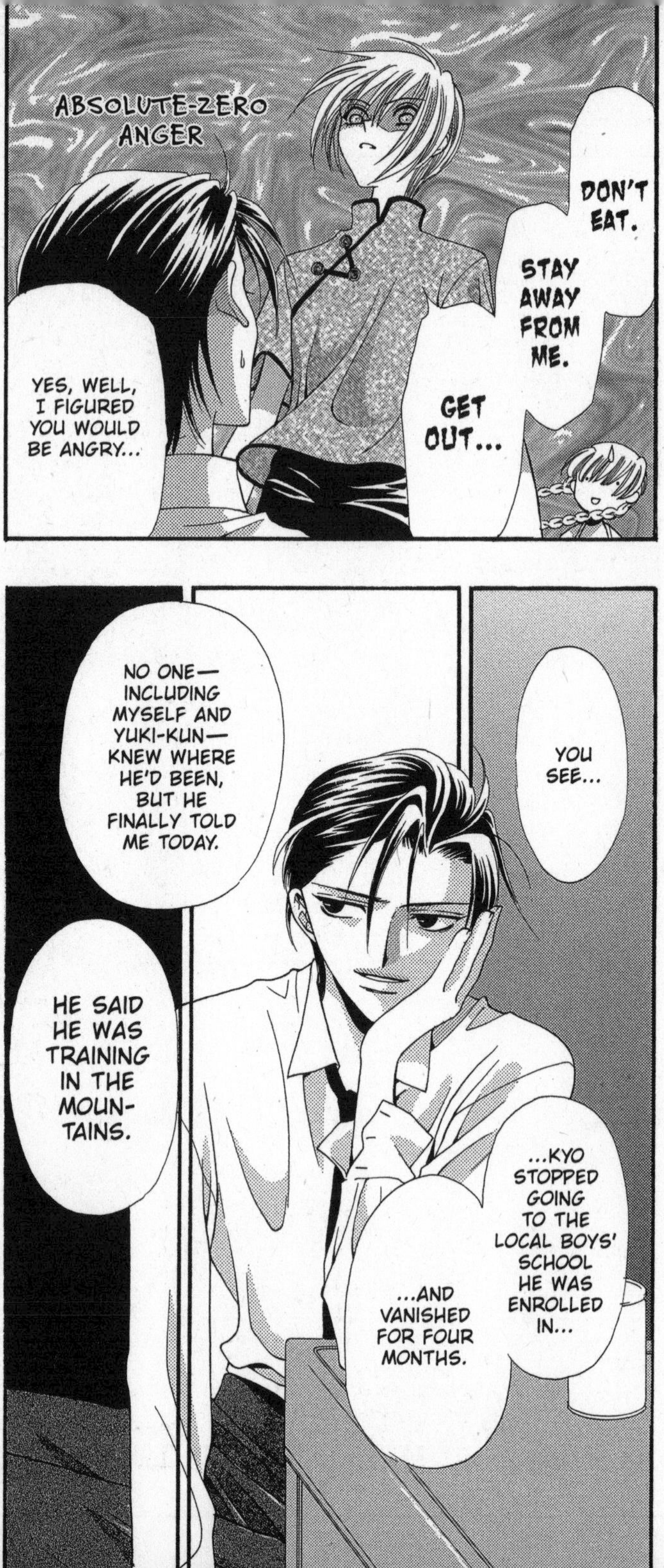
DON'T EAT.
STAY AWAY FROM ME.
GET OUT...
ABSOLUTE-ZERO ANGER
YES, WELL, I FIGURED YOU WOULD BE ANGRY...
YOU SEE...
...KYO STOPPED GOING TO THE LOCAL BOYS' SCHOOL HE WAS ENROLLED IN...
...AND VANISHED FOR FOUR MONTHS.
NO ONE—INCLUDING MYSELF AND YUKI-KUN—KNEW WHERE HE'D BEEN, BUT HE FINALLY TOLD ME TODAY.
HE SAID HE WAS TRAINING IN THE MOUNTAINS.
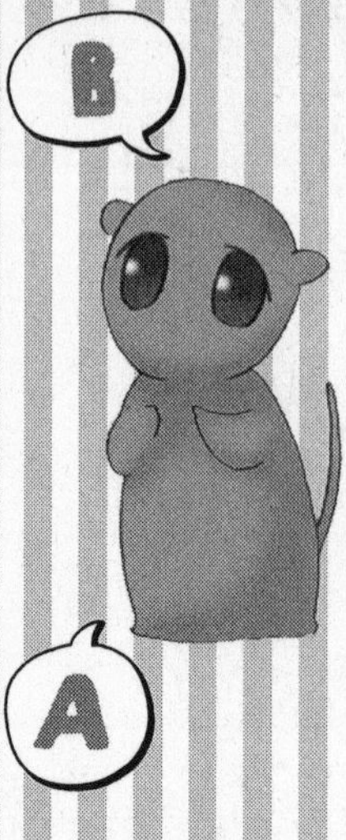
B
A

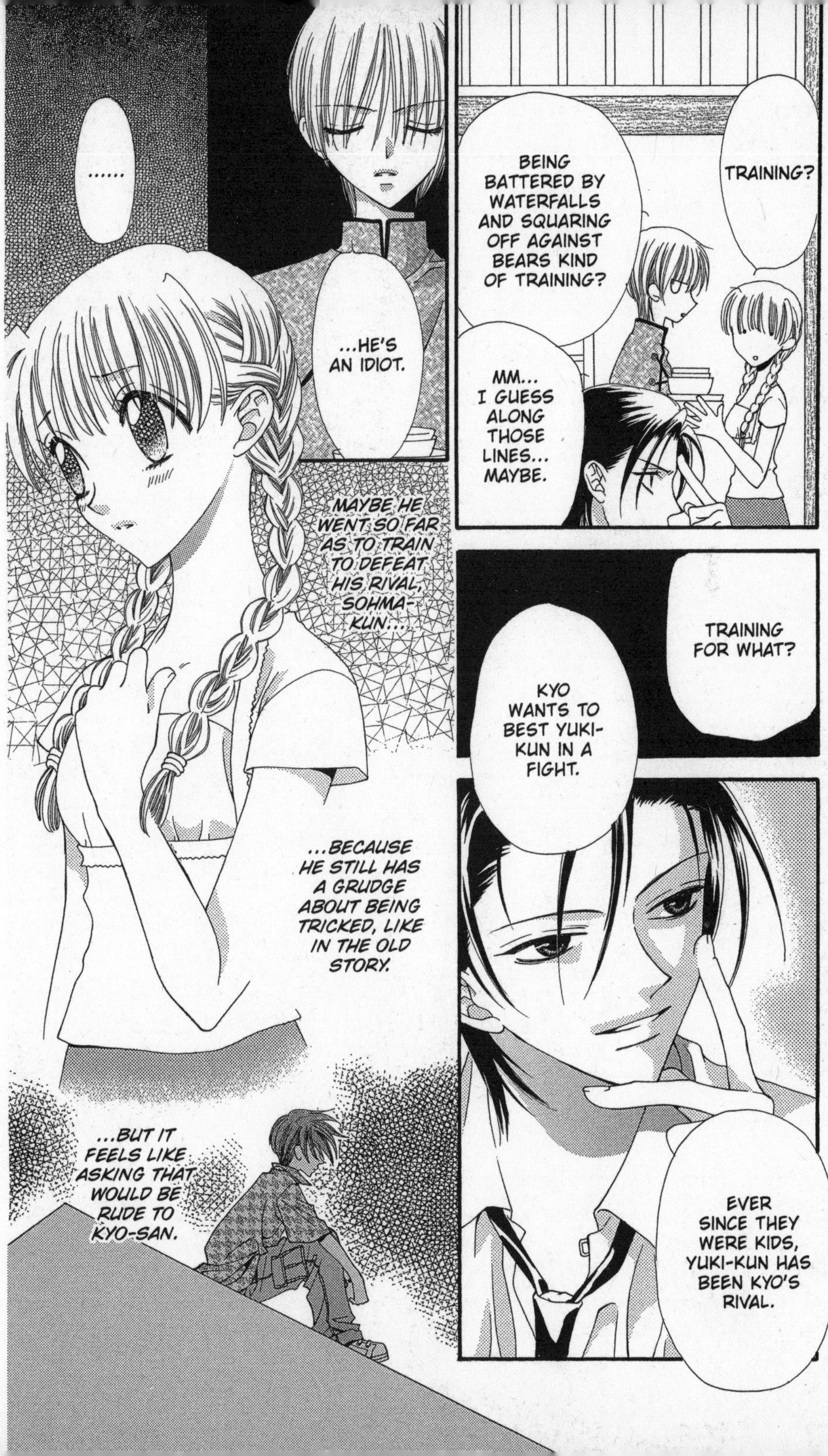

TRAINING?
BEING BATTERED BY WATERFALLS AND SQUARING OFF AGAINST BEARS KIND OF TRAINING?
MM... I GUESS ALONG THOSE LINES... MAYBE.
TRAINING FOR WHAT?
KYO WANTS TO BEST YUKI-KUN IN A FIGHT.
EVER SINCE THEY WERE KIDS, YUKI-KUN HAS BEEN KYO'S RIVAL.
......
...HE'S AN IDIOT.
MAYBE HE WENT SO FAR AS TO TRAIN TO DEFEAT HIS RIVAL, SOHMA-KUN...
...BECAUSE HE STILL HAS A GRUDGE ABOUT BEING TRICKED, LIKE IN THE OLD STORY.
...BUT IT FEELS LIKE ASKING THAT WOULD BE RUDE TO KYO-SAN.

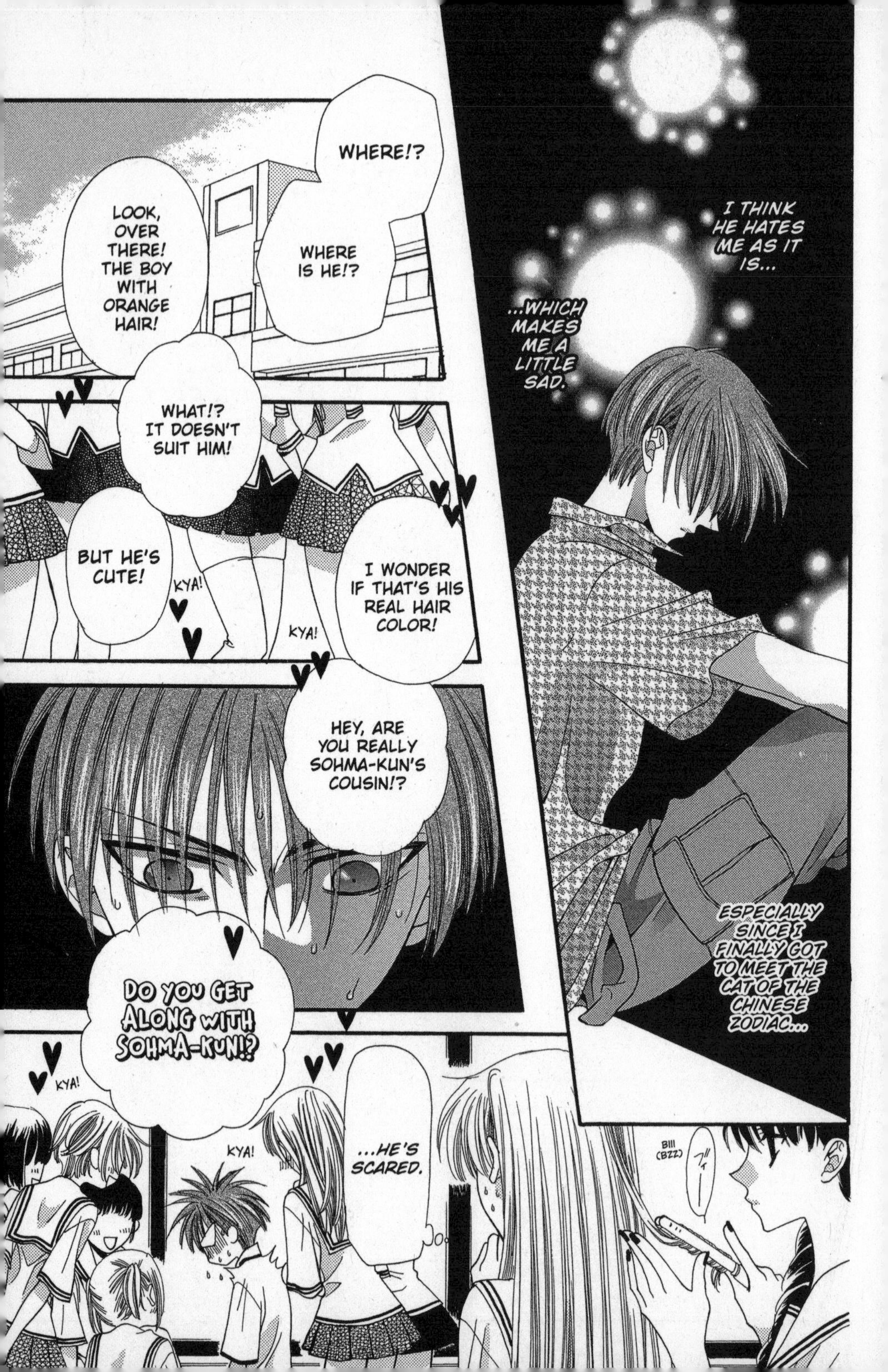

I THINK HE HATES ME AS IT IS...
...WHICH MAKES ME A LITTLE SAD.
ESPECIALLY SINCE I FINALLY GOT TO MEET THE CAT OF THE CHINESE ZODIAC...
WHERE!?
WHERE IS HE!?
LOOK, OVER THERE! THE BOY WITH ORANGE HAIR!
I WONDER IF THAT'S HIS REAL HAIR COLOR!
KYA!
WHAT!? IT DOESN'T SUIT HIM!
KYA!
BUT HE'S CUTE!
HEY, ARE YOU REALLY SOHMA-KUN'S COUSIN!?
DO YOU GET ALONG WITH SOHMA-KUN!?
BIII (BZZ)
...HE'S SCARED.
KYA!
KYA!

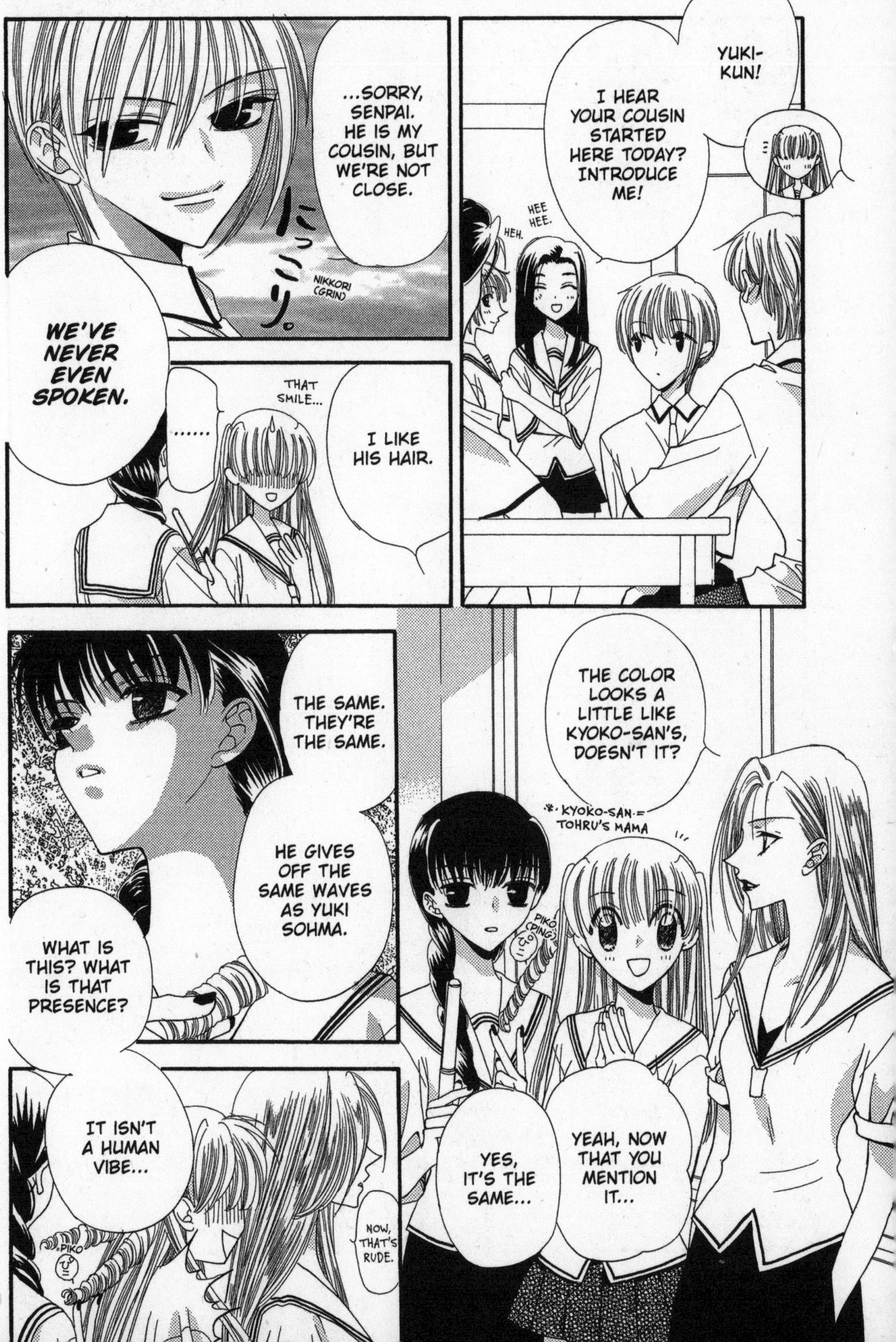
YUKI-KUN!
I HEAR YOUR COUSIN STARTED HERE TODAY? INTRODUCE ME!
HEE HEE.
HEH.
...SORRY, SENPAI. HE IS MY COUSIN, BUT WE'RE NOT CLOSE.
NIKKORI (GRIN)
WE'VE NEVER EVEN SPOKEN.
THAT SMILE...
I LIKE HIS HAIR.
......
THE COLOR LOOKS A LITTLE LIKE KYOKO-SAN'S, DOESN'T IT?
*KYOKO-SAN = TOHRU'S MAMA
PIKO (PING)
YEAH, NOW THAT YOU MENTION IT...
YES, IT'S THE SAME...
THE SAME. THEY'RE THE SAME.
HE GIVES OFF THE SAME WAVES AS YUKI SOHMA.
WHAT IS THIS? WHAT IS THAT PRESENCE?
NOW, THAT'S RUDE.
IT ISN'T A HUMAN VIBE...
PIKO

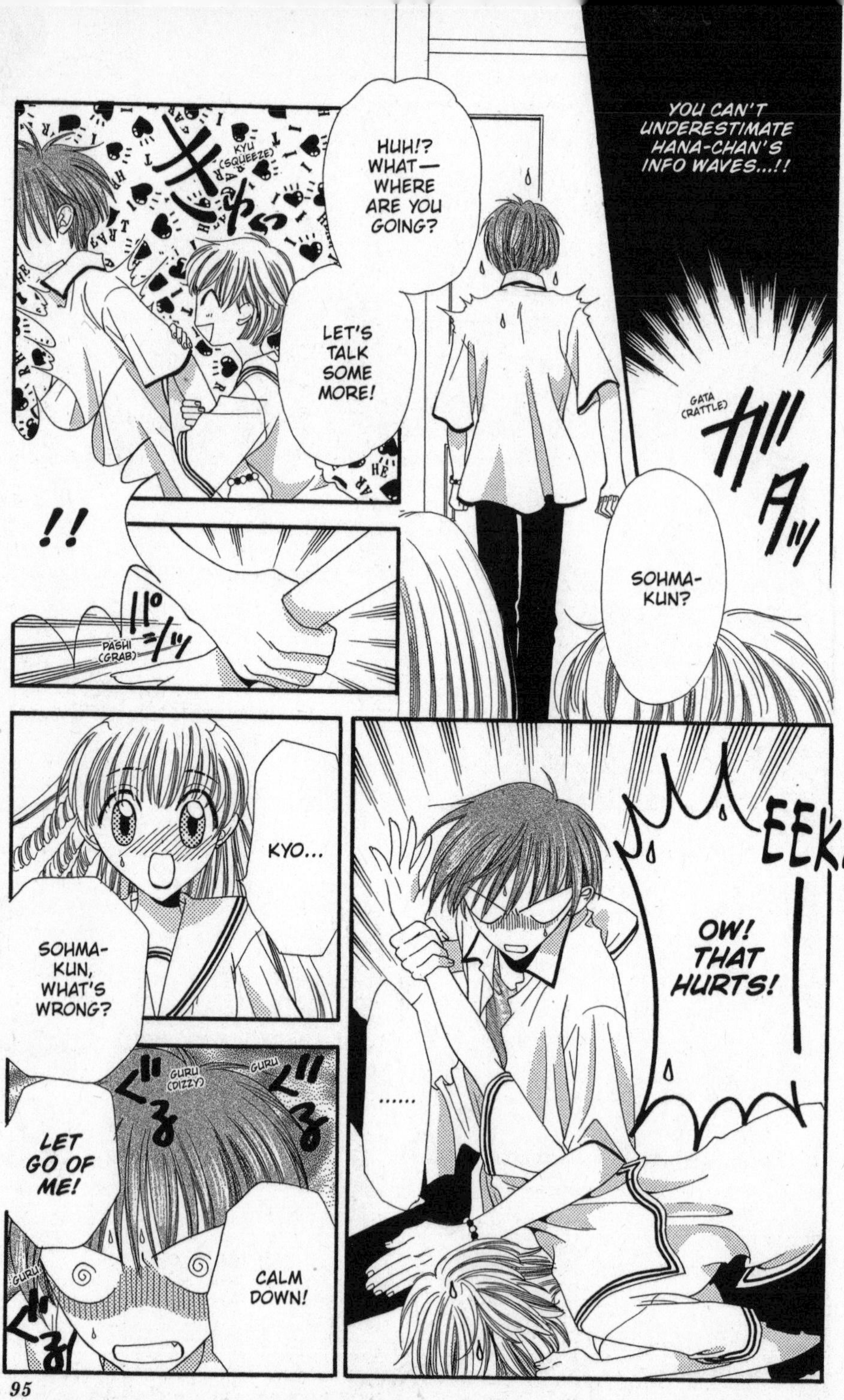
YOU CAN'T UNDERESTIMATE HANA-CHAN'S INFO WAVES...!!
GATA (RATTLE)
SOHMA-KUN?
HUH!? WHAT— WHERE ARE YOU GOING?
LET'S TALK SOME MORE!
KYU (SQUEEZE)
!!
PASHI (GRAB)
EEK!
OW! THAT HURTS!
......
KYO...
SOHMA-KUN, WHAT'S WRONG?
GURU (DIZZY)
GURU
LET GO OF ME!
CALM DOWN!
GURU

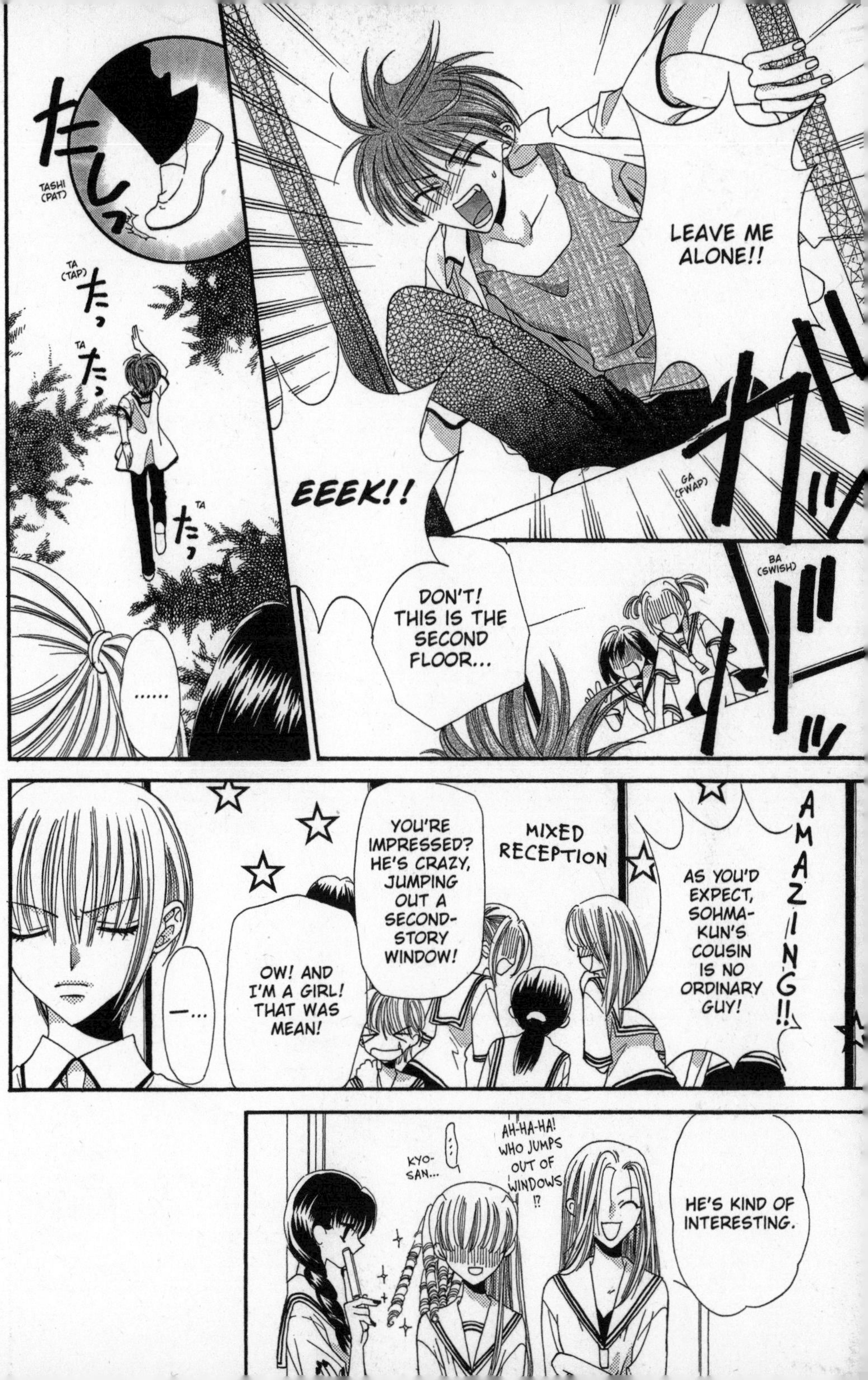
LEAVE ME ALONE!!
ガッ
GA (FWAP)
EEEK!!
バッ
BA (SWISH)
DON'T! THIS IS THE SECOND FLOOR...
たしっ
TASHI (PAT)
たっ
TA (TAP)
たっ
TA
たっ
TA
......
AMAZING!!
AS YOU'D EXPECT, SOHMA-KUN'S COUSIN IS NO ORDINARY GUY!
MIXED RECEPTION
YOU'RE IMPRESSED? HE'S CRAZY, JUMPING OUT A SECOND-STORY WINDOW!
OW! AND I'M A GIRL! THAT WAS MEAN!
—...
HE'S KIND OF INTERESTING.
AH-HA-HA! WHO JUMPS OUT OF WINDOWS!?
!...
KYO-SAN...

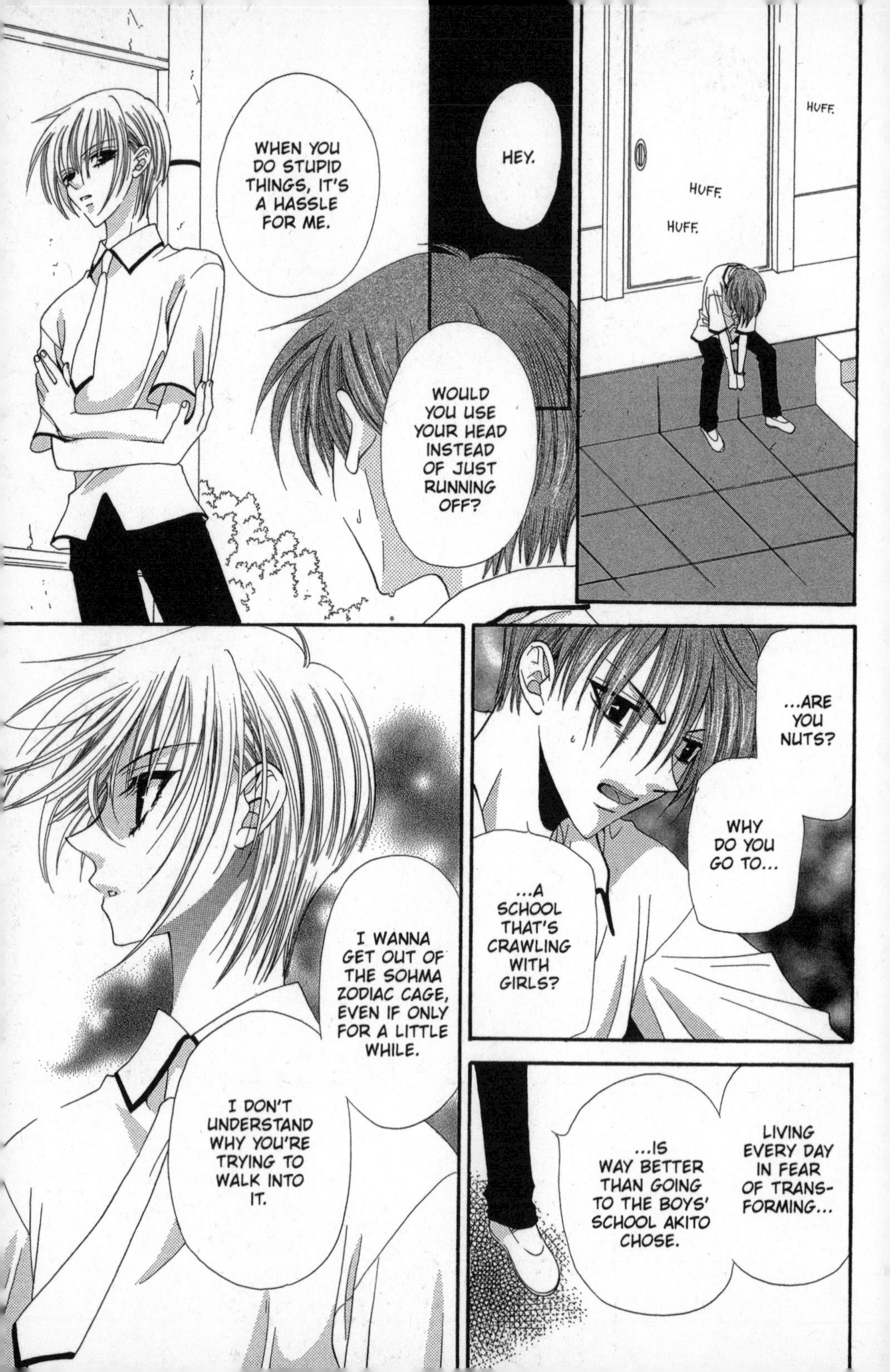
HUFF.
HUFF.
HUFF.
HEY.
WHEN YOU DO STUPID THINGS, IT'S A HASSLE FOR ME.
WOULD YOU USE YOUR HEAD INSTEAD OF JUST RUNNING OFF?
...ARE YOU NUTS?
WHY DO YOU GO TO...
...A SCHOOL THAT'S CRAWLING WITH GIRLS?
LIVING EVERY DAY IN FEAR OF TRANS-FORMING...
...IS WAY BETTER THAN GOING TO THE BOYS' SCHOOL AKITO CHOSE.
I WANNA GET OUT OF THE SOHMA ZODIAC CAGE, EVEN IF ONLY FOR A LITTLE WHILE.
I DON'T UNDERSTAND WHY YOU'RE TRYING TO WALK INTO IT.

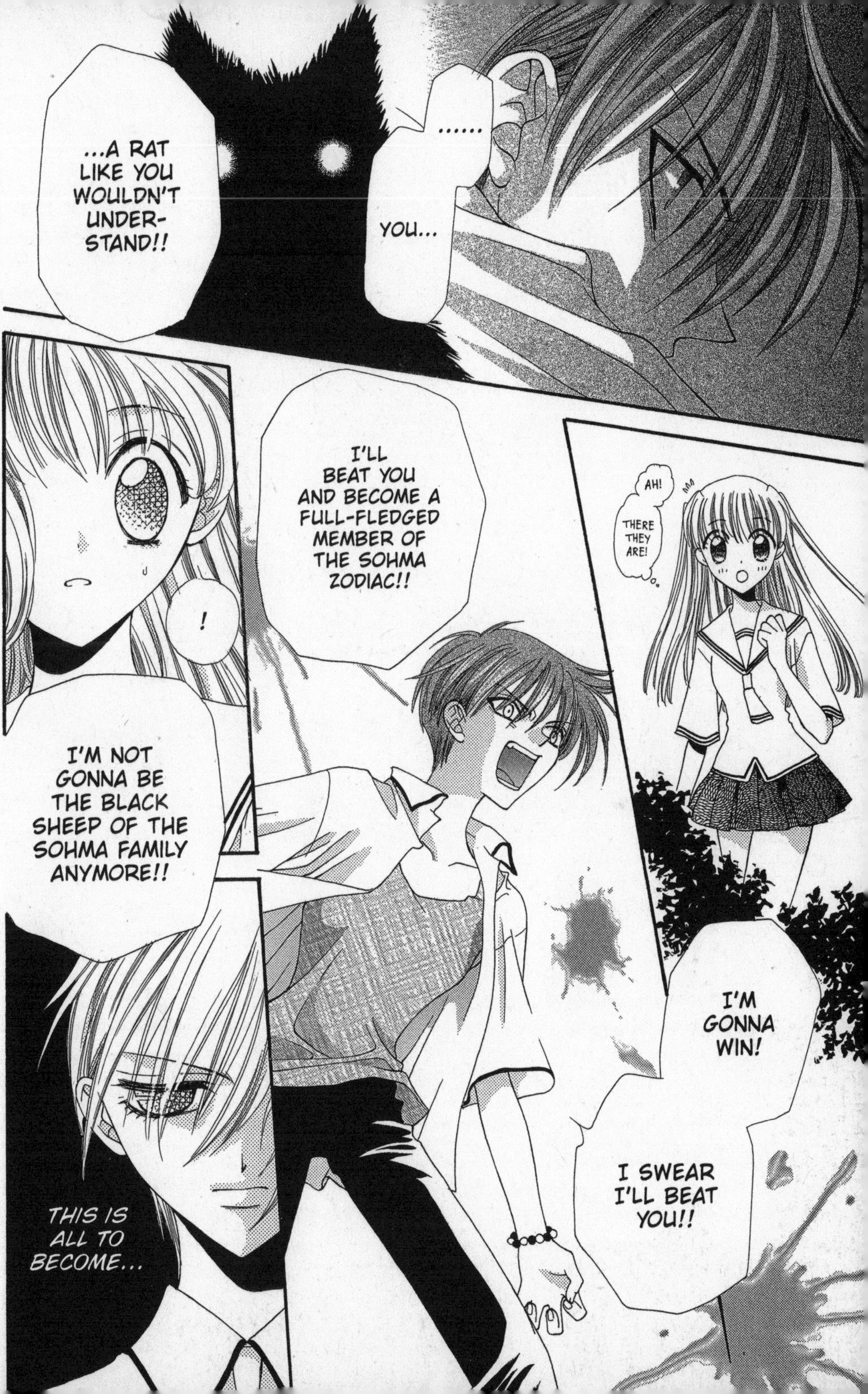
......
YOU...
...A RAT LIKE YOU WOULDN'T UNDER-STAND!!
AH!
THERE THEY ARE!
I'LL BEAT YOU AND BECOME A FULL-FLEDGED MEMBER OF THE SOHMA ZODIAC!!
I'M NOT GONNA BE THE BLACK SHEEP OF THE SOHMA FAMILY ANYMORE!!
!
I'M GONNA WIN!
I SWEAR I'LL BEAT YOU!!
THIS IS ALL TO BECOME...

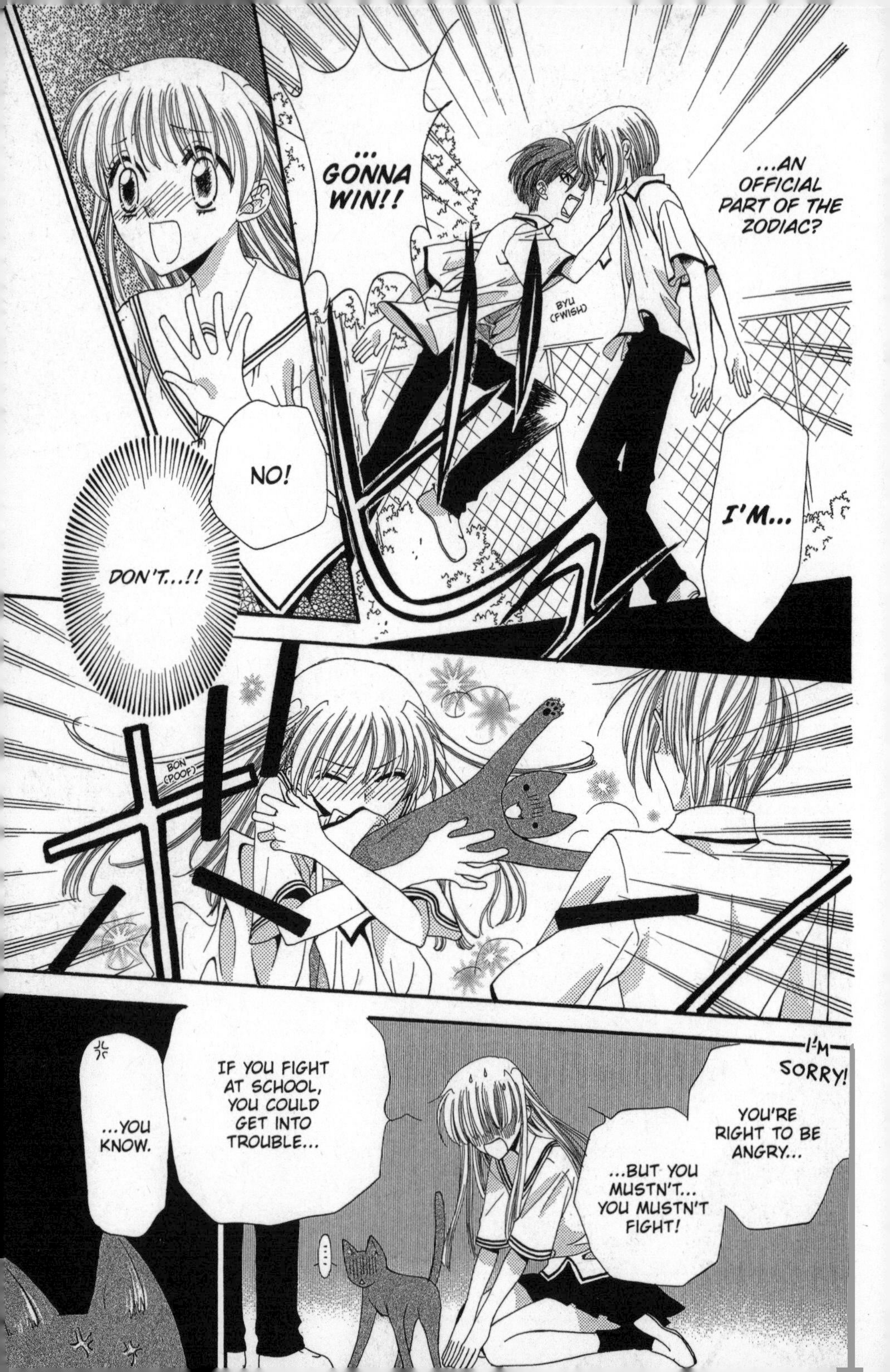
...AN OFFICIAL PART OF THE ZODIAC?
... GONNA WIN!!
BYU (FWISH)
I'M...
NO!
DON'T...!!
BON (POOF)
I'M SORRY!
YOU'RE RIGHT TO BE ANGRY...
...BUT YOU MUSTN'T... YOU MUSTN'T FIGHT!
IF YOU FIGHT AT SCHOOL, YOU COULD GET INTO TROUBLE...
...YOU KNOW.

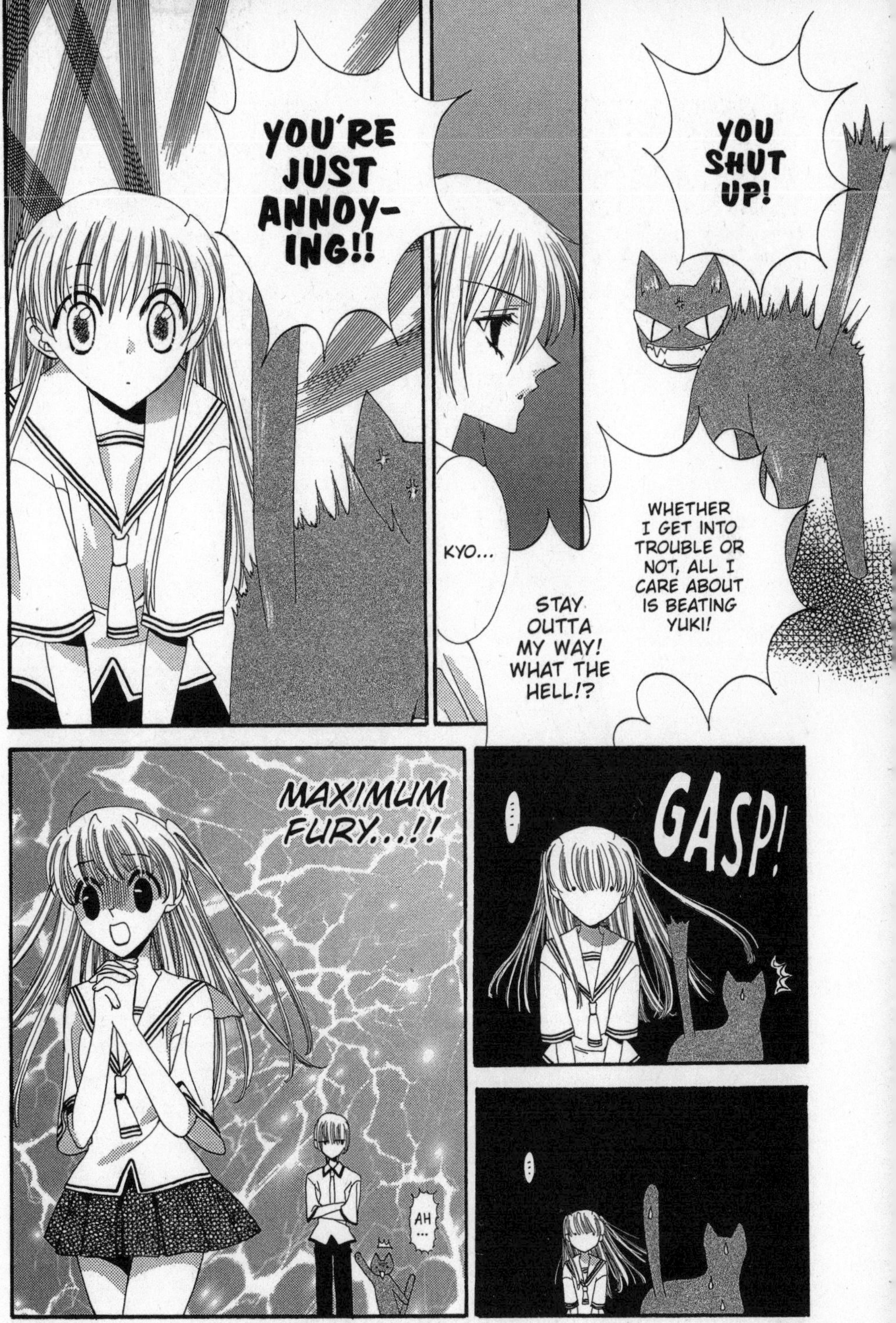

YOU SHUT UP!
WHETHER I GET INTO TROUBLE OR NOT, ALL I CARE ABOUT IS BEATING YUKI!
STAY OUTTA MY WAY! WHAT THE HELL!?
KYO...
YOU'RE JUST ANNOY-ING!!
GASP!
...
...
MAXIMUM FURY...!!
AH...

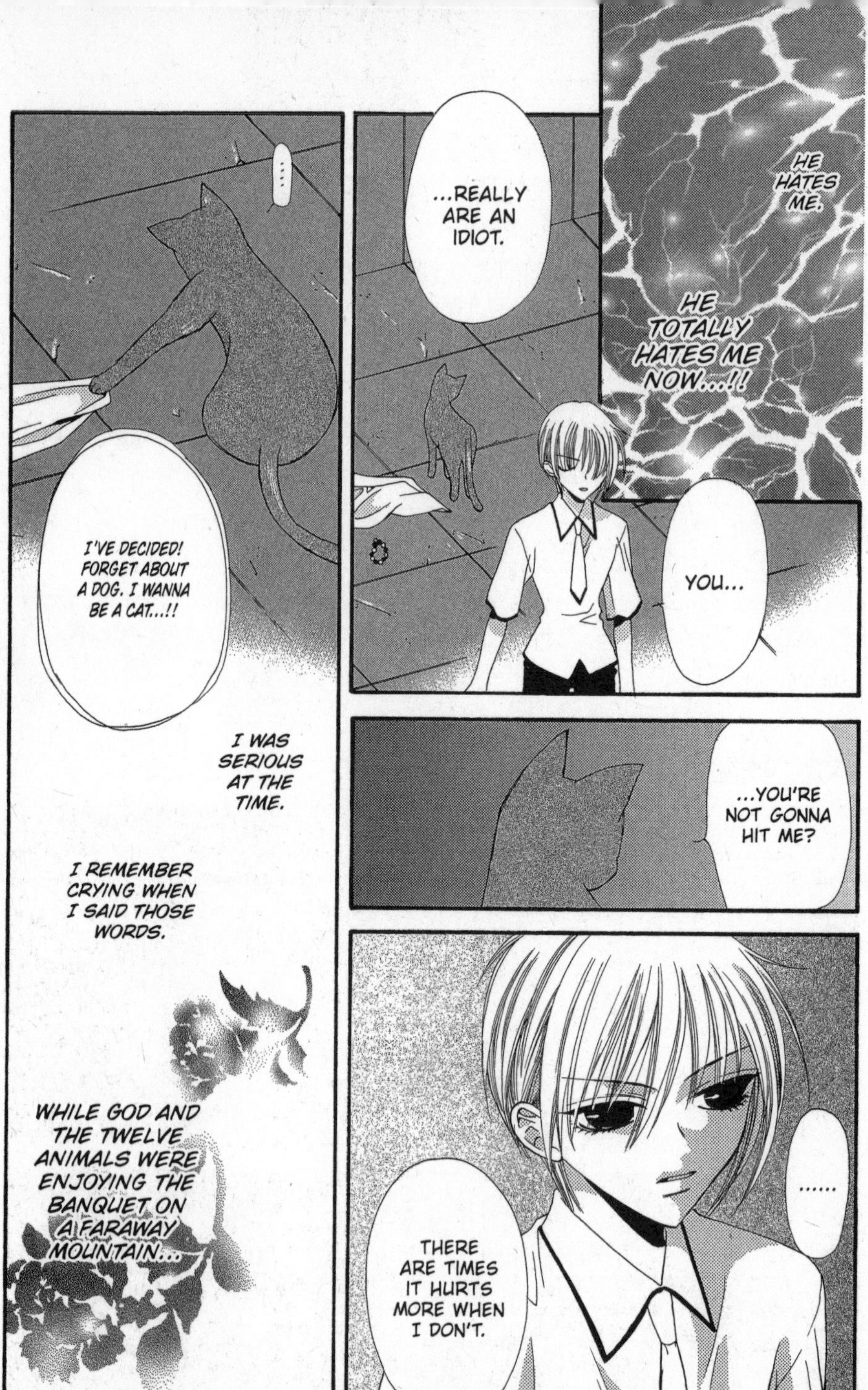
HE HATES ME.
HE TOTALLY HATES ME NOW...!!
YOU...
...REALLY ARE AN IDIOT.
...YOU'RE NOT GONNA HIT ME?
......
THERE ARE TIMES IT HURTS MORE WHEN I DON'T.
.....
I'VE DECIDED! FORGET ABOUT A DOG. I WANNA BE A CAT...!!
I WAS SERIOUS AT THE TIME.
I REMEMBER CRYING WHEN I SAID THOSE WORDS.
WHILE GOD AND THE TWELVE ANIMALS WERE ENJOYING THE BANQUET ON A FARAWAY MOUNTAIN...

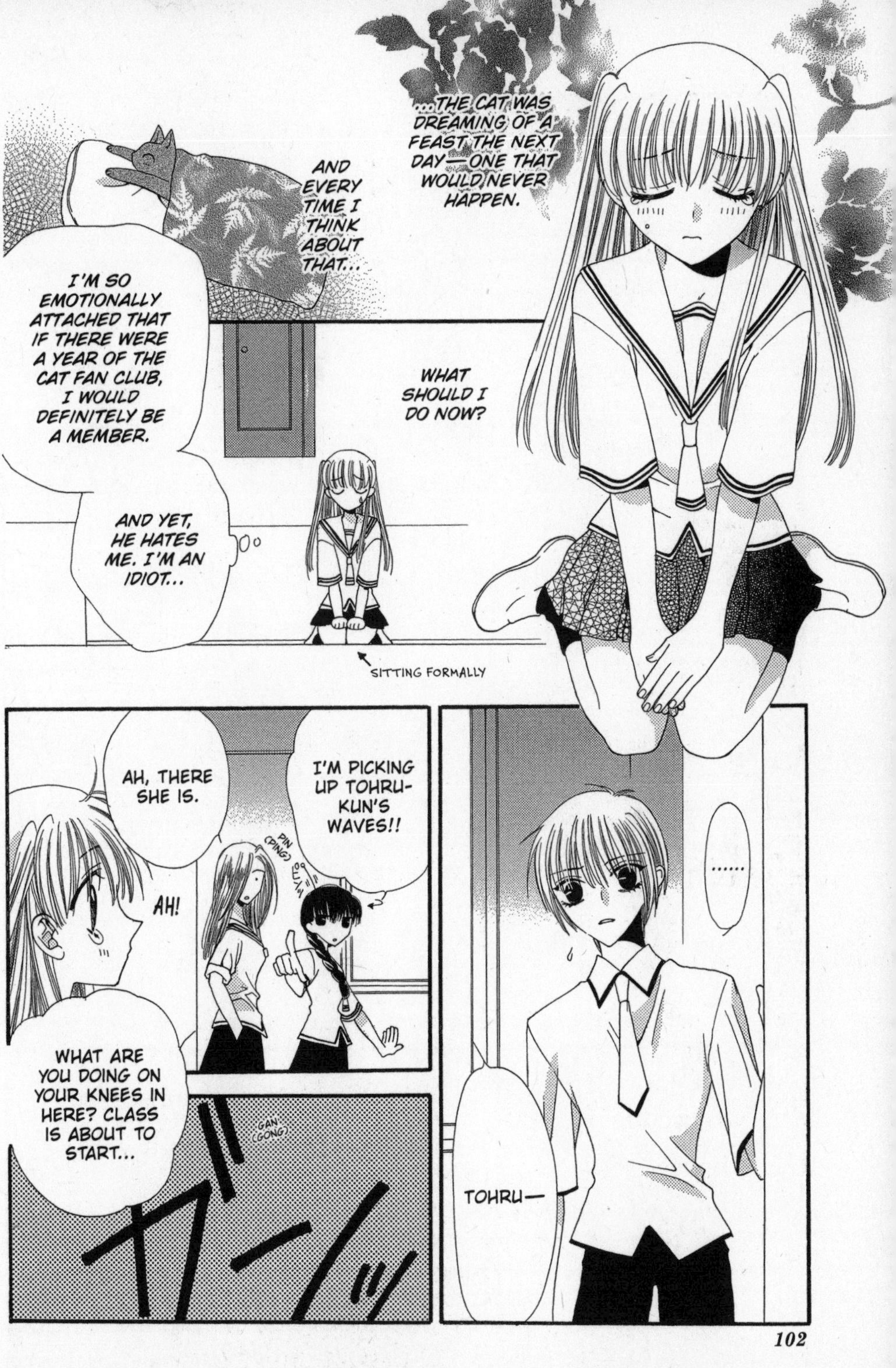

...THE CAT WAS DREAMING OF A FEAST THE NEXT DAY—ONE THAT WOULD NEVER HAPPEN.
AND EVERY TIME I THINK ABOUT THAT...
I'M SO EMOTIONALLY ATTACHED THAT IF THERE WERE A YEAR OF THE CAT FAN CLUB, I WOULD DEFINITELY BE A MEMBER.
WHAT SHOULD I DO NOW?
AND YET, HE HATES ME. I'M AN IDIOT...
SITTING FORMALLY
......
TOHRU—
I'M PICKING UP TOHRU-KUN'S WAVES!!
PIN (PING)
AH, THERE SHE IS.
AH!
WHAT ARE YOU DOING ON YOUR KNEES IN HERE? CLASS IS ABOUT TO START...
GAN (GONG)

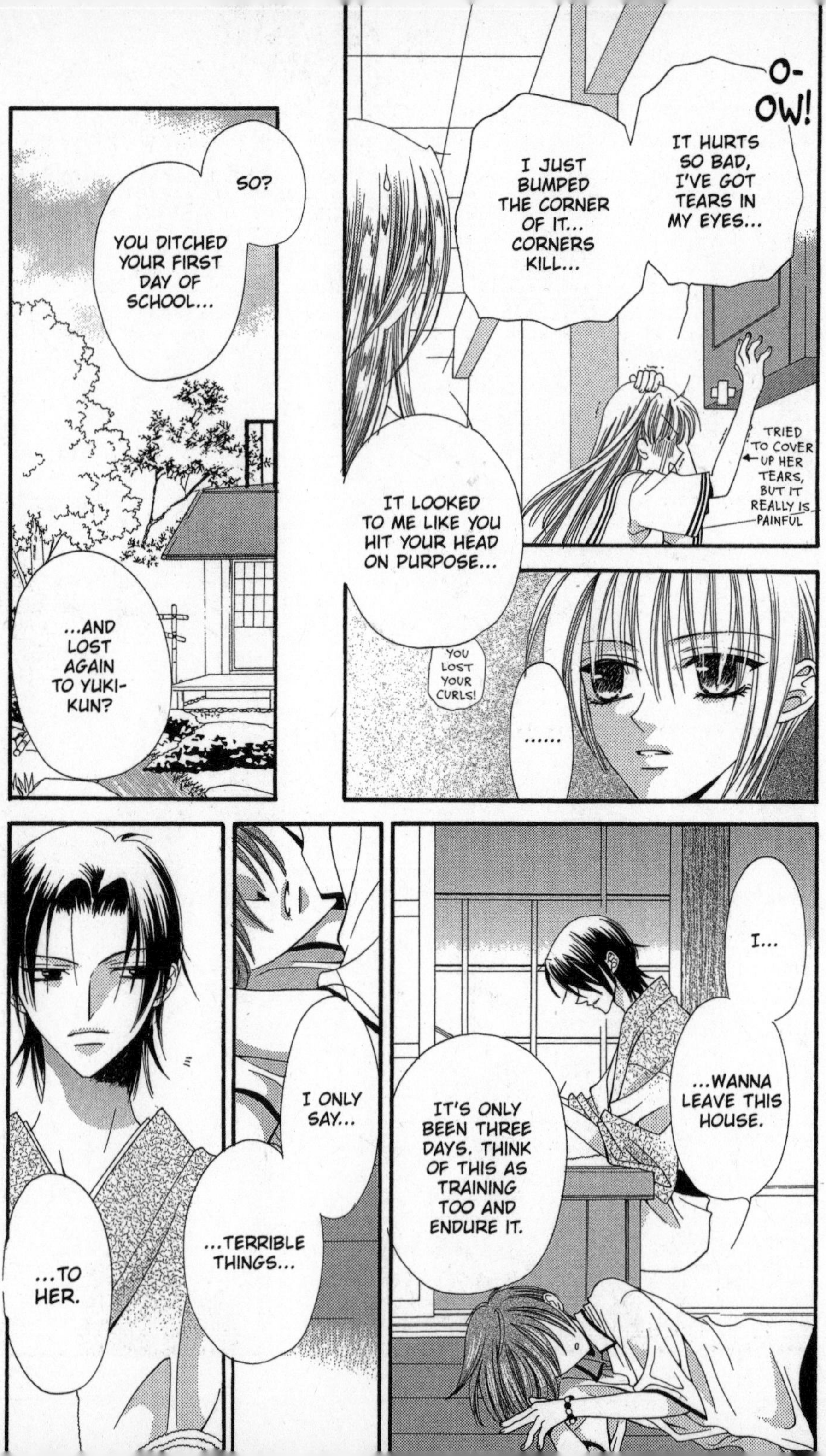
O-OW!
IT HURTS SO BAD, I'VE GOT TEARS IN MY EYES...
I JUST BUMPED THE CORNER OF IT... CORNERS KILL...
TRIED TO COVER UP HER TEARS, BUT IT REALLY IS PAINFUL
IT LOOKED TO ME LIKE YOU HIT YOUR HEAD ON PURPOSE...
YOU LOST YOUR CURLS!
......
SO?
YOU DITCHED YOUR FIRST DAY OF SCHOOL...
...AND LOST AGAIN TO YUKI-KUN?
I...
...WANNA LEAVE THIS HOUSE.
IT'S ONLY BEEN THREE DAYS. THINK OF THIS AS TRAINING TOO AND ENDURE IT.
I ONLY SAY...
...TERRIBLE THINGS...
...TO HER.

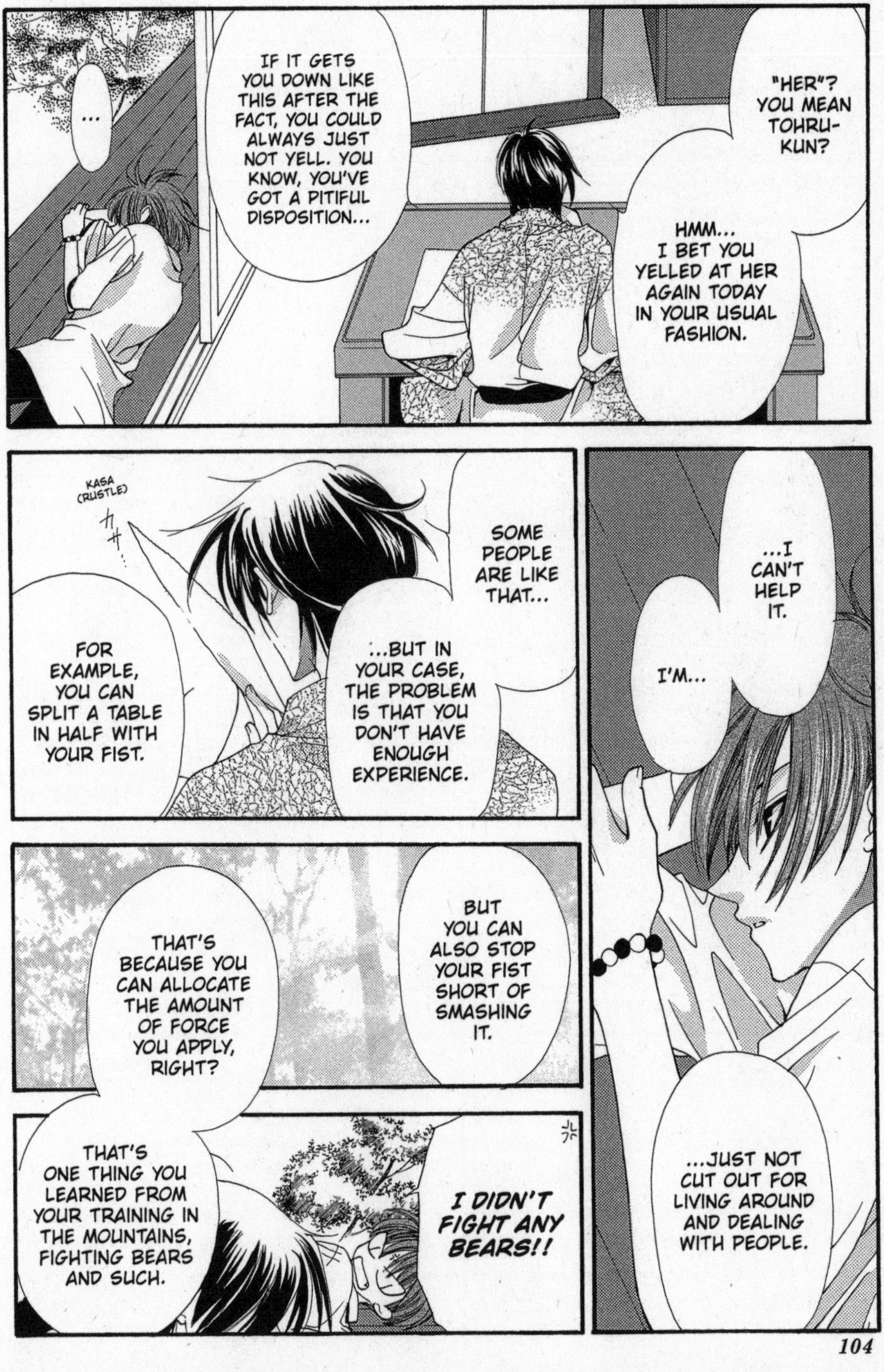
"HER"? YOU MEAN TOHRU-KUN?
HMM... I BET YOU YELLED AT HER AGAIN TODAY IN YOUR USUAL FASHION.
IF IT GETS YOU DOWN LIKE THIS AFTER THE FACT, YOU COULD ALWAYS JUST NOT YELL. YOU KNOW, YOU'VE GOT A PITIFUL DISPOSITION...
...
...I CAN'T HELP IT.
I'M...
...JUST NOT CUT OUT FOR LIVING AROUND AND DEALING WITH PEOPLE.
SOME PEOPLE ARE LIKE THAT...
...BUT IN YOUR CASE, THE PROBLEM IS THAT YOU DON'T HAVE ENOUGH EXPERIENCE.
KASA (RUSTLE)
FOR EXAMPLE, YOU CAN SPLIT A TABLE IN HALF WITH YOUR FIST.
BUT YOU CAN ALSO STOP YOUR FIST SHORT OF SMASHING IT.
THAT'S BECAUSE YOU CAN ALLOCATE THE AMOUNT OF FORCE YOU APPLY, RIGHT?
THAT'S ONE THING YOU LEARNED FROM YOUR TRAINING IN THE MOUNTAINS, FIGHTING BEARS AND SUCH.
I DIDN'T FIGHT ANY BEARS!!

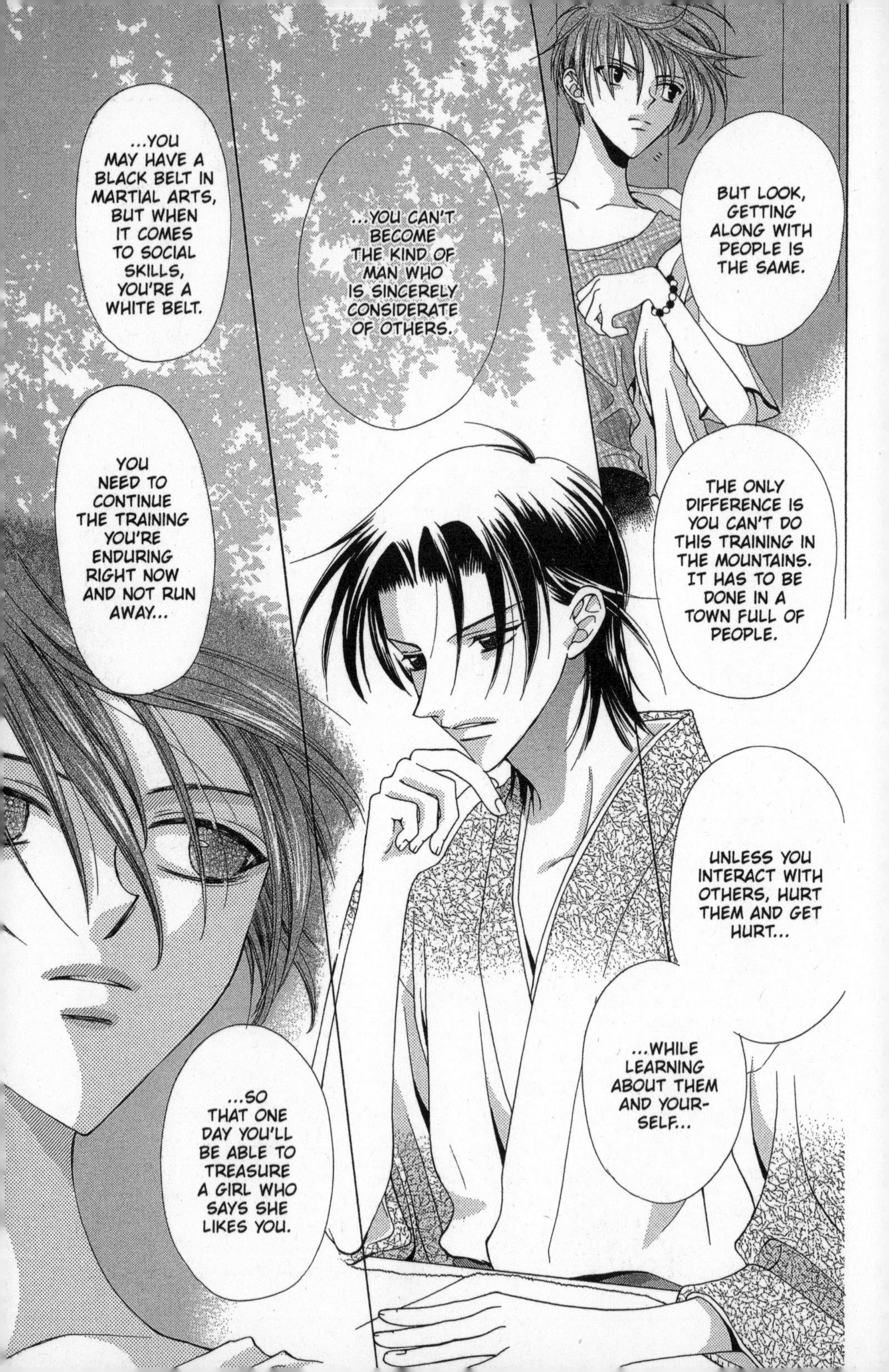
BUT LOOK, GETTING ALONG WITH PEOPLE IS THE SAME.
THE ONLY DIFFERENCE IS YOU CAN'T DO THIS TRAINING IN THE MOUNTAINS. IT HAS TO BE DONE IN A TOWN FULL OF PEOPLE.
UNLESS YOU INTERACT WITH OTHERS, HURT THEM AND GET HURT...
...WHILE LEARNING ABOUT THEM AND YOUR-SELF...
...YOU CAN'T BECOME THE KIND OF MAN WHO IS SINCERELY CONSIDERATE OF OTHERS.
...YOU MAY HAVE A BLACK BELT IN MARTIAL ARTS, BUT WHEN IT COMES TO SOCIAL SKILLS, YOU'RE A WHITE BELT.
YOU NEED TO CONTINUE THE TRAINING YOU'RE ENDURING RIGHT NOW AND NOT RUN AWAY...
...SO THAT ONE DAY YOU'LL BE ABLE TO TREASURE A GIRL WHO SAYS SHE LIKES YOU.

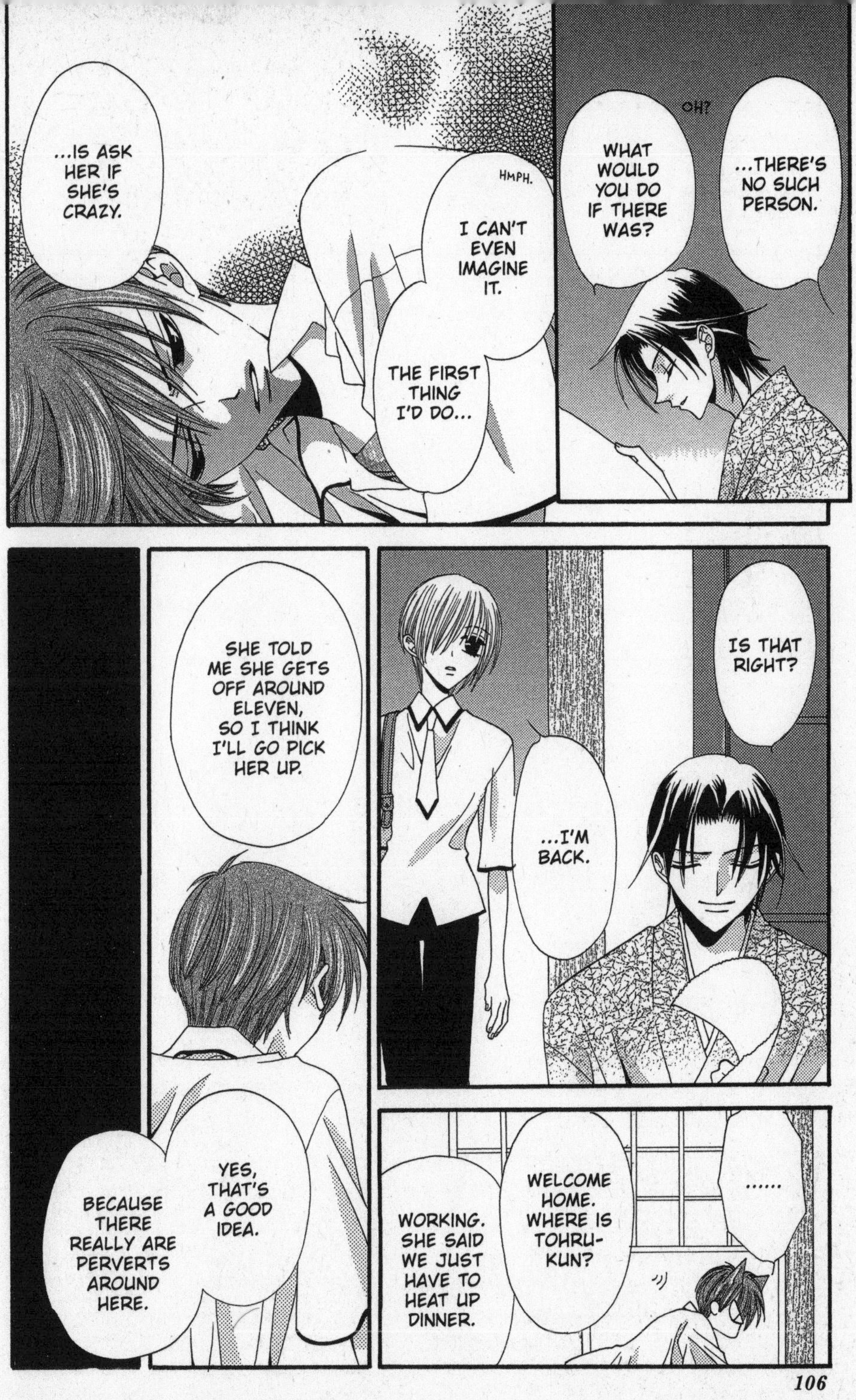
OH?
...THERE'S NO SUCH PERSON.
WHAT WOULD YOU DO IF THERE WAS?
HMPH.
I CAN'T EVEN IMAGINE IT.
THE FIRST THING I'D DO...
...IS ASK HER IF SHE'S CRAZY.
IS THAT RIGHT?
...I'M BACK.
......
WELCOME HOME. WHERE IS TOHRU-KUN?
WORKING. SHE SAID WE JUST HAVE TO HEAT UP DINNER.
SHE TOLD ME SHE GETS OFF AROUND ELEVEN, SO I THINK I'LL GO PICK HER UP.
YES, THAT'S A GOOD IDEA.
BECAUSE THERE REALLY ARE PERVERTS AROUND HERE.

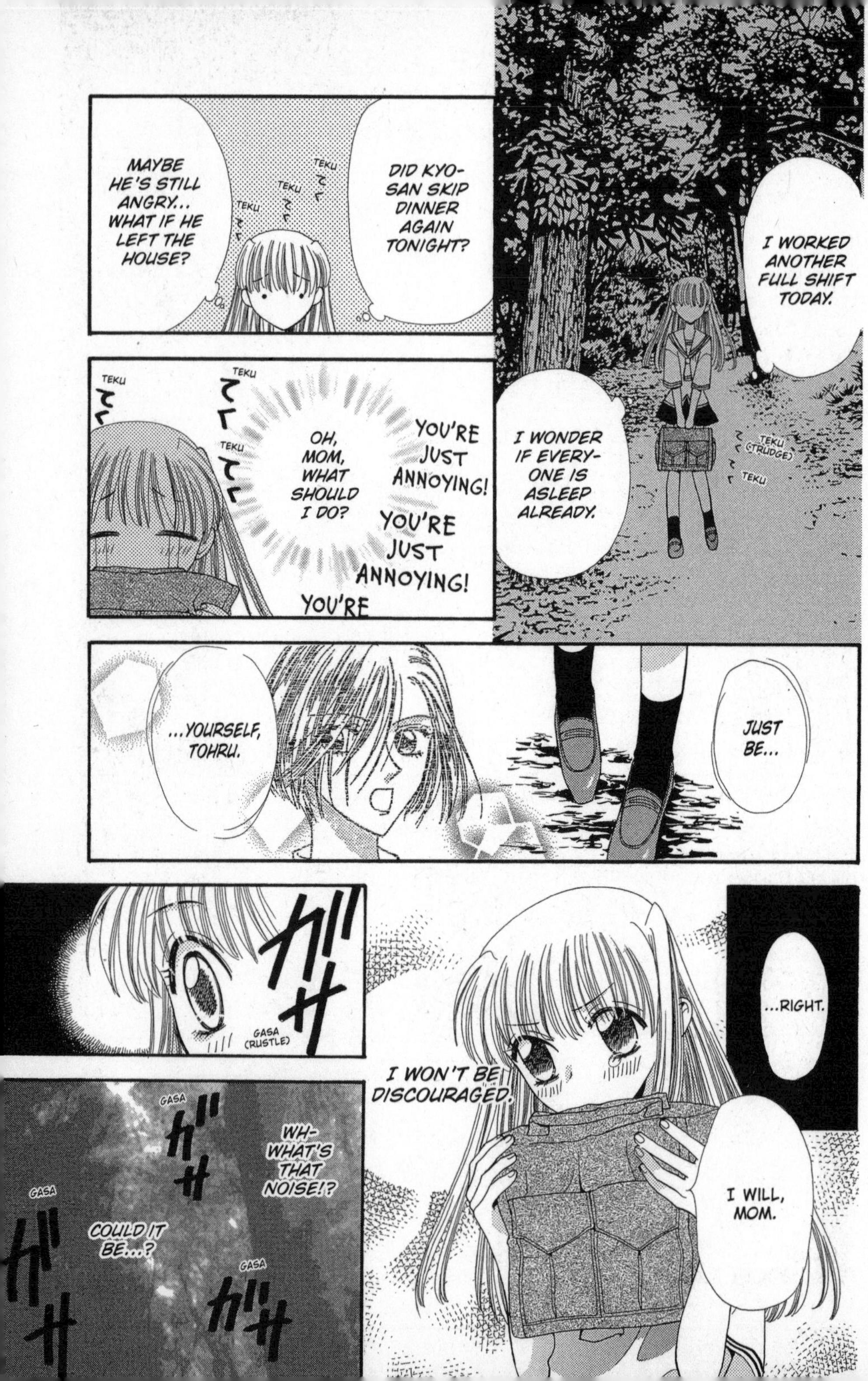
I WORKED ANOTHER FULL SHIFT TODAY.
I WONDER IF EVERY-ONE IS ASLEEP ALREADY.
TEKU (TRUDGE)
TEKU
DID KYO-SAN SKIP DINNER AGAIN TONIGHT?
TEKU
TEKU
TEKU
MAYBE HE'S STILL ANGRY... WHAT IF HE LEFT THE HOUSE?
YOU'RE JUST ANNOYING!
YOU'RE JUST ANNOYING!
YOU'RE
OH, MOM, WHAT SHOULD I DO?
TEKU
TEKU
TEKU
JUST BE...
...YOURSELF, TOHRU.
...RIGHT.
I WILL, MOM.
I WON'T BE DISCOURAGED.
GASA (RUSTLE)
WH-WHAT'S THAT NOISE!?
GASA
COULD IT BE...?
GASA
GASA

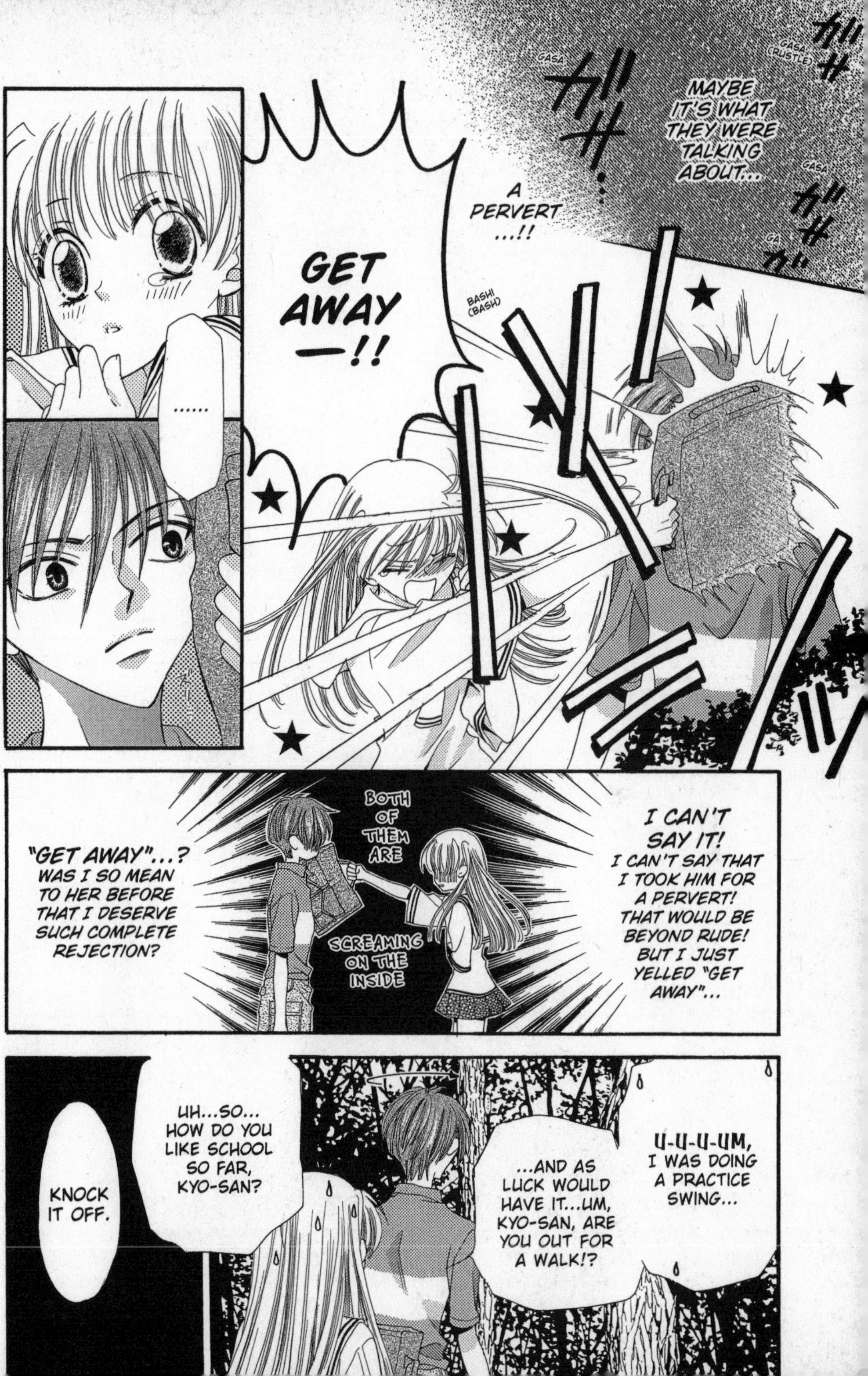

GASA (RUSTLE)
GASA
MAYBE IT'S WHAT THEY WERE TALKING ABOUT...
GASA
GA
A PERVERT ...!!
BASHI (BASH)
GET AWAY—!!
......
I CAN'T SAY IT! I CAN'T SAY THAT I TOOK HIM FOR A PERVERT! THAT WOULD BE BEYOND RUDE! BUT I JUST YELLED "GET AWAY"...
BOTH OF THEM ARE SCREAMING ON THE INSIDE
"GET AWAY"...? WAS I SO MEAN TO HER BEFORE THAT I DESERVE SUCH COMPLETE REJECTION?
U-U-U-UM, I WAS DOING A PRACTICE SWING...
...AND AS LUCK WOULD HAVE IT...UM, KYO-SAN, ARE YOU OUT FOR A WALK!?
UH...SO... HOW DO YOU LIKE SCHOOL SO FAR, KYO-SAN?
KNOCK IT OFF.

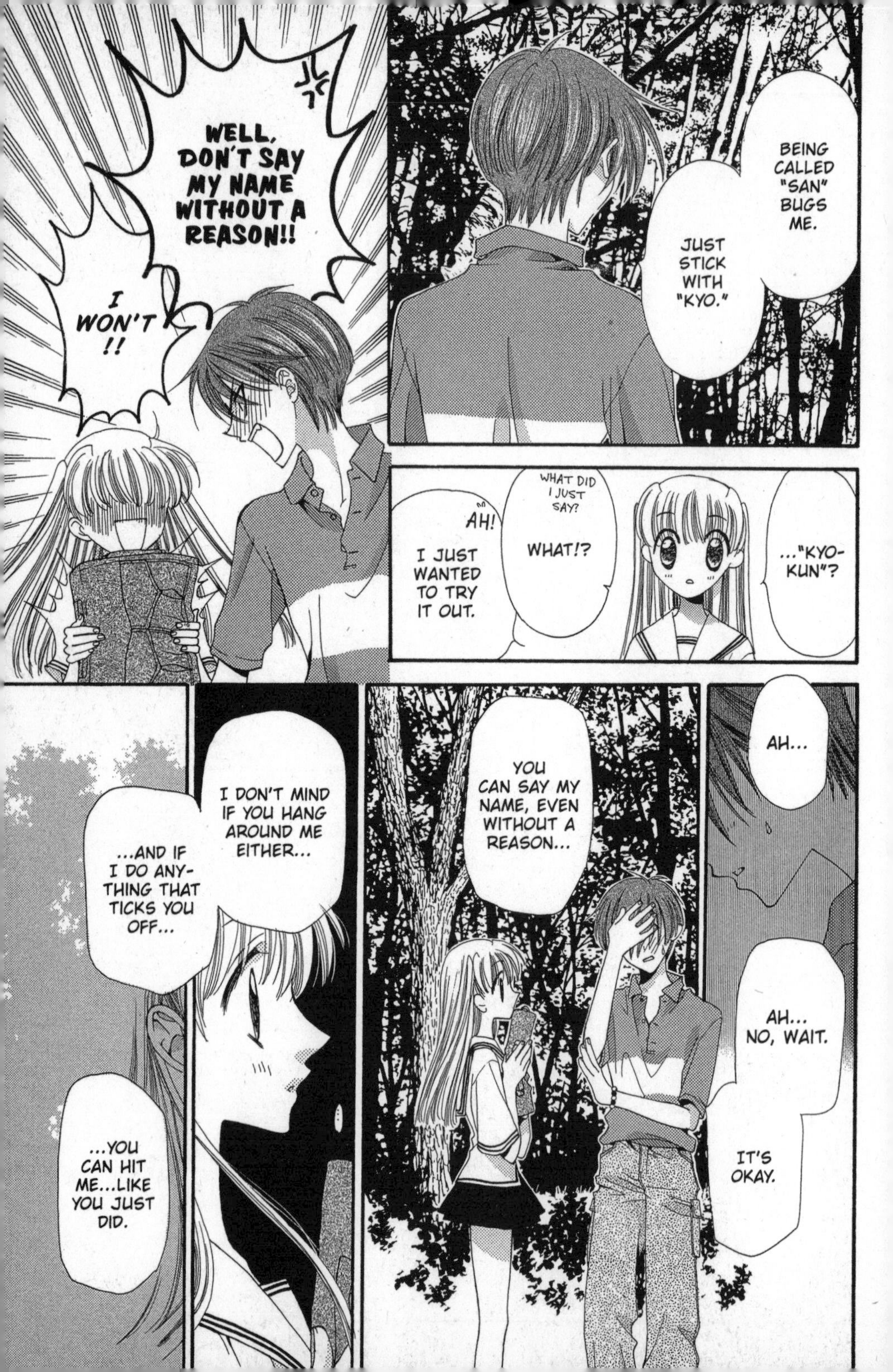
BEING CALLED "SAN" BUGS ME.
JUST STICK WITH "KYO."
..."KYO-KUN"?
WHAT!?
WHAT DID I JUST SAY?
AH!
I JUST WANTED TO TRY IT OUT.
WELL, DON'T SAY MY NAME WITHOUT A REASON!!
I WON'T!!
AH...
AH... NO, WAIT.
IT'S OKAY.
YOU CAN SAY MY NAME, EVEN WITHOUT A REASON...
I DON'T MIND IF YOU HANG AROUND ME EITHER...
...AND IF I DO ANYTHING THAT TICKS YOU OFF...
...YOU CAN HIT ME...LIKE YOU JUST DID.

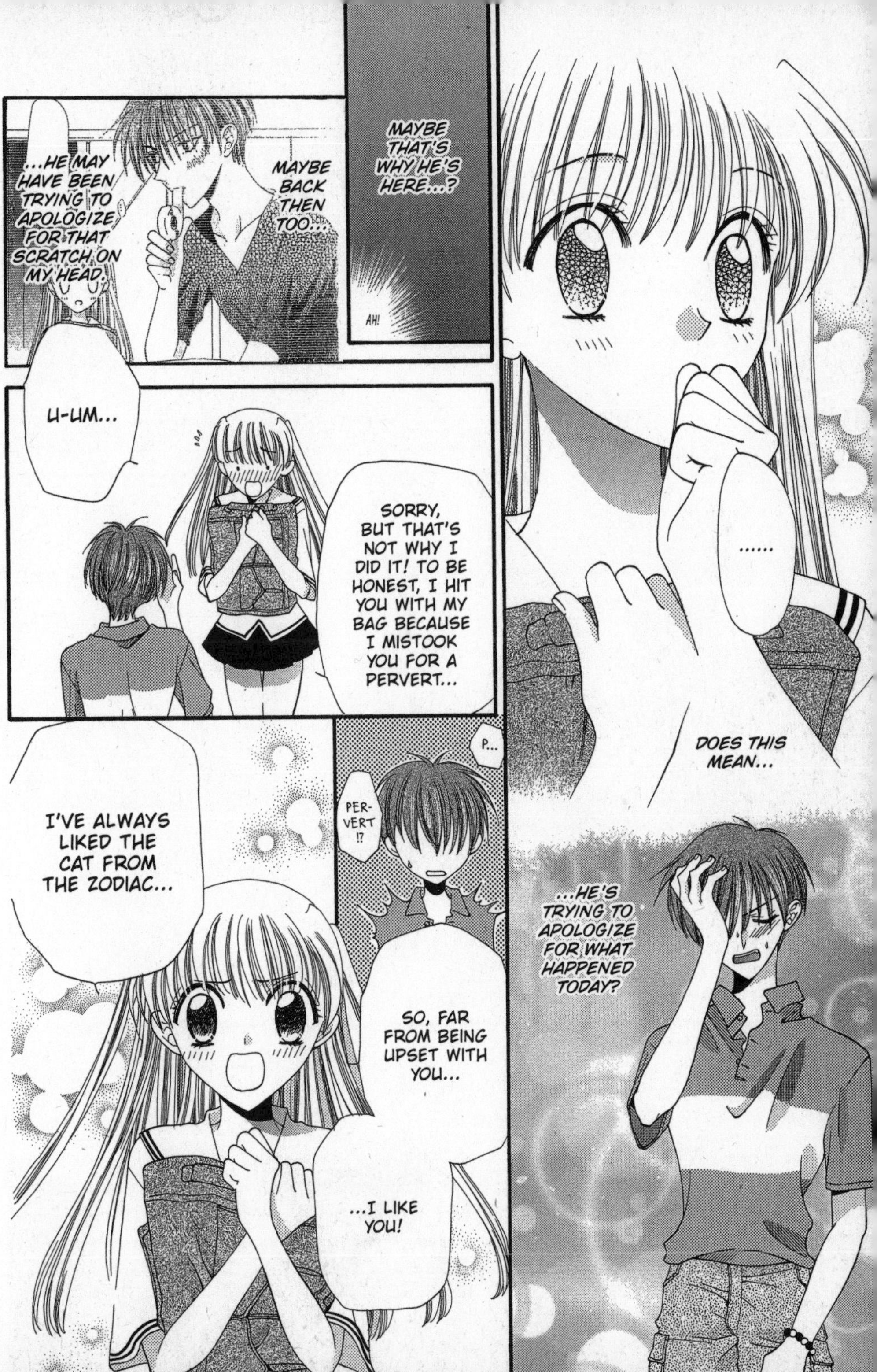
......
DOES THIS MEAN...
...HE'S TRYING TO APOLOGIZE FOR WHAT HAPPENED TODAY?
MAYBE THAT'S WHY HE'S HERE...?
AH!
MAYBE BACK THEN TOO...
...HE MAY HAVE BEEN TRYING TO APOLOGIZE FOR THAT SCRATCH ON MY HEAD.
U-UM...
SORRY, BUT THAT'S NOT WHY I DID IT! TO BE HONEST, I HIT YOU WITH MY BAG BECAUSE I MISTOOK YOU FOR A PERVERT...
P...
PER-VERT!?
I'VE ALWAYS LIKED THE CAT FROM THE ZODIAC...
SO, FAR FROM BEING UPSET WITH YOU...
...I LIKE YOU!

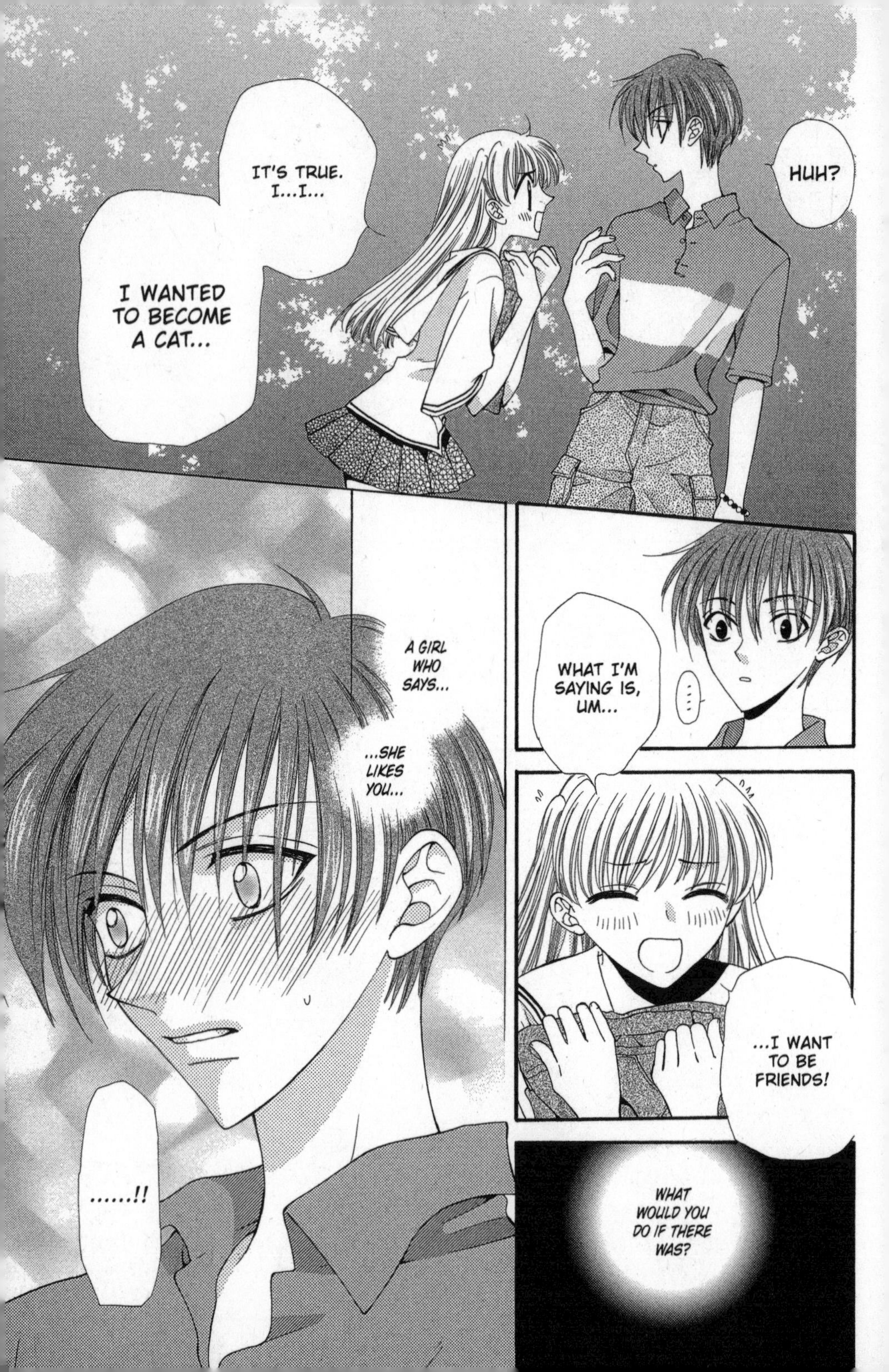
HUH?
IT'S TRUE. I...I...
I WANTED TO BECOME A CAT...
WHAT I'M SAYING IS, UM...
...
...I WANT TO BE FRIENDS!
WHAT WOULD YOU DO IF THERE WAS?
A GIRL WHO SAYS...
...SHE LIKES YOU...
......!!

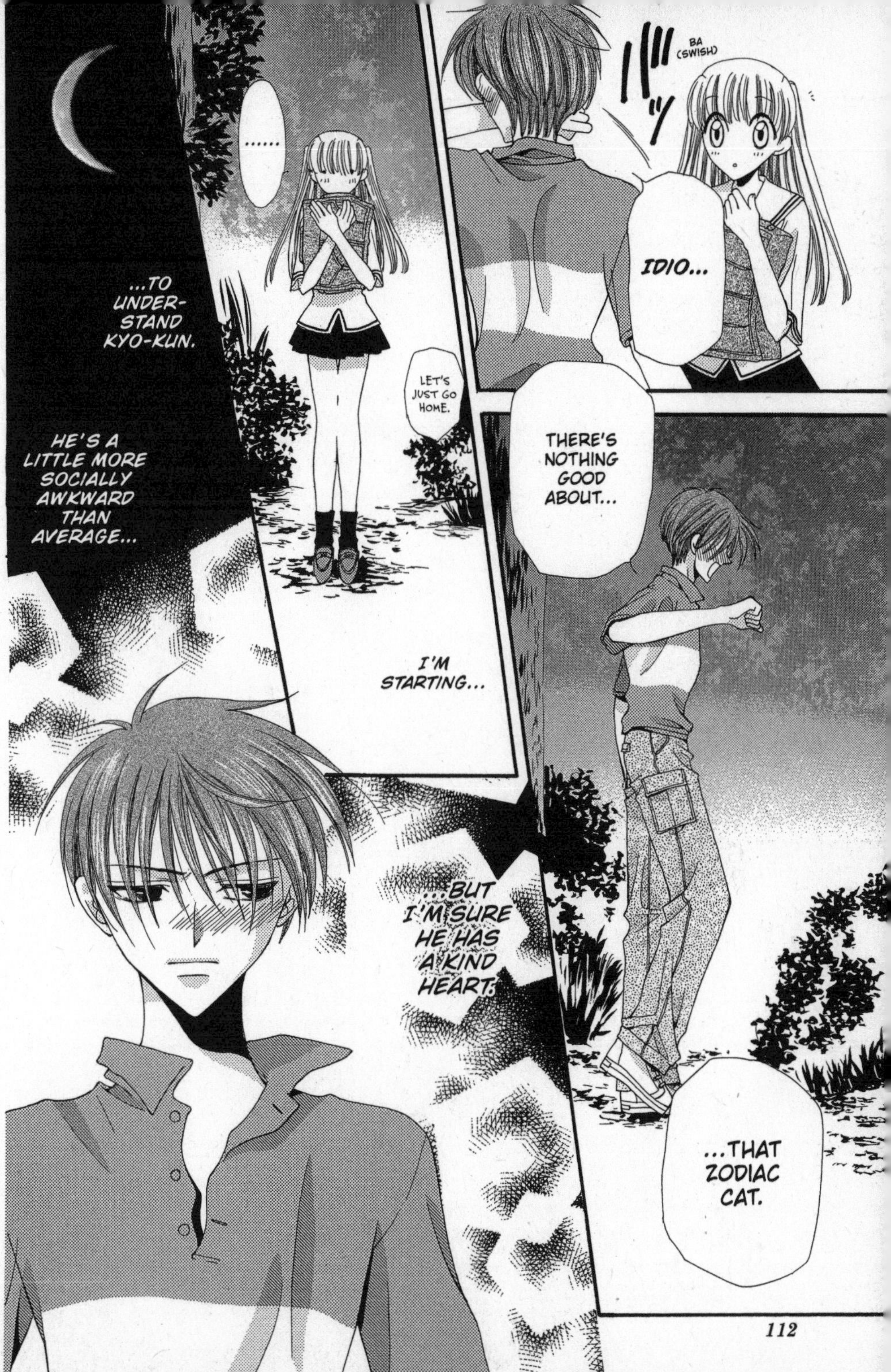
BA (SWISH)
IDIO...
THERE'S NOTHING GOOD ABOUT...
...THAT ZODIAC CAT.
......
LET'S JUST GO HOME.
I'M STARTING...
...TO UNDERSTAND KYO-KUN.
HE'S A LITTLE MORE SOCIALLY AWKWARD THAN AVERAGE...
...BUT I'M SURE HE HAS A KIND HEART.

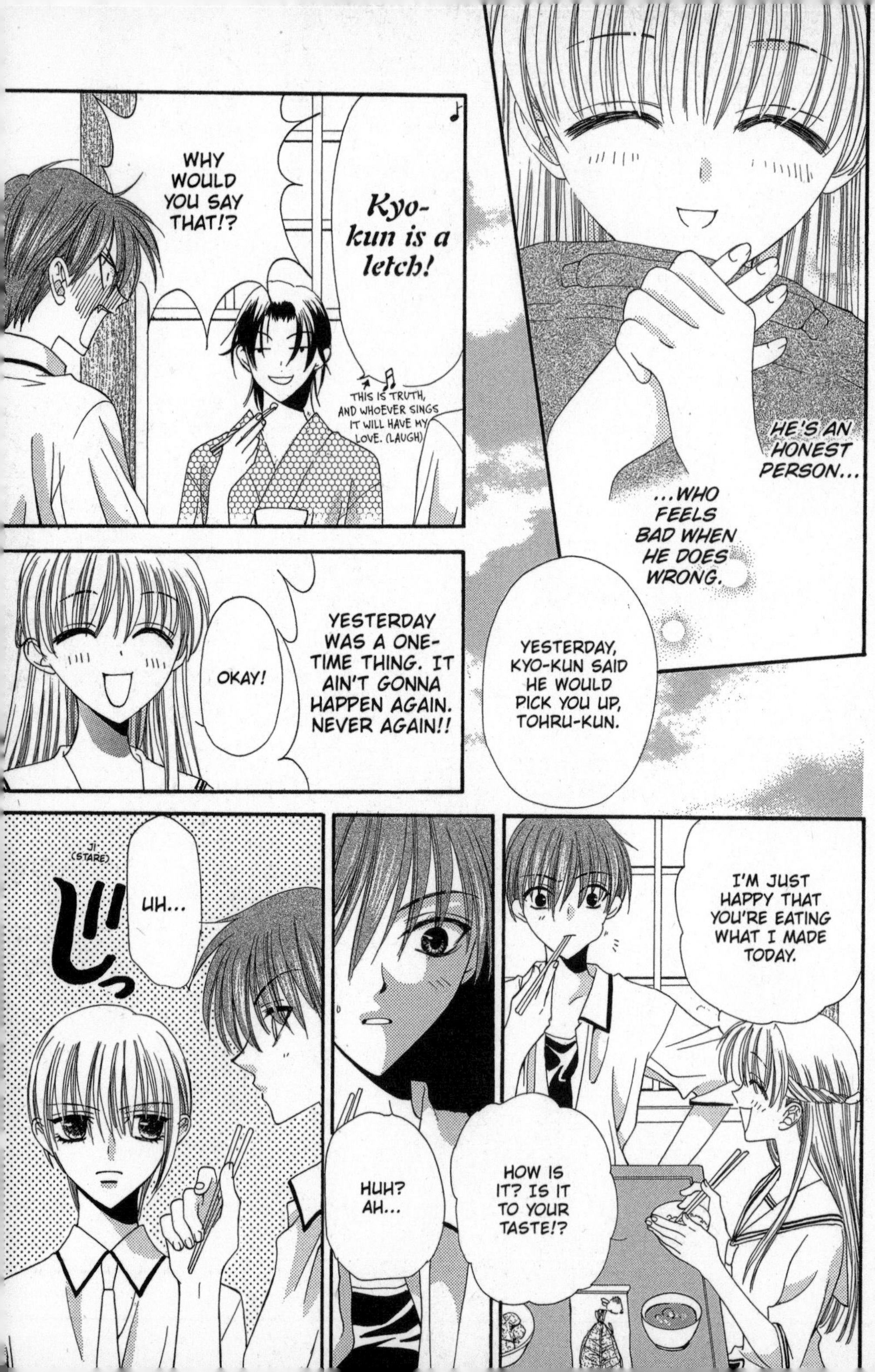
HE'S AN HONEST PERSON...
...WHO FEELS BAD WHEN HE DOES WRONG.
YESTERDAY, KYO-KUN SAID HE WOULD PICK YOU UP, TOHRU-KUN.
Kyo-kun is a letch!
THIS IS TRUTH, AND WHOEVER SINGS IT WILL HAVE MY LOVE. (LAUGH)
WHY WOULD YOU SAY THAT!?
YESTERDAY WAS A ONE-TIME THING. IT AIN'T GONNA HAPPEN AGAIN. NEVER AGAIN!!
OKAY!
I'M JUST HAPPY THAT YOU'RE EATING WHAT I MADE TODAY.
HOW IS IT? IS IT TO YOUR TASTE!?
HUH? AH...
UH...
じっ
JI (STARE)

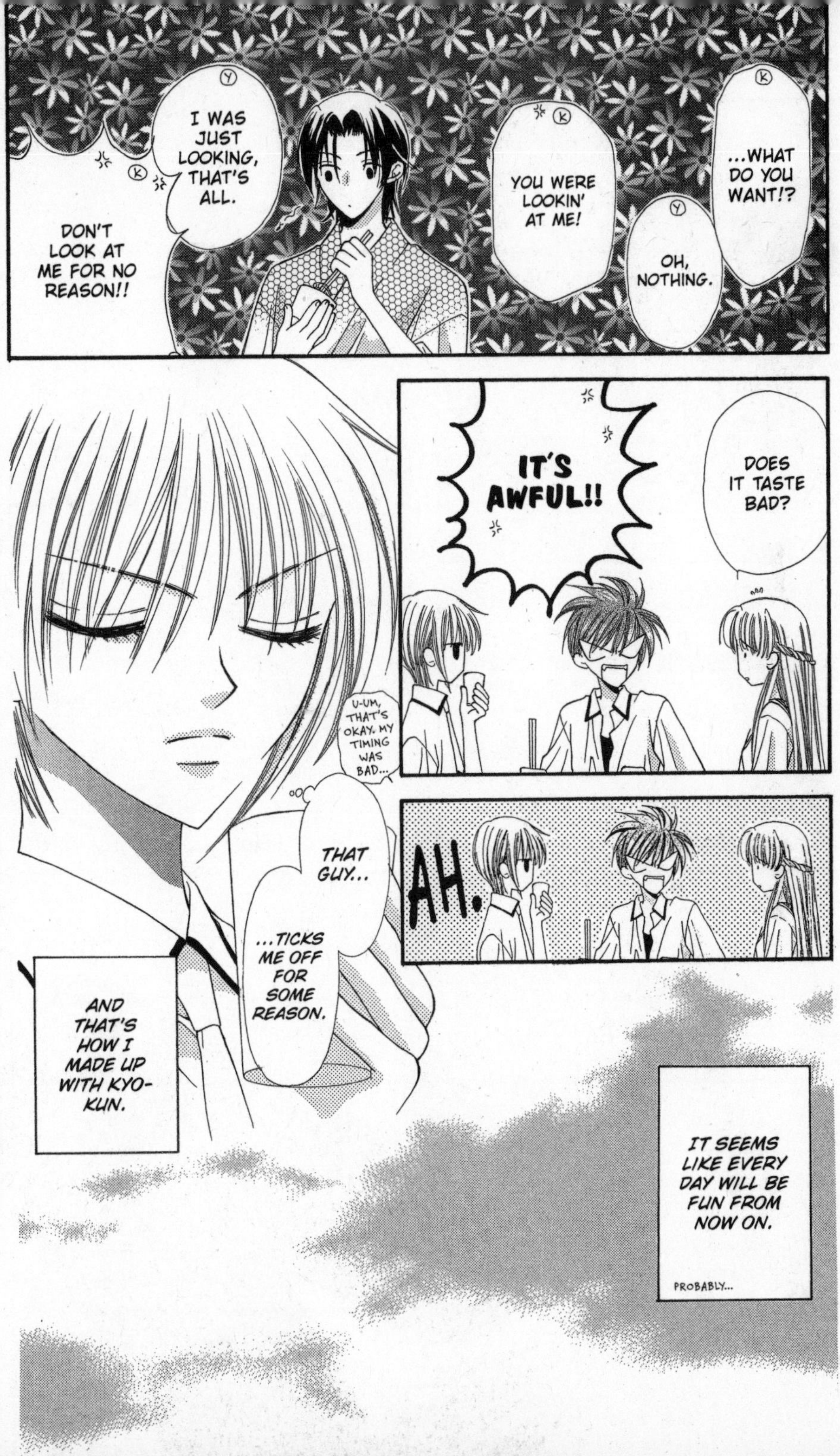
...WHAT DO YOU WANT!?
OH, NOTHING.
YOU WERE LOOKIN' AT ME!
I WAS JUST LOOKING, THAT'S ALL.
DON'T LOOK AT ME FOR NO REASON!!
DOES IT TASTE BAD?
IT'S AWFUL!!
U-UM, THAT'S OKAY. MY TIMING WAS BAD...
AH.
THAT GUY...
...TICKS ME OFF FOR SOME REASON.
AND THAT'S HOW I MADE UP WITH KYO-KUN.
IT SEEMS LIKE EVERY DAY WILL BE FUN FROM NOW ON.
PROBABLY...

Chapter 4

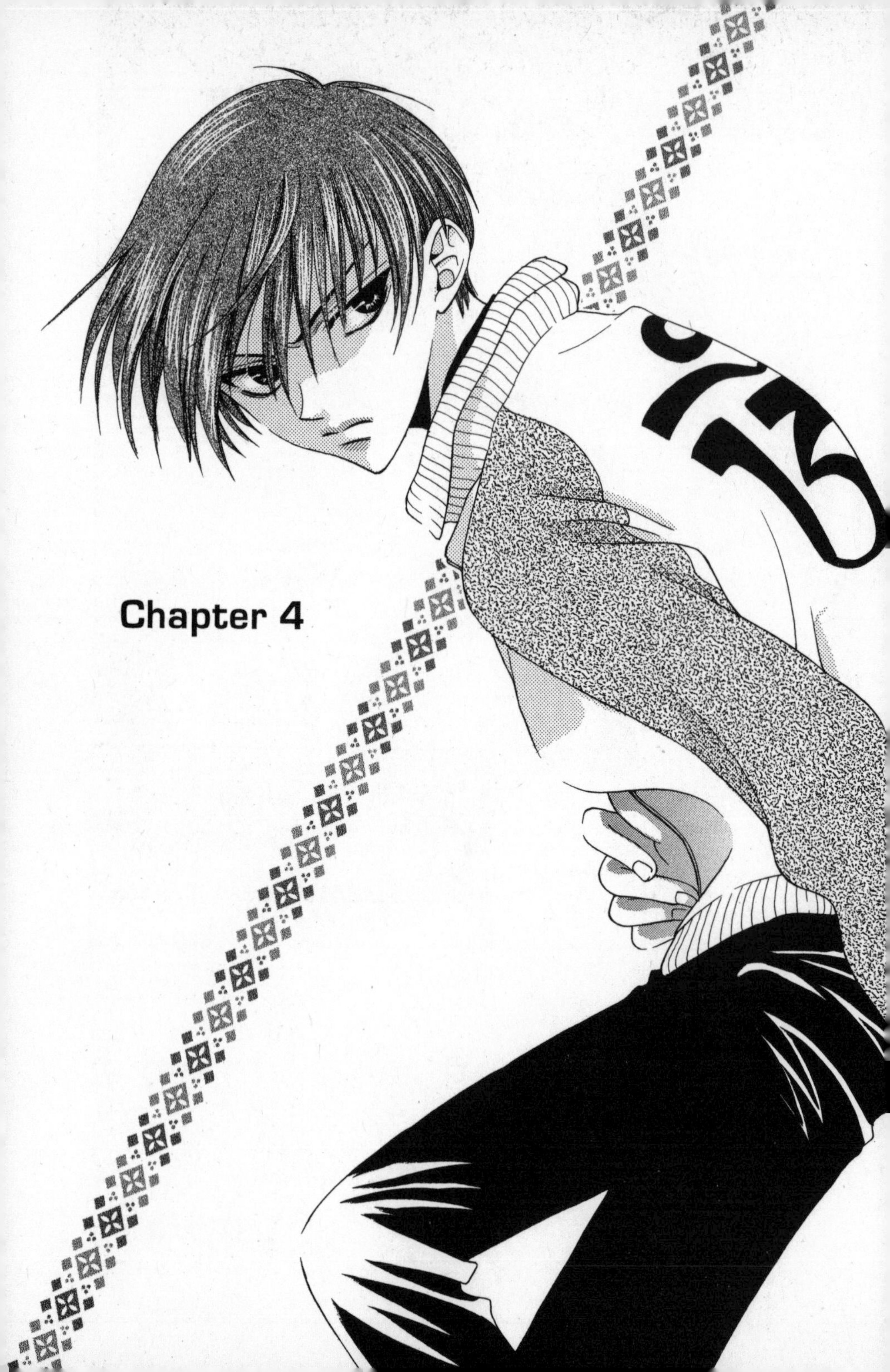

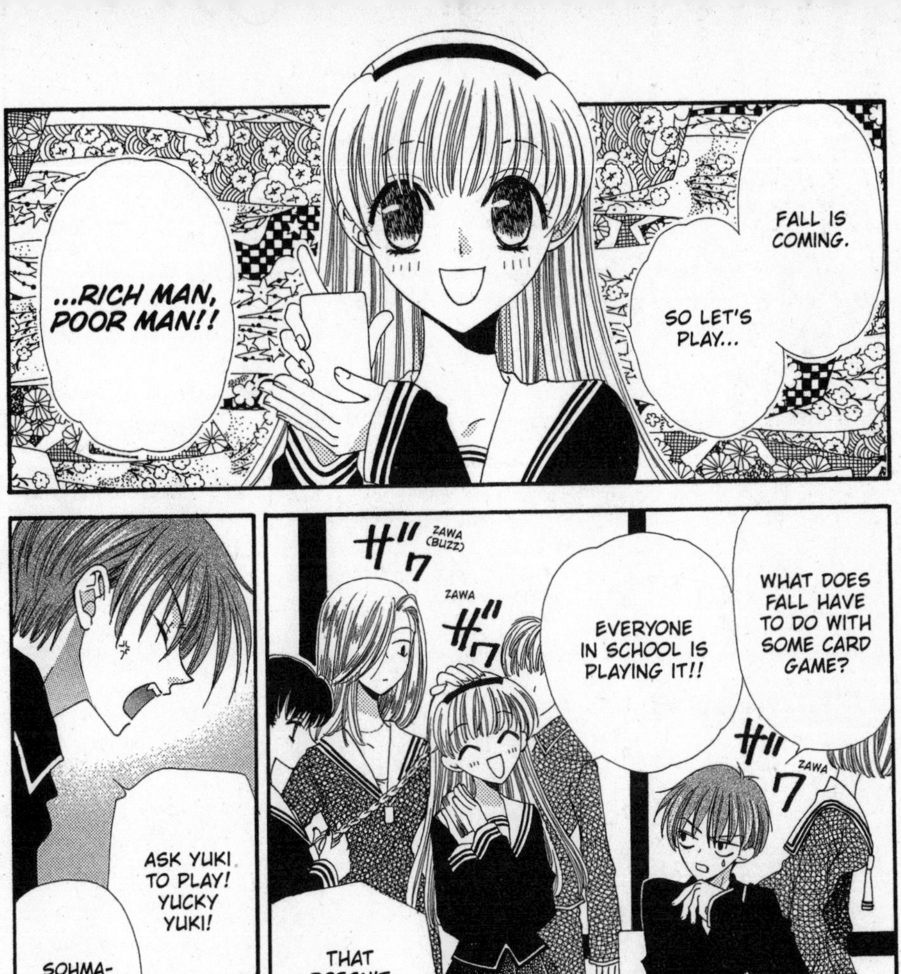
FALL IS COMING.
SO LET'S PLAY...
...RICH MAN, POOR MAN!!
WHAT DOES FALL HAVE TO DO WITH SOME CARD GAME?
ザワ ZAWA (BUZZ)
EVERYONE IN SCHOOL IS PLAYING IT!!
ザワ ZAWA
ザワ ZAWA
THAT DOESN'T ANSWER MY QUESTION.
ASK YUKI TO PLAY! YUCKY YUKI!
SOHMA-KUN ISN'T AROUND...
WHAT DO I CARE!?
WHERE I'M FROM, THEY CALLED THE GAME "RICH MAN, POOR MAN" INSTEAD OF "PRESIDENT."

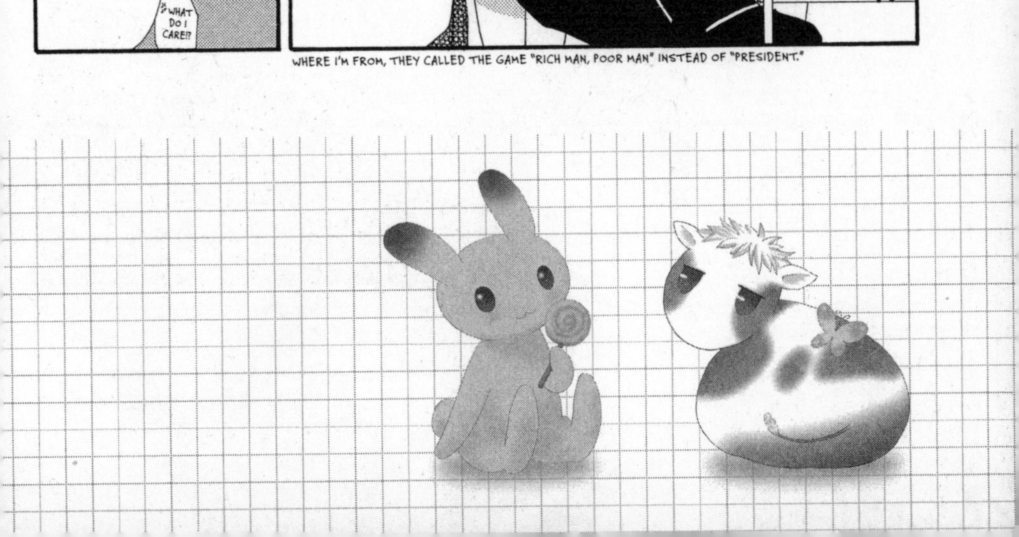

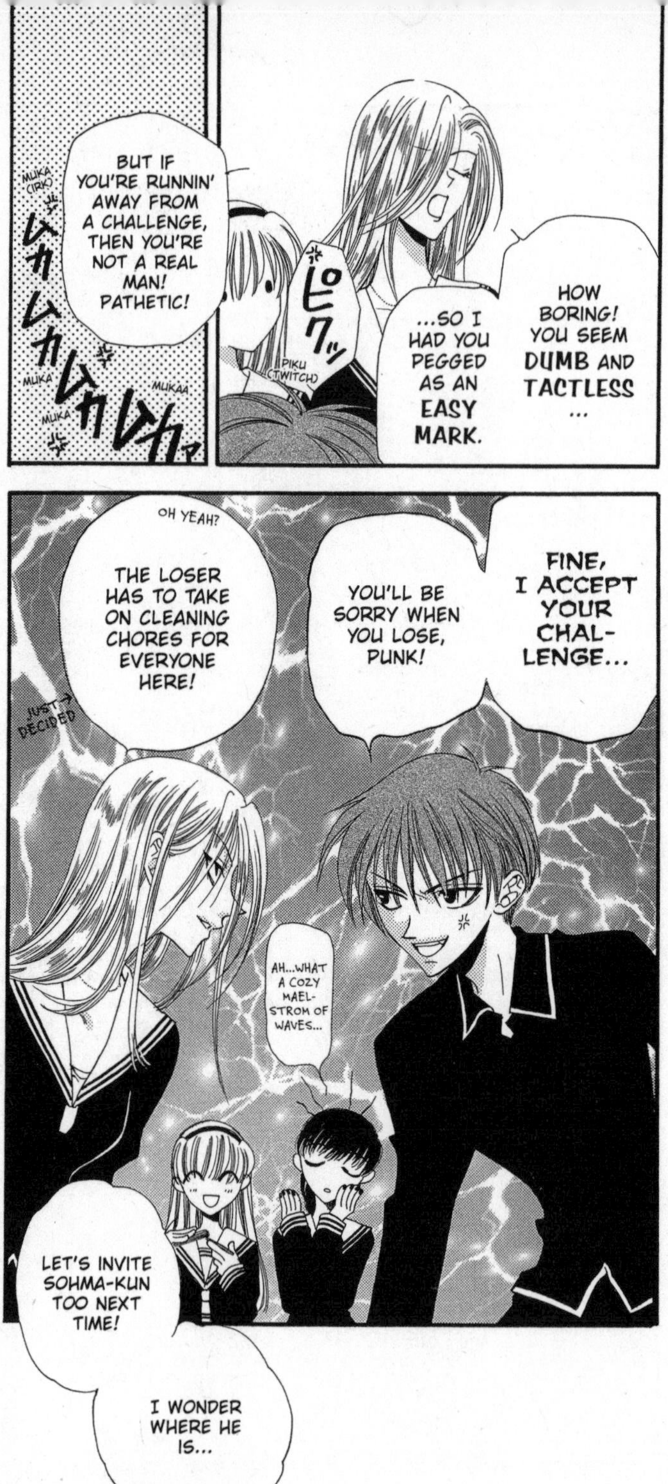
HOW BORING! YOU SEEM DUMB AND TACTLESS...
...SO I HAD YOU PEGGED AS AN EASY MARK.
PIKU (TWITCH)
BUT IF YOU'RE RUNNIN' AWAY FROM A CHALLENGE, THEN YOU'RE NOT A REAL MAN! PATHETIC!
MUKA (IRK)
MUKA
MUKA
MUKAA
FINE, I ACCEPT YOUR CHAL-LENGE...
YOU'LL BE SORRY WHEN YOU LOSE, PUNK!
OH YEAH?
THE LOSER HAS TO TAKE ON CLEANING CHORES FOR EVERYONE HERE!
JUST DECIDED
AH...WHAT A COZY MAEL-STROM OF WAVES...
LET'S INVITE SOHMA-KUN TOO NEXT TIME!
I WONDER WHERE HE IS...

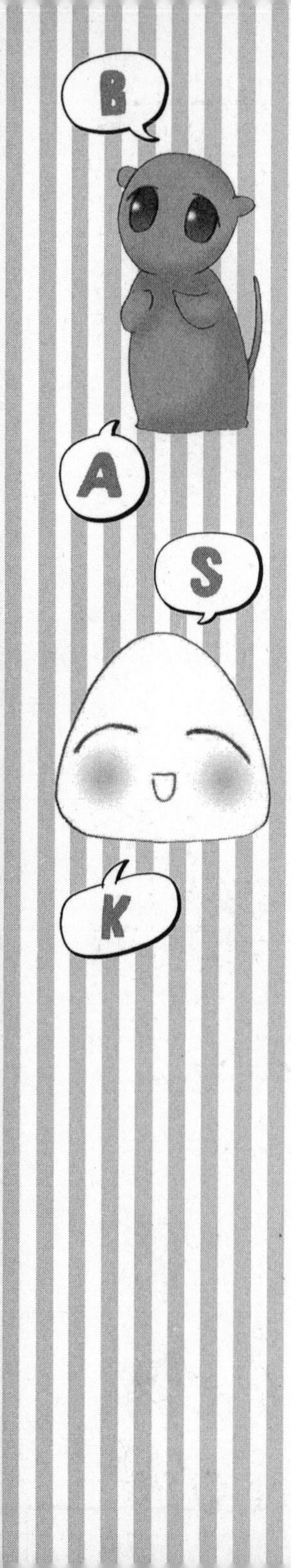
B
A
S
K

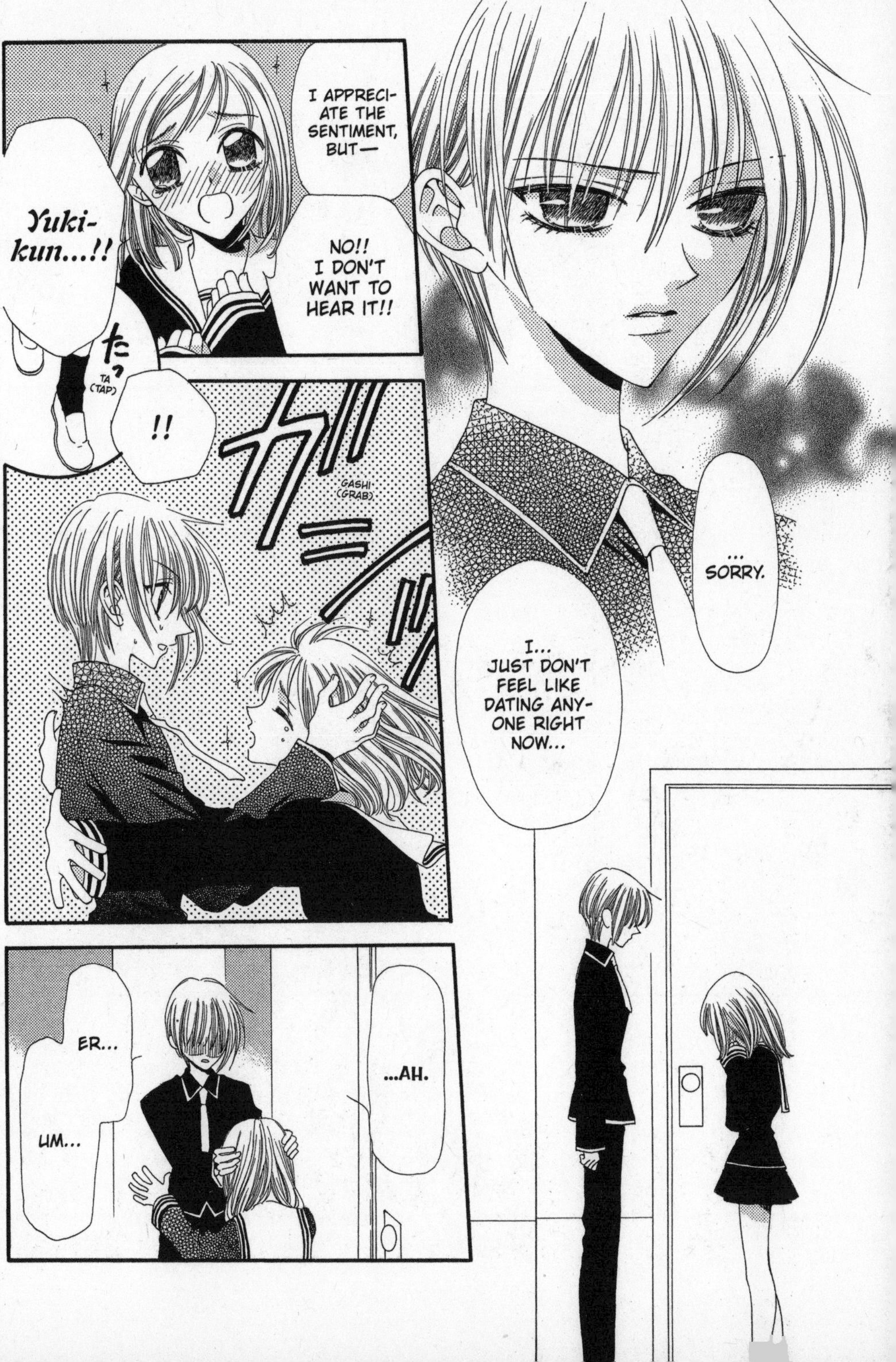
...SORRY.
I... JUST DON'T FEEL LIKE DATING ANY-ONE RIGHT NOW...
I APPRECI-ATE THE SENTIMENT, BUT—
NO!! I DON'T WANT TO HEAR IT!!
Yuki-kun...!!
たっ
TA (TAP)
!!
GASHI (GRAB)
...AH.
ER...
UM...

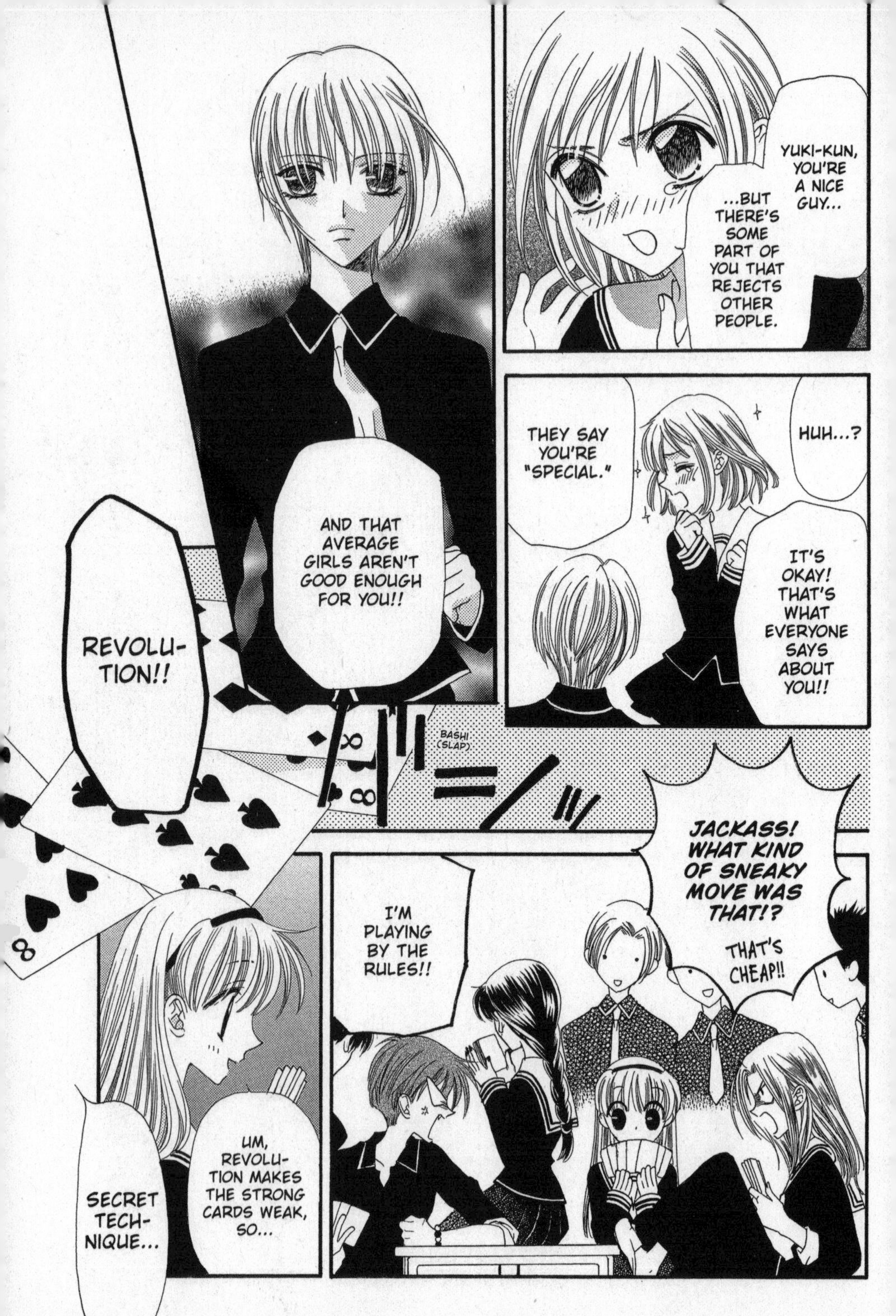
YUKI-KUN, YOU'RE A NICE GUY...
...BUT THERE'S SOME PART OF YOU THAT REJECTS OTHER PEOPLE.
HUH...?
THEY SAY YOU'RE "SPECIAL."
IT'S OKAY! THAT'S WHAT EVERYONE SAYS ABOUT YOU!!
AND THAT AVERAGE GIRLS AREN'T GOOD ENOUGH FOR YOU!!
REVOLU-TION!!
BASHI (SLAP)
JACKASS! WHAT KIND OF SNEAKY MOVE WAS THAT!?
THAT'S CHEAP!!
I'M PLAYING BY THE RULES!!
UM, REVOLU-TION MAKES THE STRONG CARDS WEAK, SO...
SECRET TECH-NIQUE...

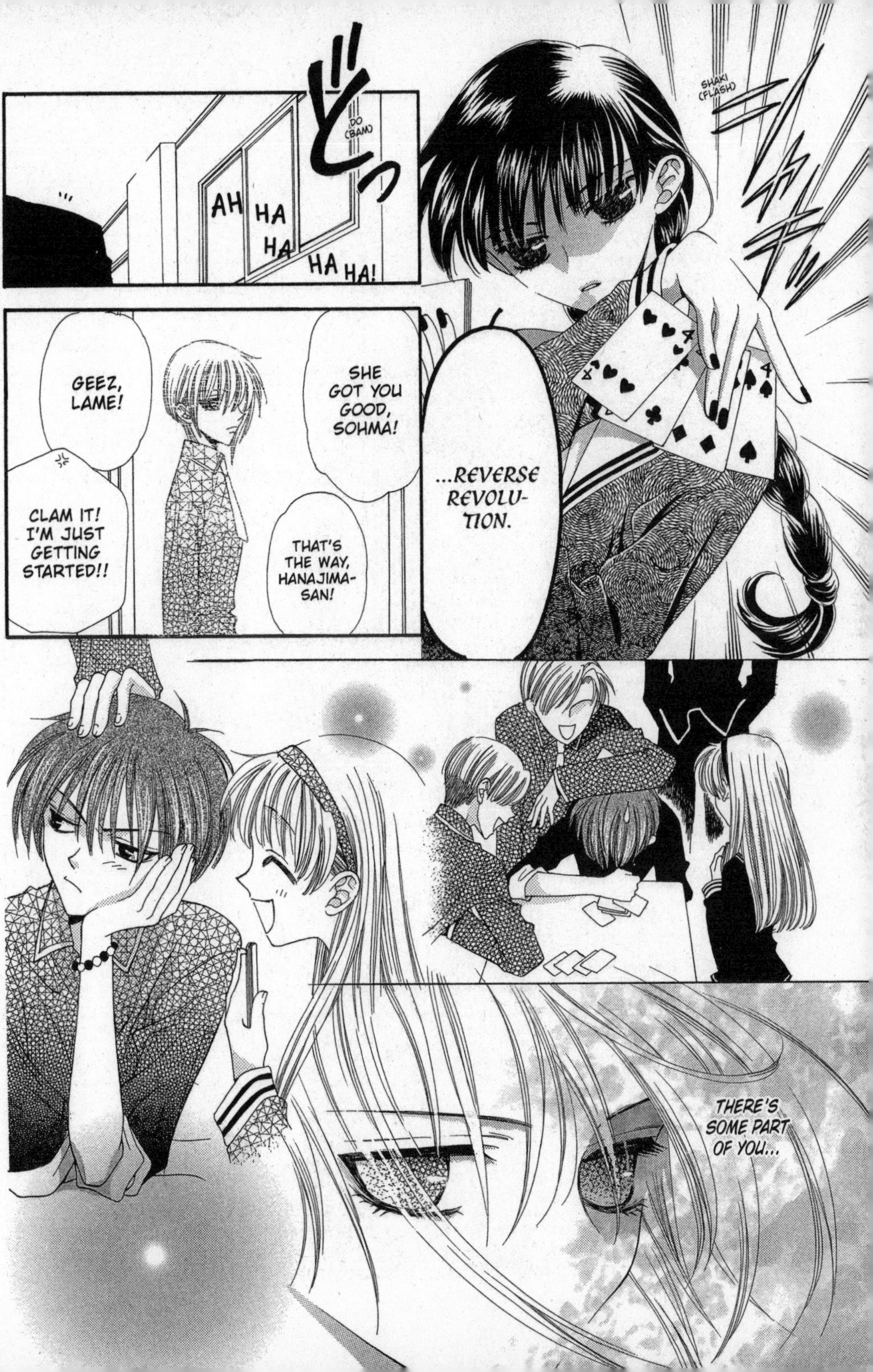
SHAKI (FLASH)
...REVERSE REVOLUTION.
...
DO (BAM)
AH HA HA HA HA!
SHE GOT YOU GOOD, SOHMA!
GEEZ, LAME!
THAT'S THE WAY, HANAJIMA-SAN!
CLAM IT! I'M JUST GETTING STARTED!!
THERE'S SOME PART OF YOU...

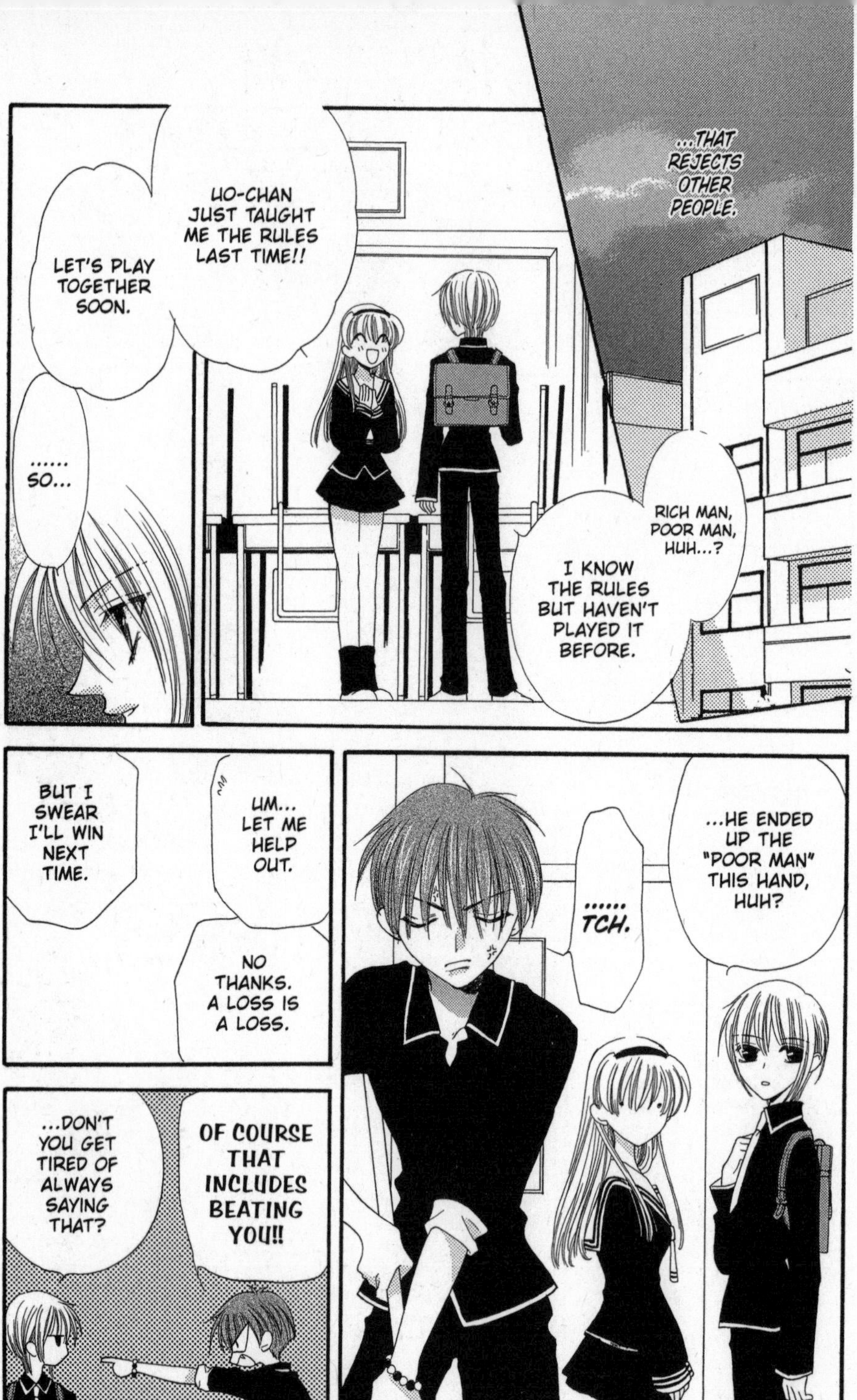
...THAT REJECTS OTHER PEOPLE.
RICH MAN, POOR MAN, HUH...?
I KNOW THE RULES BUT HAVEN'T PLAYED IT BEFORE.
UO-CHAN JUST TAUGHT ME THE RULES LAST TIME!!
LET'S PLAY TOGETHER SOON.
...... SO...
...HE ENDED UP THE "POOR MAN" THIS HAND, HUH?
...... TCH.
UM... LET ME HELP OUT.
NO THANKS. A LOSS IS A LOSS.
BUT I SWEAR I'LL WIN NEXT TIME.
OF COURSE THAT INCLUDES BEATING YOU!!
...DON'T YOU GET TIRED OF ALWAYS SAYING THAT?

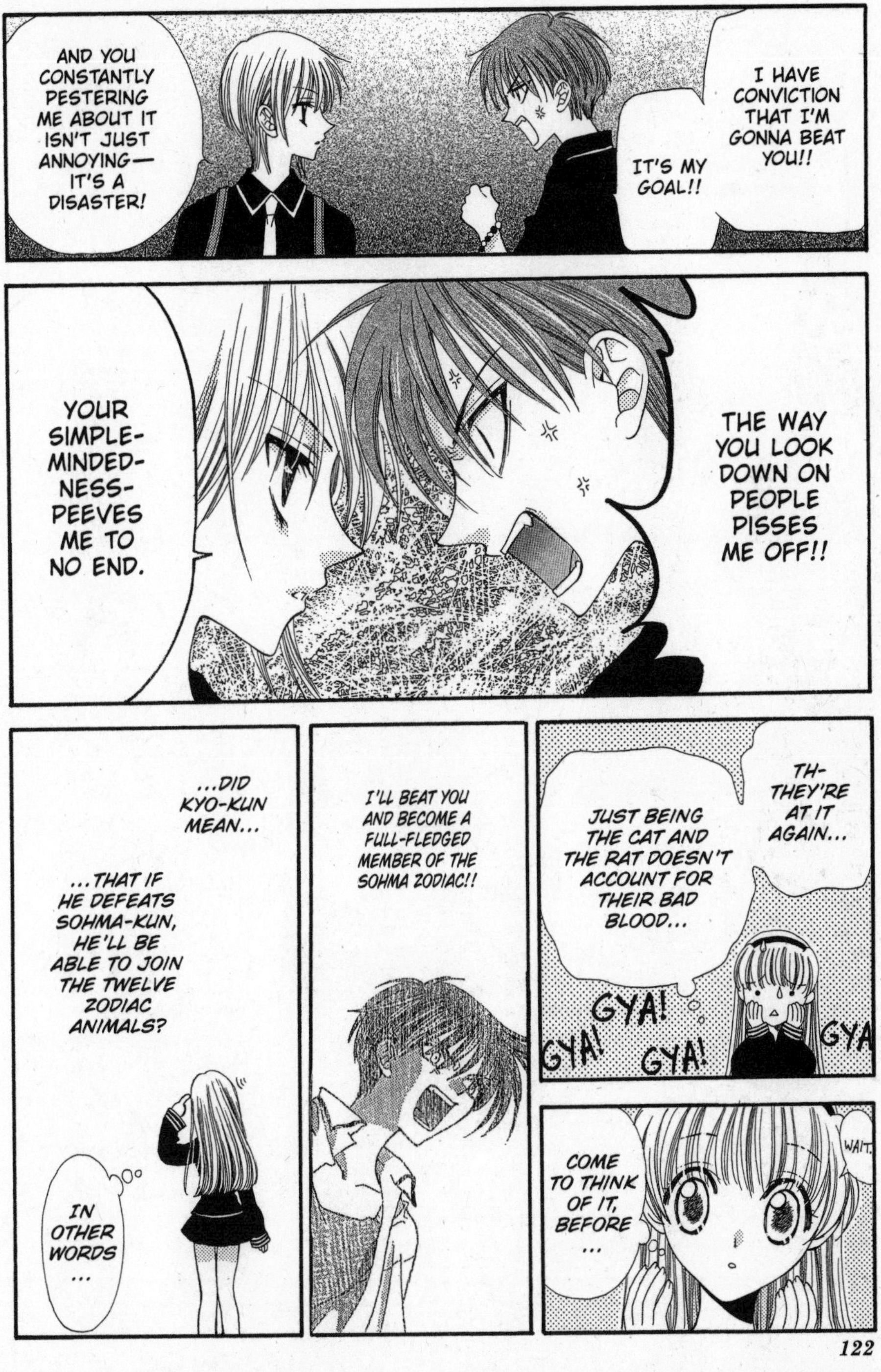
I HAVE CONVICTION THAT I'M GONNA BEAT YOU!!
IT'S MY GOAL!!
AND YOU CONSTANTLY PESTERING ME ABOUT IT ISN'T JUST ANNOYING— IT'S A DISASTER!
THE WAY YOU LOOK DOWN ON PEOPLE PISSES ME OFF!!
YOUR SIMPLE-MINDED-NESS-PEEVES ME TO NO END.
TH- THEY'RE AT IT AGAIN...
JUST BEING THE CAT AND THE RAT DOESN'T ACCOUNT FOR THEIR BAD BLOOD...
GYA!
GYA!
GYA!
GYA
WAIT.
COME TO THINK OF IT, BEFORE ...
I'LL BEAT YOU AND BECOME A FULL-FLEDGED MEMBER OF THE SOHMA ZODIAC!!
...DID KYO-KUN MEAN...
...THAT IF HE DEFEATS SOHMA-KUN, HE'LL BE ABLE TO JOIN THE TWELVE ZODIAC ANIMALS?
IN OTHER WORDS ...

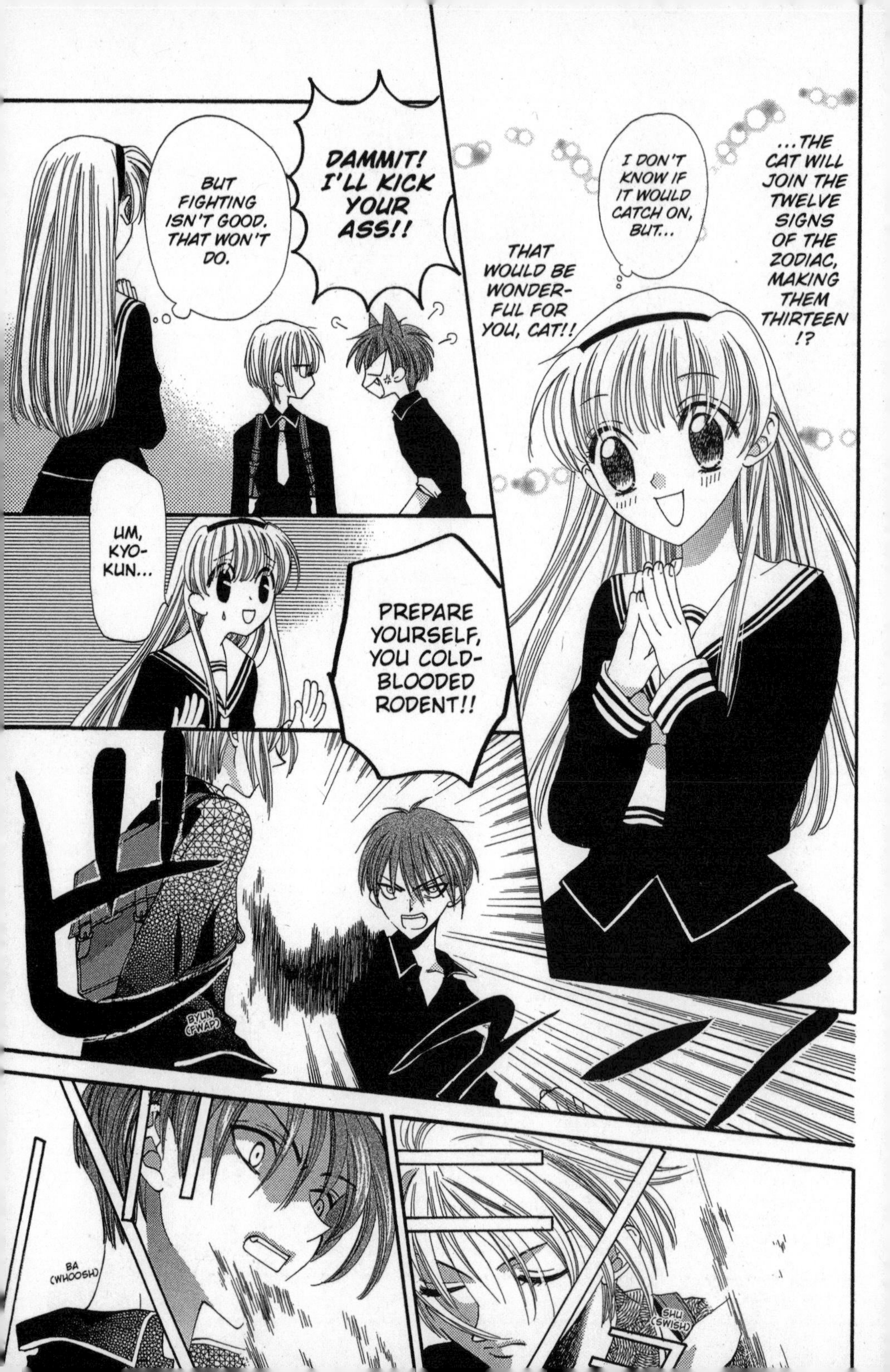
...THE CAT WILL JOIN THE TWELVE SIGNS OF THE ZODIAC, MAKING THEM THIRTEEN!?
I DON'T KNOW IF IT WOULD CATCH ON, BUT...
THAT WOULD BE WONDERFUL FOR YOU, CAT!!
DAMMIT! I'LL KICK YOUR ASS!!
BUT FIGHTING ISN'T GOOD. THAT WON'T DO.
PREPARE YOURSELF, YOU COLD-BLOODED RODENT!!
UM, KYO-KUN...
BYUN (FWAP)
SHU (SWISH)
BA (WHOOSH)

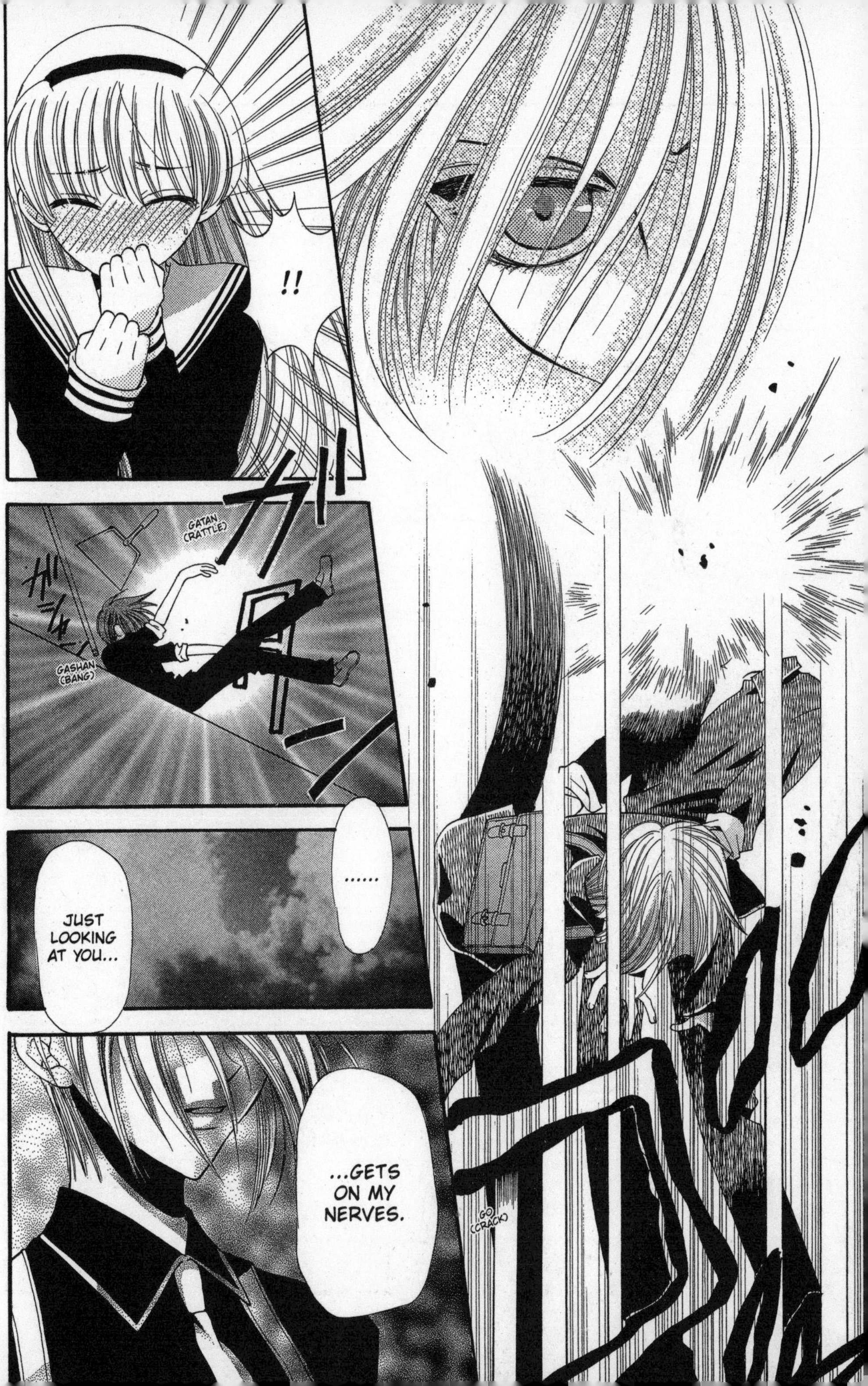
!!
GO (CRACK)
GATAN (RATTLE)
GASHAN (BANG)
......
JUST LOOKING AT YOU...
...GETS ON MY NERVES.

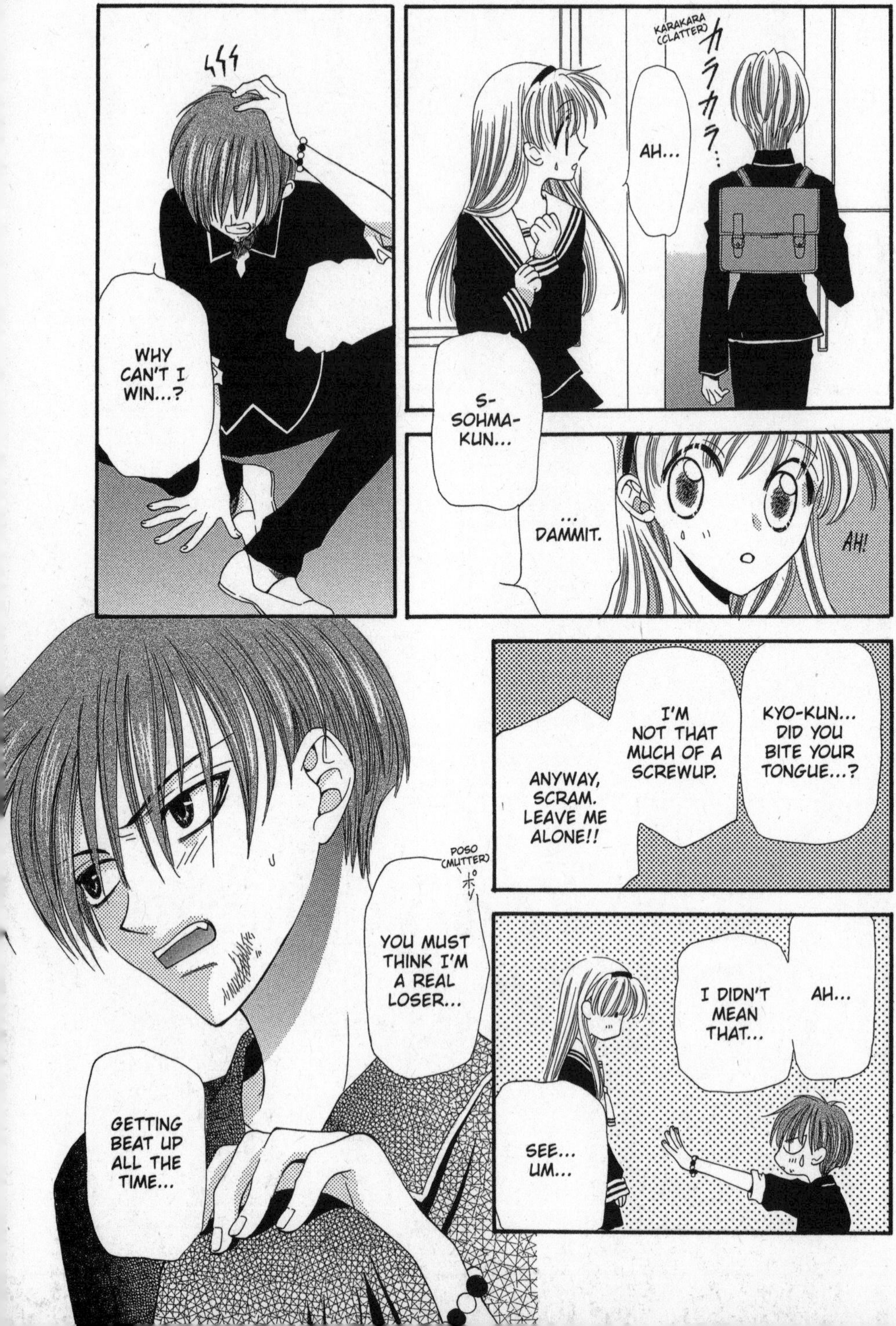
KARAKARA (CLATTER)
カラカラ…
AH…
S-SOHMA-KUN…
AH!
… DAMMIT.
WHY CAN'T I WIN…?
KYO-KUN… DID YOU BITE YOUR TONGUE…?
I'M NOT THAT MUCH OF A SCREWUP.
ANYWAY, SCRAM. LEAVE ME ALONE!!
AH…
I DIDN'T MEAN THAT…
SEE… UM…
POSO (MUTTER)
ポソ
YOU MUST THINK I'M A REAL LOSER…
GETTING BEAT UP ALL THE TIME…

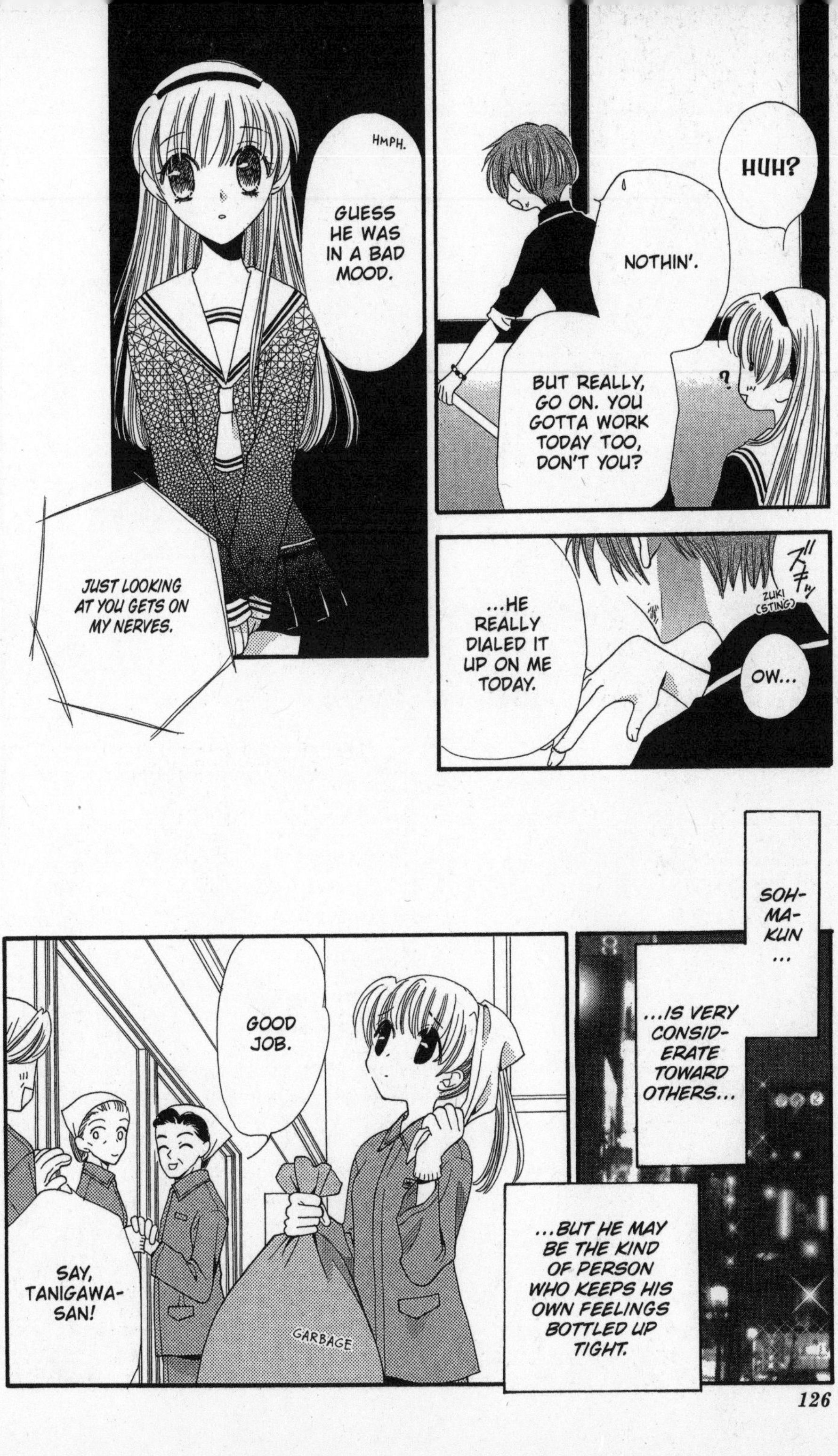
HUH?
NOTHIN'.
BUT REALLY, GO ON. YOU GOTTA WORK TODAY TOO, DON'T YOU?
?
ズキッ
ZUKI (STING)
OW...
...HE REALLY DIALED IT UP ON ME TODAY.
HMPH.
GUESS HE WAS IN A BAD MOOD.
JUST LOOKING AT YOU GETS ON MY NERVES.
SOH-MA-KUN...
...IS VERY CONSID-ERATE TOWARD OTHERS...
...BUT HE MAY BE THE KIND OF PERSON WHO KEEPS HIS OWN FEELINGS BOTTLED UP TIGHT.
GOOD JOB.
SAY, TANIGAWA-SAN!
GARBAGE

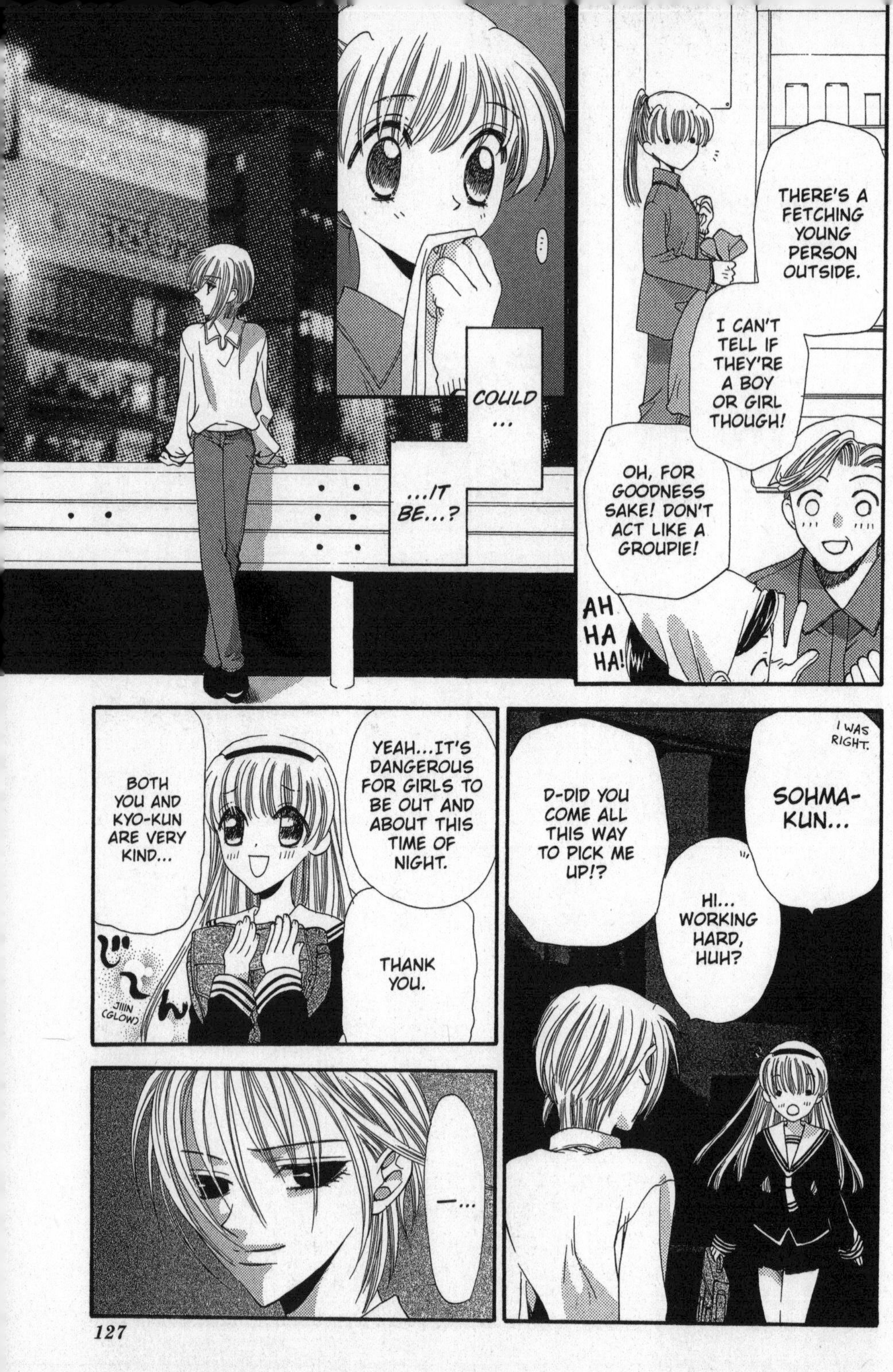
THERE'S A FETCHING YOUNG PERSON OUTSIDE.
I CAN'T TELL IF THEY'RE A BOY OR GIRL THOUGH!
OH, FOR GOODNESS SAKE! DON'T ACT LIKE A GROUPIE!
AH HA HA!
...
COULD ...
...IT BE...?
I WAS RIGHT.
SOHMA-KUN...
HI... WORKING HARD, HUH?
D-DID YOU COME ALL THIS WAY TO PICK ME UP!?
YEAH...IT'S DANGEROUS FOR GIRLS TO BE OUT AND ABOUT THIS TIME OF NIGHT.
THANK YOU.
BOTH YOU AND KYO-KUN ARE VERY KIND...
JIIIN (GLOW)
—...

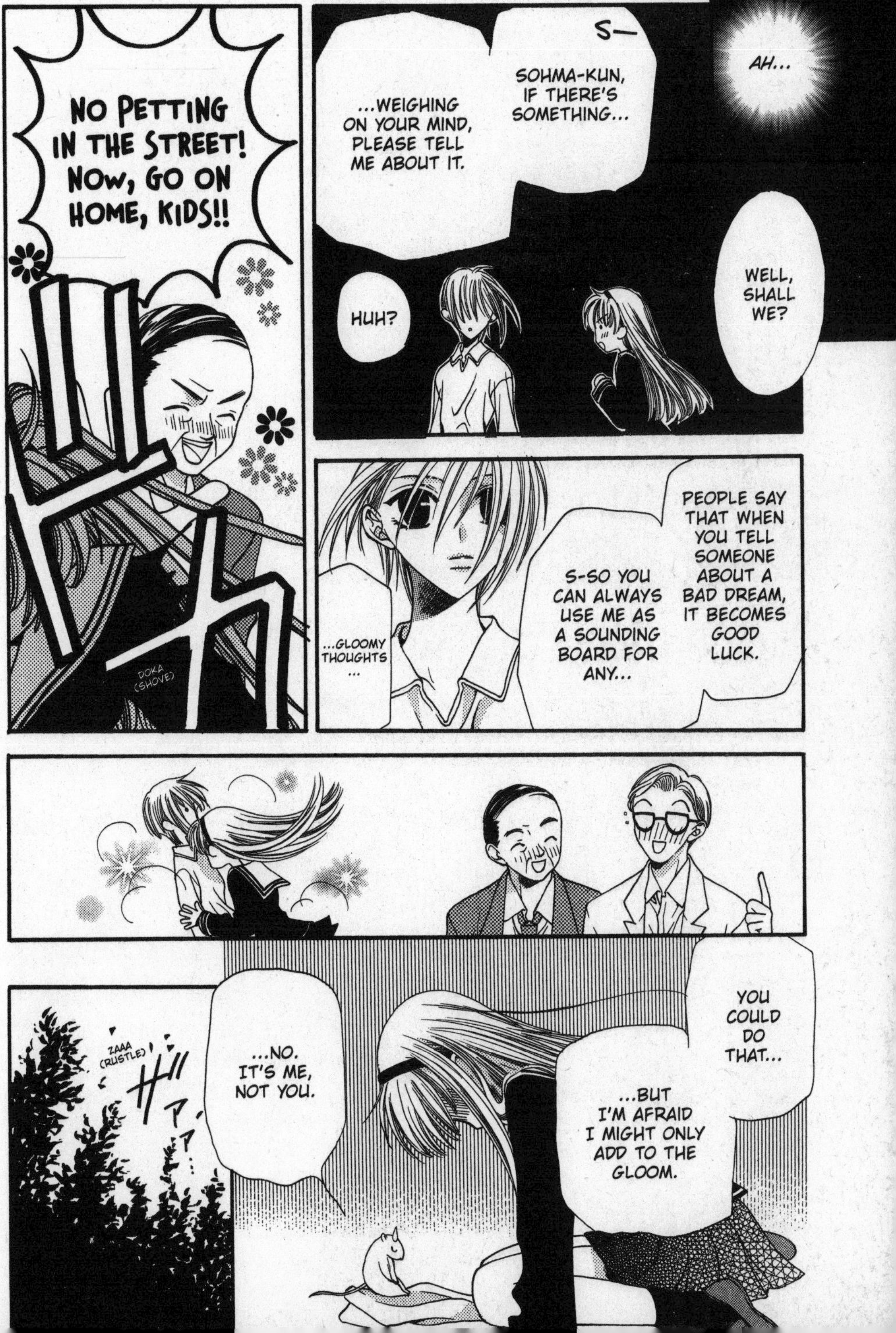
AH...
WELL, SHALL WE?
S—
SOHMA-KUN, IF THERE'S SOMETHING...
...WEIGHING ON YOUR MIND, PLEASE TELL ME ABOUT IT.
HUH?
PEOPLE SAY THAT WHEN YOU TELL SOMEONE ABOUT A BAD DREAM, IT BECOMES GOOD LUCK.
S-SO YOU CAN ALWAYS USE ME AS A SOUNDING BOARD FOR ANY...
...GLOOMY THOUGHTS...
NO PETTING IN THE STREET! NOW, GO ON HOME, KIDS!!
DOKA (SHOVE)
YOU COULD DO THAT...
...BUT I'M AFRAID I MIGHT ONLY ADD TO THE GLOOM.
...NO. IT'S ME, NOT YOU.
ZAAA (RUSTLE)

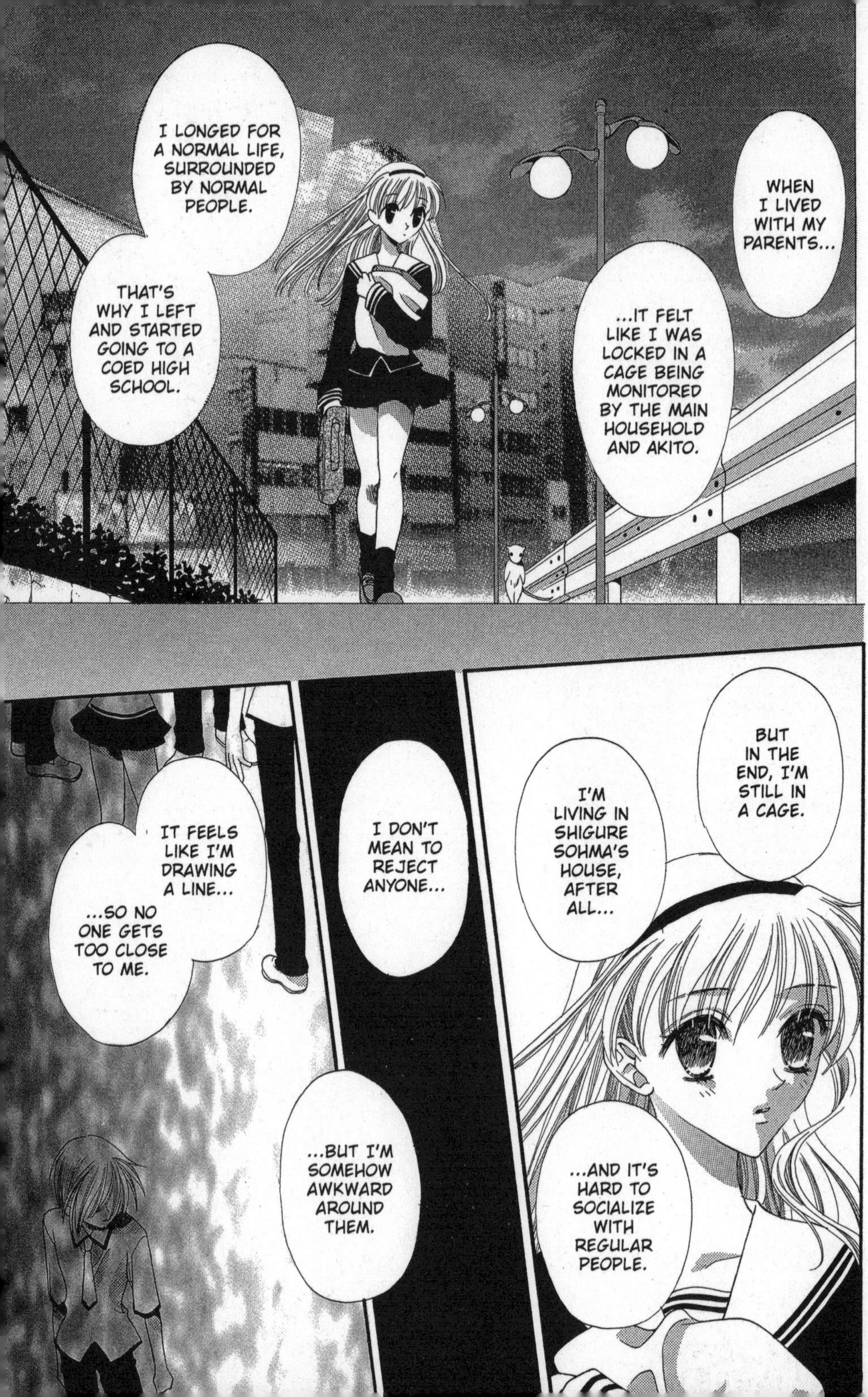
WHEN I LIVED WITH MY PARENTS...
...IT FELT LIKE I WAS LOCKED IN A CAGE BEING MONITORED BY THE MAIN HOUSEHOLD AND AKITO.
I LONGED FOR A NORMAL LIFE, SURROUNDED BY NORMAL PEOPLE.
THAT'S WHY I LEFT AND STARTED GOING TO A COED HIGH SCHOOL.
BUT IN THE END, I'M STILL IN A CAGE.
I'M LIVING IN SHIGURE SOHMA'S HOUSE, AFTER ALL...
...AND IT'S HARD TO SOCIALIZE WITH REGULAR PEOPLE.
I DON'T MEAN TO REJECT ANYONE...
...BUT I'M SOMEHOW AWKWARD AROUND THEM.
IT FEELS LIKE I'M DRAWING A LINE...
...SO NO ONE GETS TOO CLOSE TO ME.

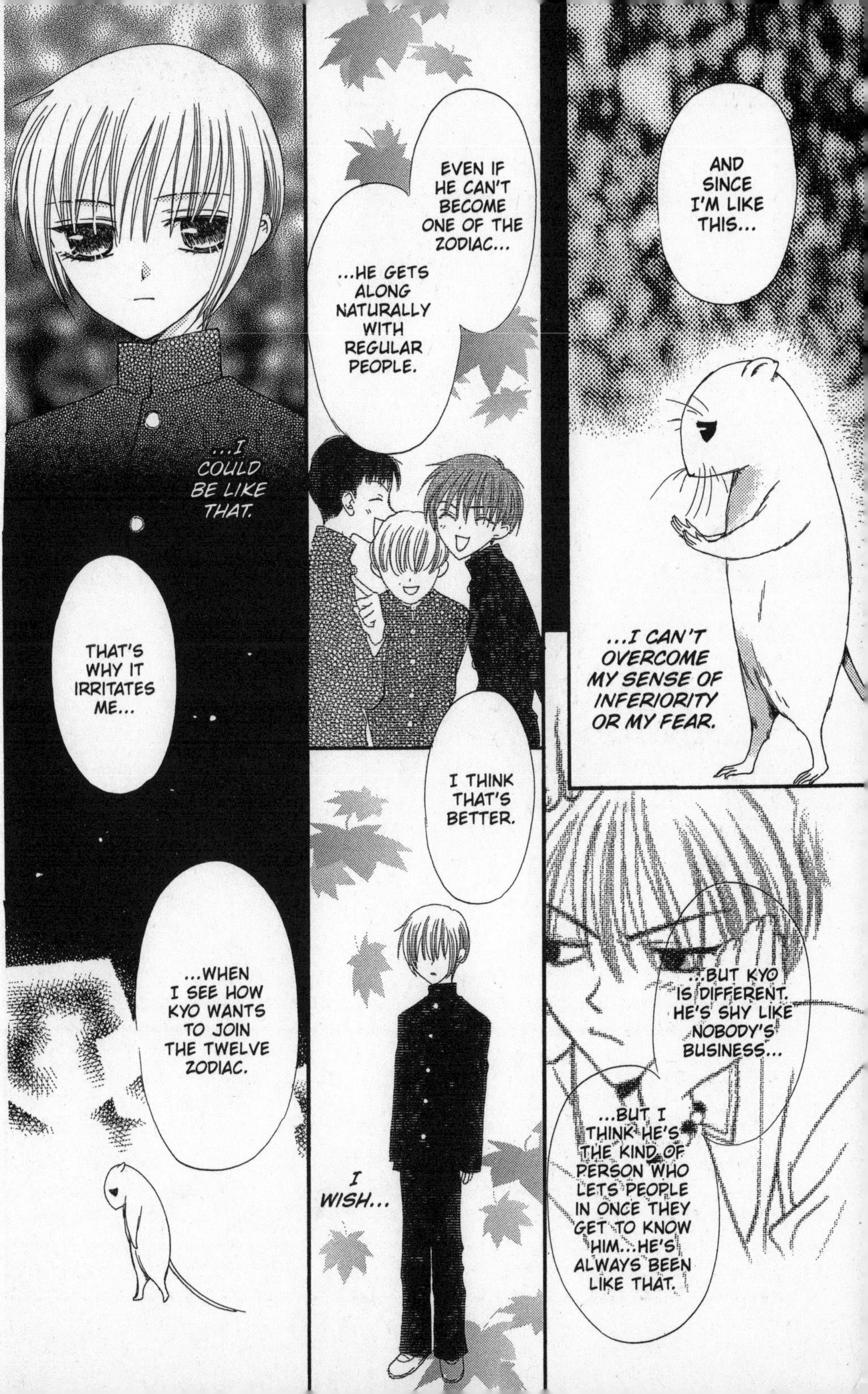
AND SINCE I'M LIKE THIS...
...I CAN'T OVERCOME MY SENSE OF INFERIORITY OR MY FEAR.
...BUT KYO IS DIFFERENT. HE'S SHY LIKE NOBODY'S BUSINESS...
...BUT I THINK HE'S THE KIND OF PERSON WHO LETS PEOPLE IN ONCE THEY GET TO KNOW HIM...HE'S ALWAYS BEEN LIKE THAT.
EVEN IF HE CAN'T BECOME ONE OF THE ZODIAC...
...HE GETS ALONG NATURALLY WITH REGULAR PEOPLE.
I THINK THAT'S BETTER.
I WISH...
...I COULD BE LIKE THAT.
THAT'S WHY IT IRRITATES ME...
...WHEN I SEE HOW KYO WANTS TO JOIN THE TWELVE ZODIAC.

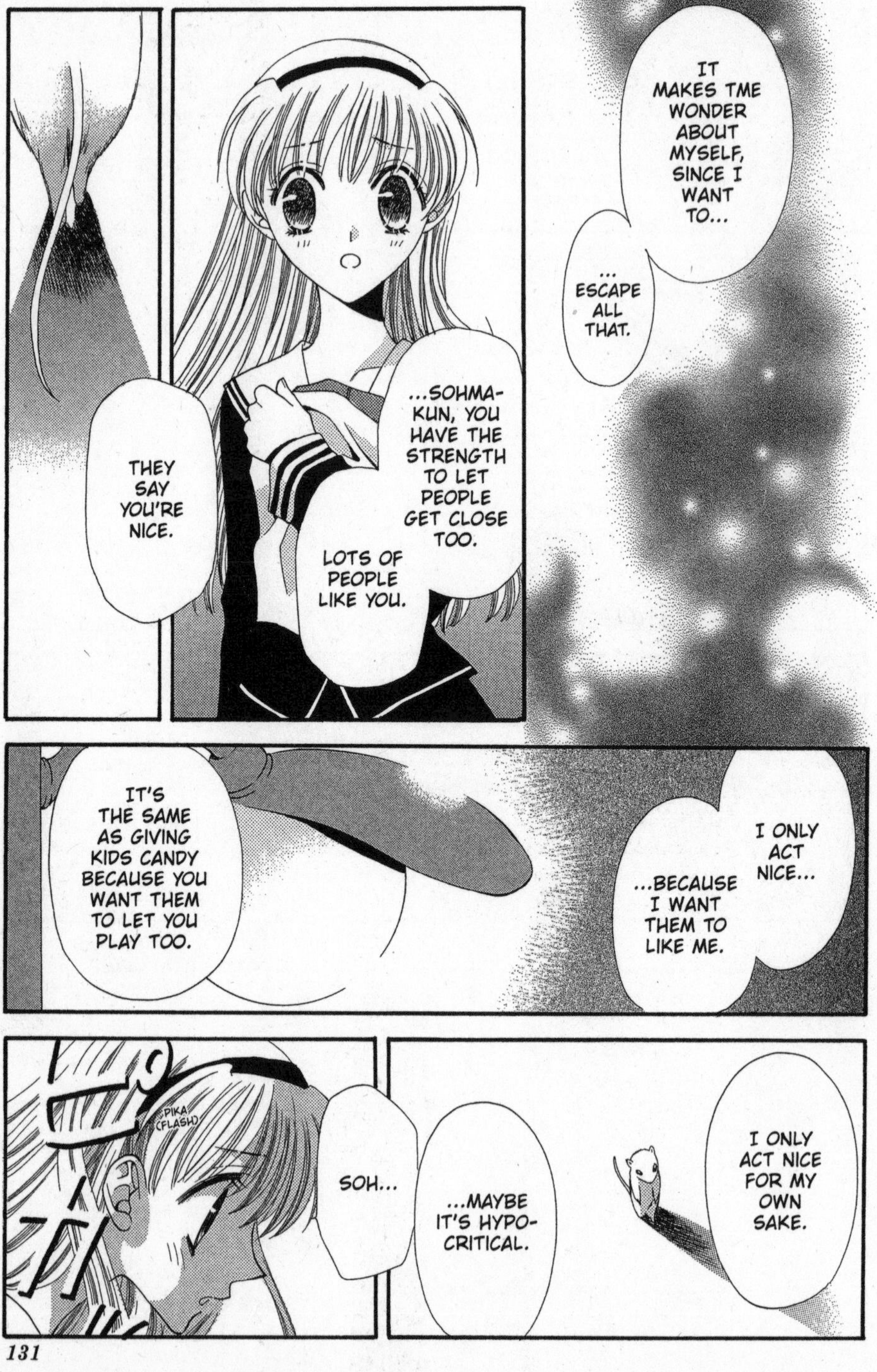
IT MAKES TME WONDER ABOUT MYSELF, SINCE I WANT TO...
...ESCAPE ALL THAT.
...SOHMA-KUN, YOU HAVE THE STRENGTH TO LET PEOPLE GET CLOSE TOO.
LOTS OF PEOPLE LIKE YOU.
THEY SAY YOU'RE NICE.
I ONLY ACT NICE...
...BECAUSE I WANT THEM TO LIKE ME.
IT'S THE SAME AS GIVING KIDS CANDY BECAUSE YOU WANT THEM TO LET YOU PLAY TOO.
I ONLY ACT NICE FOR MY OWN SAKE.
...MAYBE IT'S HYPO-CRITICAL.
SOH...
PIKA (FLASH)

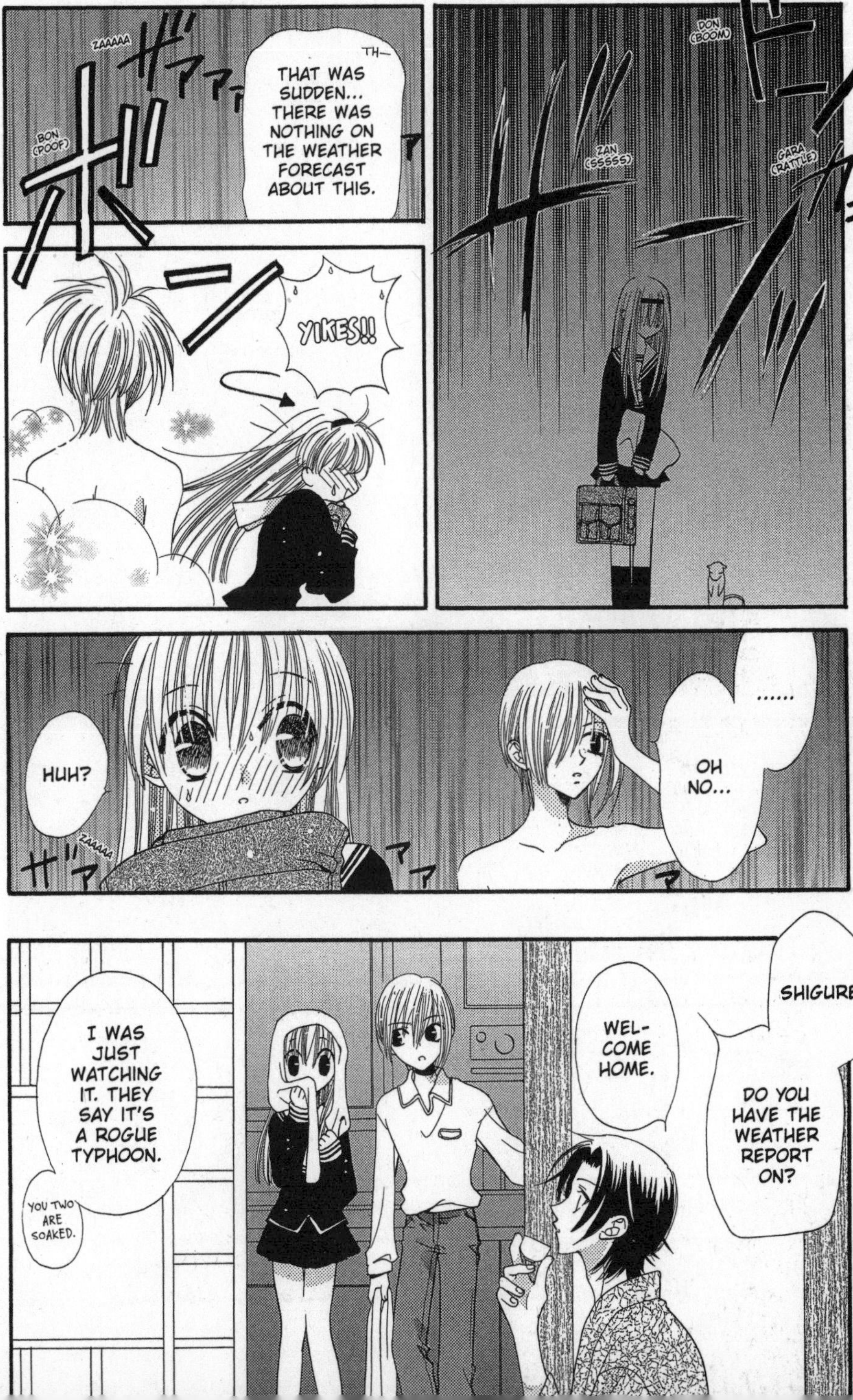
DON (BOOM)
GARA (RATTLE)
ZAN (SSSSS)
TH—
THAT WAS SUDDEN... THERE WAS NOTHING ON THE WEATHER FORECAST ABOUT THIS.
ZAAAAA
BON (POOF)
YIKES!!
......
OH NO...
HUH?
ZAAAAA
SHIGURE.
DO YOU HAVE THE WEATHER REPORT ON?
WEL-COME HOME.
I WAS JUST WATCHING IT. THEY SAY IT'S A ROGUE TYPHOON.
YOU TWO ARE SOAKED.

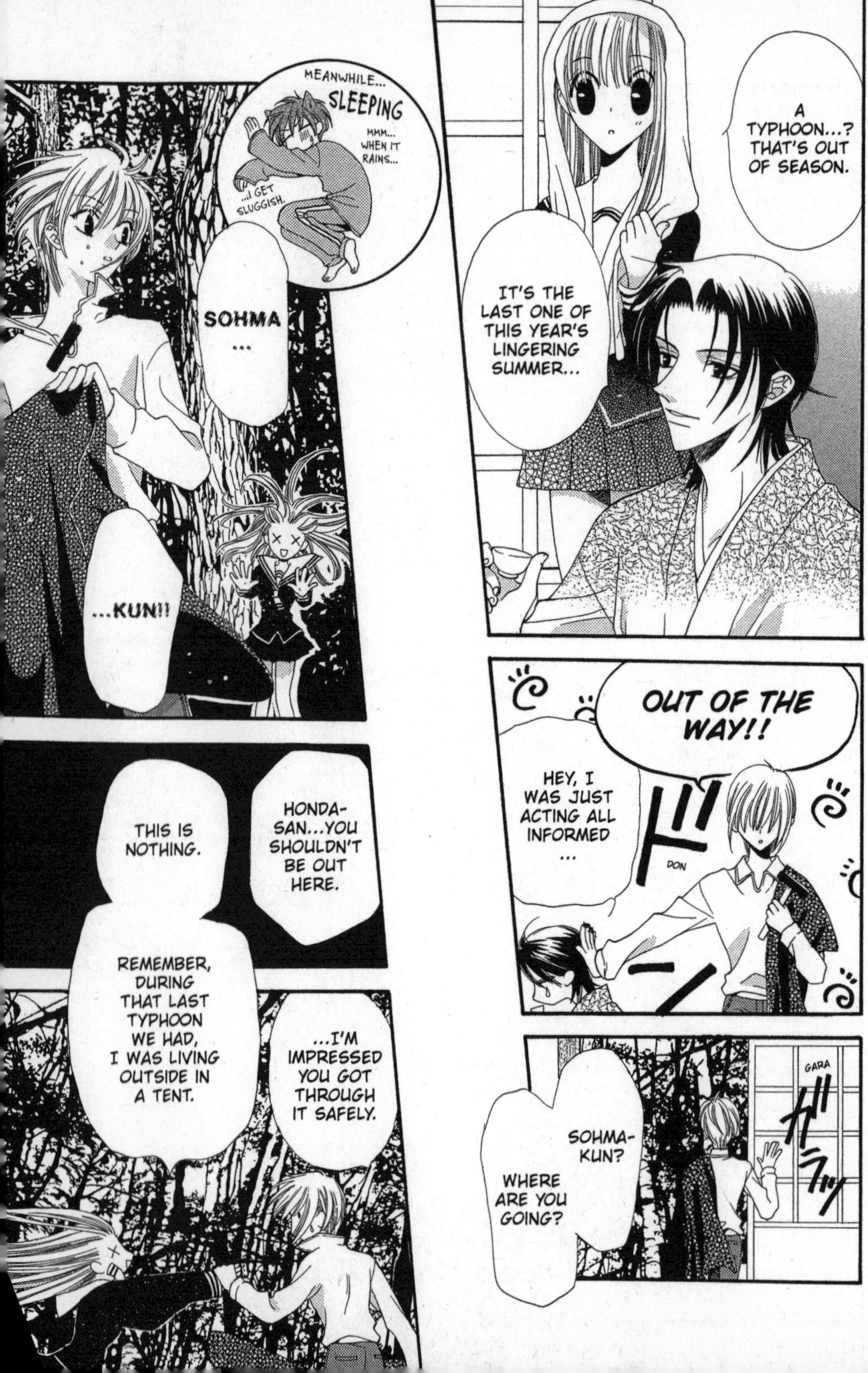
A TYPHOON...? THAT'S OUT OF SEASON.
IT'S THE LAST ONE OF THIS YEAR'S LINGERING SUMMER...
OUT OF THE WAY!!
HEY, I WAS JUST ACTING ALL INFORMED ...
DON
GARA
SOHMA-KUN?
WHERE ARE YOU GOING?
MEANWHILE... SLEEPING
MMM... WHEN IT RAINS...
...I GET SLUGGISH.
SOHMA ...
...KUN!!
HONDA-SAN...YOU SHOULDN'T BE OUT HERE.
THIS IS NOTHING.
REMEMBER, DURING THAT LAST TYPHOON WE HAD, I WAS LIVING OUTSIDE IN A TENT.
...I'M IMPRESSED YOU GOT THROUGH IT SAFELY.

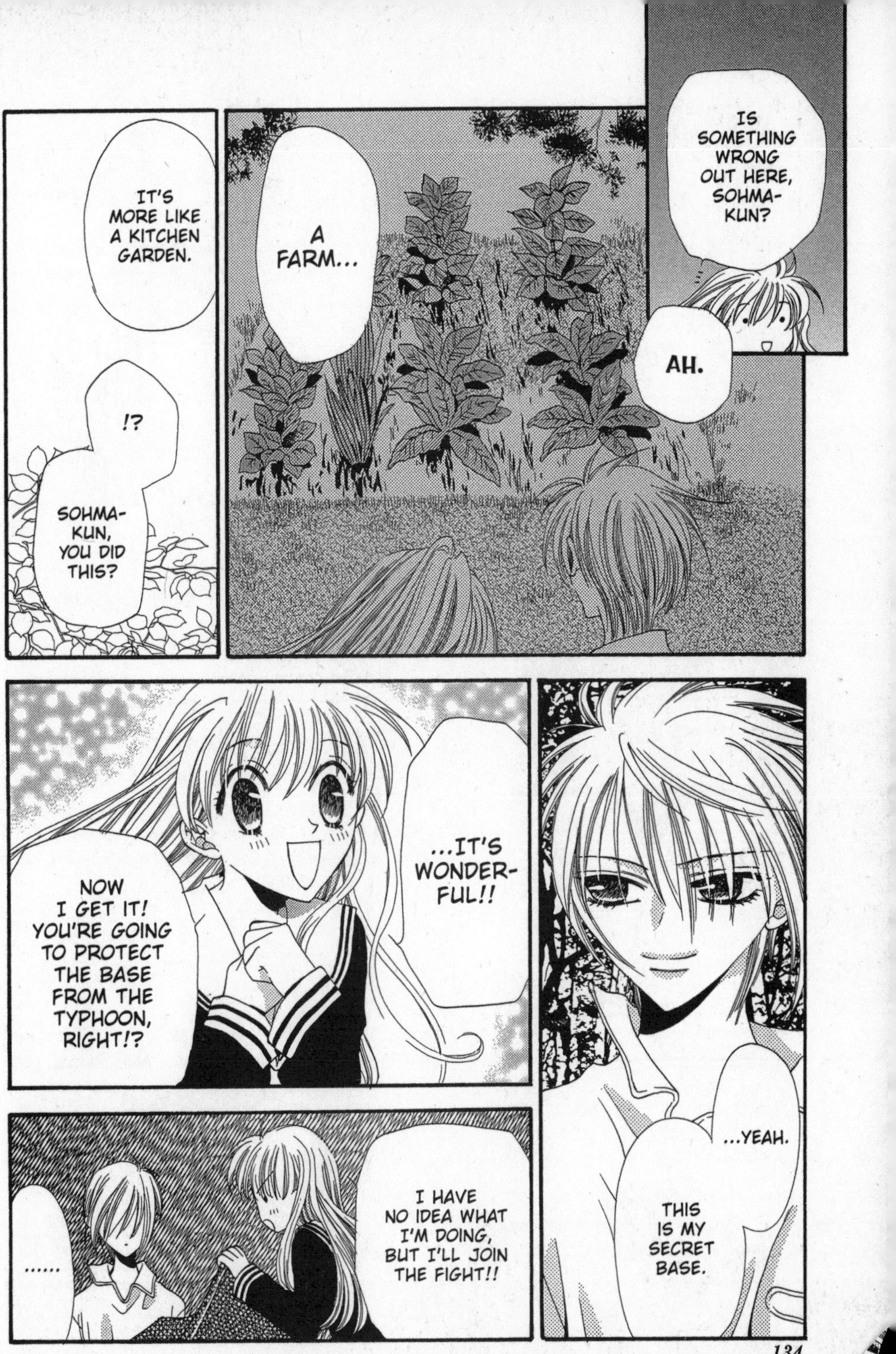
IS SOMETHING WRONG OUT HERE, SOHMA-KUN?
AH.
A FARM...
IT'S MORE LIKE A KITCHEN GARDEN.
!?
SOHMA-KUN, YOU DID THIS?
...YEAH.
THIS IS MY SECRET BASE.
...IT'S WONDERFUL!!
NOW I GET IT! YOU'RE GOING TO PROTECT THE BASE FROM THE TYPHOON, RIGHT!?
I HAVE NO IDEA WHAT I'M DOING, BUT I'LL JOIN THE FIGHT!!
......

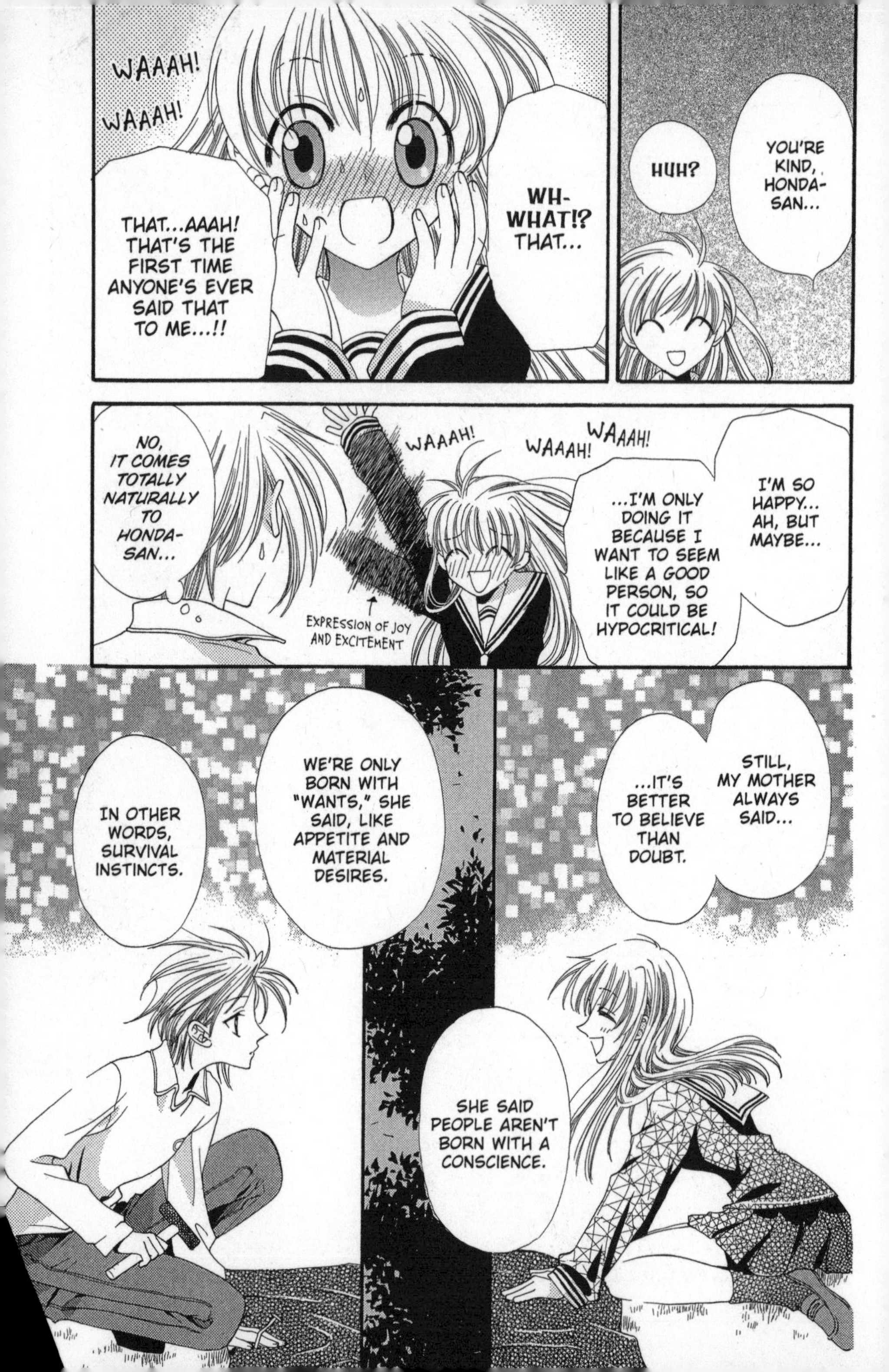

YOU'RE KIND, HONDA-SAN...
HUH?
WH-WHAT!? THAT...
WAAAH!
WAAAH!
THAT...AAAH! THAT'S THE FIRST TIME ANYONE'S EVER SAID THAT TO ME...!!
I'M SO HAPPY... AH, BUT MAYBE...
...I'M ONLY DOING IT BECAUSE I WANT TO SEEM LIKE A GOOD PERSON, SO IT COULD BE HYPOCRITICAL!
WAAAH!
WAAAH!
WAAAH!
EXPRESSION OF JOY AND EXCITEMENT
NO, IT COMES TOTALLY NATURALLY TO HONDA-SAN...
STILL, MY MOTHER ALWAYS SAID...
...IT'S BETTER TO BELIEVE THAN DOUBT.
SHE SAID PEOPLE AREN'T BORN WITH A CONSCIENCE.
WE'RE ONLY BORN WITH "WANTS," SHE SAID, LIKE APPETITE AND MATERIAL DESIRES.
IN OTHER WORDS, SURVIVAL INSTINCTS.

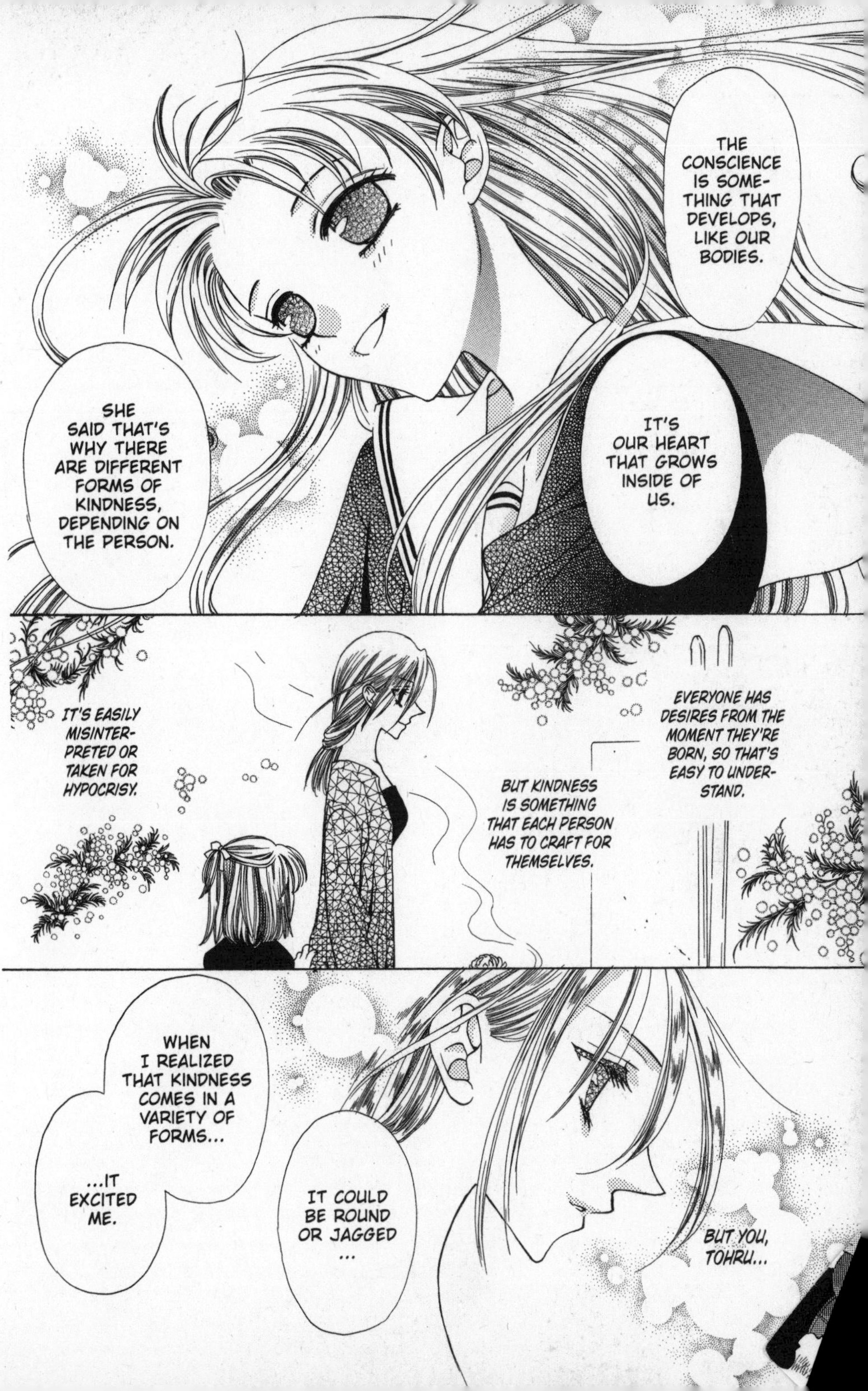
THE CONSCIENCE IS SOME-THING THAT DEVELOPS, LIKE OUR BODIES.
IT'S OUR HEART THAT GROWS INSIDE OF US.
SHE SAID THAT'S WHY THERE ARE DIFFERENT FORMS OF KINDNESS, DEPENDING ON THE PERSON.
EVERYONE HAS DESIRES FROM THE MOMENT THEY'RE BORN, SO THAT'S EASY TO UNDER-STAND.
BUT KINDNESS IS SOMETHING THAT EACH PERSON HAS TO CRAFT FOR THEMSELVES.
IT'S EASILY MISINTER-PRETED OR TAKEN FOR HYPOCRISY.
WHEN I REALIZED THAT KINDNESS COMES IN A VARIETY OF FORMS...
...IT EXCITED ME.
IT COULD BE ROUND OR JAGGED ...
BUT YOU, TOHRU...

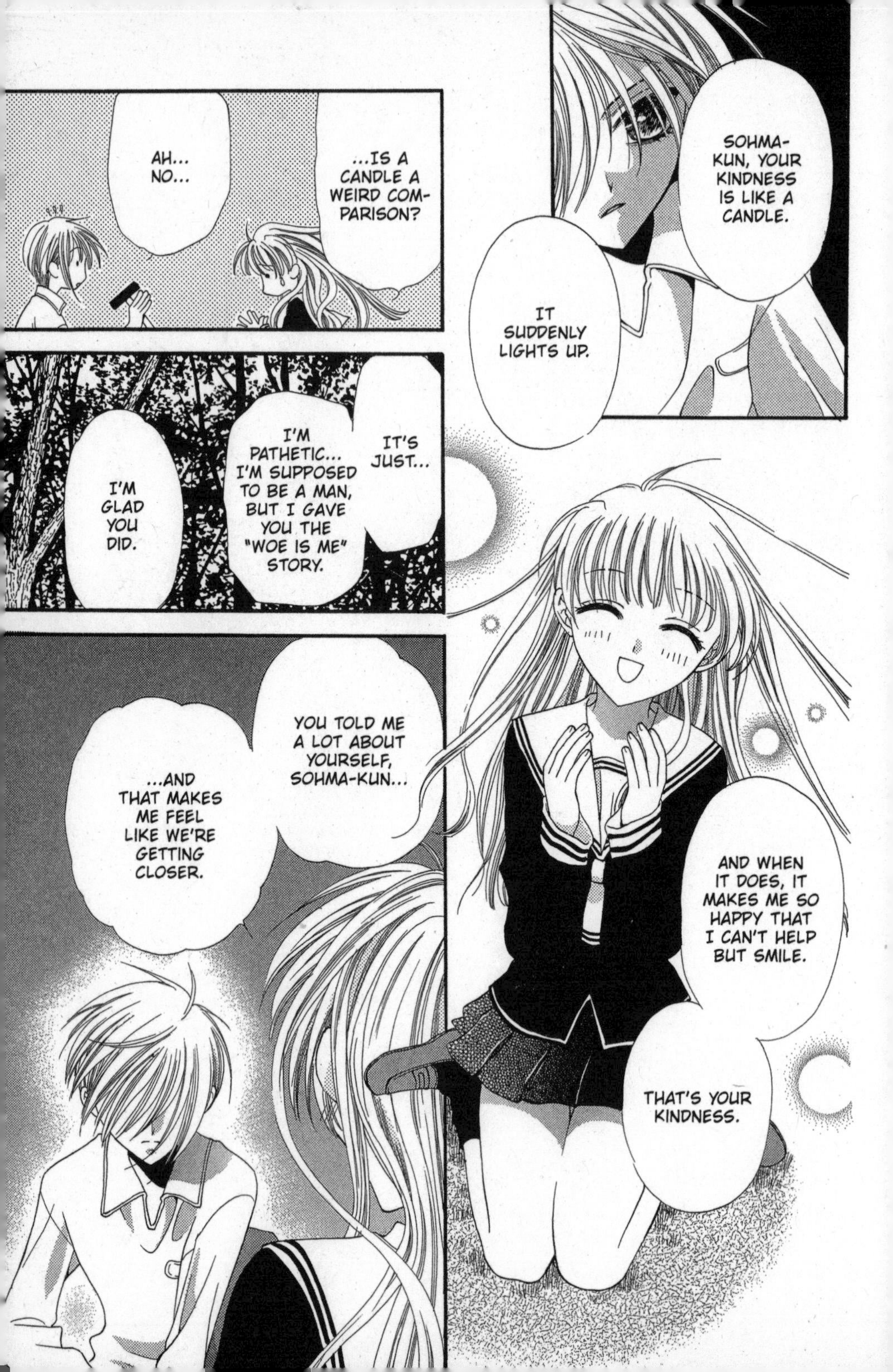
SOHMA-KUN, YOUR KINDNESS IS LIKE A CANDLE.
IT SUDDENLY LIGHTS UP.
AND WHEN IT DOES, IT MAKES ME SO HAPPY THAT I CAN'T HELP BUT SMILE.
THAT'S YOUR KINDNESS.
...IS A CANDLE A WEIRD COMPARISON?
AH... NO...
IT'S JUST...
I'M PATHETIC... I'M SUPPOSED TO BE A MAN, BUT I GAVE YOU THE "WOE IS ME" STORY.
I'M GLAD YOU DID.
YOU TOLD ME A LOT ABOUT YOURSELF, SOHMA-KUN...
...AND THAT MAKES ME FEEL LIKE WE'RE GETTING CLOSER.

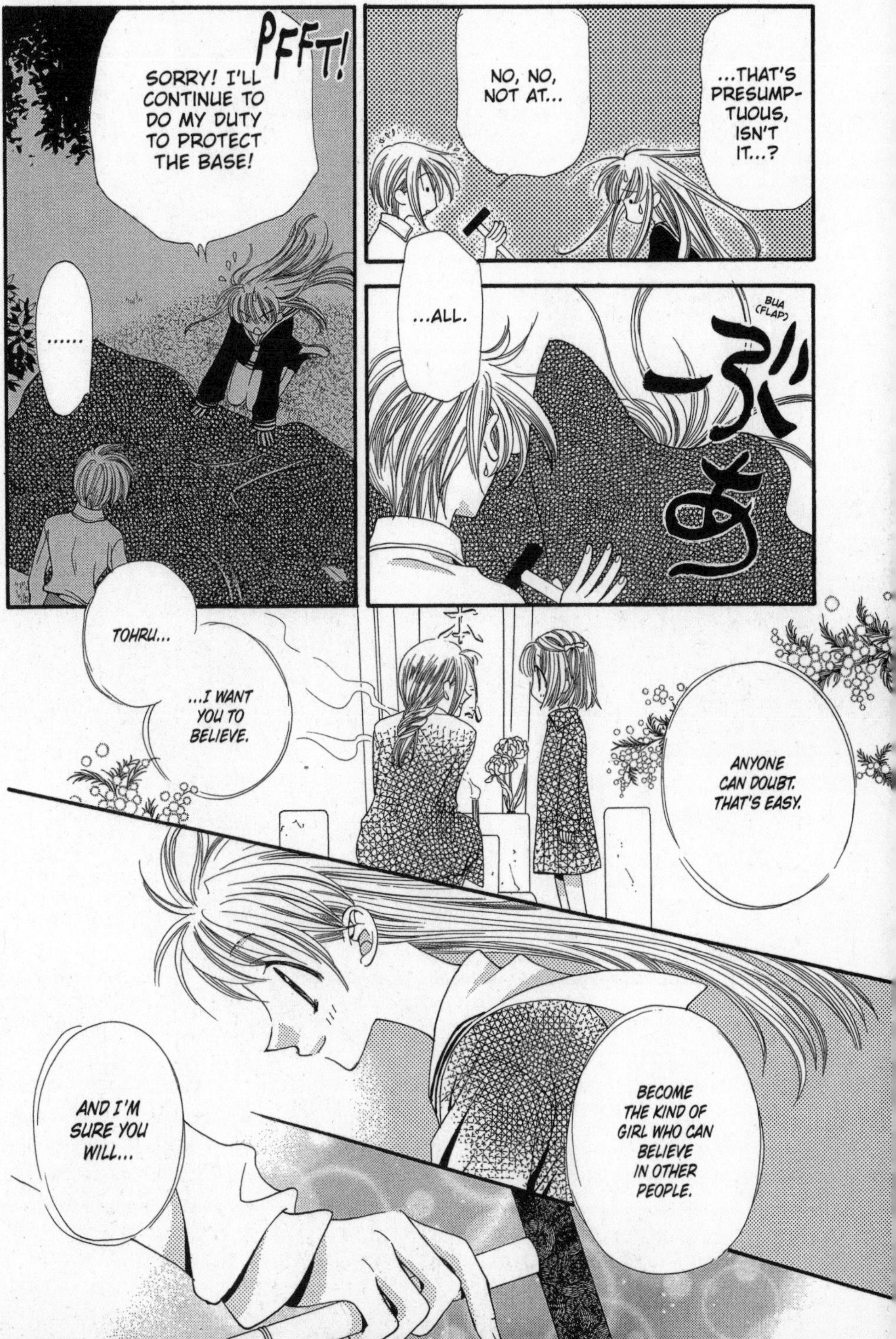
...THAT'S PRESUMPTUOUS, ISN'T IT...?
NO, NO, NOT AT...
...ALL.
ぶあ
BUA (FLAP)
PFFT!
SORRY! I'LL CONTINUE TO DO MY DUTY TO PROTECT THE BASE!
......
ANYONE CAN DOUBT. THAT'S EASY.
TOHRU...
...I WANT YOU TO BELIEVE.
BECOME THE KIND OF GIRL WHO CAN BELIEVE IN OTHER PEOPLE.
AND I'M SURE YOU WILL...

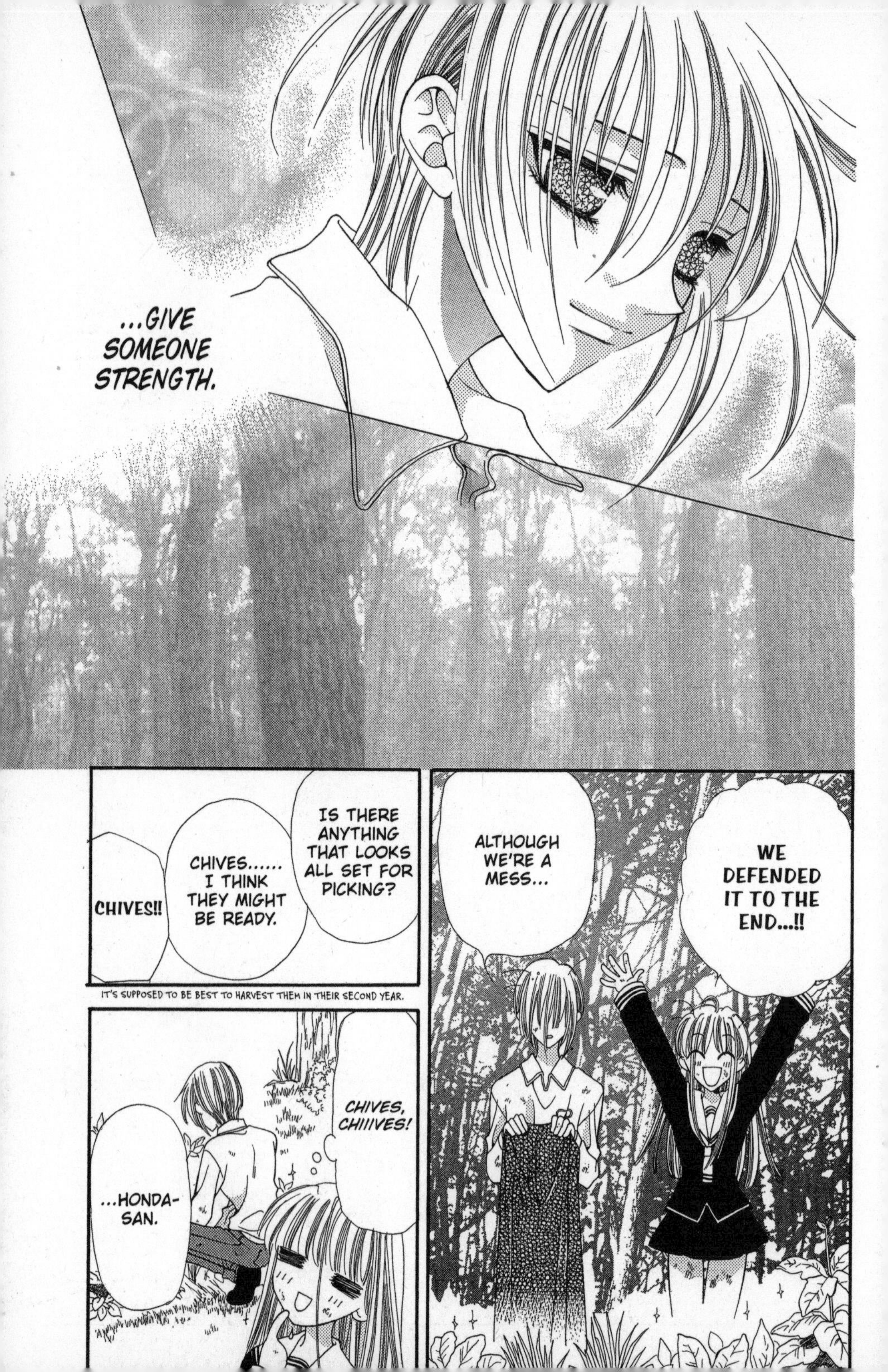
...GIVE SOMEONE STRENGTH.
WE DEFENDED IT TO THE END...!!
ALTHOUGH WE'RE A MESS...
IS THERE ANYTHING THAT LOOKS ALL SET FOR PICKING?
CHIVES...... I THINK THEY MIGHT BE READY.
CHIVES!!
IT'S SUPPOSED TO BE BEST TO HARVEST THEM IN THEIR SECOND YEAR.
CHIVES, CHIIIVES!
...HONDA-SAN.

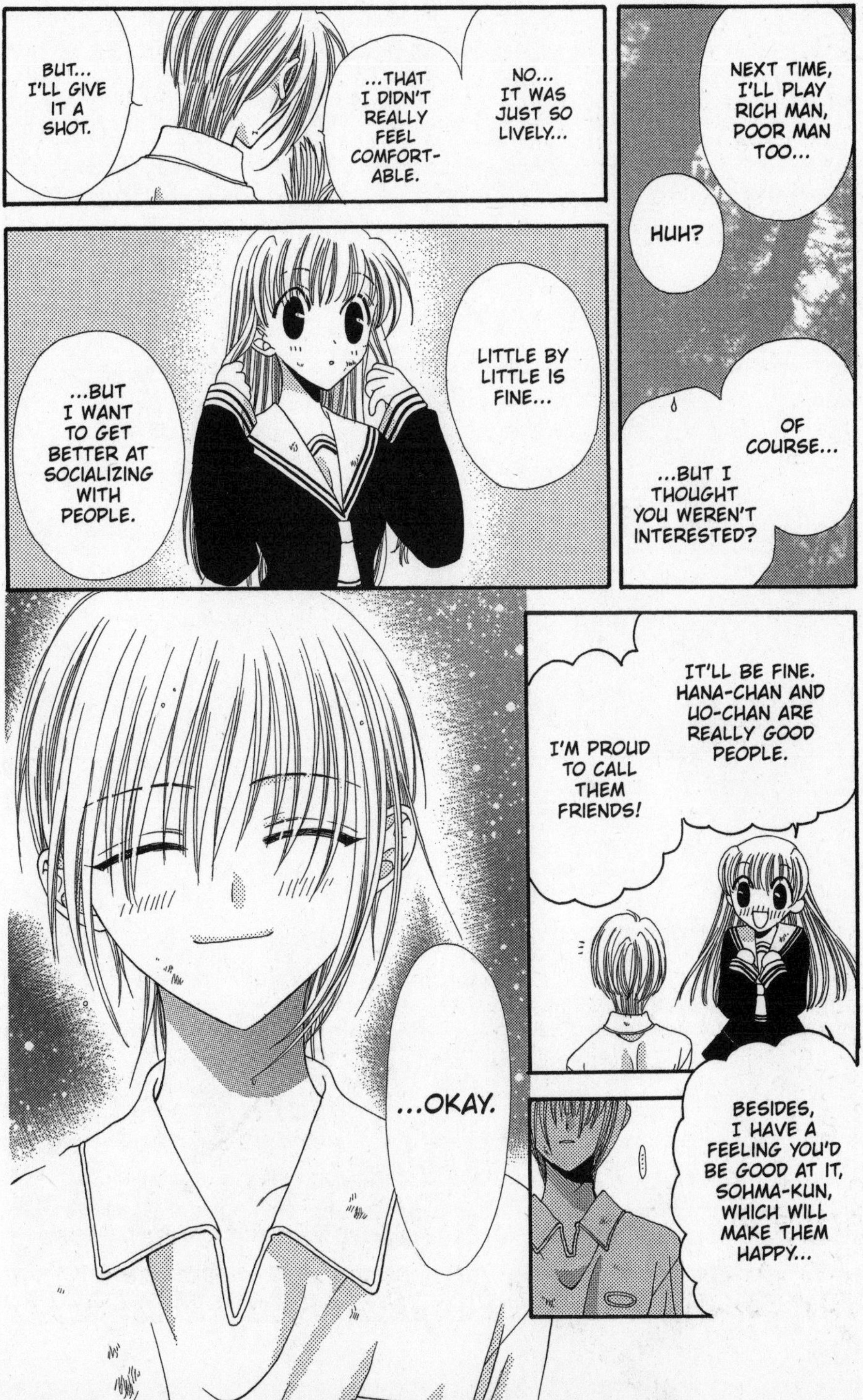

NEXT TIME, I'LL PLAY RICH MAN, POOR MAN TOO...
HUH?
OF COURSE...
...BUT I THOUGHT YOU WEREN'T INTERESTED?
NO... IT WAS JUST SO LIVELY...
...THAT I DIDN'T REALLY FEEL COMFORT-ABLE.
BUT... I'LL GIVE IT A SHOT.
LITTLE BY LITTLE IS FINE...
...BUT I WANT TO GET BETTER AT SOCIALIZING WITH PEOPLE.
IT'LL BE FINE. HANA-CHAN AND UO-CHAN ARE REALLY GOOD PEOPLE.
I'M PROUD TO CALL THEM FRIENDS!
BESIDES, I HAVE A FEELING YOU'D BE GOOD AT IT, SOHMA-KUN, WHICH WILL MAKE THEM HAPPY...
...OKAY.

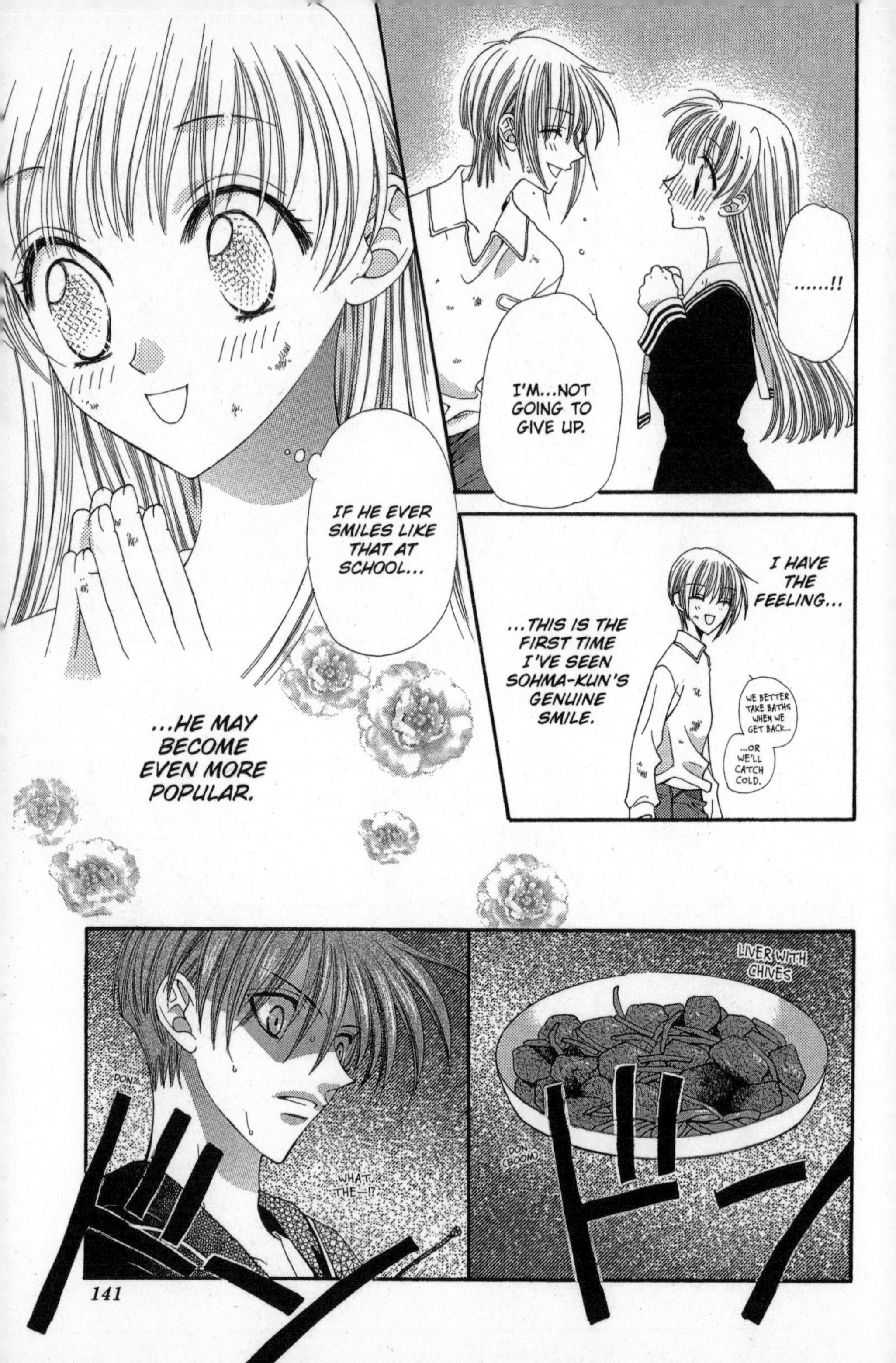
......!!
I'M...NOT GOING TO GIVE UP.
I HAVE THE FEELING...
...THIS IS THE FIRST TIME I'VE SEEN SOHMA-KUN'S GENUINE SMILE.
WE BETTER TAKE BATHS WHEN WE GET BACK...
...OR WE'LL CATCH COLD.
IF HE EVER SMILES LIKE THAT AT SCHOOL...
...HE MAY BECOME EVEN MORE POPULAR.
LIVER WITH CHIVES
DON (BOOM)
DON
WHAT THE—!?

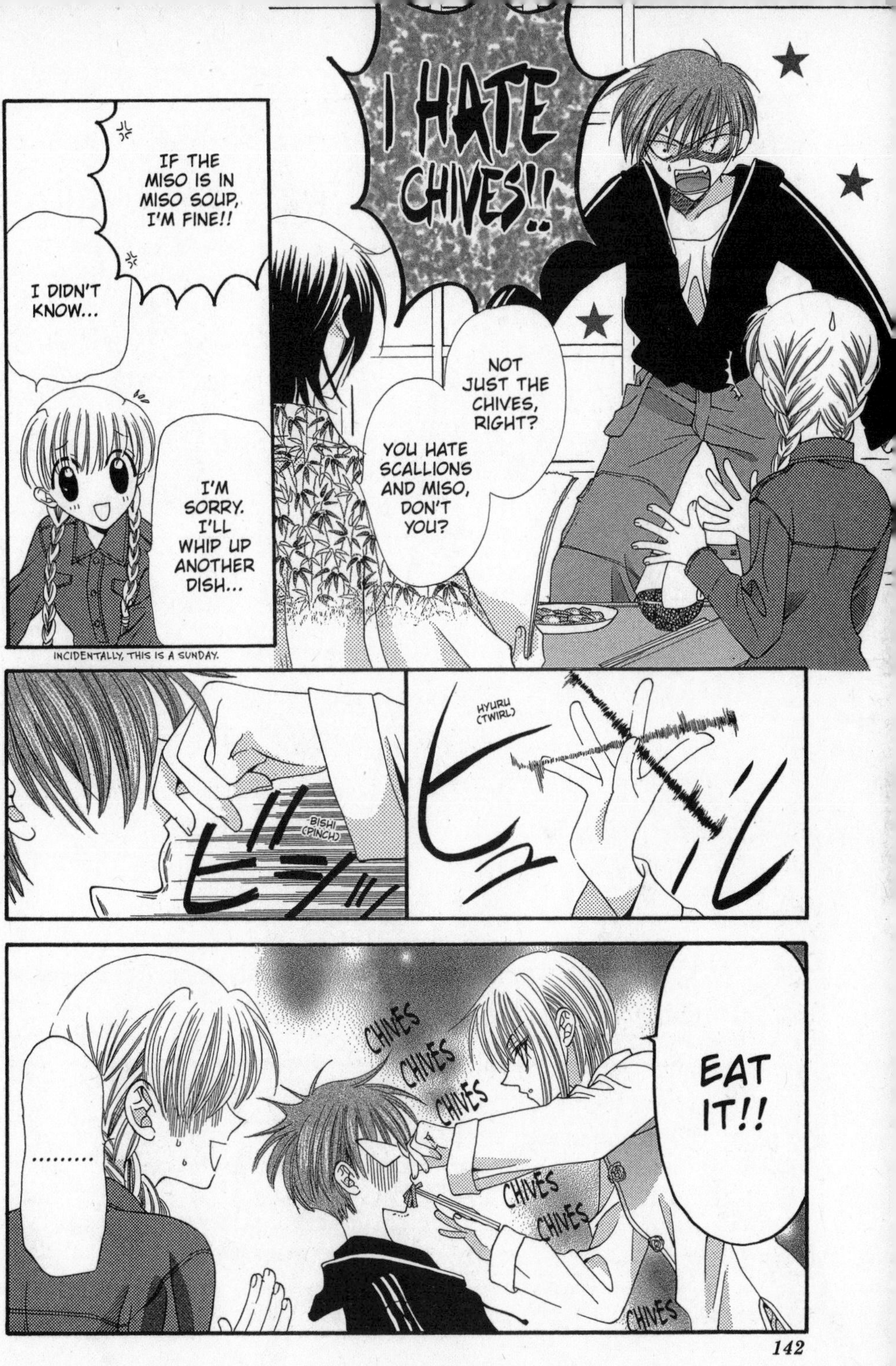
I HATE CHIVES!!
NOT JUST THE CHIVES, RIGHT?
YOU HATE SCALLIONS AND MISO, DON'T YOU?
IF THE MISO IS IN MISO SOUP, I'M FINE!!
I DIDN'T KNOW...
I'M SORRY. I'LL WHIP UP ANOTHER DISH...
INCIDENTALLY, THIS IS A SUNDAY.
HYURU (TWIRL)
BISHI (PINCH)
EAT IT!!
CHIVES CHIVES CHIVES
CHIVES CHIVES
CHIVES
....

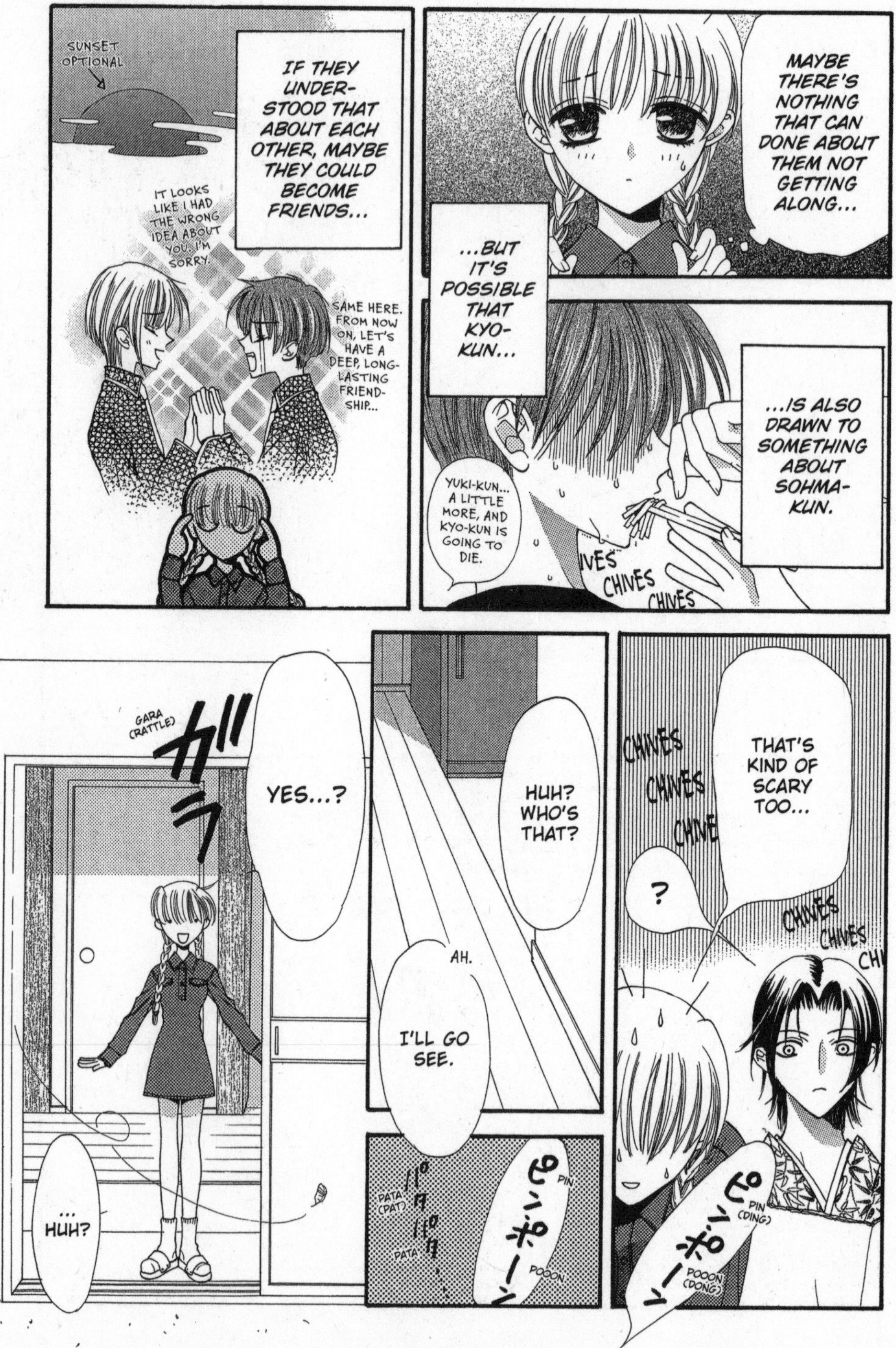
MAYBE THERE'S NOTHING THAT CAN DONE ABOUT THEM NOT GETTING ALONG...
...BUT IT'S POSSIBLE THAT KYO-KUN...
...IS ALSO DRAWN TO SOMETHING ABOUT SOHMA-KUN.
YUKI-KUN... A LITTLE MORE, AND KYO-KUN IS GOING TO DIE.
CHIVES CHIVES CHIVES
IF THEY UNDERSTOOD THAT ABOUT EACH OTHER, MAYBE THEY COULD BECOME FRIENDS...
SUNSET OPTIONAL
IT LOOKS LIKE I HAD THE WRONG IDEA ABOUT YOU. I'M SORRY.
SAME HERE. FROM NOW ON, LET'S HAVE A DEEP, LONG-LASTING FRIENDSHIP...
CHIVES CHIVES CHIVE
THAT'S KIND OF SCARY TOO...
?
CHIVES CHIVES
PIN (DING) POOON (DONG)
HUH? WHO'S THAT?
AH.
I'LL GO SEE.
PATA (PAT) PATA
PIN POOON
GARA (RATTLE)
YES...?
... HUH?

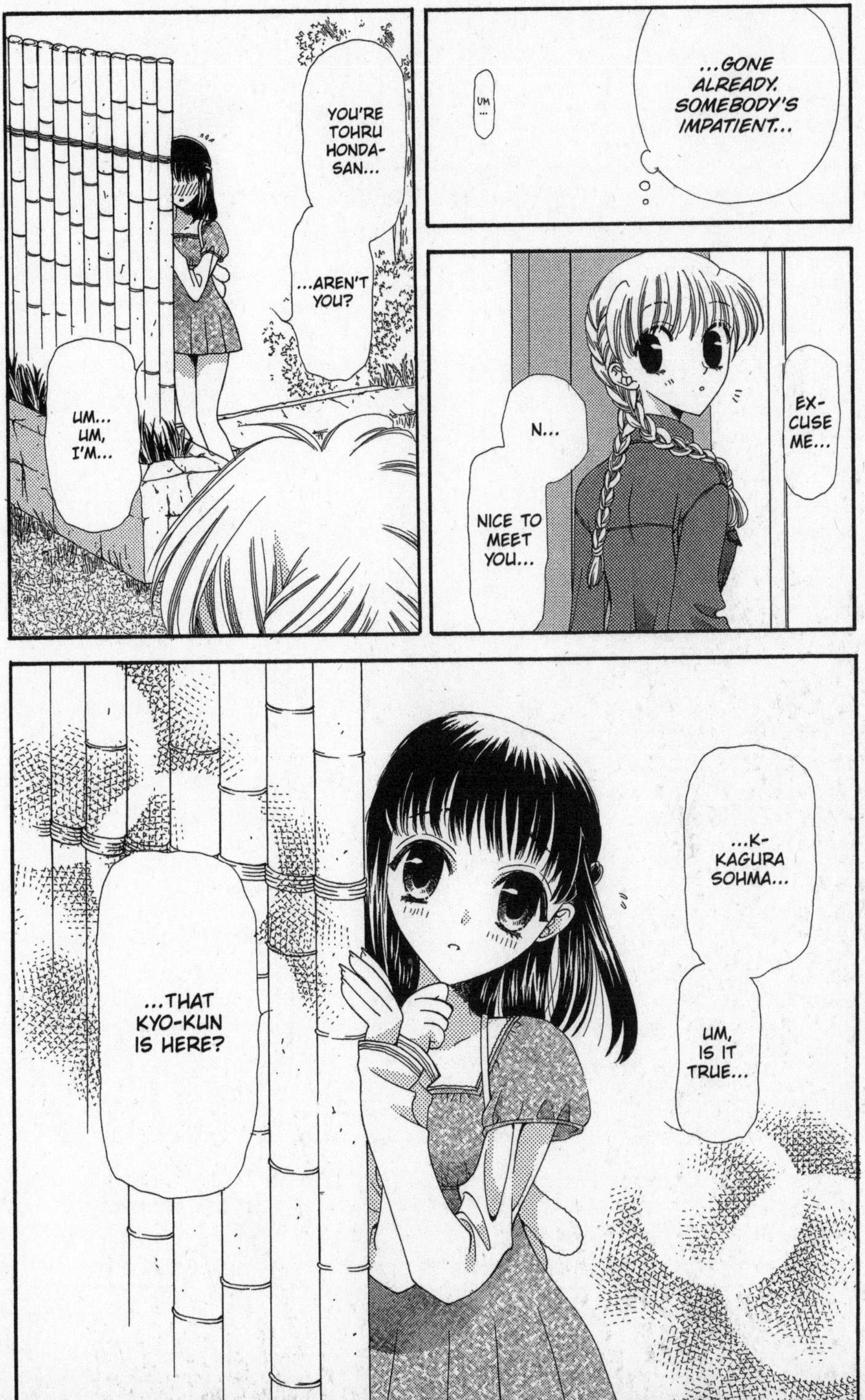
...GONE ALREADY. SOMEBODY'S IMPATIENT...
UM ...
EX-CUSE ME...
N...
NICE TO MEET YOU...
YOU'RE TOHRU HONDA-SAN...
...AREN'T YOU?
UM... UM, I'M...
...K-KAGURA SOHMA...
UM, IS IT TRUE...
...THAT KYO-KUN IS HERE?

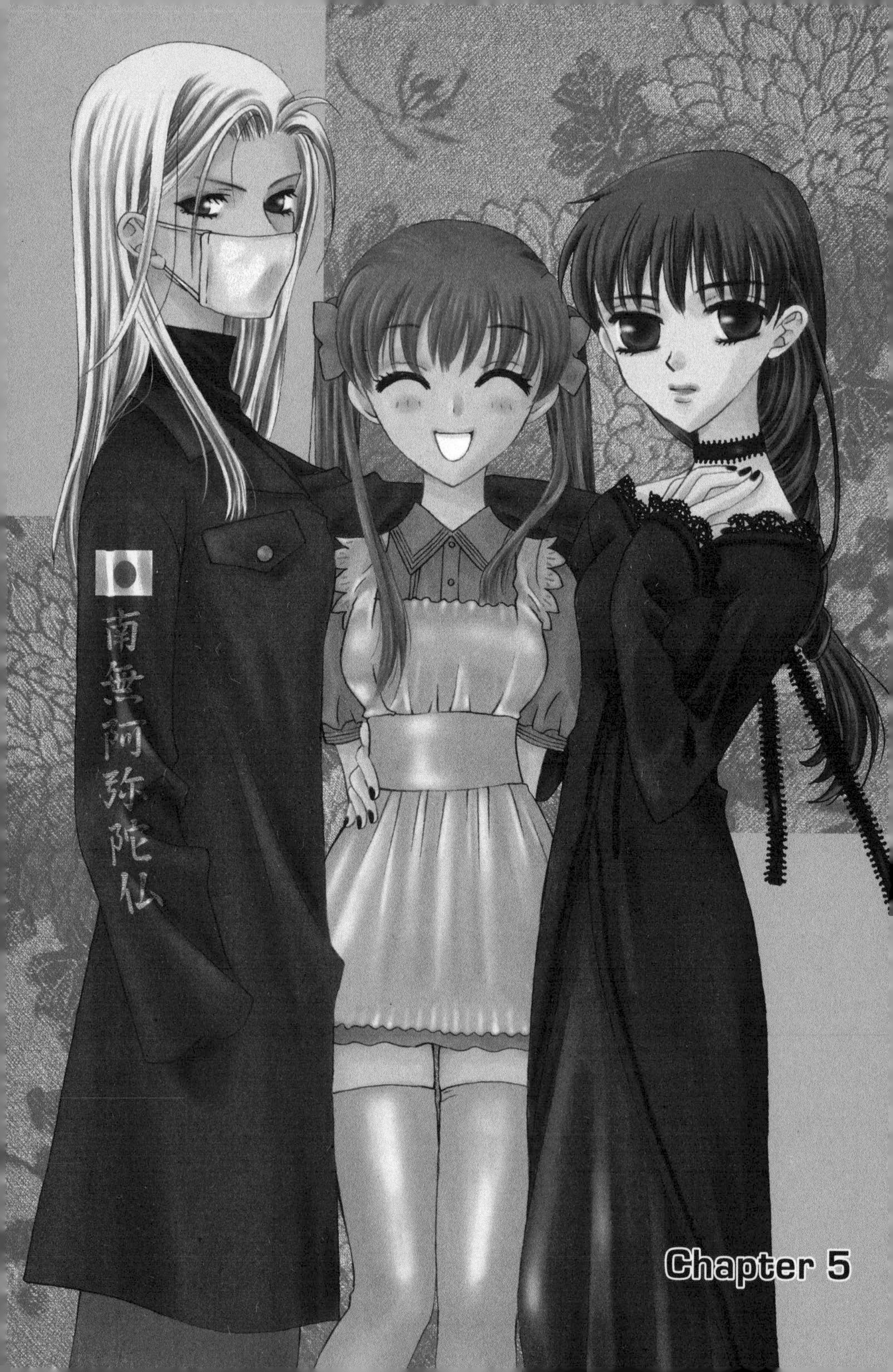
南無阿弥陀仏

Chapter 5

SCREWING AROUND OR SERIOUS?

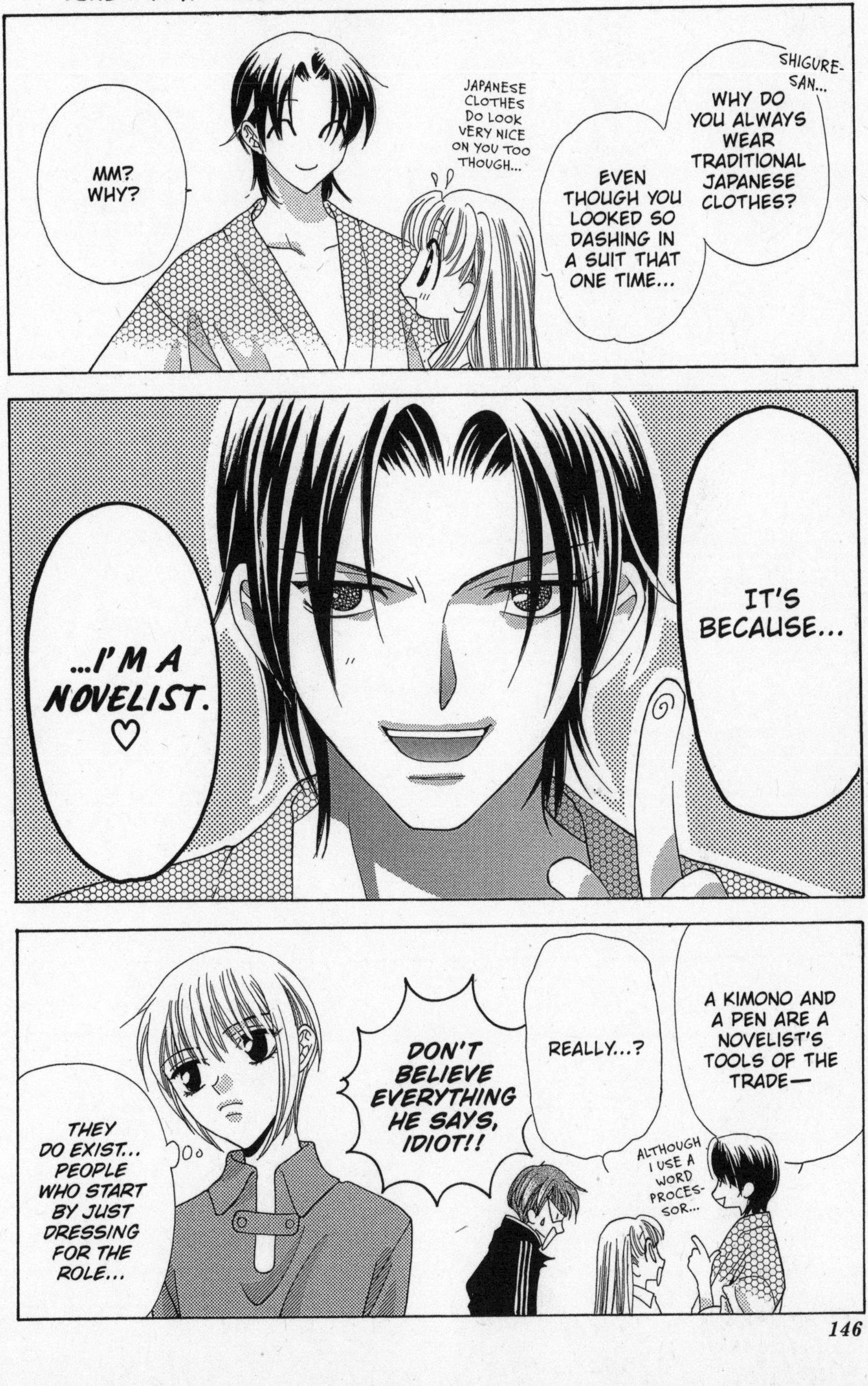
SHIGURE-SAN...
WHY DO YOU ALWAYS WEAR TRADITIONAL JAPANESE CLOTHES?
EVEN THOUGH YOU LOOKED SO DASHING IN A SUIT THAT ONE TIME...
JAPANESE CLOTHES DO LOOK VERY NICE ON YOU TOO THOUGH...
MM? WHY?
IT'S BECAUSE...
...I'M A NOVELIST. ♡
A KIMONO AND A PEN ARE A NOVELIST'S TOOLS OF THE TRADE—
ALTHOUGH I USE A WORD PROCES-SOR...
REALLY...?
DON'T BELIEVE EVERYTHING HE SAYS, IDIOT!!
THEY DO EXIST... PEOPLE WHO START BY JUST DRESSING FOR THE ROLE...

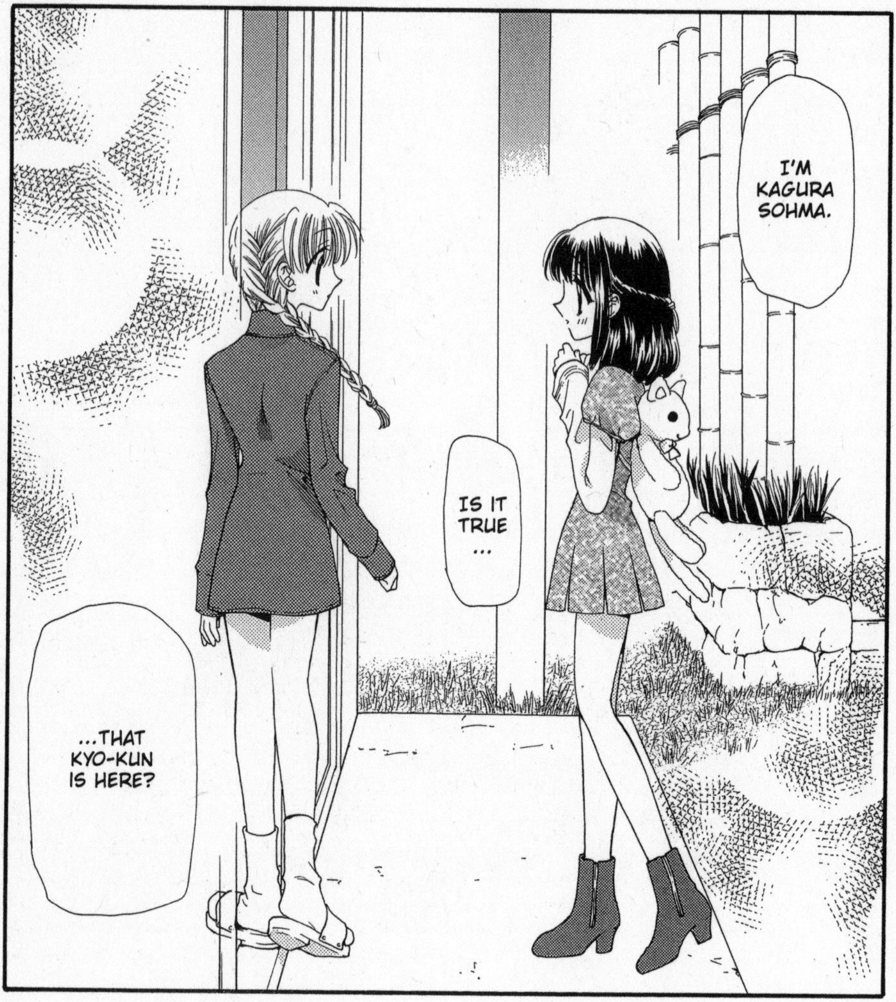
I'M KAGURA SOHMA.
IS IT TRUE ...
...THAT KYO-KUN IS HERE?

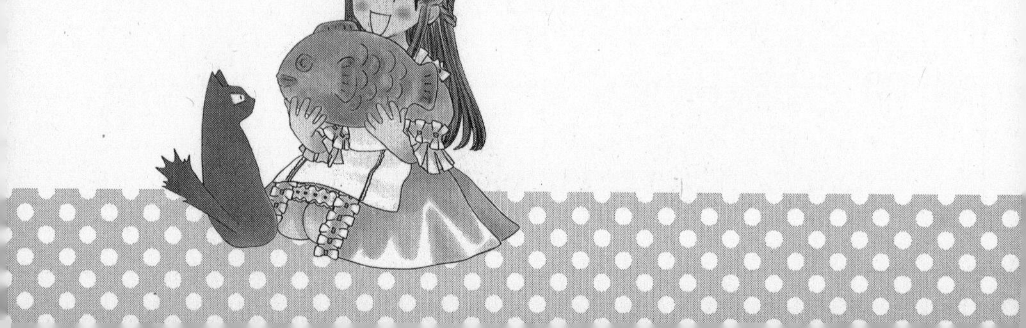

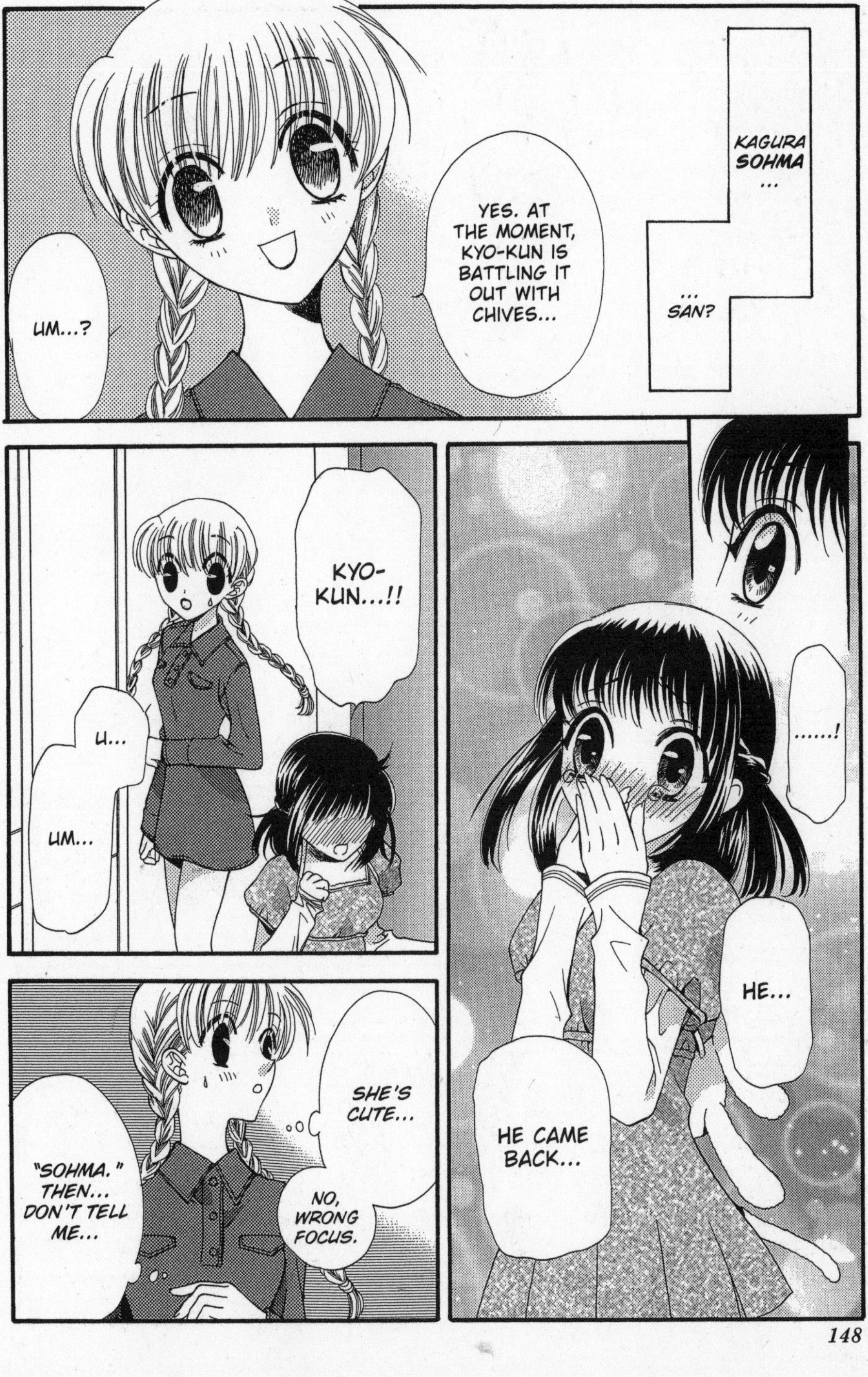
KAGURA SOHMA ...
... SAN?
YES. AT THE MOMENT, KYO-KUN IS BATTLING IT OUT WITH CHIVES...
UM...?
......!
HE...
HE CAME BACK...
KYO-KUN...!!
U...
UM...
SHE'S CUTE...
NO, WRONG FOCUS.
"SOHMA." THEN... DON'T TELL ME...

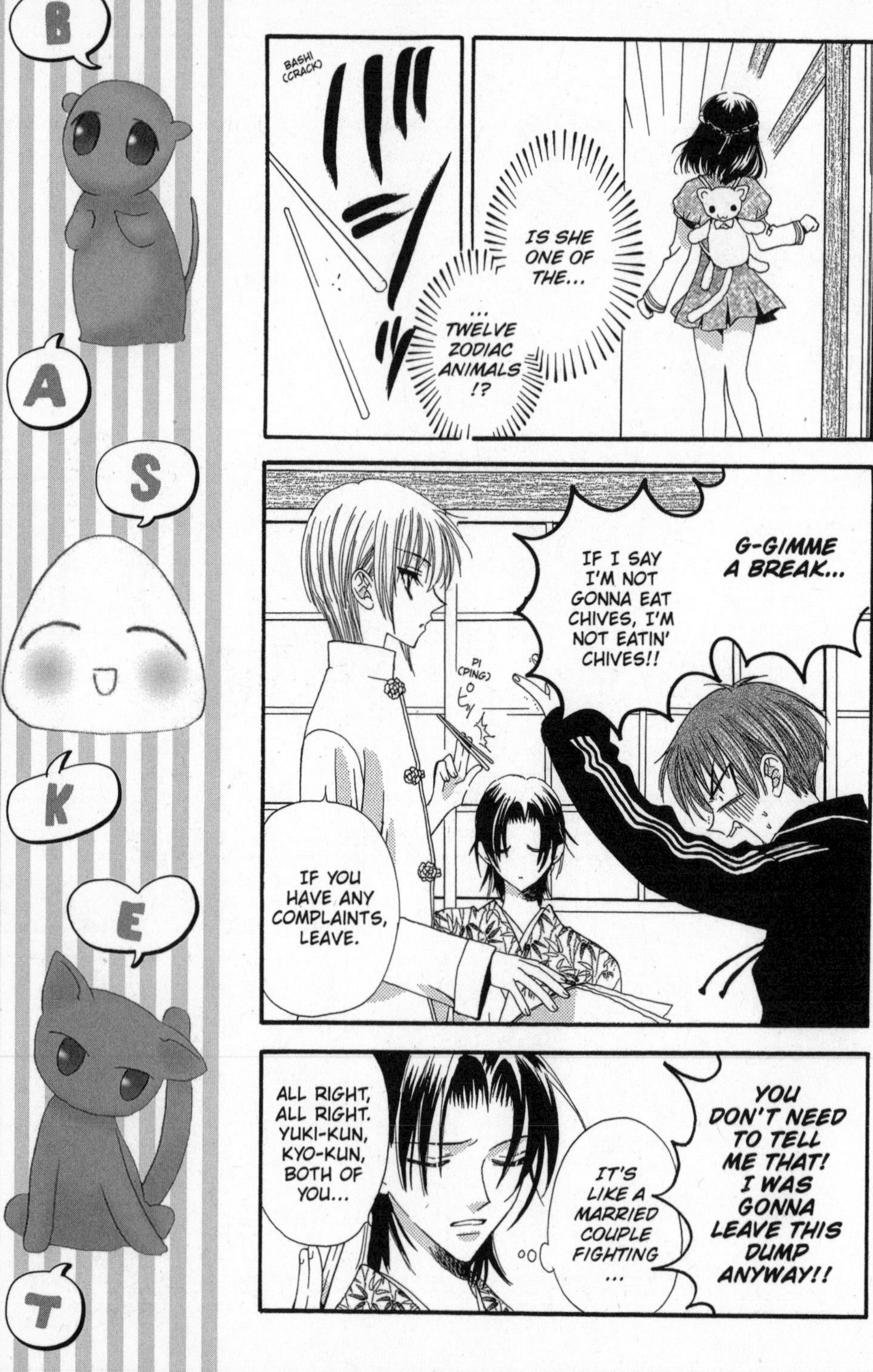
B
A
S
K
E
T
IS SHE ONE OF THE...
... TWELVE ZODIAC ANIMALS !?
BASHI (CRACK)
G-GIMME A BREAK...
IF I SAY I'M NOT GONNA EAT CHIVES, I'M NOT EATIN' CHIVES!!
PI (PING)
IF YOU HAVE ANY COMPLAINTS, LEAVE.
YOU DON'T NEED TO TELL ME THAT! I WAS GONNA LEAVE THIS DUMP ANYWAY!!
IT'S LIKE A MARRIED COUPLE FIGHTING ...
ALL RIGHT, ALL RIGHT. YUKI-KUN, KYO-KUN, BOTH OF YOU...

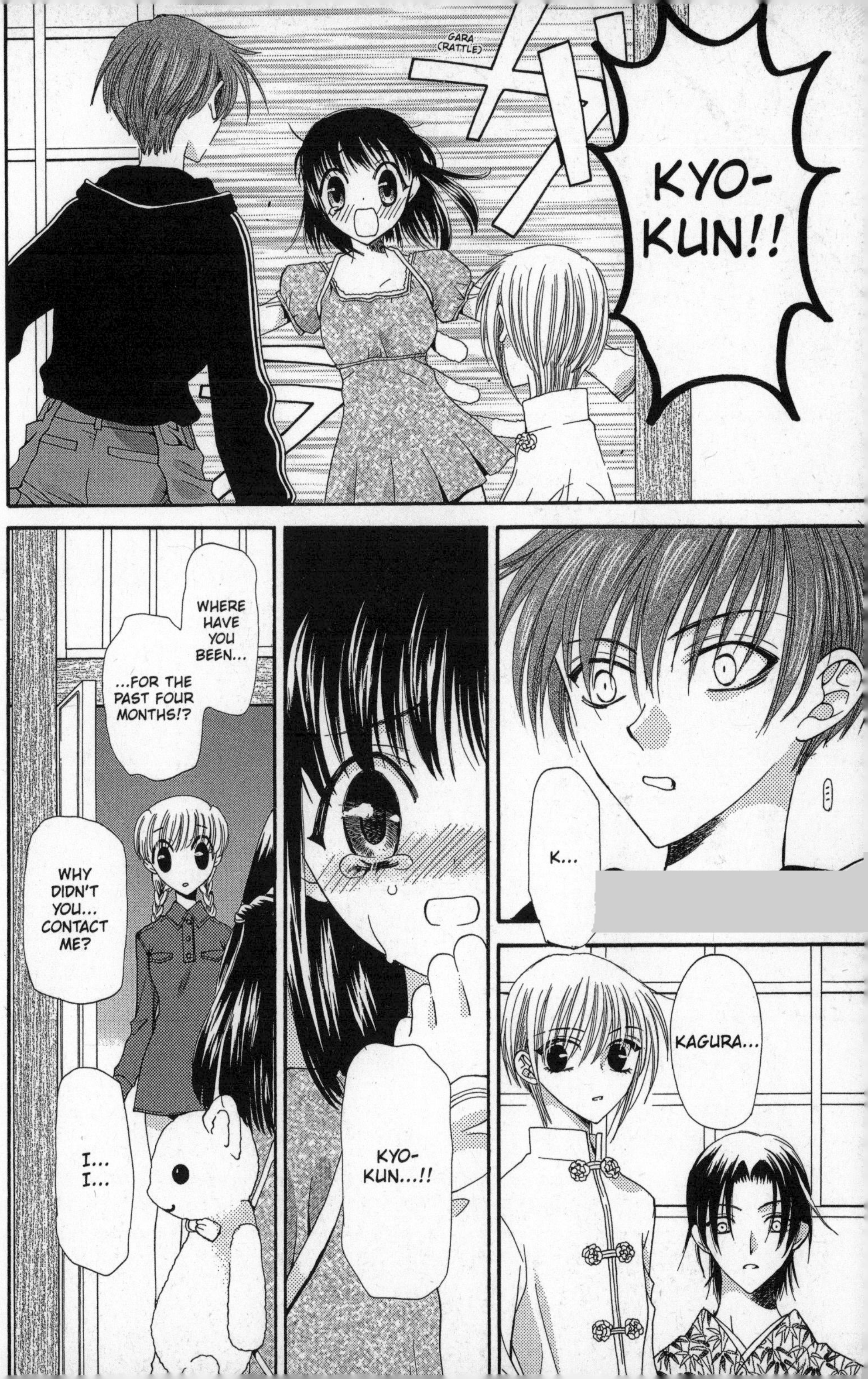

GARA (RATTLE)
KYO-KUN!!
...
K...
KAGURA...
KYO-KUN...!!
WHERE HAVE YOU BEEN...
...FOR THE PAST FOUR MONTHS!?
WHY DIDN'T YOU... CONTACT ME?
I... I...

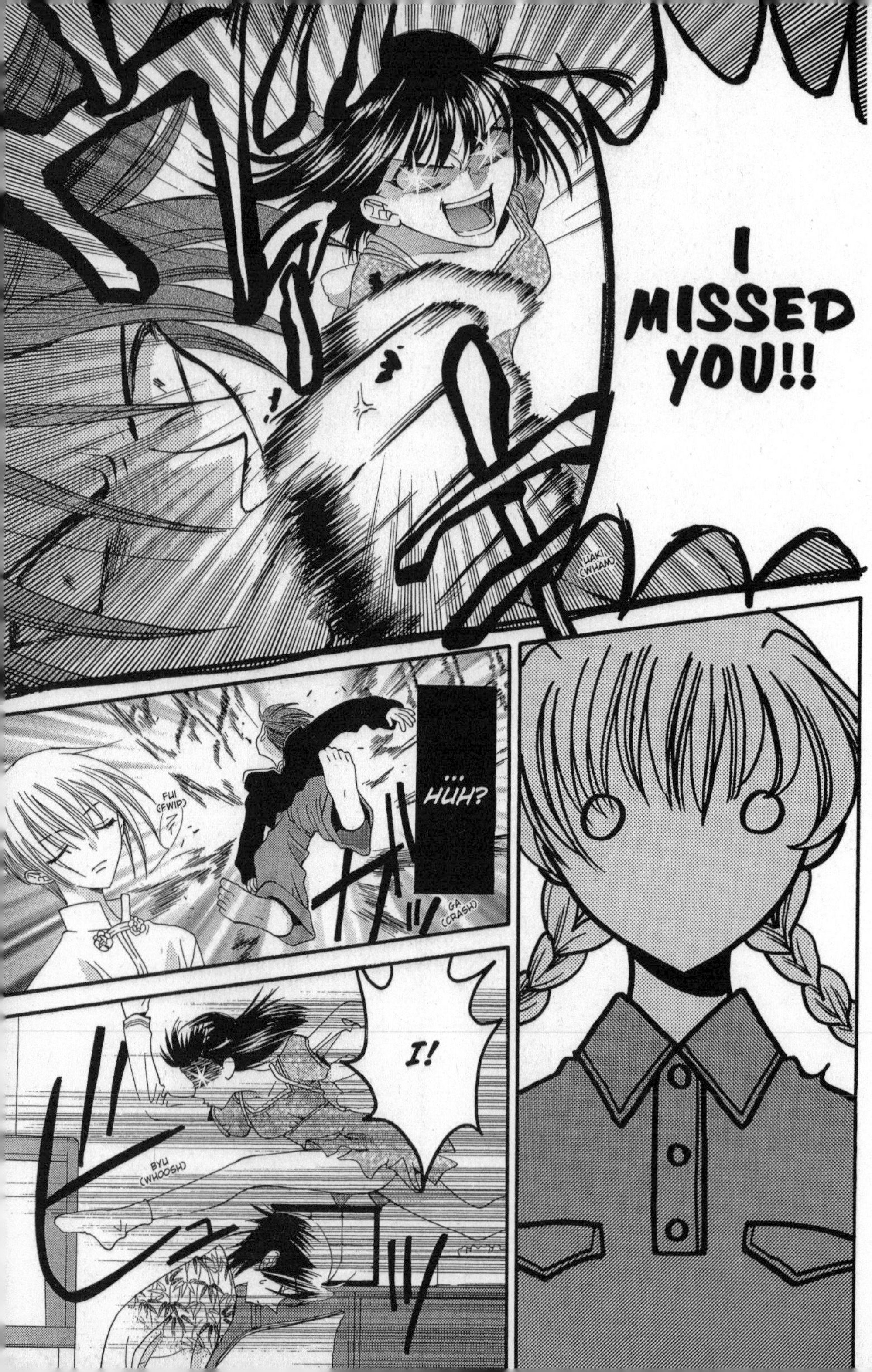
I MISSED YOU!!
WAKI (WHAM)
... HUH?
GA (CRASH)
FUI (FWIP)
I!
BYU (WHOOSH)

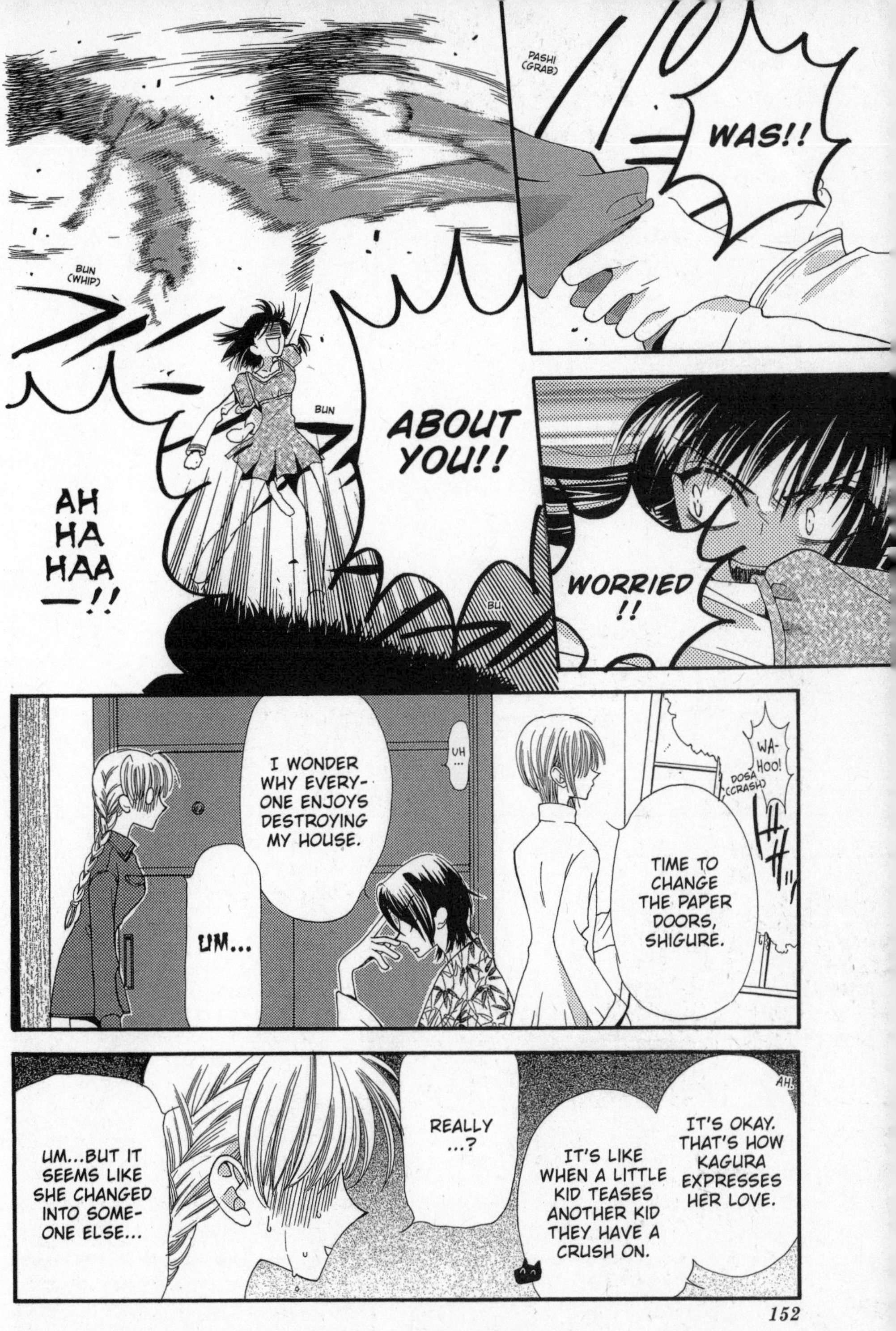
PASHI (GRAB)
WAS!!
WORRIED!!
ABOUT YOU!!
BUN (WHIP)
BUN
BU
AH HA HAA—!!
WA-HOO!
DOSA (CRASH)
TIME TO CHANGE THE PAPER DOORS, SHIGURE.
I WONDER WHY EVERY-ONE ENJOYS DESTROYING MY HOUSE.
UH...
UM...
AH.
IT'S OKAY. THAT'S HOW KAGURA EXPRESSES HER LOVE.
IT'S LIKE WHEN A LITTLE KID TEASES ANOTHER KID THEY HAVE A CRUSH ON.
REALLY...?
UM...BUT IT SEEMS LIKE SHE CHANGED INTO SOME-ONE ELSE...

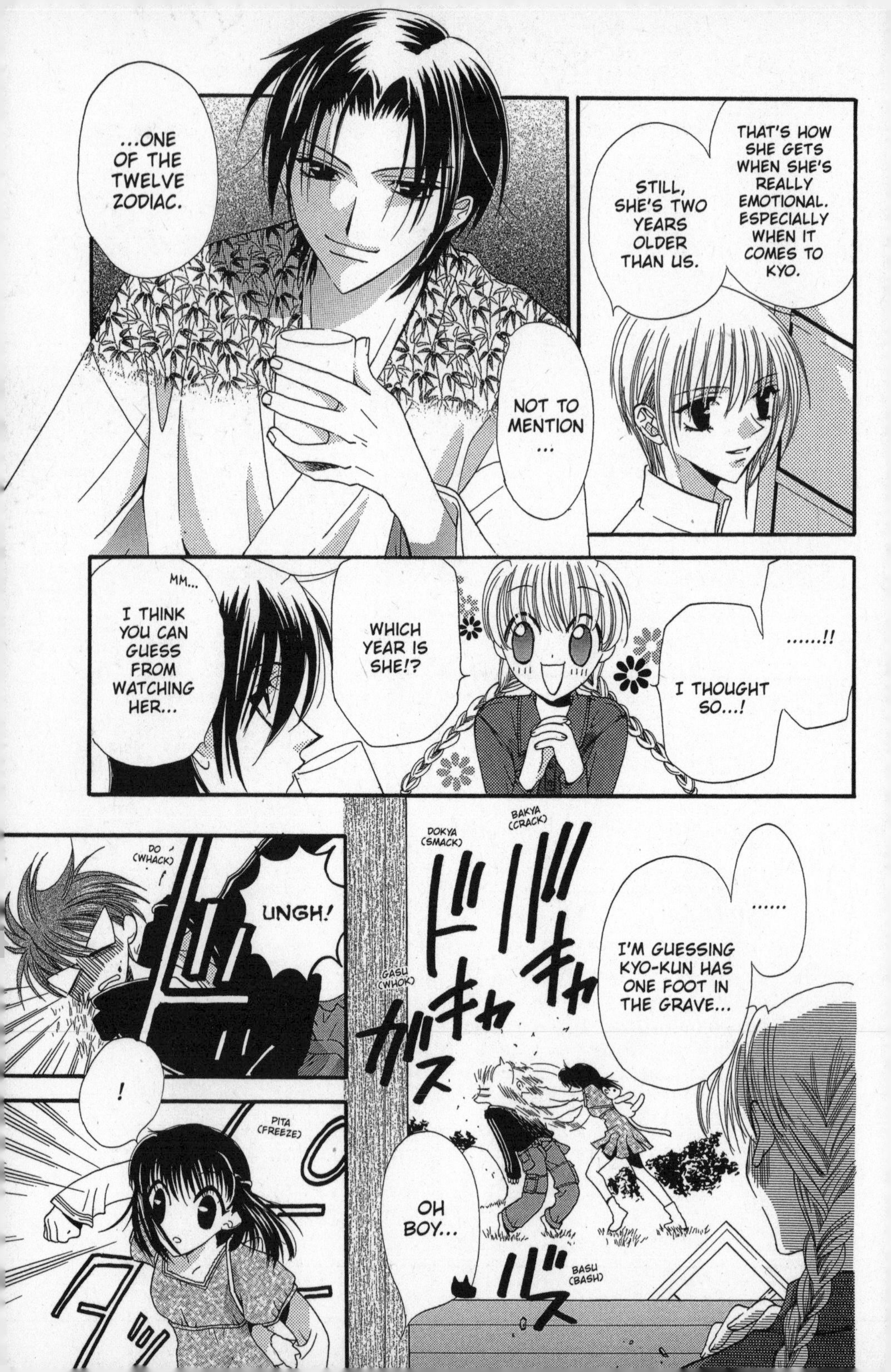
THAT'S HOW SHE GETS WHEN SHE'S REALLY EMOTIONAL. ESPECIALLY WHEN IT COMES TO KYO.
STILL, SHE'S TWO YEARS OLDER THAN US.
NOT TO MENTION ...
...ONE OF THE TWELVE ZODIAC.
......!!
I THOUGHT SO...!
WHICH YEAR IS SHE!?
MM...
I THINK YOU CAN GUESS FROM WATCHING HER...
......
I'M GUESSING KYO-KUN HAS ONE FOOT IN THE GRAVE...
BAKYA (CRACK)
DOKYA (SMACK)
GASU (WHOK)
OH BOY...
BASU (BASH)
DO (WHACK)
UNGH!
!
PITA (FREEZE)

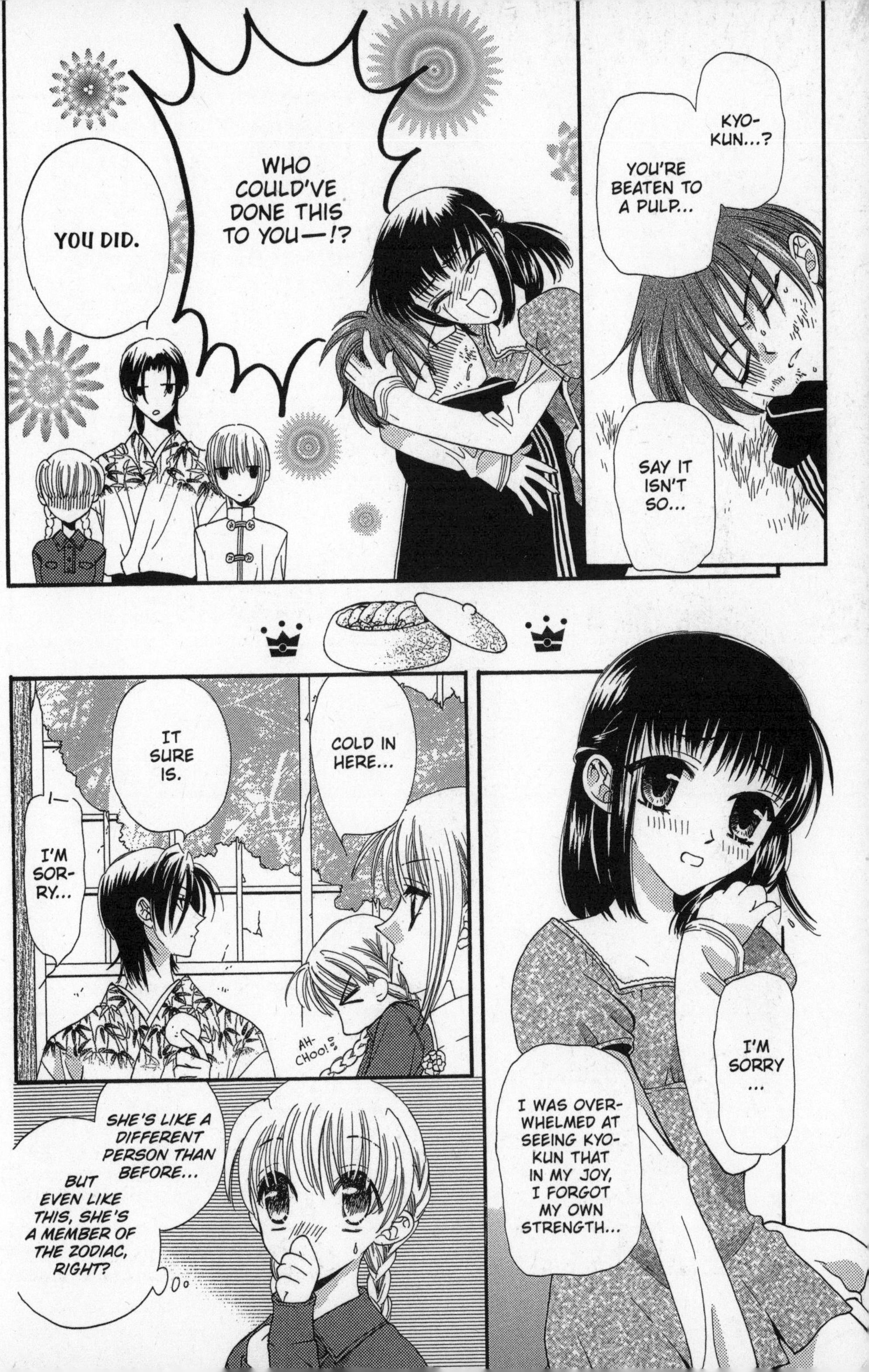
KYO-KUN...?
YOU'RE BEATEN TO A PULP...
SAY IT ISN'T SO...
WHO COULD'VE DONE THIS TO YOU—!?
YOU DID.
I'M SORRY ...
I WAS OVER-WHELMED AT SEEING KYO-KUN THAT IN MY JOY, I FORGOT MY OWN STRENGTH...
COLD IN HERE...
IT SURE IS.
I— I'M SOR-RY...
AH-CHOO!
SHE'S LIKE A DIFFERENT PERSON THAN BEFORE...
BUT EVEN LIKE THIS, SHE'S A MEMBER OF THE ZODIAC, RIGHT?

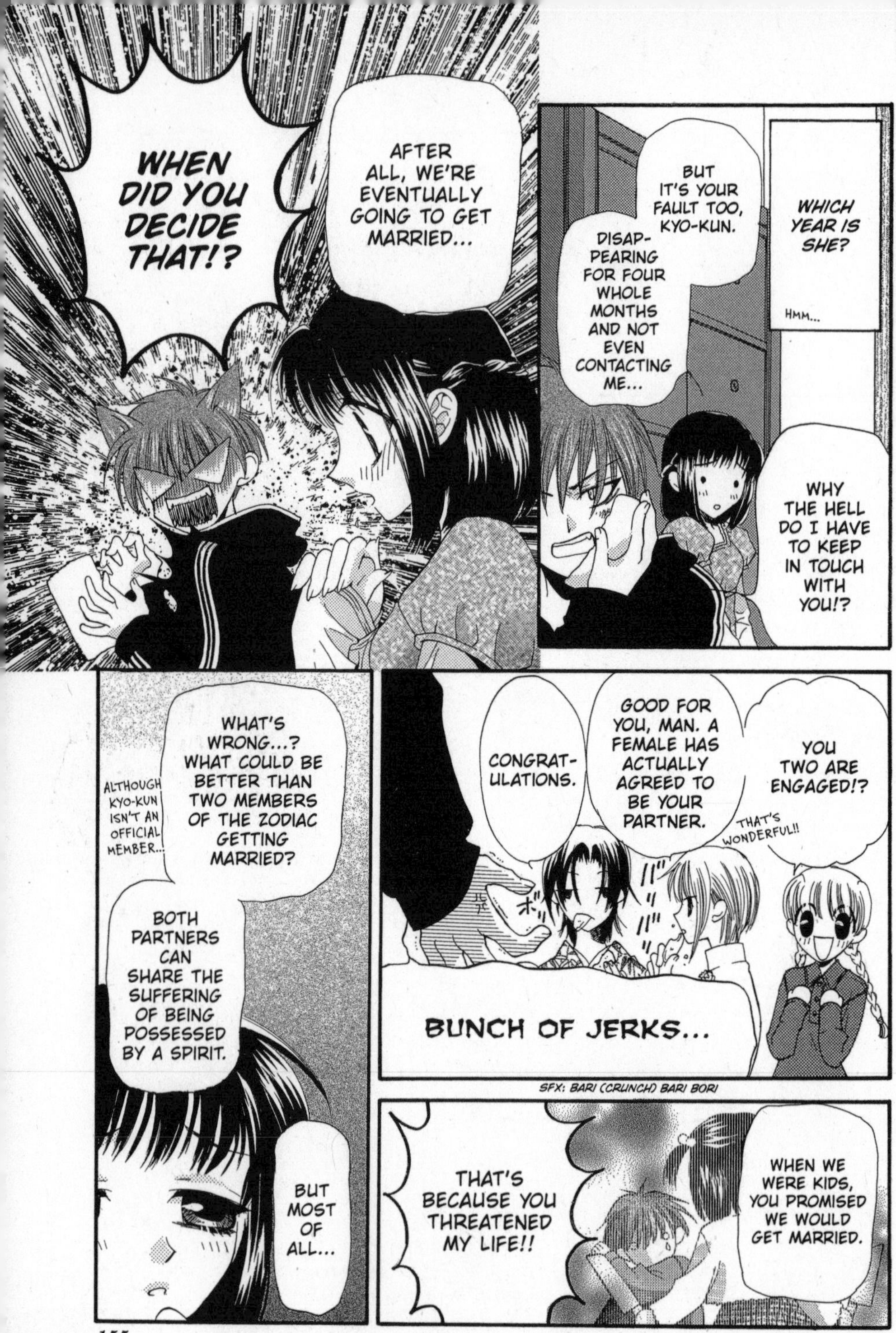
WHICH YEAR IS SHE?
HMM...
BUT IT'S YOUR FAULT TOO, KYO-KUN.
DISAPPEARING FOR FOUR WHOLE MONTHS AND NOT EVEN CONTACTING ME...
WHY THE HELL DO I HAVE TO KEEP IN TOUCH WITH YOU!?
AFTER ALL, WE'RE EVENTUALLY GOING TO GET MARRIED...
WHEN DID YOU DECIDE THAT!?
YOU TWO ARE ENGAGED!?
THAT'S WONDERFUL!!
GOOD FOR YOU, MAN. A FEMALE HAS ACTUALLY AGREED TO BE YOUR PARTNER.
CONGRATULATIONS.
BUNCH OF JERKS...
SFX: BARI (CRUNCH) BARI BORI
WHEN WE WERE KIDS, YOU PROMISED WE WOULD GET MARRIED.
THAT'S BECAUSE YOU THREATENED MY LIFE!!
WHAT'S WRONG...? WHAT COULD BE BETTER THAN TWO MEMBERS OF THE ZODIAC GETTING MARRIED?
ALTHOUGH KYO-KUN ISN'T AN OFFICIAL MEMBER...
BOTH PARTNERS CAN SHARE THE SUFFERING OF BEING POSSESSED BY A SPIRIT.
BUT MOST OF ALL...

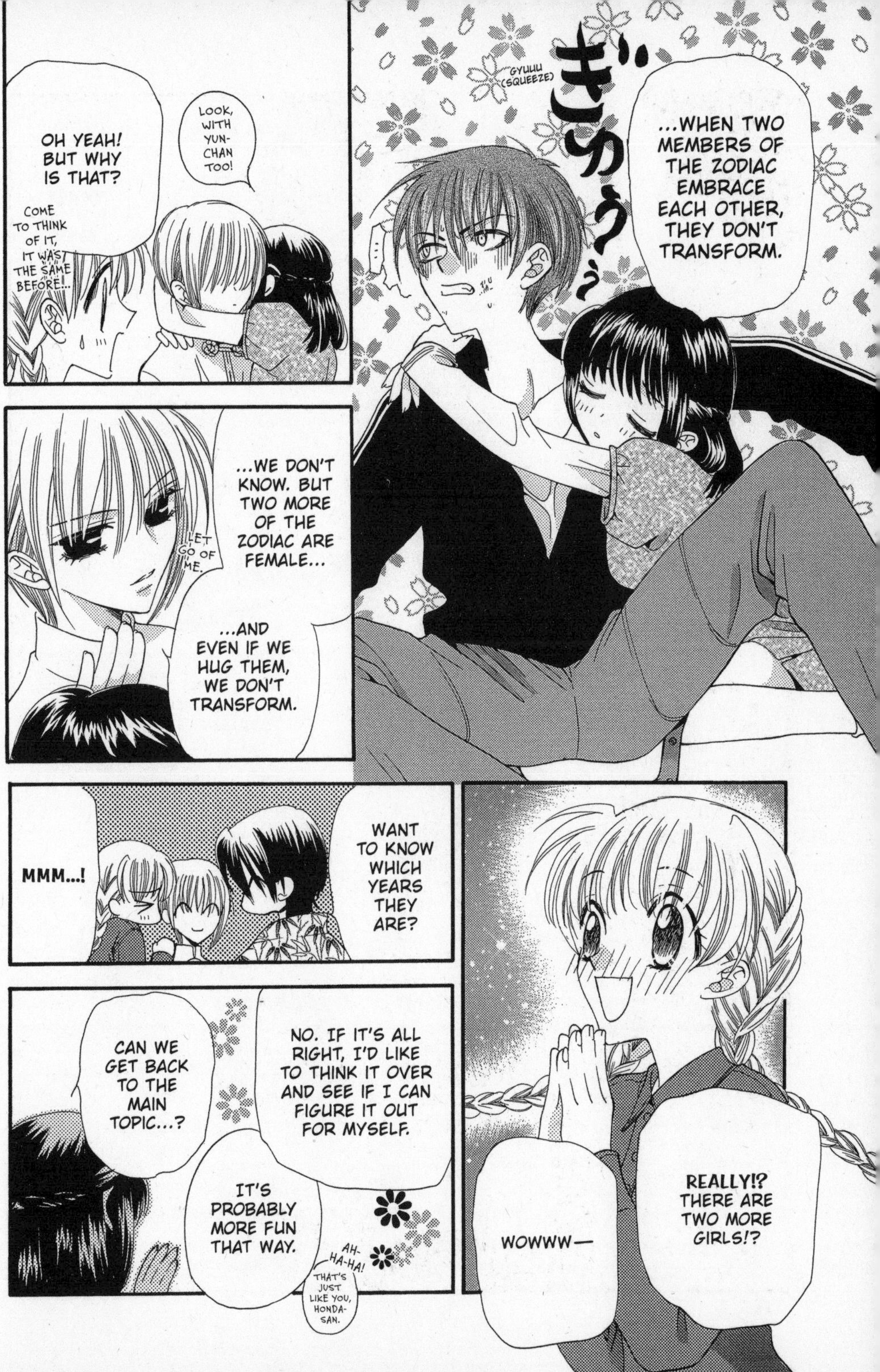
ぎゅうう
GYUUU (SQUEEZE)
...WHEN TWO MEMBERS OF THE ZODIAC EMBRACE EACH OTHER, THEY DON'T TRANSFORM.
LOOK, WITH YUN-CHAN TOO!
OH YEAH! BUT WHY IS THAT?
COME TO THINK OF IT, IT WAS THE SAME BEFORE!...
...WE DON'T KNOW. BUT TWO MORE OF THE ZODIAC ARE FEMALE...
LET GO OF ME.
...AND EVEN IF WE HUG THEM, WE DON'T TRANSFORM.
REALLY!? THERE ARE TWO MORE GIRLS!?
WOWWW—
WANT TO KNOW WHICH YEARS THEY ARE?
MMM...!
NO. IF IT'S ALL RIGHT, I'D LIKE TO THINK IT OVER AND SEE IF I CAN FIGURE IT OUT FOR MYSELF.
CAN WE GET BACK TO THE MAIN TOPIC...?
IT'S PROBABLY MORE FUN THAT WAY.
AH-HA-HA! THAT'S JUST LIKE YOU, HONDA-SAN.

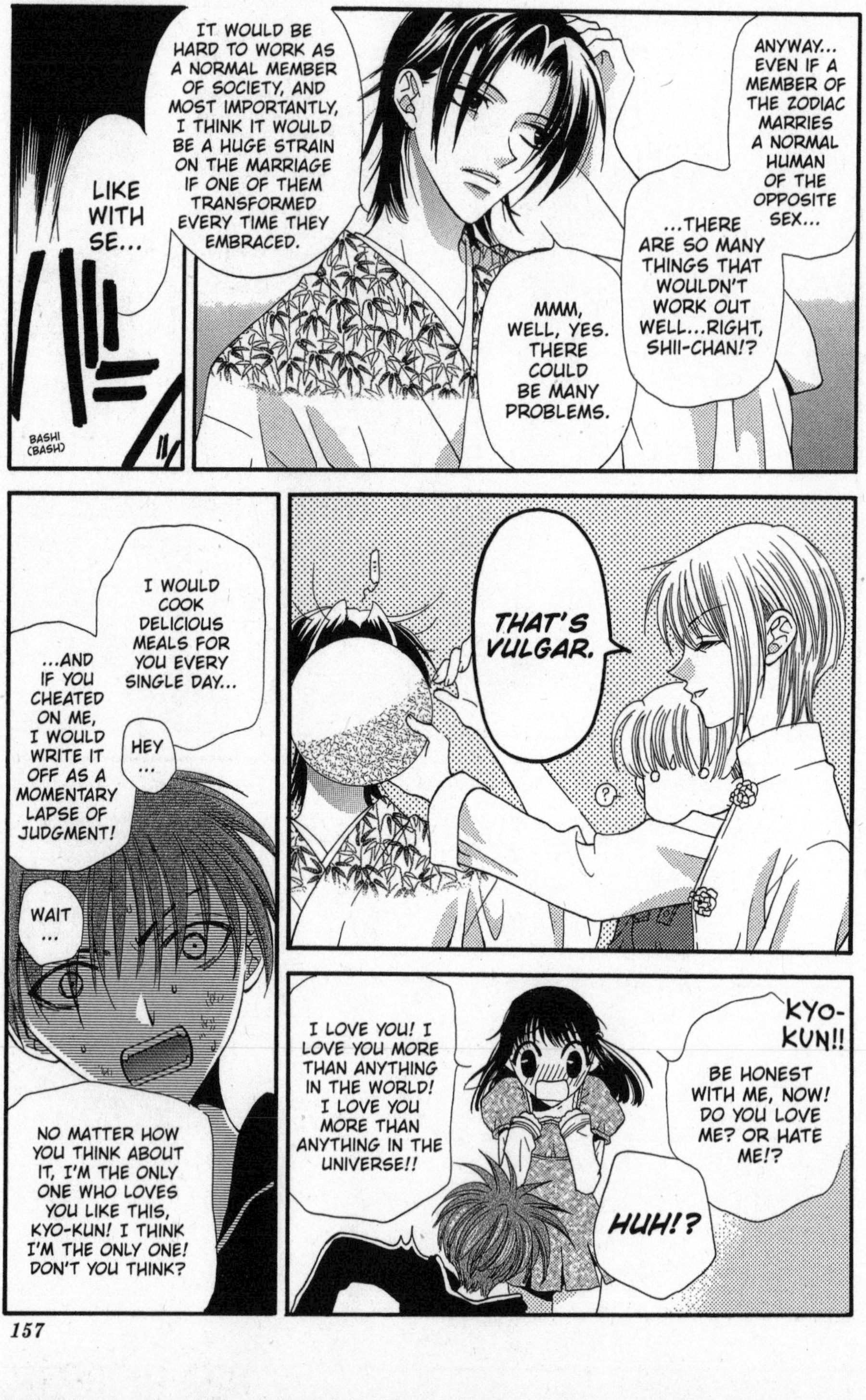
ANYWAY... EVEN IF A MEMBER OF THE ZODIAC MARRIES A NORMAL HUMAN OF THE OPPOSITE SEX...
...THERE ARE SO MANY THINGS THAT WOULDN'T WORK OUT WELL...RIGHT, SHII-CHAN!?
MMM, WELL, YES. THERE COULD BE MANY PROBLEMS.
IT WOULD BE HARD TO WORK AS A NORMAL MEMBER OF SOCIETY, AND MOST IMPORTANTLY, I THINK IT WOULD BE A HUGE STRAIN ON THE MARRIAGE IF ONE OF THEM TRANSFORMED EVERY TIME THEY EMBRACED.
LIKE WITH SE...
BASHI (BASH)
THAT'S VULGAR.
?
KYO-KUN!!
BE HONEST WITH ME, NOW! DO YOU LOVE ME? OR HATE ME!?
I LOVE YOU! I LOVE YOU MORE THAN ANYTHING IN THE WORLD! I LOVE YOU MORE THAN ANYTHING IN THE UNIVERSE!!
HUH!?
I WOULD COOK DELICIOUS MEALS FOR YOU EVERY SINGLE DAY...
...AND IF YOU CHEATED ON ME, I WOULD WRITE IT OFF AS A MOMENTARY LAPSE OF JUDGMENT!
HEY ...
WAIT ...
NO MATTER HOW YOU THINK ABOUT IT, I'M THE ONLY ONE WHO LOVES YOU LIKE THIS, KYO-KUN! I THINK I'M THE ONLY ONE! DON'T YOU THINK?

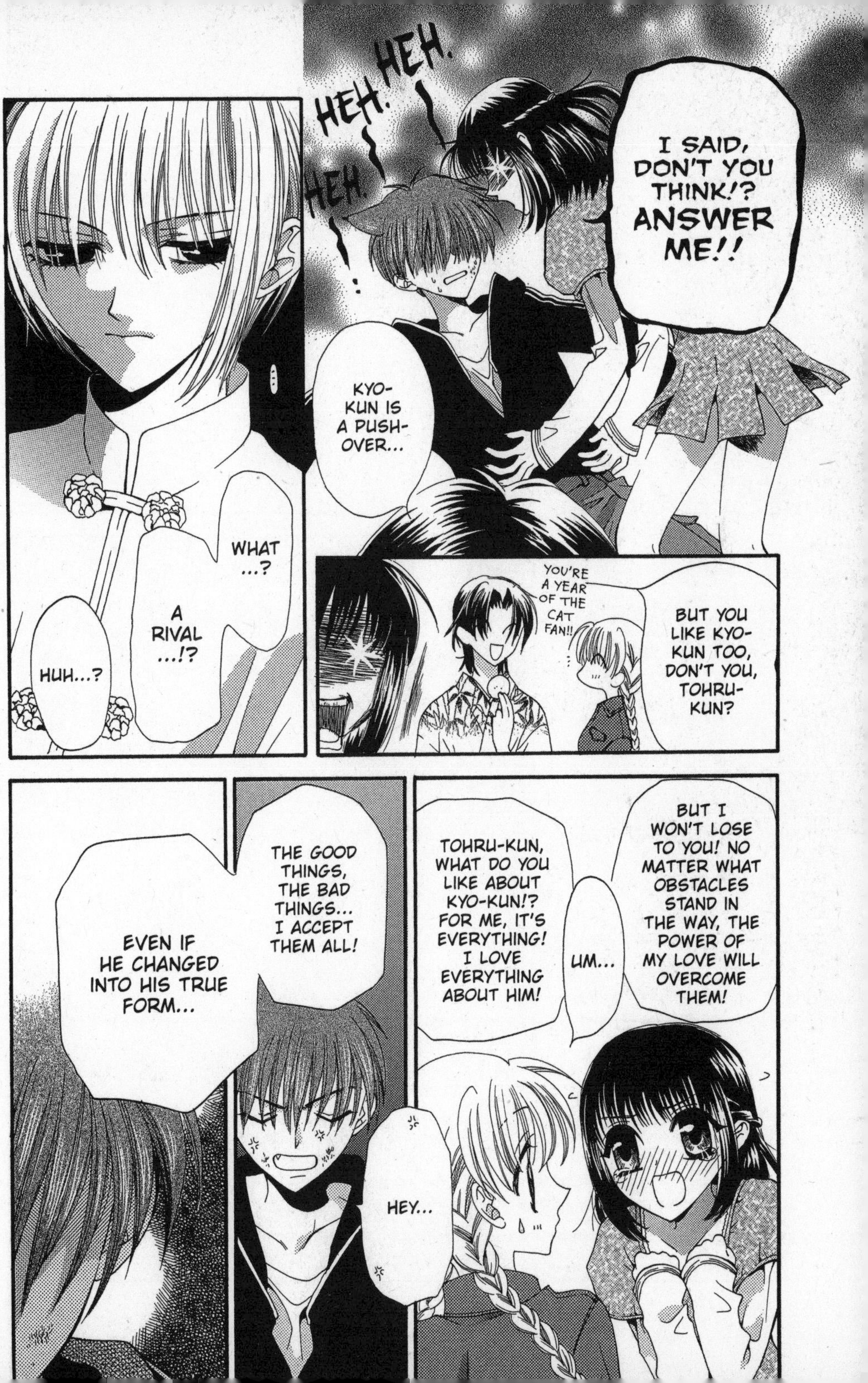
I SAID, DON'T YOU THINK!? ANSWER ME!!
HEH. HEH. HEH.
KYO-KUN IS A PUSH-OVER...
BUT YOU LIKE KYO-KUN TOO, DON'T YOU, TOHRU-KUN?
YOU'RE A YEAR OF THE CAT FAN!!
WHAT ...?
A RIVAL ...!?
HUH...?
BUT I WON'T LOSE TO YOU! NO MATTER WHAT OBSTACLES STAND IN THE WAY, THE POWER OF MY LOVE WILL OVERCOME THEM!
UM...
TOHRU-KUN, WHAT DO YOU LIKE ABOUT KYO-KUN!? FOR ME, IT'S EVERYTHING! I LOVE EVERYTHING ABOUT HIM!
THE GOOD THINGS, THE BAD THINGS... I ACCEPT THEM ALL!
HEY...
EVEN IF HE CHANGED INTO HIS TRUE FORM...

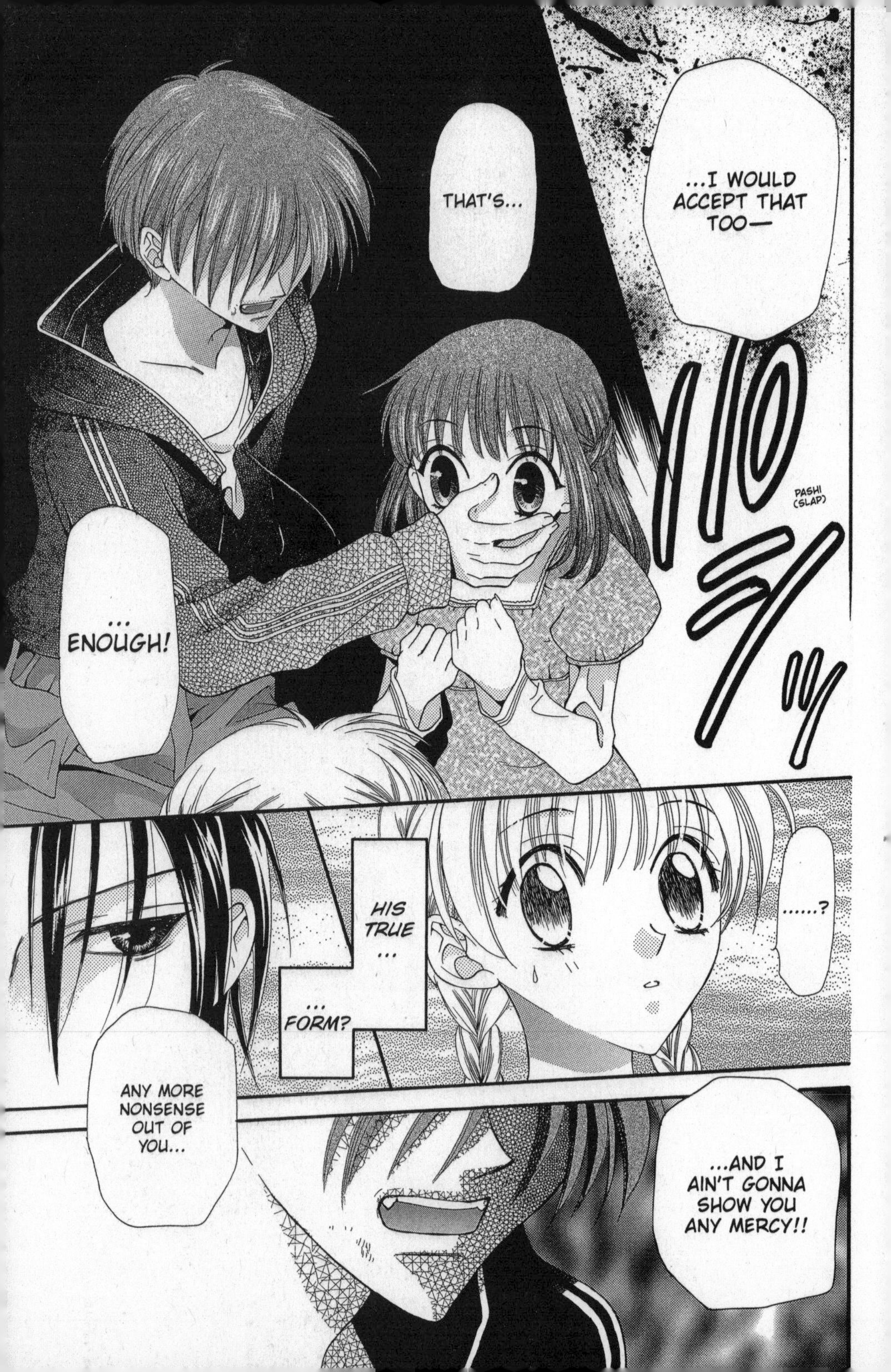
...I WOULD ACCEPT THAT TOO—
PASHI (SLAP)
THAT'S...
... ENOUGH!
......?
HIS TRUE ...
... FORM?
ANY MORE NONSENSE OUT OF YOU...
...AND I AIN'T GONNA SHOW YOU ANY MERCY!!

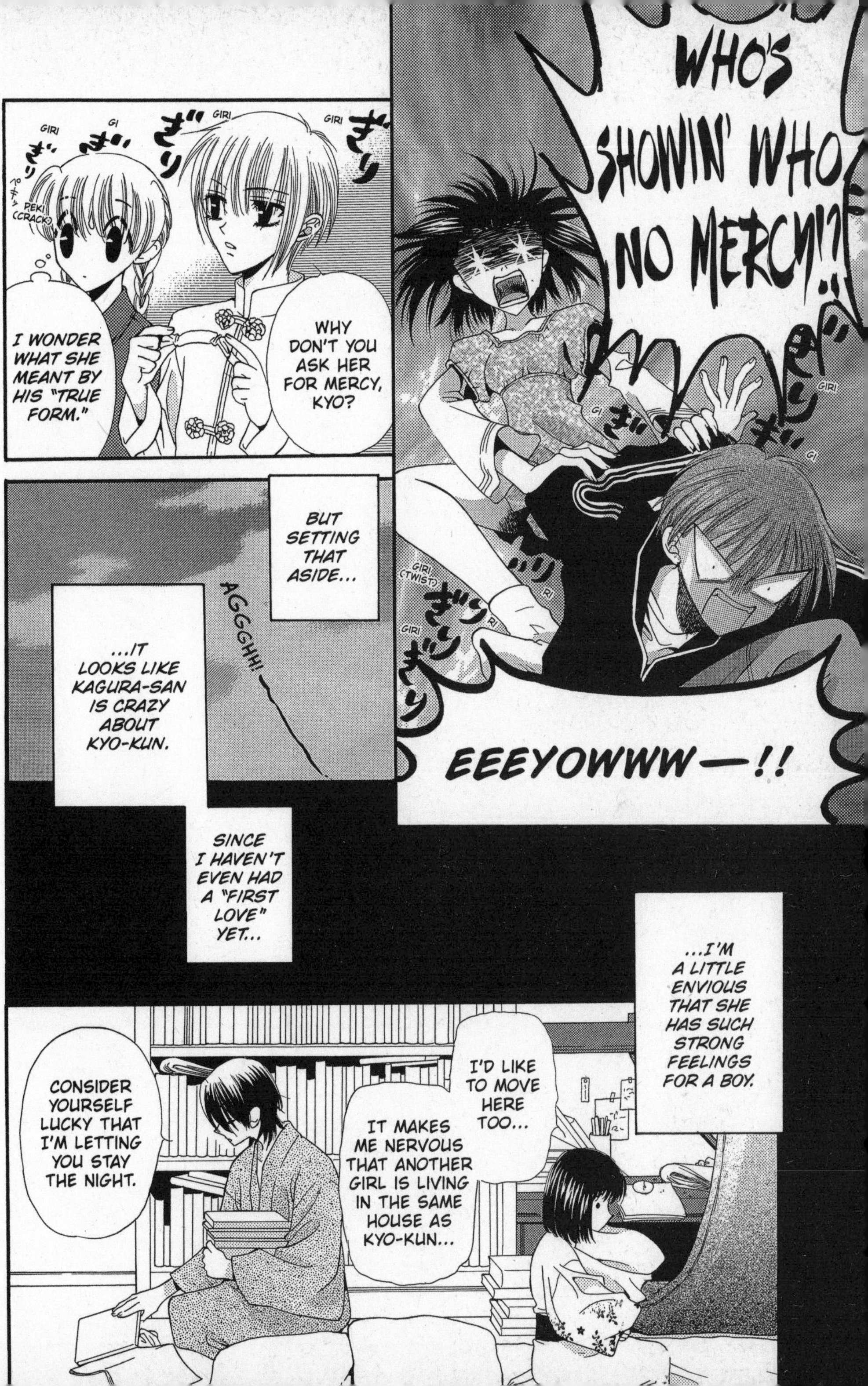

WHO'S SHOWIN' WHO NO MERCY!?
GIRI
GI
GIRI (TWIST)
RI
RI
GIRI
EEEYOWWW—!!
GIRI
GI
GIRI
GIRI
PEKI (CRACK)
WHY DON'T YOU ASK HER FOR MERCY, KYO?
I WONDER WHAT SHE MEANT BY HIS "TRUE FORM."
BUT SETTING THAT ASIDE...
AGGGHH!
...IT LOOKS LIKE KAGURA-SAN IS CRAZY ABOUT KYO-KUN.
SINCE I HAVEN'T EVEN HAD A "FIRST LOVE" YET...
...I'M A LITTLE ENVIOUS THAT SHE HAS SUCH STRONG FEELINGS FOR A BOY.
I'D LIKE TO MOVE HERE TOO...
IT MAKES ME NERVOUS THAT ANOTHER GIRL IS LIVING IN THE SAME HOUSE AS KYO-KUN...
CONSIDER YOURSELF LUCKY THAT I'M LETTING YOU STAY THE NIGHT.

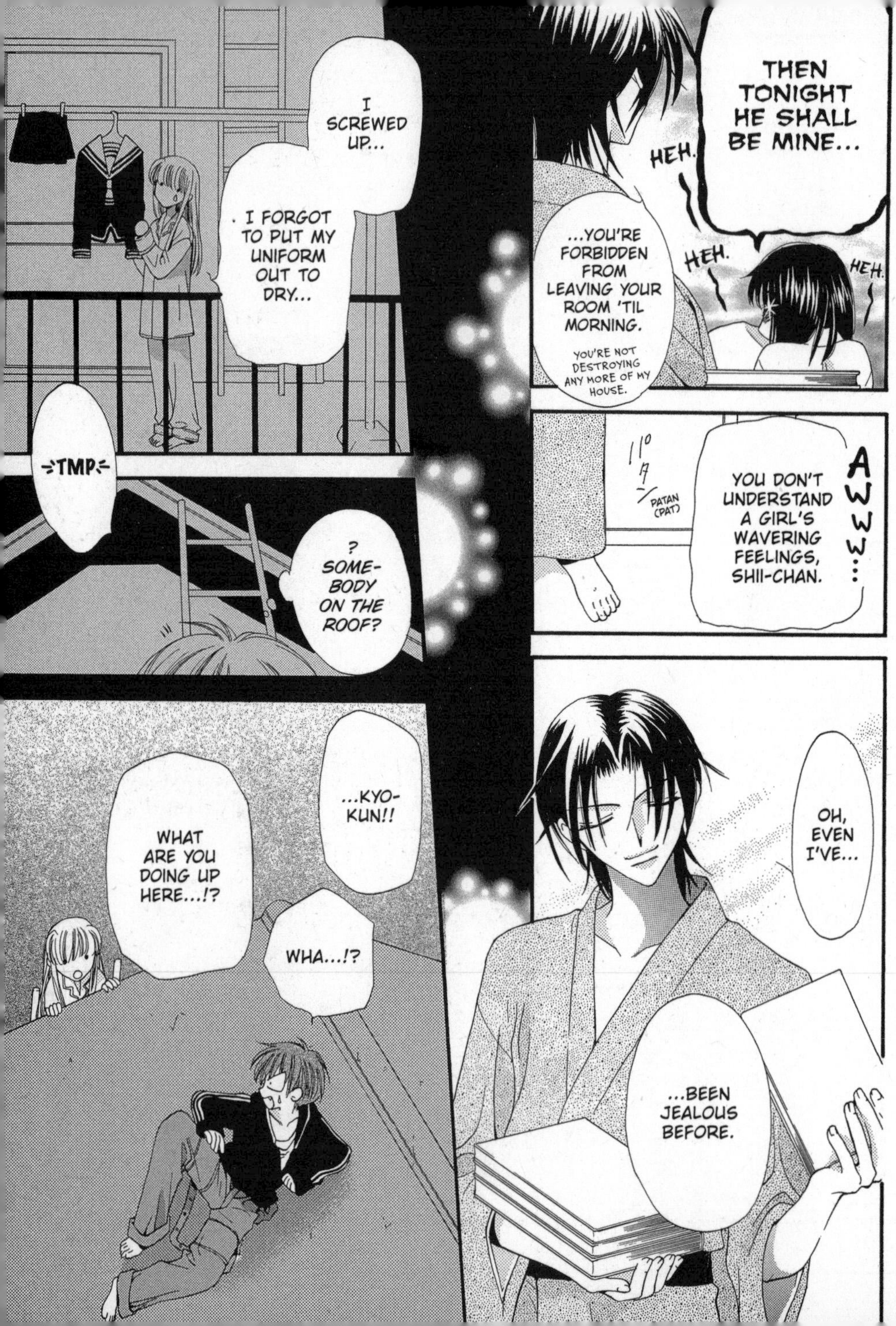
THEN TONIGHT HE SHALL BE MINE...
HEH.
HEH.
HEH.
...YOU'RE FORBIDDEN FROM LEAVING YOUR ROOM 'TIL MORNING.
YOU'RE NOT DESTROYING ANY MORE OF MY HOUSE.
AWWW...
YOU DON'T UNDERSTAND A GIRL'S WAVERING FEELINGS, SHII-CHAN.
PATAN (PAT)
OH, EVEN I'VE...
...BEEN JEALOUS BEFORE.
I SCREWED UP...
I FORGOT TO PUT MY UNIFORM OUT TO DRY...
TMP
? SOMEBODY ON THE ROOF?
...KYO-KUN!!
WHAT ARE YOU DOING UP HERE...!?
WHA...!?

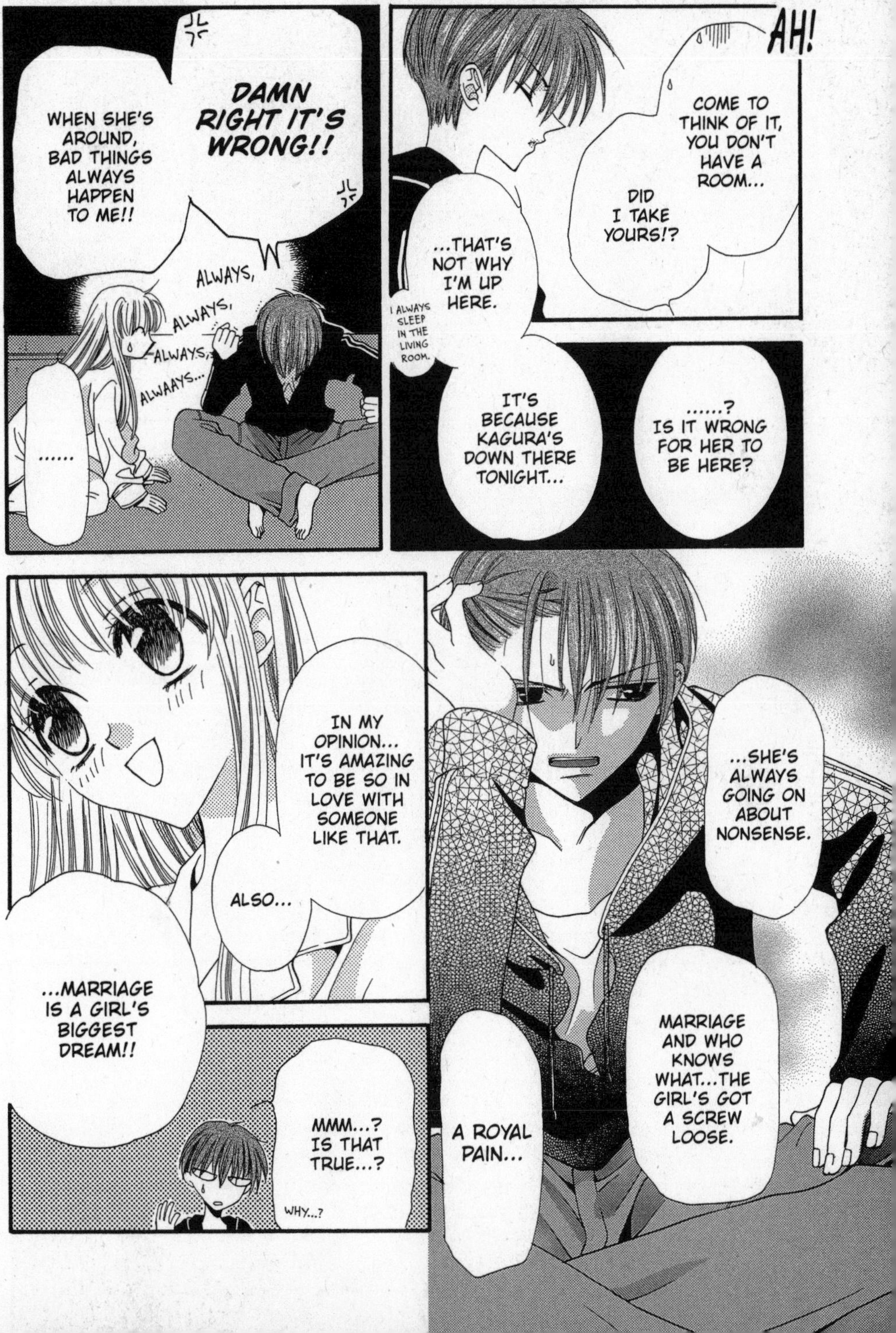
AH!
COME TO THINK OF IT, YOU DON'T HAVE A ROOM...
DID I TAKE YOURS!?
...THAT'S NOT WHY I'M UP HERE.
I ALWAYS SLEEP IN THE LIVING ROOM.
IT'S BECAUSE KAGURA'S DOWN THERE TONIGHT...
......? IS IT WRONG FOR HER TO BE HERE?
DAMN RIGHT IT'S WRONG!!
WHEN SHE'S AROUND, BAD THINGS ALWAYS HAPPEN TO ME!!
ALWAYS, ALWAYS, ALWAYS, ALWAAYS...
......
...SHE'S ALWAYS GOING ON ABOUT NONSENSE.
MARRIAGE AND WHO KNOWS WHAT...THE GIRL'S GOT A SCREW LOOSE.
A ROYAL PAIN...
IN MY OPINION... IT'S AMAZING TO BE SO IN LOVE WITH SOMEONE LIKE THAT.
ALSO...
...MARRIAGE IS A GIRL'S BIGGEST DREAM!!
MMM...? IS THAT TRUE...?
WHY...?

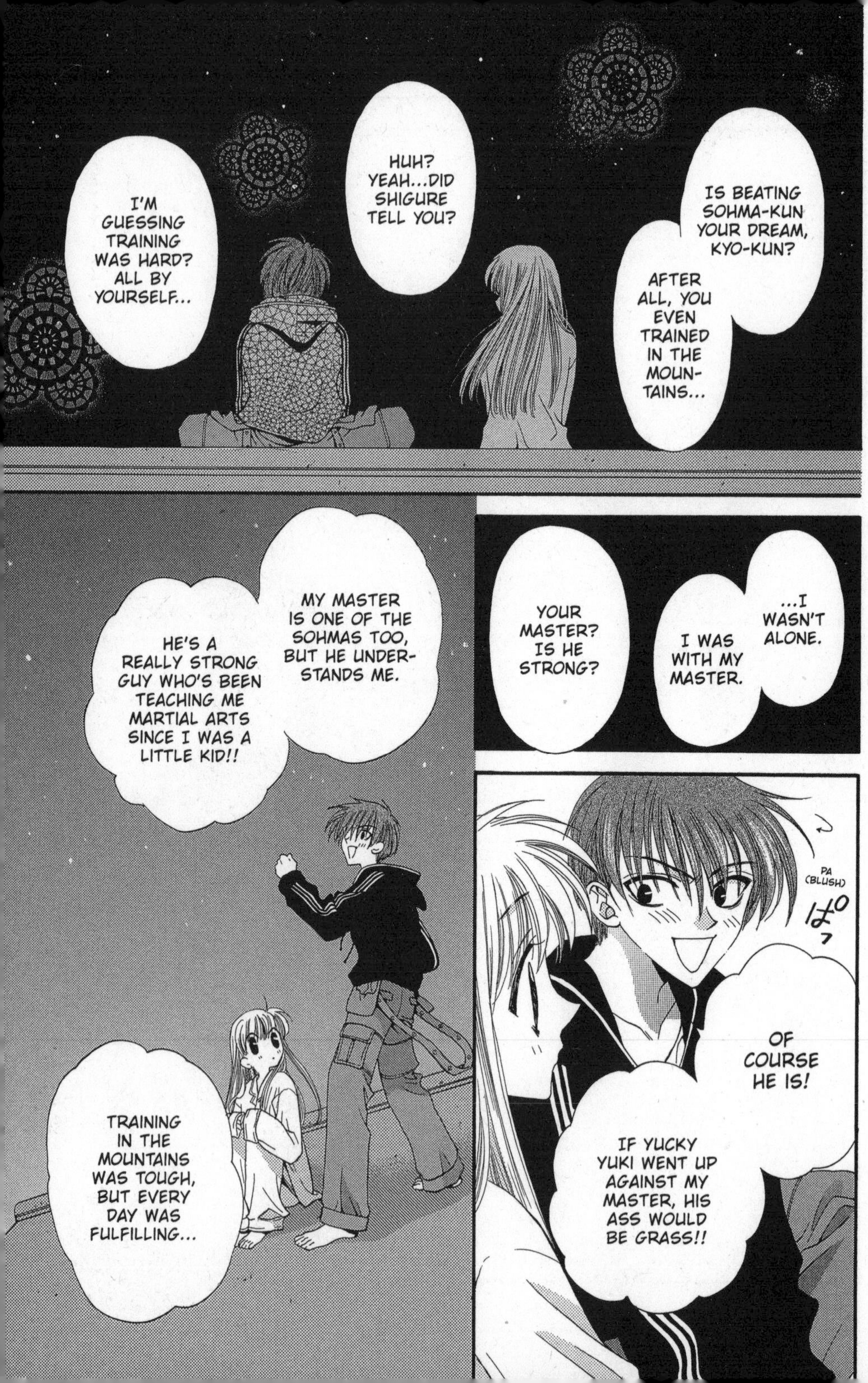
IS BEATING SOHMA-KUN YOUR DREAM, KYO-KUN?
AFTER ALL, YOU EVEN TRAINED IN THE MOUNTAINS...
HUH? YEAH...DID SHIGURE TELL YOU?
I'M GUESSING TRAINING WAS HARD? ALL BY YOURSELF...
...I WASN'T ALONE.
I WAS WITH MY MASTER.
YOUR MASTER? IS HE STRONG?
PA (BLUSH)
ぱっ
OF COURSE HE IS!
IF YUCKY YUKI WENT UP AGAINST MY MASTER, HIS ASS WOULD BE GRASS!!
MY MASTER IS ONE OF THE SOHMAS TOO, BUT HE UNDERSTANDS ME.
HE'S A REALLY STRONG GUY WHO'S BEEN TEACHING ME MARTIAL ARTS SINCE I WAS A LITTLE KID!!
TRAINING IN THE MOUNTAINS WAS TOUGH, BUT EVERY DAY WAS FULFILLING...

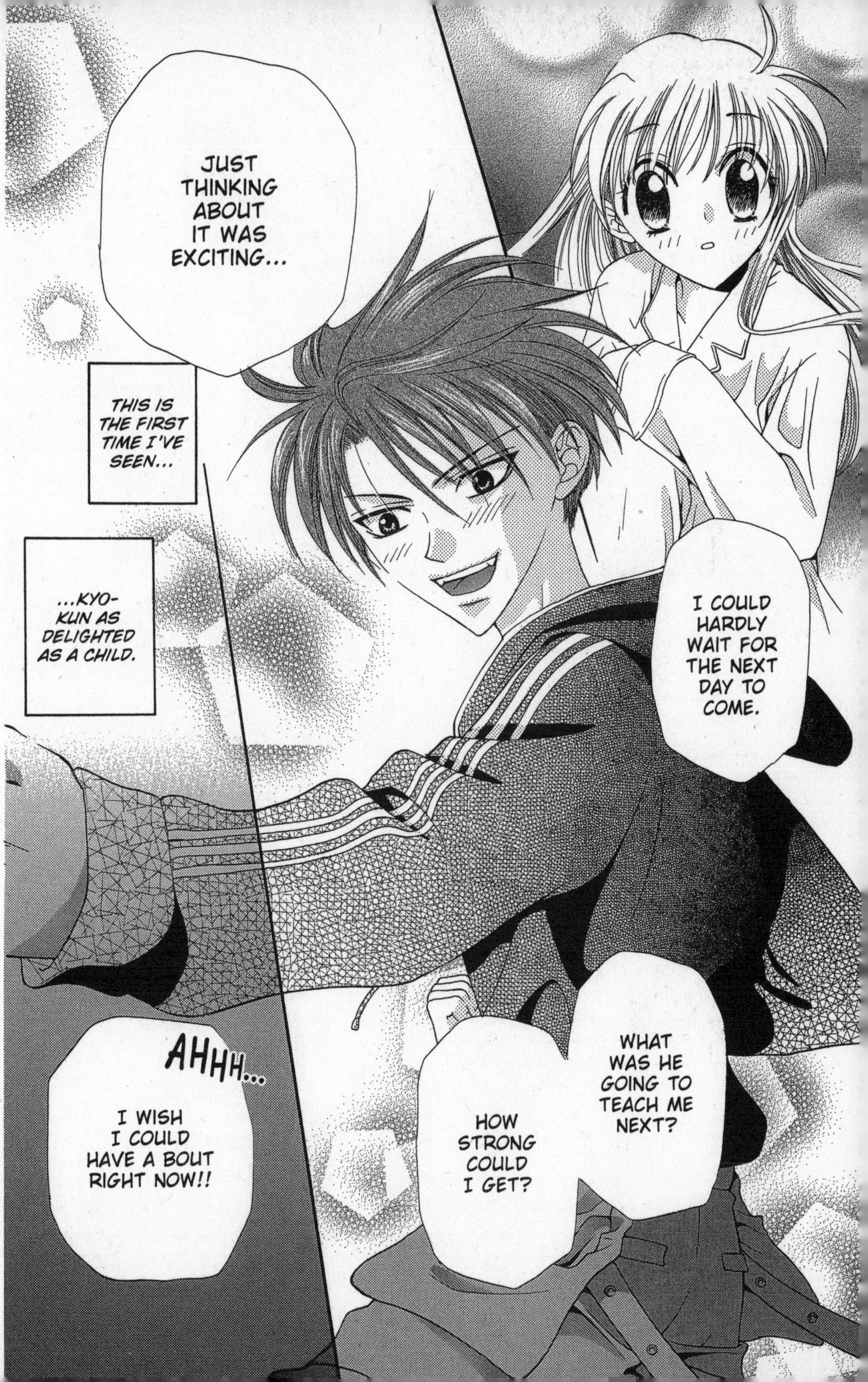
JUST THINKING ABOUT IT WAS EXCITING...
I COULD HARDLY WAIT FOR THE NEXT DAY TO COME.
WHAT WAS HE GOING TO TEACH ME NEXT?
HOW STRONG COULD I GET?
AHHH...
I WISH I COULD HAVE A BOUT RIGHT NOW!!
THIS IS THE FIRST TIME I'VE SEEN...
...KYO-KUN AS DELIGHTED AS A CHILD.

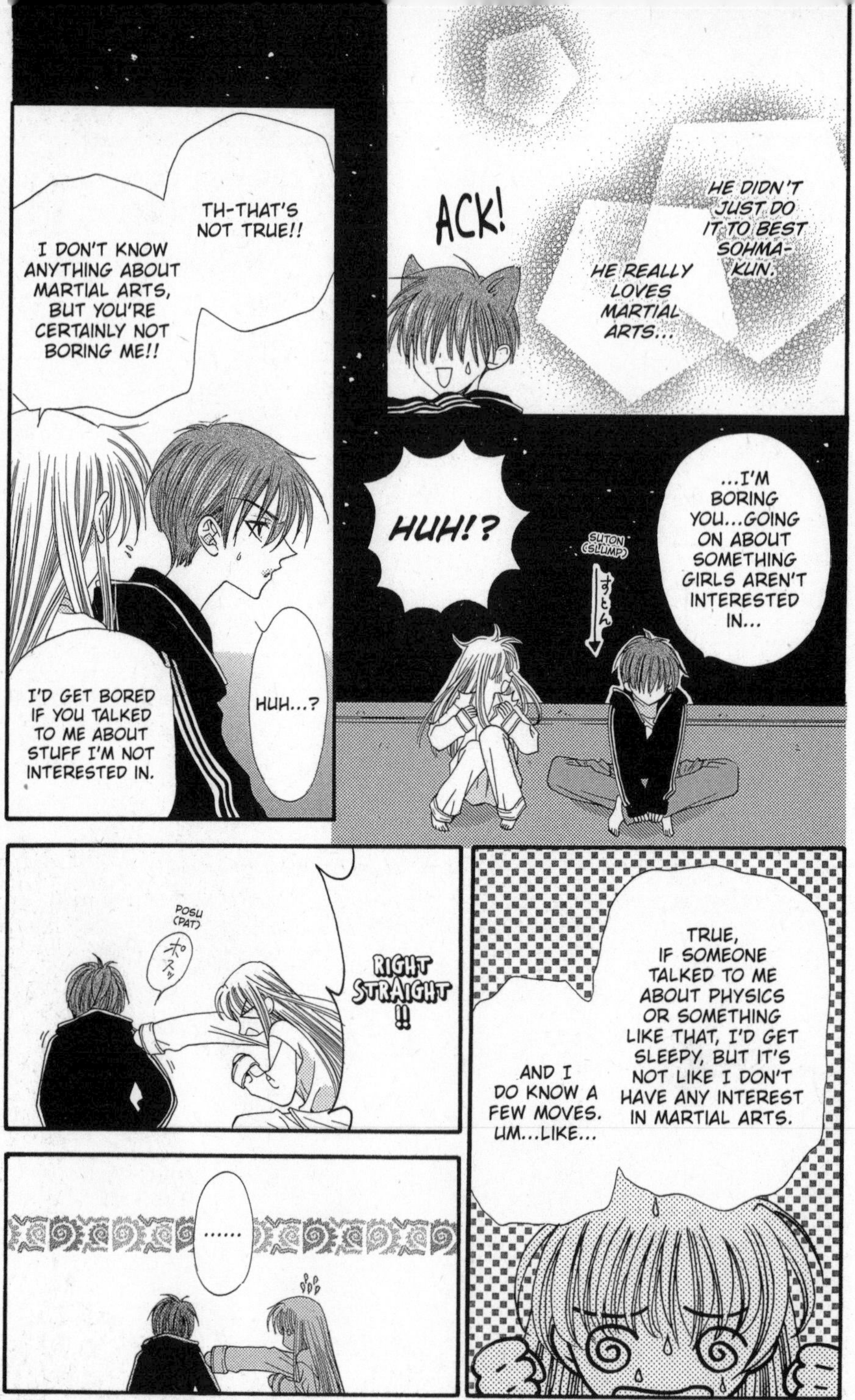
HE DIDN'T JUST DO IT TO BEST SOHMA-KUN.
HE REALLY LOVES MARTIAL ARTS...
ACK!
...I'M BORING YOU...GOING ON ABOUT SOMETHING GIRLS AREN'T INTERESTED IN...
SUTON (SLUMP)
すとん
HUH!?
TH-THAT'S NOT TRUE!!
I DON'T KNOW ANYTHING ABOUT MARTIAL ARTS, BUT YOU'RE CERTAINLY NOT BORING ME!!
HUH...?
I'D GET BORED IF YOU TALKED TO ME ABOUT STUFF I'M NOT INTERESTED IN.
TRUE, IF SOMEONE TALKED TO ME ABOUT PHYSICS OR SOMETHING LIKE THAT, I'D GET SLEEPY, BUT IT'S NOT LIKE I DON'T HAVE ANY INTEREST IN MARTIAL ARTS.
AND I DO KNOW A FEW MOVES. UM...LIKE...
RIGHT STRAIGHT!!
POSU (PAT)
ポスッ
......

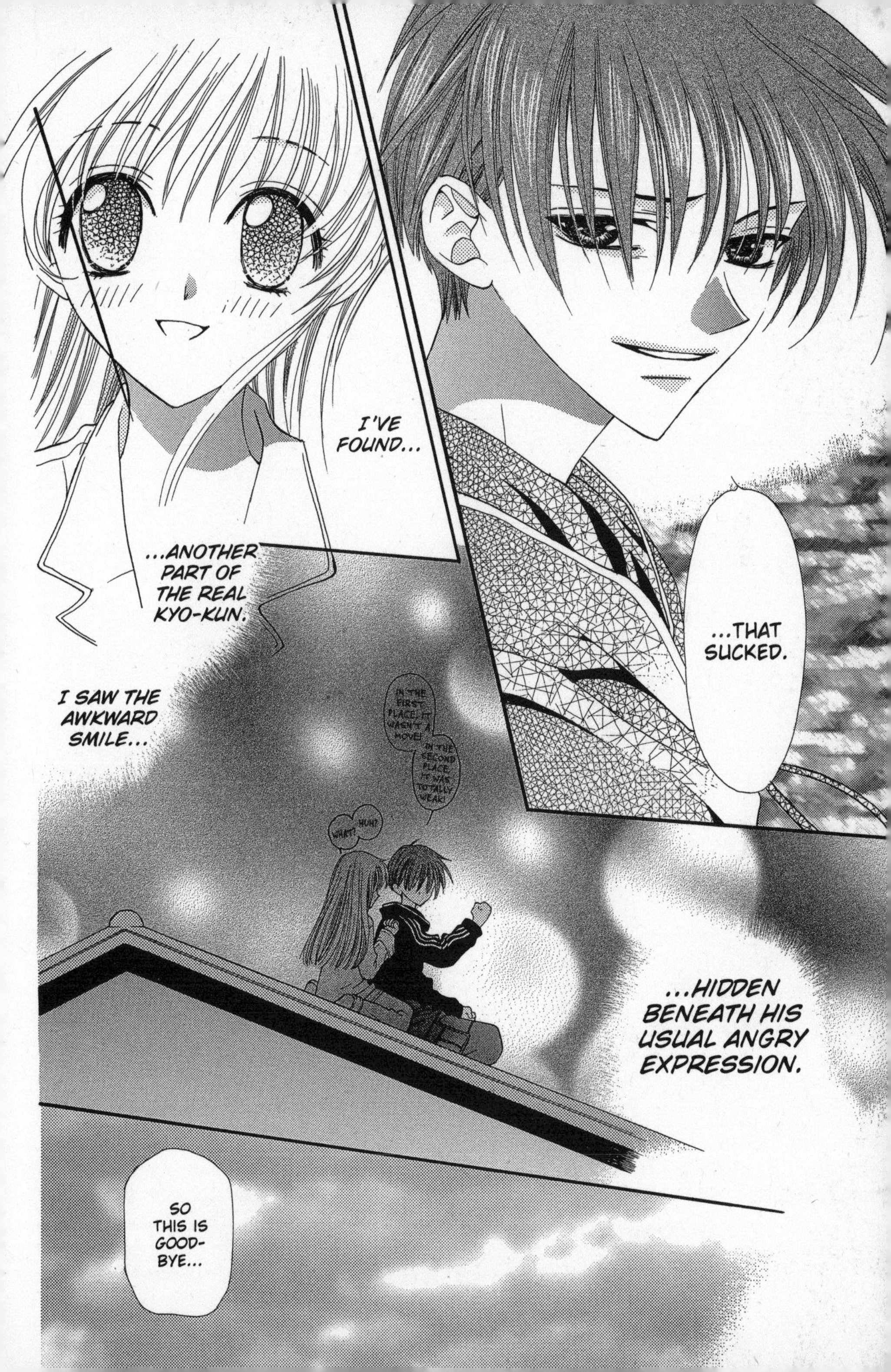
...THAT SUCKED.
I'VE FOUND...
...ANOTHER PART OF THE REAL KYO-KUN.
I SAW THE AWKWARD SMILE...
IN THE FIRST PLACE, IT WASN'T A MOVE!
IN THE SECOND PLACE, IT WAS TOTALLY WEAK!
HUH?
WHAT?
...HIDDEN BENEATH HIS USUAL ANGRY EXPRESSION.
SO THIS IS GOOD-BYE...

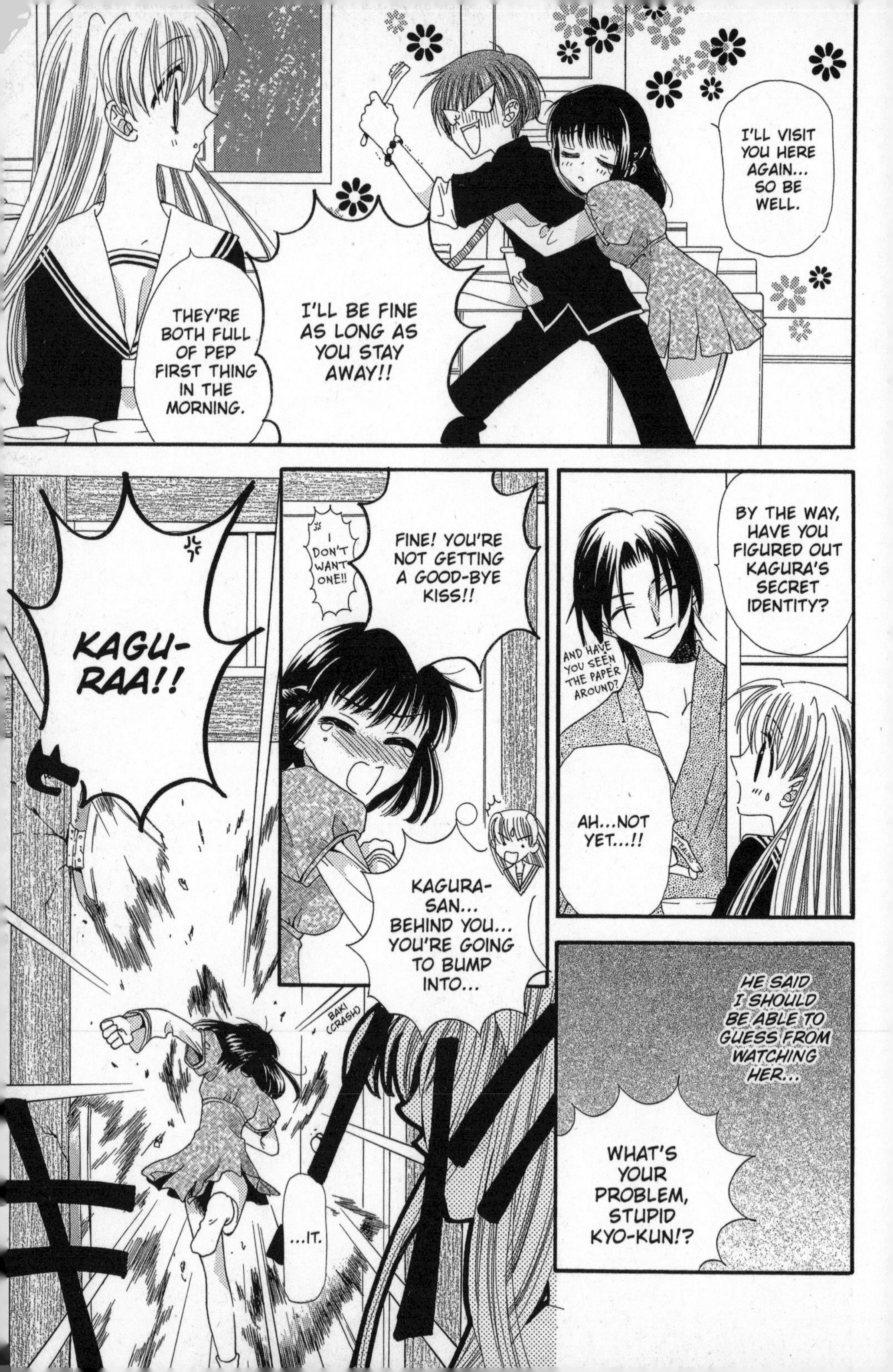

I'LL VISIT YOU HERE AGAIN... SO BE WELL.
I'LL BE FINE AS LONG AS YOU STAY AWAY!!
THEY'RE BOTH FULL OF PEP FIRST THING IN THE MORNING.
BY THE WAY, HAVE YOU FIGURED OUT KAGURA'S SECRET IDENTITY?
AND HAVE YOU SEEN THE PAPER AROUND?
AH...NOT YET...!!
STEALING
FINE! YOU'RE NOT GETTING A GOOD-BYE KISS!!
I DON'T WANT ONE!!
KAGURA-SAN... BEHIND YOU... YOU'RE GOING TO BUMP INTO...
KAGU-RAA!!
BAKI (CRASH)
...IT.
HE SAID I SHOULD BE ABLE TO GUESS FROM WATCHING HER...
WHAT'S YOUR PROBLEM, STUPID KYO-KUN!?

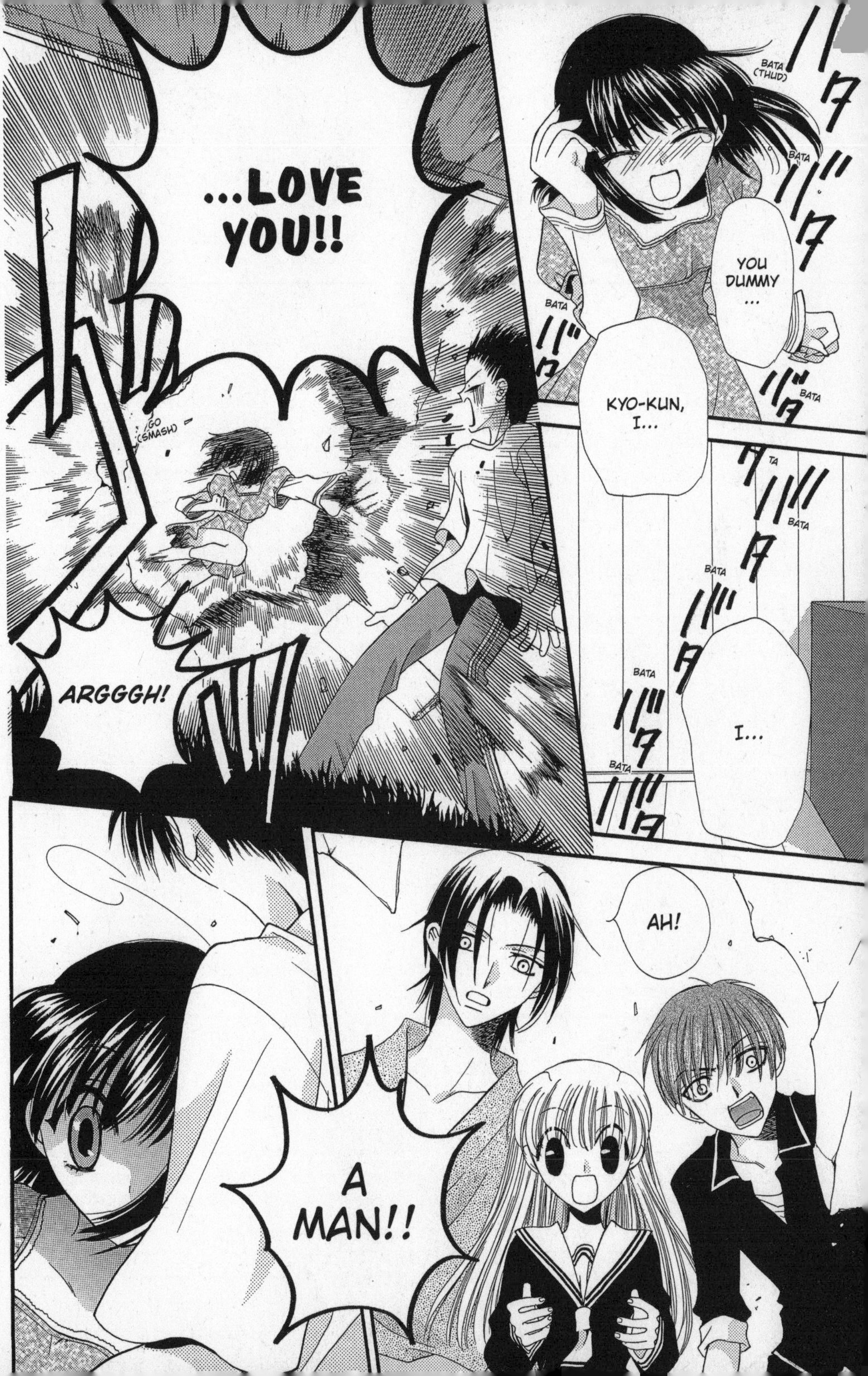
BATA (THUD)
BATA
YOU DUMMY ...
BATA
KYO-KUN, I...
BATA
TA
BATA
BATA
I...
BATA
BATA
...LOVE YOU!!
GO (SMASH)
ARGGGH!
AH!
A MAN!!

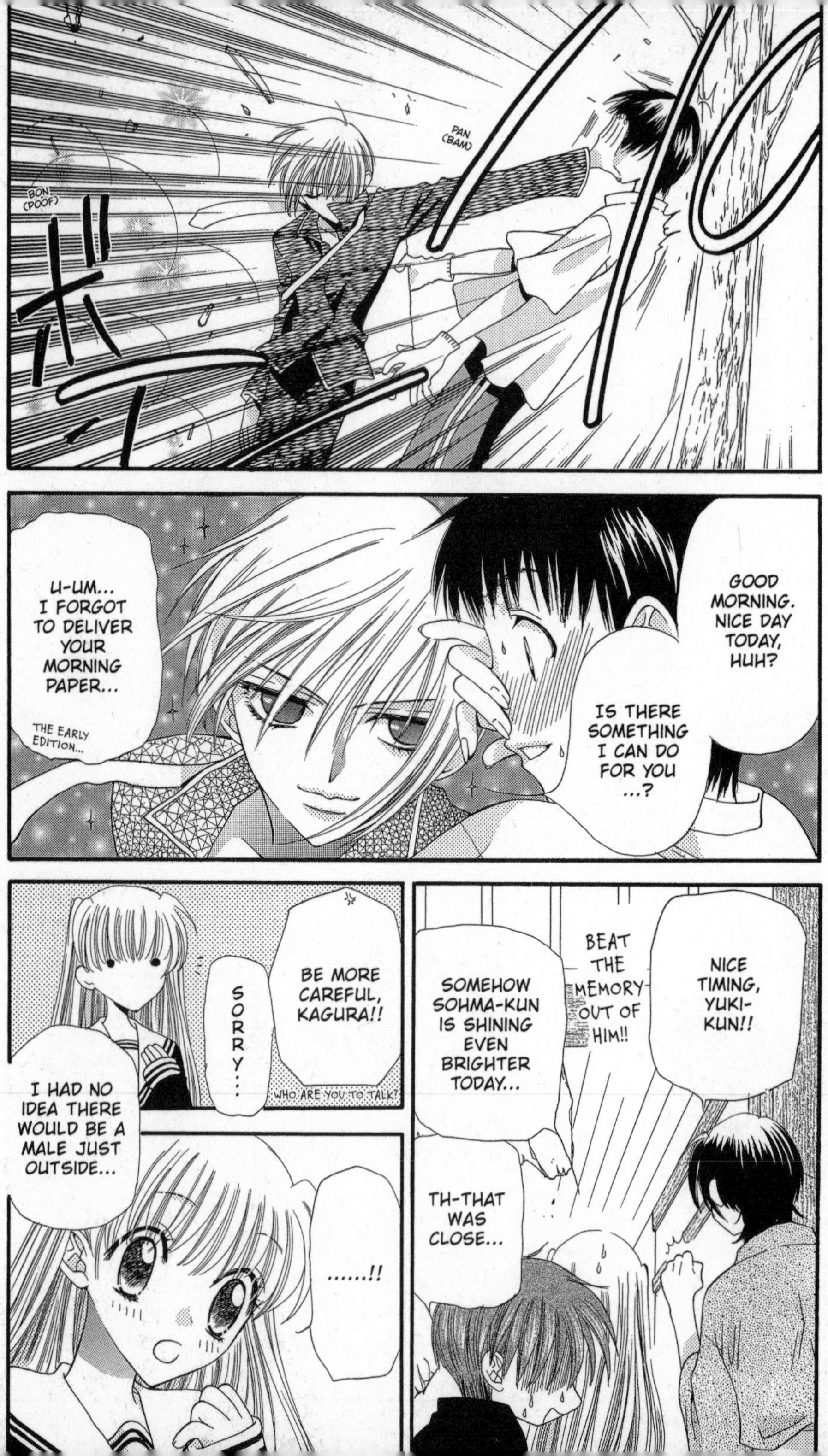
PAN (BAM)
BON (POOF)
GOOD MORNING. NICE DAY TODAY, HUH?
IS THERE SOMETHING I CAN DO FOR YOU ...?
U-UM... I FORGOT TO DELIVER YOUR MORNING PAPER...
THE EARLY EDITION...
NICE TIMING, YUKI-KUN!!
BEAT THE MEMORY OUT OF HIM!!
SOMEHOW SOHMA-KUN IS SHINING EVEN BRIGHTER TODAY...
TH-THAT WAS CLOSE...
BE MORE CAREFUL, KAGURA!!
SORRY...
WHO ARE YOU TO TALK?
I HAD NO IDEA THERE WOULD BE A MALE JUST OUTSIDE...
......!!

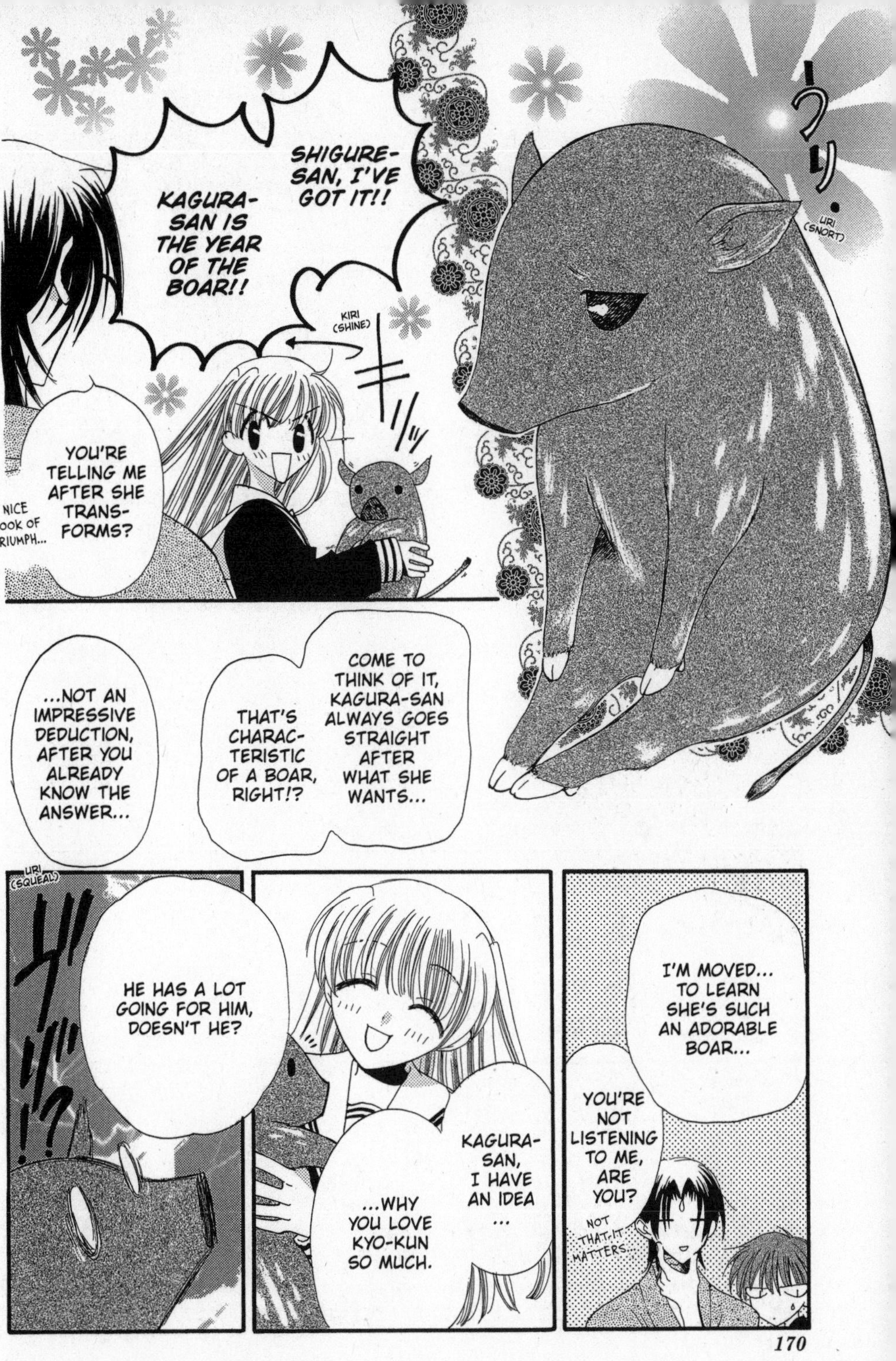

URI (SNORT)
SHIGURE-SAN, I'VE GOT IT!!
KAGURA-SAN IS THE YEAR OF THE BOAR!!
KIRI (SHINE)
YOU'RE TELLING ME AFTER SHE TRANSFORMS?
NICE LOOK OF TRIUMPH...
COME TO THINK OF IT, KAGURA-SAN ALWAYS GOES STRAIGHT AFTER WHAT SHE WANTS...
THAT'S CHARACTERISTIC OF A BOAR, RIGHT!?
...NOT AN IMPRESSIVE DEDUCTION, AFTER YOU ALREADY KNOW THE ANSWER...
I'M MOVED... TO LEARN SHE'S SUCH AN ADORABLE BOAR...
YOU'RE NOT LISTENING TO ME, ARE YOU?
NOT THAT IT MATTERS...
KAGURA-SAN, I HAVE AN IDEA...
...WHY YOU LOVE KYO-KUN SO MUCH.
HE HAS A LOT GOING FOR HIM, DOESN'T HE?
URI (SQUEAL)

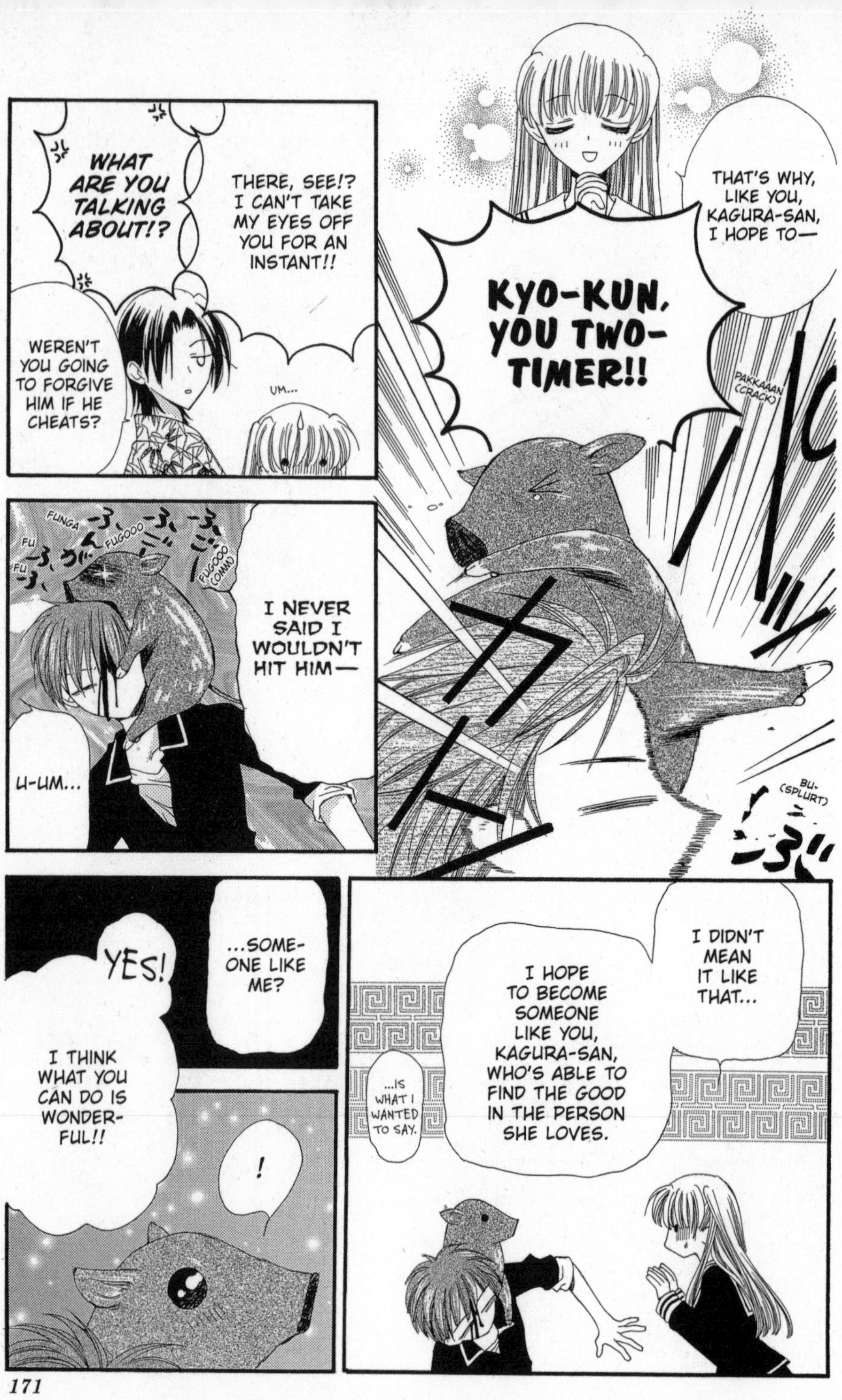
THAT'S WHY, LIKE YOU, KAGURA-SAN, I HOPE TO—
KYO-KUN, YOU TWO-TIMER!!
PAKKAAAN (CRACK)
BU- (SPLURT)
THERE, SEE!? I CAN'T TAKE MY EYES OFF YOU FOR AN INSTANT!!
WHAT ARE YOU TALKING ABOUT!?
UM...
WEREN'T YOU GOING TO FORGIVE HIM IF HE CHEATS?
I NEVER SAID I WOULDN'T HIT HIM—
FUGOOO (COMM)
FUGOOO
FUNGA
FU
FU
U-UM...
I DIDN'T MEAN IT LIKE THAT...
I HOPE TO BECOME SOMEONE LIKE YOU, KAGURA-SAN, WHO'S ABLE TO FIND THE GOOD IN THE PERSON SHE LOVES.
...IS WHAT I WANTED TO SAY.
...SOME-ONE LIKE ME?
YES!
I THINK WHAT YOU CAN DO IS WONDERFUL!!
!

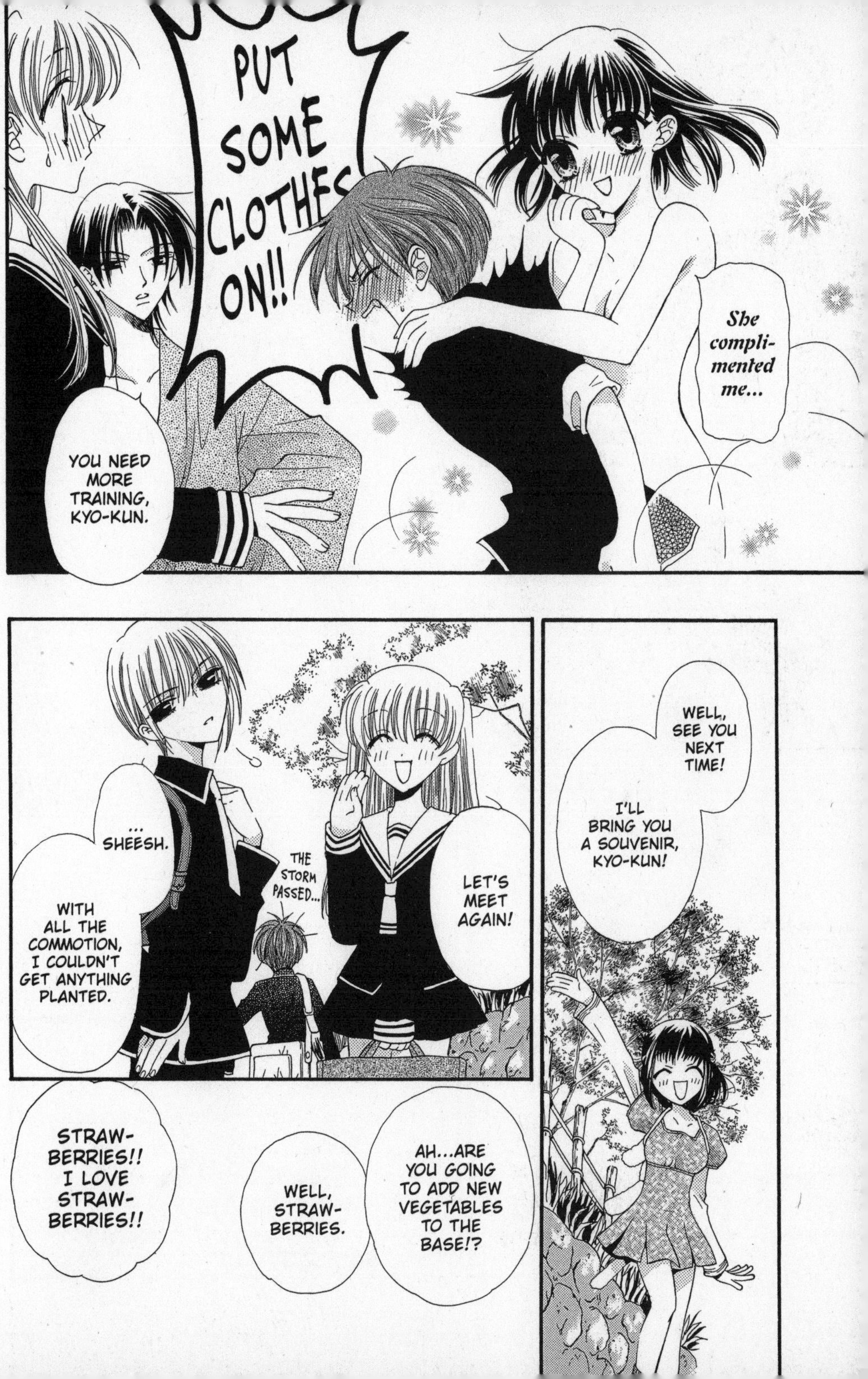
She compli-mented me...
PUT SOME CLOTHES ON!!
YOU NEED MORE TRAINING, KYO-KUN.
WELL, SEE YOU NEXT TIME!
I'LL BRING YOU A SOUVENIR, KYO-KUN!
LET'S MEET AGAIN!
THE STORM PASSED...
... SHEESH.
WITH ALL THE COMMOTION, I COULDN'T GET ANYTHING PLANTED.
AH...ARE YOU GOING TO ADD NEW VEGETABLES TO THE BASE!?
WELL, STRAW-BERRIES.
STRAW-BERRIES!! I LOVE STRAW-BERRIES!!

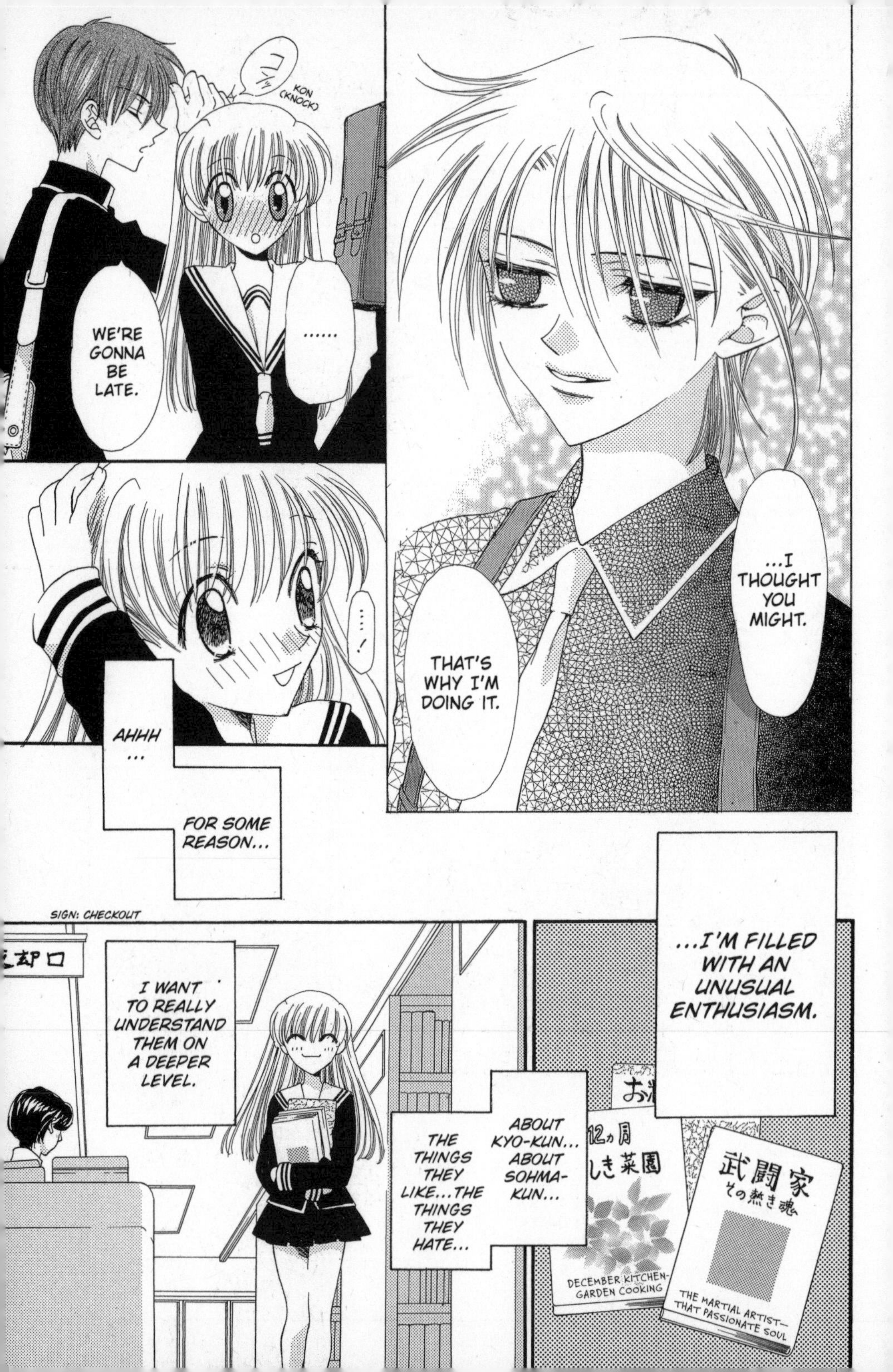
...I THOUGHT YOU MIGHT.
THAT'S WHY I'M DOING IT.
KON (KNOCK)
......
WE'RE GONNA BE LATE.
...!
AHHH ...
FOR SOME REASON...
...I'M FILLED WITH AN UNUSUAL ENTHUSIASM.
ABOUT KYO-KUN... ABOUT SOHMA-KUN...
THE THINGS THEY LIKE...THE THINGS THEY HATE...
武闘家 その熱き魂
THE MARTIAL ARTIST—THAT PASSIONATE SOUL
DECEMBER KITCHEN-GARDEN COOKING
SIGN: CHECKOUT
I WANT TO REALLY UNDERSTAND THEM ON A DEEPER LEVEL.

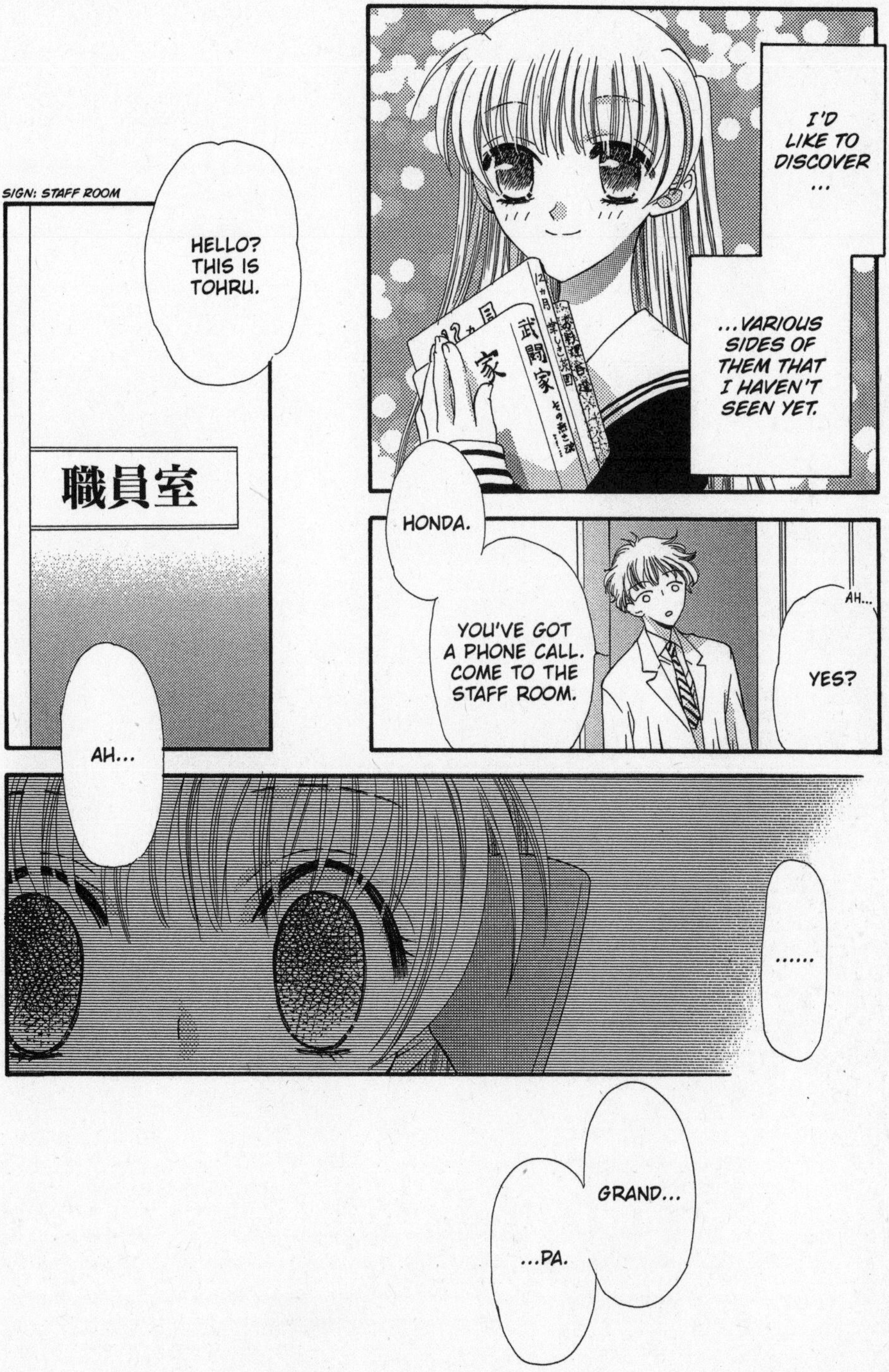
I'D LIKE TO DISCOVER ...
...VARIOUS SIDES OF THEM THAT I HAVEN'T SEEN YET.
HONDA.
YOU'VE GOT A PHONE CALL. COME TO THE STAFF ROOM.
AH...
YES?
SIGN: STAFF ROOM
職員室
HELLO? THIS IS TOHRU.
......
AH...
GRAND...
...PA.

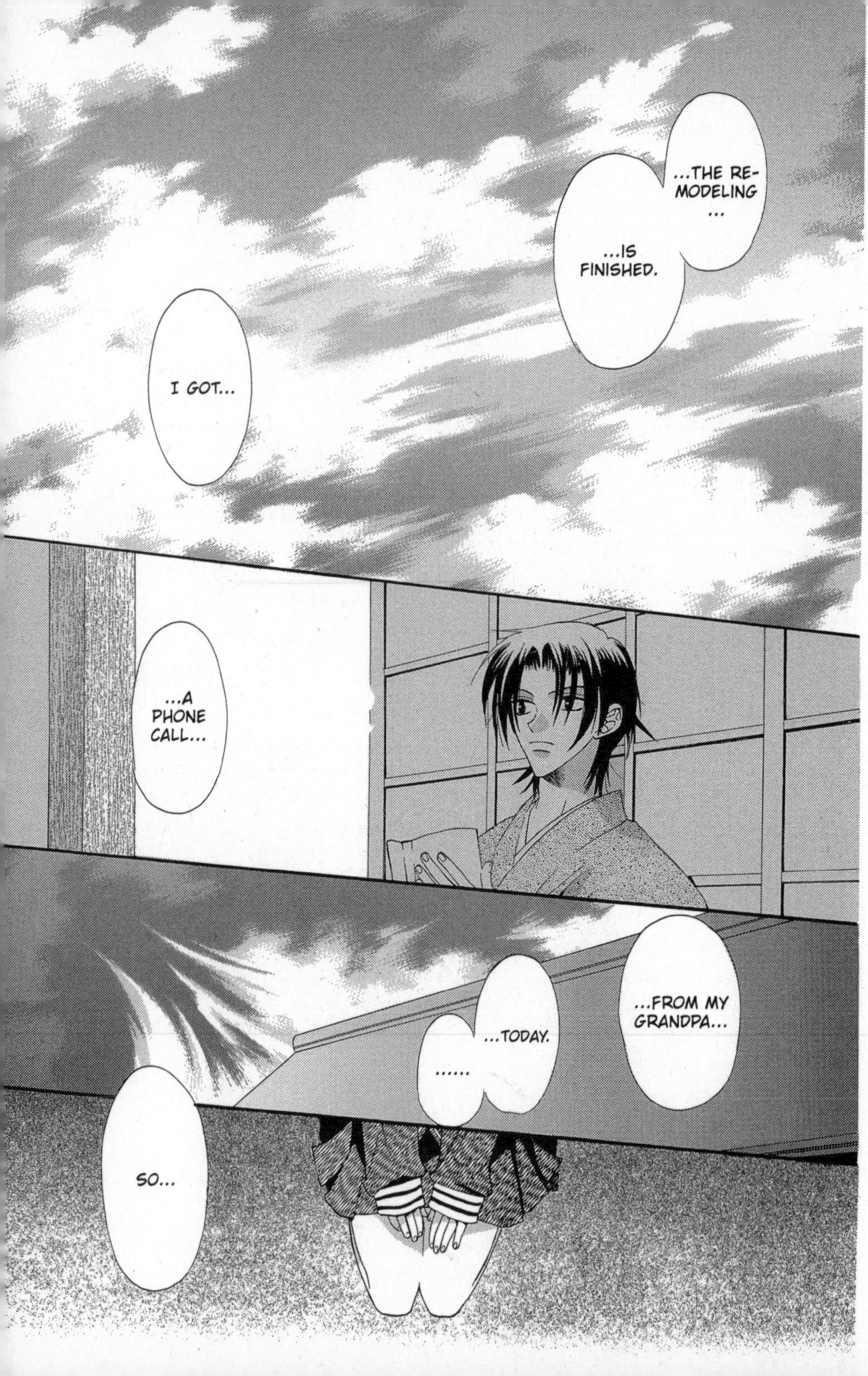
...THE RE-MODELING...
...IS FINISHED.
I GOT...
...A PHONE CALL...
...FROM MY GRANDPA...
...TODAY.
......
SO...

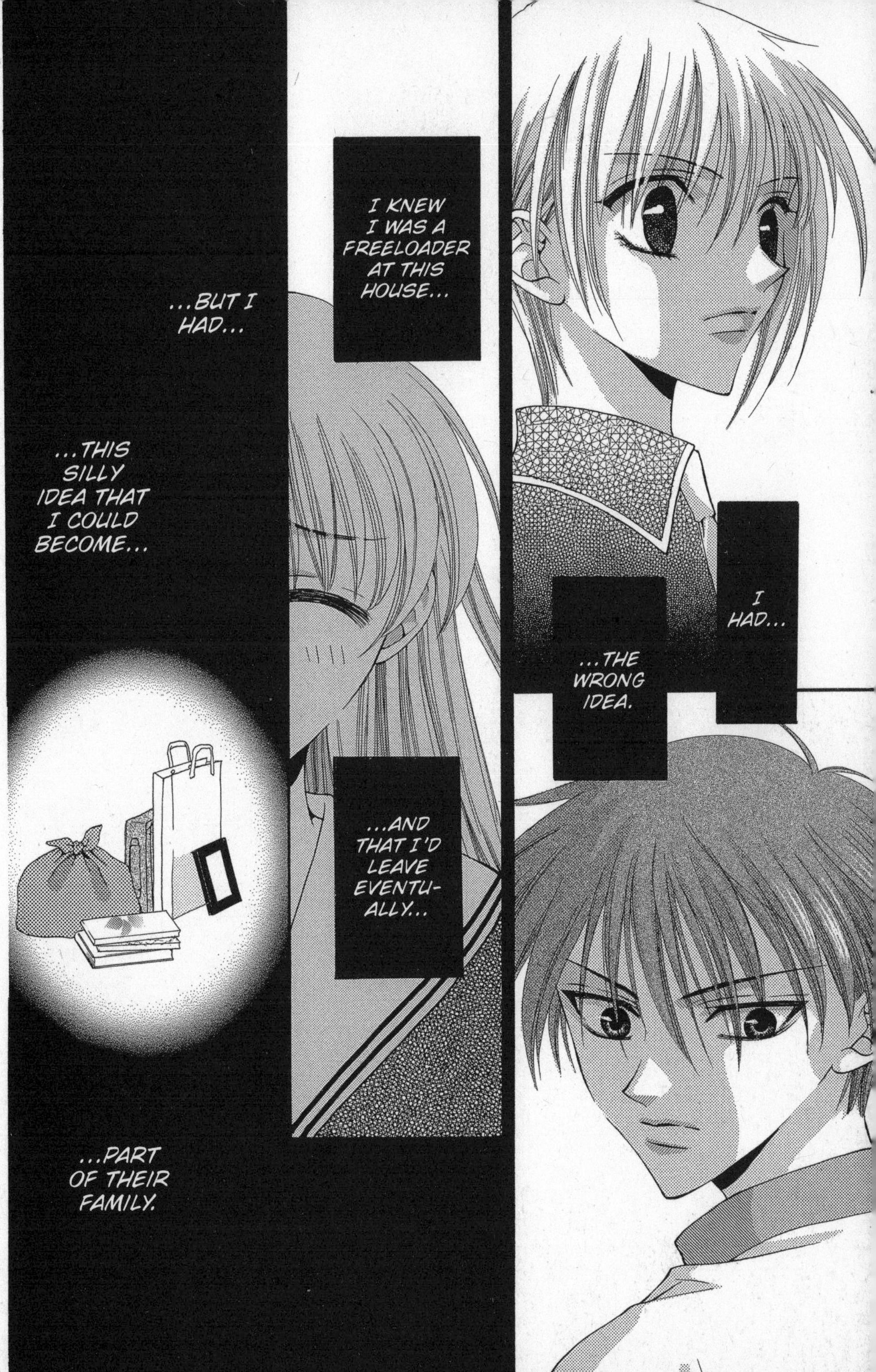
I HAD...
...THE WRONG IDEA.
I KNEW I WAS A FREELOADER AT THIS HOUSE...
...AND THAT I'D LEAVE EVENTU-ALLY...
...BUT I HAD...
...THIS SILLY IDEA THAT I COULD BECOME...
...PART OF THEIR FAMILY.

Chapter 6

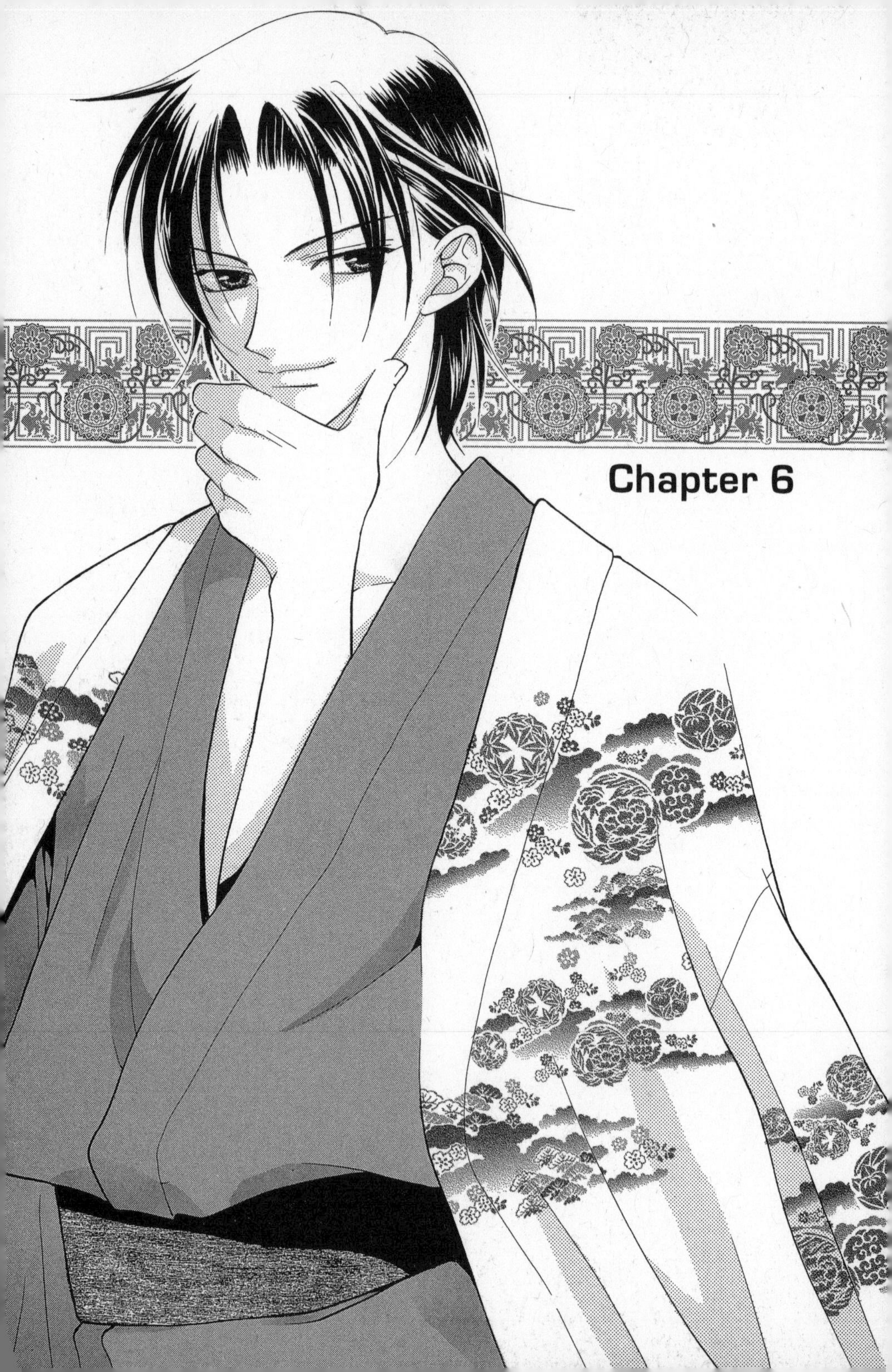

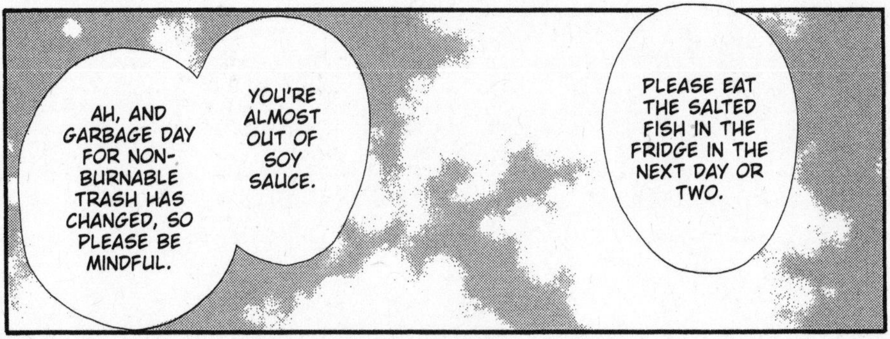
PLEASE EAT THE SALTED FISH IN THE FRIDGE IN THE NEXT DAY OR TWO.
YOU'RE ALMOST OUT OF SOY SAUCE.
AH, AND GARBAGE DAY FOR NON-BURNABLE TRASH HAS CHANGED, SO PLEASE BE MINDFUL.

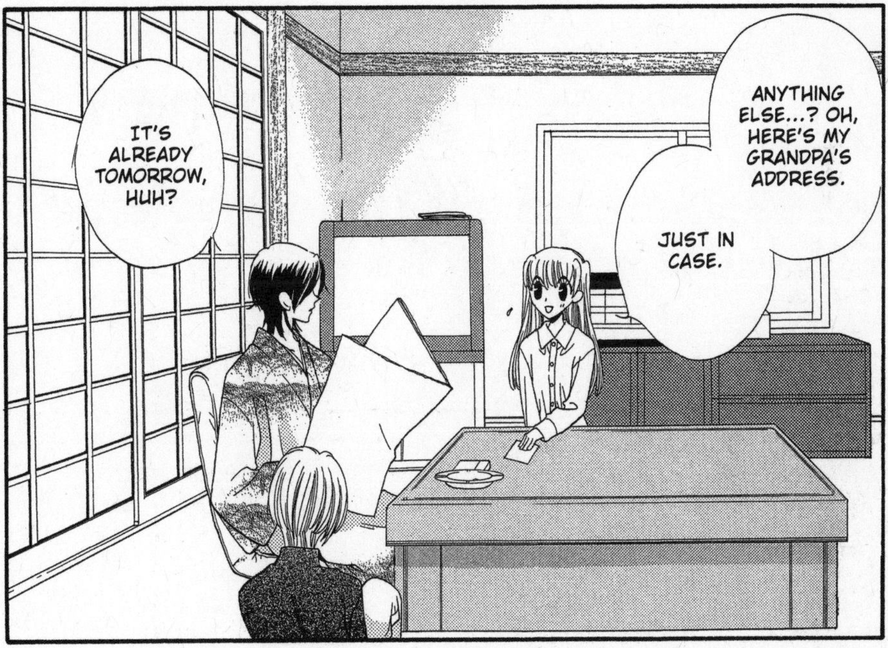
ANYTHING ELSE...? OH, HERE'S MY GRANDPA'S ADDRESS.
JUST IN CASE.
IT'S ALREADY TOMORROW, HUH?

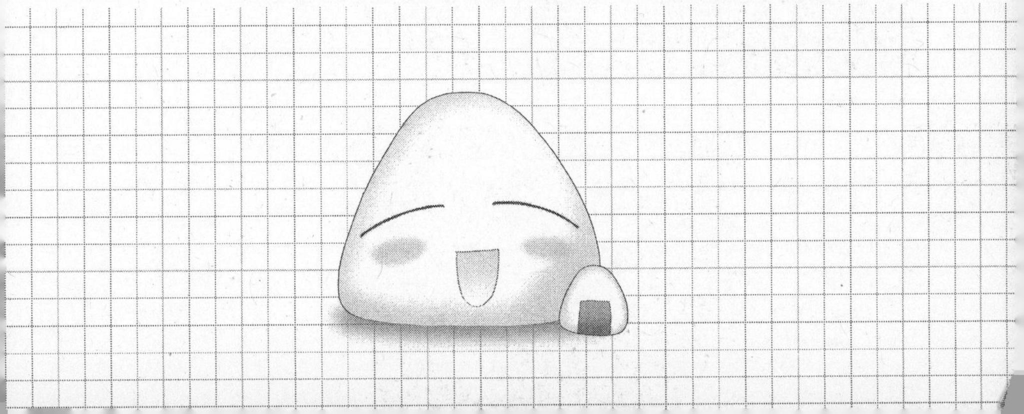

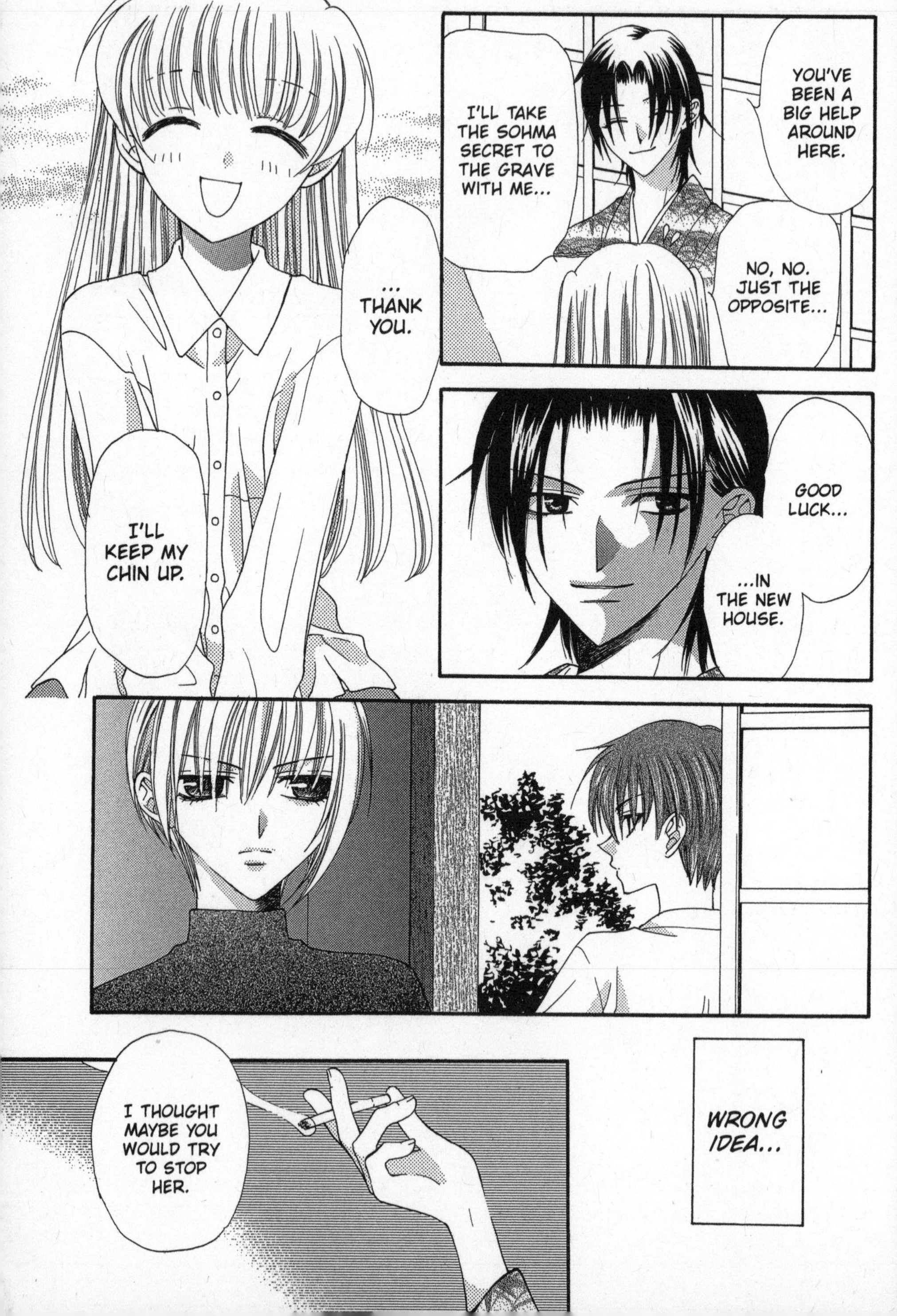
YOU'VE BEEN A BIG HELP AROUND HERE.
NO, NO. JUST THE OPPOSITE...
I'LL TAKE THE SOHMA SECRET TO THE GRAVE WITH ME...
GOOD LUCK...
...IN THE NEW HOUSE.
...THANK YOU.
I'LL KEEP MY CHIN UP.
WRONG IDEA...
I THOUGHT MAYBE YOU WOULD TRY TO STOP HER.

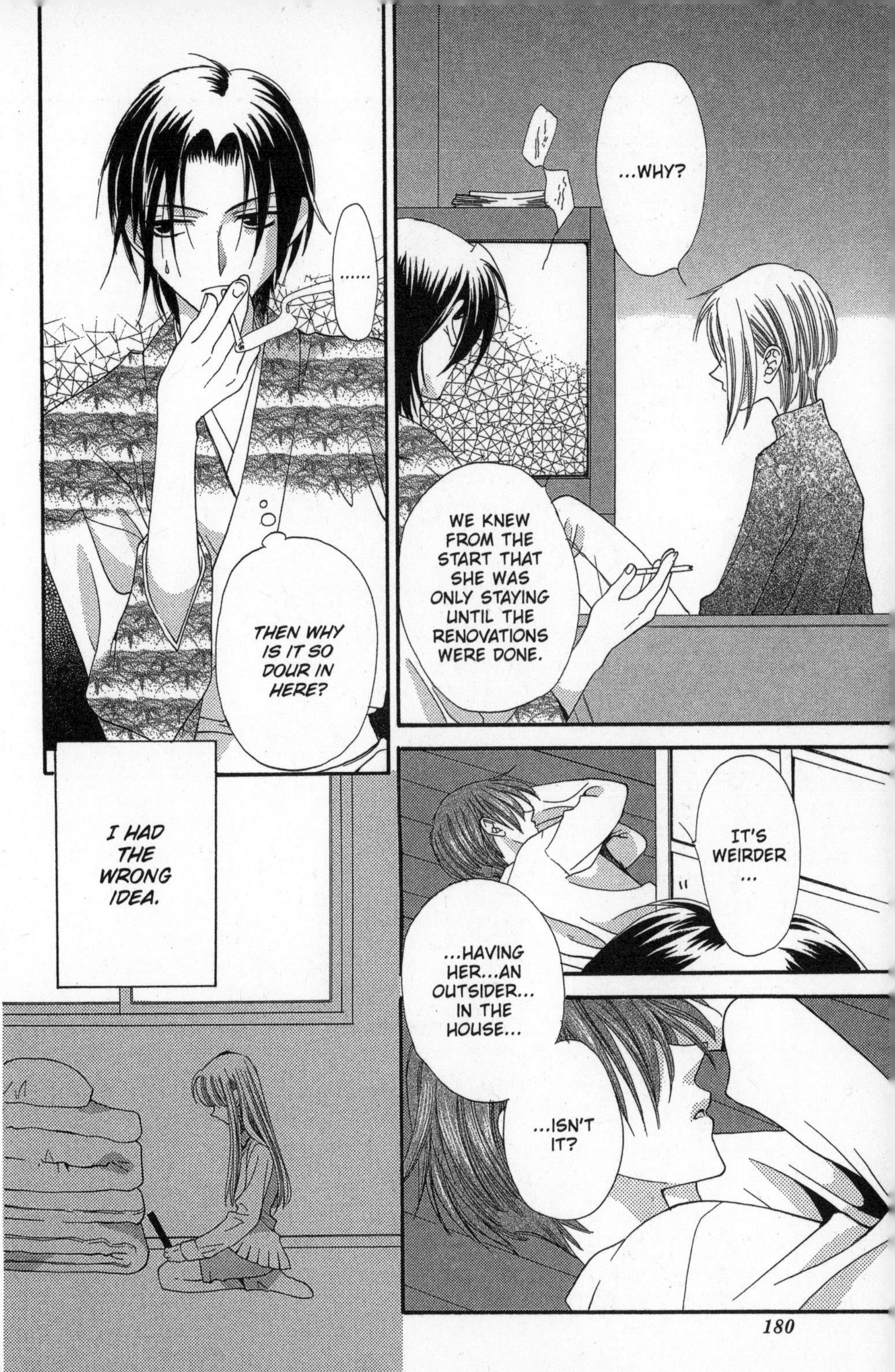
...WHY?
WE KNEW FROM THE START THAT SHE WAS ONLY STAYING UNTIL THE RENOVATIONS WERE DONE.
......
THEN WHY IS IT SO DOUR IN HERE?
IT'S WEIRDER ...
...HAVING HER...AN OUTSIDER... IN THE HOUSE...
...ISN'T IT?
I HAD THE WRONG IDEA.

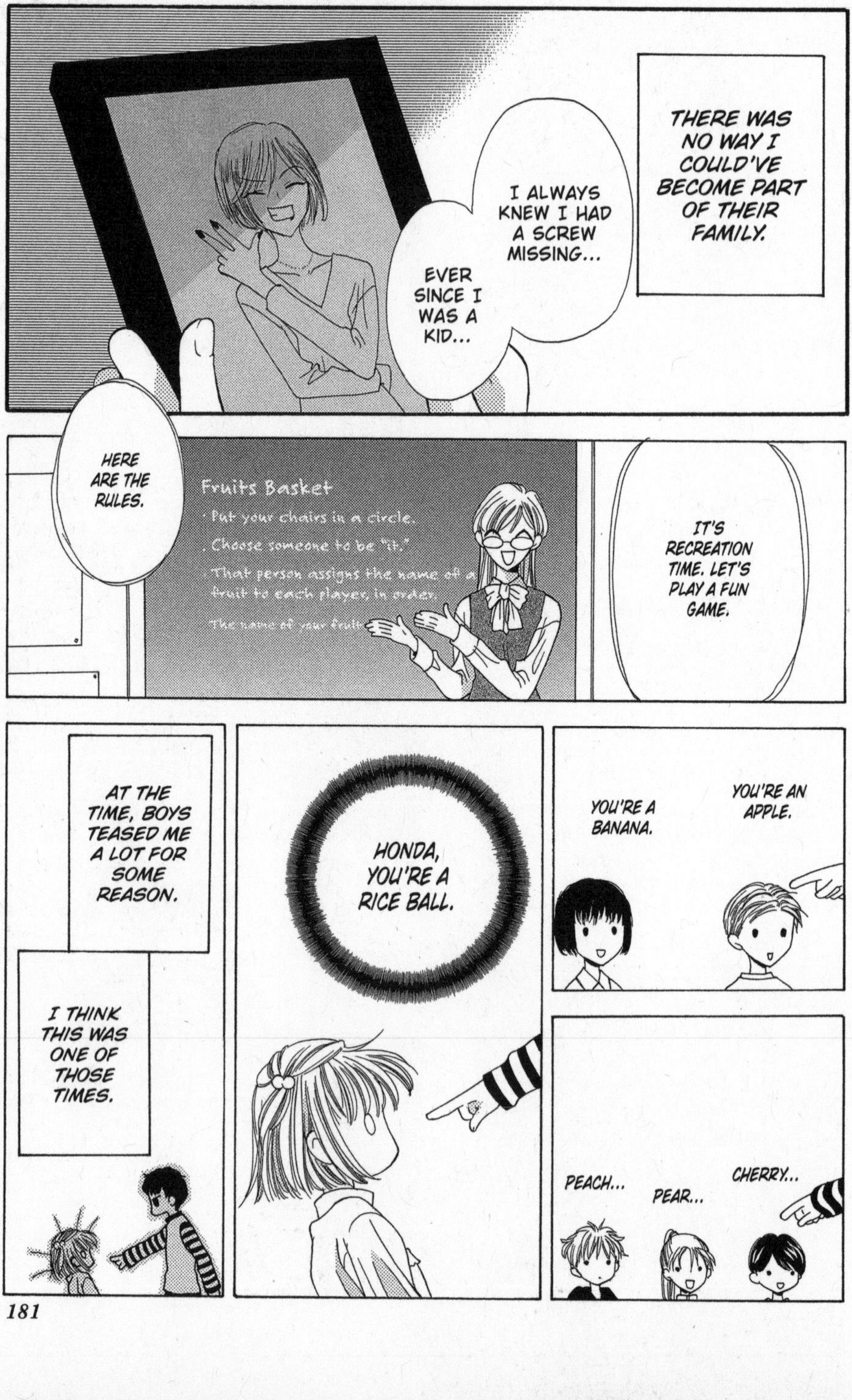
THERE WAS NO WAY I COULD'VE BECOME PART OF THEIR FAMILY.
I ALWAYS KNEW I HAD A SCREW MISSING...
EVER SINCE I WAS A KID...
IT'S RECREATION TIME. LET'S PLAY A FUN GAME.
HERE ARE THE RULES.
Fruits Basket
· Put your chairs in a circle.
· Choose someone to be "it."
· That person assigns the name of a fruit to each player, in order.
· The name of your fruit
YOU'RE AN APPLE.
YOU'RE A BANANA.
CHERRY...
PEAR...
PEACH...
HONDA, YOU'RE A RICE BALL.
AT THE TIME, BOYS TEASED ME A LOT FOR SOME REASON.
I THINK THIS WAS ONE OF THOSE TIMES.

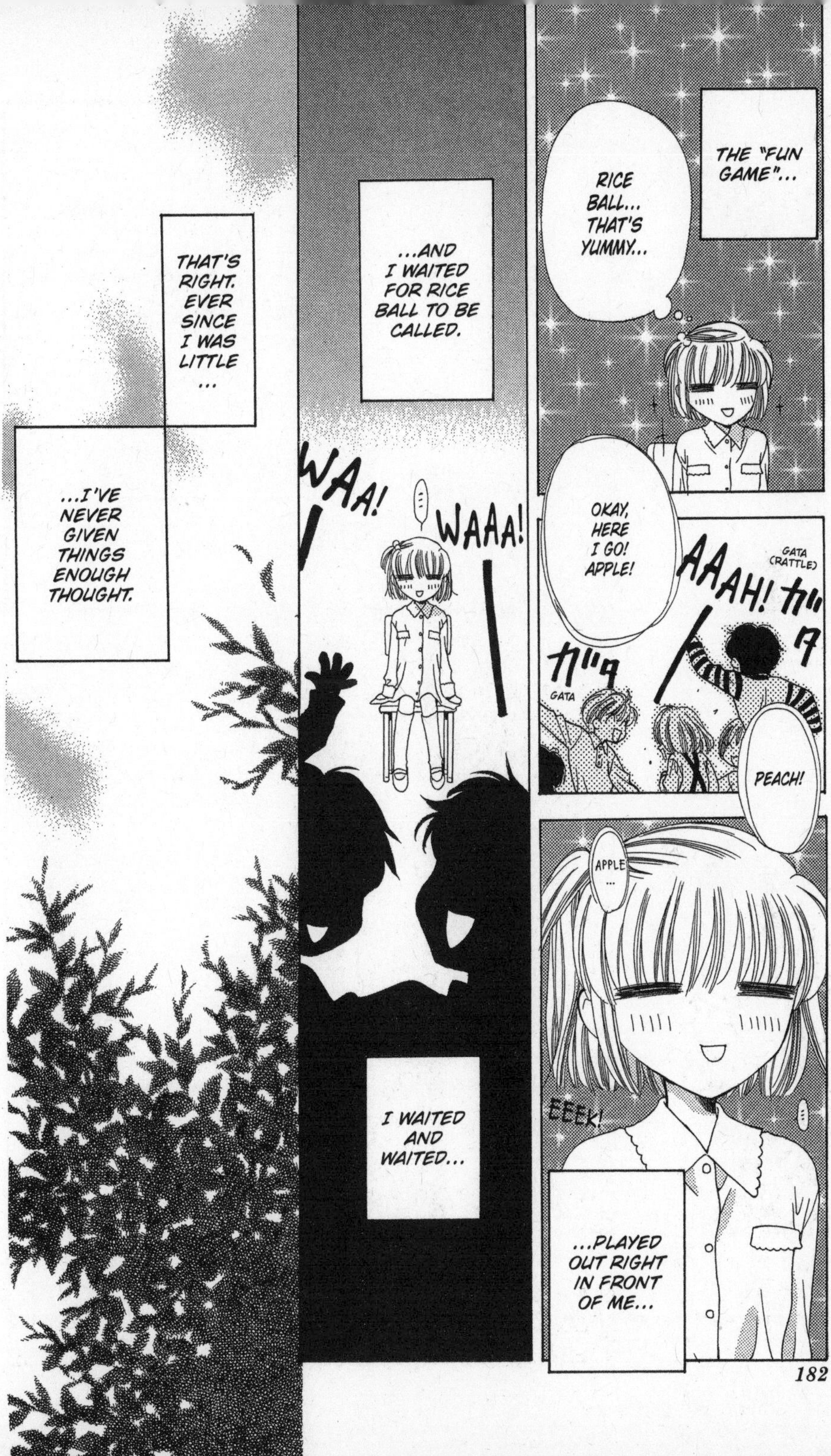
THE "FUN GAME"...
RICE BALL... THAT'S YUMMY...
OKAY, HERE I GO! APPLE!
AAAH!
GATA (RATTLE)
ガタ
ガタ
GATA
PEACH!
APPLE...
EEEK!
...PLAYED OUT RIGHT IN FRONT OF ME...
...AND I WAITED FOR RICE BALL TO BE CALLED.
WAAA!
WAAAA!
I WAITED AND WAITED...
THAT'S RIGHT. EVER SINCE I WAS LITTLE...
...I'VE NEVER GIVEN THINGS ENOUGH THOUGHT.

Fruits Basket

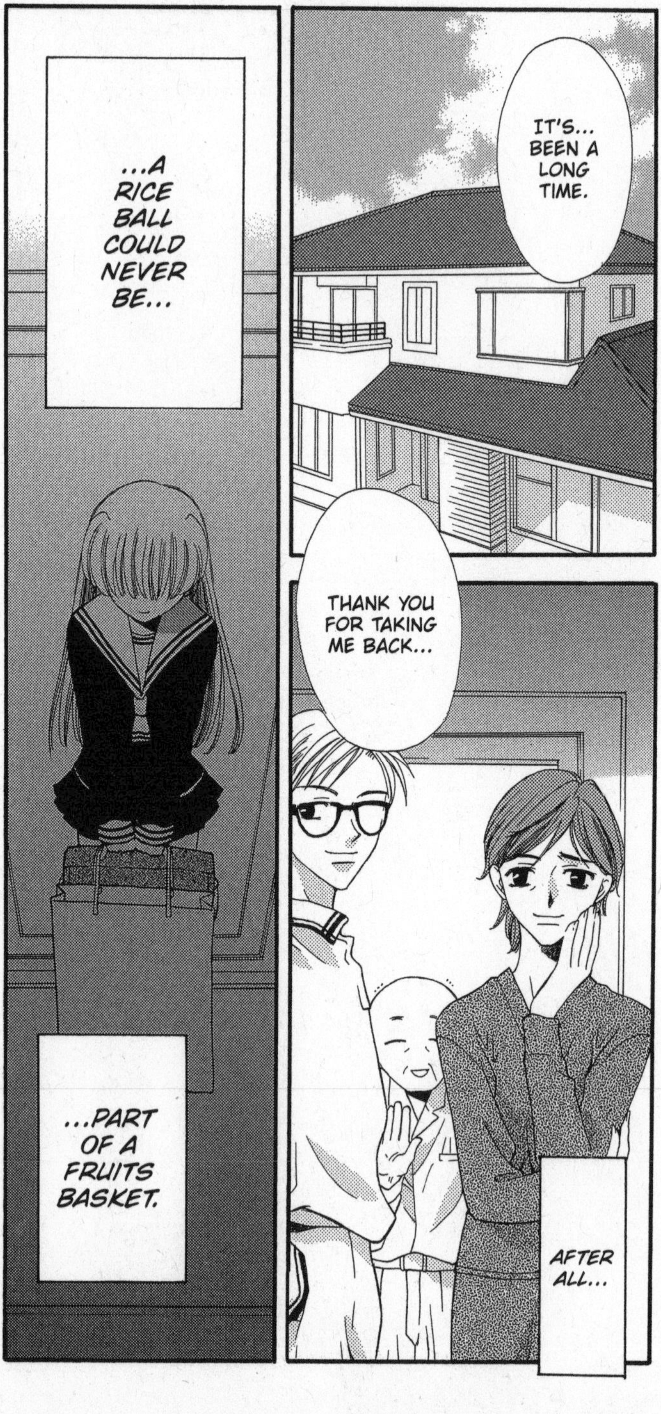

IT'S... BEEN A LONG TIME.
THANK YOU FOR TAKING ME BACK...
AFTER ALL...
...A RICE BALL COULD NEVER BE...
...PART OF A FRUITS BASKET.

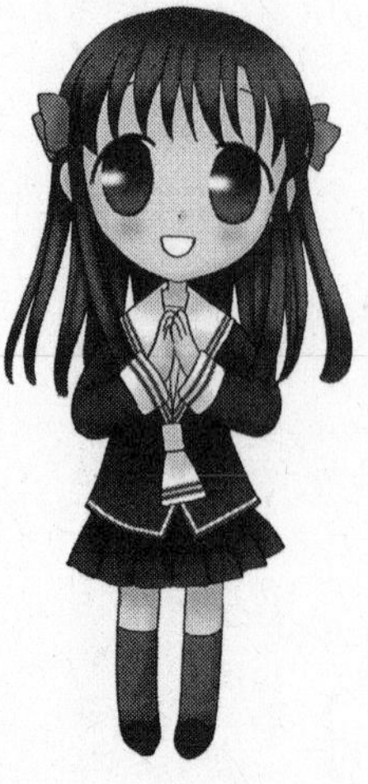

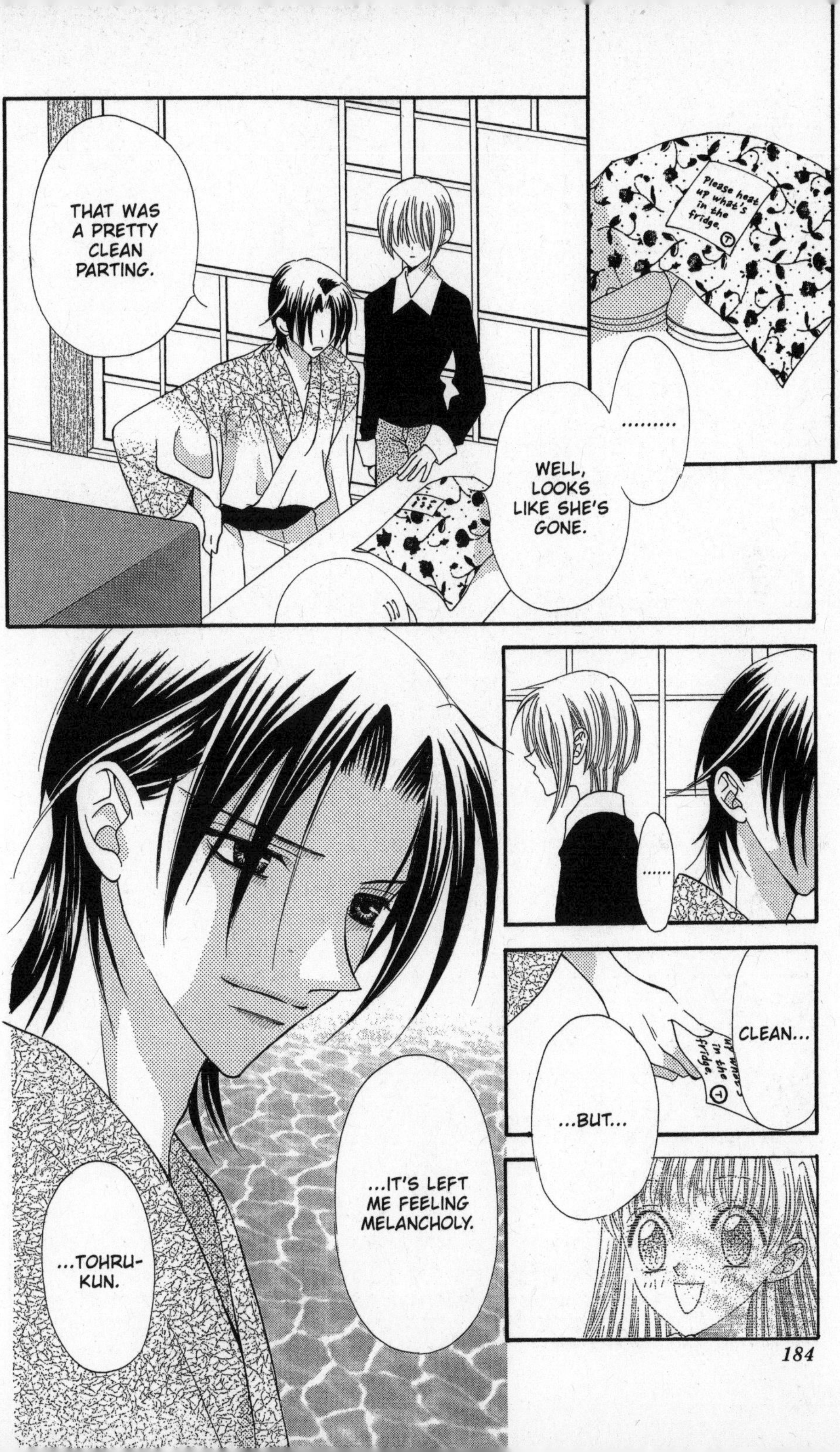
Please heat up what's in the fridge. T
....
WELL, LOOKS LIKE SHE'S GONE.
THAT WAS A PRETTY CLEAN PARTING.
......
CLEAN...
...BUT...
...IT'S LEFT ME FEELING MELANCHOLY.
...TOHRU-KUN.

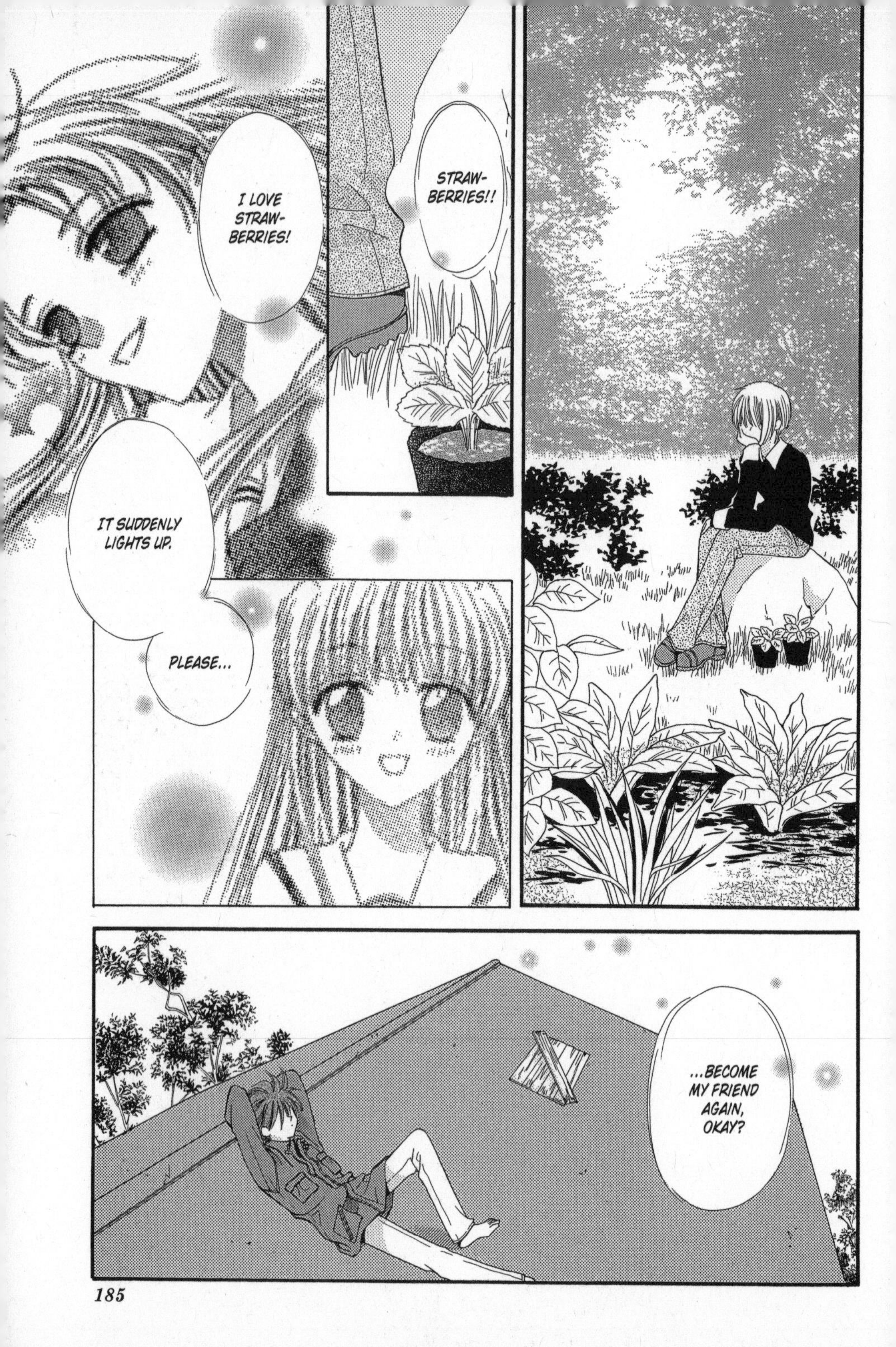
STRAW-BERRIES!!
I LOVE STRAW-BERRIES!
IT SUDDENLY LIGHTS UP.
PLEASE...
...BECOME MY FRIEND AGAIN, OKAY?

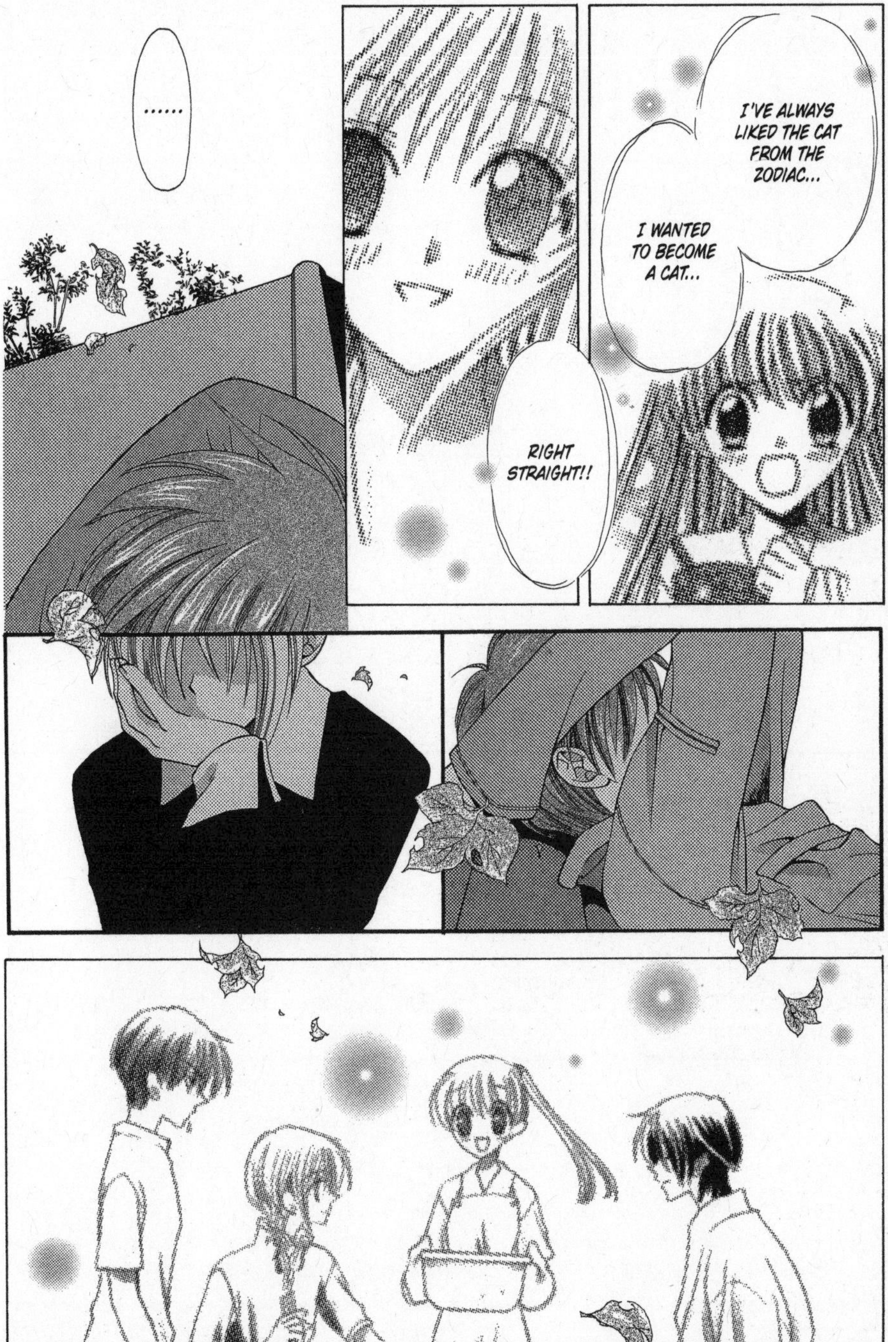
I'VE ALWAYS LIKED THE CAT FROM THE ZODIAC...
I WANTED TO BECOME A CAT...
RIGHT STRAIGHT!!
......

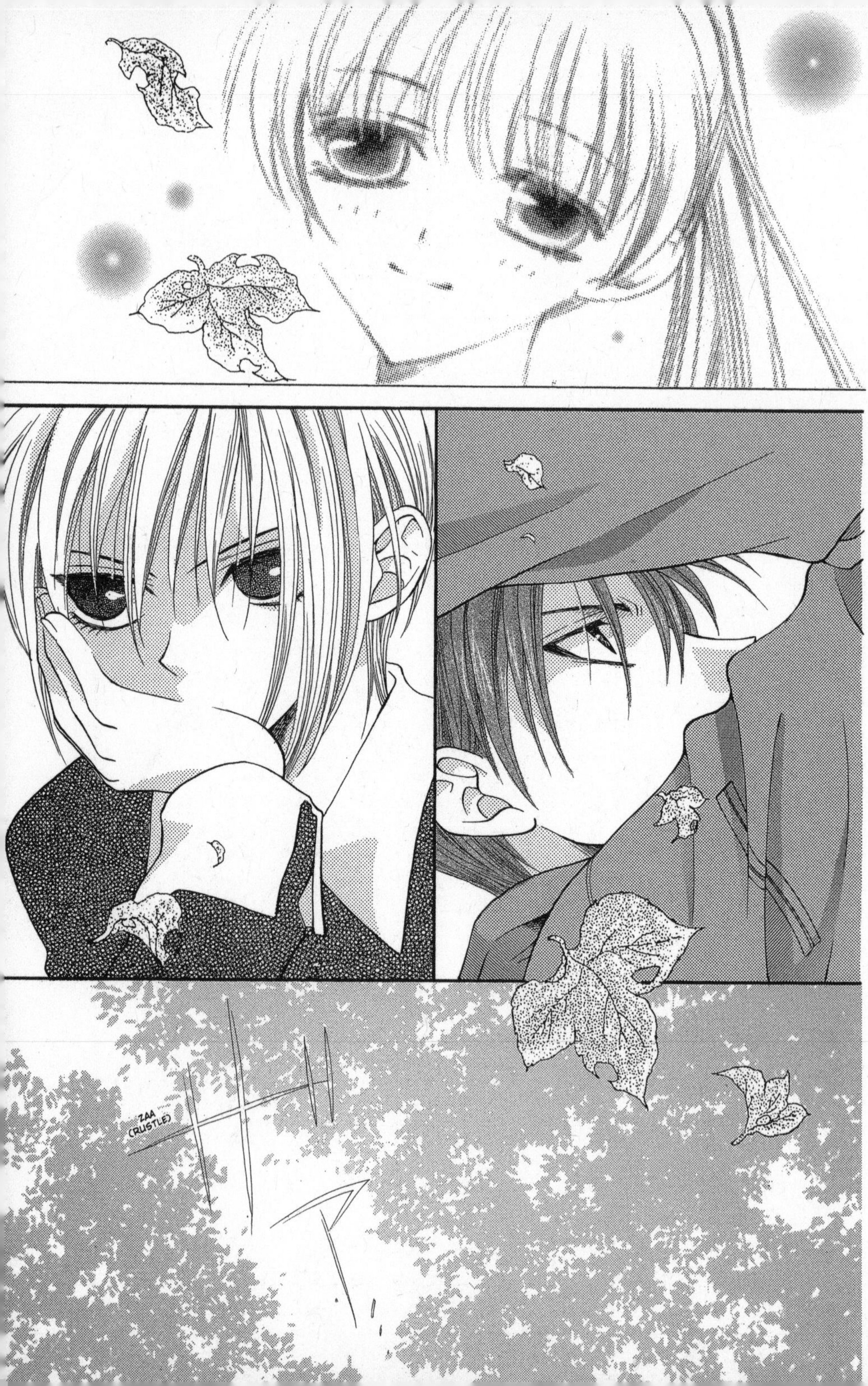
ZAA
(RUSTLE)

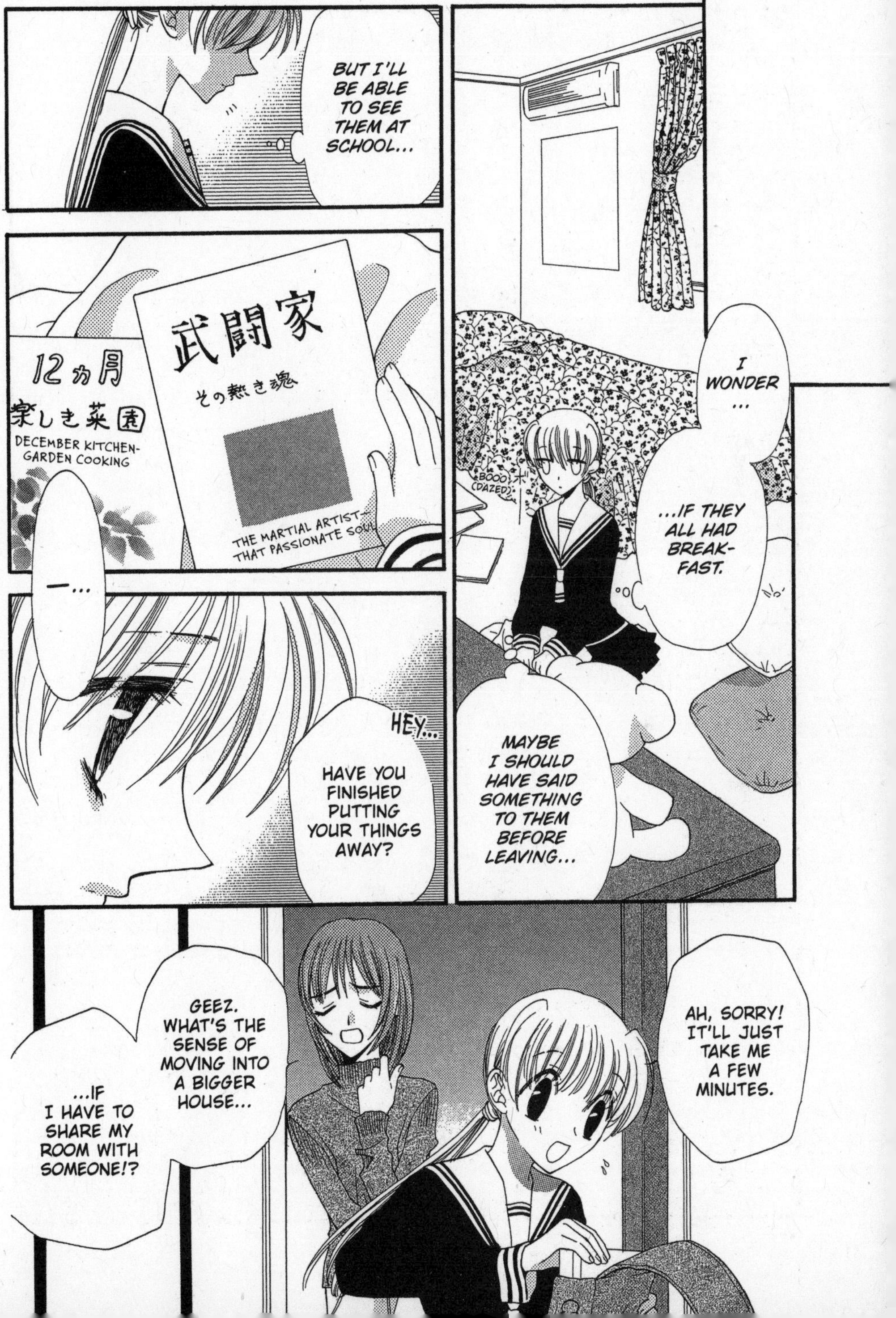

I WONDER...
...IF THEY ALL HAD BREAKFAST.
BOOO (DAZED)
MAYBE I SHOULD HAVE SAID SOMETHING TO THEM BEFORE LEAVING...
BUT I'LL BE ABLE TO SEE THEM AT SCHOOL...
武闘家
その熱き魂
THE MARTIAL ARTIST—THAT PASSIONATE SOUL
12ヵ月
楽しき菜園
DECEMBER KITCHEN-GARDEN COOKING
HEY...
HAVE YOU FINISHED PUTTING YOUR THINGS AWAY?
—...
AH, SORRY! IT'LL JUST TAKE ME A FEW MINUTES.
GEEZ. WHAT'S THE SENSE OF MOVING INTO A BIGGER HOUSE...
...IF I HAVE TO SHARE MY ROOM WITH SOMEONE!?

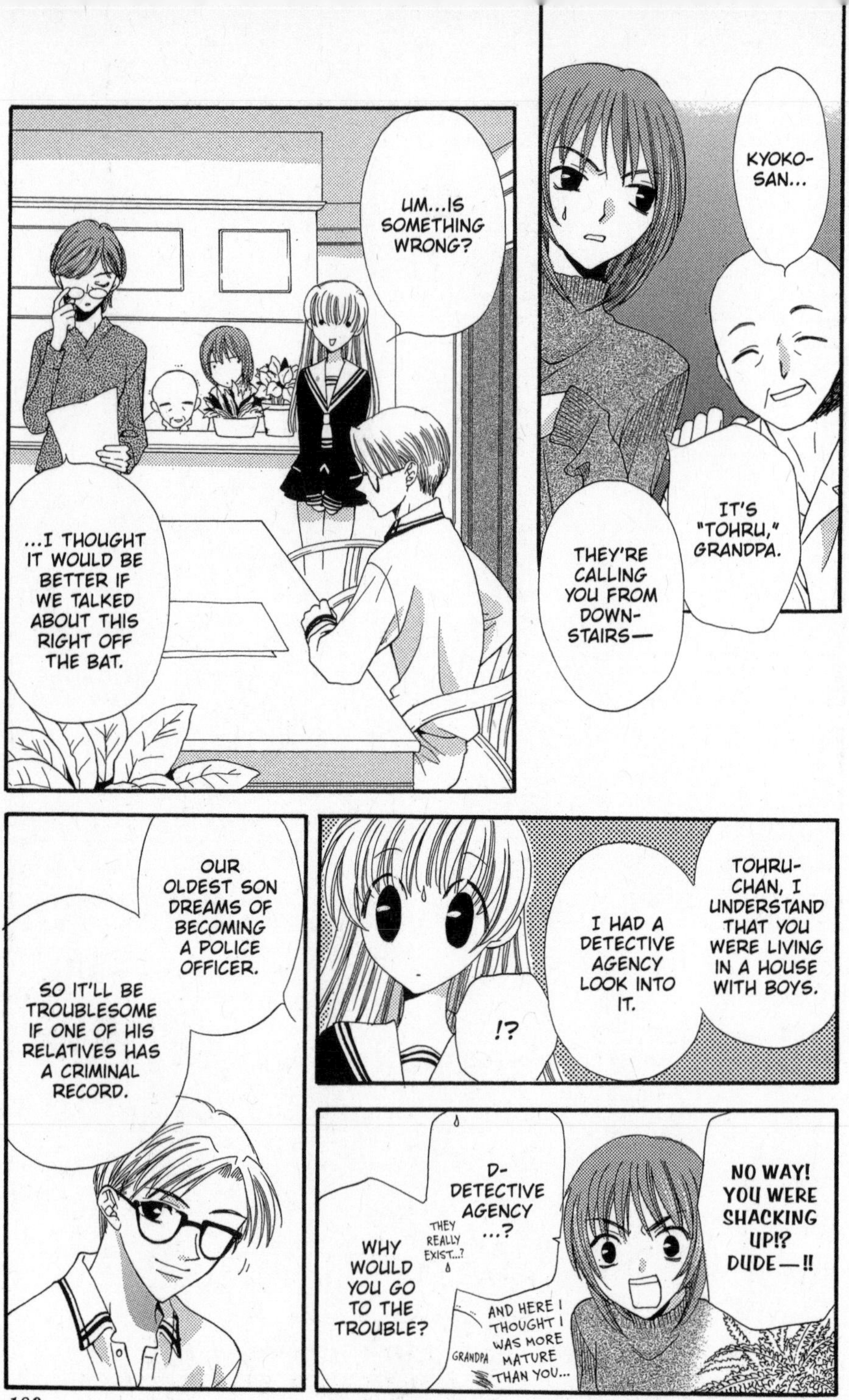
KYOKO-SAN...
IT'S "TOHRU," GRANDPA.
THEY'RE CALLING YOU FROM DOWN-STAIRS—
UM...IS SOMETHING WRONG?
...I THOUGHT IT WOULD BE BETTER IF WE TALKED ABOUT THIS RIGHT OFF THE BAT.
TOHRU-CHAN, I UNDERSTAND THAT YOU WERE LIVING IN A HOUSE WITH BOYS.
I HAD A DETECTIVE AGENCY LOOK INTO IT.
!?
NO WAY! YOU WERE SHACKING UP!? DUDE—!!
D-DETECTIVE AGENCY...?
THEY REALLY EXIST...?
WHY WOULD YOU GO TO THE TROUBLE?
AND HERE I THOUGHT I WAS MORE MATURE THAN YOU...
GRANDPA
OUR OLDEST SON DREAMS OF BECOMING A POLICE OFFICER.
SO IT'LL BE TROUBLESOME IF ONE OF HIS RELATIVES HAS A CRIMINAL RECORD.

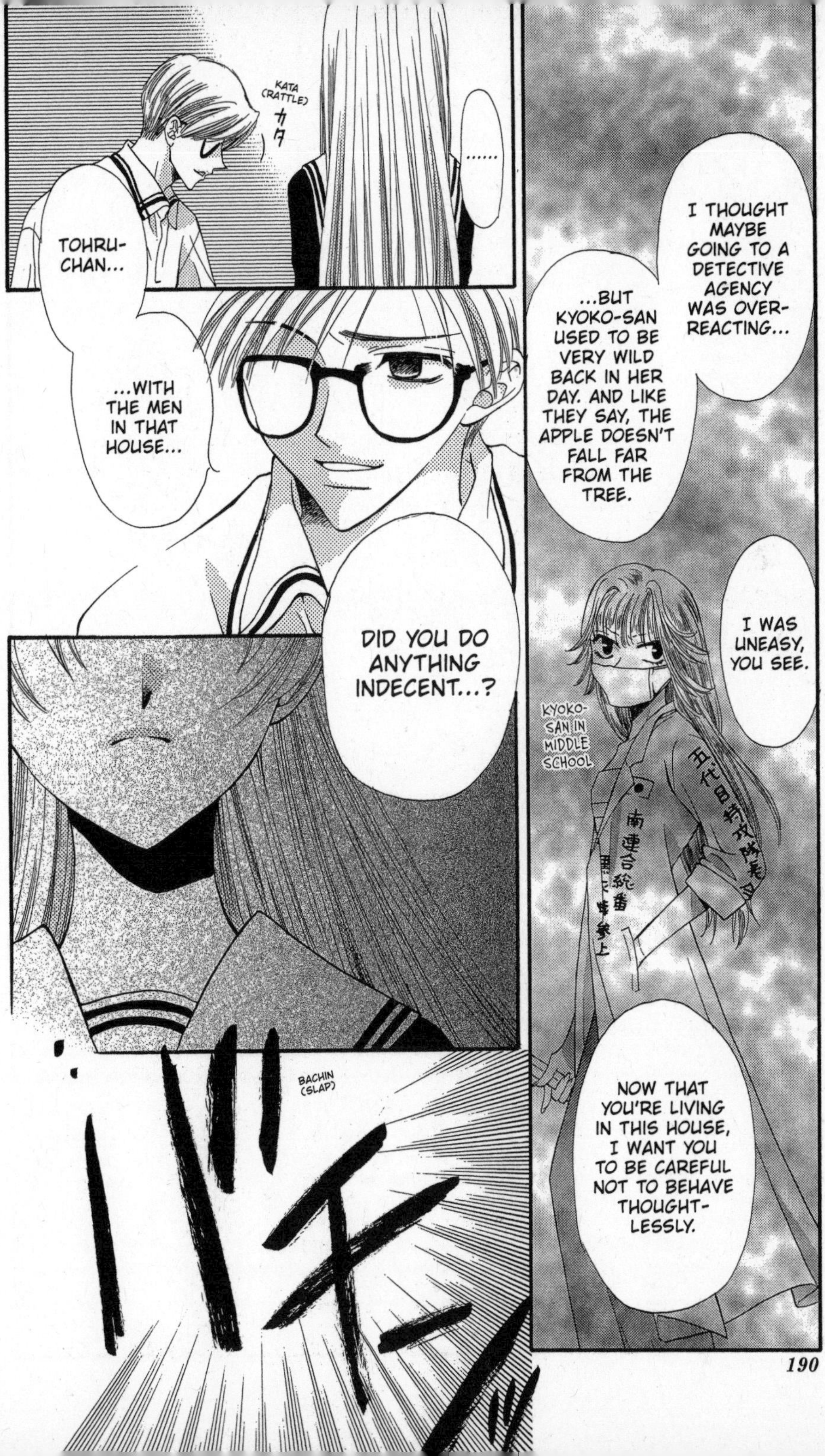

I THOUGHT MAYBE GOING TO A DETECTIVE AGENCY WAS OVER-REACTING...
...BUT KYOKO-SAN USED TO BE VERY WILD BACK IN HER DAY. AND LIKE THEY SAY, THE APPLE DOESN'T FALL FAR FROM THE TREE.
I WAS UNEASY, YOU SEE.
KYOKO-SAN IN MIDDLE SCHOOL
NOW THAT YOU'RE LIVING IN THIS HOUSE, I WANT YOU TO BE CAREFUL NOT TO BEHAVE THOUGHT-LESSLY.
KATA (RATTLE)
カタ
......
TOHRU-CHAN...
...WITH THE MEN IN THAT HOUSE...
DID YOU DO ANYTHING INDECENT...?
BACHIN (SLAP)

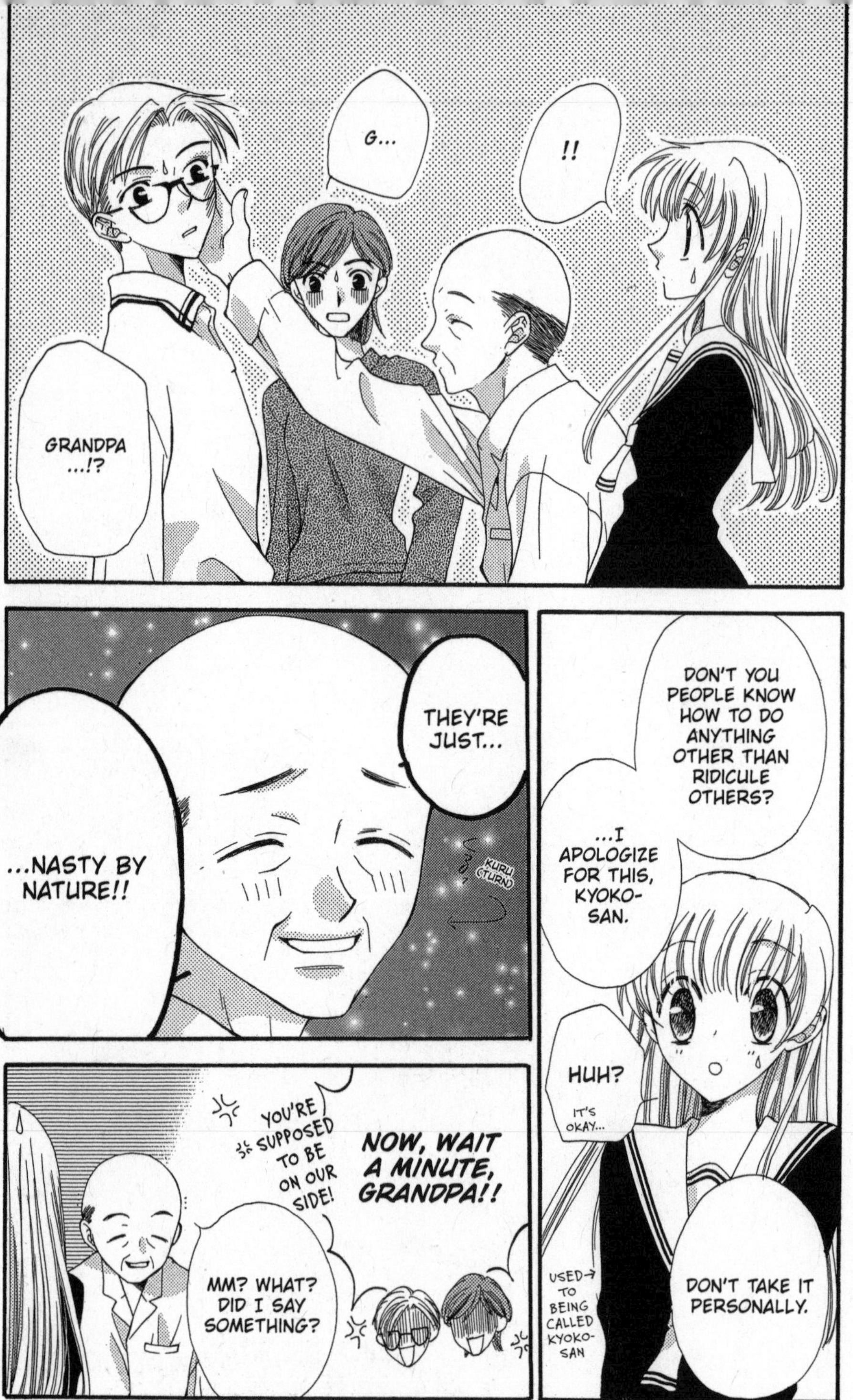
!!
G...
GRANDPA ...!?
DON'T YOU PEOPLE KNOW HOW TO DO ANYTHING OTHER THAN RIDICULE OTHERS?
...I APOLOGIZE FOR THIS, KYOKO-SAN.
HUH?
IT'S OKAY...
DON'T TAKE IT PERSONALLY.
USED TO BEING CALLED KYOKO-SAN
THEY'RE JUST...
...NASTY BY NATURE!!
KURU (TURN)
NOW, WAIT A MINUTE, GRANDPA!!
YOU'RE SUPPOSED TO BE ON OUR SIDE!
MM? WHAT? DID I SAY SOMETHING?

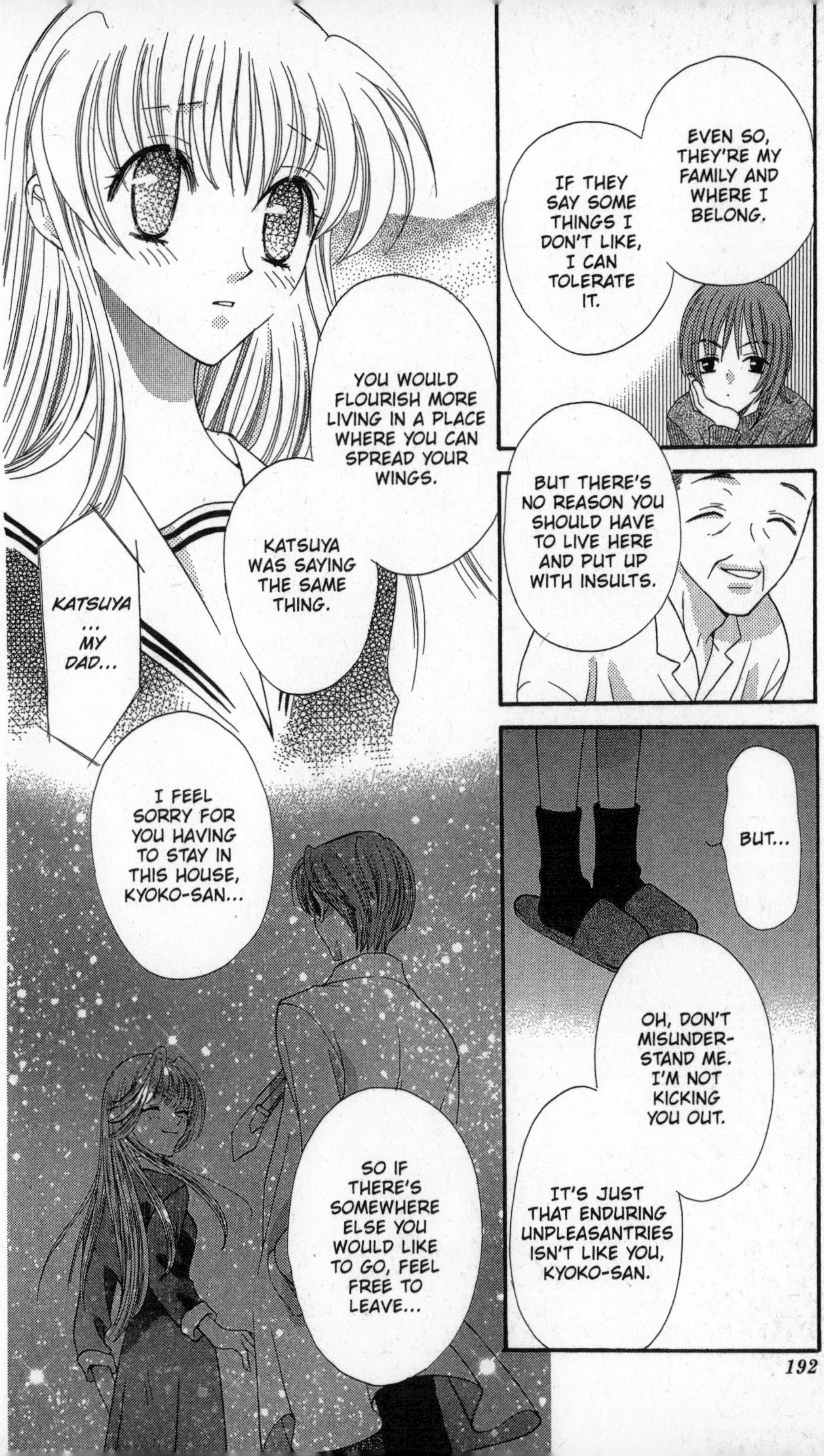
EVEN SO, THEY'RE MY FAMILY AND WHERE I BELONG.
IF THEY SAY SOME THINGS I DON'T LIKE, I CAN TOLERATE IT.
BUT THERE'S NO REASON YOU SHOULD HAVE TO LIVE HERE AND PUT UP WITH INSULTS.
BUT...
OH, DON'T MISUNDER-STAND ME. I'M NOT KICKING YOU OUT.
IT'S JUST THAT ENDURING UNPLEASANTRIES ISN'T LIKE YOU, KYOKO-SAN.
YOU WOULD FLOURISH MORE LIVING IN A PLACE WHERE YOU CAN SPREAD YOUR WINGS.
KATSUYA WAS SAYING THE SAME THING.
KATSUYA ... MY DAD...
I FEEL SORRY FOR YOU HAVING TO STAY IN THIS HOUSE, KYOKO-SAN...
SO IF THERE'S SOMEWHERE ELSE YOU WOULD LIKE TO GO, FEEL FREE TO LEAVE...

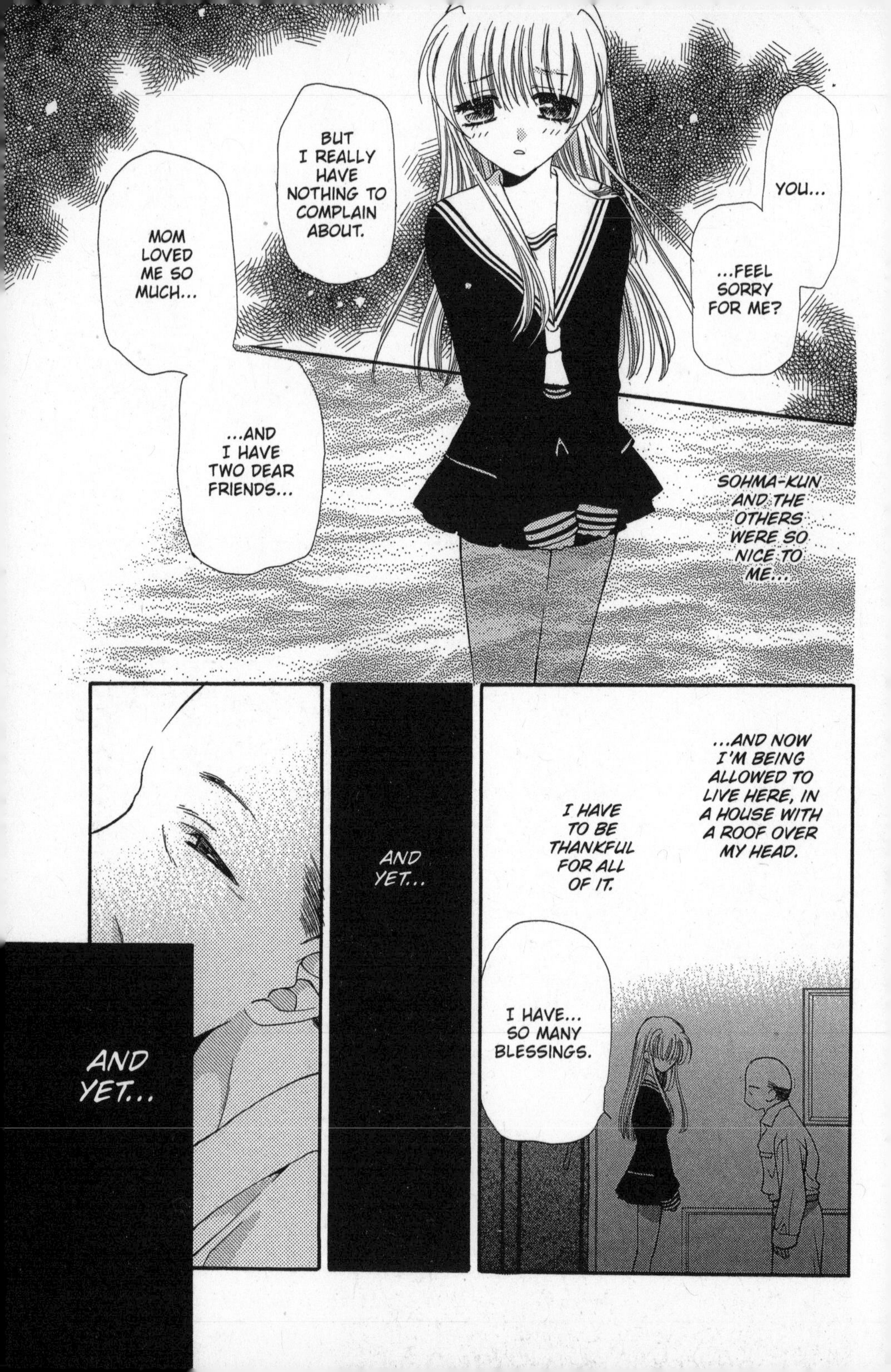
YOU...
...FEEL SORRY FOR ME?
BUT I REALLY HAVE NOTHING TO COMPLAIN ABOUT.
MOM LOVED ME SO MUCH...
...AND I HAVE TWO DEAR FRIENDS...
SOHMA-KUN AND THE OTHERS WERE SO NICE TO ME...
...AND NOW I'M BEING ALLOWED TO LIVE HERE, IN A HOUSE WITH A ROOF OVER MY HEAD.
I HAVE TO BE THANKFUL FOR ALL OF IT.
I HAVE... SO MANY BLESSINGS.
AND YET...
AND YET...

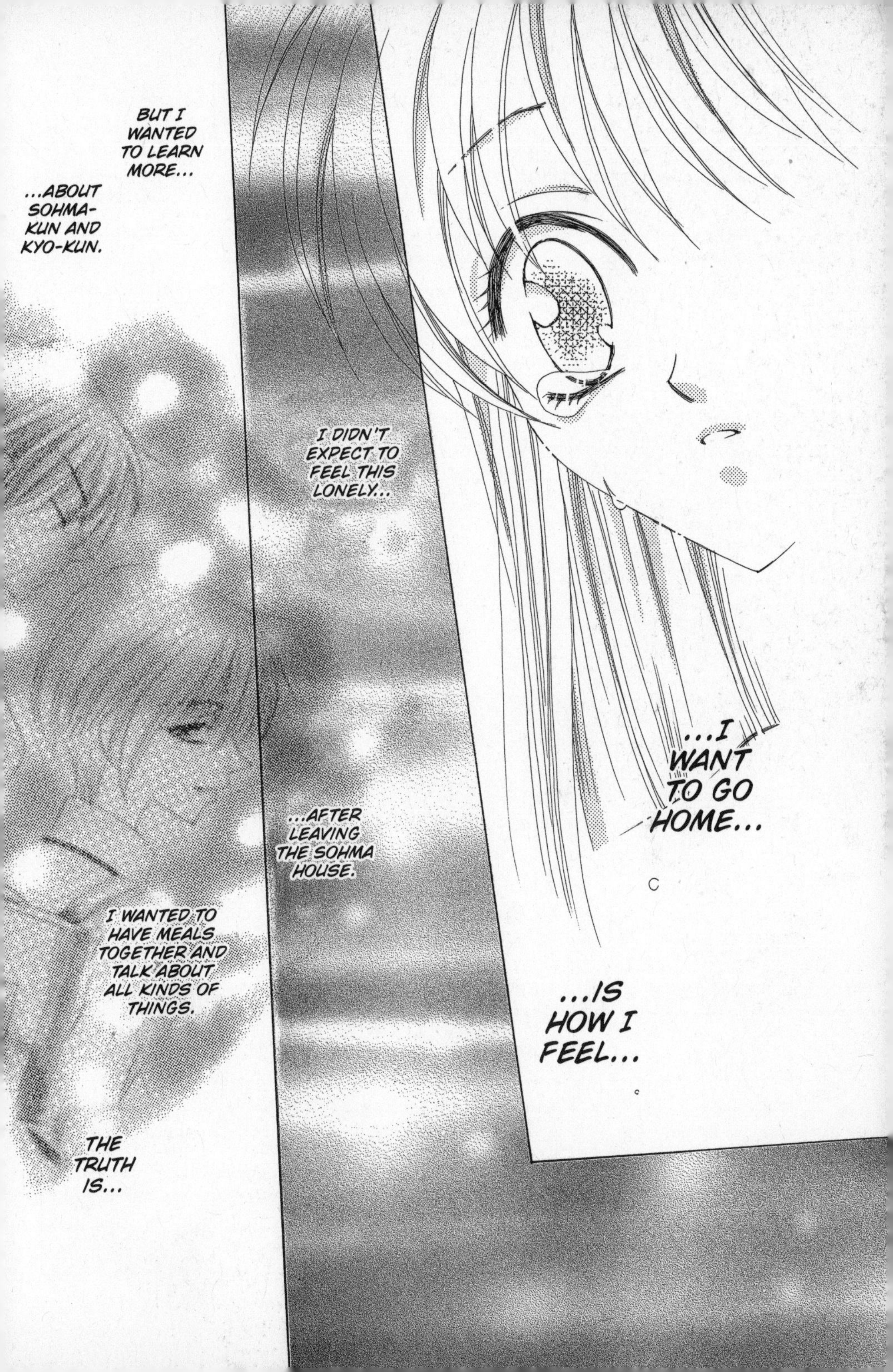
...I WANT TO GO HOME...
...IS HOW I FEEL...
I DIDN'T EXPECT TO FEEL THIS LONELY...
...AFTER LEAVING THE SOHMA HOUSE.
BUT I WANTED TO LEARN MORE...
...ABOUT SOHMA-KUN AND KYO-KUN.
I WANTED TO HAVE MEALS TOGETHER AND TALK ABOUT ALL KINDS OF THINGS.
THE TRUTH IS...

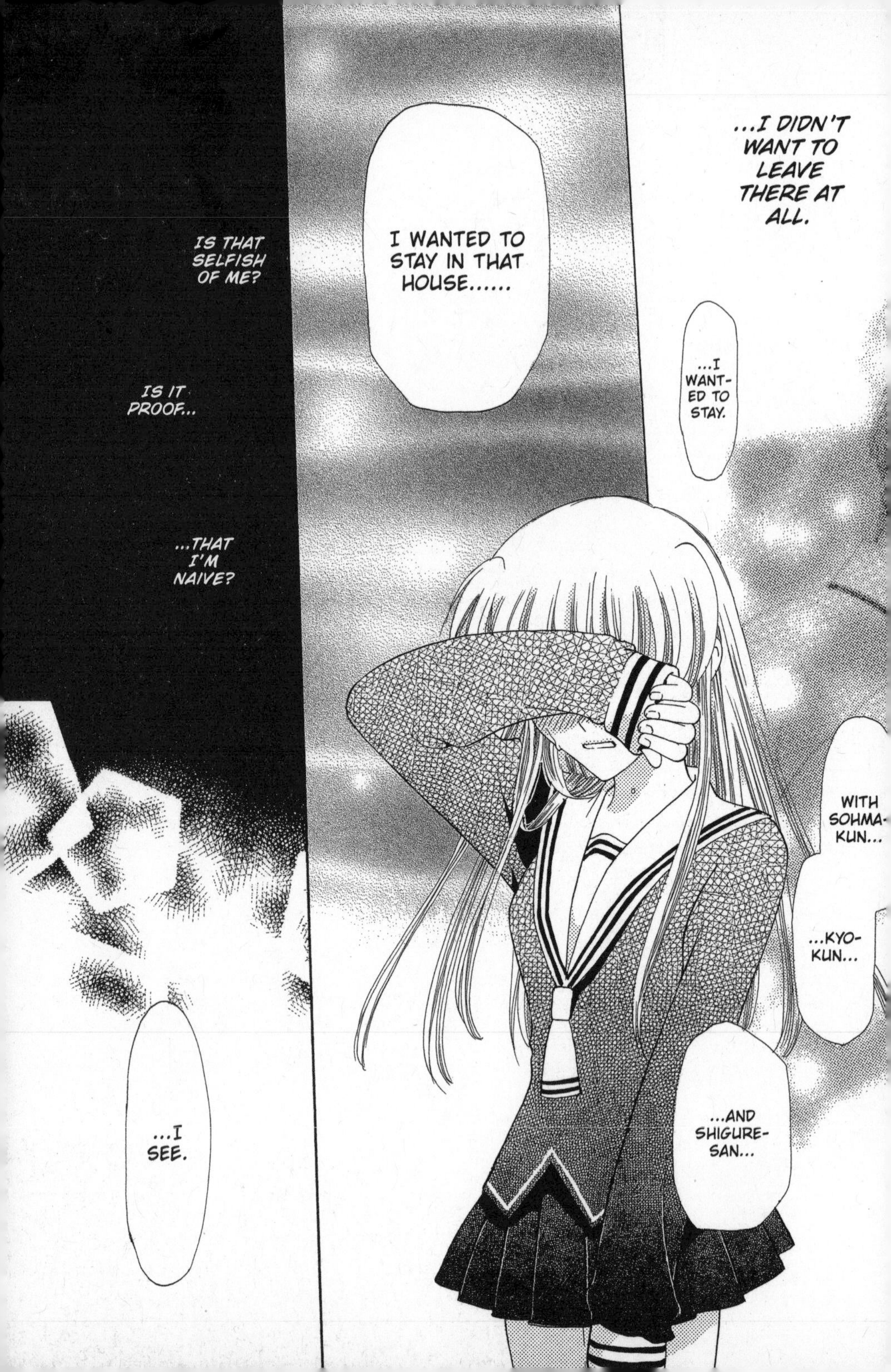
...I DIDN'T WANT TO LEAVE THERE AT ALL.
I WANTED TO STAY IN THAT HOUSE......
...I WANTED TO STAY.
WITH SOHMA-KUN...
...KYO-KUN...
...AND SHIGURE-SAN...
IS THAT SELFISH OF ME?
IS IT PROOF...
...THAT I'M NAIVE?
...I SEE.

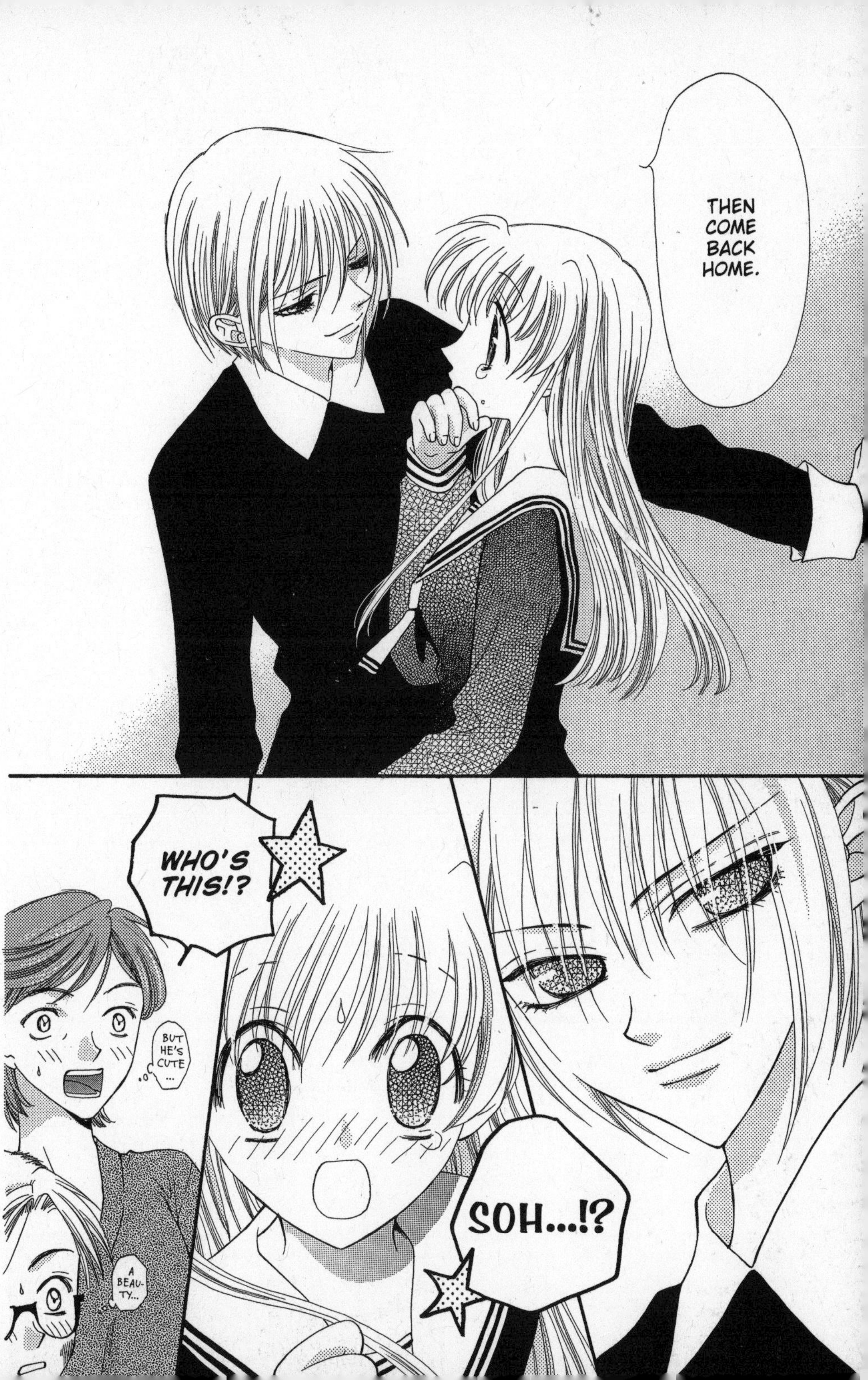
THEN COME BACK HOME.
SOH...!?
WHO'S THIS!?
BUT HE'S CUTE ...
A BEAU-TY...

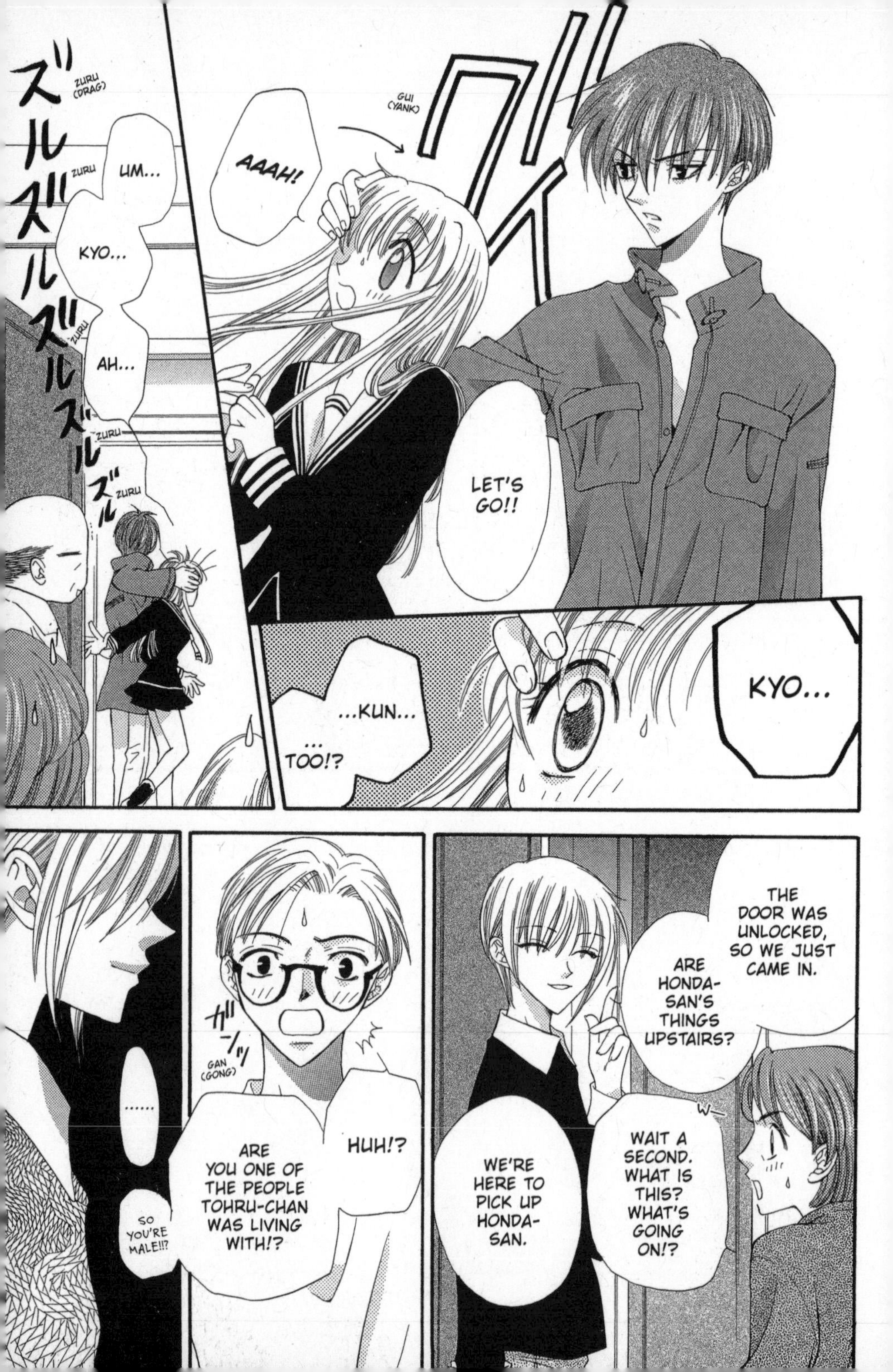

GUI (YANK)
AAAH!
LET'S GO!!
KYO...
...KUN...
... TOO!?
ZURU (DRAG)
UM...
ZURU
KYO...
ZURU
AH...
ZURU
ZURU
THE DOOR WAS UNLOCKED, SO WE JUST CAME IN.
ARE HONDA-SAN'S THINGS UPSTAIRS?
W—
WAIT A SECOND. WHAT IS THIS? WHAT'S GOING ON!?
WE'RE HERE TO PICK UP HONDA-SAN.
GAN (GONG)
HUH!?
ARE YOU ONE OF THE PEOPLE TOHRU-CHAN WAS LIVING WITH!?
......
SO YOU'RE MALE!!?

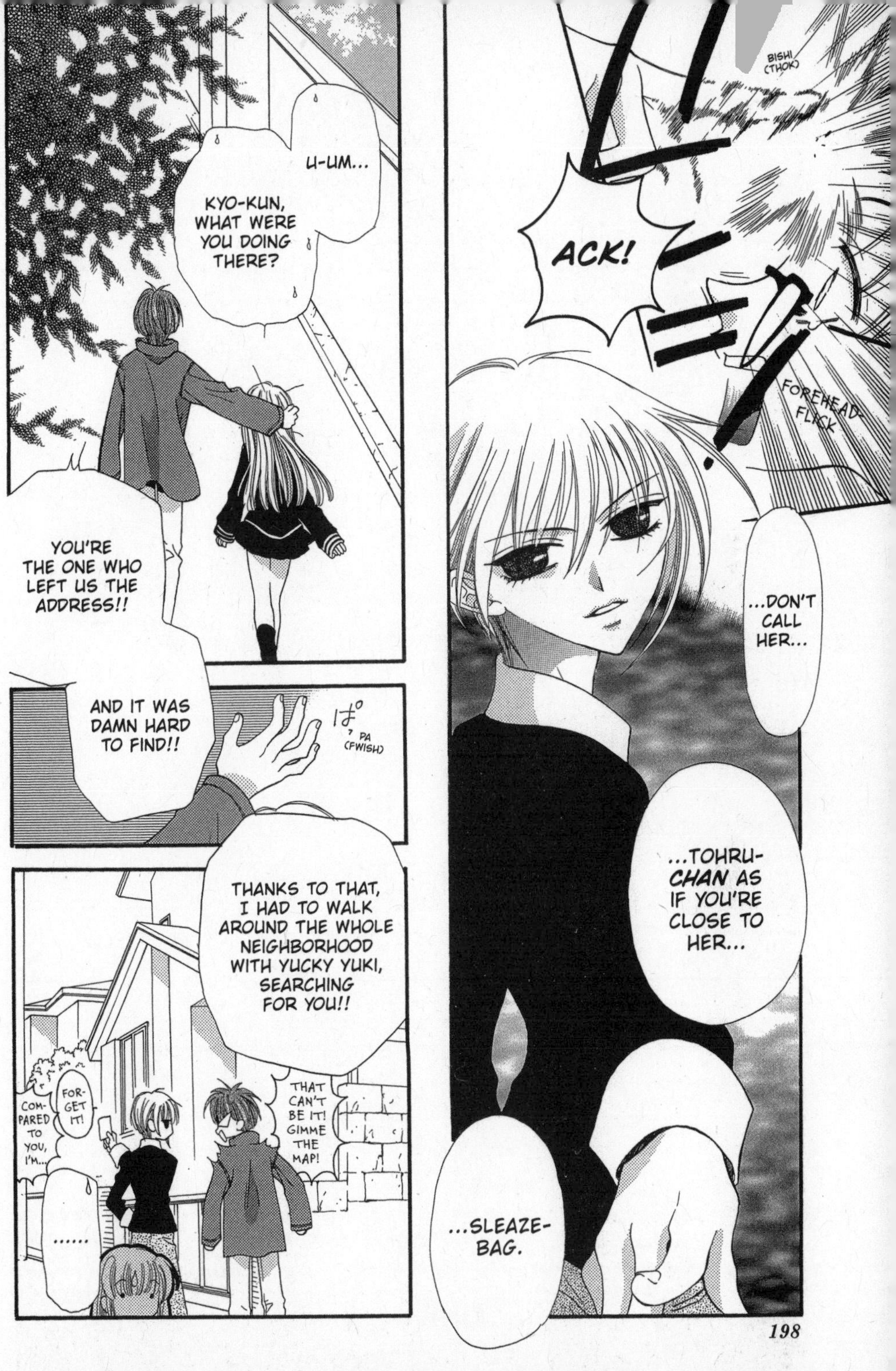
BISHI (THOK)
ACK!
FOREHEAD-FLICK
...DON'T CALL HER...
...TOHRU-*CHAN* AS IF YOU'RE CLOSE TO HER...
...SLEAZE-BAG.
U-UM...
KYO-KUN, WHAT WERE YOU DOING THERE?
YOU'RE THE ONE WHO LEFT US THE ADDRESS!!
AND IT WAS DAMN HARD TO FIND!!
ぱ PA (FWISH)
THANKS TO THAT, I HAD TO WALK AROUND THE WHOLE NEIGHBORHOOD WITH YUCKY YUKI, SEARCHING FOR YOU!!
THAT CAN'T BE IT! GIMME THE MAP!
FOR-GET IT!
COM-PARED TO YOU, I'M...
......

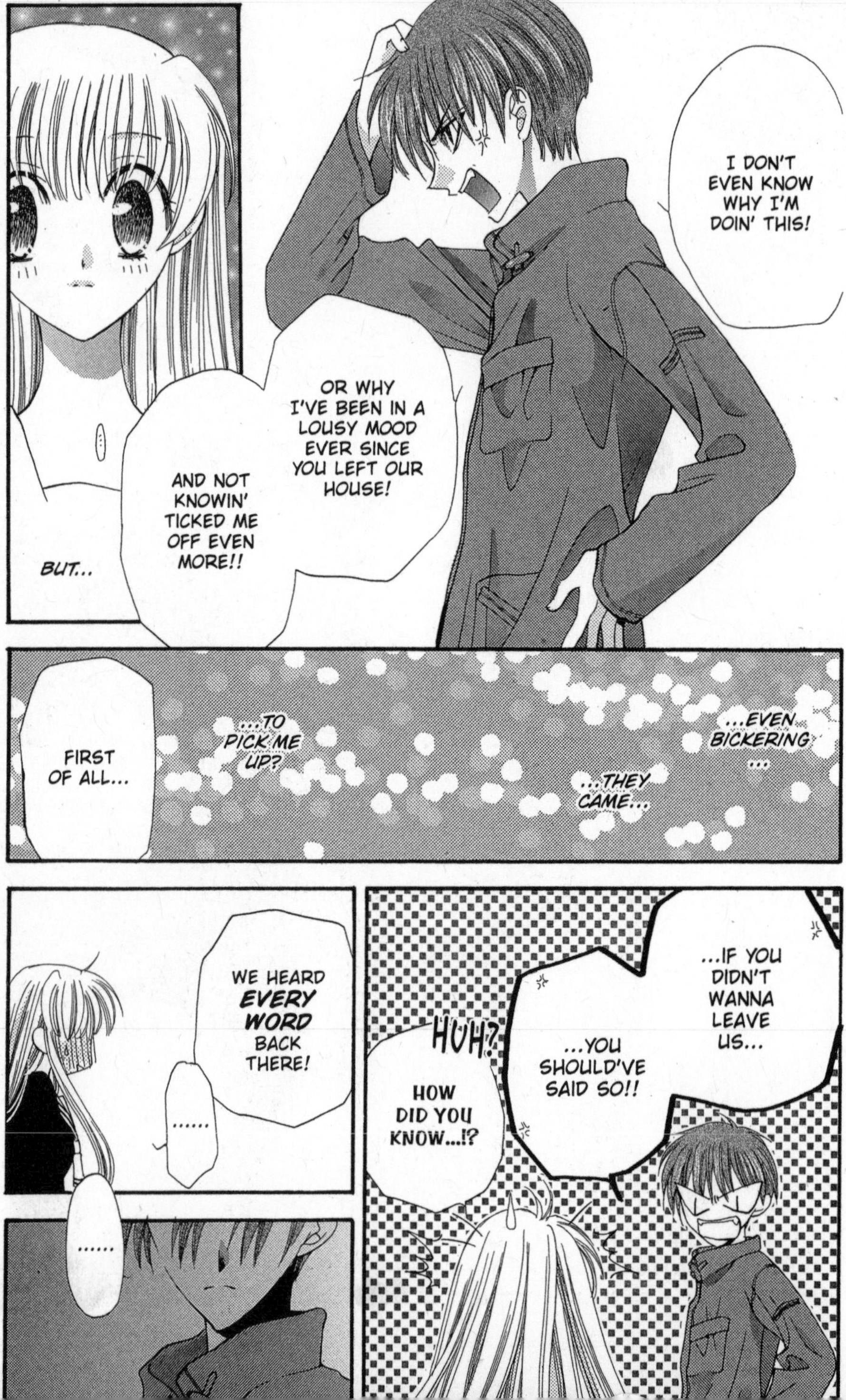
I DON'T EVEN KNOW WHY I'M DOIN' THIS!
OR WHY I'VE BEEN IN A LOUSY MOOD EVER SINCE YOU LEFT OUR HOUSE!
AND NOT KNOWIN' TICKED ME OFF EVEN MORE!!
...
BUT...
...EVEN BICKERING...
...THEY CAME...
...TO PICK ME UP?
FIRST OF ALL...
...IF YOU DIDN'T WANNA LEAVE US...
...YOU SHOULD'VE SAID SO!!
HUH?
HOW DID YOU KNOW...!?
WE HEARD EVERY WORD BACK THERE!
......
......

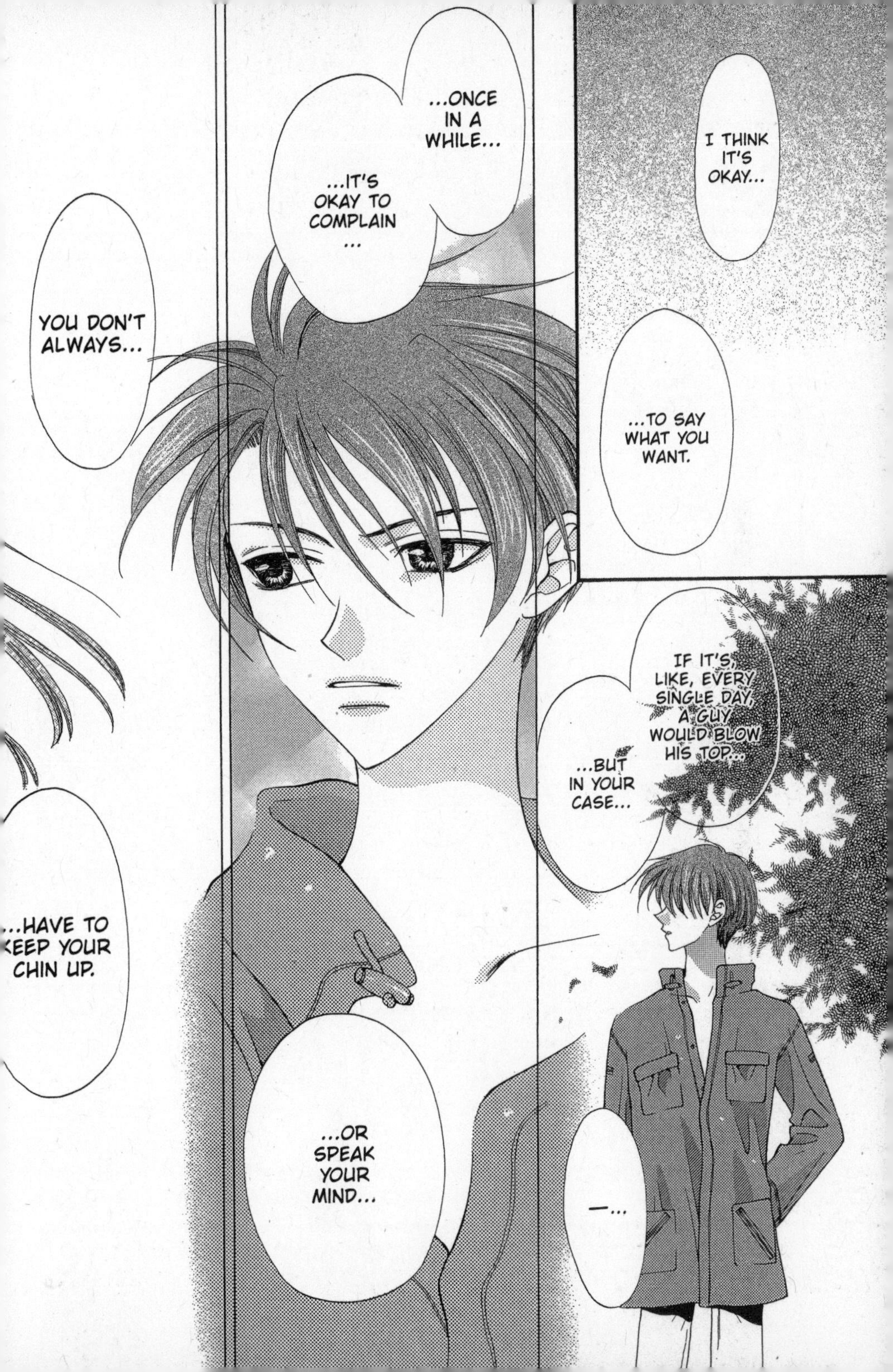
I THINK IT'S OKAY...
...TO SAY WHAT YOU WANT.
IF IT'S, LIKE, EVERY SINGLE DAY, A GUY WOULD BLOW HIS TOP...
...BUT IN YOUR CASE...
—...
...ONCE IN A WHILE...
...IT'S OKAY TO COMPLAIN ...
...OR SPEAK YOUR MIND...
YOU DON'T ALWAYS...
...HAVE TO KEEP YOUR CHIN UP.

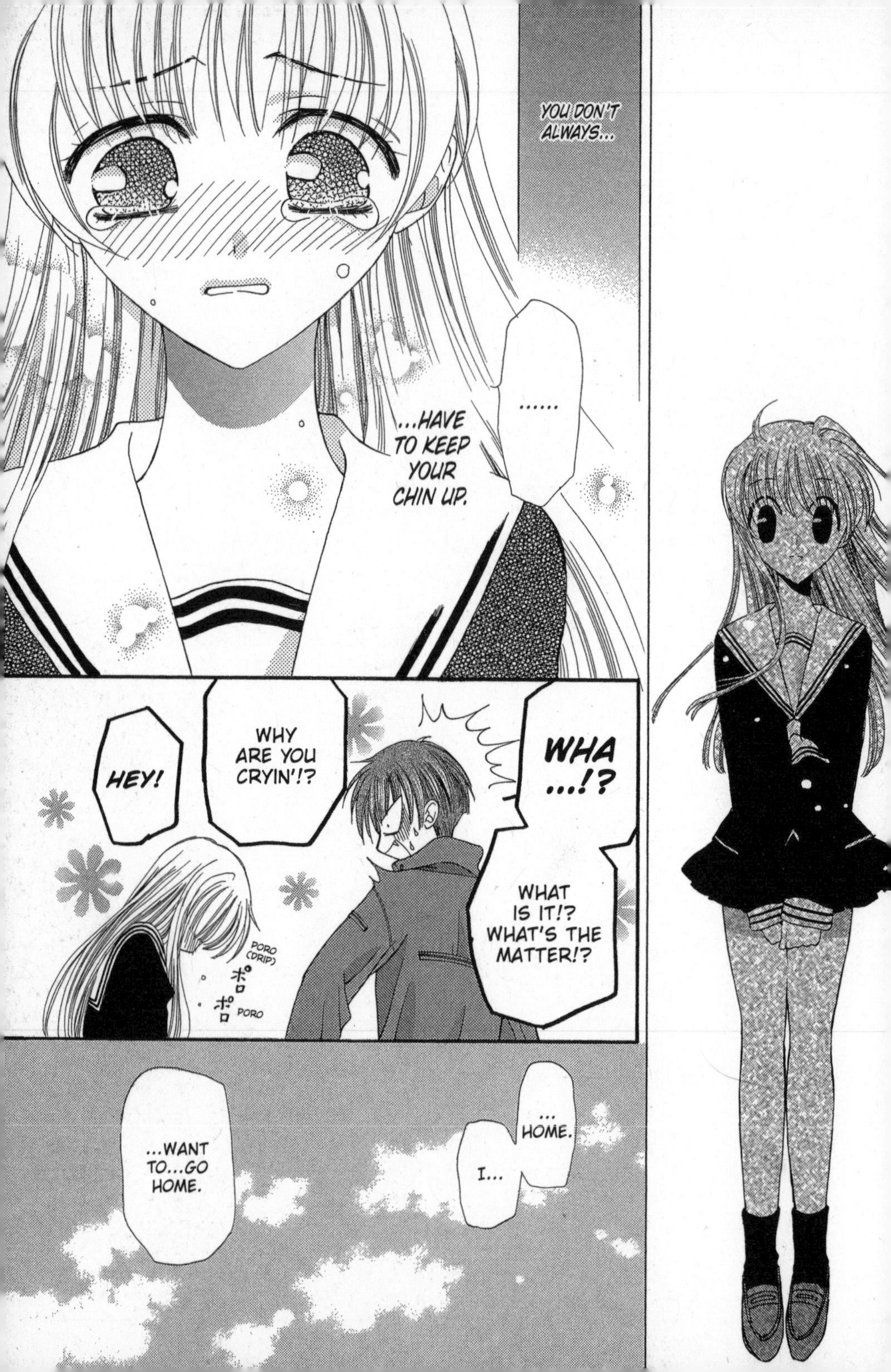
YOU DON'T ALWAYS...
...HAVE TO KEEP YOUR CHIN UP.
......
WHA ...!?
WHAT IS IT!? WHAT'S THE MATTER!?
WHY ARE YOU CRYIN'!?
HEY!
ポロ PORO (DRIP)
ポロ PORO
... HOME.
I...
...WANT TO...GO HOME.

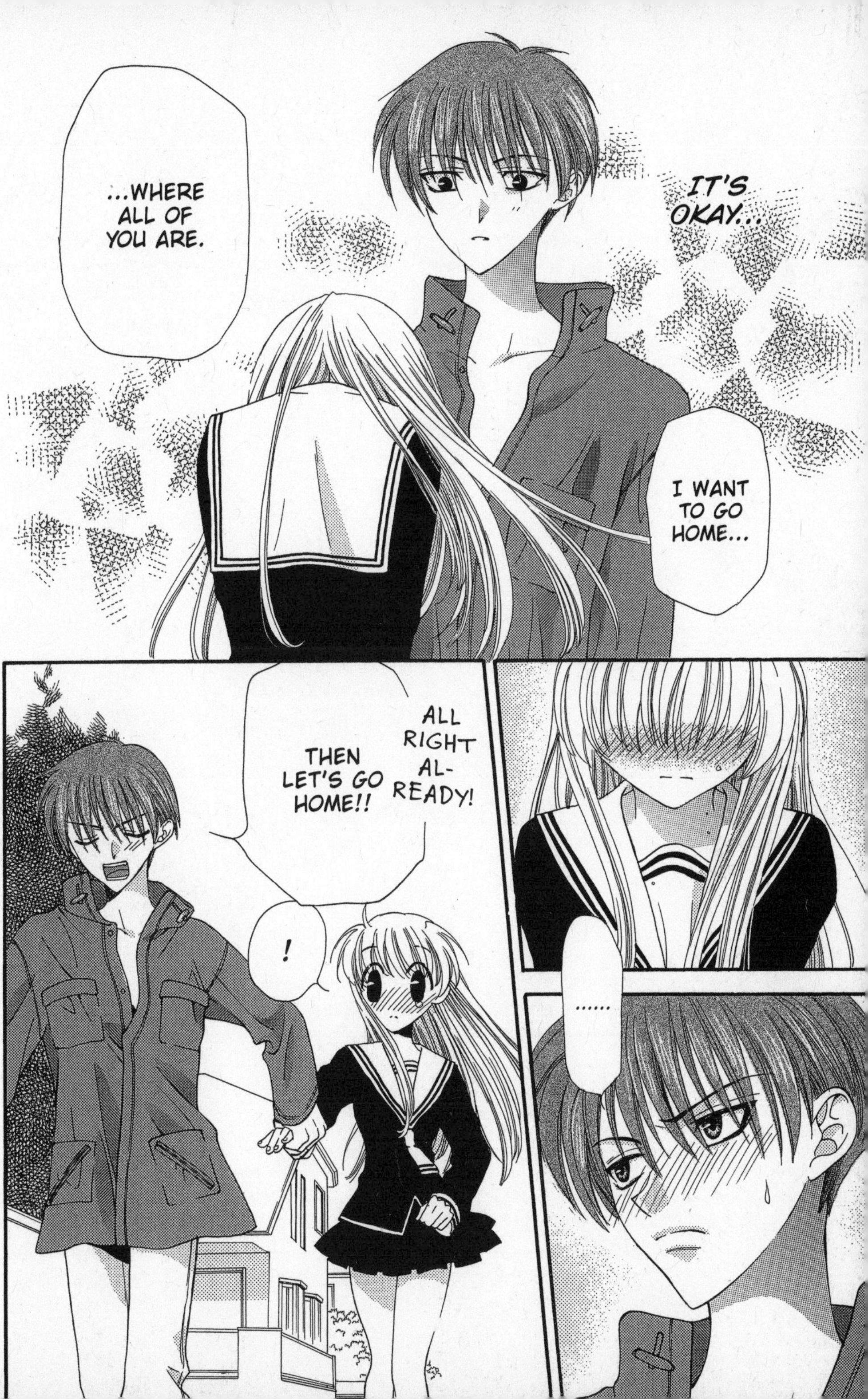
IT'S OKAY...
I WANT TO GO HOME...
...WHERE ALL OF YOU ARE.
......
ALL RIGHT AL-READY!
THEN LET'S GO HOME!!
!

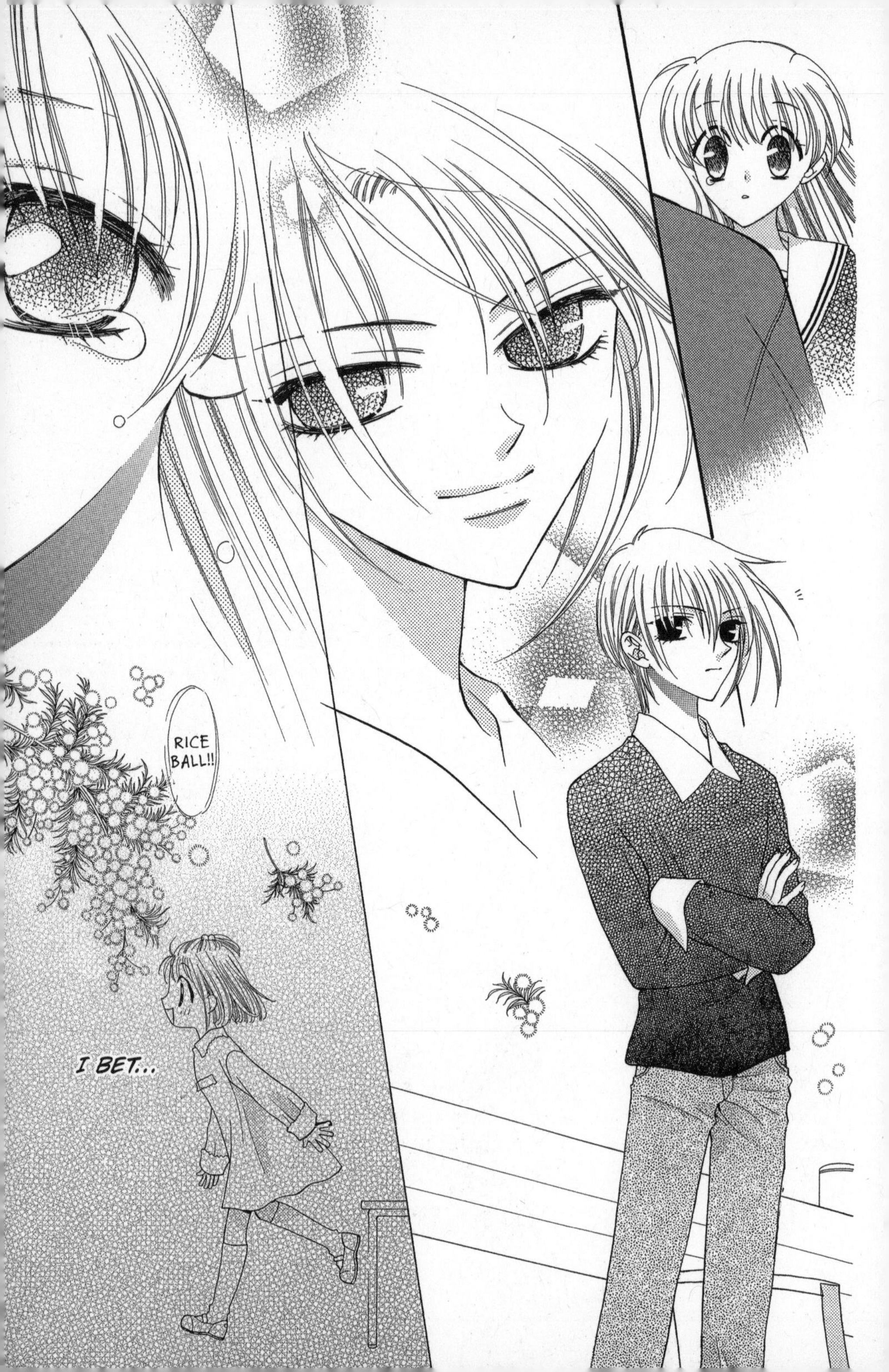
RICE BALL!!
I BET...

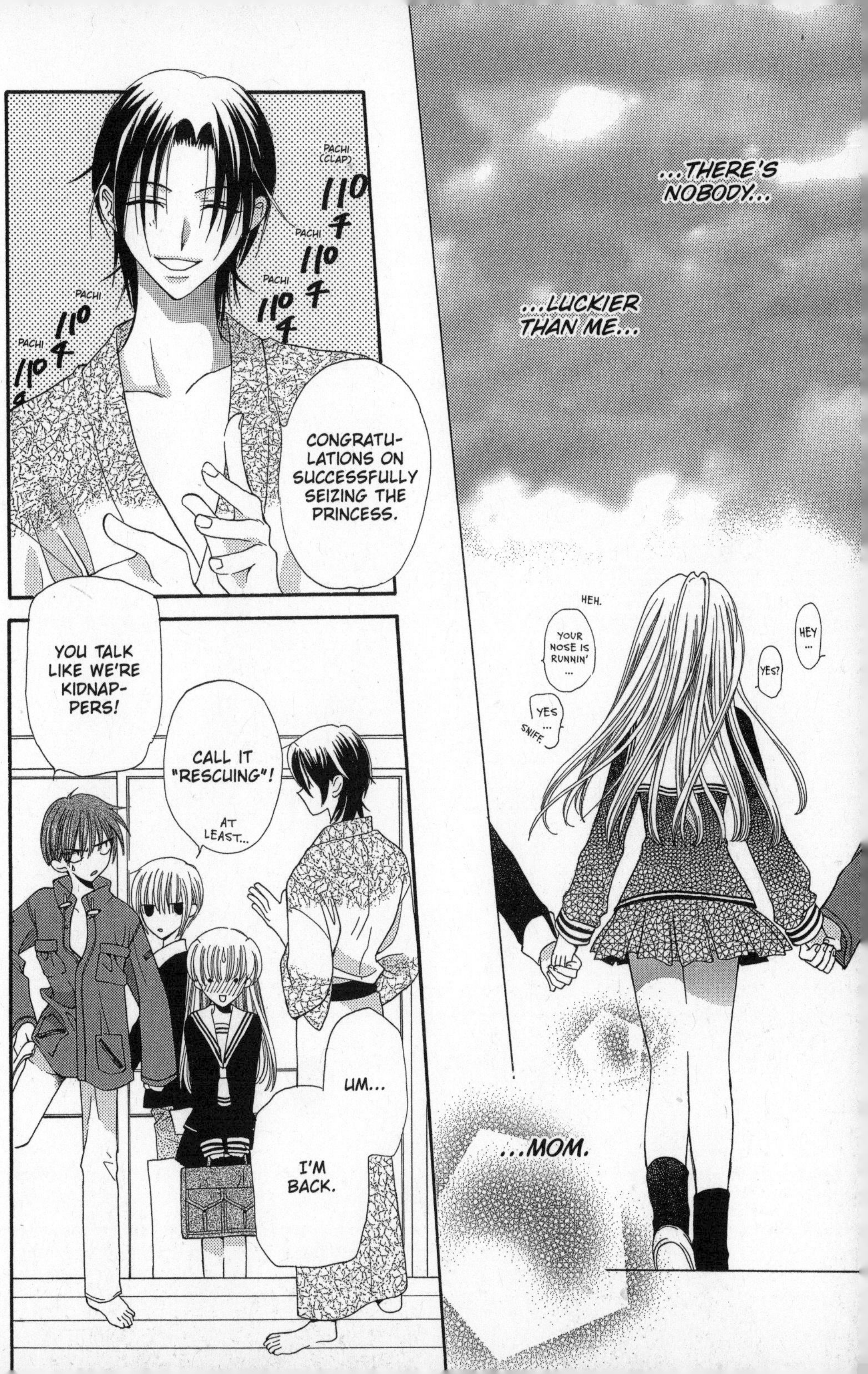
...THERE'S NOBODY...
...LUCKIER THAN ME...
HEY ...
YES?
HEH.
YOUR NOSE IS RUNNIN' ...
YES ...
SNIFF
...MOM.
PACHI (CLAP)
PACHI
PACHI
PACHI
PACHI
CONGRATULATIONS ON SUCCESSFULLY SEIZING THE PRINCESS.
YOU TALK LIKE WE'RE KIDNAPPERS!
CALL IT "RESCUING"!
AT LEAST...
UM...
I'M BACK.

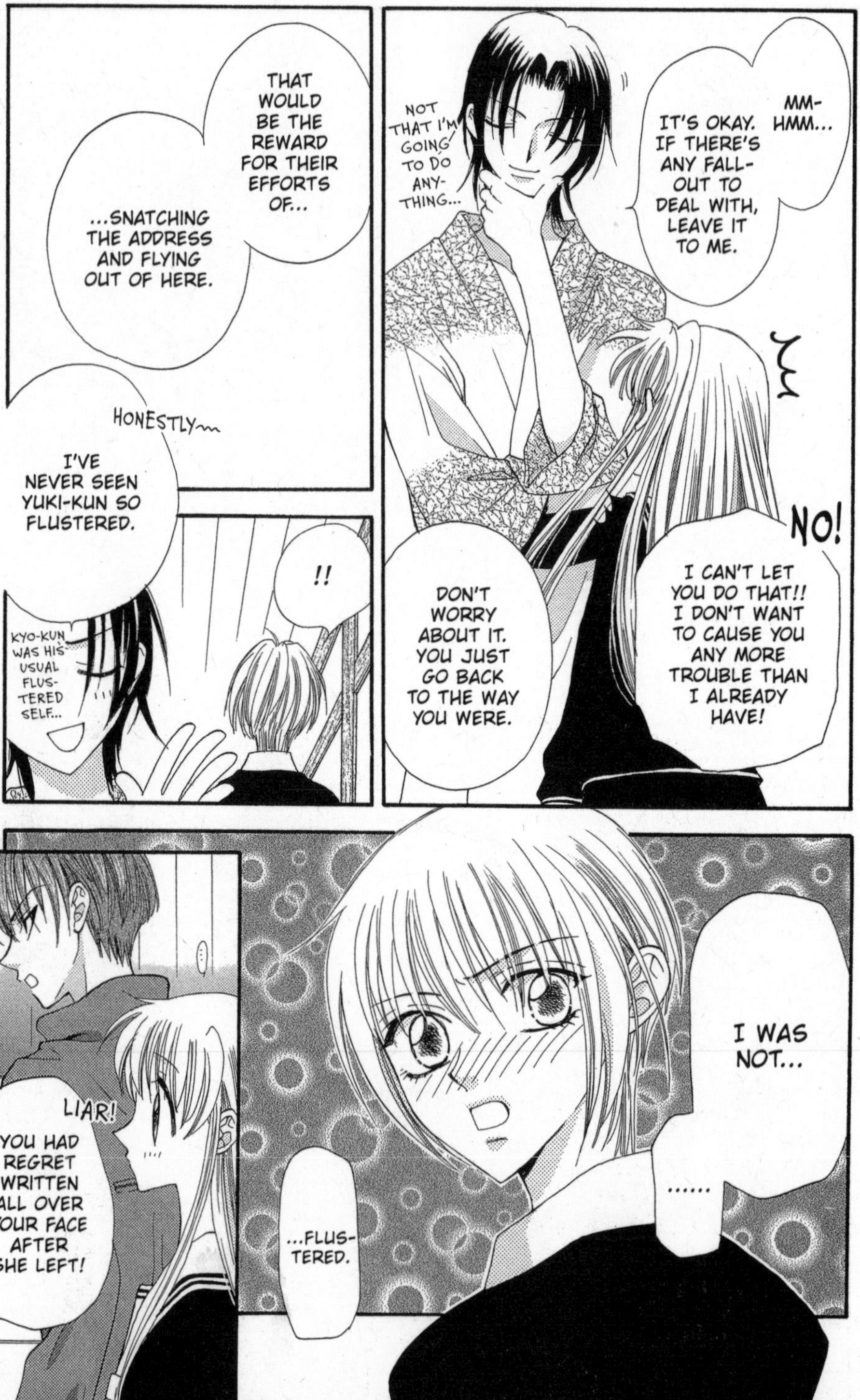
MM-HMM...
IT'S OKAY. IF THERE'S ANY FALL-OUT TO DEAL WITH, LEAVE IT TO ME.
NOT THAT I'M GOING TO DO ANYTHING...
NO!
I CAN'T LET YOU DO THAT!! I DON'T WANT TO CAUSE YOU ANY MORE TROUBLE THAN I ALREADY HAVE!
DON'T WORRY ABOUT IT. YOU JUST GO BACK TO THE WAY YOU WERE.
THAT WOULD BE THE REWARD FOR THEIR EFFORTS OF...
...SNATCHING THE ADDRESS AND FLYING OUT OF HERE.
HONESTLY~
I'VE NEVER SEEN YUKI-KUN SO FLUSTERED.
!!
KYO-KUN WAS HIS USUAL FLUSTERED SELF...
I WAS NOT...
......
...FLUSTERED.
...
LIAR!
YOU HAD REGRET WRITTEN ALL OVER YOUR FACE AFTER SHE LEFT!
...

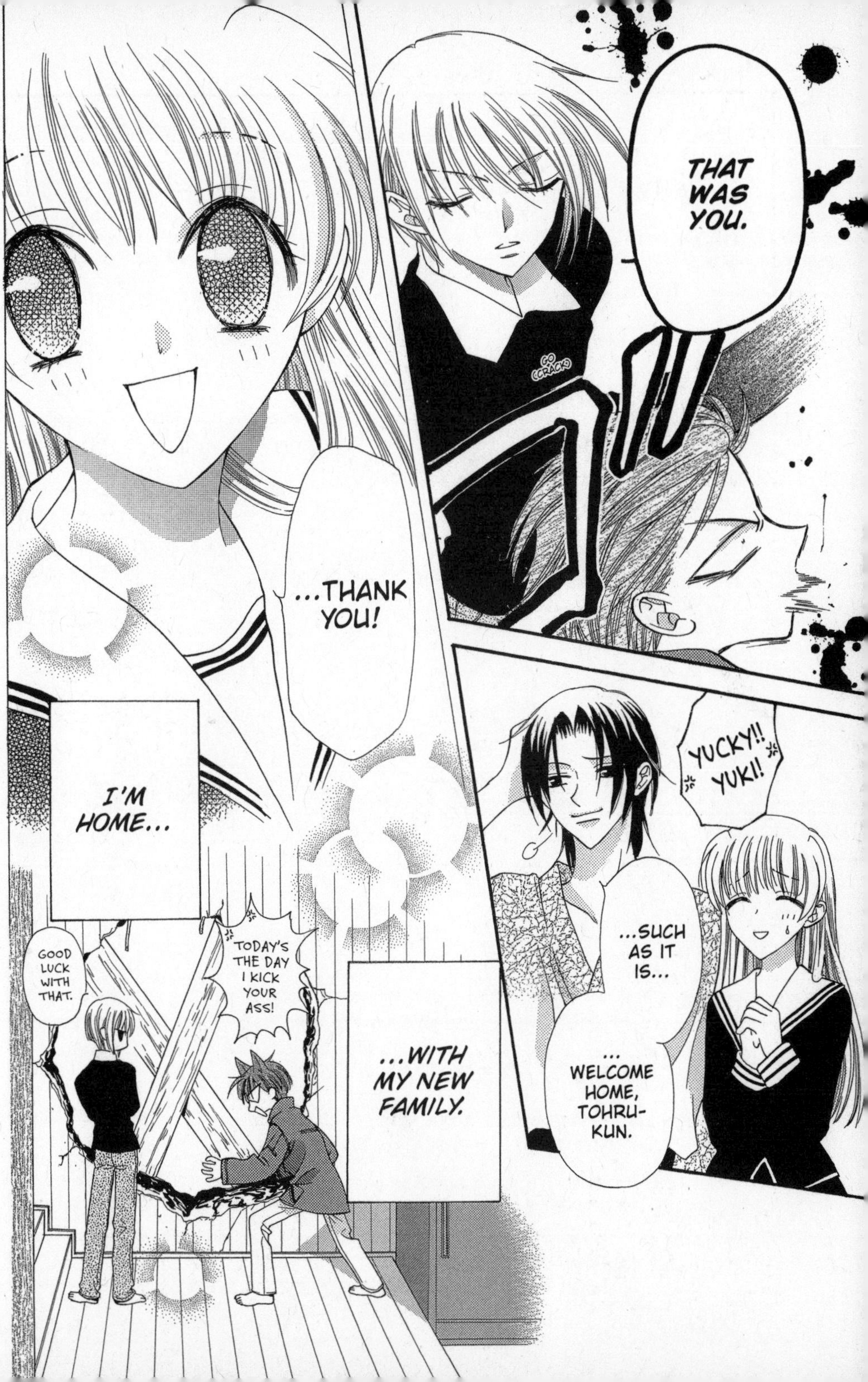
THAT WAS YOU.
GO (CRACK)
YUCKY!! YUKI!!
...SUCH AS IT IS...
... WELCOME HOME, TOHRU-KUN.
...THANK YOU!
I'M HOME...
...WITH MY NEW FAMILY.
TODAY'S THE DAY I KICK YOUR ASS!
GOOD LUCK WITH THAT.

IT ISN'T A HIGH SCHOOL-LEVEL PROBLEM, BUT ANYWAY...

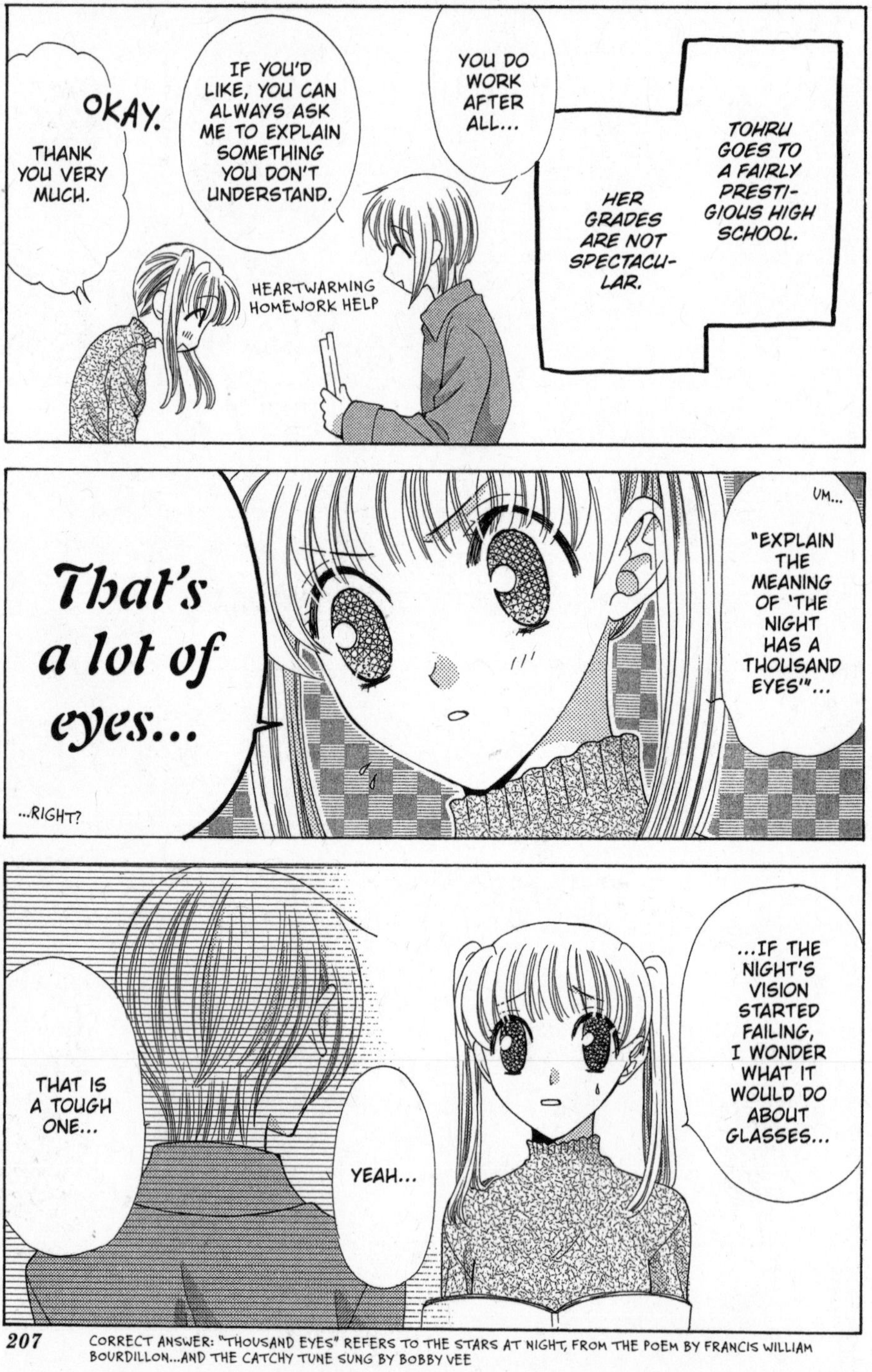
TOHRU GOES TO A FAIRLY PRESTIGIOUS HIGH SCHOOL.
HER GRADES ARE NOT SPECTACULAR.
YOU DO WORK AFTER ALL...
IF YOU'D LIKE, YOU CAN ALWAYS ASK ME TO EXPLAIN SOMETHING YOU DON'T UNDERSTAND.
HEARTWARMING HOMEWORK HELP
OKAY.
THANK YOU VERY MUCH.
UM...
"EXPLAIN THE MEANING OF 'THE NIGHT HAS A THOUSAND EYES'"...
That's a lot of eyes...
...RIGHT?
...IF THE NIGHT'S VISION STARTED FAILING, I WONDER WHAT IT WOULD DO ABOUT GLASSES...
YEAH...
THAT IS A TOUGH ONE...

CORRECT ANSWER: "THOUSAND EYES" REFERS TO THE STARS AT NIGHT, FROM THE POEM BY FRANCIS WILLIAM BOURDILLON...AND THE CATCHY TUNE SUNG BY BOBBY VEE

SHIGURE IS GUILTY OF THE SAME OFFENSE...

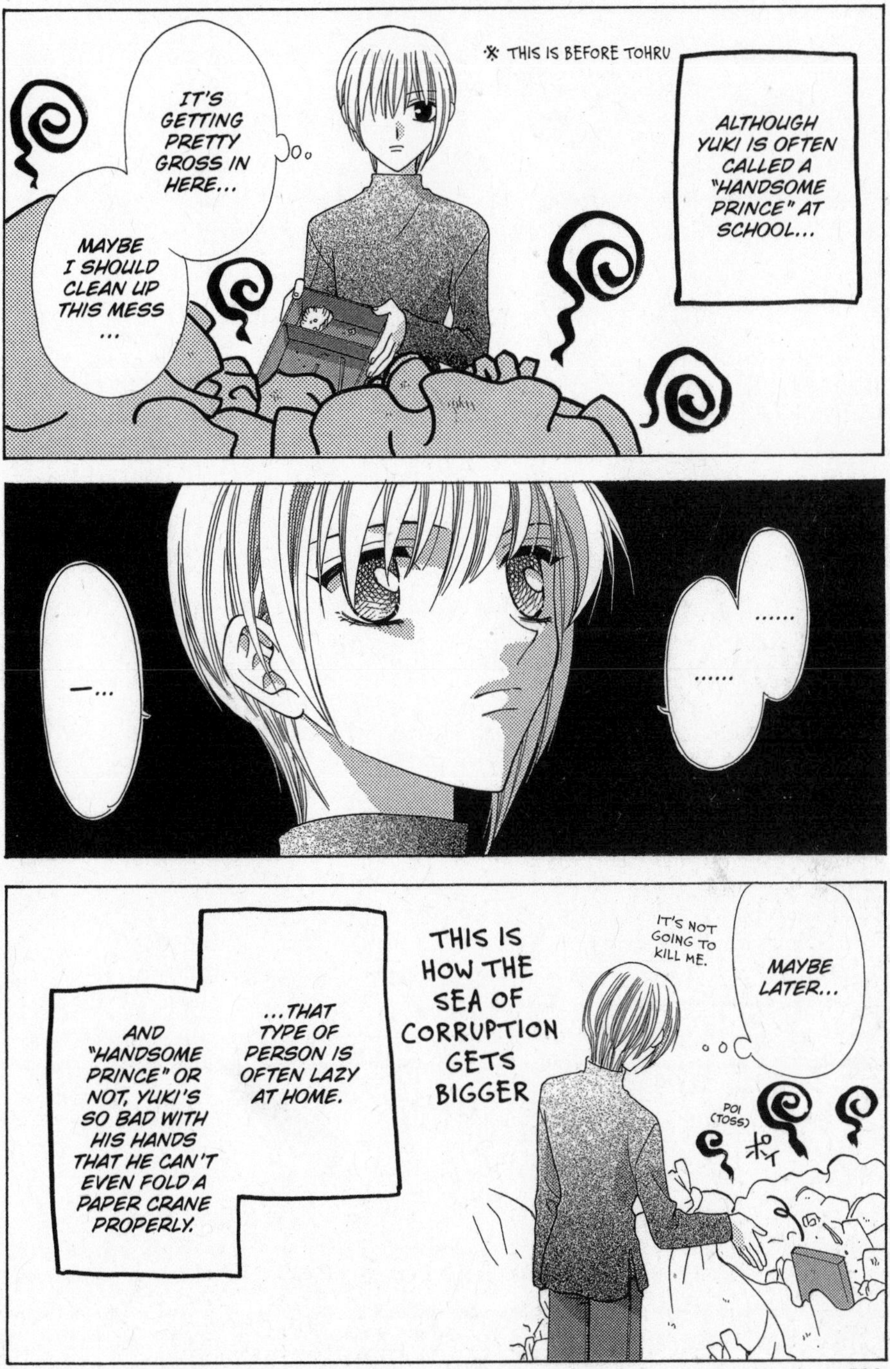

ALTHOUGH YUKI IS OFTEN CALLED A "HANDSOME PRINCE" AT SCHOOL...
※ THIS IS BEFORE TOHRU
IT'S GETTING PRETTY GROSS IN HERE...
MAYBE I SHOULD CLEAN UP THIS MESS ...
....
—...
IT'S NOT GOING TO KILL ME.
MAYBE LATER...
POI (TOSS)
THIS IS HOW THE SEA OF CORRUPTION GETS BIGGER
...THAT TYPE OF PERSON IS OFTEN LAZY AT HOME.
AND "HANDSOME PRINCE" OR NOT, YUKI'S SO BAD WITH HIS HANDS THAT HE CAN'T EVEN FOLD A PAPER CRANE PROPERLY.

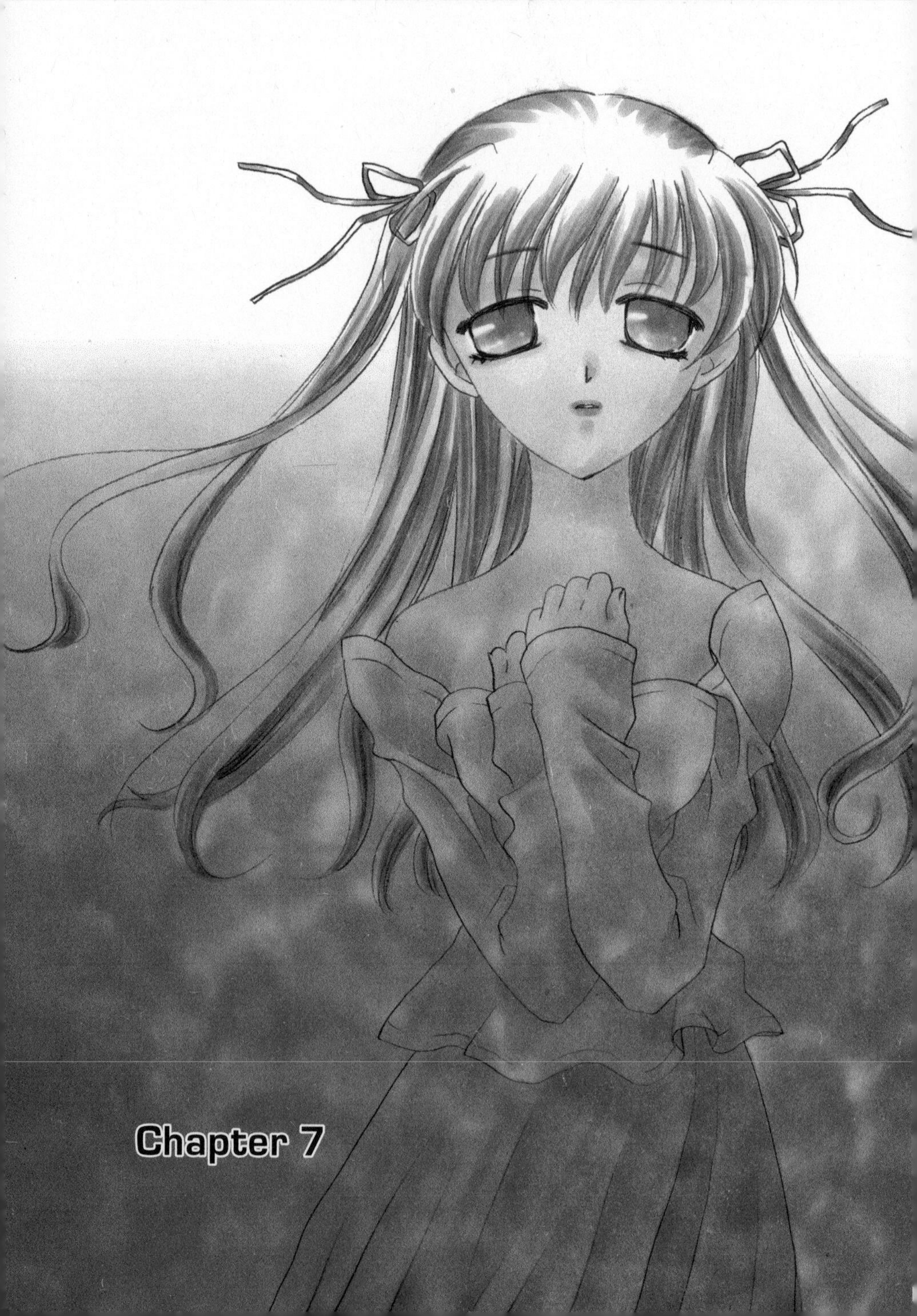

Chapter 7

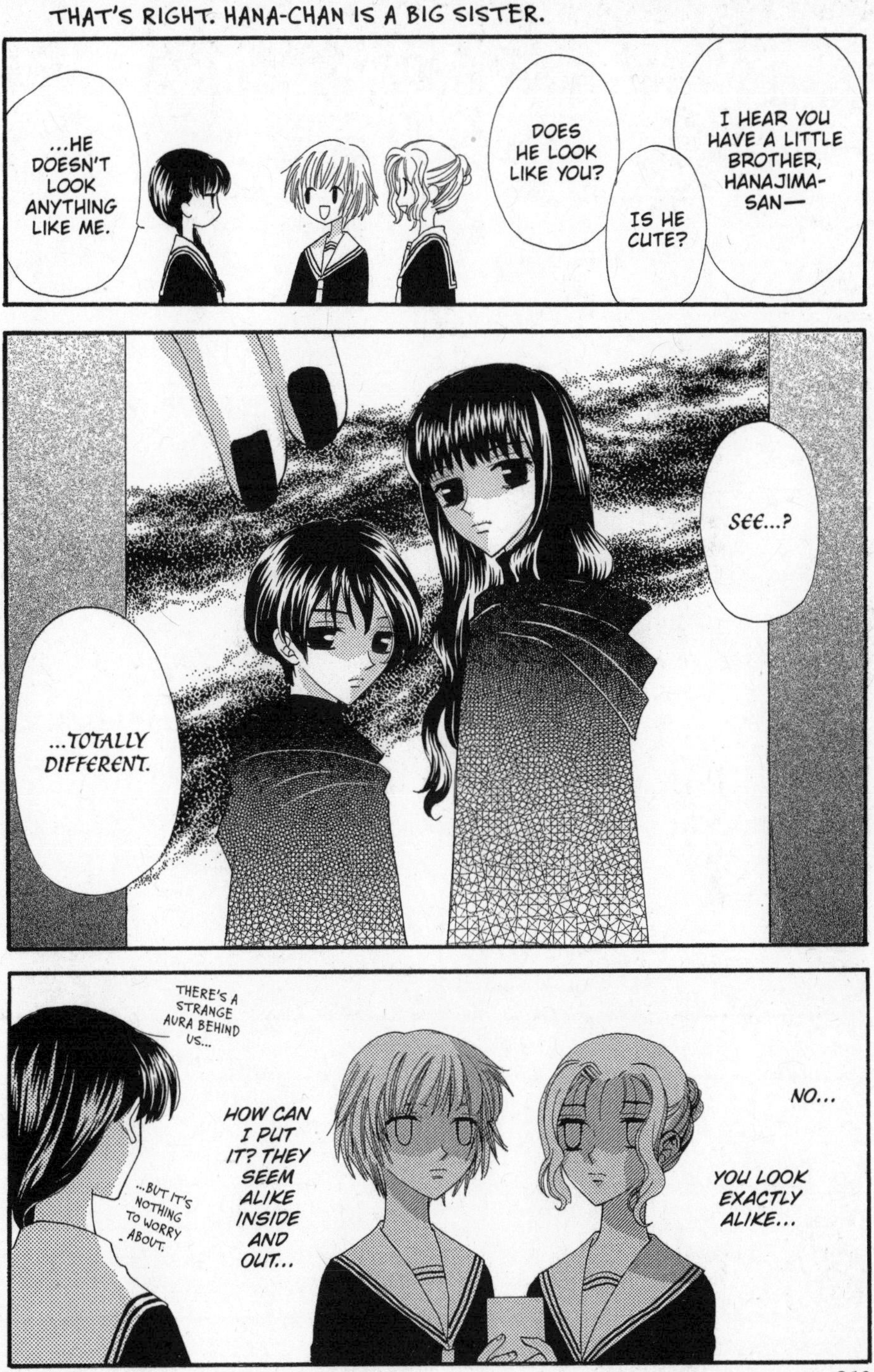
THAT'S RIGHT. HANA-CHAN IS A BIG SISTER.
I HEAR YOU HAVE A LITTLE BROTHER, HANAJIMA-SAN—
IS HE CUTE?
DOES HE LOOK LIKE YOU?
...HE DOESN'T LOOK ANYTHING LIKE ME.
SEE...?
...TOTALLY DIFFERENT.
NO...
YOU LOOK EXACTLY ALIKE...
HOW CAN I PUT IT? THEY SEEM ALIKE INSIDE AND OUT...
THERE'S A STRANGE AURA BEHIND US...
...BUT IT'S NOTHING TO WORRY ABOUT.

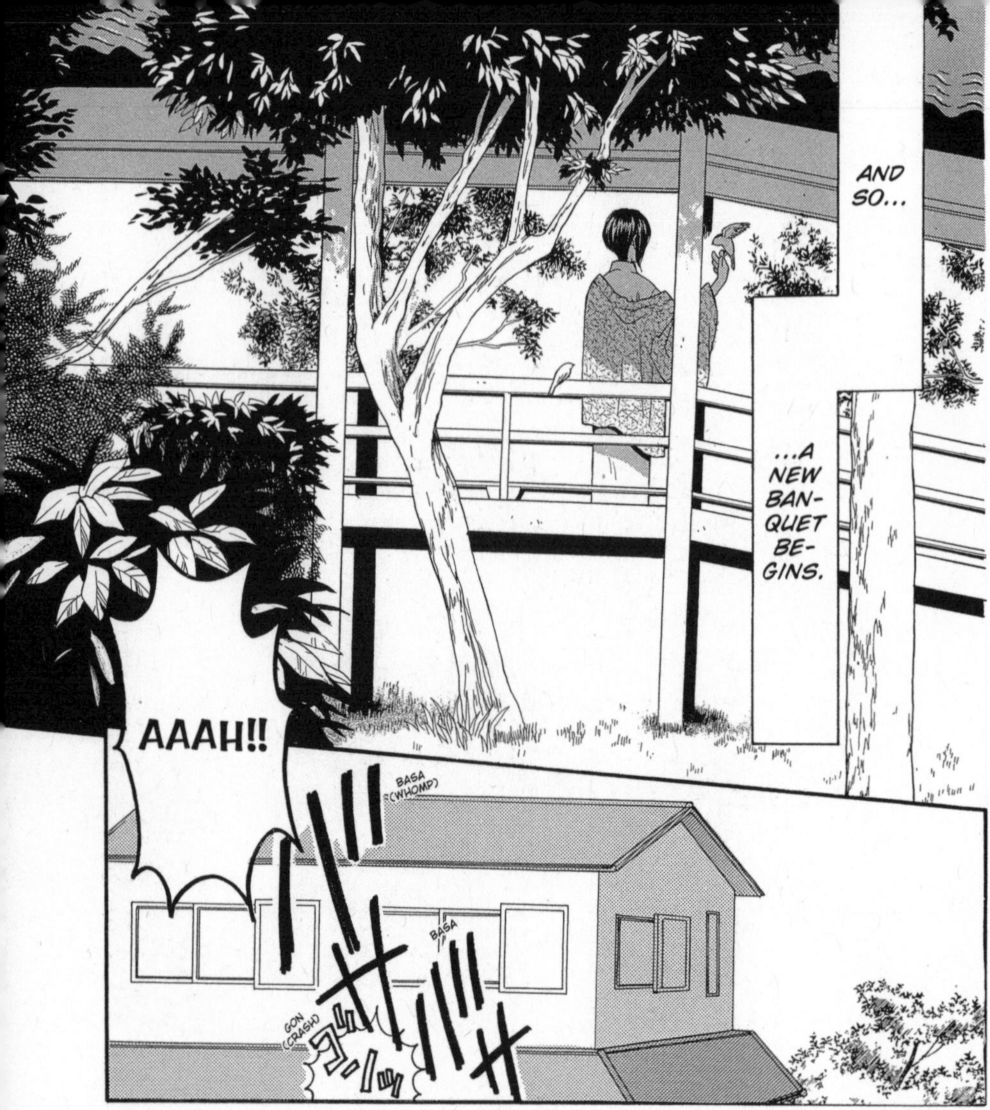
AND SO...
...A NEW BAN-QUET BE-GINS.
AAAH!!
BASA (WHOMP)
BASA
GON (CRASH)

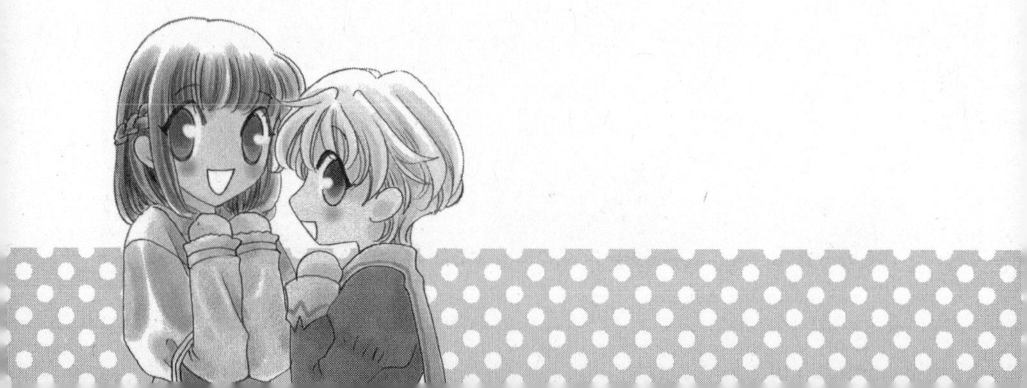

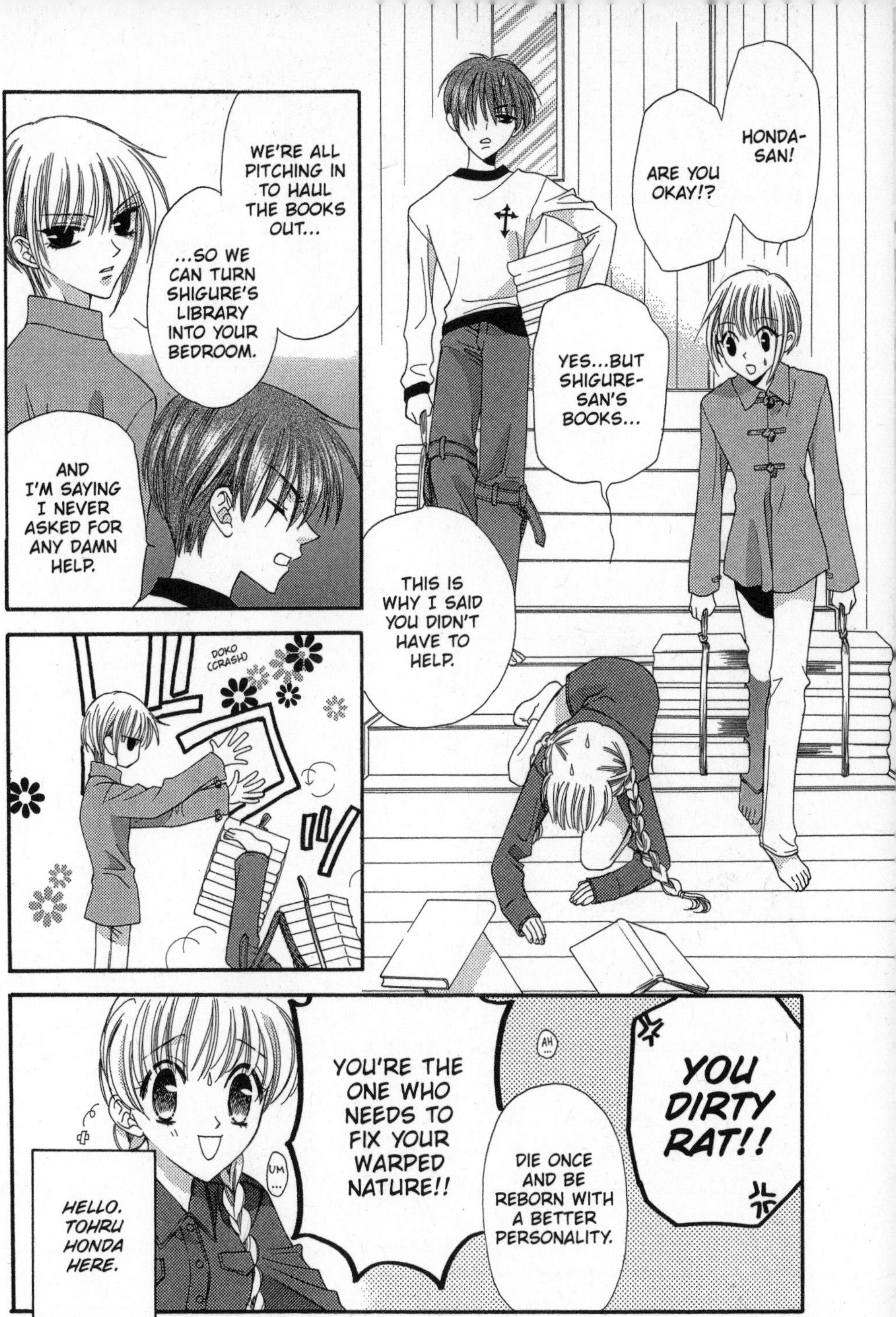
HONDA-SAN!
ARE YOU OKAY!?
YES...BUT SHIGURE-SAN'S BOOKS...
THIS IS WHY I SAID YOU DIDN'T HAVE TO HELP.
WE'RE ALL PITCHING IN TO HAUL THE BOOKS OUT...
...SO WE CAN TURN SHIGURE'S LIBRARY INTO YOUR BEDROOM.
AND I'M SAYING I NEVER ASKED FOR ANY DAMN HELP.
DOKO (CRASH)
YOU DIRTY RAT!!
DIE ONCE AND BE REBORN WITH A BETTER PERSONALITY.
AH...
YOU'RE THE ONE WHO NEEDS TO FIX YOUR WARPED NATURE!!
UM...
HELLO. TOHRU HONDA HERE.

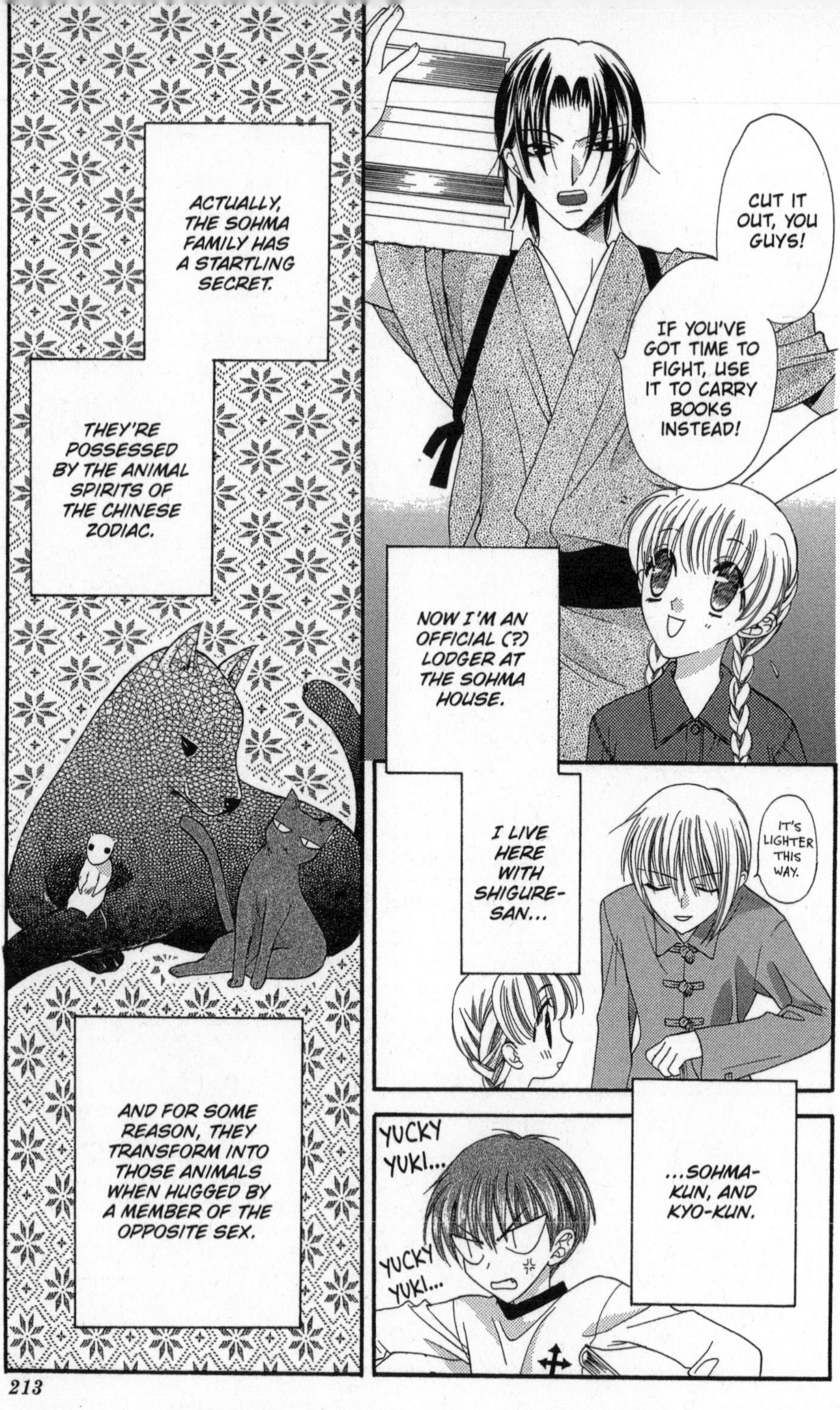
CUT IT OUT, YOU GUYS!
IF YOU'VE GOT TIME TO FIGHT, USE IT TO CARRY BOOKS INSTEAD!
NOW I'M AN OFFICIAL (?) LODGER AT THE SOHMA HOUSE.
I LIVE HERE WITH SHIGURE-SAN...
IT'S LIGHTER THIS WAY.
...SOHMA-KUN, AND KYO-KUN.
YUCKY YUKI...
YUCKY YUKI...
ACTUALLY, THE SOHMA FAMILY HAS A STARTLING SECRET.
THEY'RE POSSESSED BY THE ANIMAL SPIRITS OF THE CHINESE ZODIAC.
AND FOR SOME REASON, THEY TRANSFORM INTO THOSE ANIMALS WHEN HUGGED BY A MEMBER OF THE OPPOSITE SEX.

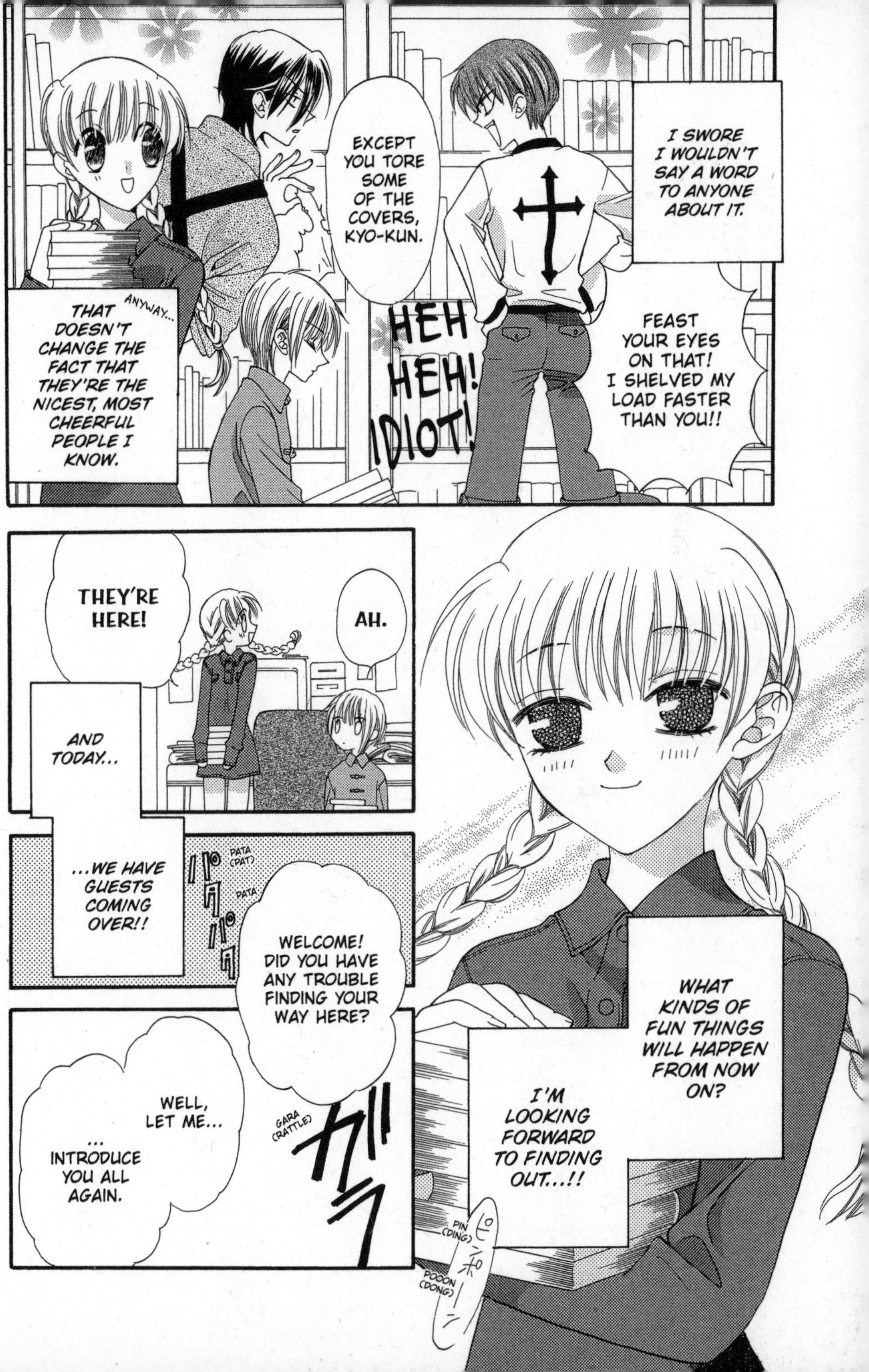
I SWORE I WOULDN'T SAY A WORD TO ANYONE ABOUT IT.
FEAST YOUR EYES ON THAT! I SHELVED MY LOAD FASTER THAN YOU!!
HEH HEH! IDIOT!
EXCEPT YOU TORE SOME OF THE COVERS, KYO-KUN.
ANYWAY...
THAT DOESN'T CHANGE THE FACT THAT THEY'RE THE NICEST, MOST CHEERFUL PEOPLE I KNOW.
WHAT KINDS OF FUN THINGS WILL HAPPEN FROM NOW ON?
I'M LOOKING FORWARD TO FINDING OUT...!!
PIN (DING)
POOON (DONG)
AH.
THEY'RE HERE!
AND TODAY...
...WE HAVE GUESTS COMING OVER!!
PATA (PAT)
PATA
WELCOME! DID YOU HAVE ANY TROUBLE FINDING YOUR WAY HERE?
GARA (RATTLE)
WELL, LET ME...
... INTRODUCE YOU ALL AGAIN.

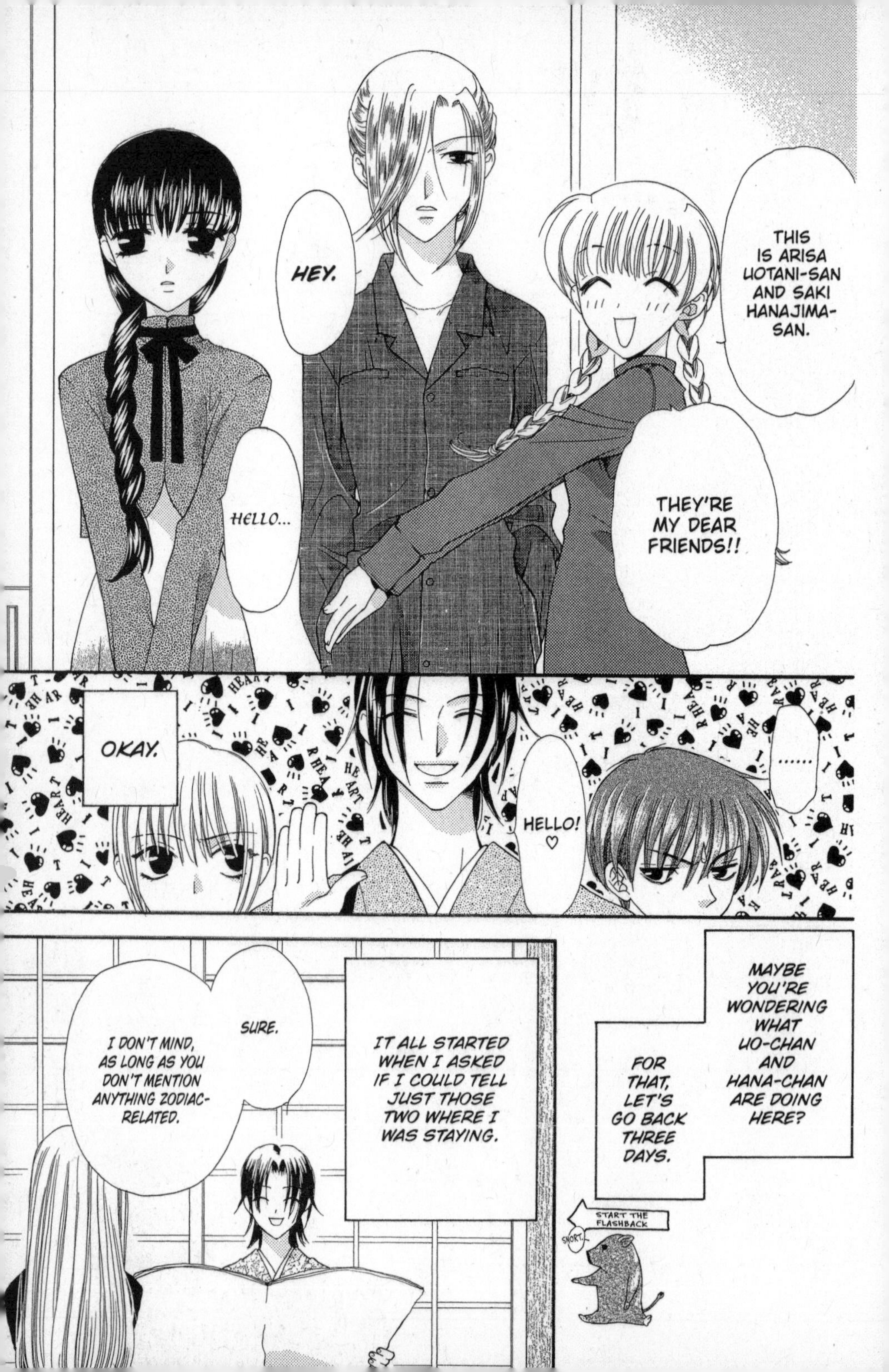
THIS IS ARISA UOTANI-SAN AND SAKI HANAJIMA-SAN.
THEY'RE MY DEAR FRIENDS!!
HEY.
HELLO...
......
HELLO! ♡
OKAY.
MAYBE YOU'RE WONDERING WHAT UO-CHAN AND HANA-CHAN ARE DOING HERE?
FOR THAT, LET'S GO BACK THREE DAYS.
START THE FLASHBACK
SNORT.
IT ALL STARTED WHEN I ASKED IF I COULD TELL JUST THOSE TWO WHERE I WAS STAYING.
SURE.
I DON'T MIND, AS LONG AS YOU DON'T MENTION ANYTHING ZODIAC-RELATED.

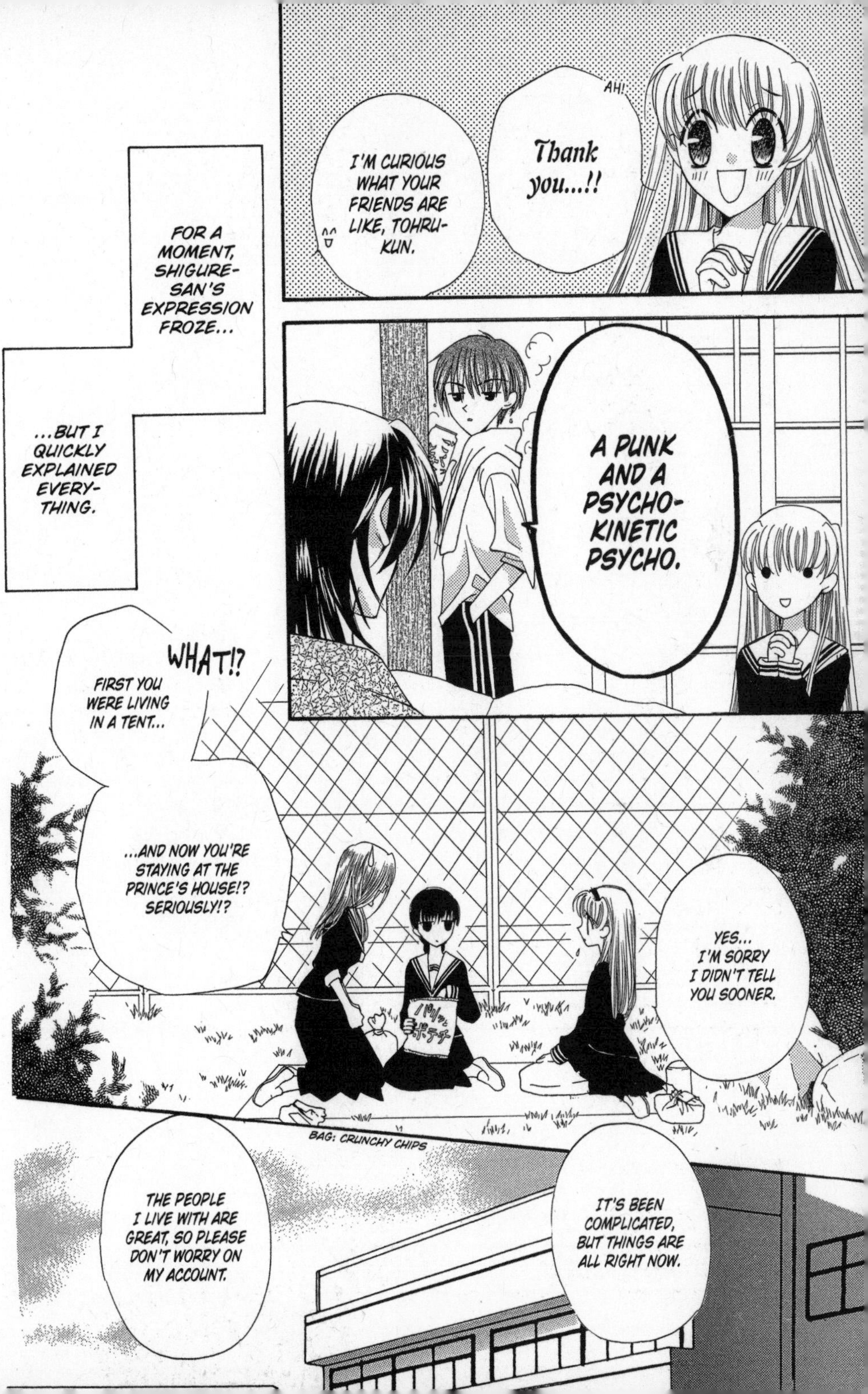
AH!
Thank you...!!
I'M CURIOUS WHAT YOUR FRIENDS ARE LIKE, TOHRU-KUN.
FOR A MOMENT, SHIGURE-SAN'S EXPRESSION FROZE...
...BUT I QUICKLY EXPLAINED EVERYTHING.
A PUNK AND A PSYCHO-KINETIC PSYCHO.
WHAT!?
FIRST YOU WERE LIVING IN A TENT...
...AND NOW YOU'RE STAYING AT THE PRINCE'S HOUSE!? SERIOUSLY!?
YES... I'M SORRY I DIDN'T TELL YOU SOONER.
BAG: CRUNCHY CHIPS
IT'S BEEN COMPLICATED, BUT THINGS ARE ALL RIGHT NOW.
THE PEOPLE I LIVE WITH ARE GREAT, SO PLEASE DON'T WORRY ON MY ACCOUNT.

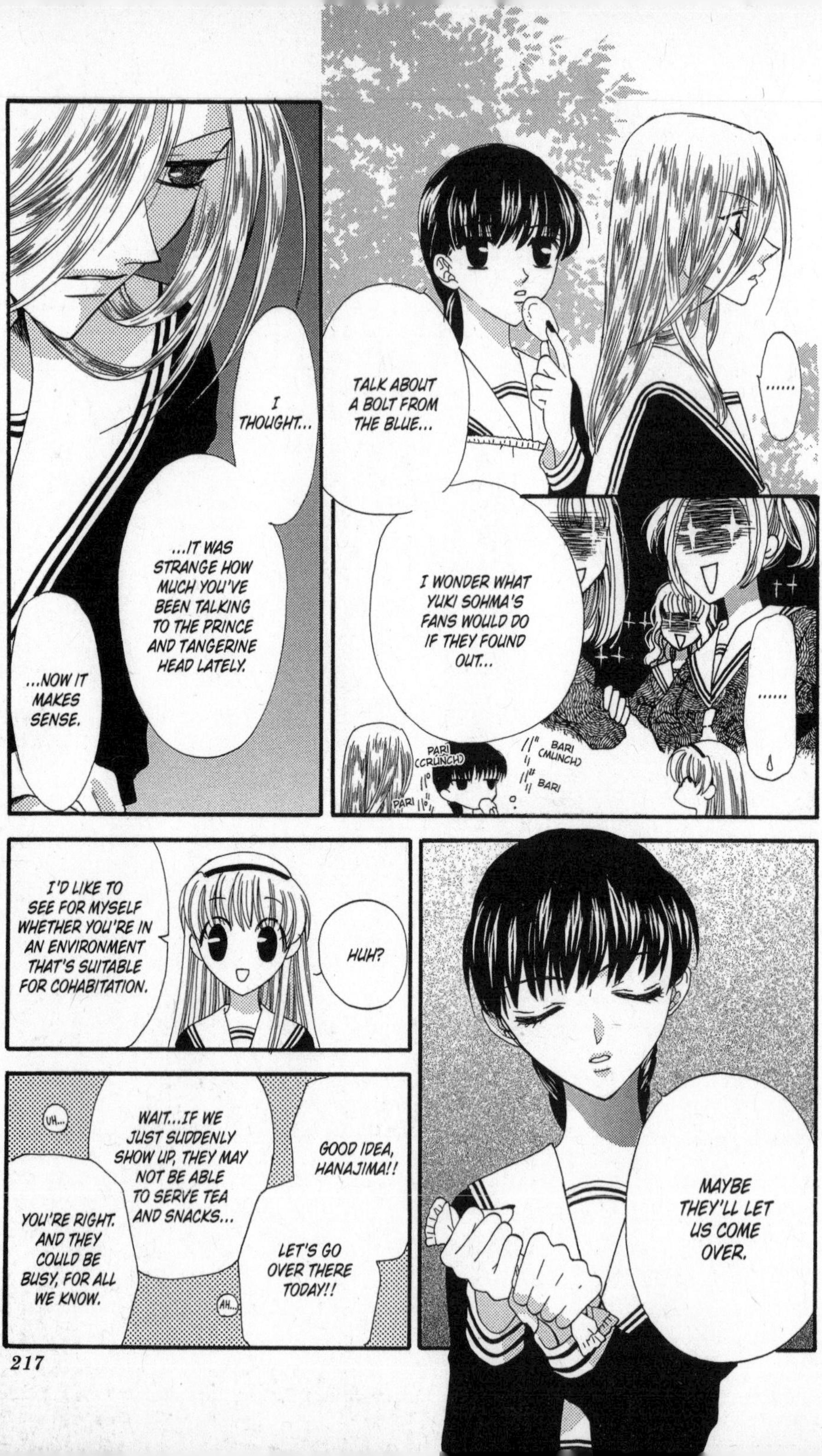
......
TALK ABOUT A BOLT FROM THE BLUE...
......
I WONDER WHAT YUKI SOHMA'S FANS WOULD DO IF THEY FOUND OUT...
BARI (MUNCH)
BARI
PARI (CRUNCH)
PARI
I THOUGHT...
...IT WAS STRANGE HOW MUCH YOU'VE BEEN TALKING TO THE PRINCE AND TANGERINE HEAD LATELY.
...NOW IT MAKES SENSE.
MAYBE THEY'LL LET US COME OVER.
HUH?
I'D LIKE TO SEE FOR MYSELF WHETHER YOU'RE IN AN ENVIRONMENT THAT'S SUITABLE FOR COHABITATION.
GOOD IDEA, HANAJIMA!!
LET'S GO OVER THERE TODAY!!
AH...
WAIT...IF WE JUST SUDDENLY SHOW UP, THEY MAY NOT BE ABLE TO SERVE TEA AND SNACKS...
UH...
YOU'RE RIGHT. AND THEY COULD BE BUSY, FOR ALL WE KNOW.

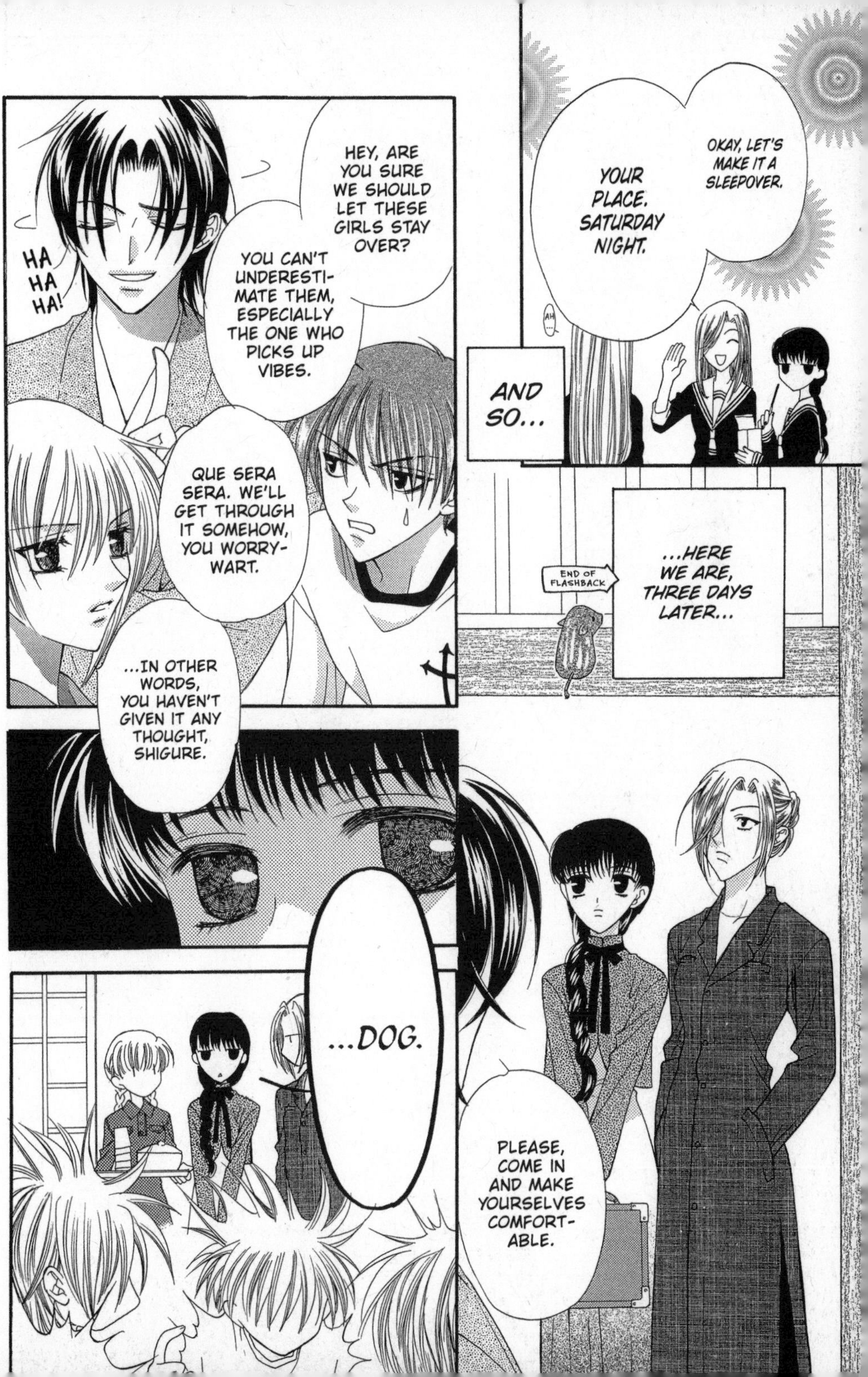

OKAY, LET'S MAKE IT A SLEEPOVER.
YOUR PLACE. SATURDAY NIGHT.
AH...
AND SO...
...HERE WE ARE, THREE DAYS LATER...
END OF FLASHBACK
HEY, ARE YOU SURE WE SHOULD LET THESE GIRLS STAY OVER?
YOU CAN'T UNDERESTIMATE THEM, ESPECIALLY THE ONE WHO PICKS UP VIBES.
HA HA HA!
QUE SERA SERA. WE'LL GET THROUGH IT SOMEHOW, YOU WORRYWART.
...IN OTHER WORDS, YOU HAVEN'T GIVEN IT ANY THOUGHT, SHIGURE.
PLEASE, COME IN AND MAKE YOURSELVES COMFORTABLE.
...DOG.

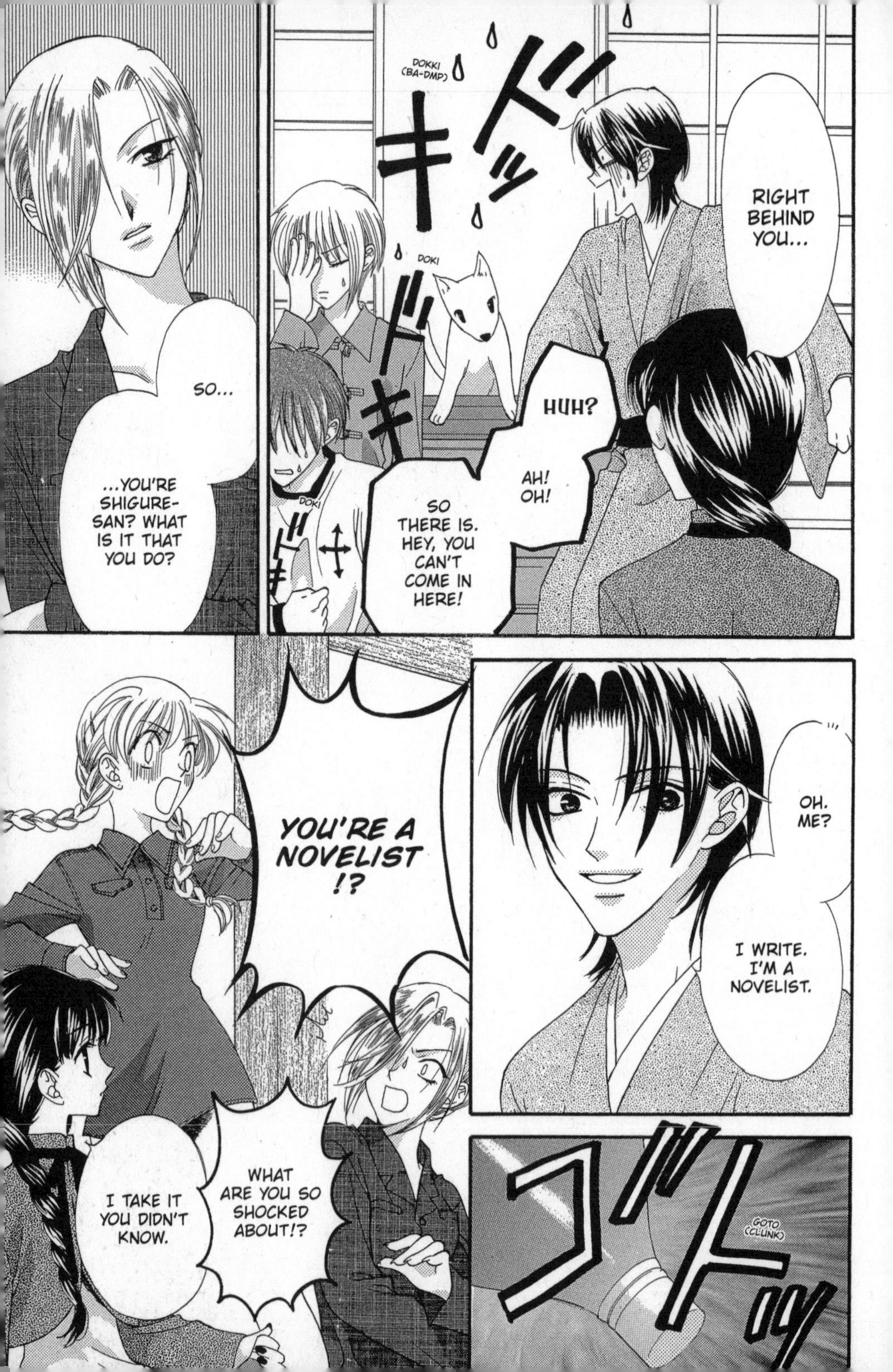
DOKI (BA-DMP)
RIGHT BEHIND YOU...
DOKI
HUH?
AH! OH!
SO THERE IS. HEY, YOU CAN'T COME IN HERE!
DOKI
SO...
...YOU'RE SHIGURE-SAN? WHAT IS IT THAT YOU DO?
OH. ME?
I WRITE. I'M A NOVELIST.
GOTO (CLUNK)
YOU'RE A NOVELIST!?
WHAT ARE YOU SO SHOCKED ABOUT!?
I TAKE IT YOU DIDN'T KNOW.

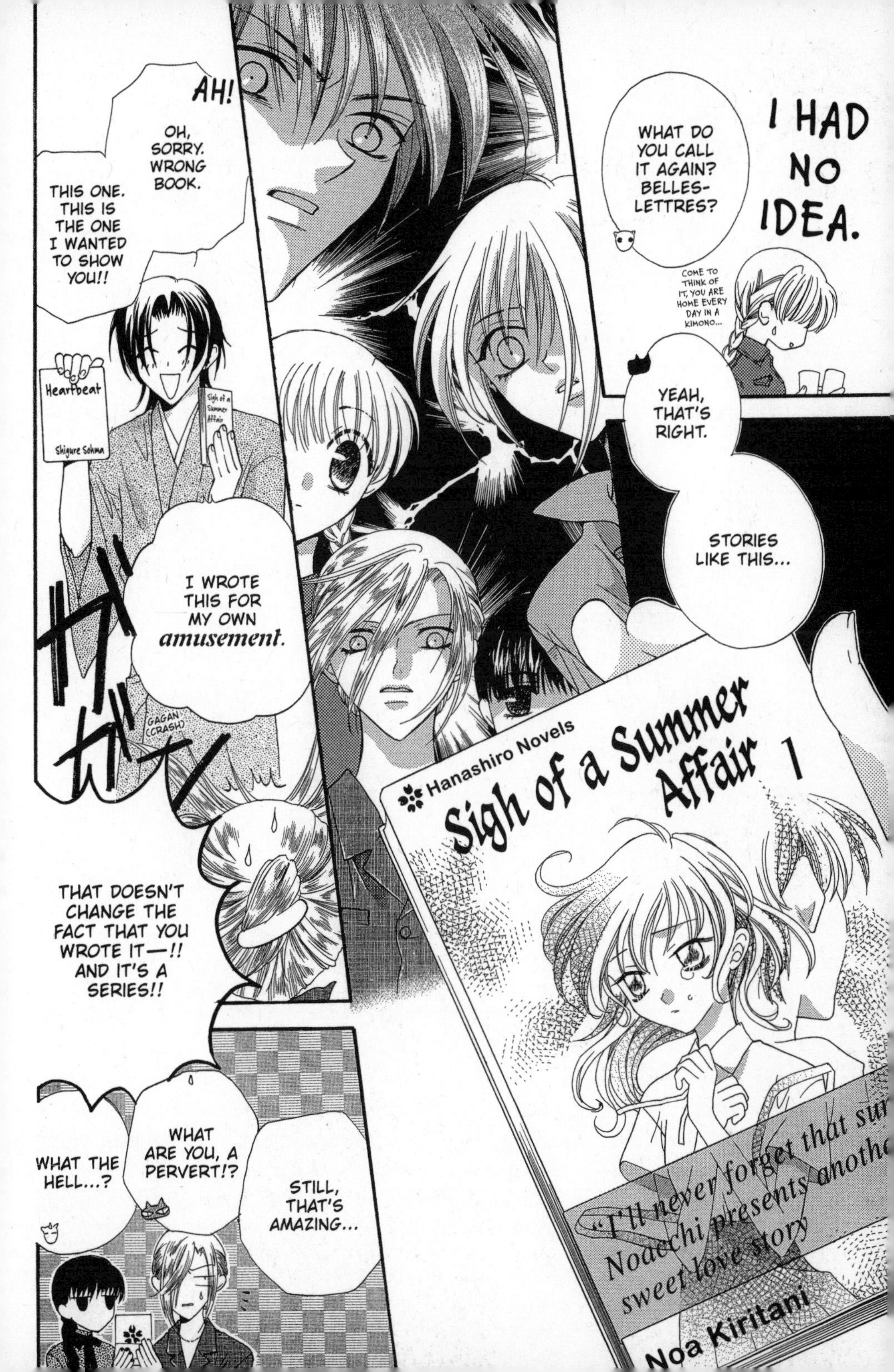

I HAD NO IDEA.
WHAT DO YOU CALL IT AGAIN? BELLES-LETTRES?
COME TO THINK OF IT, YOU ARE HOME EVERY DAY IN A KIMONO...
YEAH, THAT'S RIGHT.
STORIES LIKE THIS...
Hanashiro Novels
Sigh of a Summer Affair 1
“I'll never forget that su
Noaechi presents anothe
sweet love story
Noa Kiritani
AH!
OH, SORRY. WRONG BOOK.
THIS ONE. THIS IS THE ONE I WANTED TO SHOW YOU!!
Heartbeat
Shigure Sohma
Sigh of a Summer Affair
I WROTE THIS FOR MY OWN *amusement*.
GAGAN (CRASH)
THAT DOESN'T CHANGE THE FACT THAT YOU WROTE IT—!! AND IT'S A SERIES!!
STILL, THAT'S AMAZING...
WHAT ARE YOU, A PERVERT!?
WHAT THE HELL...?

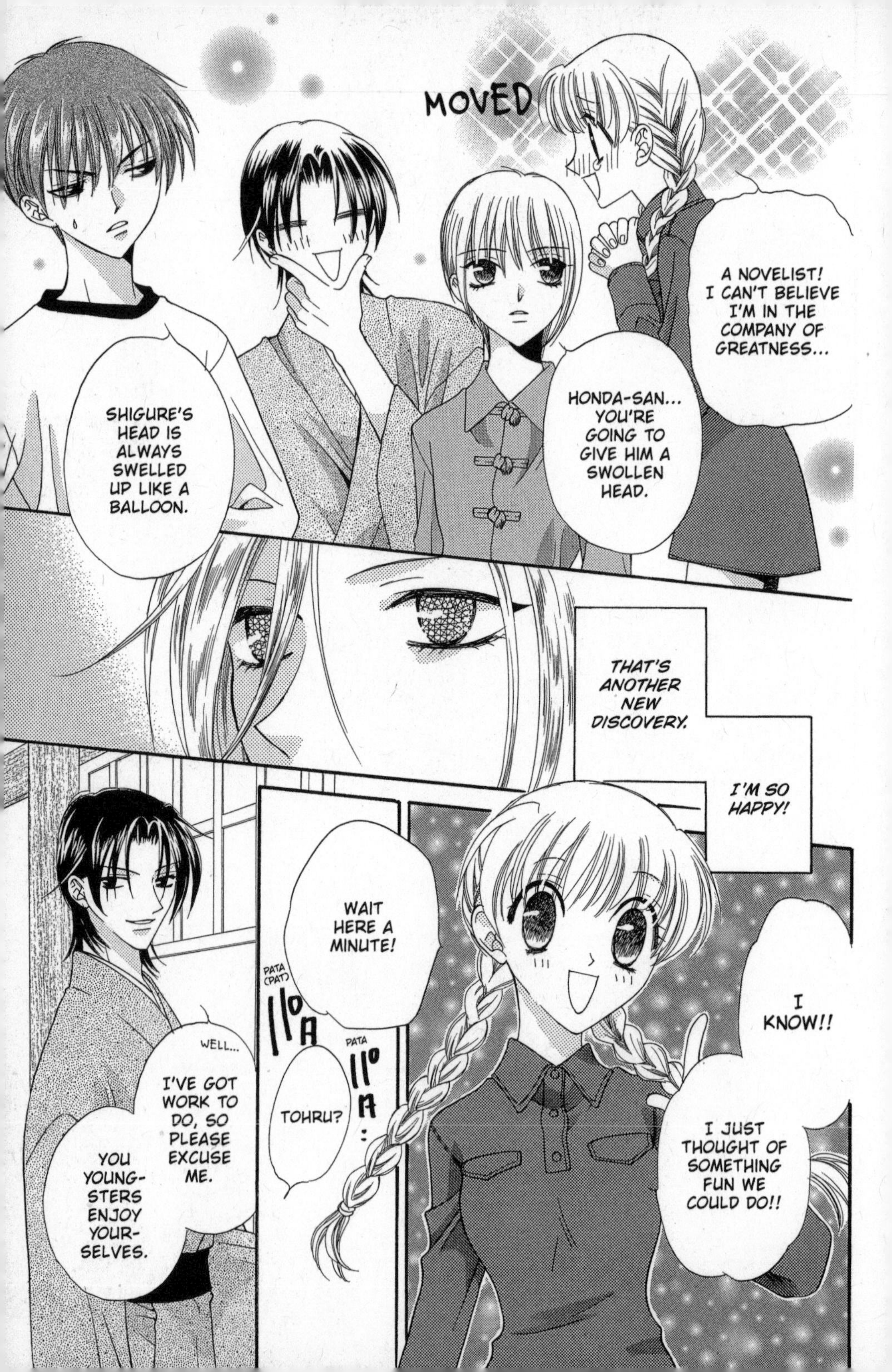
MOVED
A NOVELIST! I CAN'T BELIEVE I'M IN THE COMPANY OF GREATNESS...
HONDA-SAN... YOU'RE GOING TO GIVE HIM A SWOLLEN HEAD.
SHIGURE'S HEAD IS ALWAYS SWELLED UP LIKE A BALLOON.
THAT'S ANOTHER NEW DISCOVERY.
I'M SO HAPPY!
I KNOW!!
I JUST THOUGHT OF SOMETHING FUN WE COULD DO!!
WAIT HERE A MINUTE!
PATA (PAT)
PATA
TOHRU?
WELL...
I'VE GOT WORK TO DO, SO PLEASE EXCUSE ME.
YOU YOUNG-STERS ENJOY YOUR-SELVES.

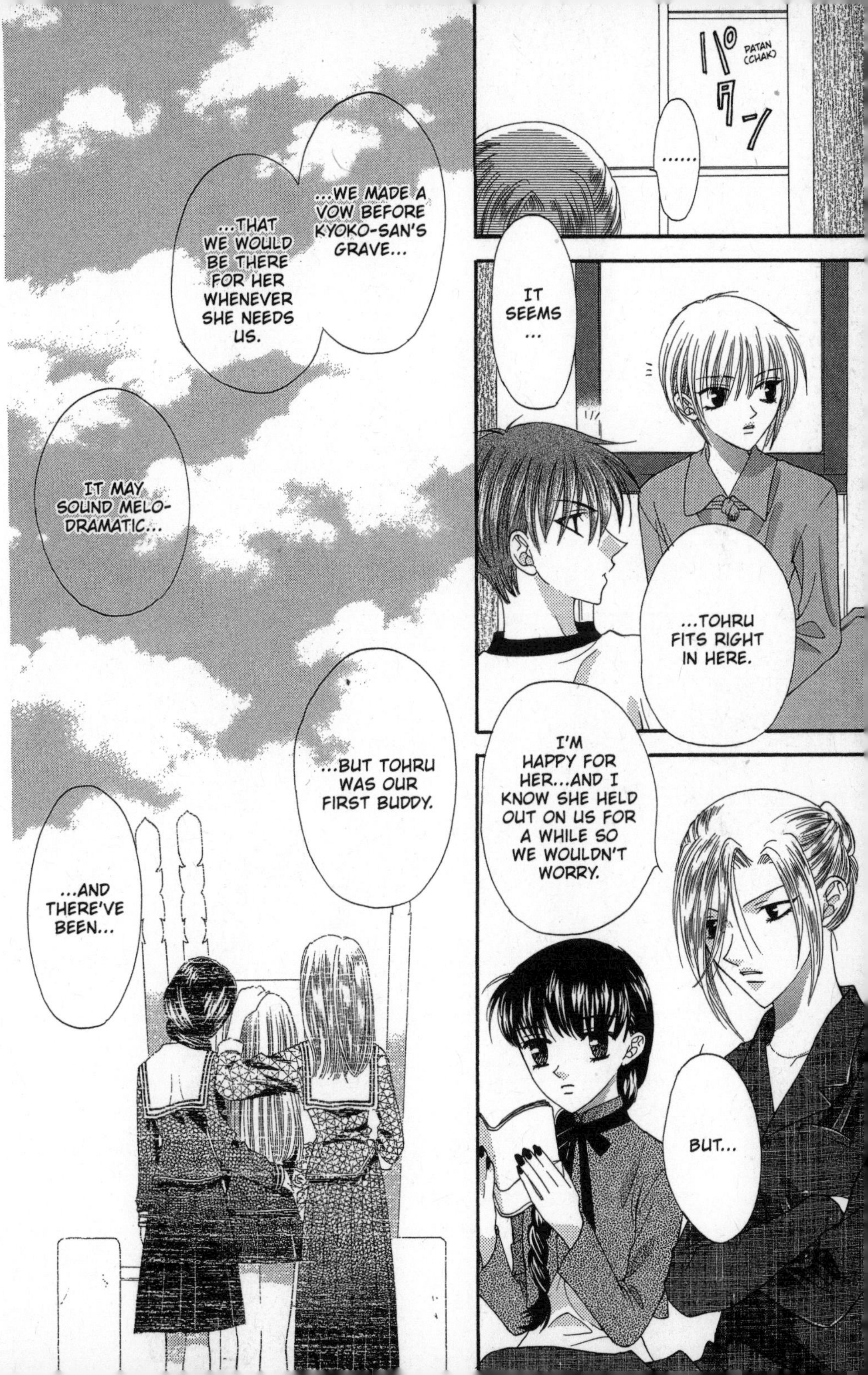
パタン
PATAN (CHAK)
......
IT SEEMS ...
...TOHRU FITS RIGHT IN HERE.
I'M HAPPY FOR HER...AND I KNOW SHE HELD OUT ON US FOR A WHILE SO WE WOULDN'T WORRY.
BUT...
...WE MADE A VOW BEFORE KYOKO-SAN'S GRAVE...
...THAT WE WOULD BE THERE FOR HER WHENEVER SHE NEEDS US.
IT MAY SOUND MELO-DRAMATIC...
...BUT TOHRU WAS OUR FIRST BUDDY.
...AND THERE'VE BEEN...

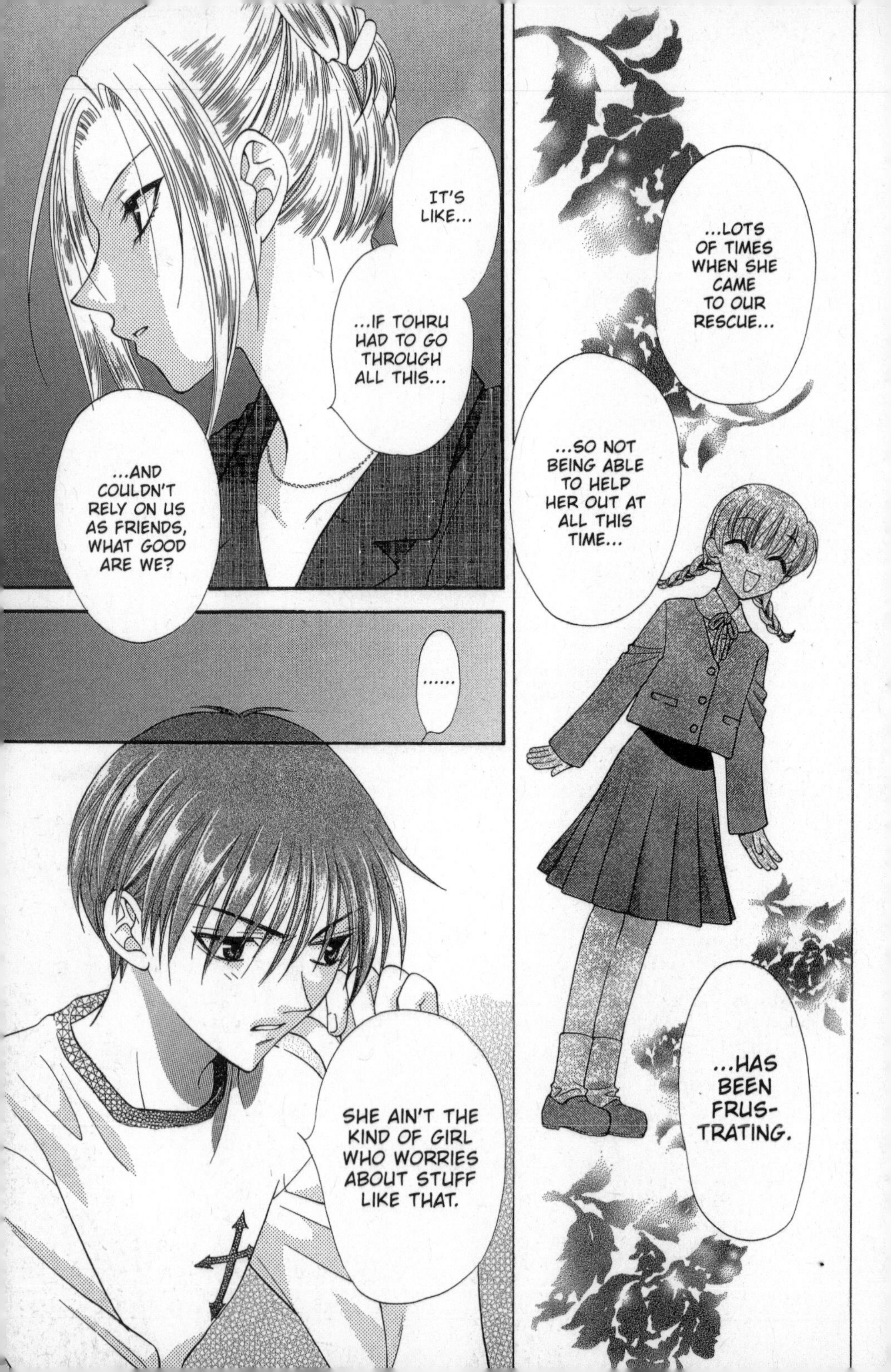
...LOTS OF TIMES WHEN SHE CAME TO OUR RESCUE...
...SO NOT BEING ABLE TO HELP HER OUT AT ALL THIS TIME...
...HAS BEEN FRUS-TRATING.
IT'S LIKE...
...IF TOHRU HAD TO GO THROUGH ALL THIS...
...AND COULDN'T RELY ON US AS FRIENDS, WHAT GOOD ARE WE?
......
SHE AIN'T THE KIND OF GIRL WHO WORRIES ABOUT STUFF LIKE THAT.

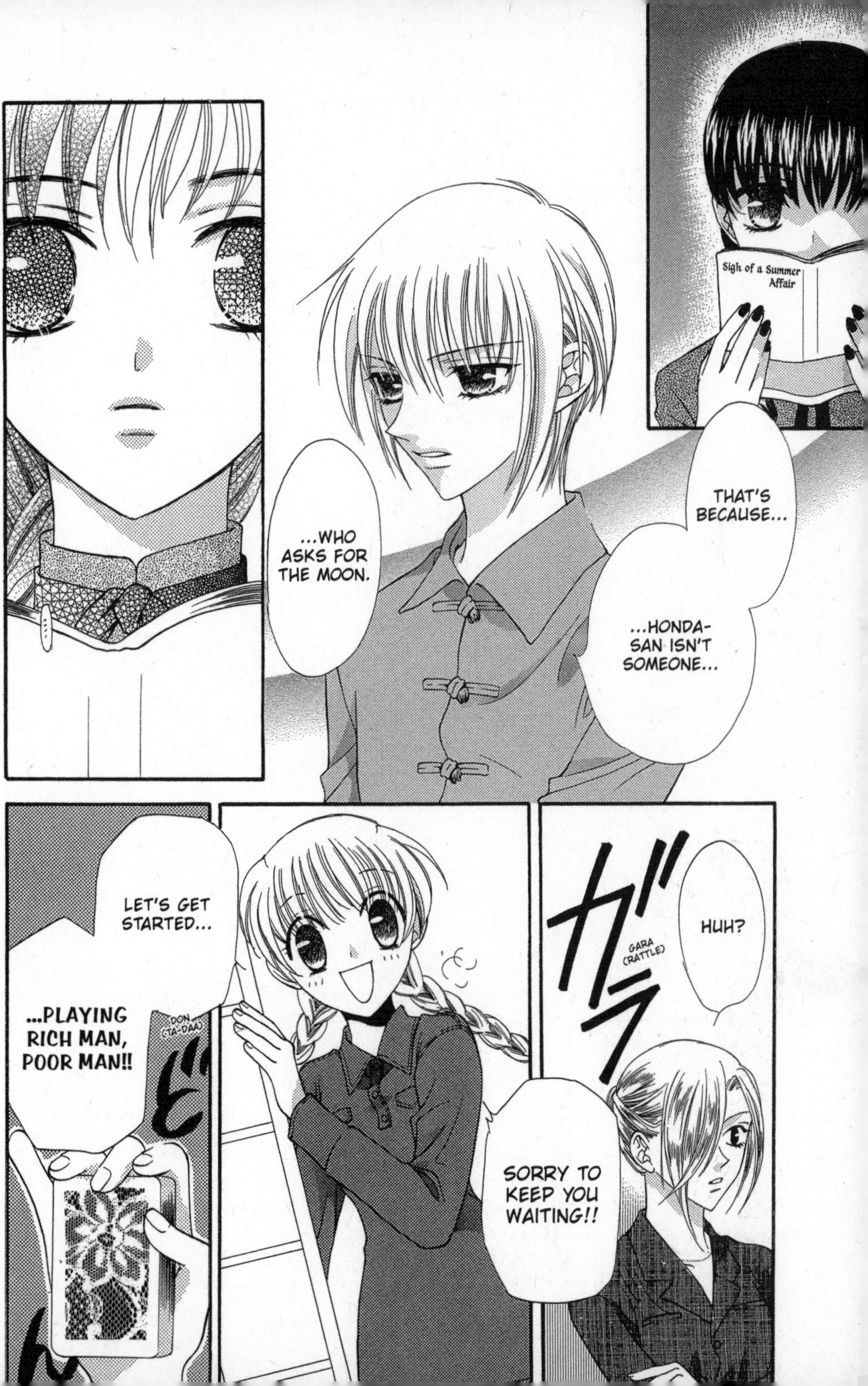
Sigh of a Summer Affair
THAT'S BECAUSE...
...HONDA-SAN ISN'T SOMEONE...
...WHO ASKS FOR THE MOON.
ガラ
GARA (RATTLE)
HUH?
SORRY TO KEEP YOU WAITING!!
LET'S GET STARTED...
...PLAYING RICH MAN, POOR MAN!!
DON (TA-DAA)

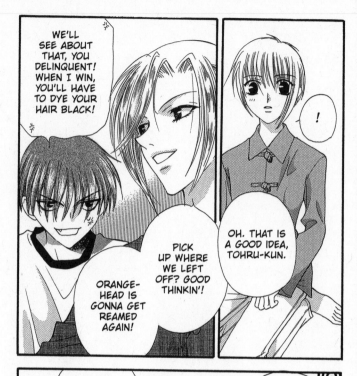

!
OH. THAT IS A GOOD IDEA, TOHRU-KUN.
PICK UP WHERE WE LEFT OFF? GOOD THINKIN'!
ORANGE-HEAD IS GONNA GET REAMED AGAIN!
WE'LL SEE ABOUT THAT, YOU DELINQUENT! WHEN I WIN, YOU'LL HAVE TO DYE YOUR HAIR BLACK!
YEAH, RIGHT, AND WHEN YOU LOSE, YOU'LL HAVE TO BLEACH ALL THE COLOR OUT AND MAKE IT WHITE!
THIS IS MY NATURAL COLOR!!
OH, IS THAT RIGHT?
SOHMA-KUN, WOULD YOU LIKE TO CUT THE DECK?
HUH?
......
AH...

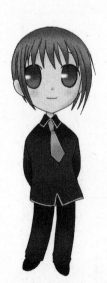

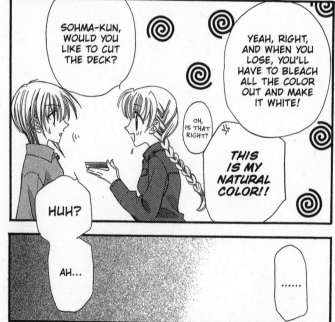

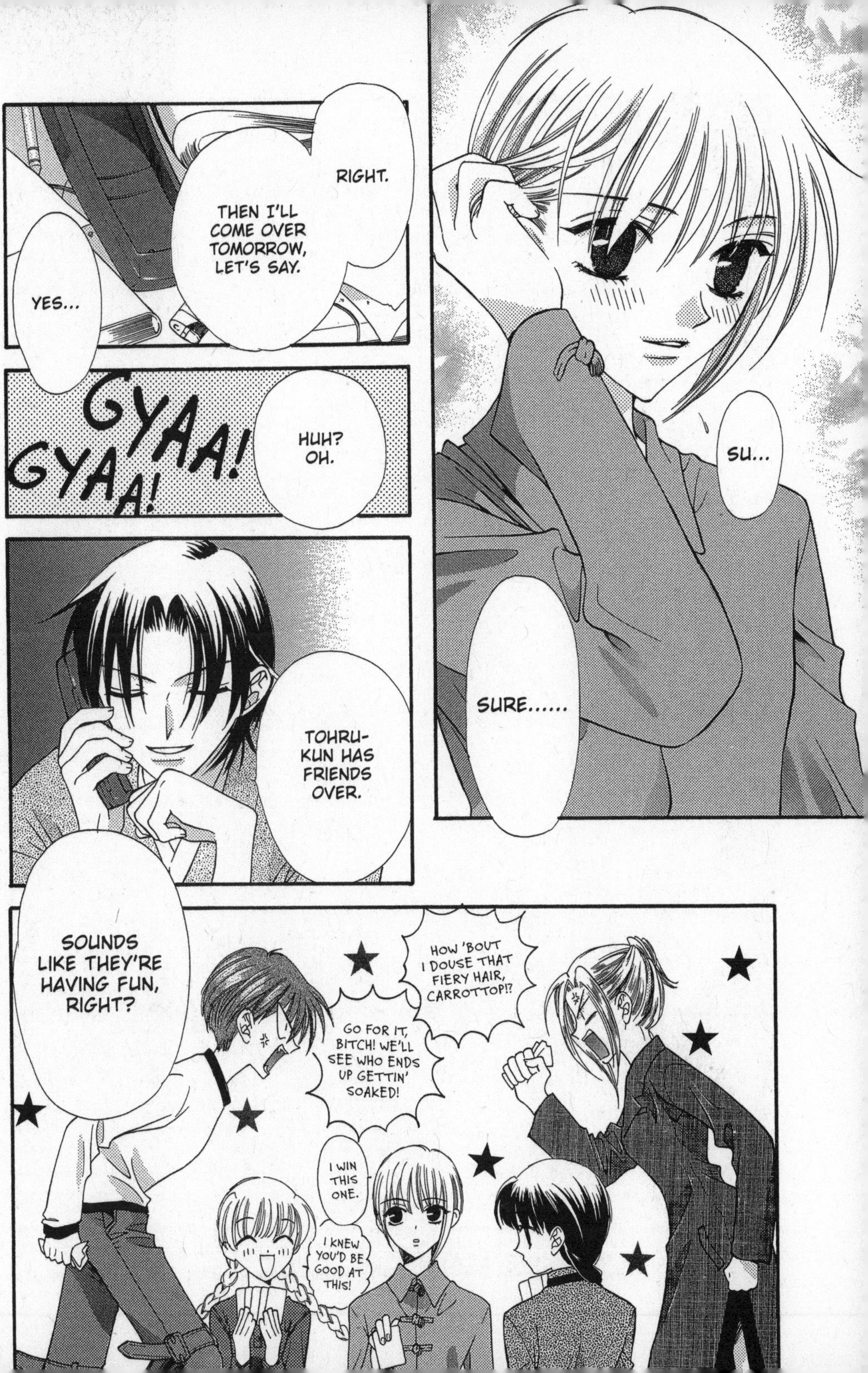
SU...
SURE......
RIGHT.
THEN I'LL COME OVER TOMORROW, LET'S SAY.
YES...
GYAA! GYAA!
HUH? OH.
TOHRU-KUN HAS FRIENDS OVER.
SOUNDS LIKE THEY'RE HAVING FUN, RIGHT?
HOW 'BOUT I DOUSE THAT FIERY HAIR, CARROTTOP!?
GO FOR IT, BITCH! WE'LL SEE WHO ENDS UP GETTIN' SOAKED!
I WIN THIS ONE.
I KNEW YOU'D BE GOOD AT THIS!

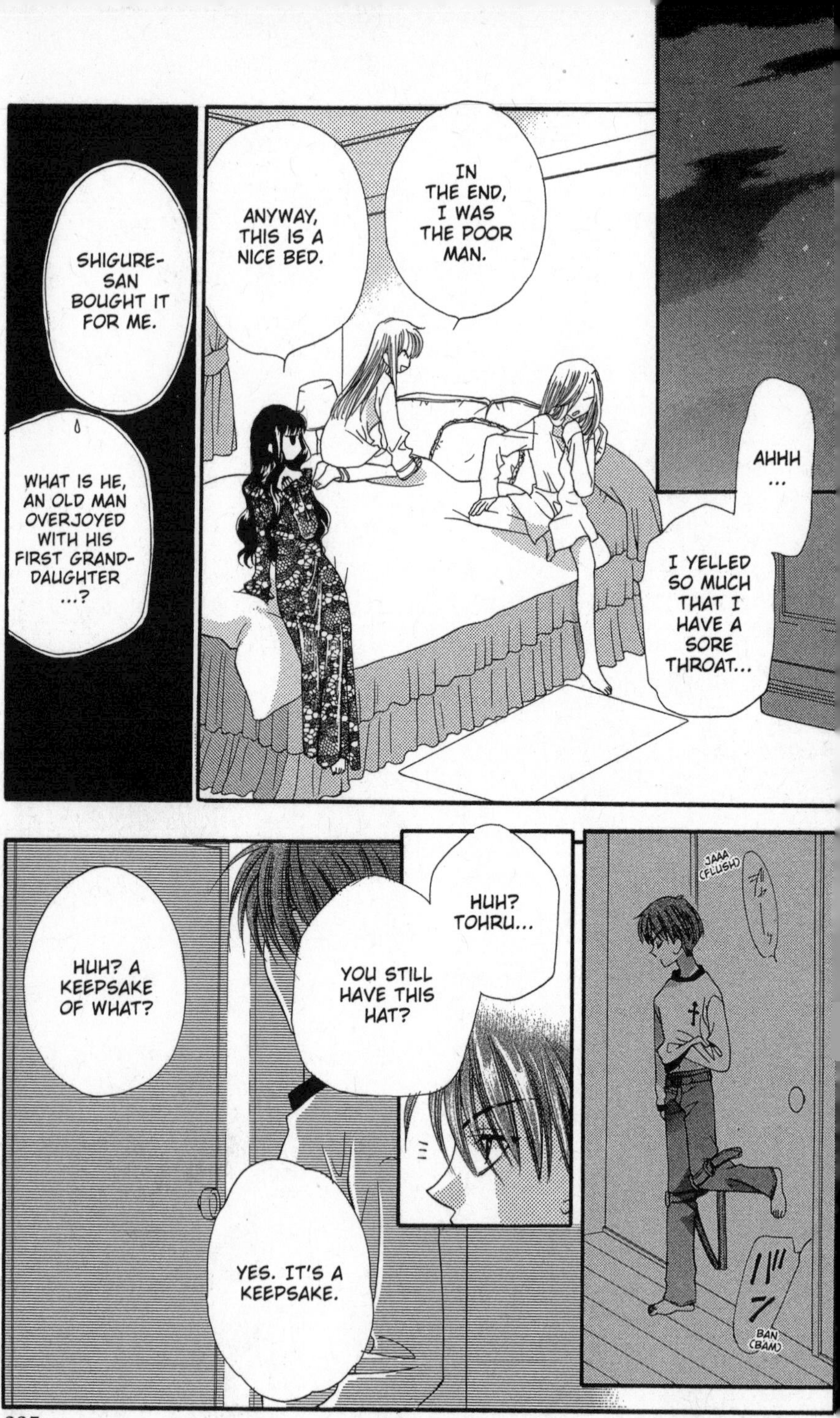
AHHH ...
I YELLED SO MUCH THAT I HAVE A SORE THROAT...
IN THE END, I WAS THE POOR MAN.
ANYWAY, THIS IS A NICE BED.
SHIGURE-SAN BOUGHT IT FOR ME.
WHAT IS HE, AN OLD MAN OVERJOYED WITH HIS FIRST GRAND-DAUGHTER ...?
JAAA (FLUSH)
BAN (BAM)
HUH? TOHRU...
YOU STILL HAVE THIS HAT?
YES. IT'S A KEEPSAKE.
HUH? A KEEPSAKE OF WHAT?

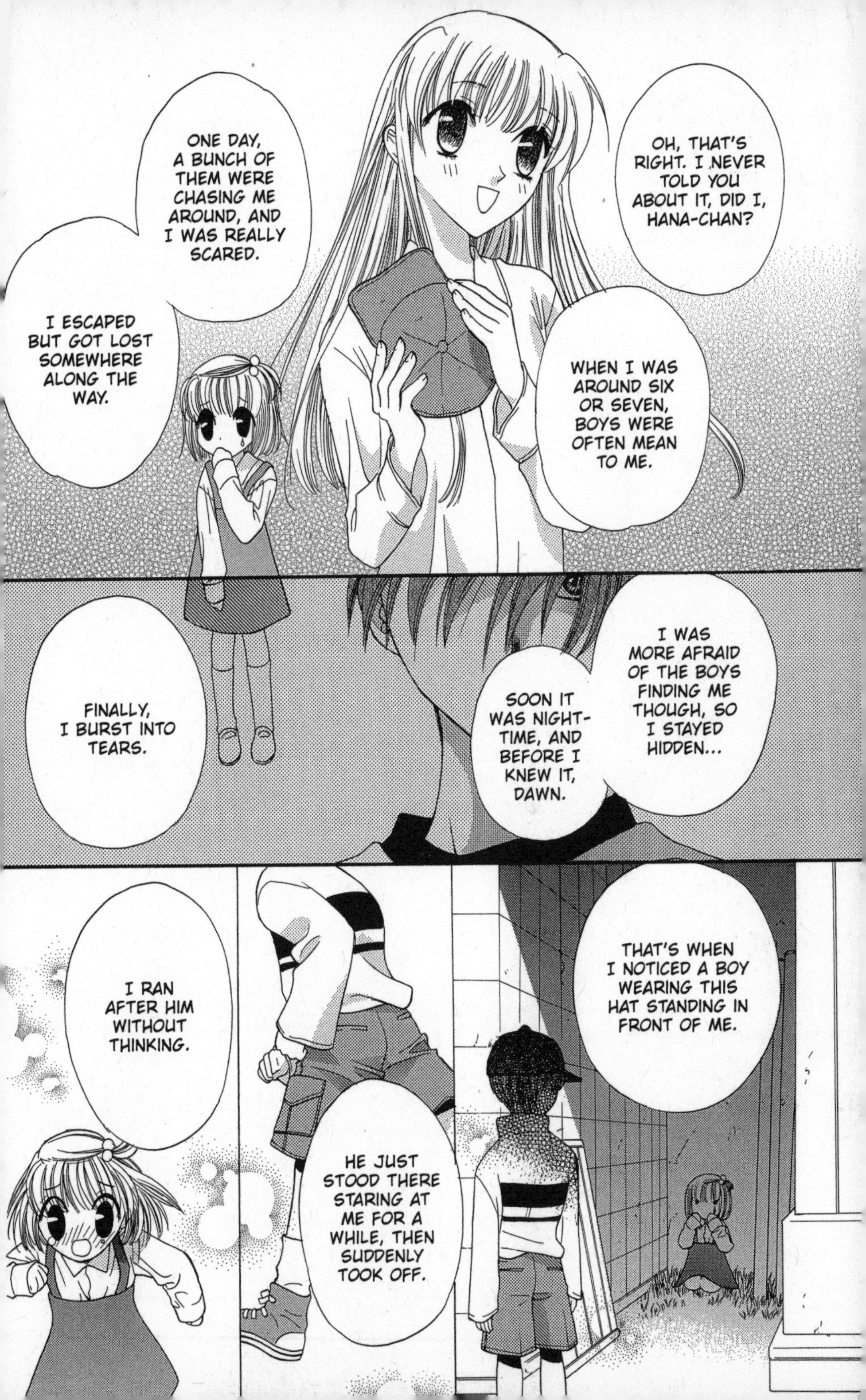
OH, THAT'S RIGHT. I NEVER TOLD YOU ABOUT IT, DID I, HANA-CHAN?
WHEN I WAS AROUND SIX OR SEVEN, BOYS WERE OFTEN MEAN TO ME.
ONE DAY, A BUNCH OF THEM WERE CHASING ME AROUND, AND I WAS REALLY SCARED.
I ESCAPED BUT GOT LOST SOMEWHERE ALONG THE WAY.
FINALLY, I BURST INTO TEARS.
I WAS MORE AFRAID OF THE BOYS FINDING ME THOUGH, SO I STAYED HIDDEN...
SOON IT WAS NIGHT-TIME, AND BEFORE I KNEW IT, DAWN.
THAT'S WHEN I NOTICED A BOY WEARING THIS HAT STANDING IN FRONT OF ME.
HE JUST STOOD THERE STARING AT ME FOR A WHILE, THEN SUDDENLY TOOK OFF.
I RAN AFTER HIM WITHOUT THINKING.

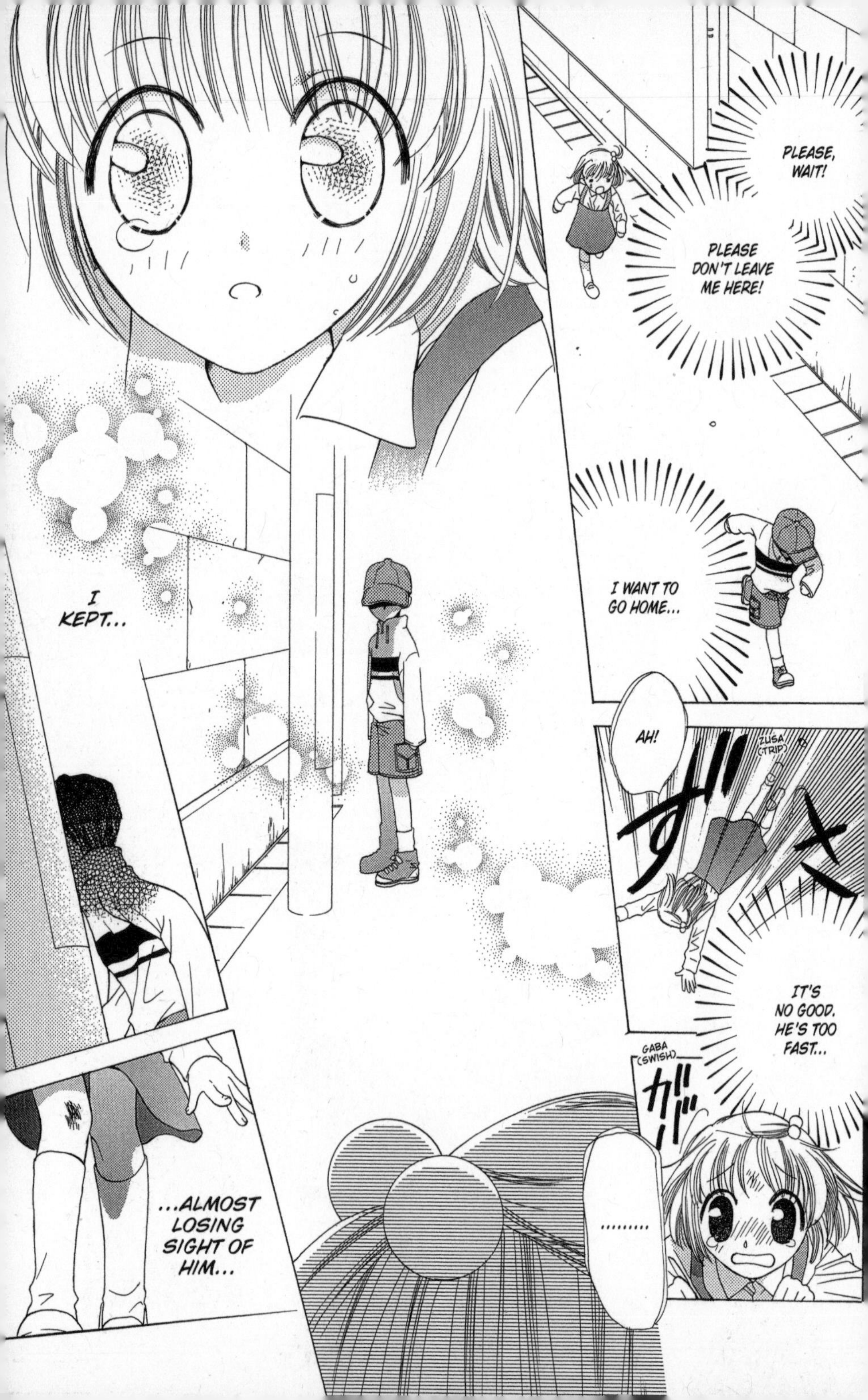
PLEASE, WAIT!
PLEASE DON'T LEAVE ME HERE!
I WANT TO GO HOME...
AH!
ZUSA (TRIP)
IT'S NO GOOD. HE'S TOO FAST...
GABA (SWISH)
....
I KEPT...
...ALMOST LOSING SIGHT OF HIM...

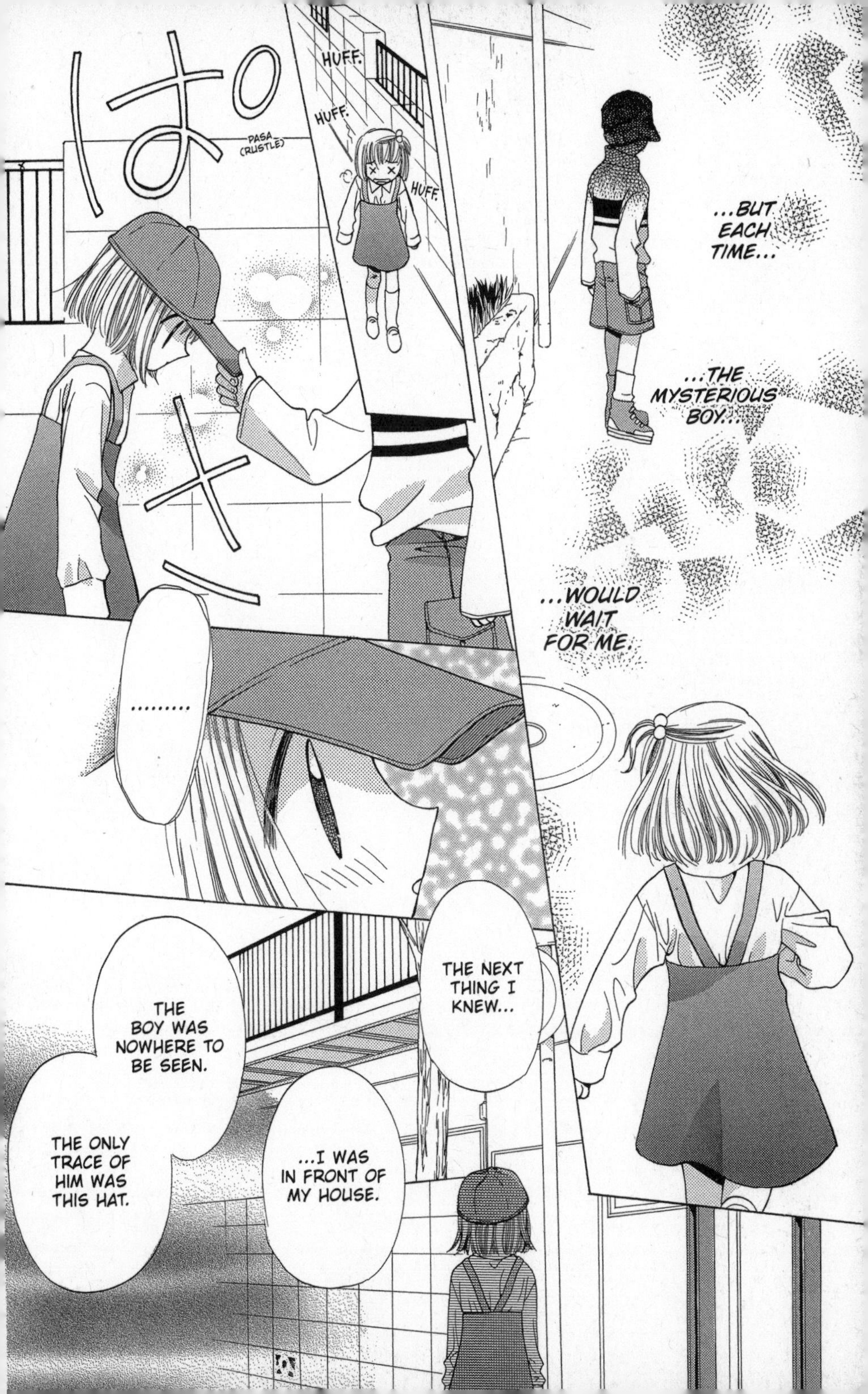
...BUT EACH TIME...
...THE MYSTERIOUS BOY...
...WOULD WAIT FOR ME.
HUFF.
HUFF.
HUFF.
PASA (RUSTLE)
....
THE NEXT THING I KNEW...
...I WAS IN FRONT OF MY HOUSE.
THE BOY WAS NOWHERE TO BE SEEN.
THE ONLY TRACE OF HIM WAS THIS HAT.

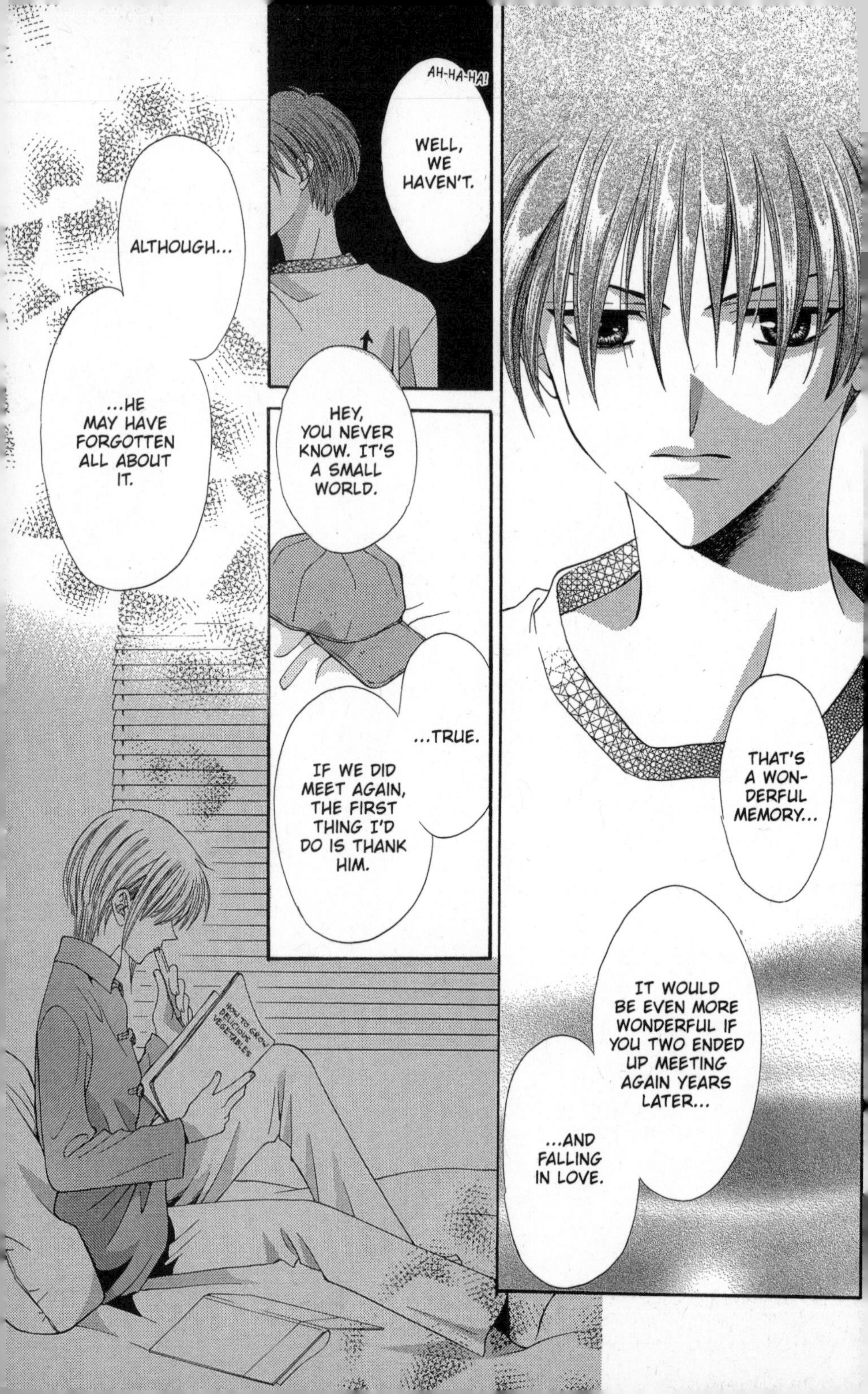
THAT'S A WON-DERFUL MEMORY...
IT WOULD BE EVEN MORE WONDERFUL IF YOU TWO ENDED UP MEETING AGAIN YEARS LATER...
...AND FALLING IN LOVE.
AH-HA-HA!
WELL, WE HAVEN'T.
HEY, YOU NEVER KNOW. IT'S A SMALL WORLD.
...TRUE.
IF WE DID MEET AGAIN, THE FIRST THING I'D DO IS THANK HIM.
ALTHOUGH...
...HE MAY HAVE FORGOTTEN ALL ABOUT IT.
HOW TO GROW DELICIOUS VEGETABLES

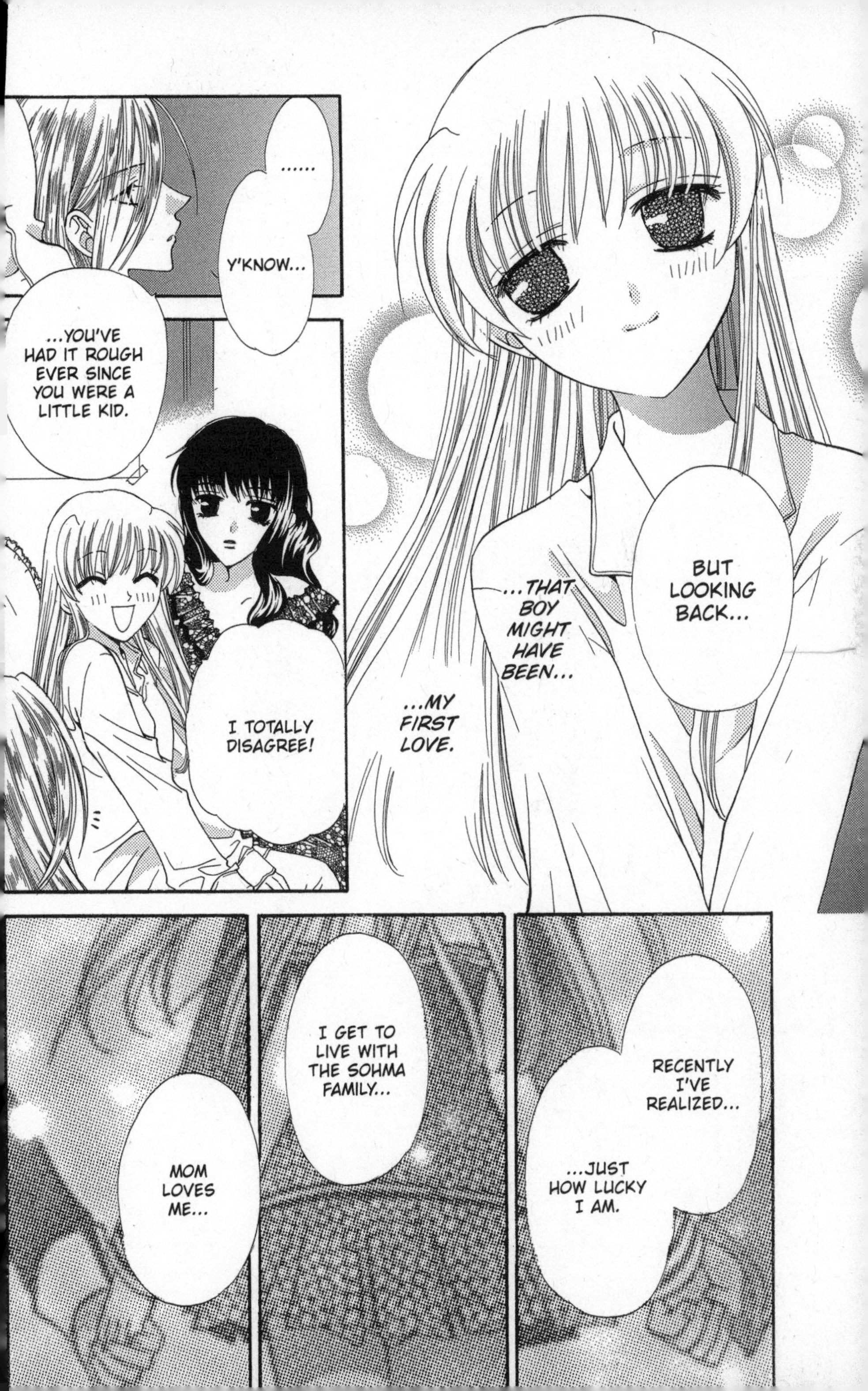
BUT LOOKING BACK...
...THAT BOY MIGHT HAVE BEEN...
...MY FIRST LOVE.
......
Y'KNOW...
...YOU'VE HAD IT ROUGH EVER SINCE YOU WERE A LITTLE KID.
I TOTALLY DISAGREE!
RECENTLY I'VE REALIZED...
...JUST HOW LUCKY I AM.
I GET TO LIVE WITH THE SOHMA FAMILY...
MOM LOVES ME...

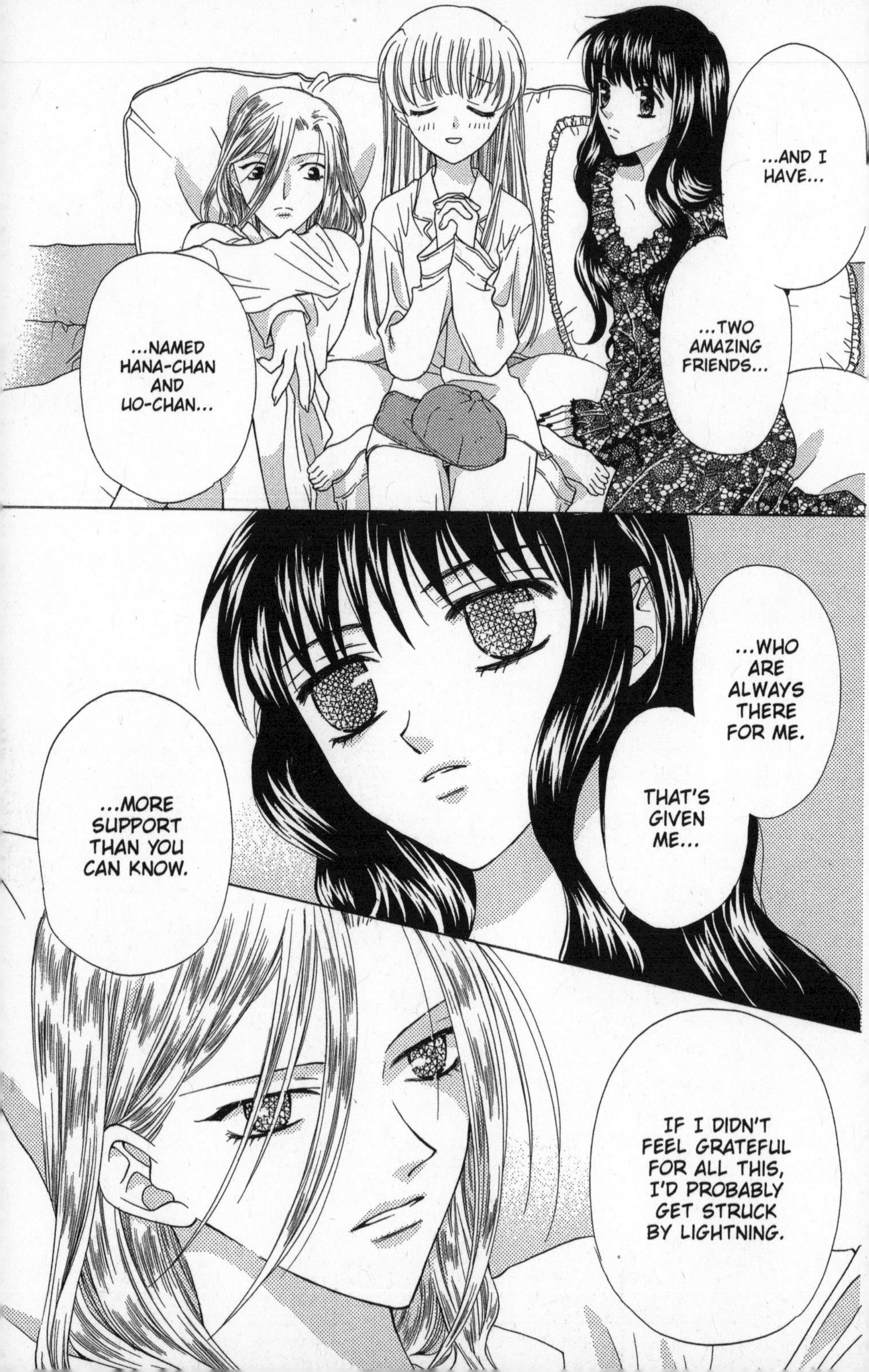
...AND I HAVE...
...TWO AMAZING FRIENDS...
...NAMED HANA-CHAN AND UO-CHAN...
...WHO ARE ALWAYS THERE FOR ME.
THAT'S GIVEN ME...
...MORE SUPPORT THAN YOU CAN KNOW.
IF I DIDN'T FEEL GRATEFUL FOR ALL THIS, I'D PROBABLY GET STRUCK BY LIGHTNING.

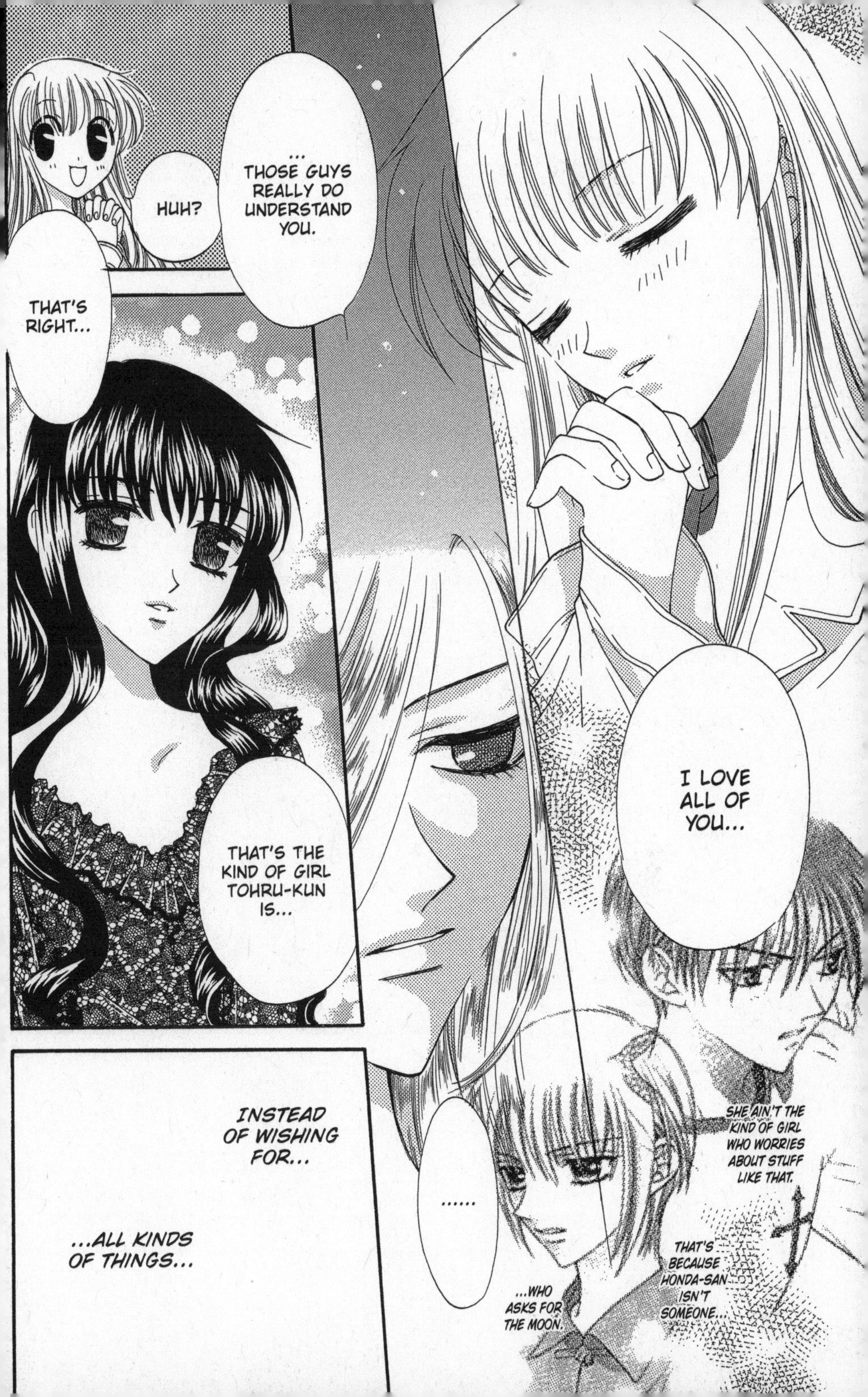
...THOSE GUYS REALLY DO UNDERSTAND YOU.
HUH?
THAT'S RIGHT...
THAT'S THE KIND OF GIRL TOHRU-KUN IS...
I LOVE ALL OF YOU...
......
SHE AIN'T THE KIND OF GIRL WHO WORRIES ABOUT STUFF LIKE THAT.
THAT'S BECAUSE HONDA-SAN ISN'T SOMEONE...
...WHO ASKS FOR THE MOON.
INSTEAD OF WISHING FOR...
...ALL KINDS OF THINGS...

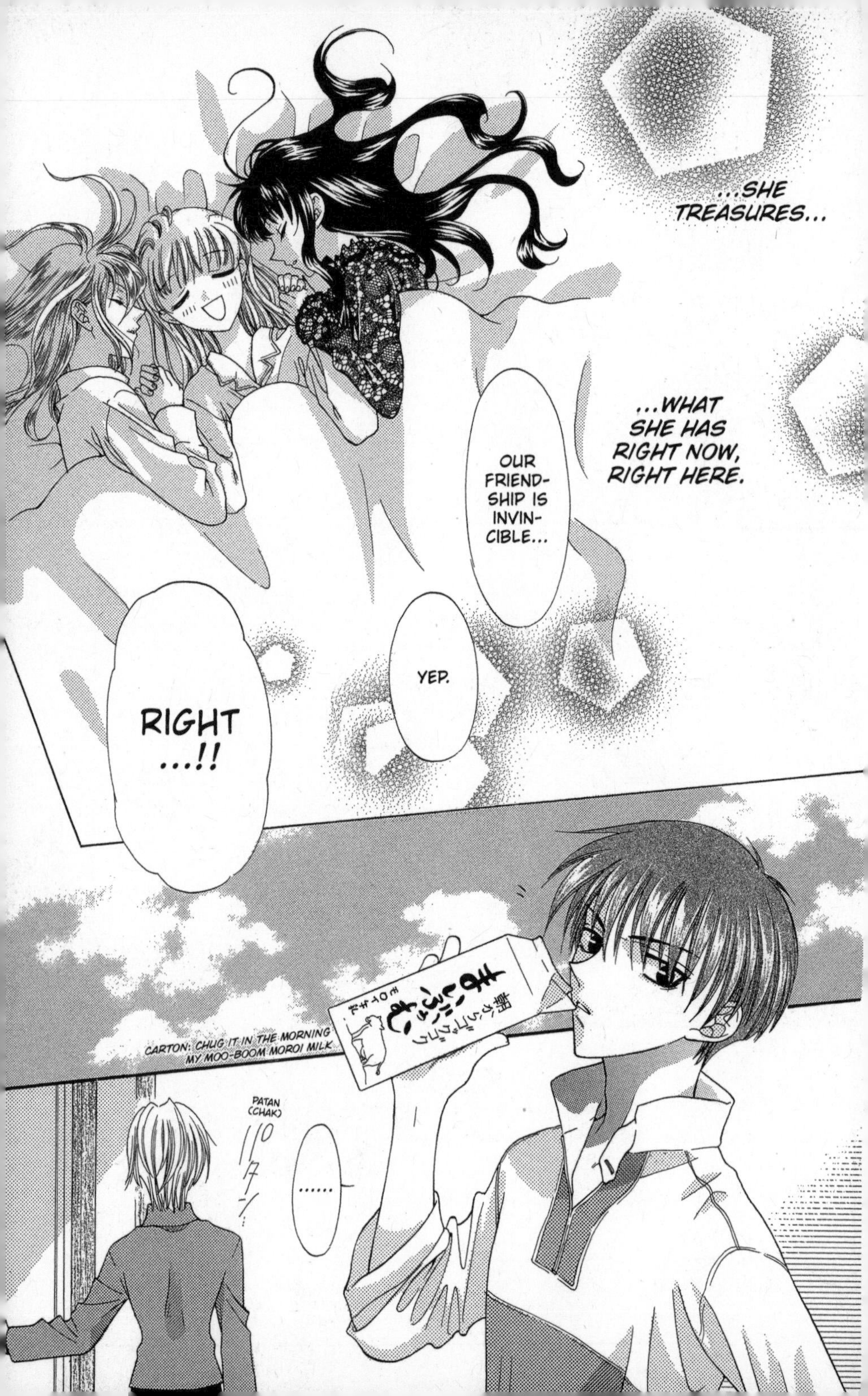
...SHE TREASURES...
...WHAT SHE HAS RIGHT NOW, RIGHT HERE.
OUR FRIEND-SHIP IS INVIN-CIBLE...
YEP.
RIGHT ...!!
CARTON: CHUG IT IN THE MORNING MY MOO-BOOM MOROI MILK
PATAN (CHAK)
......

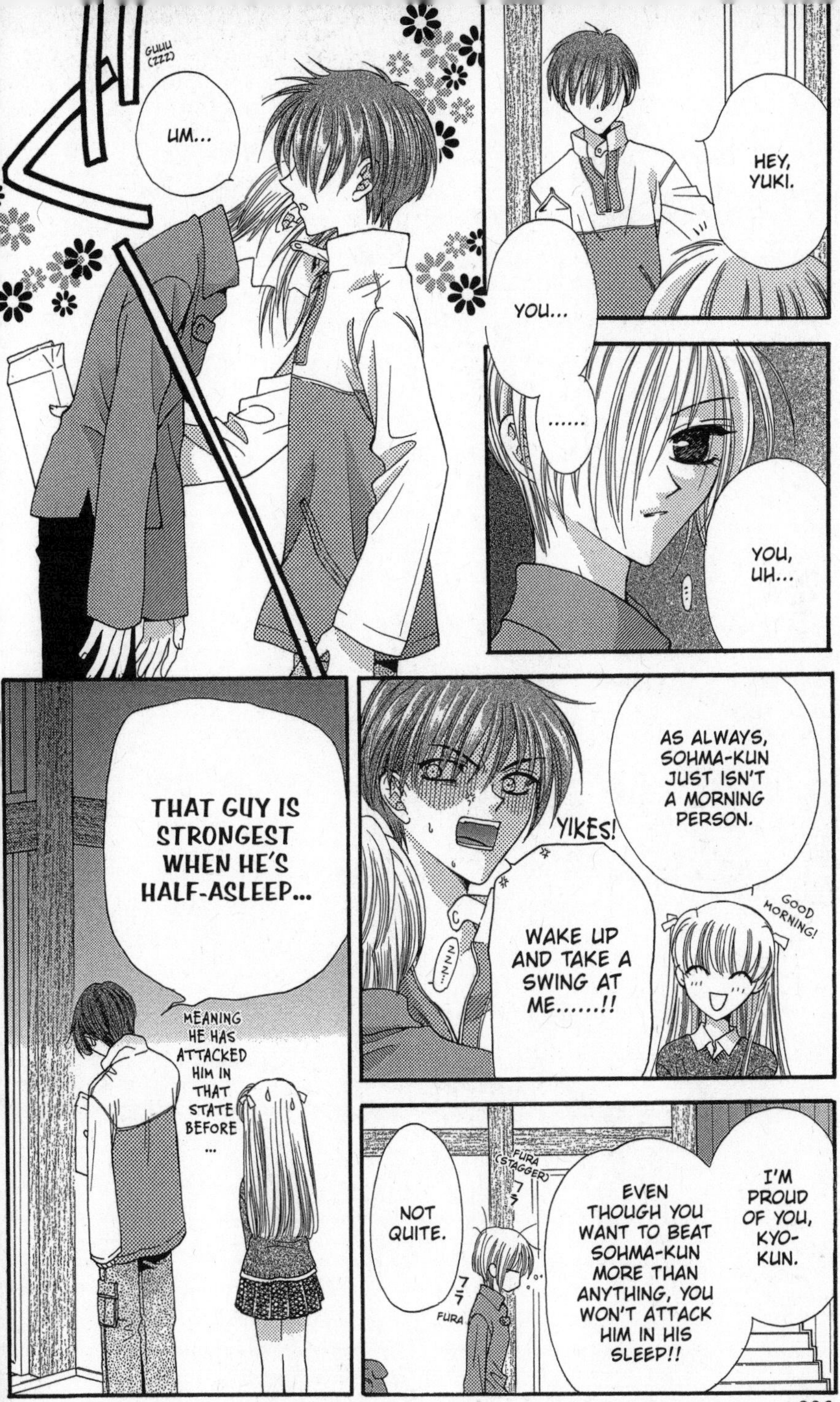
HEY, YUKI.
YOU...
......
YOU, UH...
GUUU (ZZZ)
UM...
AS ALWAYS, SOHMA-KUN JUST ISN'T A MORNING PERSON.
GOOD MORNING!
YIKES!
WAKE UP AND TAKE A SWING AT ME......!!
ZZZ...
I'M PROUD OF YOU, KYO-KUN.
EVEN THOUGH YOU WANT TO BEAT SOHMA-KUN MORE THAN ANYTHING, YOU WON'T ATTACK HIM IN HIS SLEEP!!
FURA (STAGGER)
NOT QUITE.
FURA
THAT GUY IS STRONGEST WHEN HE'S HALF-ASLEEP...
MEANING HE HAS ATTACKED HIM IN THAT STATE BEFORE ...

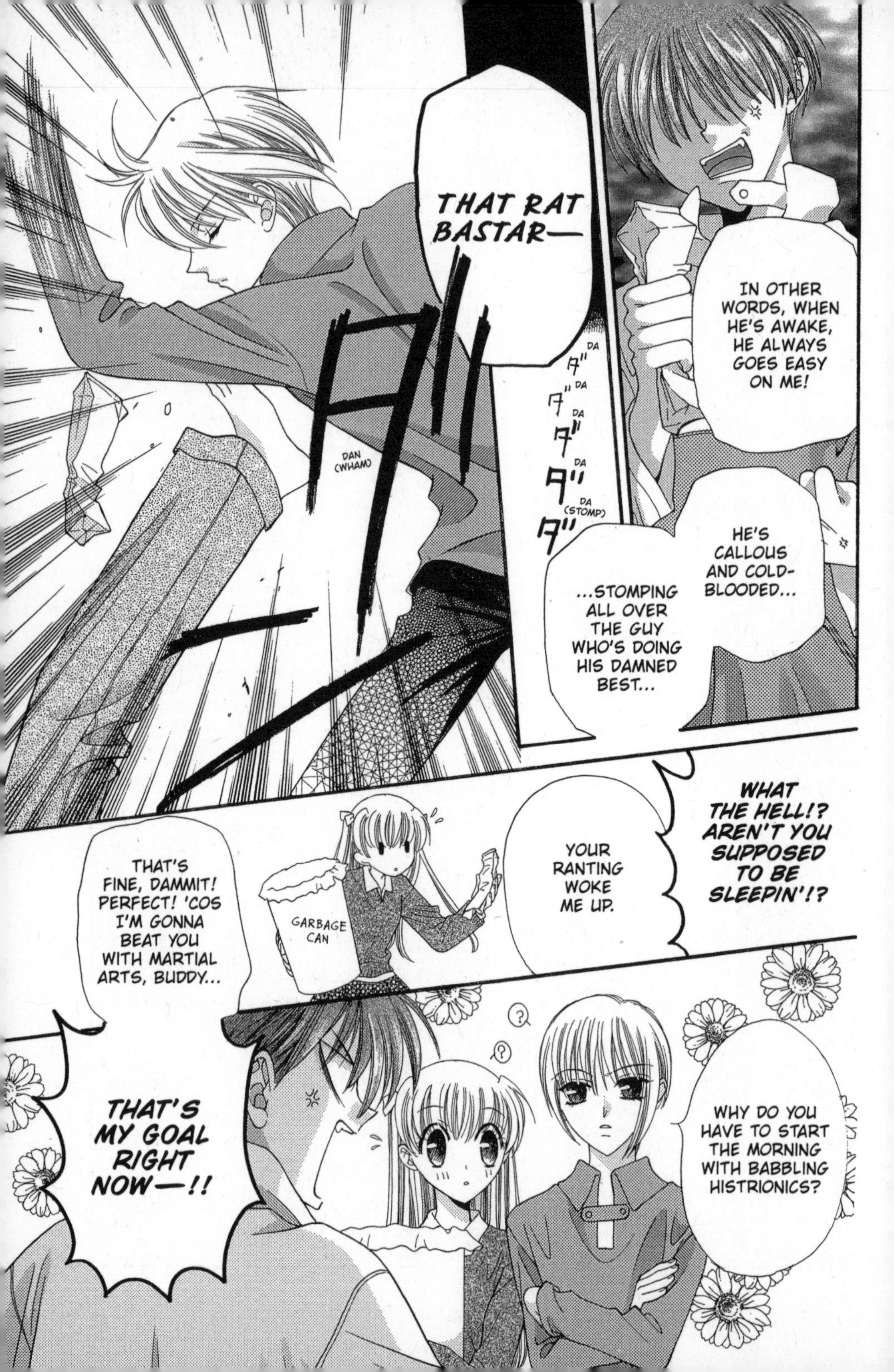
IN OTHER WORDS, WHEN HE'S AWAKE, HE ALWAYS GOES EASY ON ME!
HE'S CALLOUS AND COLD-BLOODED...
...STOMPING ALL OVER THE GUY WHO'S DOING HIS DAMNED BEST...
DA DA DA DA DA (STOMP)
THAT RAT BASTAR—
DAN (WHAM)
WHAT THE HELL!? AREN'T YOU SUPPOSED TO BE SLEEPIN'!?
YOUR RANTING WOKE ME UP.
GARBAGE CAN
THAT'S FINE, DAMMIT! PERFECT! 'COS I'M GONNA BEAT YOU WITH MARTIAL ARTS, BUDDY...
WHY DO YOU HAVE TO START THE MORNING WITH BABBLING HISTRIONICS?
THAT'S MY GOAL RIGHT NOW—!!

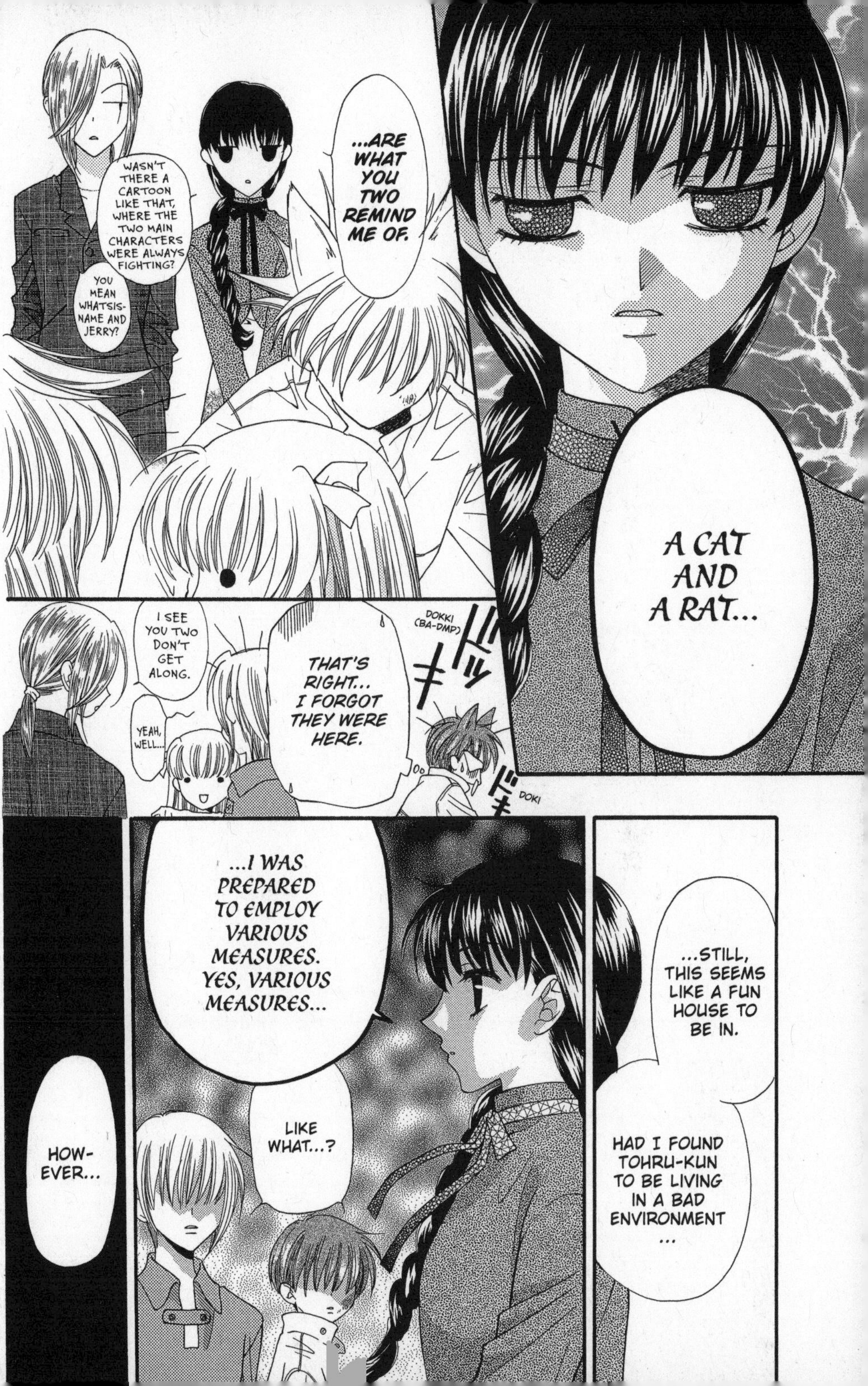
A CAT AND A RAT...
...ARE WHAT YOU TWO REMIND ME OF.
WASN'T THERE A CARTOON LIKE THAT, WHERE THE TWO MAIN CHARACTERS WERE ALWAYS FIGHTING?
YOU MEAN WHATSIS-NAME AND JERRY?
DOKKI (BA-DMP)
THAT'S RIGHT... I FORGOT THEY WERE HERE.
I SEE YOU TWO DON'T GET ALONG.
YEAH, WELL...
DOKI
...STILL, THIS SEEMS LIKE A FUN HOUSE TO BE IN.
HAD I FOUND TOHRU-KUN TO BE LIVING IN A BAD ENVIRONMENT...
...I WAS PREPARED TO EMPLOY VARIOUS MEASURES. YES, VARIOUS MEASURES...
LIKE WHAT...?
HOW-EVER...

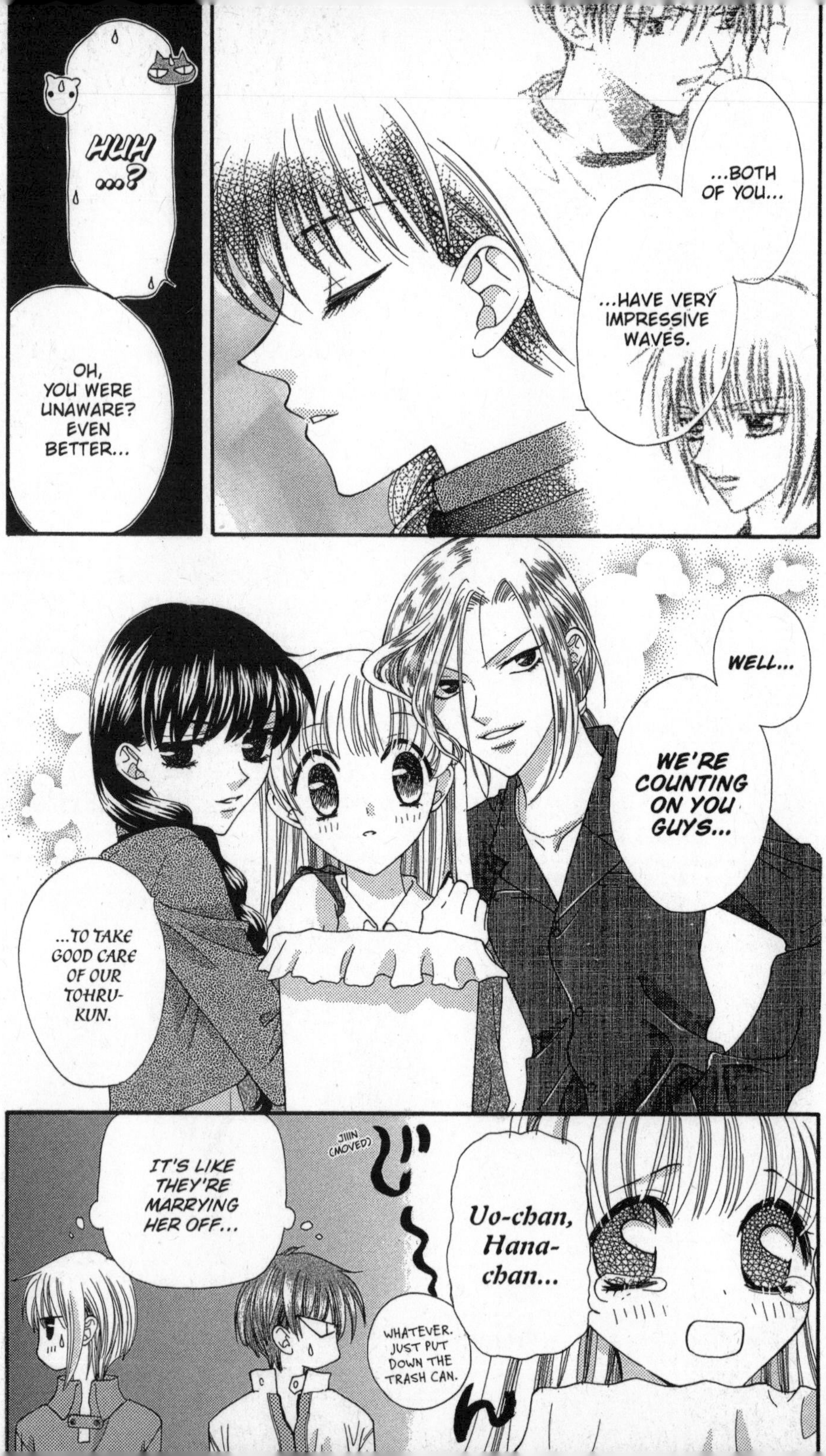
...BOTH OF YOU...
...HAVE VERY IMPRESSIVE WAVES.
HUH ...?
OH, YOU WERE UNAWARE? EVEN BETTER...
WELL...
WE'RE COUNTING ON YOU GUYS...
...TO TAKE GOOD CARE OF OUR TOHRU-KUN.
Uo-chan, Hana-chan...
JIIIN (MOVED)
IT'S LIKE THEY'RE MARRYING HER OFF...
WHATEVER. JUST PUT DOWN THE TRASH CAN.

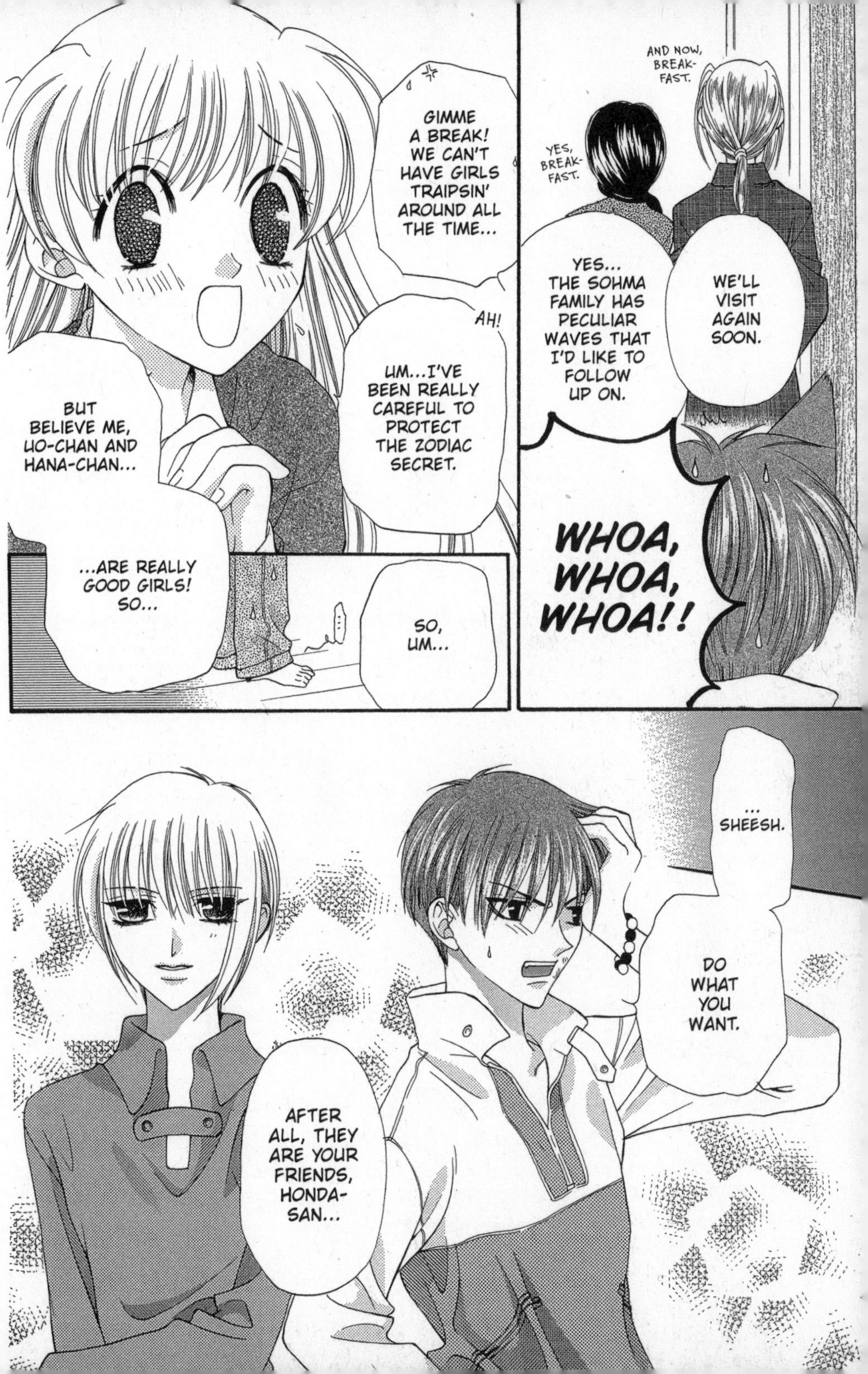
AND NOW, BREAK-FAST.
YES, BREAK-FAST.
WE'LL VISIT AGAIN SOON.
YES... THE SOHMA FAMILY HAS PECULIAR WAVES THAT I'D LIKE TO FOLLOW UP ON.
WHOA, WHOA, WHOA!!
GIMME A BREAK! WE CAN'T HAVE GIRLS TRAIPSIN' AROUND ALL THE TIME...
AH!
UM...I'VE BEEN REALLY CAREFUL TO PROTECT THE ZODIAC SECRET.
BUT BELIEVE ME, UO-CHAN AND HANA-CHAN...
...ARE REALLY GOOD GIRLS! SO...
SO, UM...
...SHEESH.
DO WHAT YOU WANT.
AFTER ALL, THEY ARE YOUR FRIENDS, HONDA-SAN...

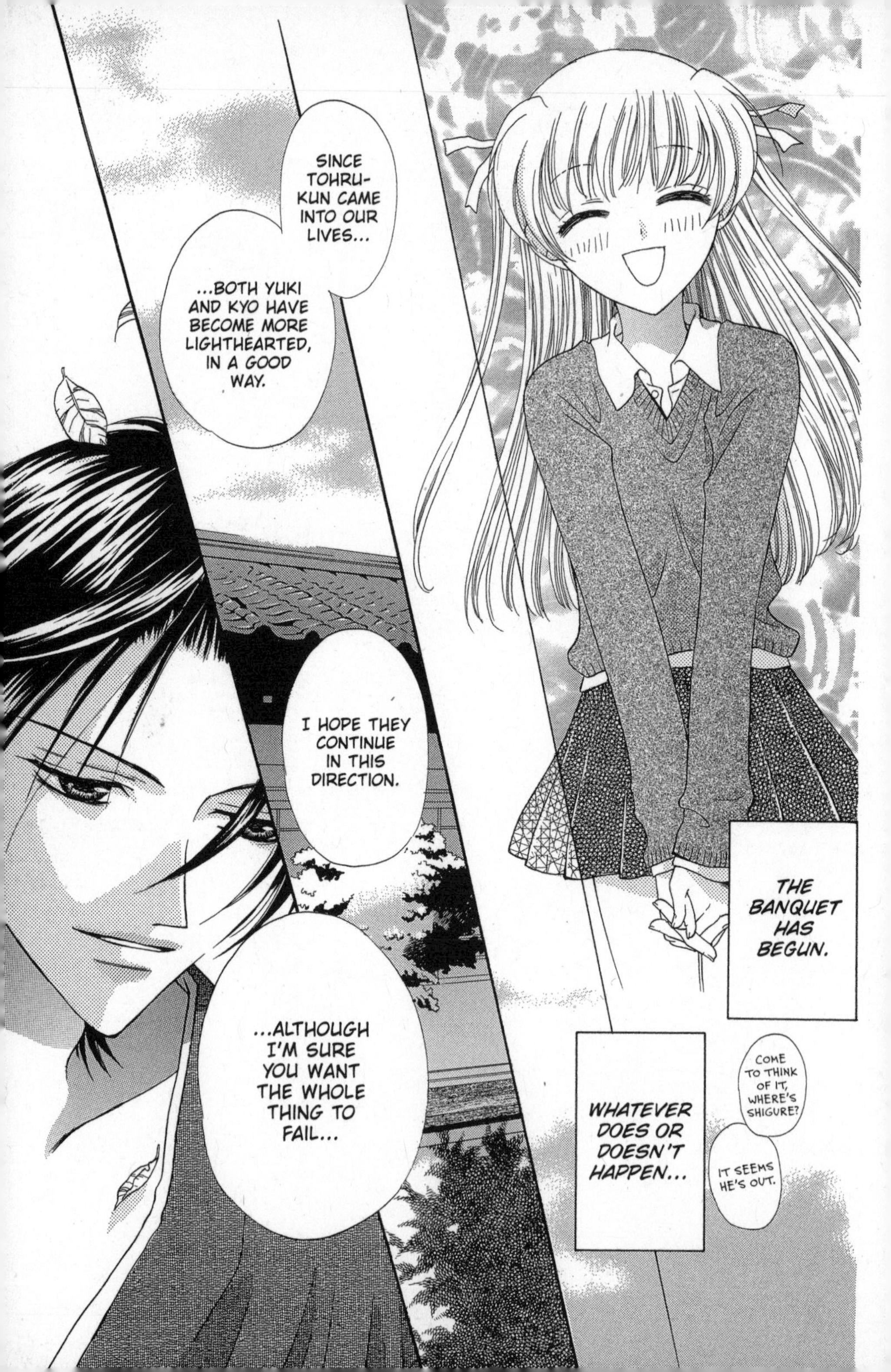
THE BANQUET HAS BEGUN.
COME TO THINK OF IT, WHERE'S SHIGURE?
IT SEEMS HE'S OUT.
WHATEVER DOES OR DOESN'T HAPPEN...
SINCE TOHRU-KUN CAME INTO OUR LIVES...
...BOTH YUKI AND KYO HAVE BECOME MORE LIGHTHEARTED, IN A GOOD WAY.
I HOPE THEY CONTINUE IN THIS DIRECTION.
...ALTHOUGH I'M SURE YOU WANT THE WHOLE THING TO FAIL...

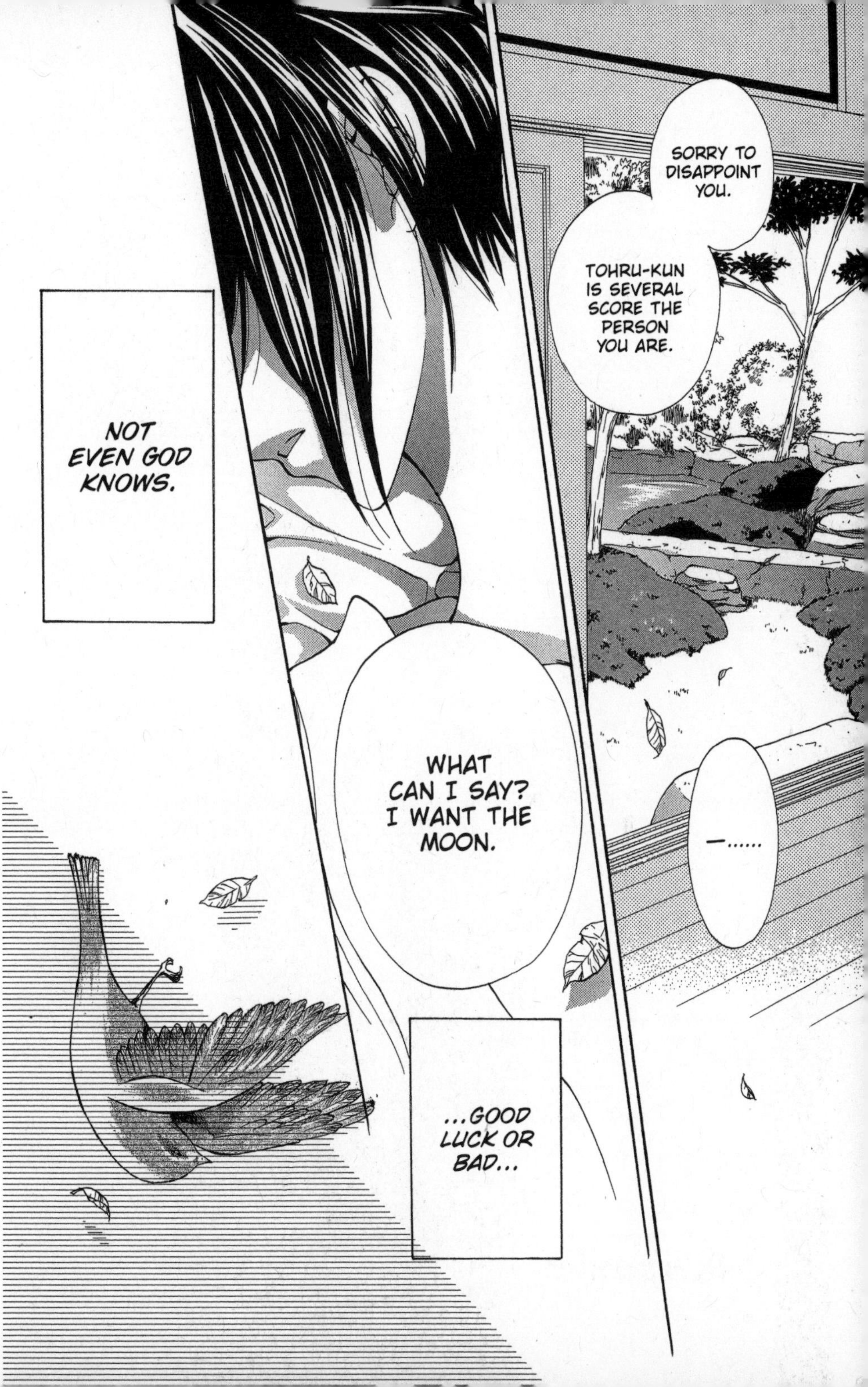
SORRY TO DISAPPOINT YOU.
TOHRU-KUN IS SEVERAL SCORE THE PERSON YOU ARE.
—......
WHAT CAN I SAY? I WANT THE MOON.
...GOOD LUCK OR BAD...
NOT EVEN GOD KNOWS.

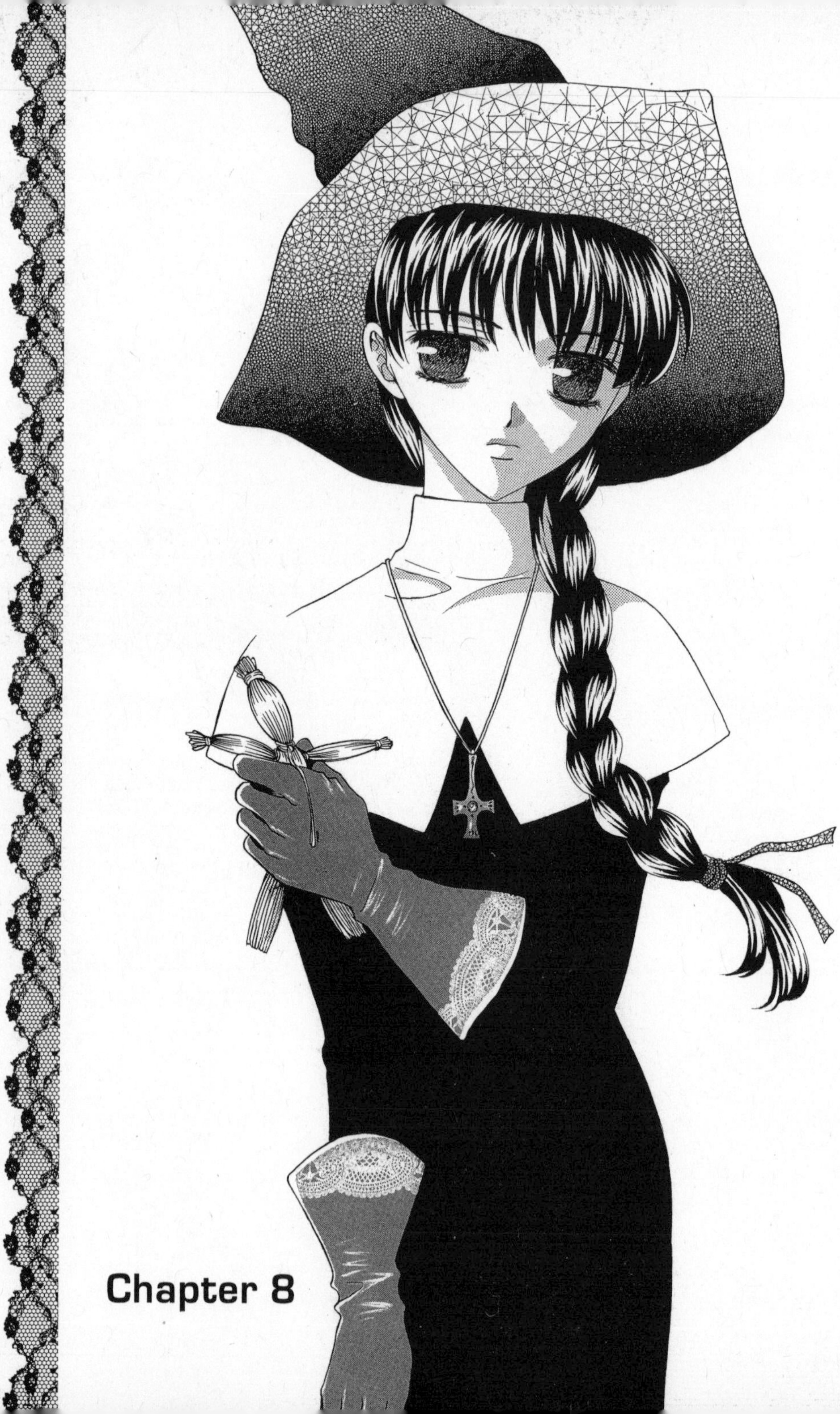

Chapter 8

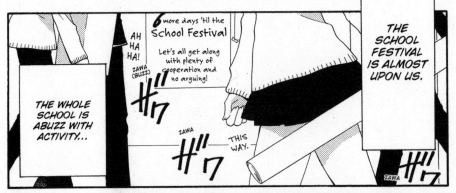

THE SCHOOL FESTIVAL IS ALMOST UPON US.
ZAWA
THIS WAY.
6 more days 'til the School Festival
Let's all get along with plenty of cooperation and no arguing!
AH HA HA!
ZAWA (BUZZ)
ZAWA
THE WHOLE SCHOOL IS ABUZZ WITH ACTIVITY...
...AND OUR CLASS, 1-D, IS NO DIFFERENT.
WE'VE PASSED THE HEALTH INSPECTION...
...SO WE CAN DO OUR RICE BALL STAND...
...BUT I'D LIKE TO GET YOUR OPINIONS AGAIN ON THE DIFFERENT FILLINGS WE'LL USE.

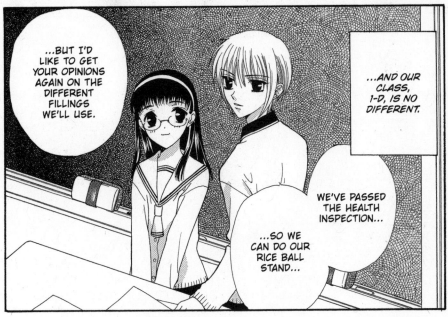

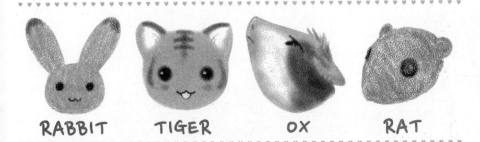

RABBIT TIGER OX RAT

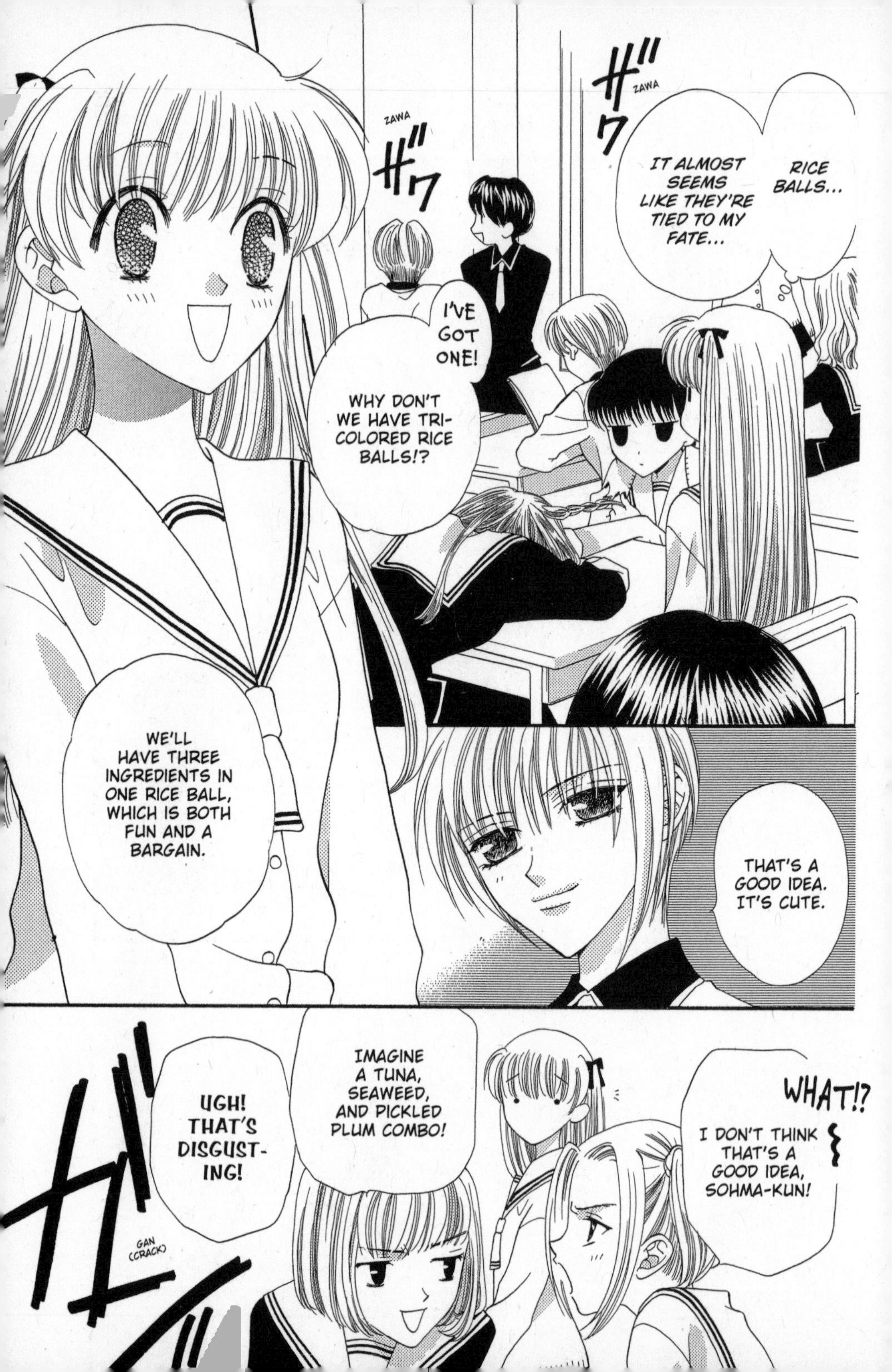
ZAWA
RICE BALLS...
IT ALMOST SEEMS LIKE THEY'RE TIED TO MY FATE...
ZAWA
I'VE GOT ONE!
WHY DON'T WE HAVE TRI-COLORED RICE BALLS!?
THAT'S A GOOD IDEA. IT'S CUTE.
WE'LL HAVE THREE INGREDIENTS IN ONE RICE BALL, WHICH IS BOTH FUN AND A BARGAIN.
WHAT!?
I DON'T THINK THAT'S A GOOD IDEA, SOHMA-KUN!
IMAGINE A TUNA, SEAWEED, AND PICKLED PLUM COMBO!
UGH! THAT'S DISGUST-ING!
GAN (CRACK)

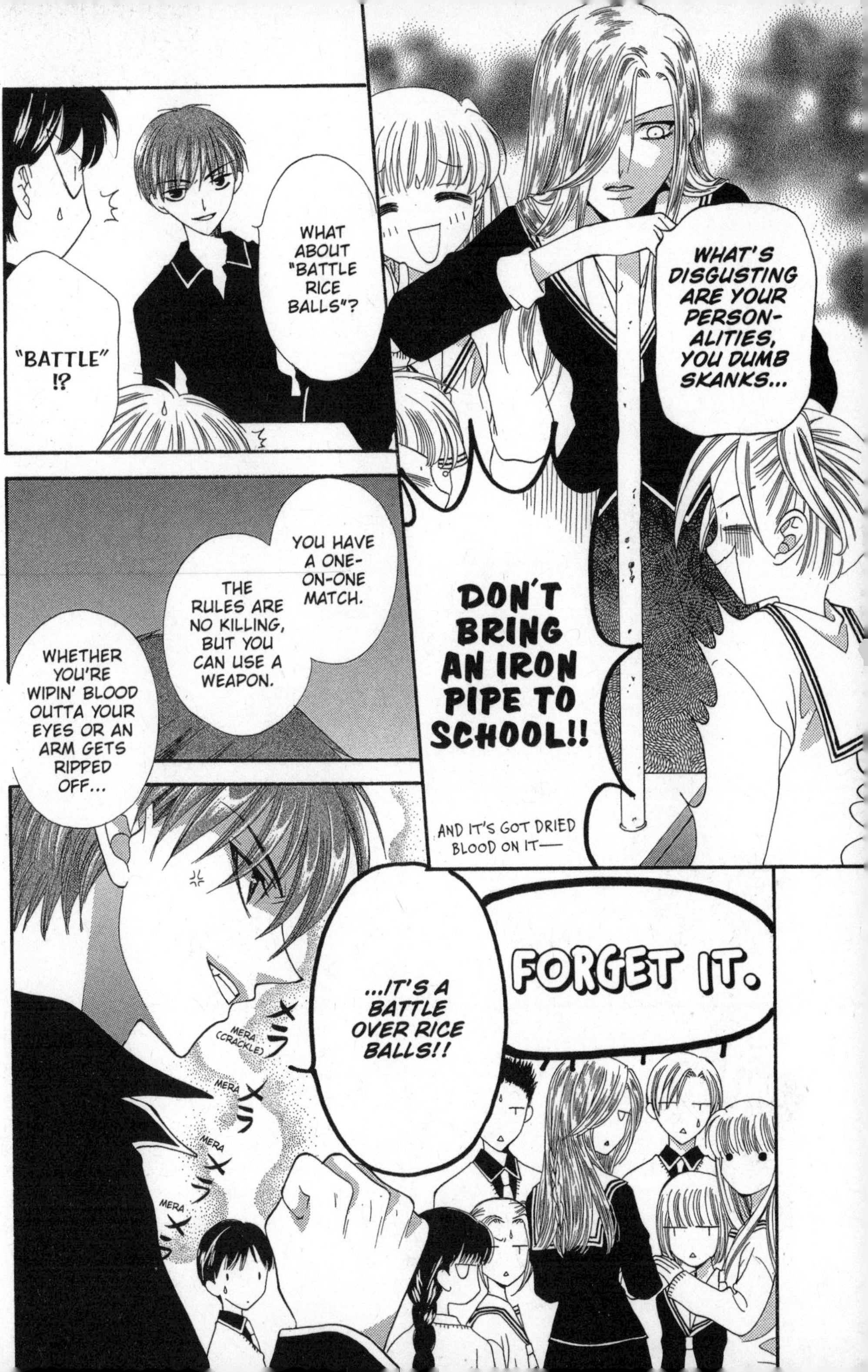
WHAT'S DISGUSTING ARE YOUR PERSON-ALITIES, YOU DUMB SKANKS...
DON'T BRING AN IRON PIPE TO SCHOOL!!
AND IT'S GOT DRIED BLOOD ON IT—
WHAT ABOUT "BATTLE RICE BALLS"?
"BATTLE" !?
YOU HAVE A ONE-ON-ONE MATCH.
THE RULES ARE NO KILLING, BUT YOU CAN USE A WEAPON.
WHETHER YOU'RE WIPIN' BLOOD OUTTA YOUR EYES OR AN ARM GETS RIPPED OFF...
FORGET IT.
...IT'S A BATTLE OVER RICE BALLS!!
MERA (CRACKLE)
MERA
MERA
MERA

Fruits Basket

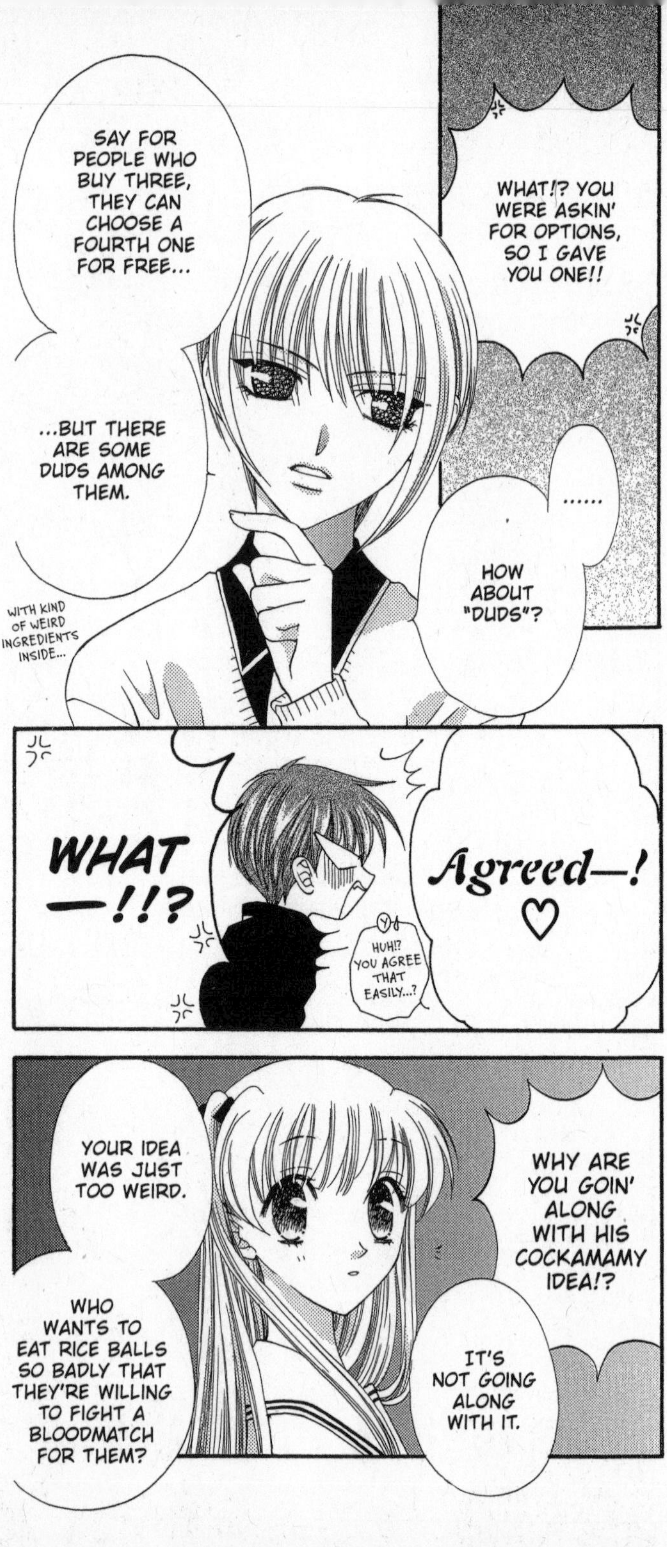
WHAT!? YOU WERE ASKIN' FOR OPTIONS, SO I GAVE YOU ONE!!
......
HOW ABOUT "DUDS"?
SAY FOR PEOPLE WHO BUY THREE, THEY CAN CHOOSE A FOURTH ONE FOR FREE...
...BUT THERE ARE SOME DUDS AMONG THEM.
WITH KIND OF WEIRD INGREDIENTS INSIDE...
Agreed—! ♡
HUH!? YOU AGREE THAT EASILY...?
WHAT—!!?
WHY ARE YOU GOIN' ALONG WITH HIS COCKAMAMY IDEA!?
IT'S NOT GOING ALONG WITH IT.
YOUR IDEA WAS JUST TOO WEIRD.
WHO WANTS TO EAT RICE BALLS SO BADLY THAT THEY'RE WILLING TO FIGHT A BLOODMATCH FOR THEM?

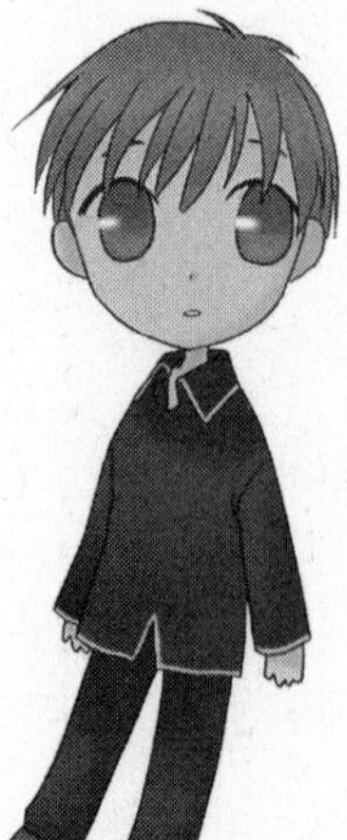

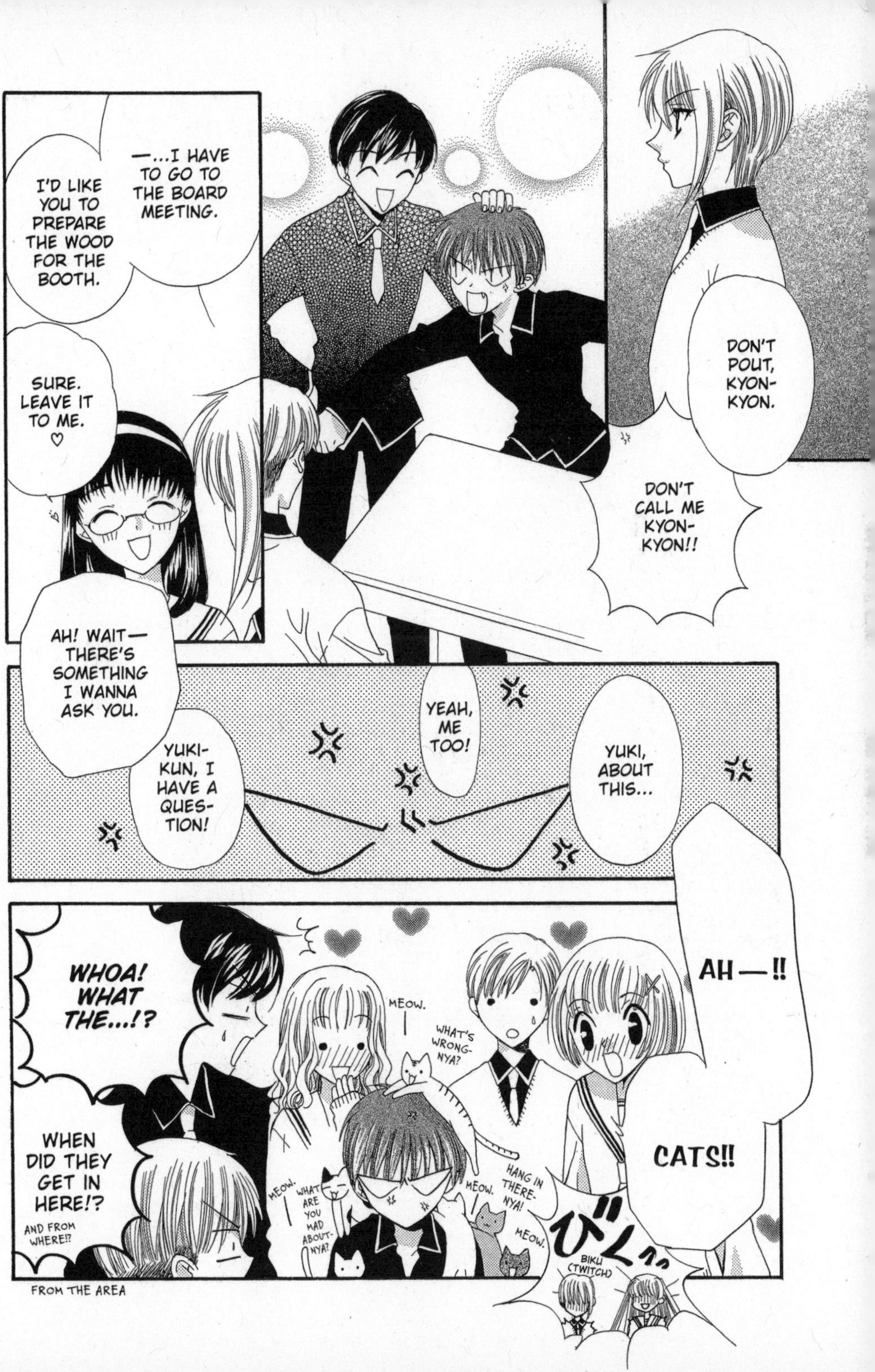
DON'T POUT, KYON-KYON.
DON'T CALL ME KYON-KYON!!
—...I HAVE TO GO TO THE BOARD MEETING.
I'D LIKE YOU TO PREPARE THE WOOD FOR THE BOOTH.
SURE. LEAVE IT TO ME. ♡
AH! WAIT— THERE'S SOMETHING I WANNA ASK YOU.
YUKI, ABOUT THIS...
YEAH, ME TOO!
YUKI-KUN, I HAVE A QUESTION!
AH—!!
CATS!!
びくっ
BIKU (TWITCH)
MEOW.
HANG IN THERE-NYA!
MEOW.
WHAT'S WRONG-NYA?
MEOW.
MEOW.
WHAT ARE YOU MAD ABOUT-NYA?
MEOW.
WHOA! WHAT THE...!?
WHEN DID THEY GET IN HERE!?
AND FROM WHERE!?
FROM THE AREA

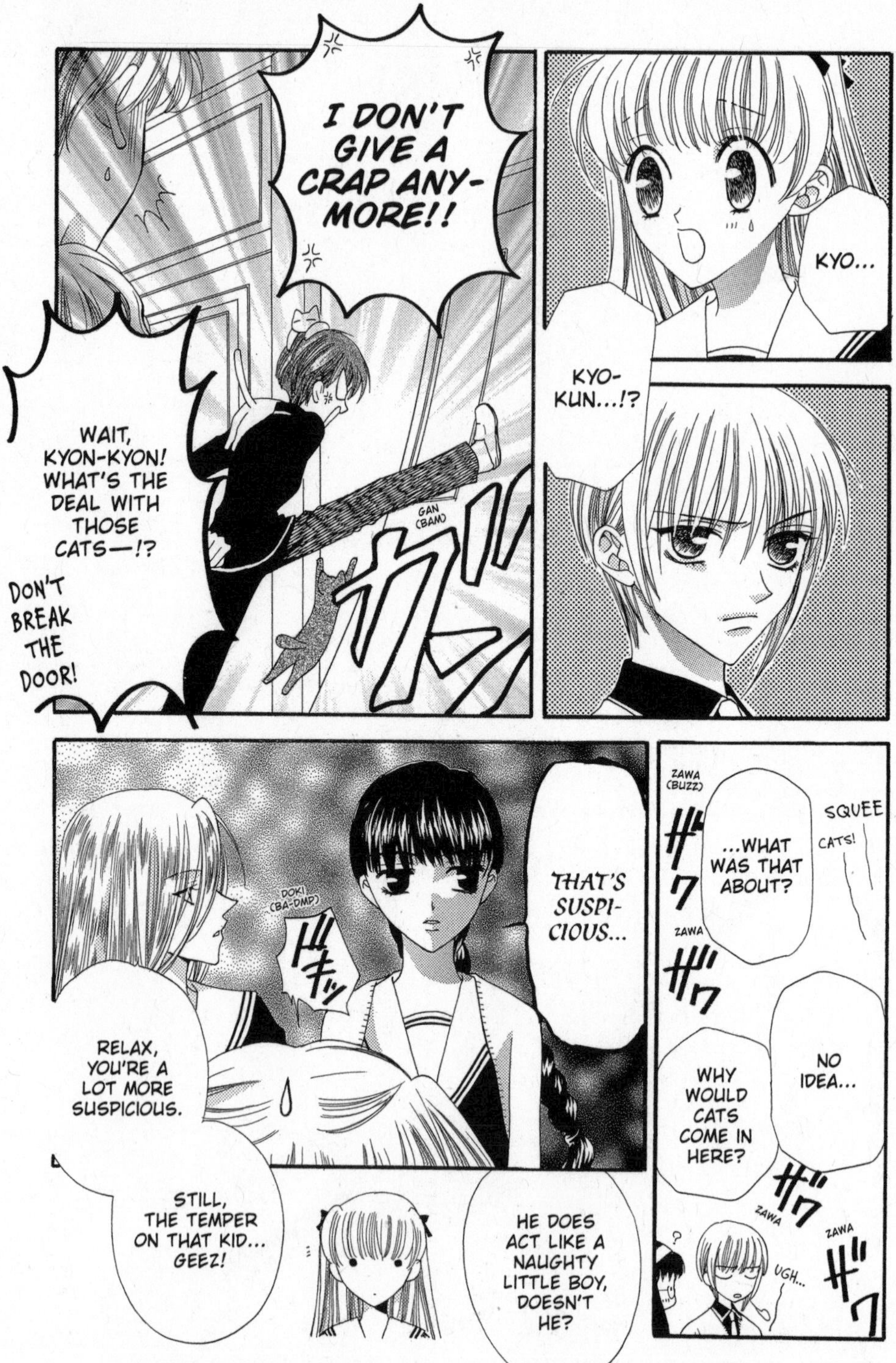
KYO...
KYO-KUN...!?
I DON'T GIVE A CRAP ANYMORE!!
GAN (BAM)
WAIT, KYON-KYON! WHAT'S THE DEAL WITH THOSE CATS—!?
DON'T BREAK THE DOOR!
SQUEE
CATS!
ZAWA (BUZZ)
...WHAT WAS THAT ABOUT?
ZAWA
NO IDEA...
WHY WOULD CATS COME IN HERE?
ZAWA
ZAWA
UGH...
THAT'S SUSPICIOUS...
DOKI (BA-DMP)
RELAX, YOU'RE A LOT MORE SUSPICIOUS.
HE DOES ACT LIKE A NAUGHTY LITTLE BOY, DOESN'T HE?
STILL, THE TEMPER ON THAT KID... GEEZ!

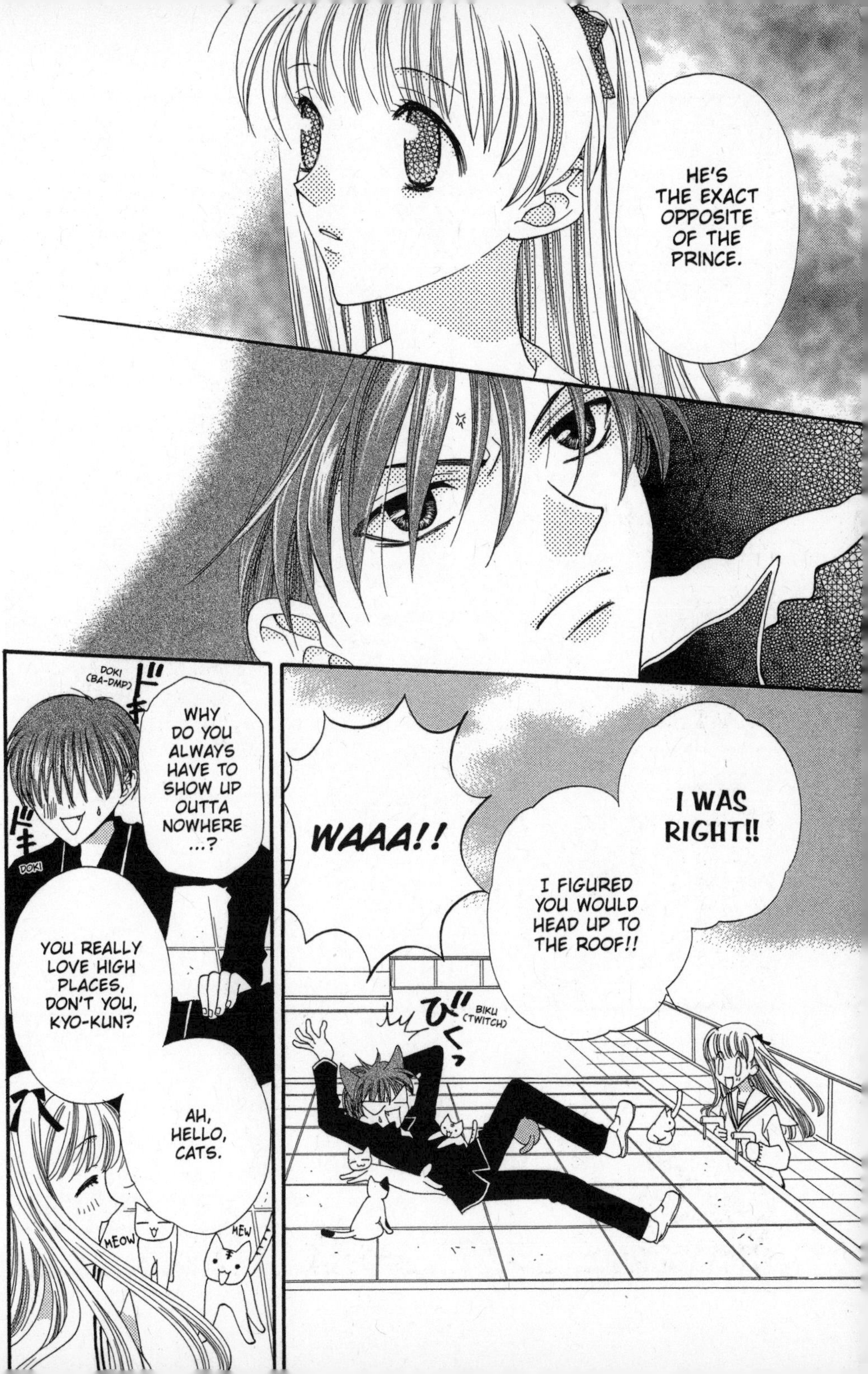
HE'S THE EXACT OPPOSITE OF THE PRINCE.
I WAS RIGHT!!
I FIGURED YOU WOULD HEAD UP TO THE ROOF!!
WAAA!!
BIKU (TWITCH)
DOKI (BA-DMP)
WHY DO YOU ALWAYS HAVE TO SHOW UP OUTTA NOWHERE ...?
DOKI
YOU REALLY LOVE HIGH PLACES, DON'T YOU, KYO-KUN?
AH, HELLO, CATS.
MEOW
MEW

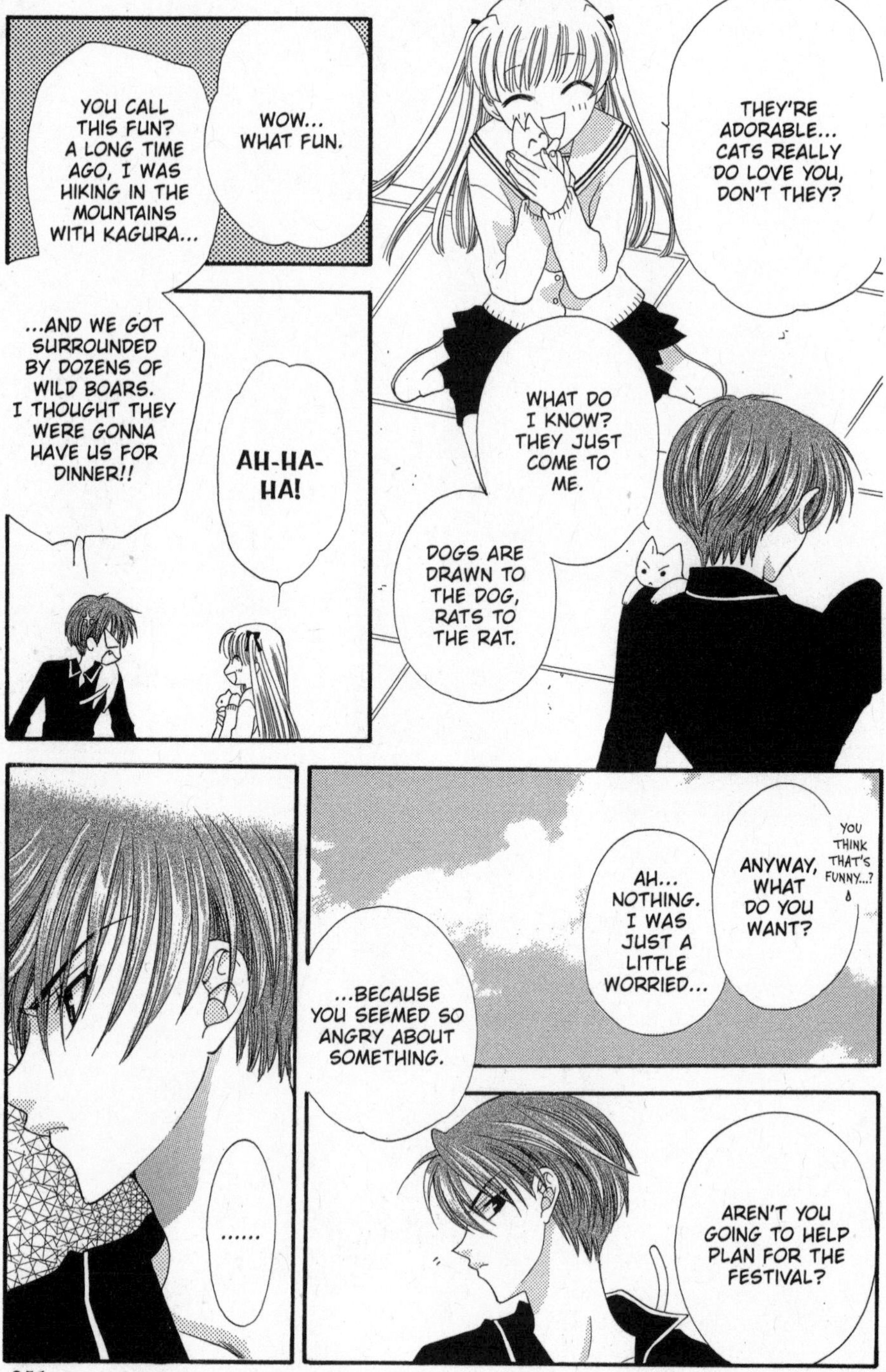
THEY'RE ADORABLE... CATS REALLY DO LOVE YOU, DON'T THEY?
WHAT DO I KNOW? THEY JUST COME TO ME.
DOGS ARE DRAWN TO THE DOG, RATS TO THE RAT.
WOW... WHAT FUN.
YOU CALL THIS FUN? A LONG TIME AGO, I WAS HIKING IN THE MOUNTAINS WITH KAGURA...
...AND WE GOT SURROUNDED BY DOZENS OF WILD BOARS. I THOUGHT THEY WERE GONNA HAVE US FOR DINNER!!
AH-HA-HA!
YOU THINK THAT'S FUNNY...?
ANYWAY, WHAT DO YOU WANT?
AH... NOTHING. I WAS JUST A LITTLE WORRIED...
...BECAUSE YOU SEEMED SO ANGRY ABOUT SOMETHING.
AREN'T YOU GOING TO HELP PLAN FOR THE FESTIVAL?
......

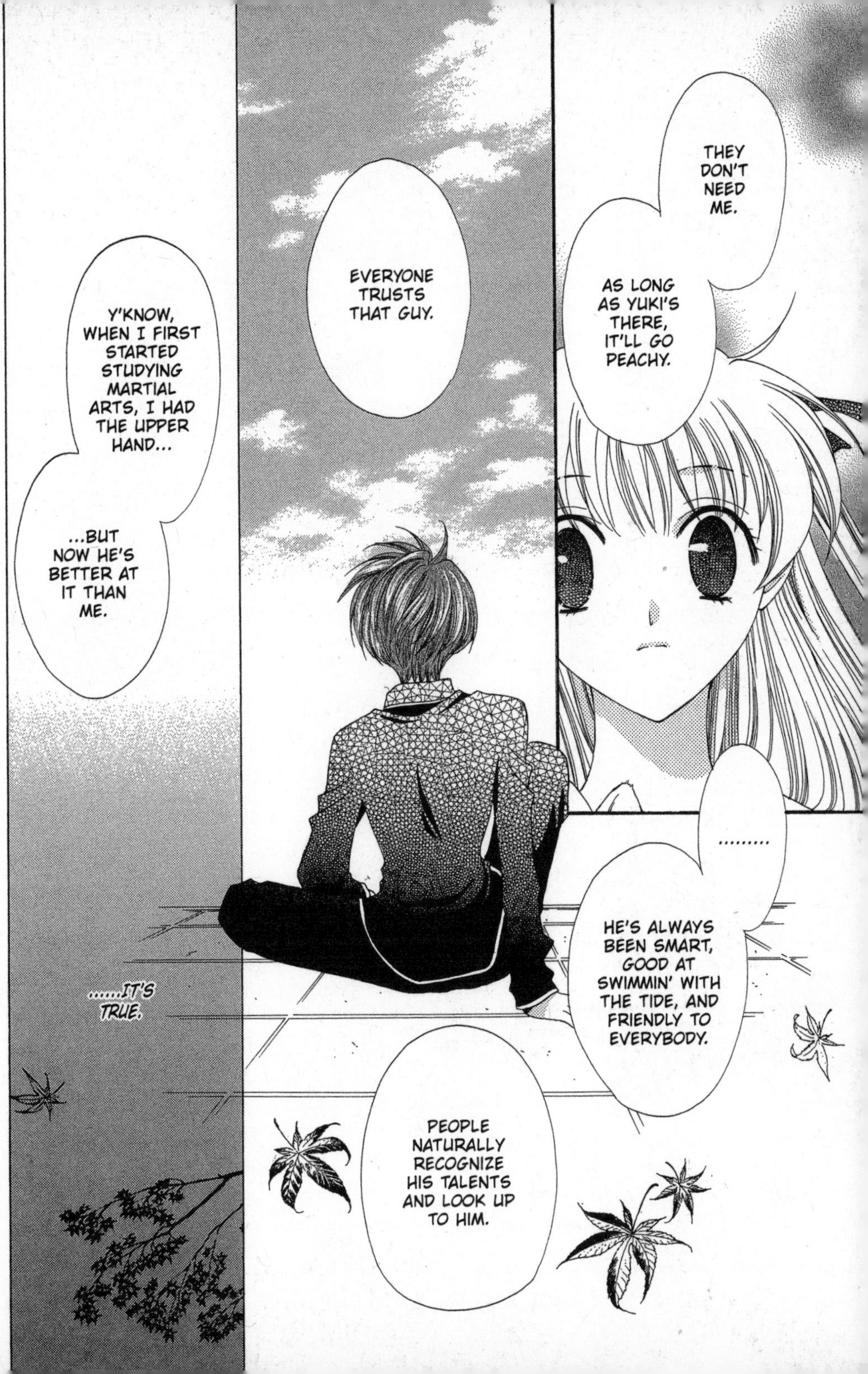
THEY DON'T NEED ME.
AS LONG AS YUKI'S THERE, IT'LL GO PEACHY.
....
HE'S ALWAYS BEEN SMART, GOOD AT SWIMMIN' WITH THE TIDE, AND FRIENDLY TO EVERYBODY.
PEOPLE NATURALLY RECOGNIZE HIS TALENTS AND LOOK UP TO HIM.
EVERYONE TRUSTS THAT GUY.
Y'KNOW, WHEN I FIRST STARTED STUDYING MARTIAL ARTS, I HAD THE UPPER HAND...
...BUT NOW HE'S BETTER AT IT THAN ME.
......IT'S TRUE.

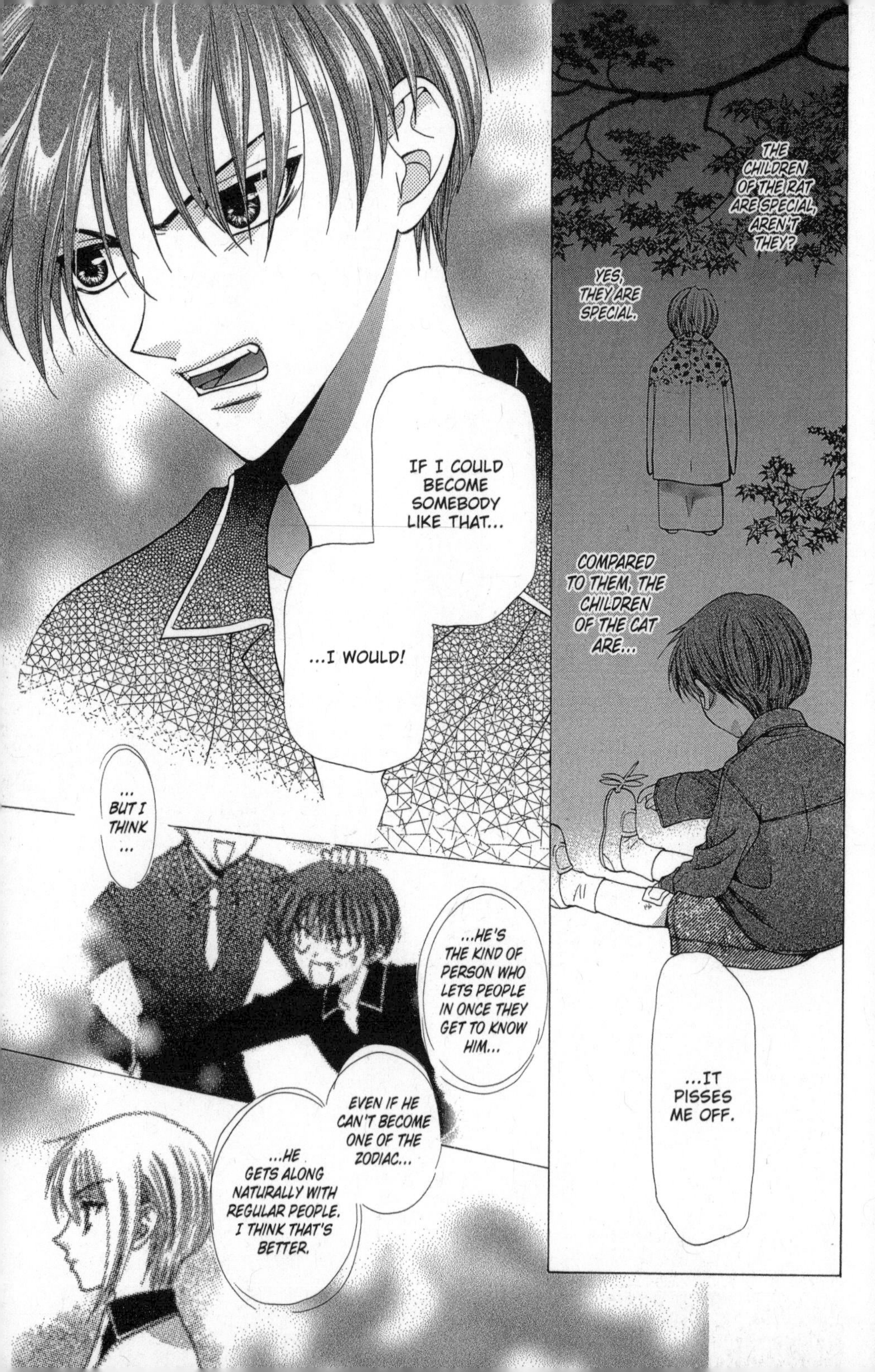
THE CHILDREN OF THE RAT ARE SPECIAL, AREN'T THEY?
YES, THEY ARE SPECIAL.
COMPARED TO THEM, THE CHILDREN OF THE CAT ARE...
...IT PISSES ME OFF.
IF I COULD BECOME SOMEBODY LIKE THAT...
...I WOULD!
...BUT I THINK...
...HE'S THE KIND OF PERSON WHO LETS PEOPLE IN ONCE THEY GET TO KNOW HIM...
EVEN IF HE CAN'T BECOME ONE OF THE ZODIAC...
...HE GETS ALONG NATURALLY WITH REGULAR PEOPLE. I THINK THAT'S BETTER.

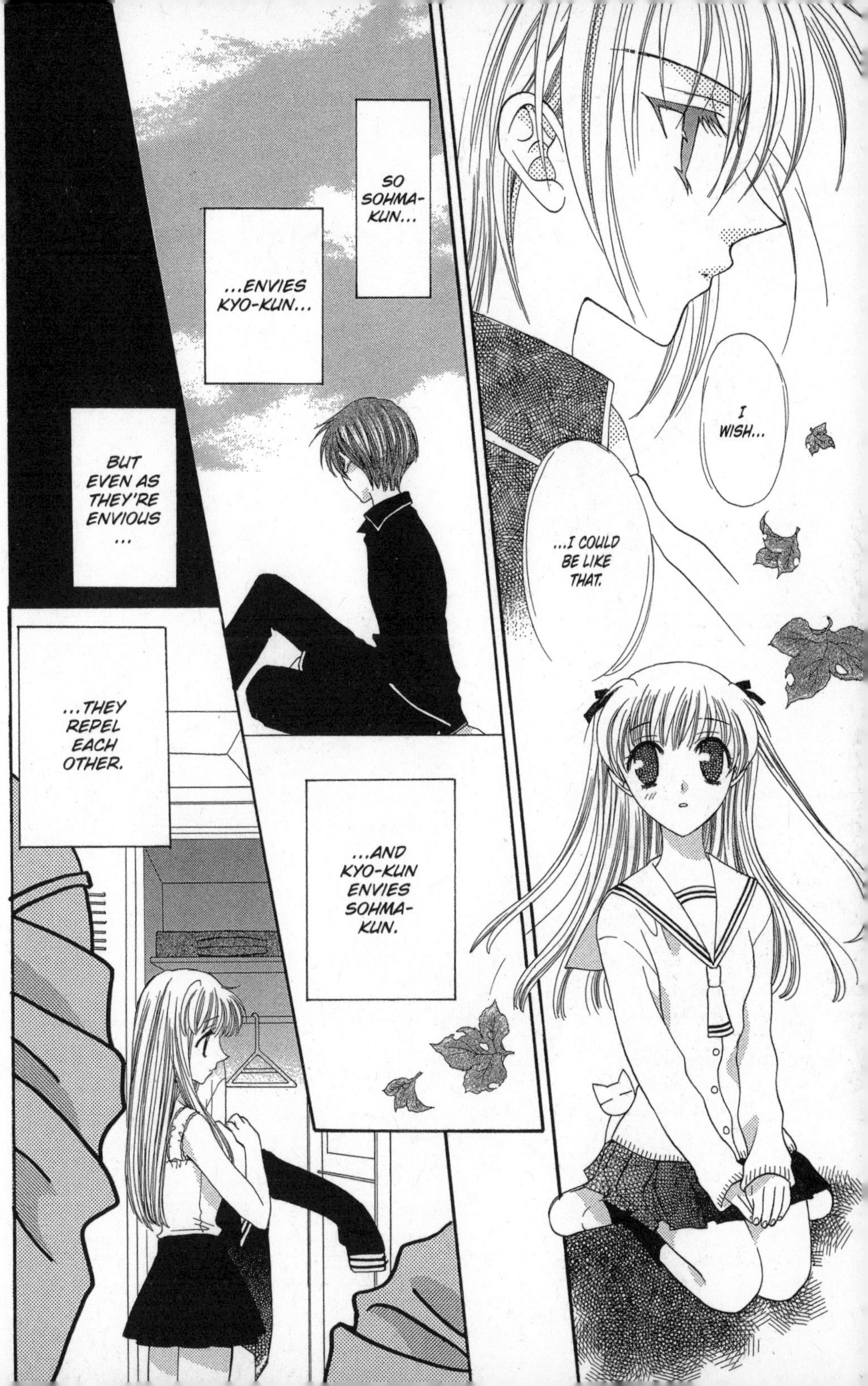
SO SOHMA-KUN...
...ENVIES KYO-KUN...
...AND KYO-KUN ENVIES SOHMA-KUN.
BUT EVEN AS THEY'RE ENVIOUS...
...THEY REPEL EACH OTHER.
I WISH...
...I COULD BE LIKE THAT.

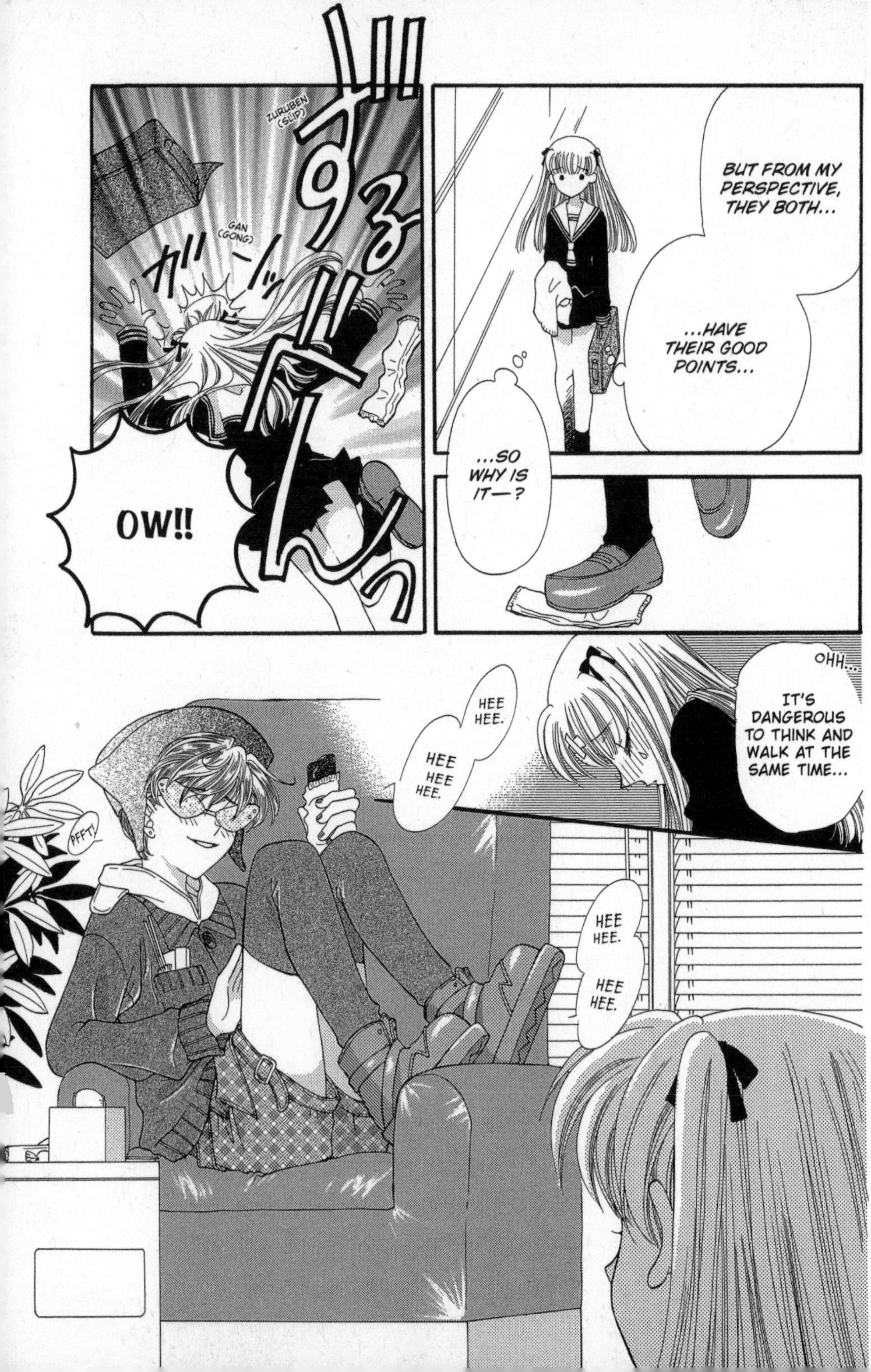
BUT FROM MY PERSPECTIVE, THEY BOTH...
...HAVE THEIR GOOD POINTS...
...SO WHY IS IT—?
ZURUBEN (SLIP)
GAN (GONG)
OW!!
OHH...
IT'S DANGEROUS TO THINK AND WALK AT THE SAME TIME...
HEE HEE.
HEE HEE HEE.
PFFT!
HEE HEE.
HEE HEE.

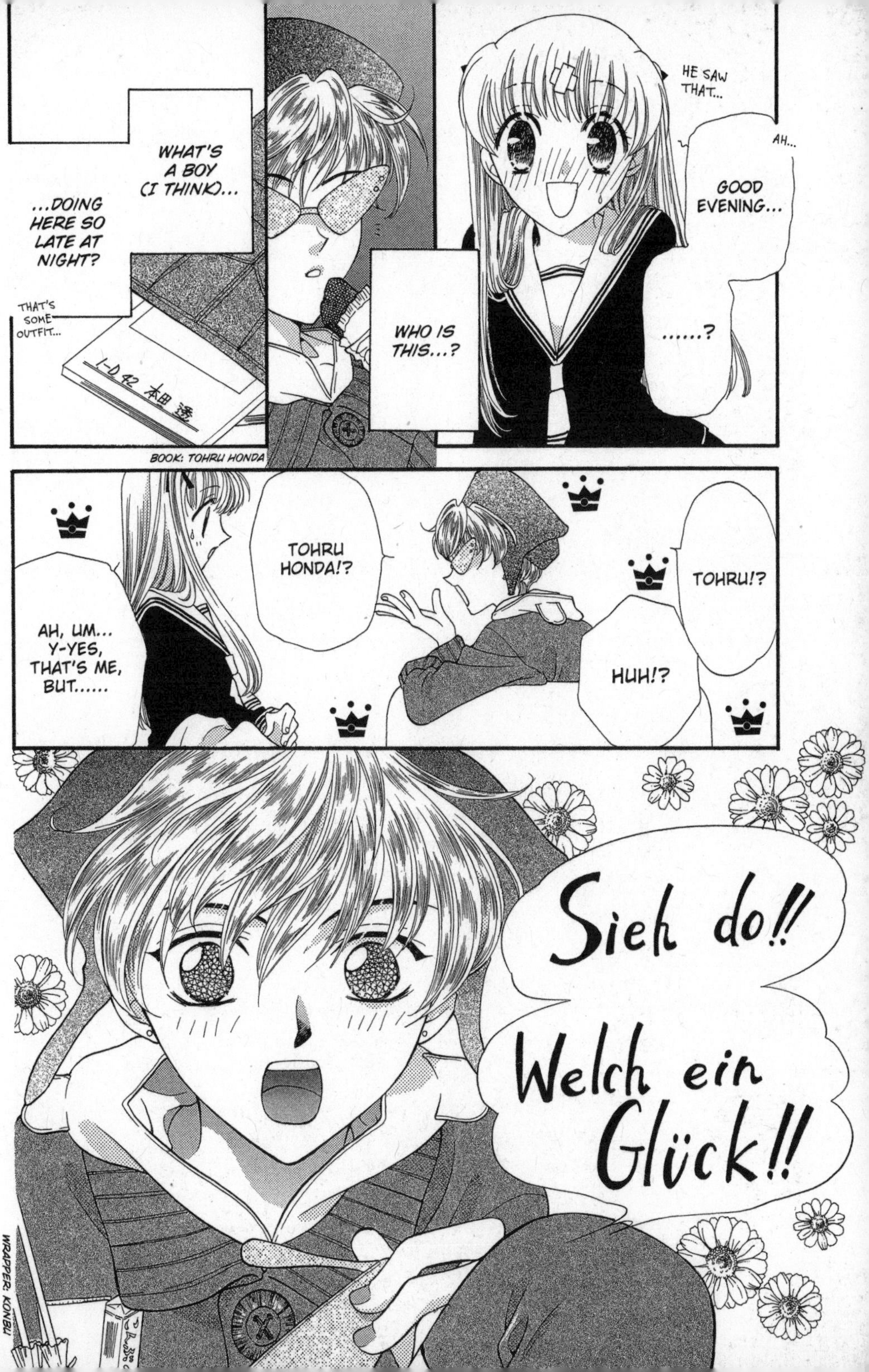
HE SAW THAT...
AH...
GOOD EVENING...
......?
WHO IS THIS...?
WHAT'S A BOY (I THINK)...
...DOING HERE SO LATE AT NIGHT?
THAT'S SOME OUTFIT...
1-D 42 本田 透
BOOK: TOHRU HONDA
TOHRU!?
HUH!?
TOHRU HONDA!?
AH, UM... Y-YES, THAT'S ME, BUT......
Sieh do!!
Welch ein Glück!!
WRAPPER: KONBU

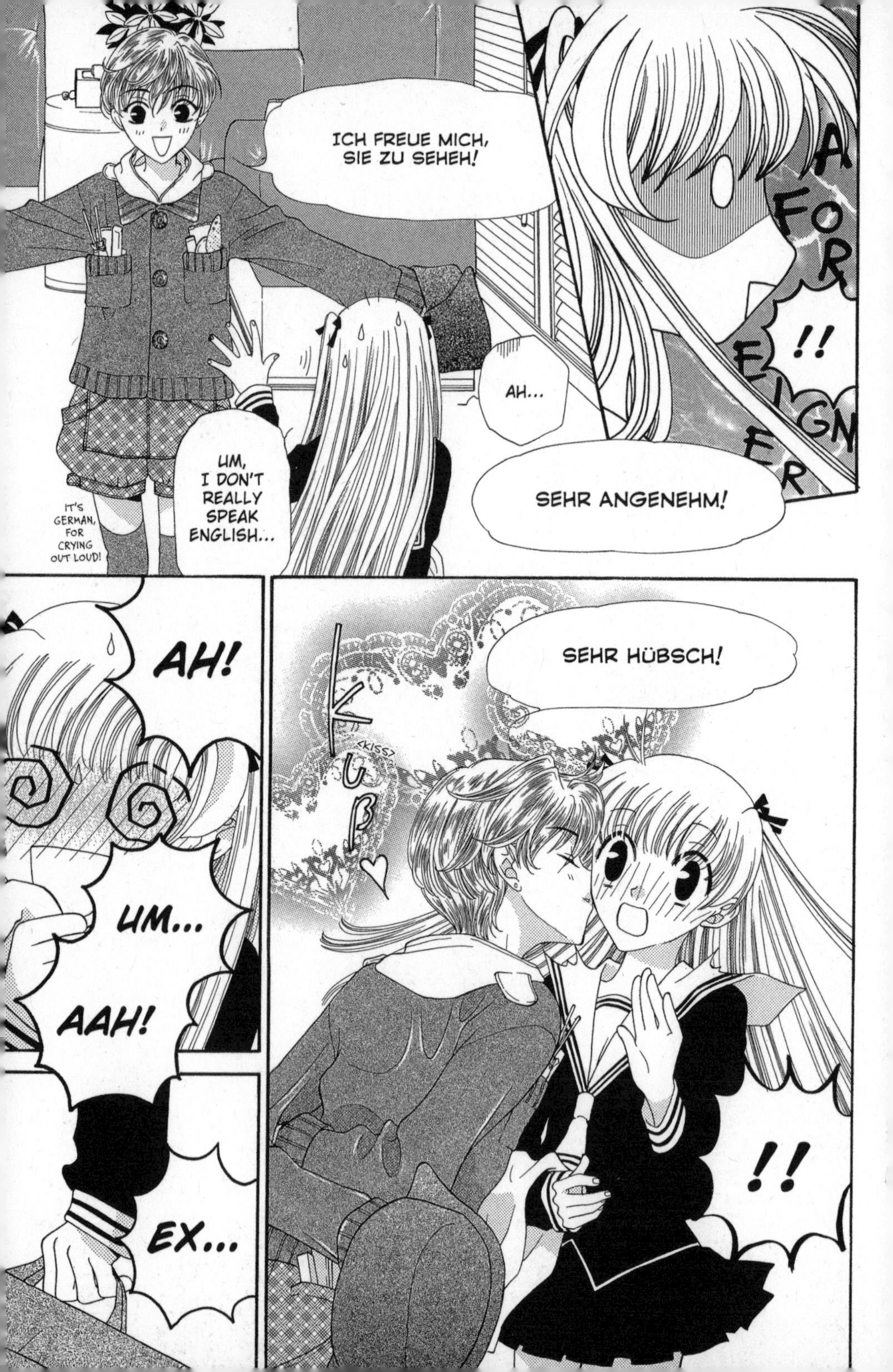
A FOREIGNER!!
ICH FREUE MICH, SIE ZU SEHEH!
AH...
SEHR ANGENEHM!
UM, I DON'T REALLY SPEAK ENGLISH...
IT'S GERMAN, FOR CRYING OUT LOUD!
SEHR HÜBSCH!
KUß
<KISS>
!!
AH!
UM...
AAH!
EX...

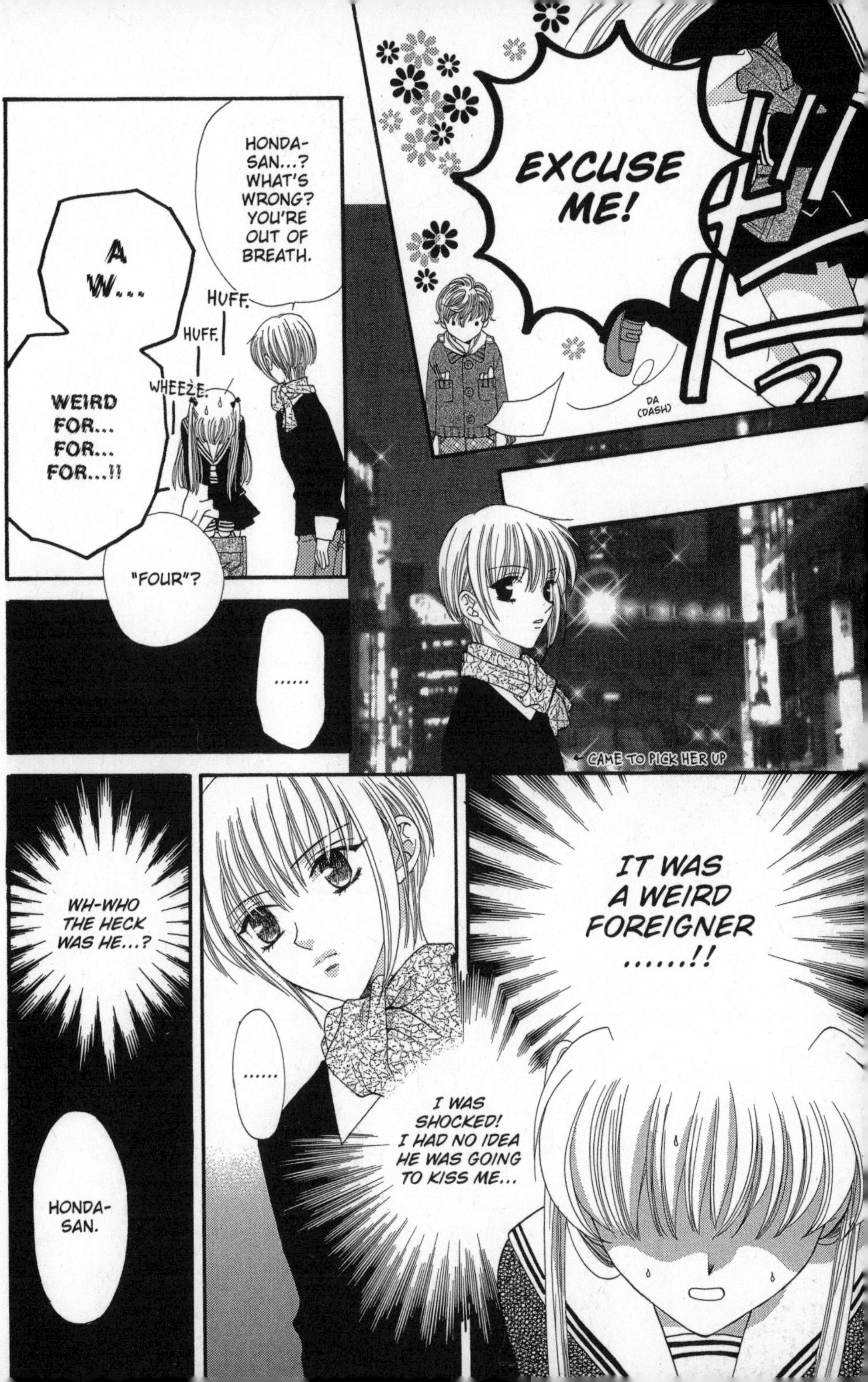
EXCUSE ME!
DA (DASH)
HONDA-SAN...? WHAT'S WRONG? YOU'RE OUT OF BREATH.
HUFF.
HUFF.
WHEEZE.
A W...
WEIRD FOR... FOR... FOR...!!
"FOUR"?
......
← CAME TO PICK HER UP
IT WAS A WEIRD FOREIGNER ......!!
I WAS SHOCKED! I HAD NO IDEA HE WAS GOING TO KISS ME...
......
WH-WHO THE HECK WAS HE...?
HONDA-SAN.

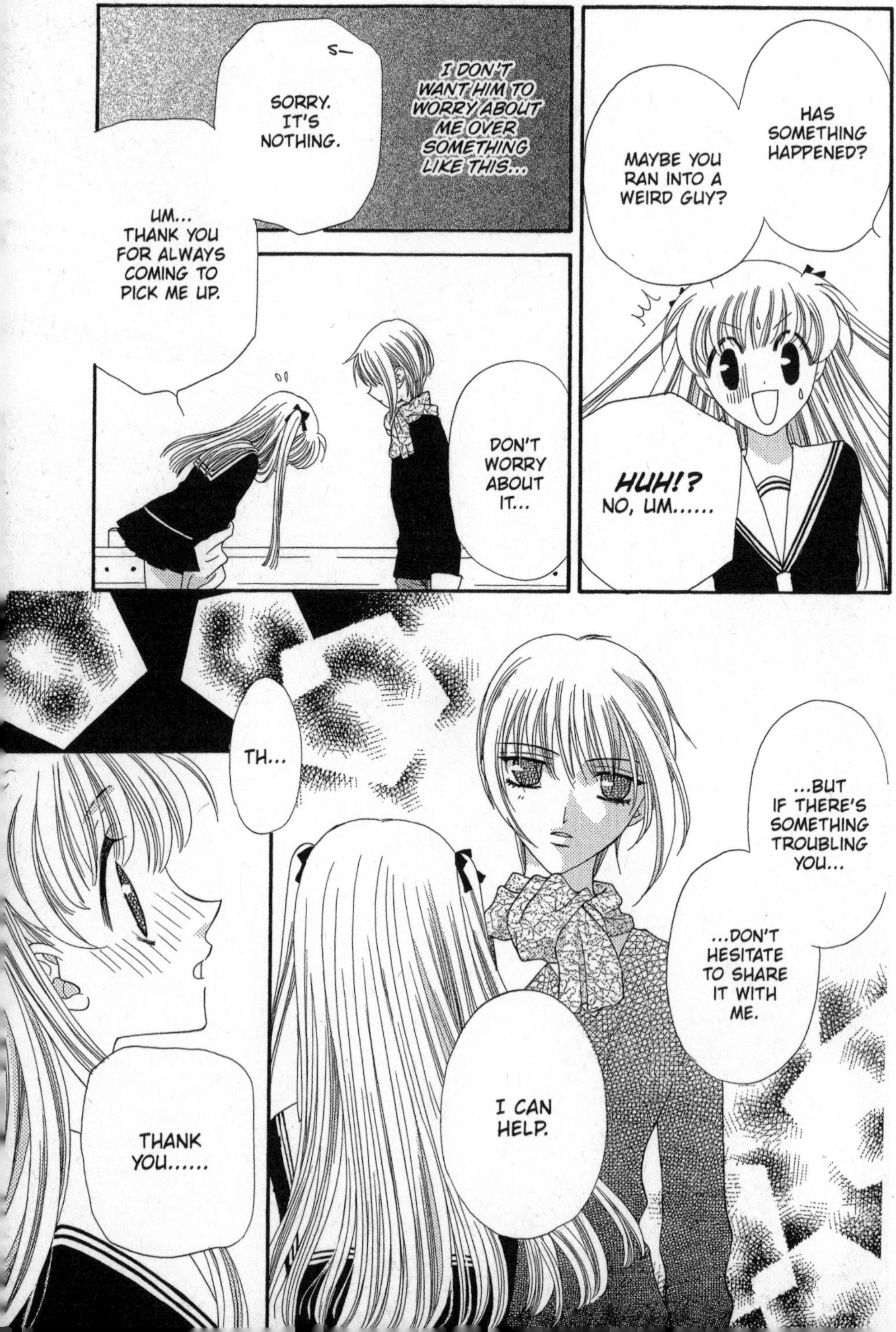
HAS SOMETHING HAPPENED?
MAYBE YOU RAN INTO A WEIRD GUY?
HUH!? NO, UM......
I DON'T WANT HIM TO WORRY ABOUT ME OVER SOMETHING LIKE THIS...
S—
SORRY. IT'S NOTHING.
UM... THANK YOU FOR ALWAYS COMING TO PICK ME UP.
DON'T WORRY ABOUT IT...
...BUT IF THERE'S SOMETHING TROUBLING YOU...
...DON'T HESITATE TO SHARE IT WITH ME.
I CAN HELP.
TH...
THANK YOU......

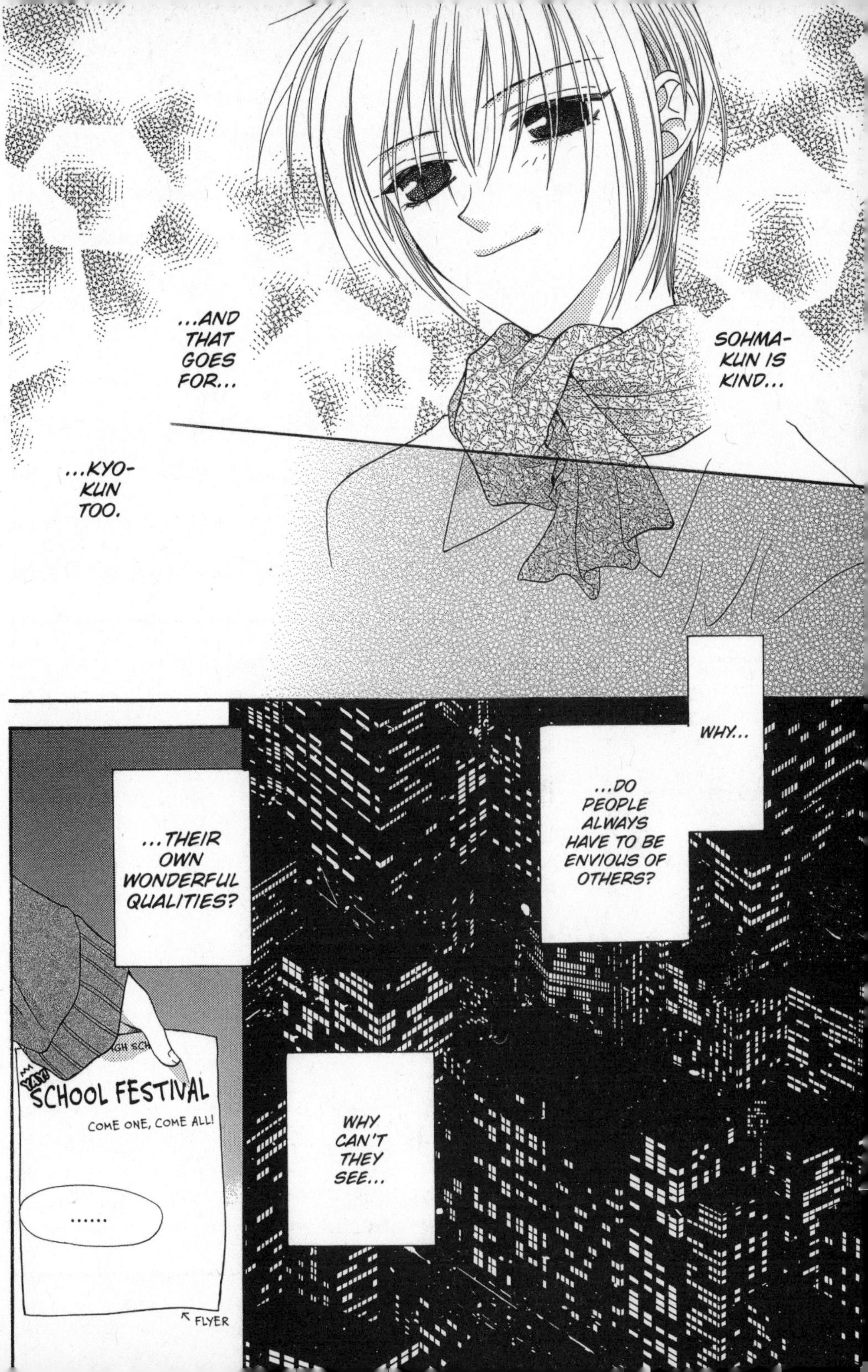
SOHMA-KUN IS KIND...
...AND THAT GOES FOR...
...KYO-KUN TOO.
WHY...
...DO PEOPLE ALWAYS HAVE TO BE ENVIOUS OF OTHERS?
WHY CAN'T THEY SEE...
...THEIR OWN WONDERFUL QUALITIES?
SCHOOL FESTIVAL
COME ONE, COME ALL!
......
FLYER

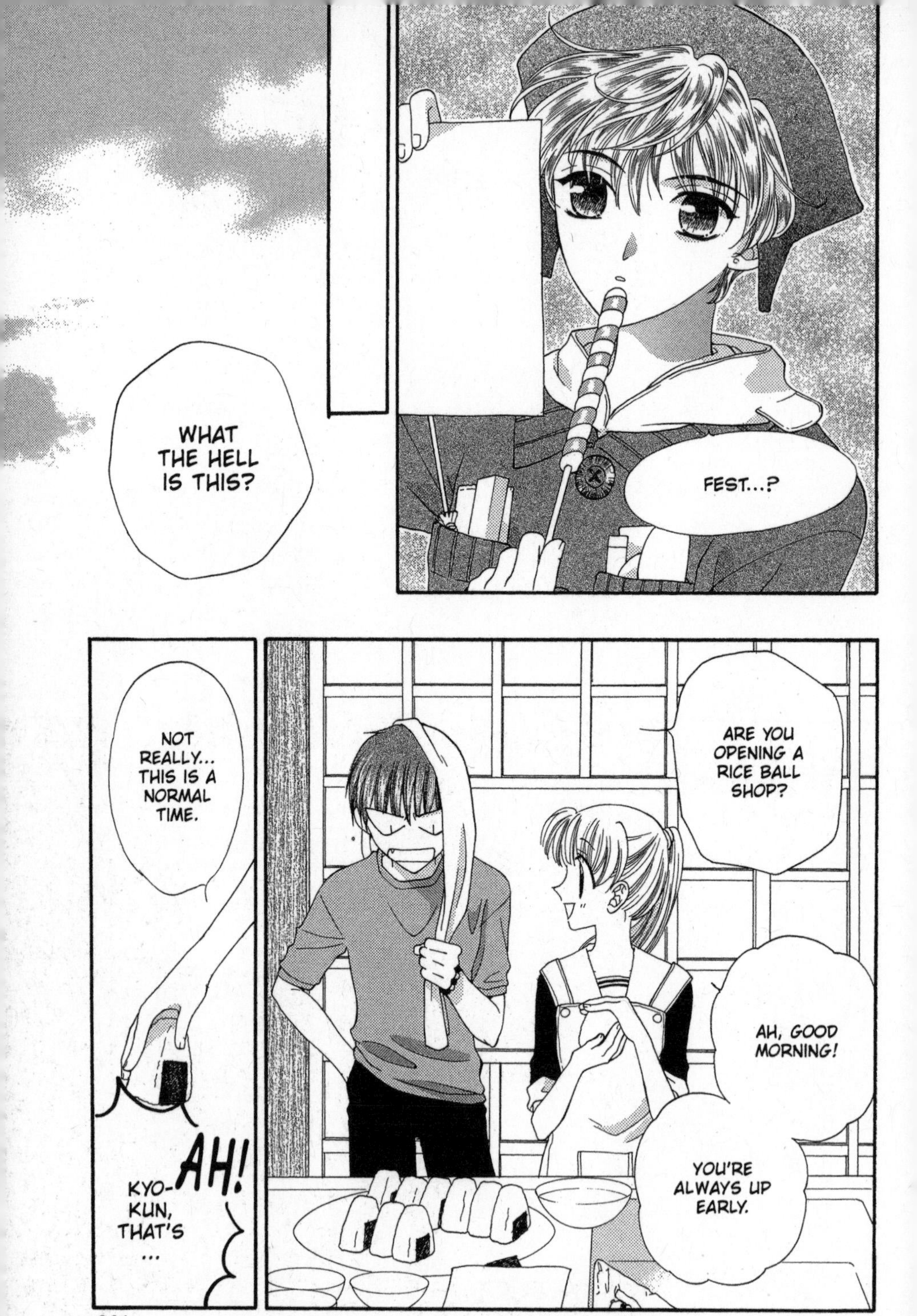
FEST...?
WHAT THE HELL IS THIS?
ARE YOU OPENING A RICE BALL SHOP?
AH, GOOD MORNING!
YOU'RE ALWAYS UP EARLY.
NOT REALLY... THIS IS A NORMAL TIME.
AH!
KYO-KUN, THAT'S...

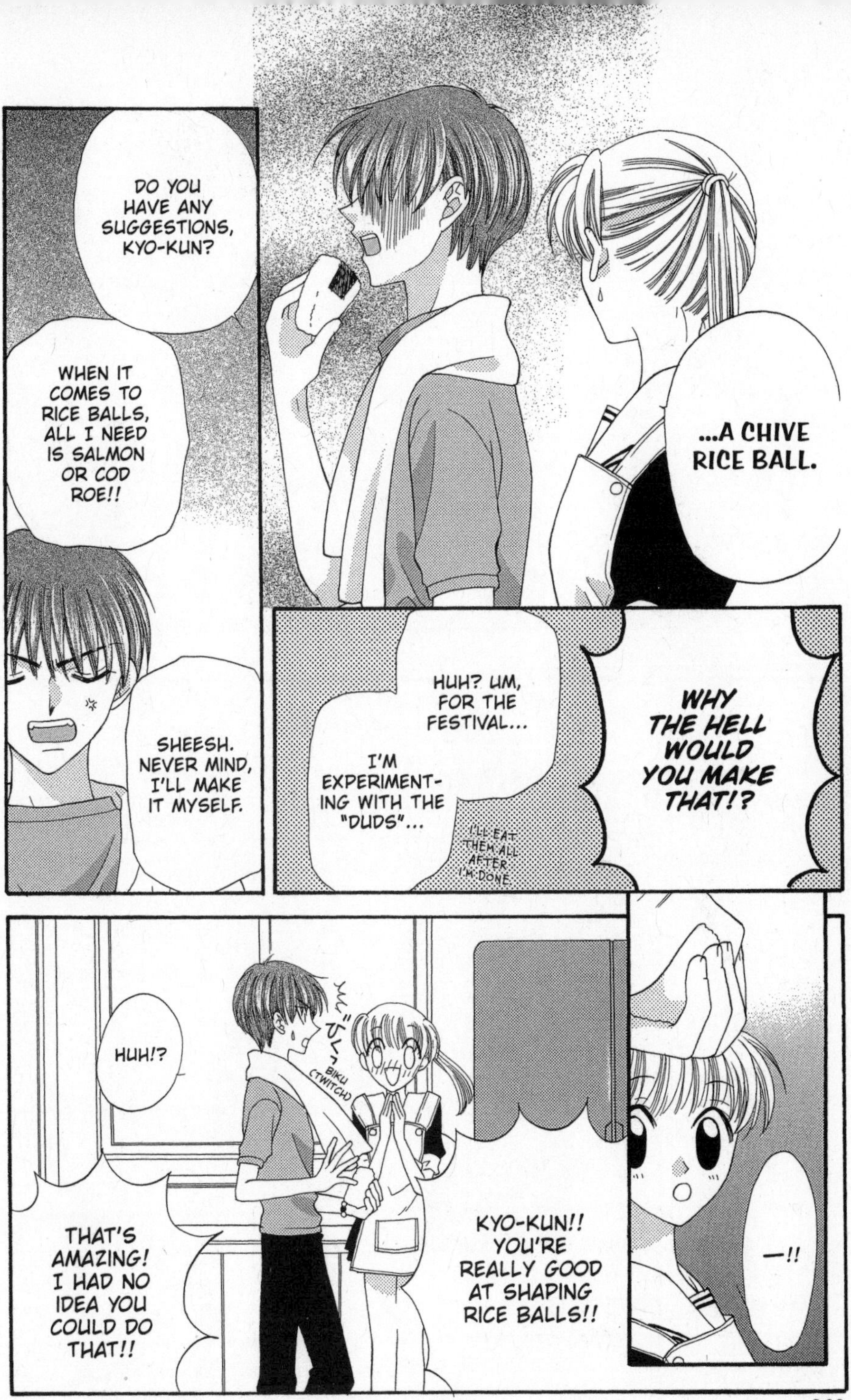
...A CHIVE RICE BALL.
WHY THE HELL WOULD YOU MAKE THAT!?
HUH? UM, FOR THE FESTIVAL...
I'M EXPERIMENT-ING WITH THE "DUDS"...
I'LL EAT THEM ALL AFTER I'M DONE
DO YOU HAVE ANY SUGGESTIONS, KYO-KUN?
WHEN IT COMES TO RICE BALLS, ALL I NEED IS SALMON OR COD ROE!!
SHEESH. NEVER MIND, I'LL MAKE IT MYSELF.
—!!
KYO-KUN!! YOU'RE REALLY GOOD AT SHAPING RICE BALLS!!
THAT'S AMAZING! I HAD NO IDEA YOU COULD DO THAT!!
BIKU (TWITCH)
HUH!?

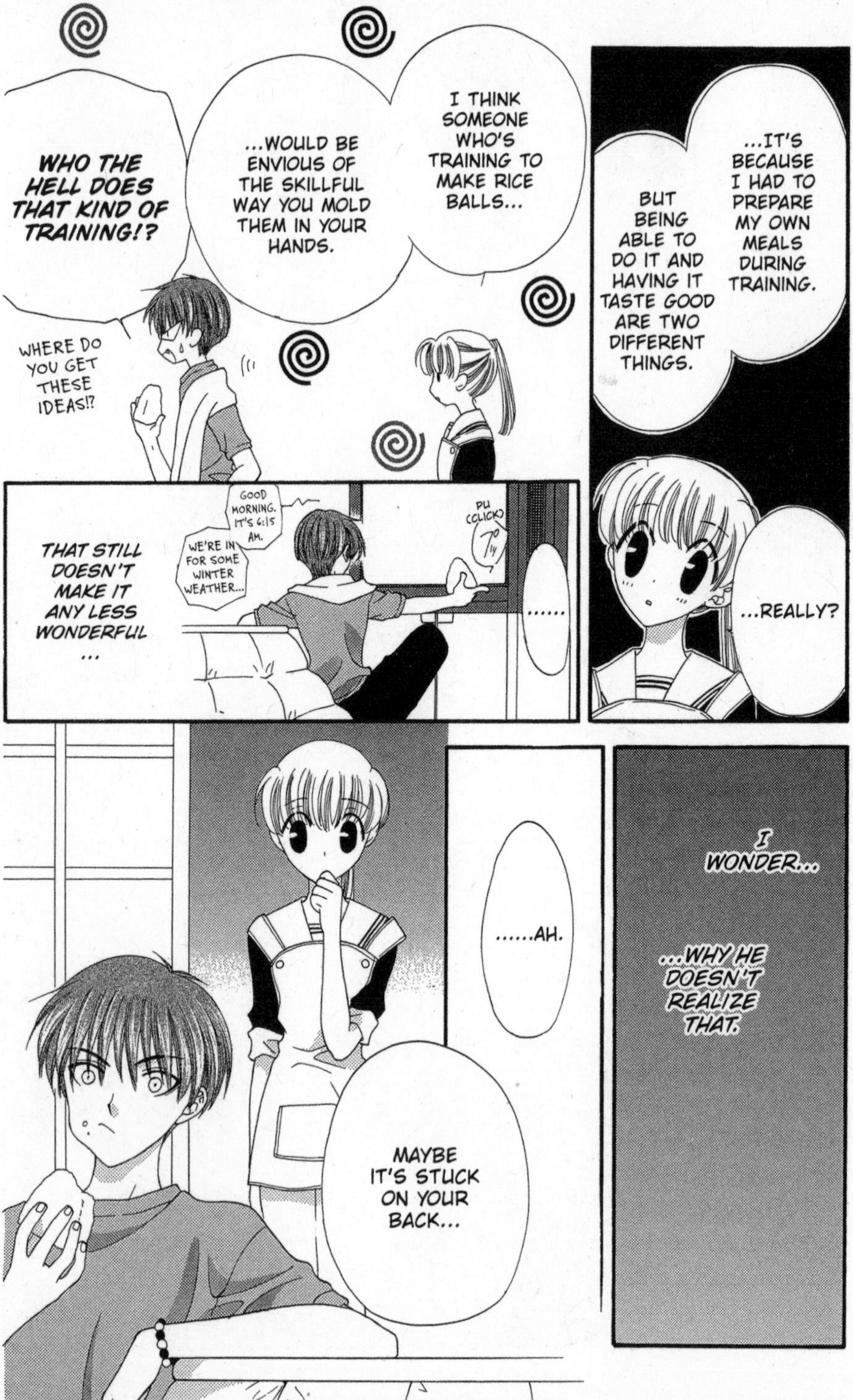
...IT'S BECAUSE I HAD TO PREPARE MY OWN MEALS DURING TRAINING.
BUT BEING ABLE TO DO IT AND HAVING IT TASTE GOOD ARE TWO DIFFERENT THINGS.
...REALLY?
I THINK SOMEONE WHO'S TRAINING TO MAKE RICE BALLS...
...WOULD BE ENVIOUS OF THE SKILLFUL WAY YOU MOLD THEM IN YOUR HANDS.
WHO THE HELL DOES THAT KIND OF TRAINING!?
WHERE DO YOU GET THESE IDEAS!?
......
PU (CLICK)
GOOD MORNING. IT'S 6:15 AM.
WE'RE IN FOR SOME WINTER WEATHER...
THAT STILL DOESN'T MAKE IT ANY LESS WONDERFUL...
I WONDER...
...WHY HE DOESN'T REALIZE THAT.
......AH.
MAYBE IT'S STUCK ON YOUR BACK...

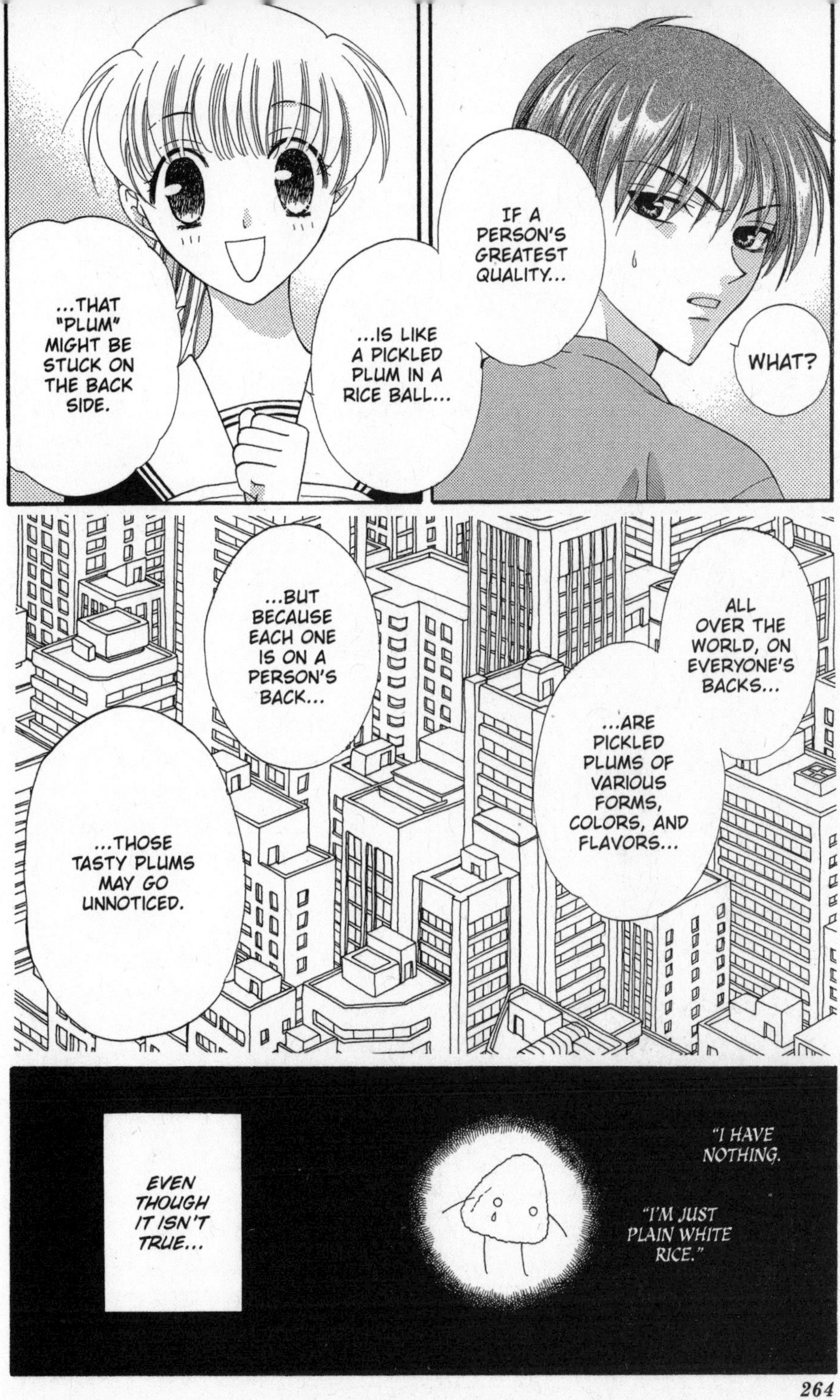
WHAT?
IF A PERSON'S GREATEST QUALITY...
...IS LIKE A PICKLED PLUM IN A RICE BALL...
...THAT "PLUM" MIGHT BE STUCK ON THE BACK SIDE.
ALL OVER THE WORLD, ON EVERYONE'S BACKS...
...ARE PICKLED PLUMS OF VARIOUS FORMS, COLORS, AND FLAVORS...
...BUT BECAUSE EACH ONE IS ON A PERSON'S BACK...
...THOSE TASTY PLUMS MAY GO UNNOTICED.
"I HAVE NOTHING.
"I'M JUST PLAIN WHITE RICE."
EVEN THOUGH IT ISN'T TRUE...

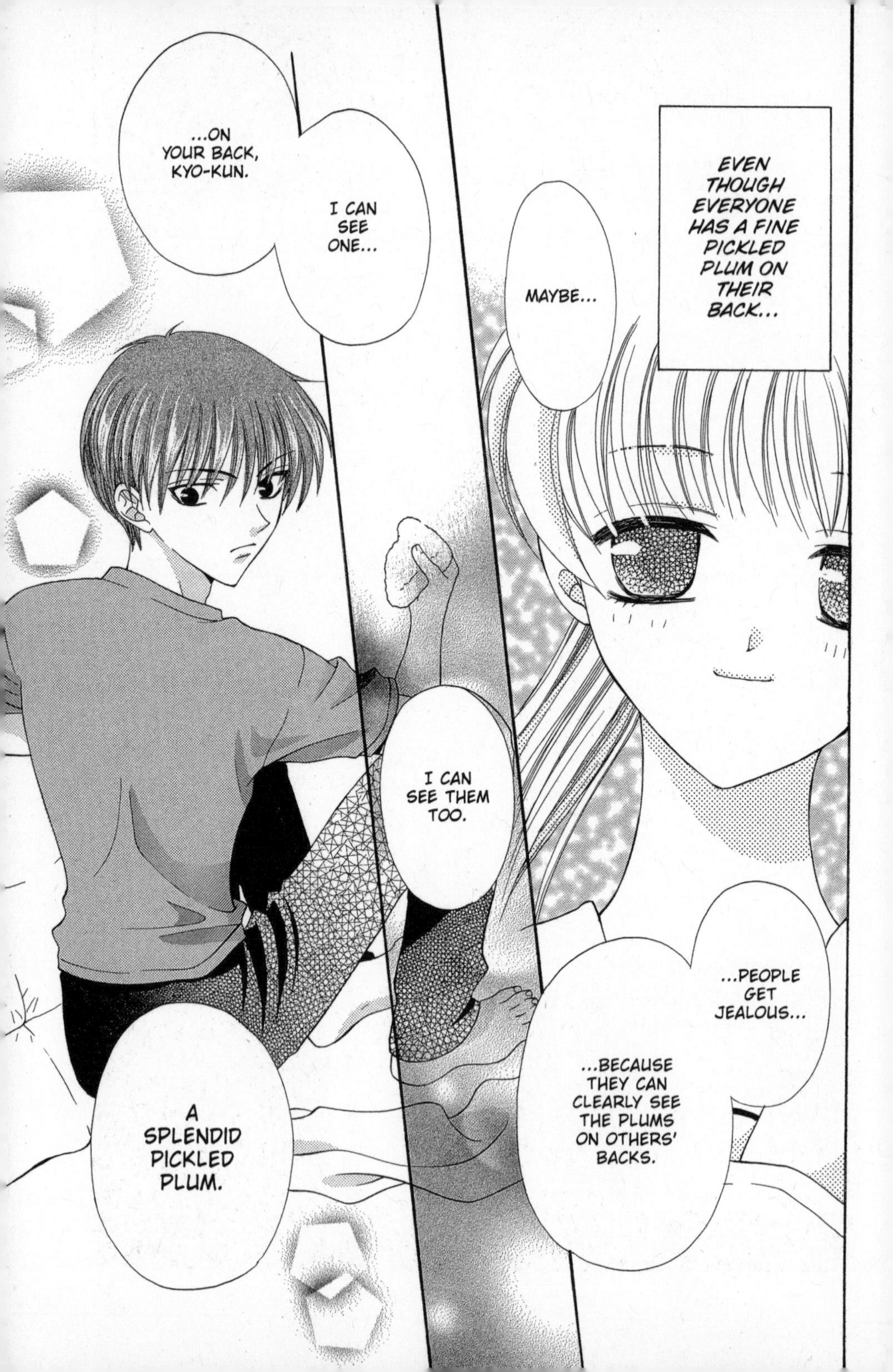
EVEN THOUGH EVERYONE HAS A FINE PICKLED PLUM ON THEIR BACK...
MAYBE...
...PEOPLE GET JEALOUS...
...BECAUSE THEY CAN CLEARLY SEE THE PLUMS ON OTHERS' BACKS.
I CAN SEE THEM TOO.
I CAN SEE ONE...
...ON YOUR BACK, KYO-KUN.
A SPLENDID PICKLED PLUM.

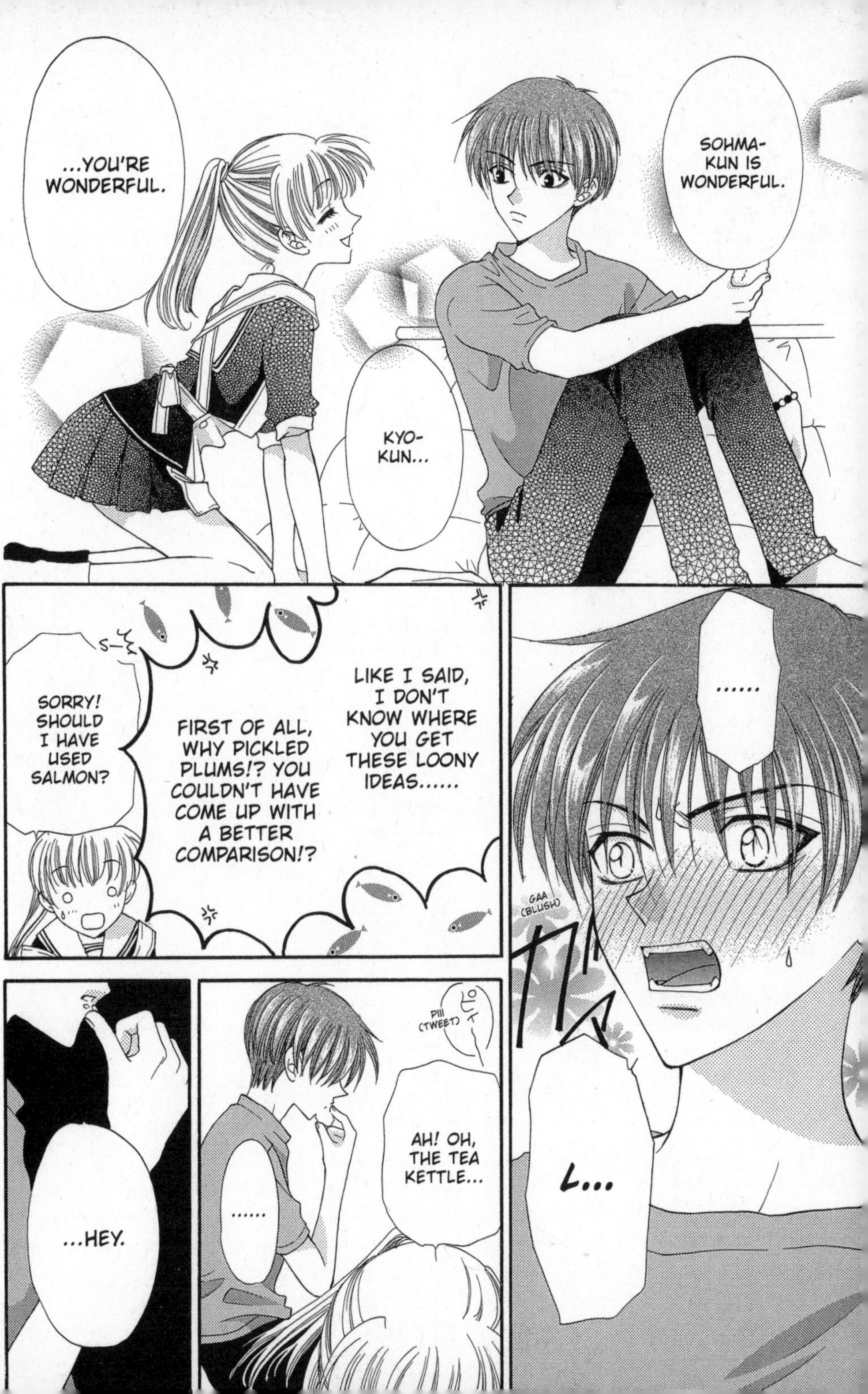
SOHMA-KUN IS WONDERFUL.
KYO-KUN...
...YOU'RE WONDERFUL.
......
GAA (BLUSH)
L...
LIKE I SAID, I DON'T KNOW WHERE YOU GET THESE LOONY IDEAS......
FIRST OF ALL, WHY PICKLED PLUMS!? YOU COULDN'T HAVE COME UP WITH A BETTER COMPARISON!?
S—
SORRY! SHOULD I HAVE USED SALMON?
PIII (TWEET)
AH! OH, THE TEA KETTLE...
......
...HEY.

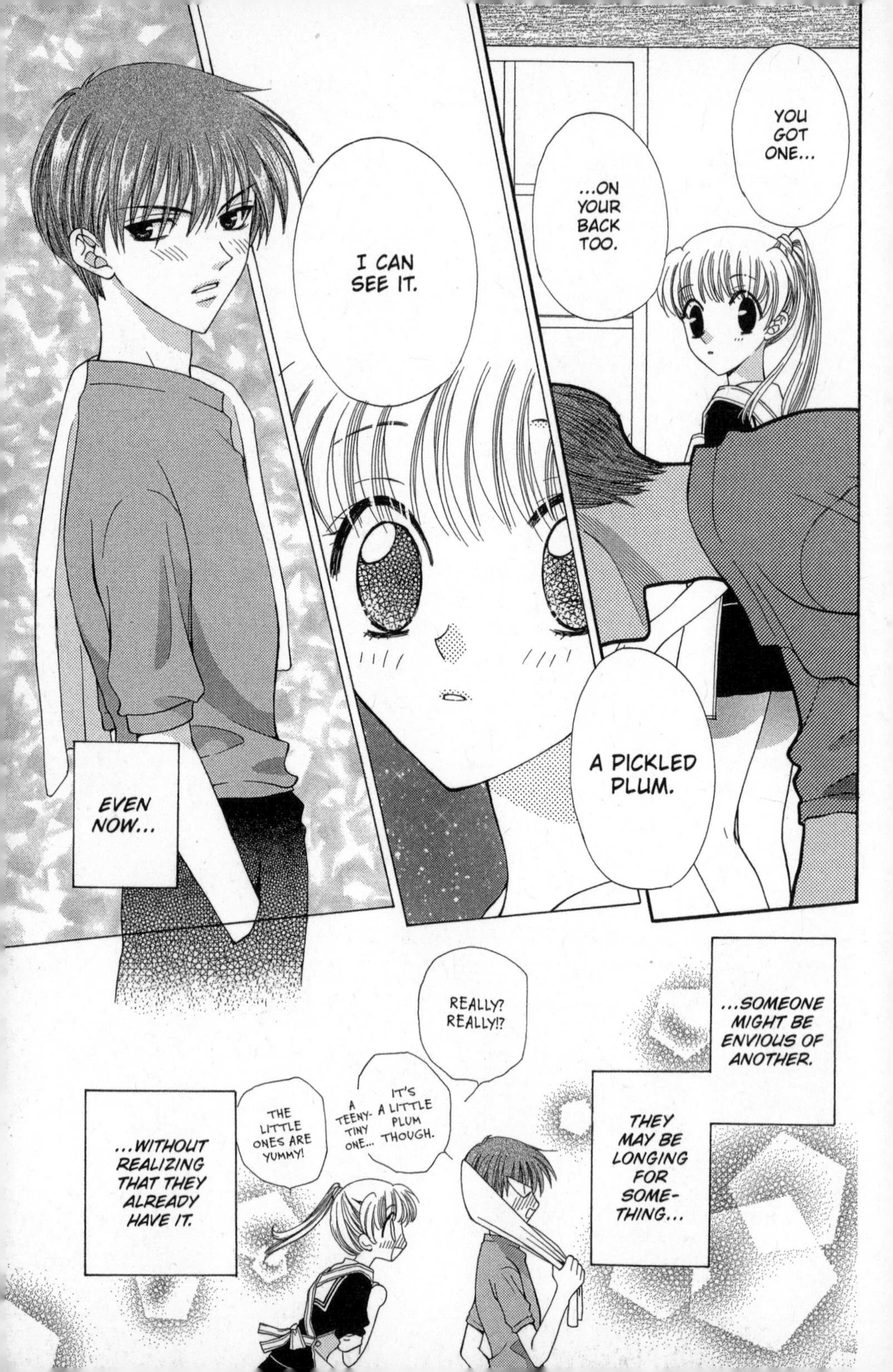
YOU GOT ONE...
...ON YOUR BACK TOO.
A PICKLED PLUM.
I CAN SEE IT.
EVEN NOW...
...SOMEONE MIGHT BE ENVIOUS OF ANOTHER.
THEY MAY BE LONGING FOR SOME-THING...
REALLY? REALLY!?
IT'S A LITTLE PLUM THOUGH.
A TEENY-TINY ONE...
THE LITTLE ONES ARE YUMMY!
...WITHOUT REALIZING THAT THEY ALREADY HAVE IT.

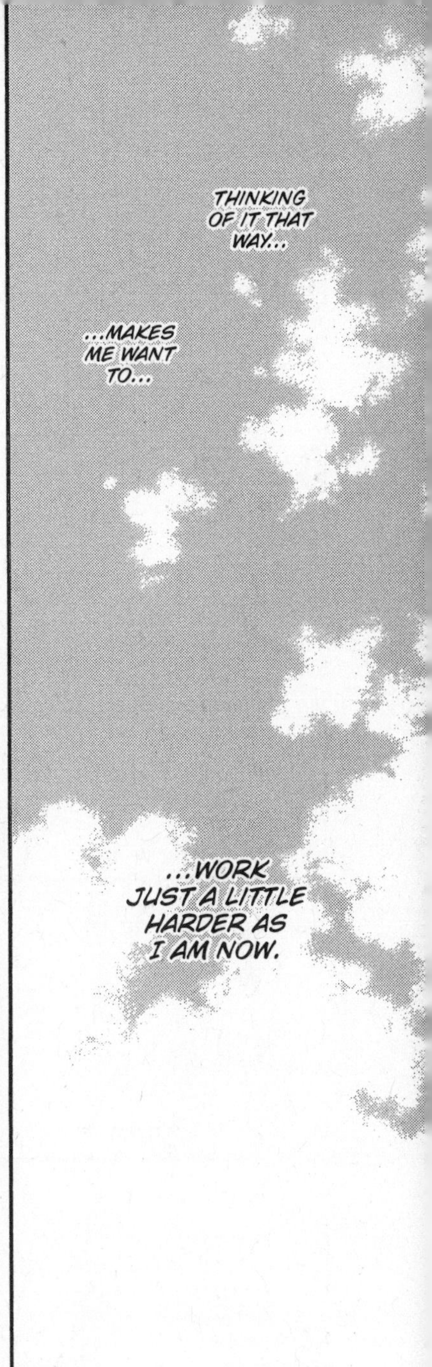
THINKING OF IT THAT WAY...
...MAKES ME WANT TO...
...WORK JUST A LITTLE HARDER AS I AM NOW.

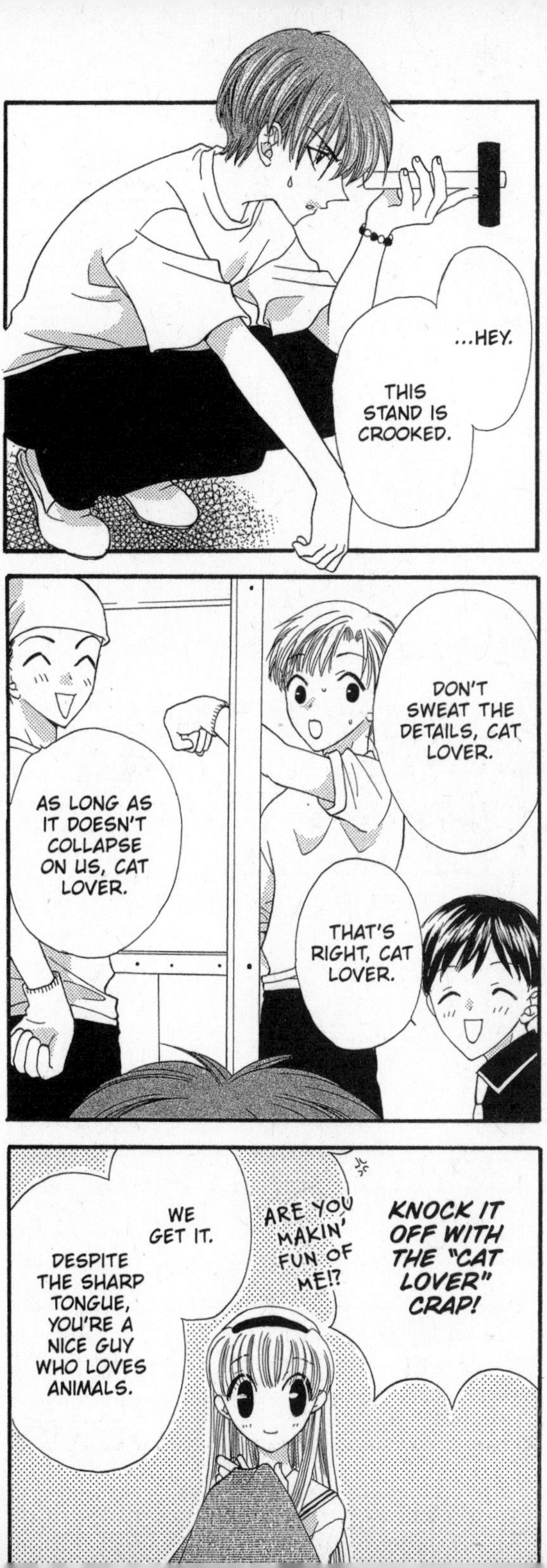
...HEY.
THIS STAND IS CROOKED.
DON'T SWEAT THE DETAILS, CAT LOVER.
AS LONG AS IT DOESN'T COLLAPSE ON US, CAT LOVER.
THAT'S RIGHT, CAT LOVER.
KNOCK IT OFF WITH THE "CAT LOVER" CRAP!
ARE YOU MAKIN' FUN OF ME!?
WE GET IT.
DESPITE THE SHARP TONGUE, YOU'RE A NICE GUY WHO LOVES ANIMALS.

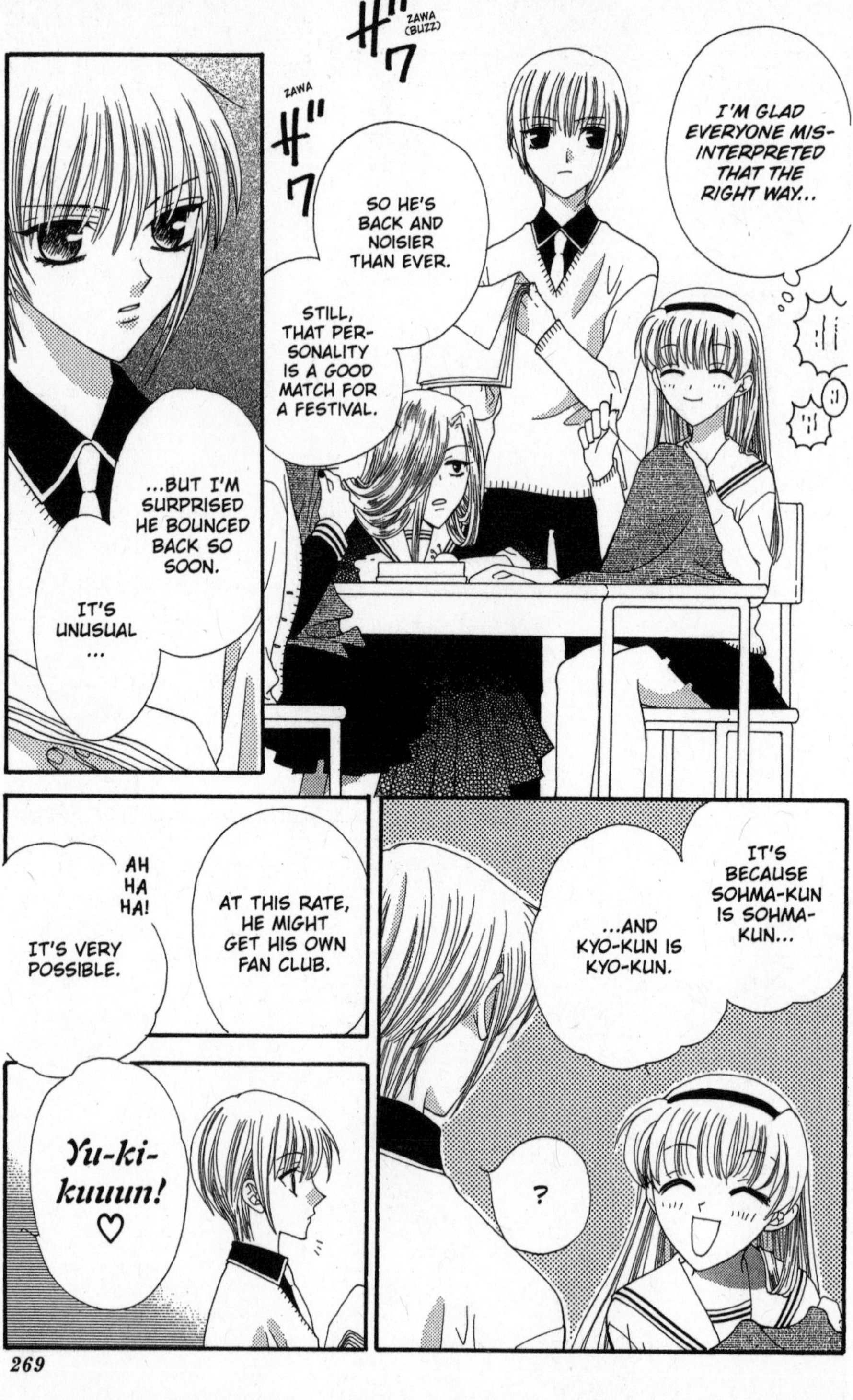
ZAWA (BUZZ)
ZAWA
SO HE'S BACK AND NOISIER THAN EVER.
STILL, THAT PERSONALITY IS A GOOD MATCH FOR A FESTIVAL.
I'M GLAD EVERYONE MIS-INTERPRETED THAT THE RIGHT WAY...
...BUT I'M SURPRISED HE BOUNCED BACK SO SOON.
IT'S UNUSUAL...
IT'S BECAUSE SOHMA-KUN IS SOHMA-KUN...
...AND KYO-KUN IS KYO-KUN.
?
AT THIS RATE, HE MIGHT GET HIS OWN FAN CLUB.
AH HA HA!
IT'S VERY POSSIBLE.
Yu-ki-kuuun! ♡

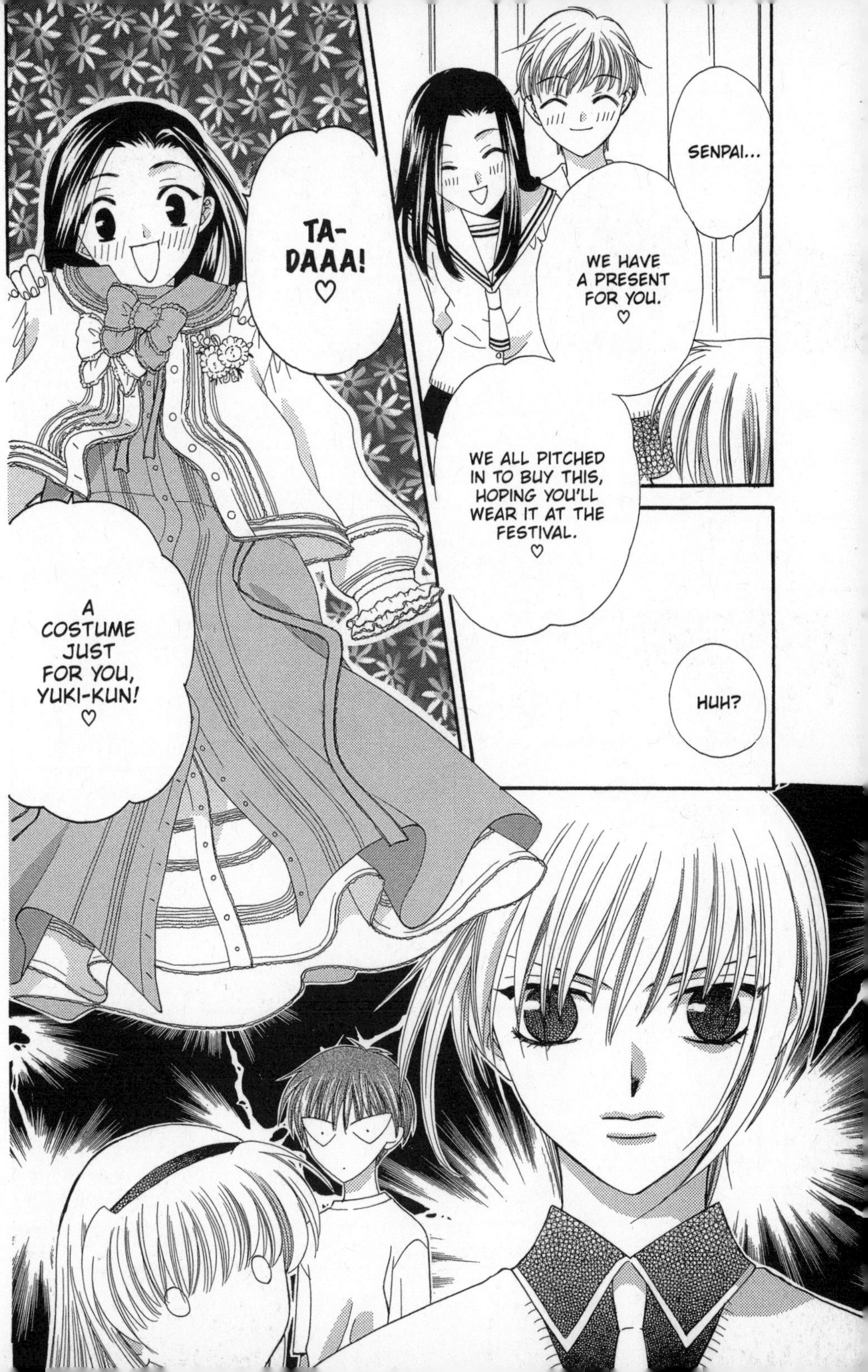
SENPAI...
WE HAVE A PRESENT FOR YOU. ♡
WE ALL PITCHED IN TO BUY THIS, HOPING YOU'LL WEAR IT AT THE FESTIVAL. ♡
HUH?
TA-DAAA! ♡
A COSTUME JUST FOR YOU, YUKI-KUN! ♡

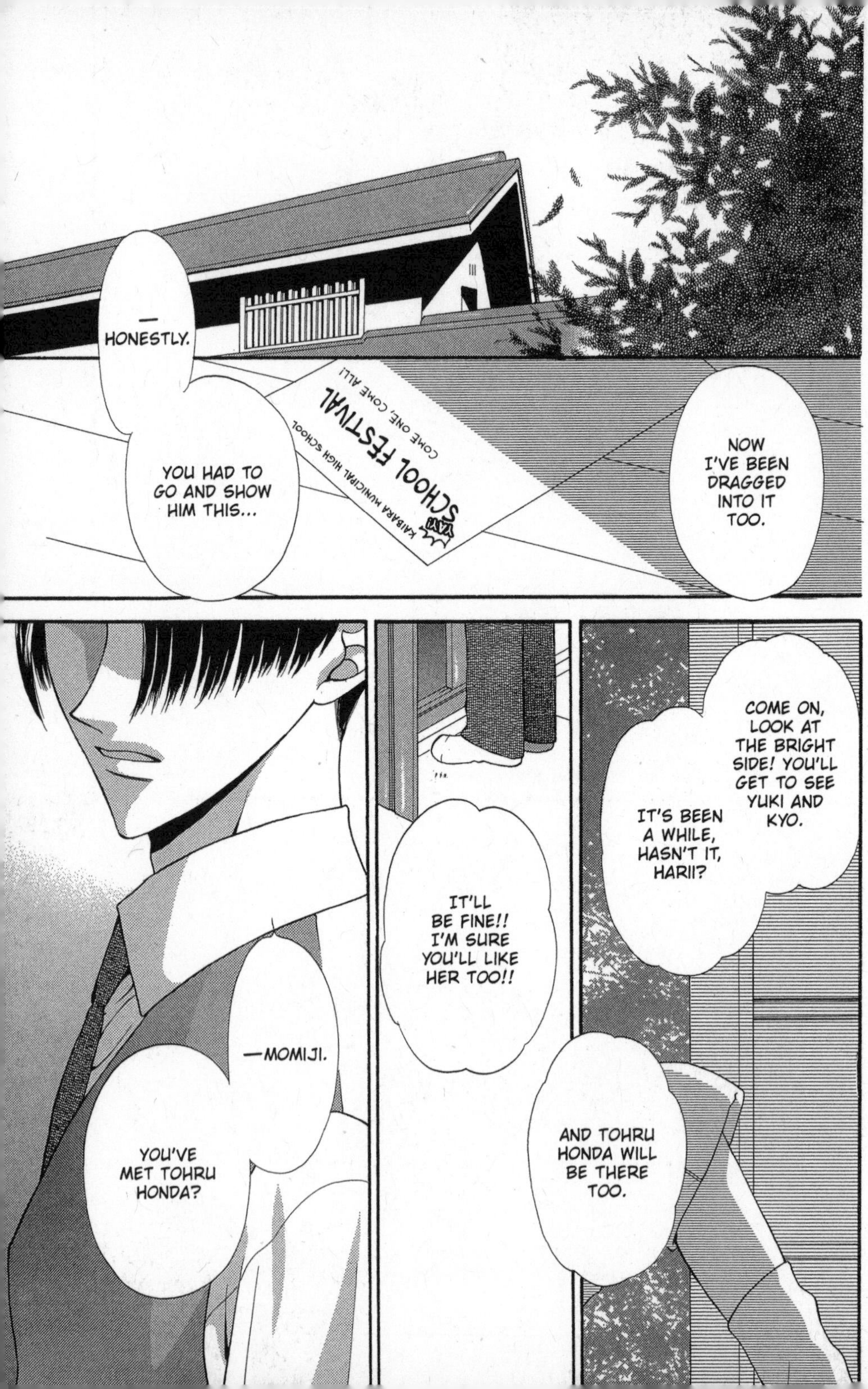
—HONESTLY.
NOW I'VE BEEN DRAGGED INTO IT TOO.
YOU HAD TO GO AND SHOW HIM THIS...
YAY! SCHOOL FESTIVAL
KAIBARA MUNICIPAL HIGH SCHOOL
COME ONE, COME ALL!
COME ON, LOOK AT THE BRIGHT SIDE! YOU'LL GET TO SEE YUKI AND KYO.
IT'S BEEN A WHILE, HASN'T IT, HARII?
AND TOHRU HONDA WILL BE THERE TOO.
IT'LL BE FINE!! I'M SURE YOU'LL LIKE HER TOO!!
—MOMIJI.
YOU'VE MET TOHRU HONDA?

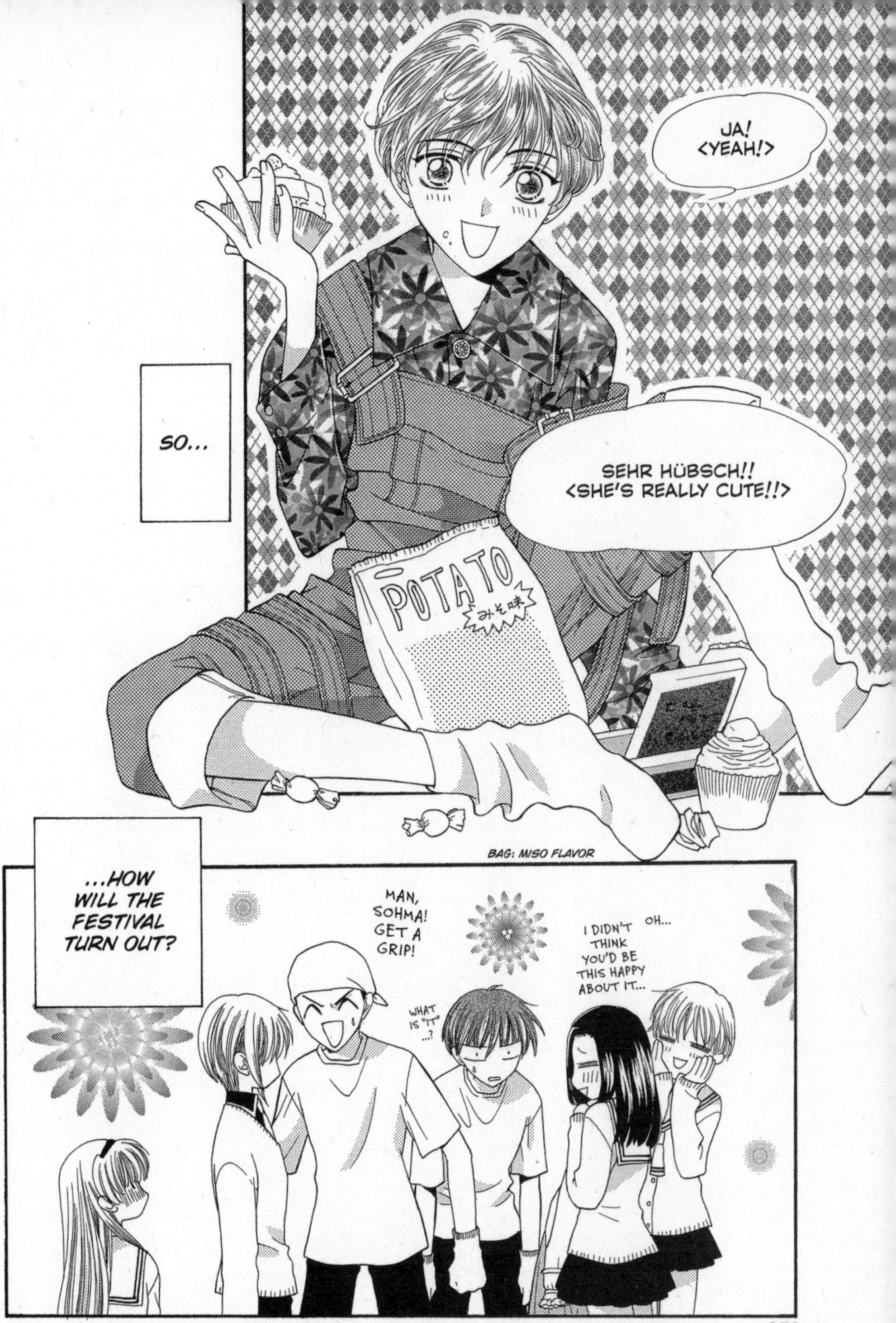
JA!
<YEAH!>
SEHR HÜBSCH!!
<SHE'S REALLY CUTE!!>
SO...
POTATO
みそ味
BAG: MISO FLAVOR
OH...
I DIDN'T THINK YOU'D BE THIS HAPPY ABOUT IT...
WHAT IS "IT" ...?
MAN, SOHMA! GET A GRIP!
...HOW WILL THE FESTIVAL TURN OUT?

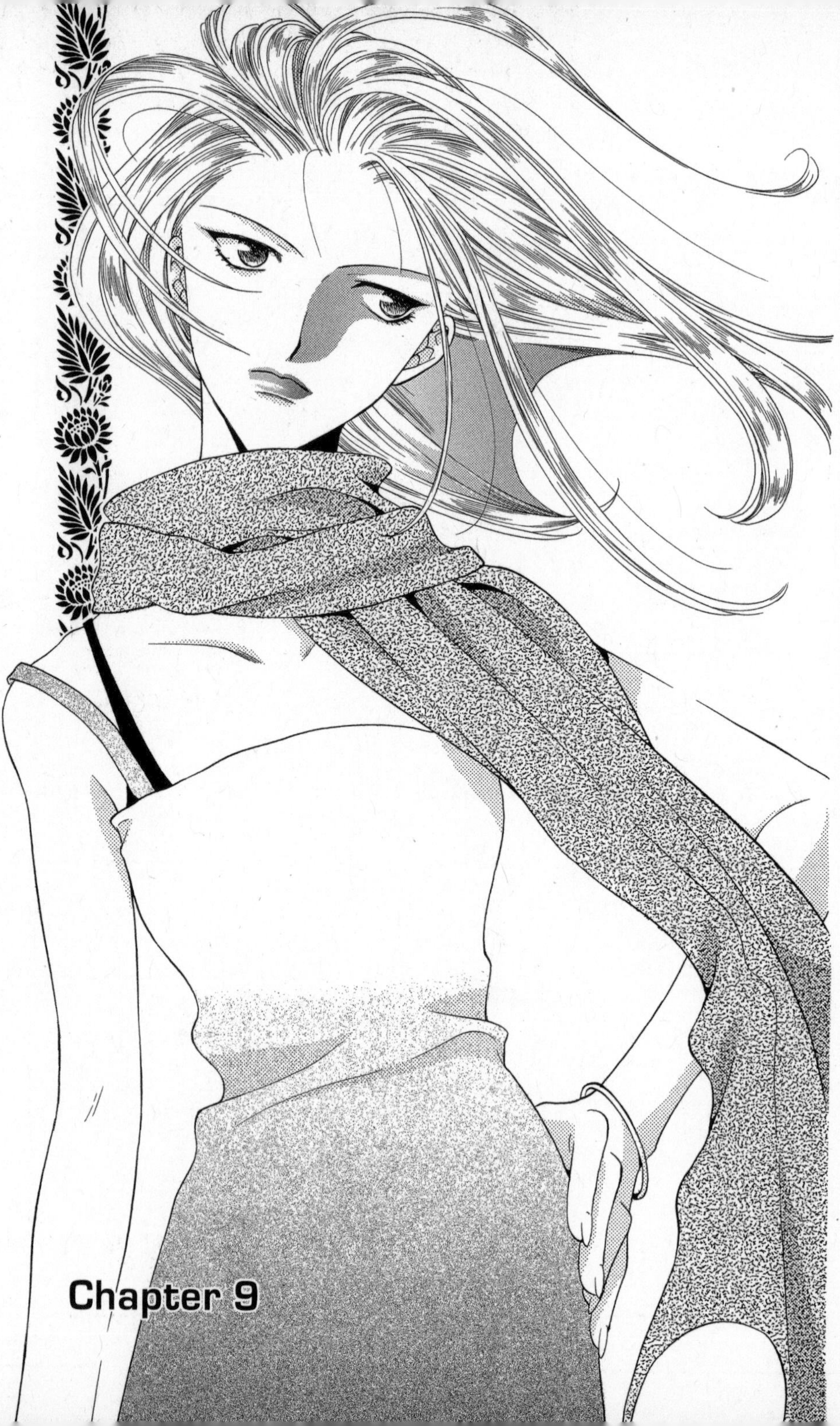

Chapter 9

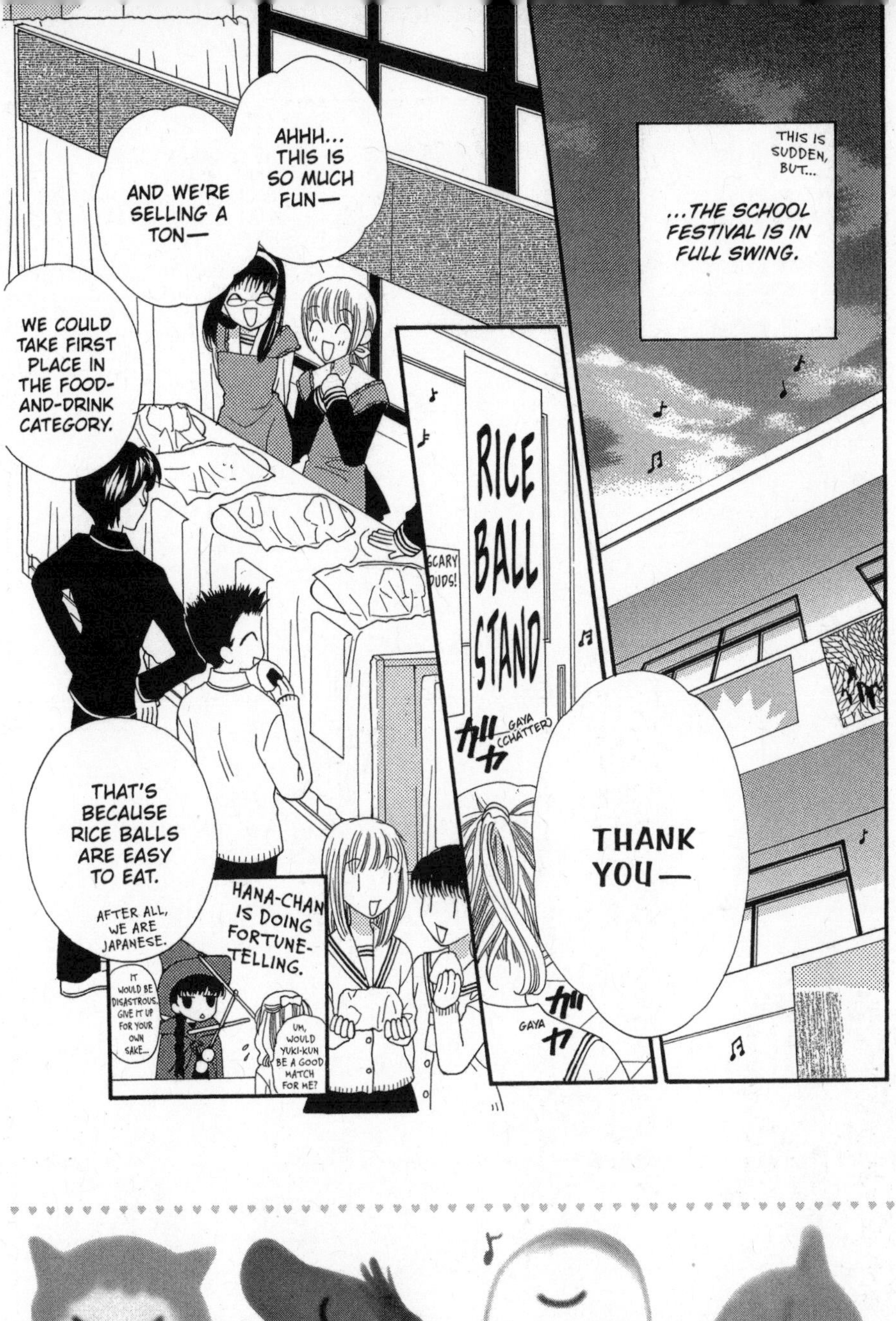
THIS IS SUDDEN, BUT...
...THE SCHOOL FESTIVAL IS IN FULL SWING.
RICE BALL STAND
GAYA (CHATTER)
THANK YOU—
GAYA
AHHH... THIS IS SO MUCH FUN—
AND WE'RE SELLING A TON—
WE COULD TAKE FIRST PLACE IN THE FOOD-AND-DRINK CATEGORY.
SCARY DUDS!
THAT'S BECAUSE RICE BALLS ARE EASY TO EAT.
AFTER ALL, WE ARE JAPANESE.
HANA-CHAN IS DOING FORTUNE-TELLING.
UM, WOULD YUKI-KUN BE A GOOD MATCH FOR ME?
IT WOULD BE DISASTROUS. GIVE IT UP FOR YOUR OWN SAKE...

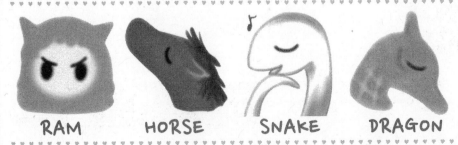

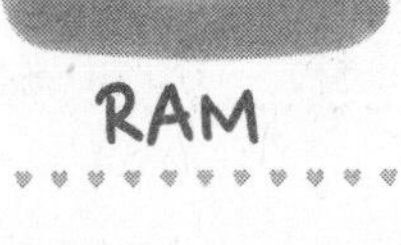
RAM

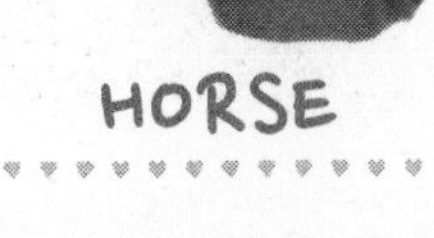
HORSE

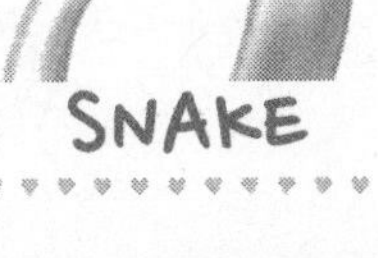
SNAKE

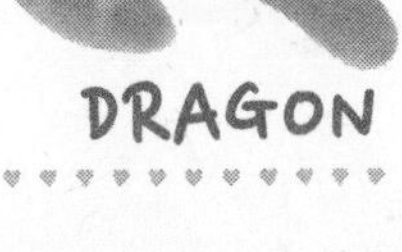
DRAGON

Fruits Basket

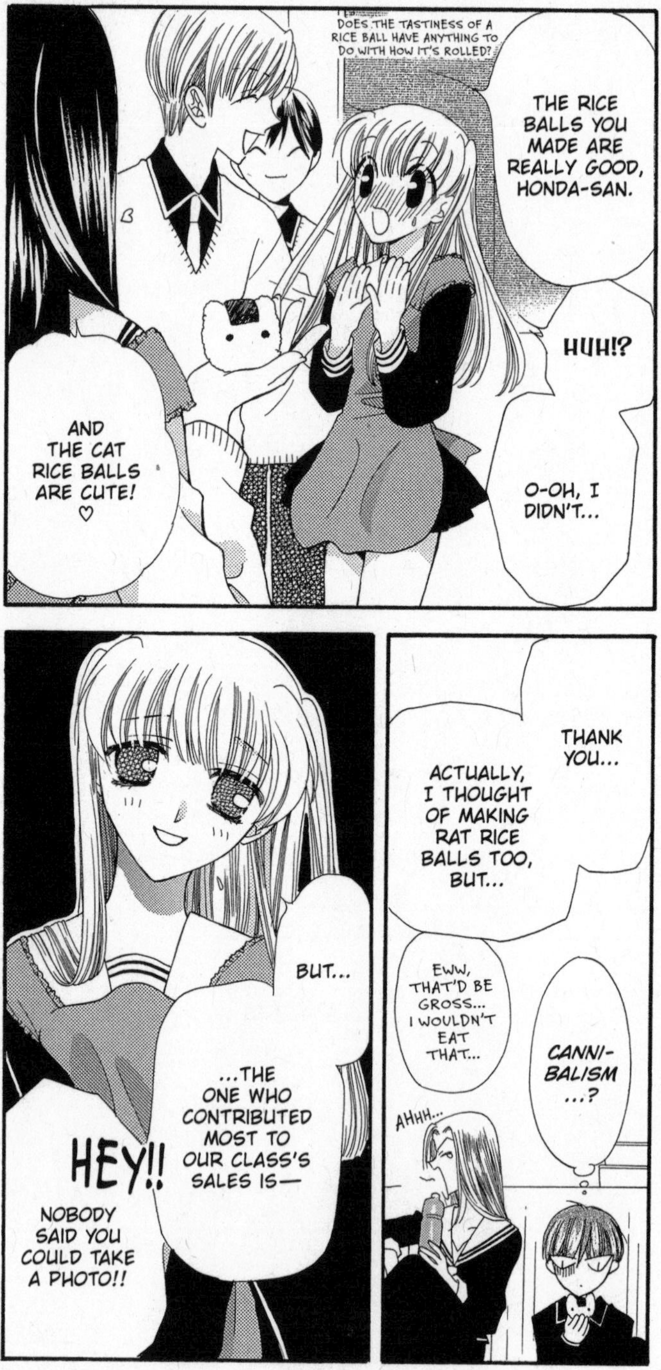
DOES THE TASTINESS OF A RICE BALL HAVE ANYTHING TO DO WITH HOW IT'S ROLLED?
THE RICE BALLS YOU MADE ARE REALLY GOOD, HONDA-SAN.
HUH!?
O-OH, I DIDN'T...
AND THE CAT RICE BALLS ARE CUTE! ♡
THANK YOU...
ACTUALLY, I THOUGHT OF MAKING RAT RICE BALLS TOO, BUT...
CANNI-BALISM ...?
EWW, THAT'D BE GROSS... I WOULDN'T EAT THAT...
AHHH...
BUT...
...THE ONE WHO CONTRIBUTED MOST TO OUR CLASS'S SALES IS—
HEY!!
NOBODY SAID YOU COULD TAKE A PHOTO!!

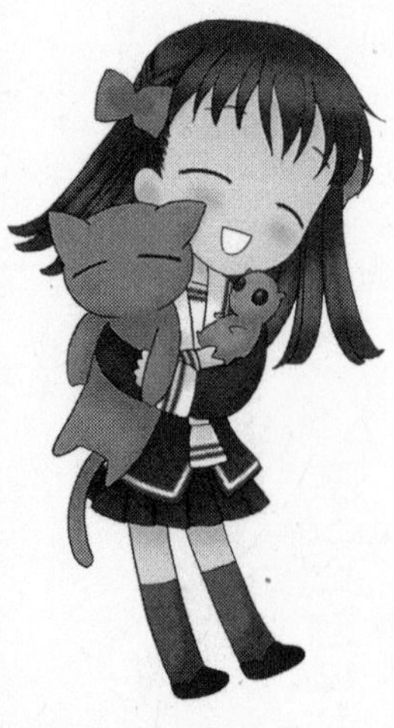

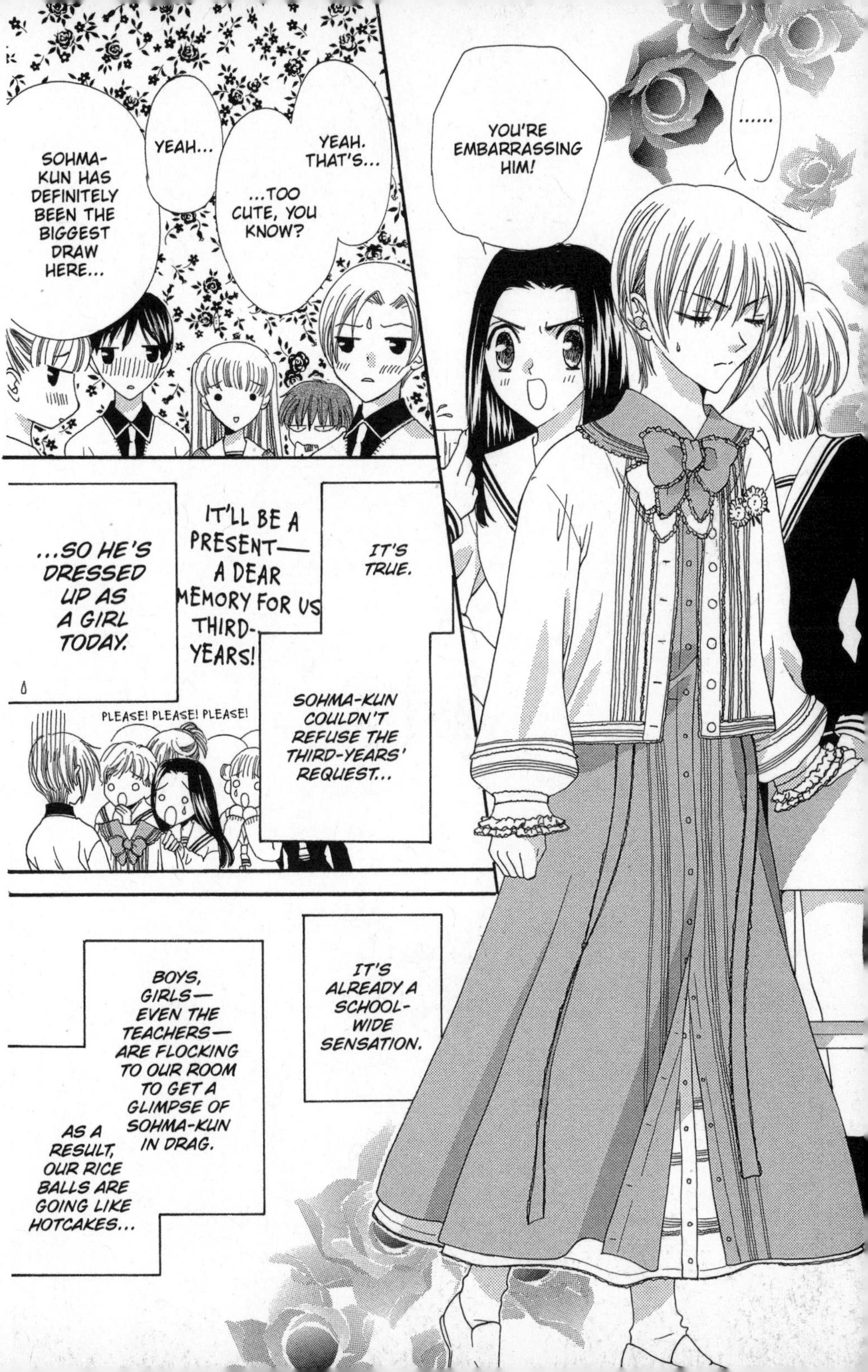
......
YOU'RE EMBARRASSING HIM!
YEAH. THAT'S...
...TOO CUTE, YOU KNOW?
YEAH...
SOHMA-KUN HAS DEFINITELY BEEN THE BIGGEST DRAW HERE...
IT'S TRUE.
IT'LL BE A PRESENT— A DEAR MEMORY FOR US THIRD-YEARS!
...SO HE'S DRESSED UP AS A GIRL TODAY.
SOHMA-KUN COULDN'T REFUSE THE THIRD-YEARS' REQUEST...
PLEASE! PLEASE! PLEASE!
IT'S ALREADY A SCHOOL-WIDE SENSATION.
BOYS, GIRLS— EVEN THE TEACHERS— ARE FLOCKING TO OUR ROOM TO GET A GLIMPSE OF SOHMA-KUN IN DRAG.
AS A RESULT, OUR RICE BALLS ARE GOING LIKE HOTCAKES...

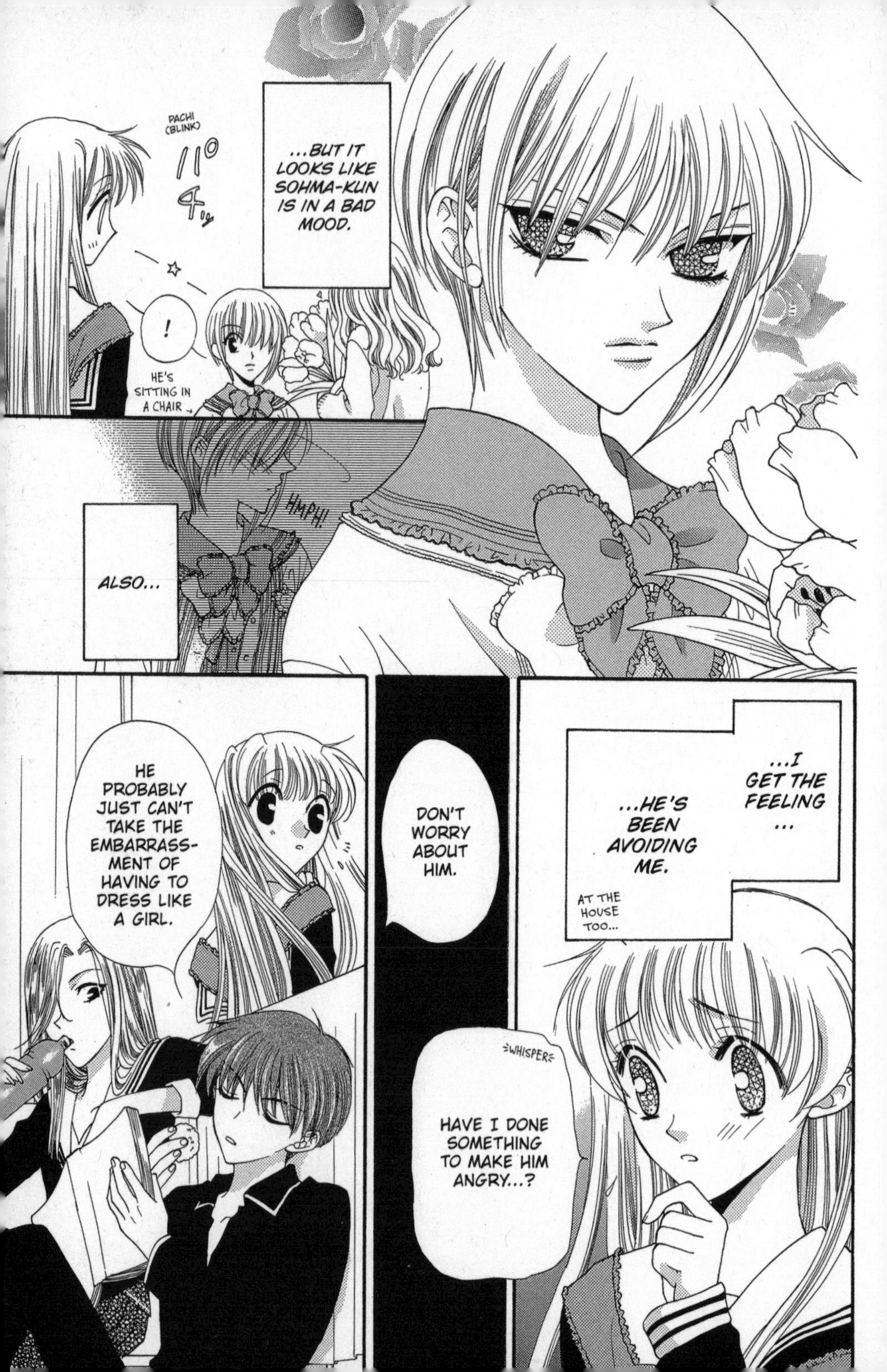
...BUT IT LOOKS LIKE SOHMA-KUN IS IN A BAD MOOD.
PACHI (BLINK)
!
HE'S SITTING IN A CHAIR
HMPH!
ALSO...
...I GET THE FEELING...
...HE'S BEEN AVOIDING ME.
AT THE HOUSE TOO...
WHISPER
HAVE I DONE SOMETHING TO MAKE HIM ANGRY...?
DON'T WORRY ABOUT HIM.
HE PROBABLY JUST CAN'T TAKE THE EMBARRASSMENT OF HAVING TO DRESS LIKE A GIRL.

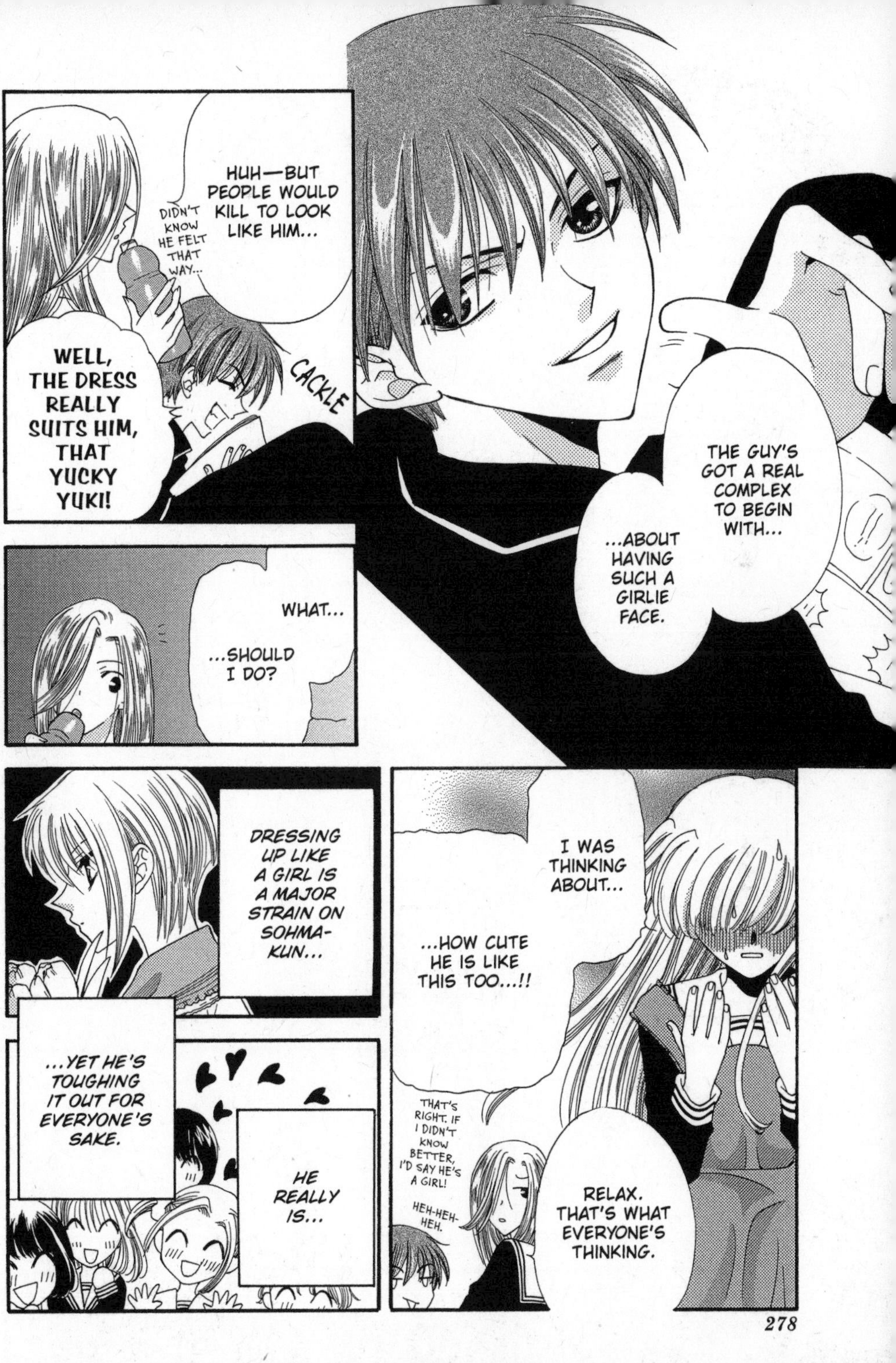
THE GUY'S GOT A REAL COMPLEX TO BEGIN WITH...
...ABOUT HAVING SUCH A GIRLIE FACE.
HUH—BUT PEOPLE WOULD KILL TO LOOK LIKE HIM...
DIDN'T KNOW HE FELT THAT WAY...
CACKLE
WELL, THE DRESS REALLY SUITS HIM, THAT YUCKY YUKI!
WHAT...
...SHOULD I DO?
I WAS THINKING ABOUT...
...HOW CUTE HE IS LIKE THIS TOO...!!
RELAX. THAT'S WHAT EVERYONE'S THINKING.
THAT'S RIGHT. IF I DIDN'T KNOW BETTER, I'D SAY HE'S A GIRL!
HEH-HEH-HEH.
DRESSING UP LIKE A GIRL IS A MAJOR STRAIN ON SOHMA-KUN...
...YET HE'S TOUGHING IT OUT FOR EVERYONE'S SAKE.
HE REALLY IS...

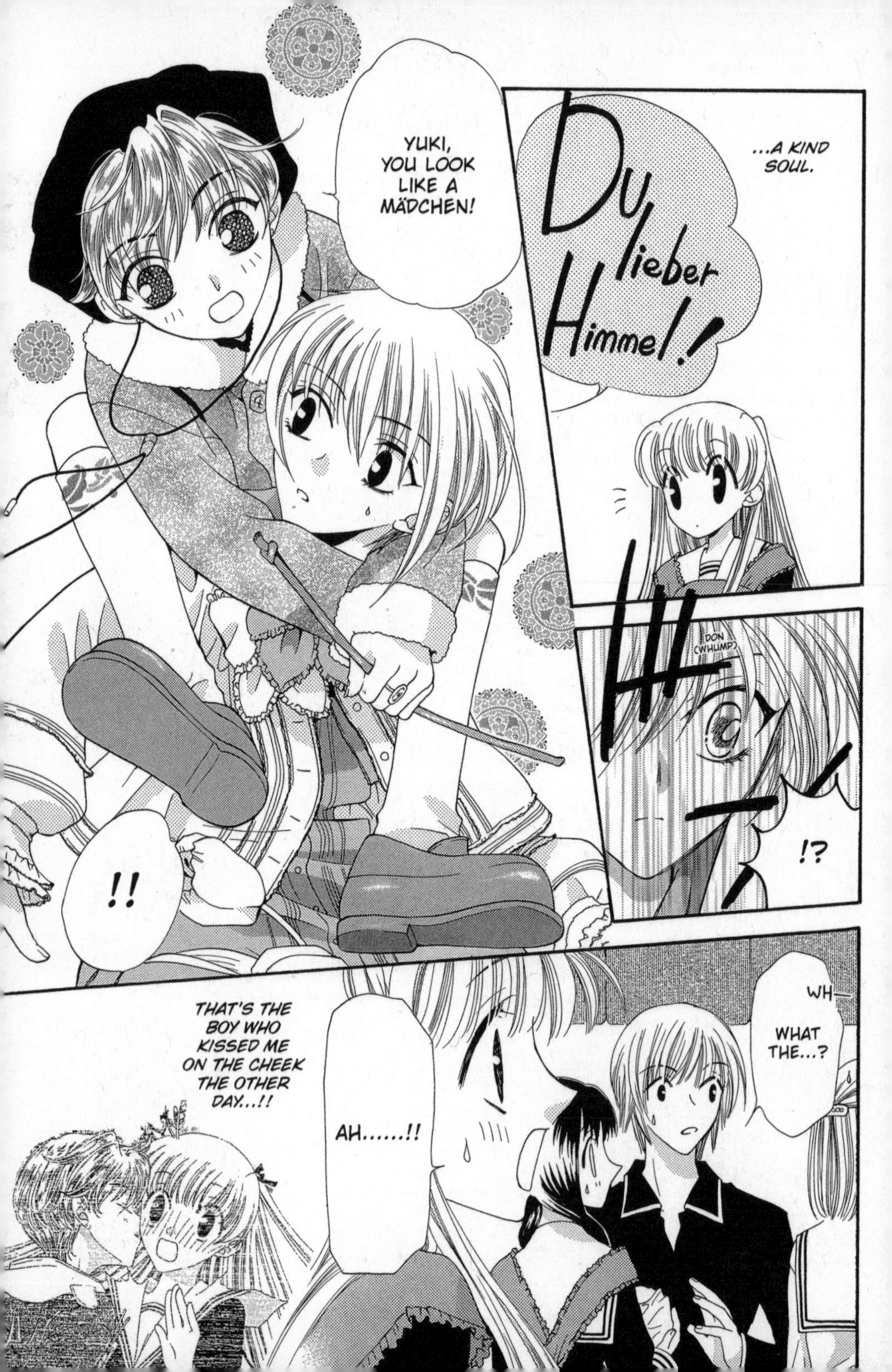
...A KIND SOUL.
Du lieber Himmel!!
DON (WHUMP)
!?
YUKI, YOU LOOK LIKE A MÄDCHEN!
!!
WH— WHAT THE...?
AH......!!
THAT'S THE BOY WHO KISSED ME ON THE CHEEK THE OTHER DAY...!!

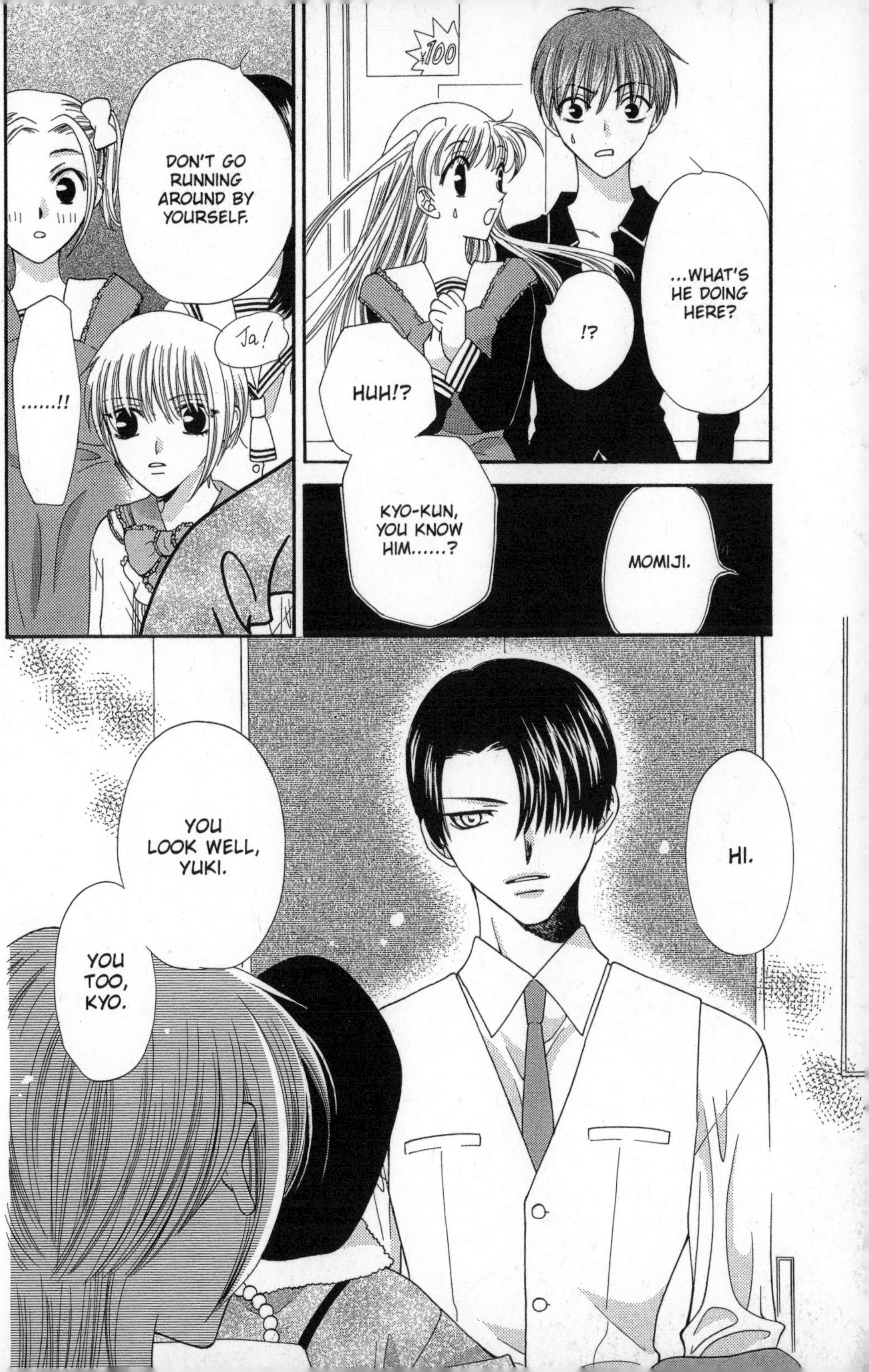
...WHAT'S HE DOING HERE?
!?
HUH!?
MOMIJI.
KYO-KUN, YOU KNOW HIM......?
DON'T GO RUNNING AROUND BY YOURSELF.
Ja!
......!!
HI.
YOU LOOK WELL, YUKI.
YOU TOO, KYO.

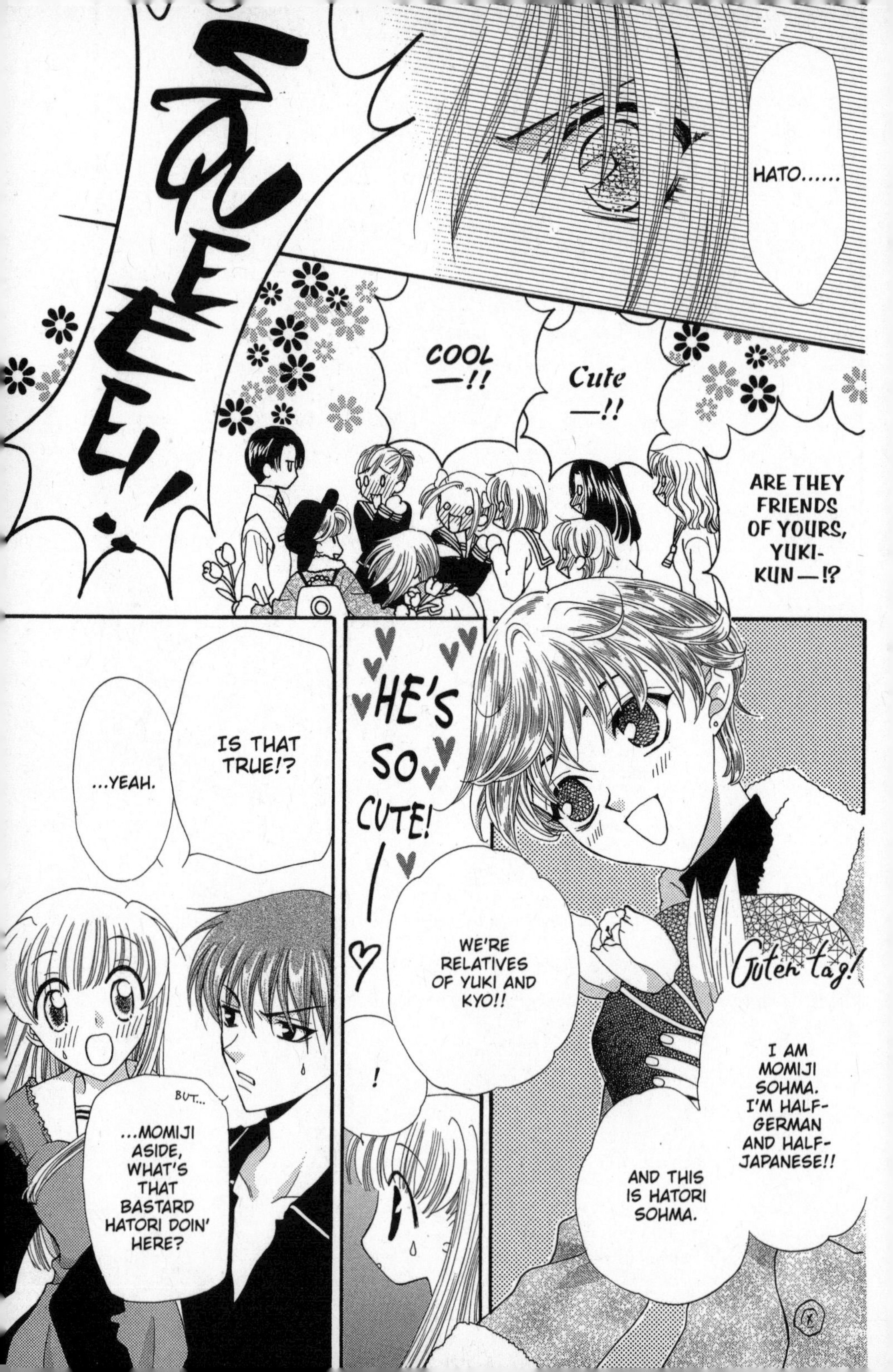
HATO......
SQUEEEE!!
ARE THEY FRIENDS OF YOURS, YUKI-KUN—!?
Cute—!!
COOL—!!
Guten tag!
I AM MOMIJI SOHMA. I'M HALF-GERMAN AND HALF-JAPANESE!!
AND THIS IS HATORI SOHMA.
WE'RE RELATIVES OF YUKI AND KYO!!
HE'S SO CUTE!
!
IS THAT TRUE!?
...YEAH.
BUT...
...MOMIJI ASIDE, WHAT'S THAT BASTARD HATORI DOIN' HERE?

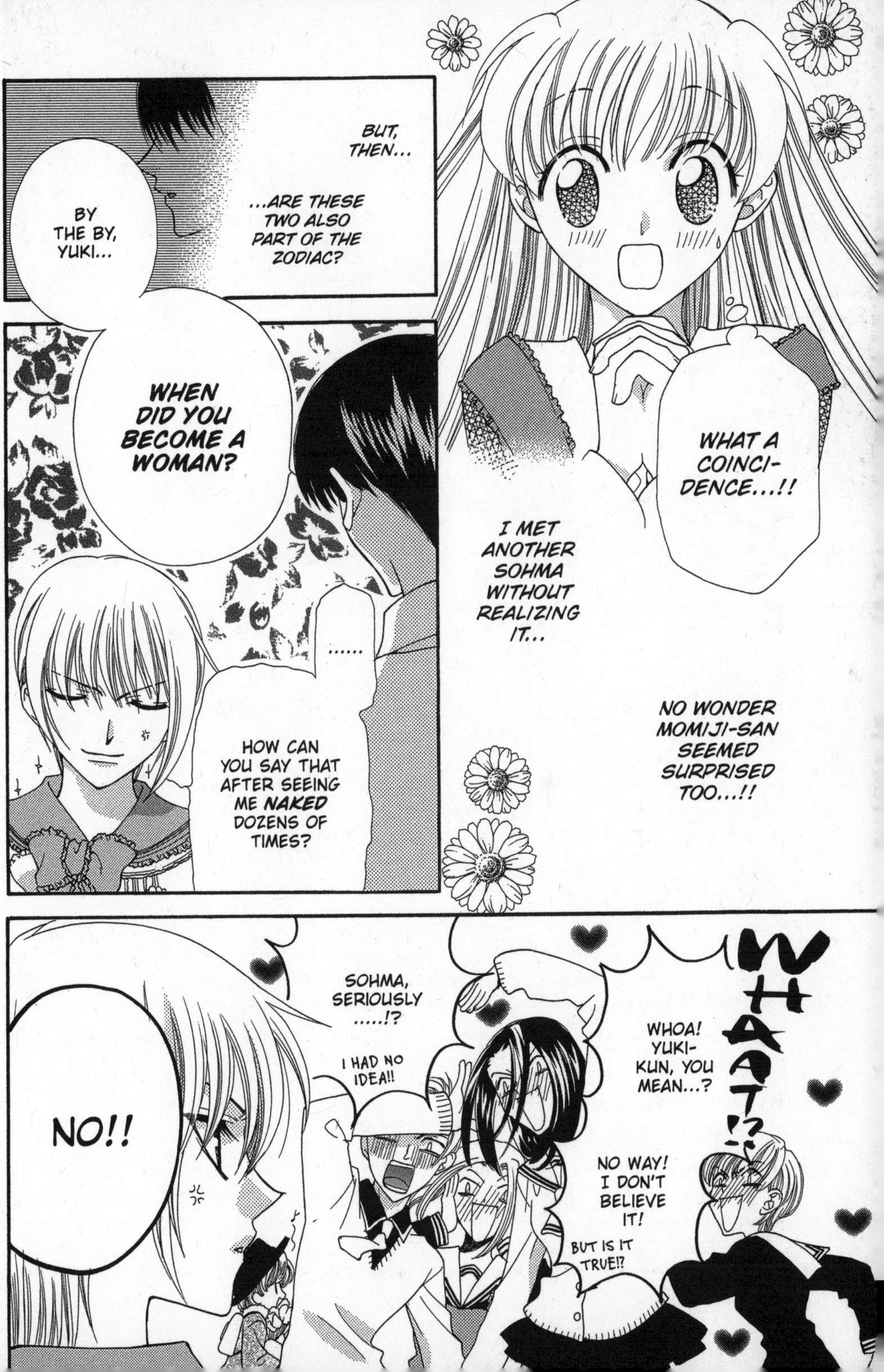
WHAT A COINCI-DENCE...!!
I MET ANOTHER SOHMA WITHOUT REALIZING IT...
NO WONDER MOMIJI-SAN SEEMED SURPRISED TOO...!!
BUT, THEN...
...ARE THESE TWO ALSO PART OF THE ZODIAC?
BY THE BY, YUKI...
WHEN DID YOU BECOME A WOMAN?
......
HOW CAN YOU SAY THAT AFTER SEEING ME NAKED DOZENS OF TIMES?
WHAAT!?
WHOA! YUKI-KUN, YOU MEAN...?
NO WAY! I DON'T BELIEVE IT!
BUT IS IT TRUE!?
SOHMA, SERIOUSLY .....!?
I HAD NO IDEA!!
NO!!

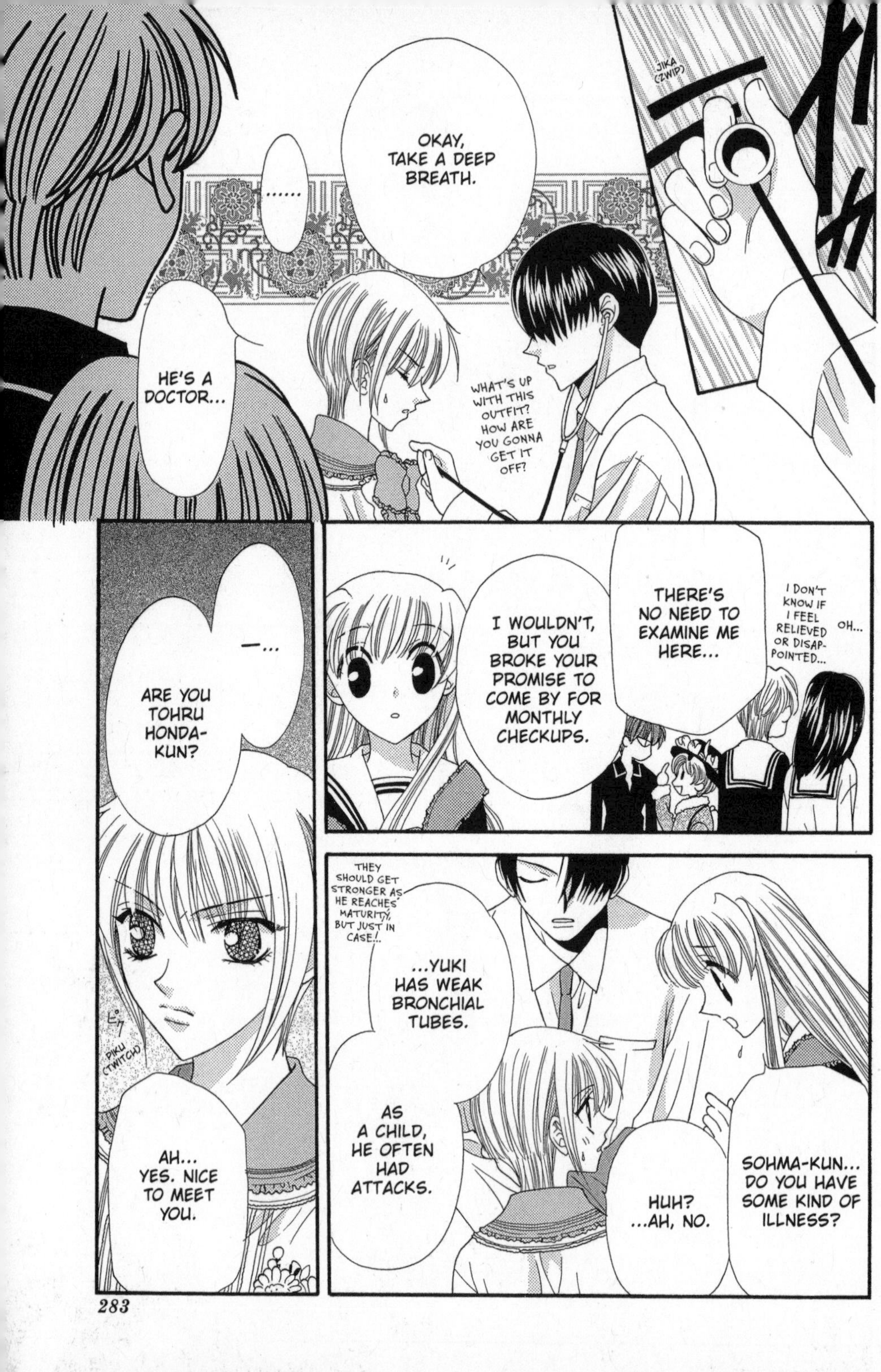
JIKA (ZWIP)
OKAY, TAKE A DEEP BREATH.
......
WHAT'S UP WITH THIS OUTFIT? HOW ARE YOU GONNA GET IT OFF?
HE'S A DOCTOR...
OH...
I DON'T KNOW IF I FEEL RELIEVED OR DISAPPOINTED...
THERE'S NO NEED TO EXAMINE ME HERE...
I WOULDN'T, BUT YOU BROKE YOUR PROMISE TO COME BY FOR MONTHLY CHECKUPS.
SOHMA-KUN... DO YOU HAVE SOME KIND OF ILLNESS?
HUH? ...AH, NO.
...YUKI HAS WEAK BRONCHIAL TUBES.
AS A CHILD, HE OFTEN HAD ATTACKS.
THEY SHOULD GET STRONGER AS HE REACHES MATURITY, BUT JUST IN CASE...
—...
ARE YOU TOHRU HONDA-KUN?
PIKU (TWITCH)
AH... YES. NICE TO MEET YOU.

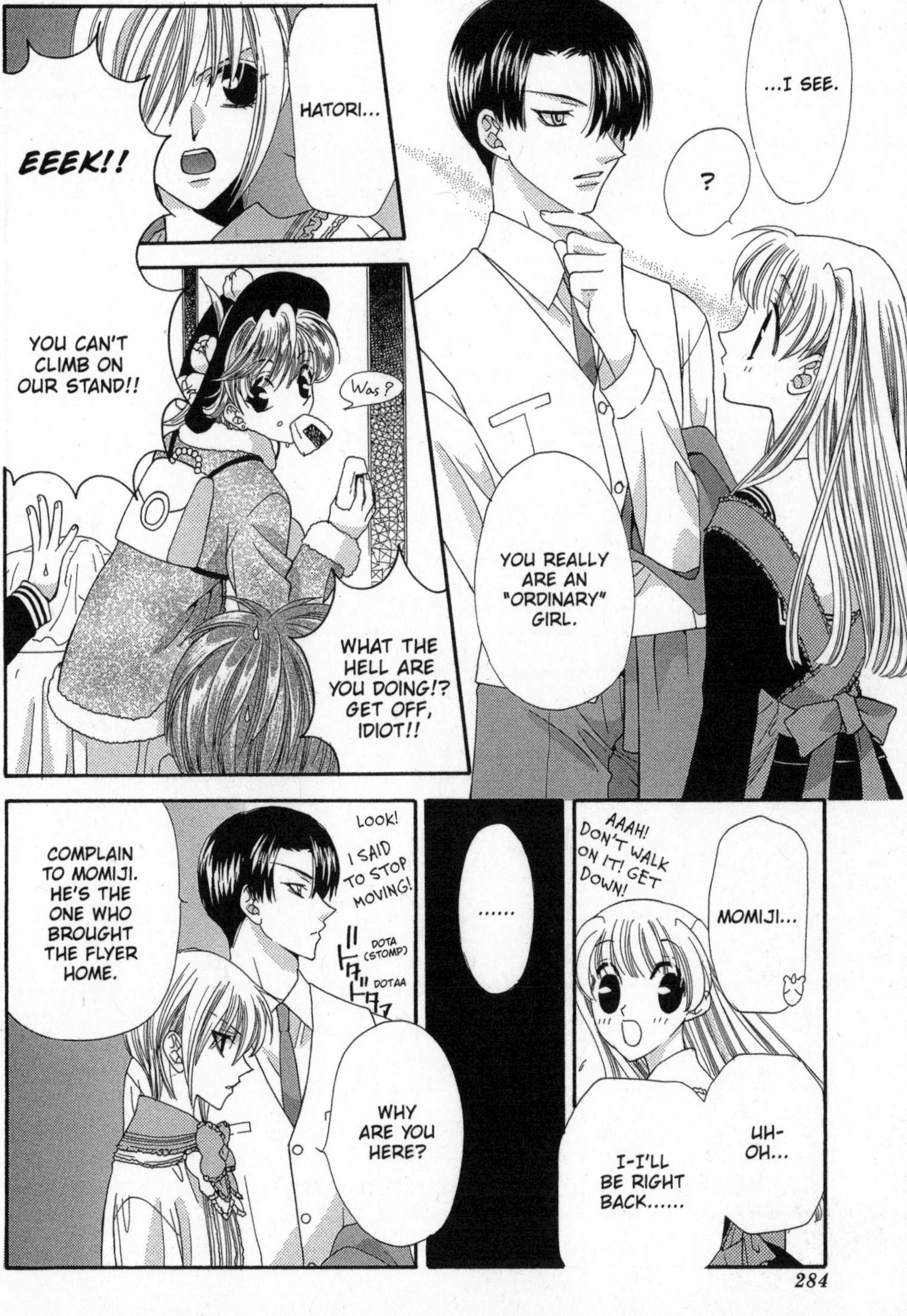
...I SEE.
?
YOU REALLY ARE AN "ORDINARY" GIRL.
HATORI...
EEEK!!
YOU CAN'T CLIMB ON OUR STAND!!
Was?
WHAT THE HELL ARE YOU DOING!? GET OFF, IDIOT!!
MOMIJI...
AAAH! DON'T WALK ON IT! GET DOWN!
UH-OH...
I-I'LL BE RIGHT BACK......
......
LOOK! I SAID TO STOP MOVING!
COMPLAIN TO MOMIJI. HE'S THE ONE WHO BROUGHT THE FLYER HOME.
DOTA (STOMP)
DOTAA
WHY ARE YOU HERE?

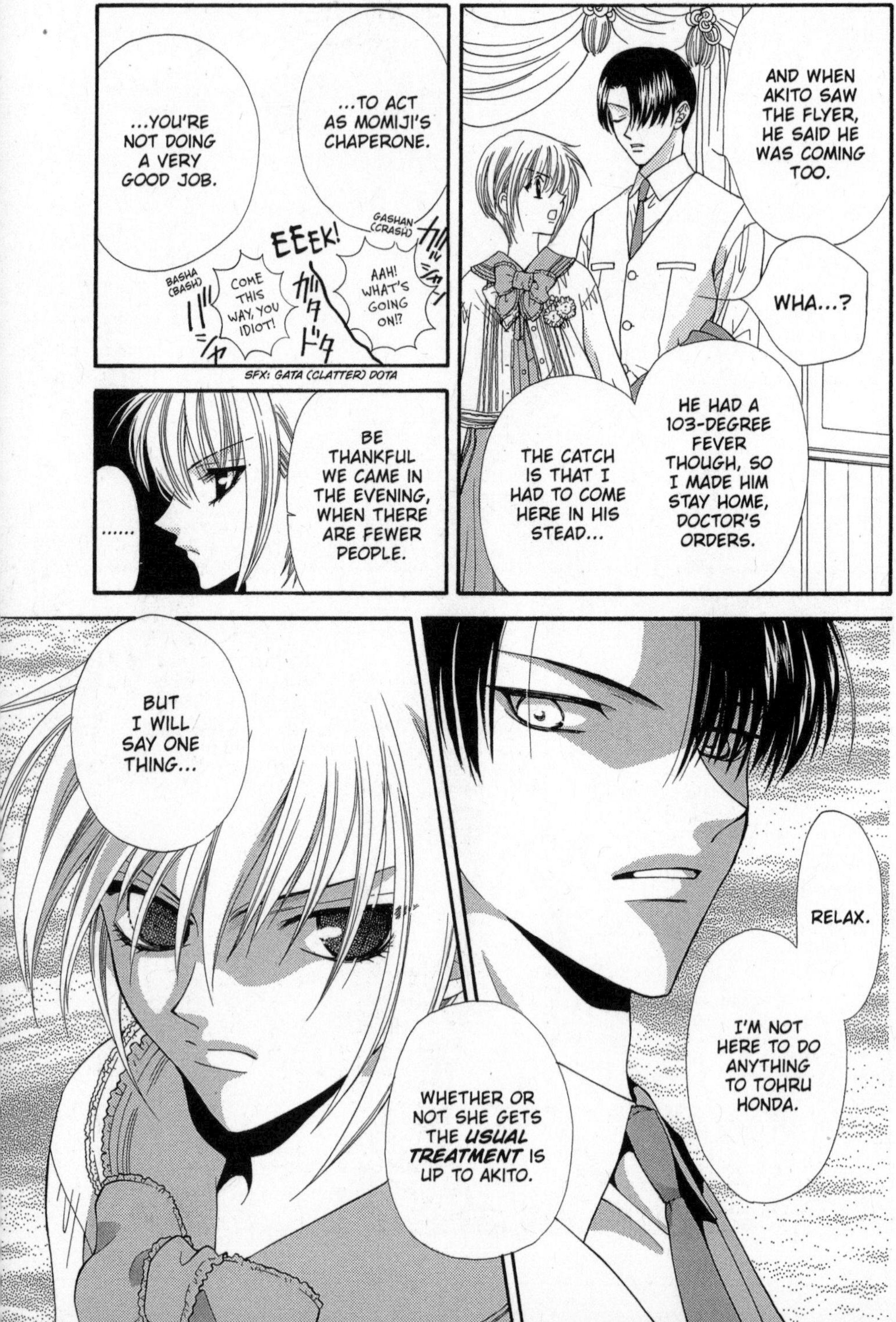
AND WHEN AKITO SAW THE FLYER, HE SAID HE WAS COMING TOO.
WHA...?
HE HAD A 103-DEGREE FEVER THOUGH, SO I MADE HIM STAY HOME, DOCTOR'S ORDERS.
THE CATCH IS THAT I HAD TO COME HERE IN HIS STEAD...
...TO ACT AS MOMIJI'S CHAPERONE.
...YOU'RE NOT DOING A VERY GOOD JOB.
GASHAN (CRASH)
AAH! WHAT'S GOING ON!?
EEEK!
COME THIS WAY, YOU IDIOT!
BASHA (BASH)
SFX: GATA (CLATTER) DOTA
BE THANKFUL WE CAME IN THE EVENING, WHEN THERE ARE FEWER PEOPLE.
......
RELAX.
I'M NOT HERE TO DO ANYTHING TO TOHRU HONDA.
WHETHER OR NOT SHE GETS THE *USUAL TREATMENT* IS UP TO AKITO.
BUT I WILL SAY ONE THING...

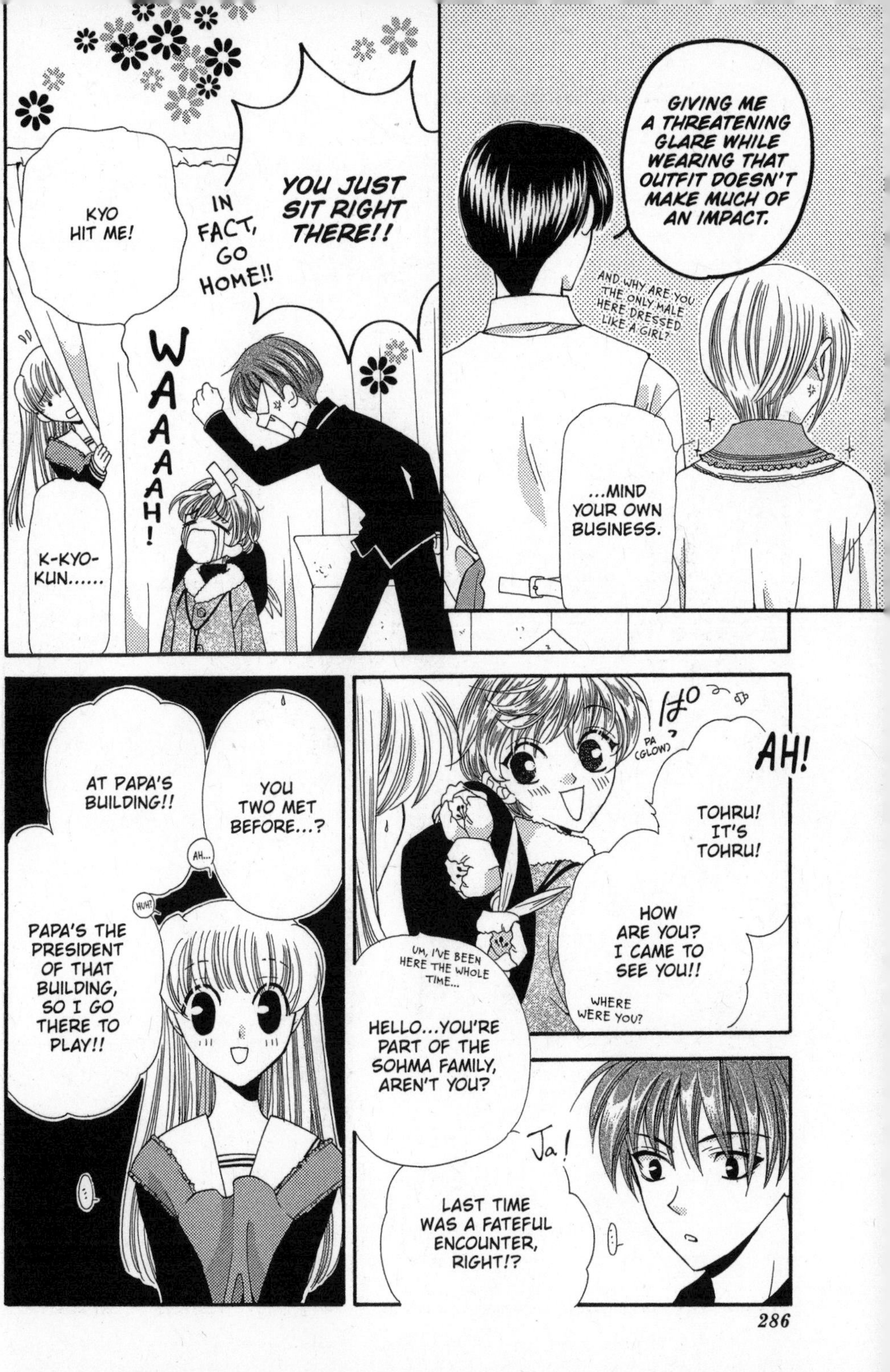
GIVING ME A THREATENING GLARE WHILE WEARING THAT OUTFIT DOESN'T MAKE MUCH OF AN IMPACT.
AND WHY ARE YOU THE ONLY MALE HERE DRESSED LIKE A GIRL?
...MIND YOUR OWN BUSINESS.
YOU JUST SIT RIGHT THERE!!
IN FACT, GO HOME!!
KYO HIT ME!
WAAAAAH!
K-KYO-KUN......
AH!
ぱ
PA (GLOW)
TOHRU! IT'S TOHRU!
HOW ARE YOU? I CAME TO SEE YOU!!
WHERE WERE YOU?
UM, I'VE BEEN HERE THE WHOLE TIME...
HELLO...YOU'RE PART OF THE SOHMA FAMILY, AREN'T YOU?
Ja!
LAST TIME WAS A FATEFUL ENCOUNTER, RIGHT!?
YOU TWO MET BEFORE...?
AH...
HUH?
AT PAPA'S BUILDING!!
PAPA'S THE PRESIDENT OF THAT BUILDING, SO I GO THERE TO PLAY!!

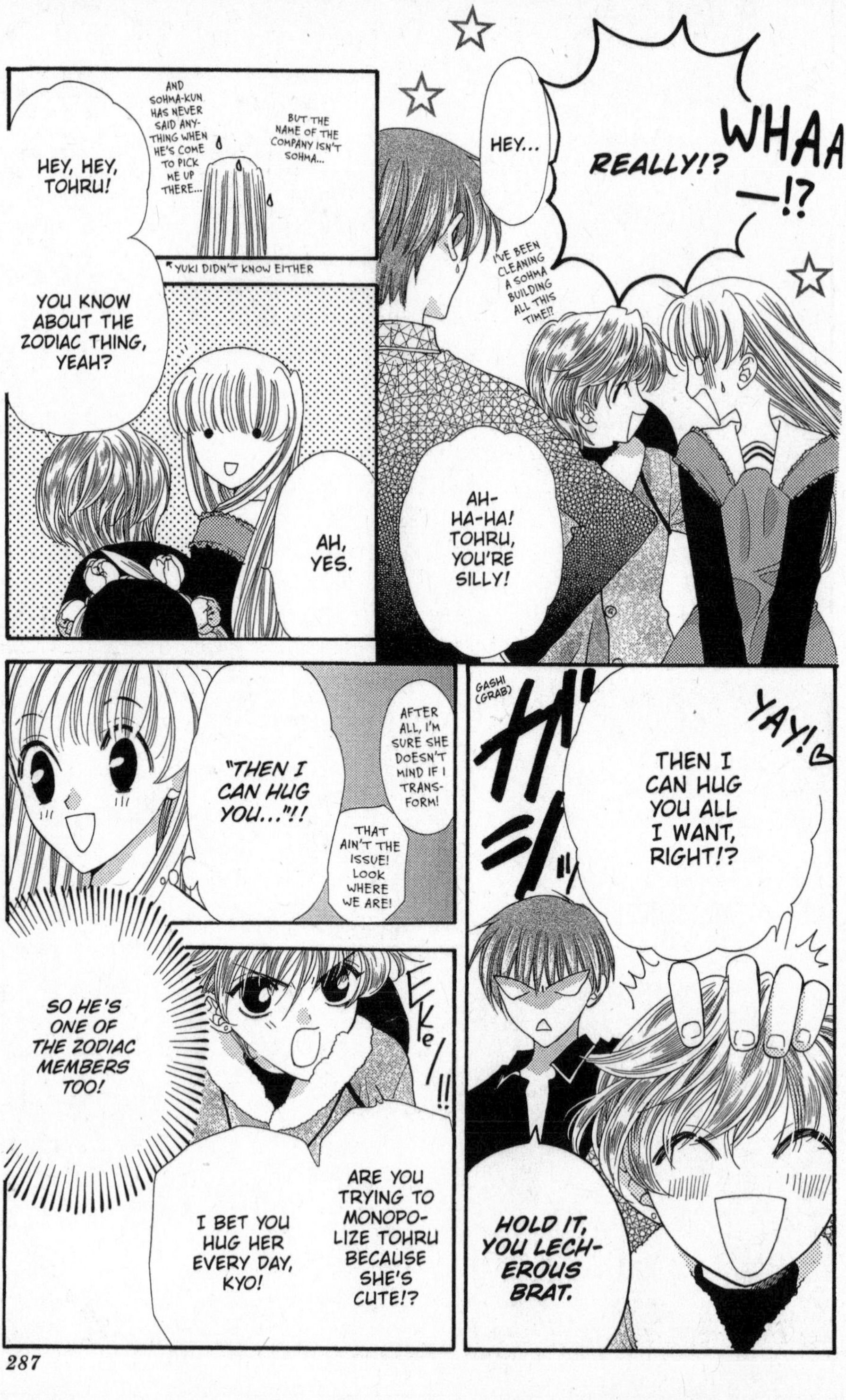
WHAA—!?
REALLY!?
HEY...
I'VE BEEN CLEANING A SOHMA BUILDING ALL THIS TIME!?
AH-HA-HA! TOHRU, YOU'RE SILLY!
BUT THE NAME OF THE COMPANY ISN'T SOHMA...
AND SOHMA-KUN HAS NEVER SAID ANYTHING WHEN HE'S COME TO PICK ME UP THERE...
HEY, HEY, TOHRU!
↖YUKI DIDN'T KNOW EITHER
YOU KNOW ABOUT THE ZODIAC THING, YEAH?
AH, YES.
GASHI (GRAB)
YAY!♡
THEN I CAN HUG YOU ALL I WANT, RIGHT!?
HOLD IT, YOU LECHEROUS BRAT.
AFTER ALL, I'M SURE SHE DOESN'T MIND IF I TRANSFORM!
THAT AIN'T THE ISSUE! LOOK WHERE WE ARE!
"THEN I CAN HUG YOU..."!!
EKE!!
ARE YOU TRYING TO MONOPOLIZE TOHRU BECAUSE SHE'S CUTE!?
I BET YOU HUG HER EVERY DAY, KYO!
SO HE'S ONE OF THE ZODIAC MEMBERS TOO!

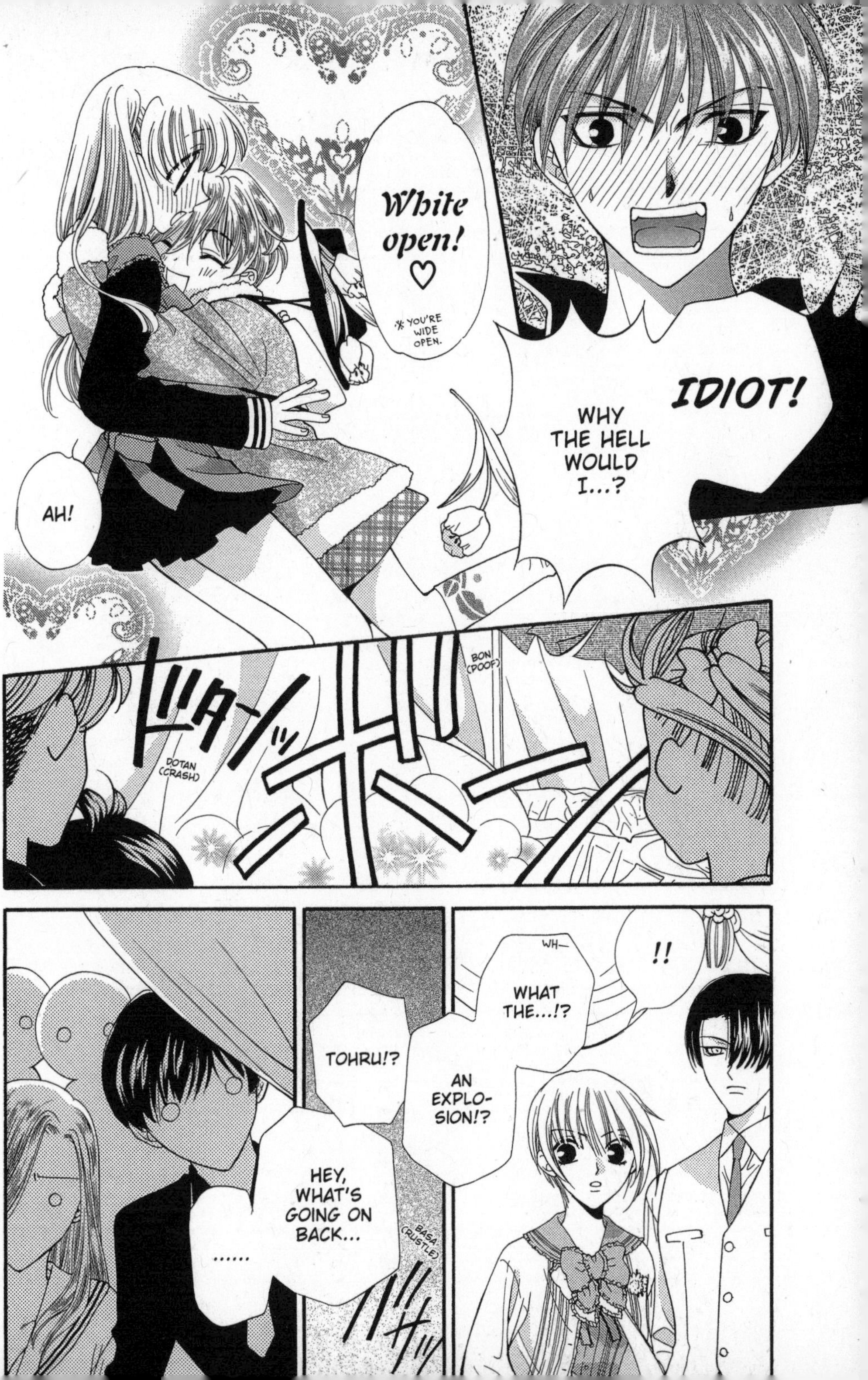
IDIOT!
WHY THE HELL WOULD I...?
White open! ♡
*YOU'RE WIDE OPEN.
AH!
BON (POOF)
DOTAN (CRASH)
!!
WH— WHAT THE...!?
AN EXPLOSION!?
TOHRU!?
HEY, WHAT'S GOING ON BACK...
BASA (RUSTLE)
......

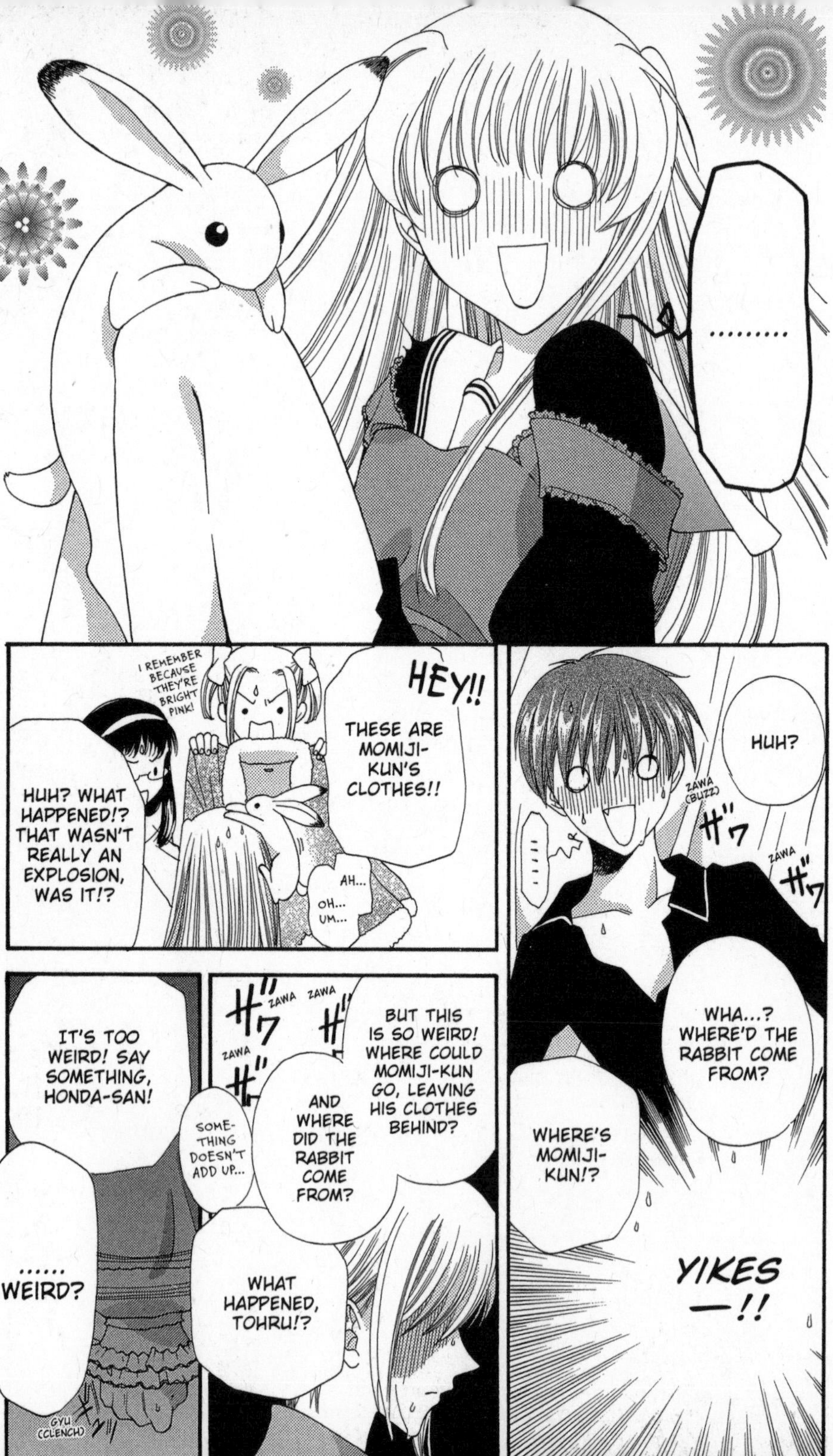
....
HUH?
ZAWA (BUZZ)
ザワ
ZAWA
ザワ
......
WHA...? WHERE'D THE RABBIT COME FROM?
WHERE'S MOMIJI-KUN!?
YIKES—!!
HEY!!
THESE ARE MOMIJI-KUN'S CLOTHES!!
I REMEMBER BECAUSE THEY'RE BRIGHT PINK!
HUH? WHAT HAPPENED!? THAT WASN'T REALLY AN EXPLOSION, WAS IT!?
AH... OH... UM...
BUT THIS IS SO WEIRD! WHERE COULD MOMIJI-KUN GO, LEAVING HIS CLOTHES BEHIND?
ZAWA ZAWA
ZAWA
AND WHERE DID THE RABBIT COME FROM?
SOMETHING DOESN'T ADD UP...
WHAT HAPPENED, TOHRU!?
IT'S TOO WEIRD! SAY SOMETHING, HONDA-SAN!
......WEIRD?
GYU (CLENCH)

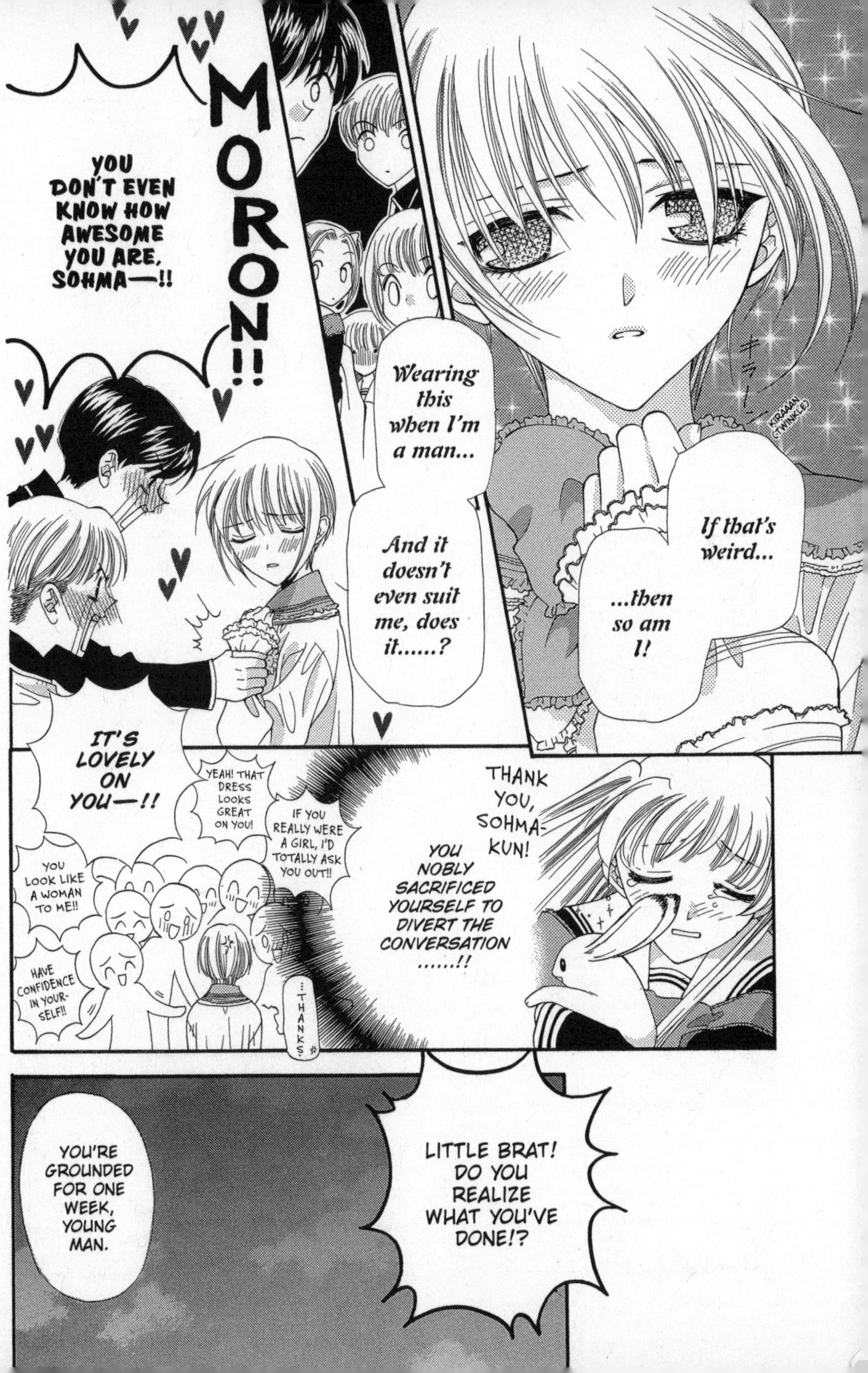
Wearing this when I'm a man...
And it doesn't even suit me, does it......?
KIRAAAN (TWINKLE)
If that's weird...
...then so am I!
MORON!!
YOU DON'T EVEN KNOW HOW AWESOME YOU ARE, SOHMA—!!
THANK YOU, SOHMA-KUN!
YOU NOBLY SACRIFICED YOURSELF TO DIVERT THE CONVERSATION ......!!
IT'S LOVELY ON YOU—!!
YEAH! THAT DRESS LOOKS GREAT ON YOU!
IF YOU REALLY WERE A GIRL, I'D TOTALLY ASK YOU OUT!!
YOU LOOK LIKE A WOMAN TO ME!!
HAVE CONFIDENCE IN YOURSELF!!
...THANKS.
LITTLE BRAT! DO YOU REALIZE WHAT YOU'VE DONE!?
YOU'RE GROUNDED FOR ONE WEEK, YOUNG MAN.

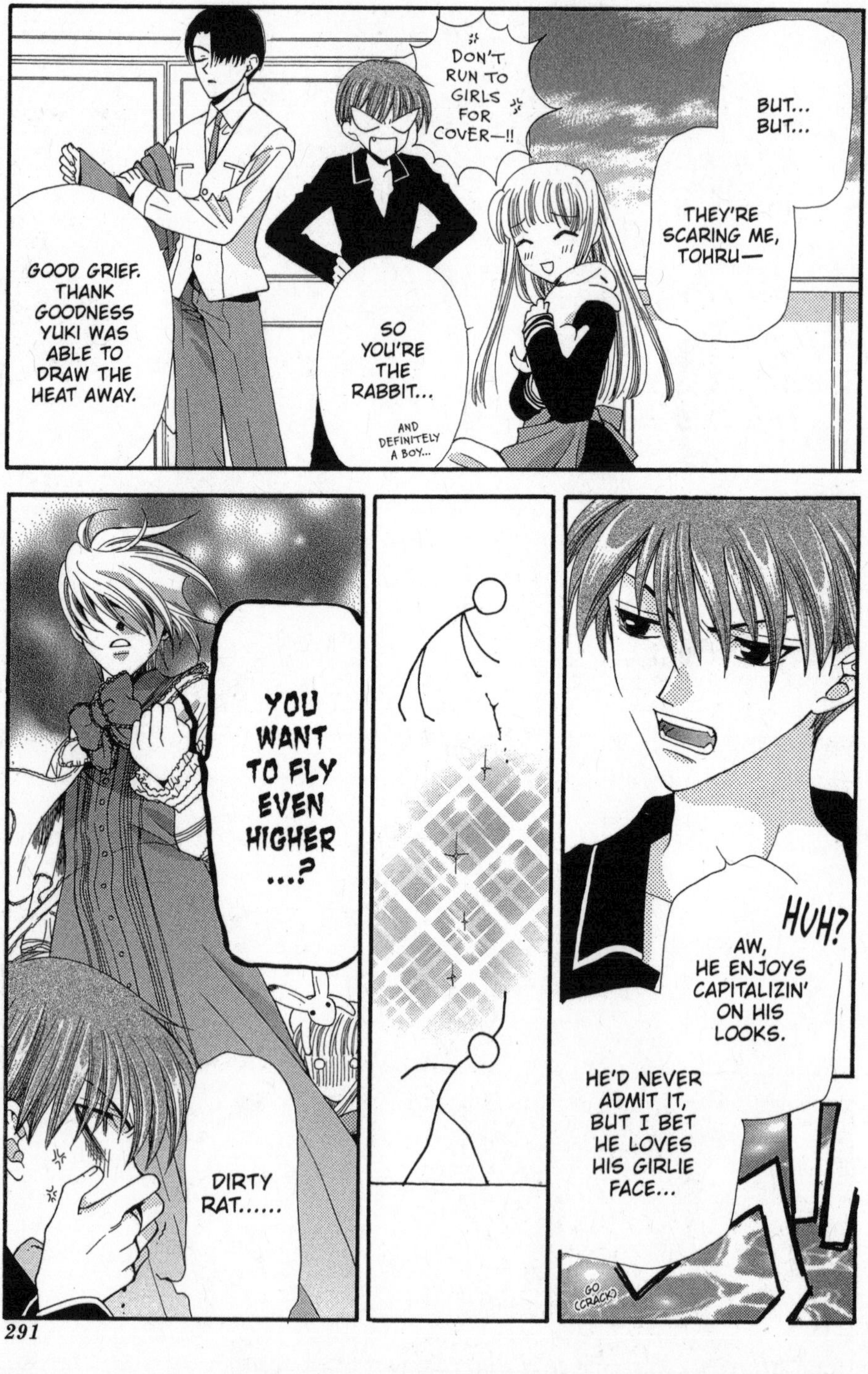
BUT... BUT...
THEY'RE SCARING ME, TOHRU—
DON'T RUN TO GIRLS FOR COVER—!!
SO YOU'RE THE RABBIT...
AND DEFINITELY A BOY...
GOOD GRIEF. THANK GOODNESS YUKI WAS ABLE TO DRAW THE HEAT AWAY.
HUH?
AW, HE ENJOYS CAPITALIZIN' ON HIS LOOKS.
HE'D NEVER ADMIT IT, BUT I BET HE LOVES HIS GIRLIE FACE...
GO (CRACK)
YOU WANT TO FLY EVEN HIGHER ...?
DIRTY RAT......

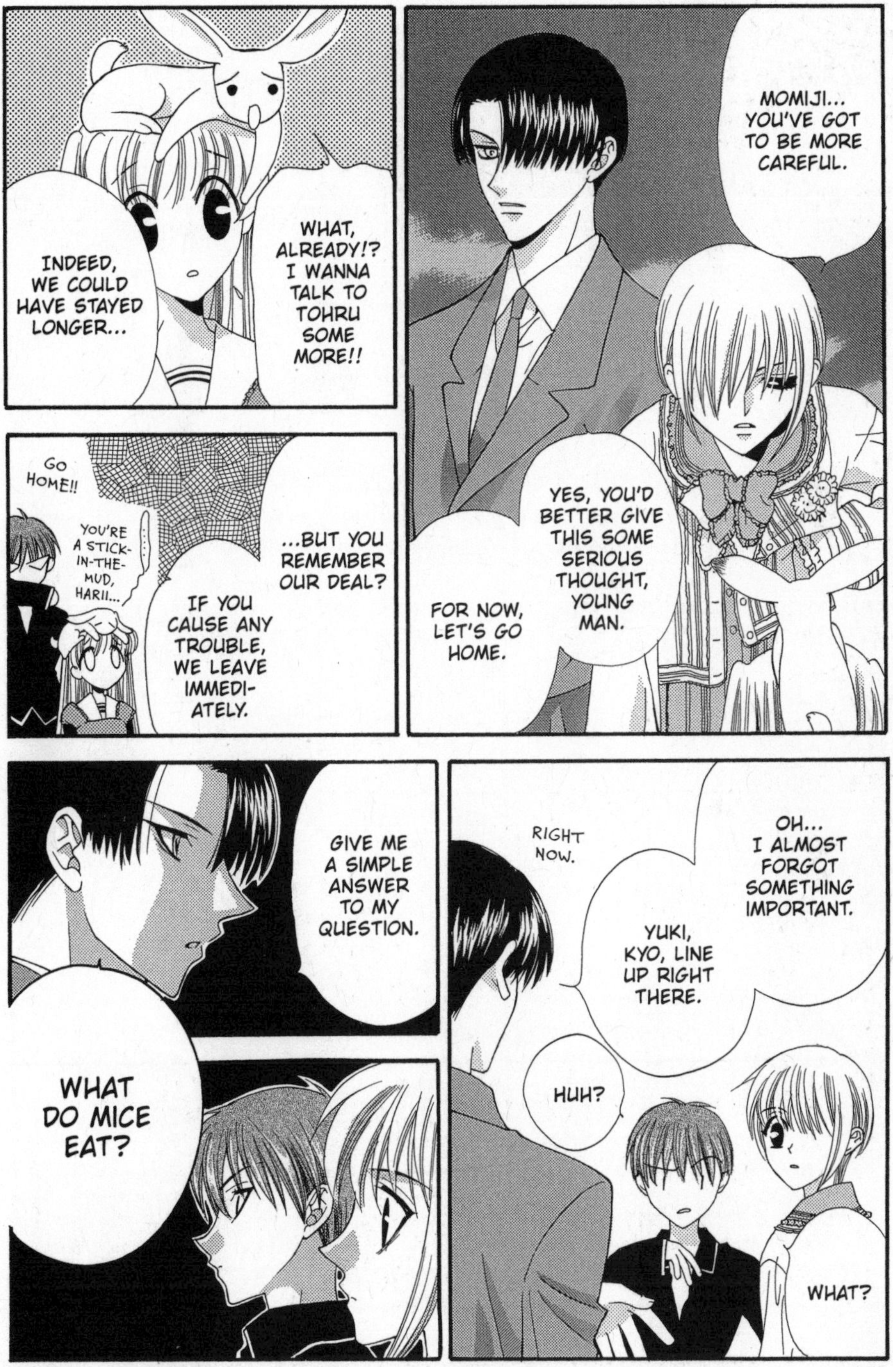
MOMIJI... YOU'VE GOT TO BE MORE CAREFUL.
YES, YOU'D BETTER GIVE THIS SOME SERIOUS THOUGHT, YOUNG MAN.
FOR NOW, LET'S GO HOME.
WHAT, ALREADY!? I WANNA TALK TO TOHRU SOME MORE!!
INDEED, WE COULD HAVE STAYED LONGER...
...BUT YOU REMEMBER OUR DEAL?
IF YOU CAUSE ANY TROUBLE, WE LEAVE IMMEDIATELY.
GO HOME!!
YOU'RE A STICK-IN-THE-MUD, HARII...
OH... I ALMOST FORGOT SOMETHING IMPORTANT.
RIGHT NOW.
YUKI, KYO, LINE UP RIGHT THERE.
HUH?
WHAT?
GIVE ME A SIMPLE ANSWER TO MY QUESTION.
WHAT DO MICE EAT?

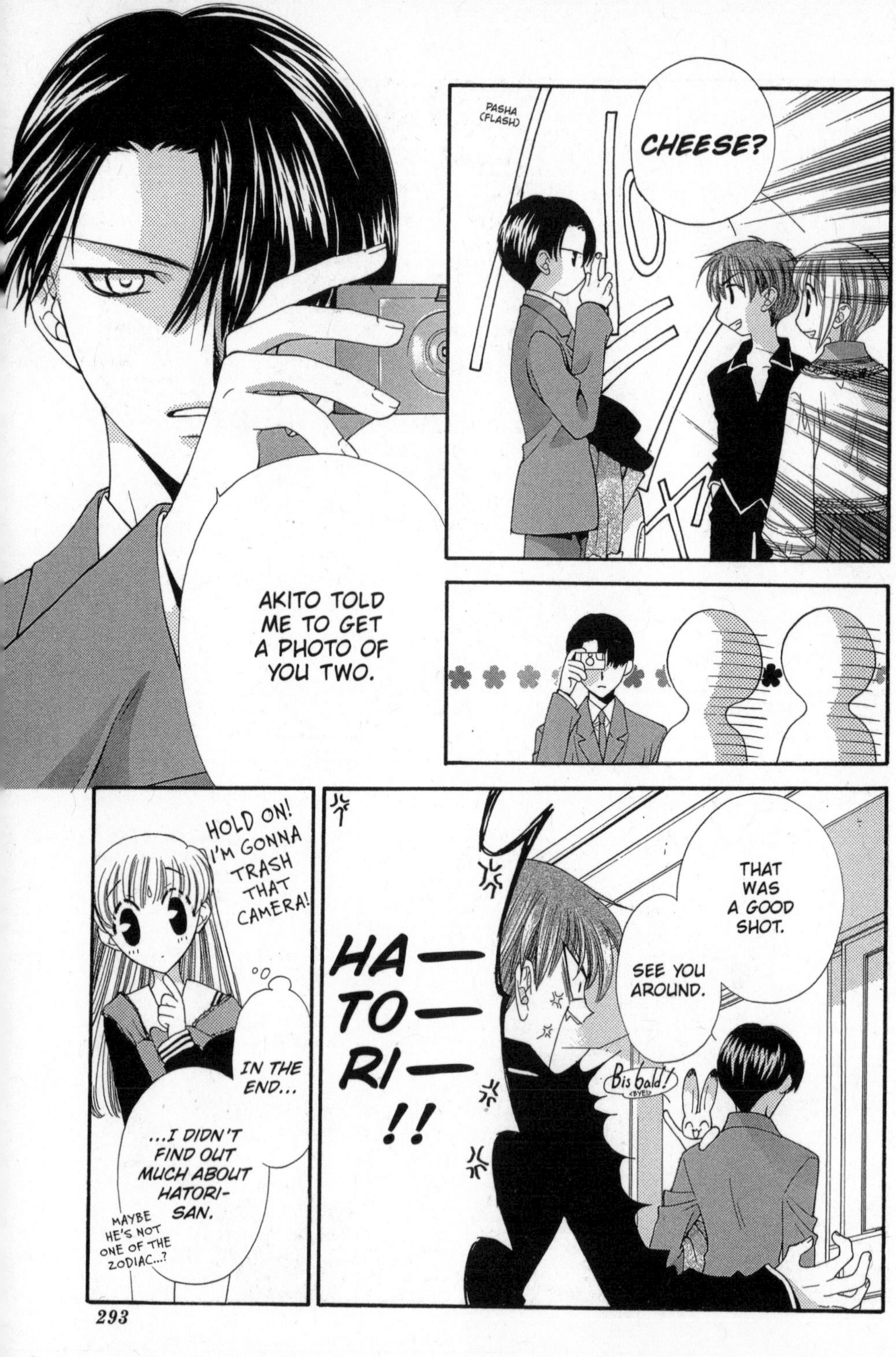
CHEESE?
PASHA (FLASH)
AKITO TOLD ME TO GET A PHOTO OF YOU TWO.
THAT WAS A GOOD SHOT.
SEE YOU AROUND.
HA— TO— RI— !!
Bis bald! <BYE!>
HOLD ON! I'M GONNA TRASH THAT CAMERA!
IN THE END...
...I DIDN'T FIND OUT MUCH ABOUT HATORI-SAN.
MAYBE HE'S NOT ONE OF THE ZODIAC...?

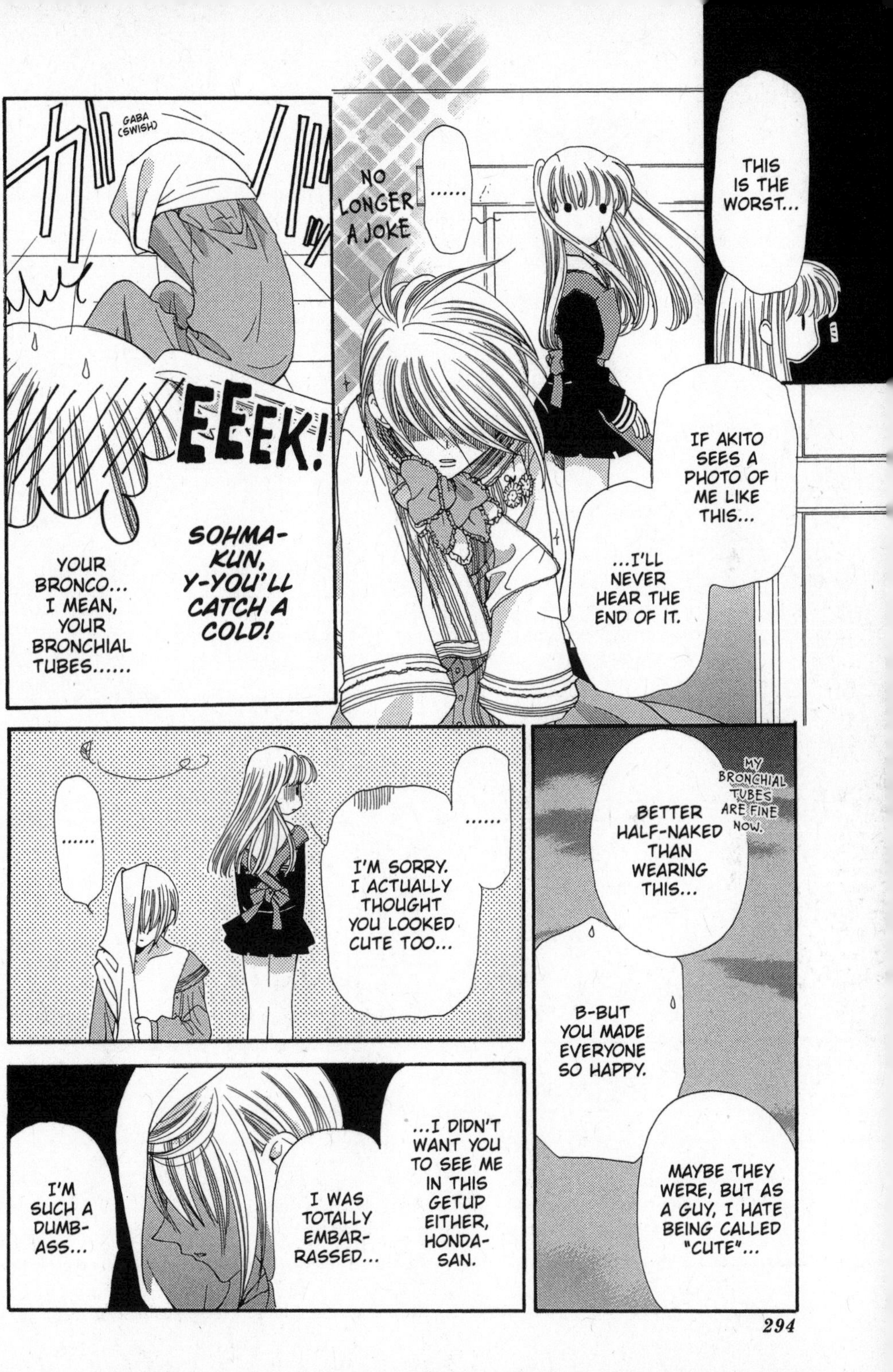
THIS IS THE WORST...
IF AKITO SEES A PHOTO OF ME LIKE THIS...
...I'LL NEVER HEAR THE END OF IT.
......
NO LONGER A JOKE
GABA (SWISH)
EEEK!
SOHMA-KUN, Y-YOU'LL CATCH A COLD!
YOUR BRONCO... I MEAN, YOUR BRONCHIAL TUBES......
BETTER HALF-NAKED THAN WEARING THIS...
MY BRONCHIAL TUBES ARE FINE NOW.
B-BUT YOU MADE EVERYONE SO HAPPY.
MAYBE THEY WERE, BUT AS A GUY, I HATE BEING CALLED "CUTE"...
......
I'M SORRY. I ACTUALLY THOUGHT YOU LOOKED CUTE TOO...
......
...I DIDN'T WANT YOU TO SEE ME IN THIS GETUP EITHER, HONDA-SAN.
I WAS TOTALLY EMBARRASSED...
I'M SUCH A DUMB-ASS...

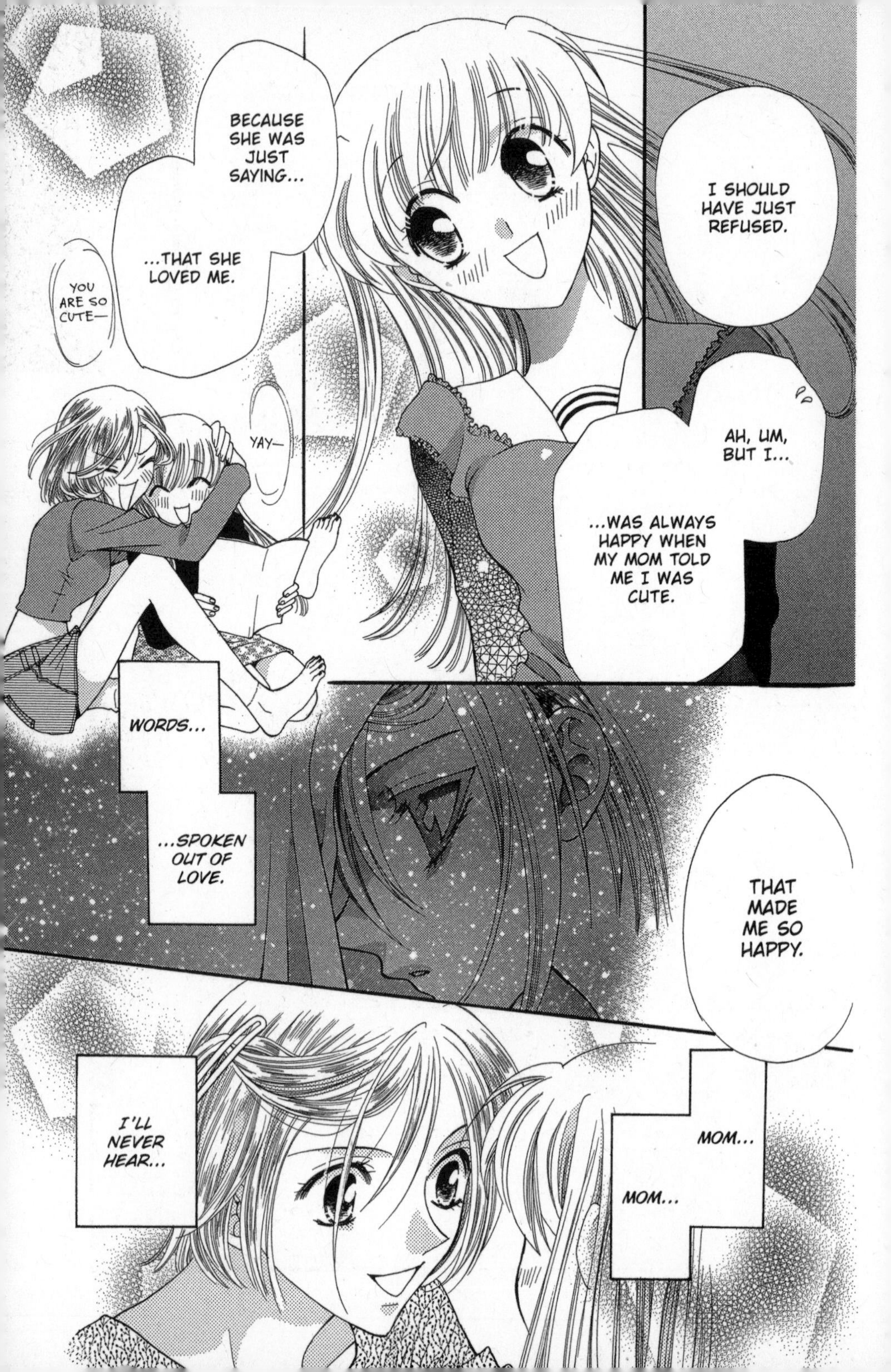
I SHOULD HAVE JUST REFUSED.
AH, UM, BUT I...
...WAS ALWAYS HAPPY WHEN MY MOM TOLD ME I WAS CUTE.
BECAUSE SHE WAS JUST SAYING...
...THAT SHE LOVED ME.
YOU ARE SO CUTE—
YAY—
THAT MADE ME SO HAPPY.
WORDS...
...SPOKEN OUT OF LOVE.
MOM...
MOM...
I'LL NEVER HEAR...

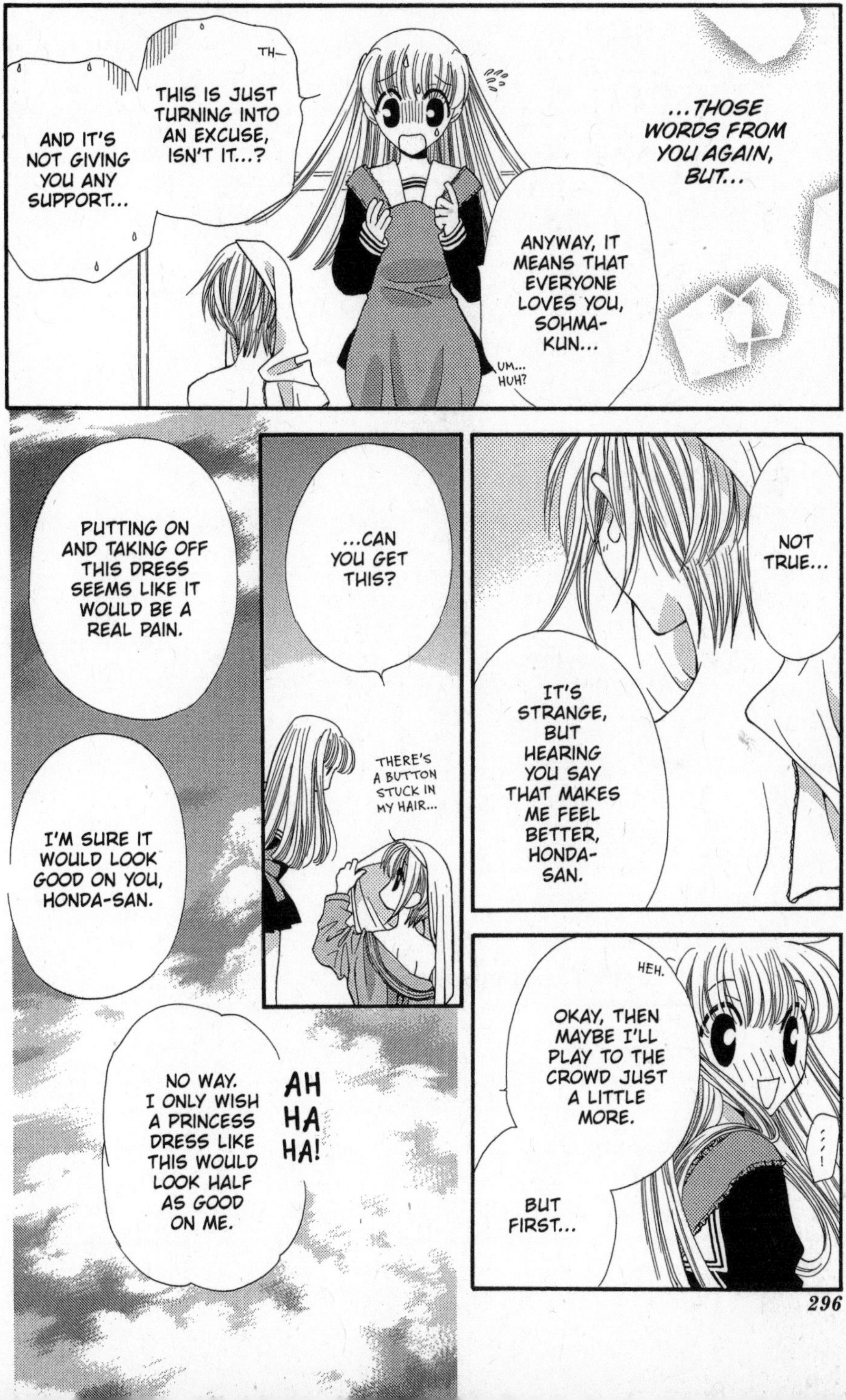
...THOSE WORDS FROM YOU AGAIN, BUT...
ANYWAY, IT MEANS THAT EVERYONE LOVES YOU, SOHMA-KUN...
UM... HUH?
TH—
THIS IS JUST TURNING INTO AN EXCUSE, ISN'T IT...?
AND IT'S NOT GIVING YOU ANY SUPPORT...
NOT TRUE...
IT'S STRANGE, BUT HEARING YOU SAY THAT MAKES ME FEEL BETTER, HONDA-SAN.
HEH.
OKAY, THEN MAYBE I'LL PLAY TO THE CROWD JUST A LITTLE MORE.
...!
BUT FIRST...
...CAN YOU GET THIS?
THERE'S A BUTTON STUCK IN MY HAIR...
PUTTING ON AND TAKING OFF THIS DRESS SEEMS LIKE IT WOULD BE A REAL PAIN.
I'M SURE IT WOULD LOOK GOOD ON YOU, HONDA-SAN.
NO WAY. I ONLY WISH A PRINCESS DRESS LIKE THIS WOULD LOOK HALF AS GOOD ON ME.
AH HA HA!

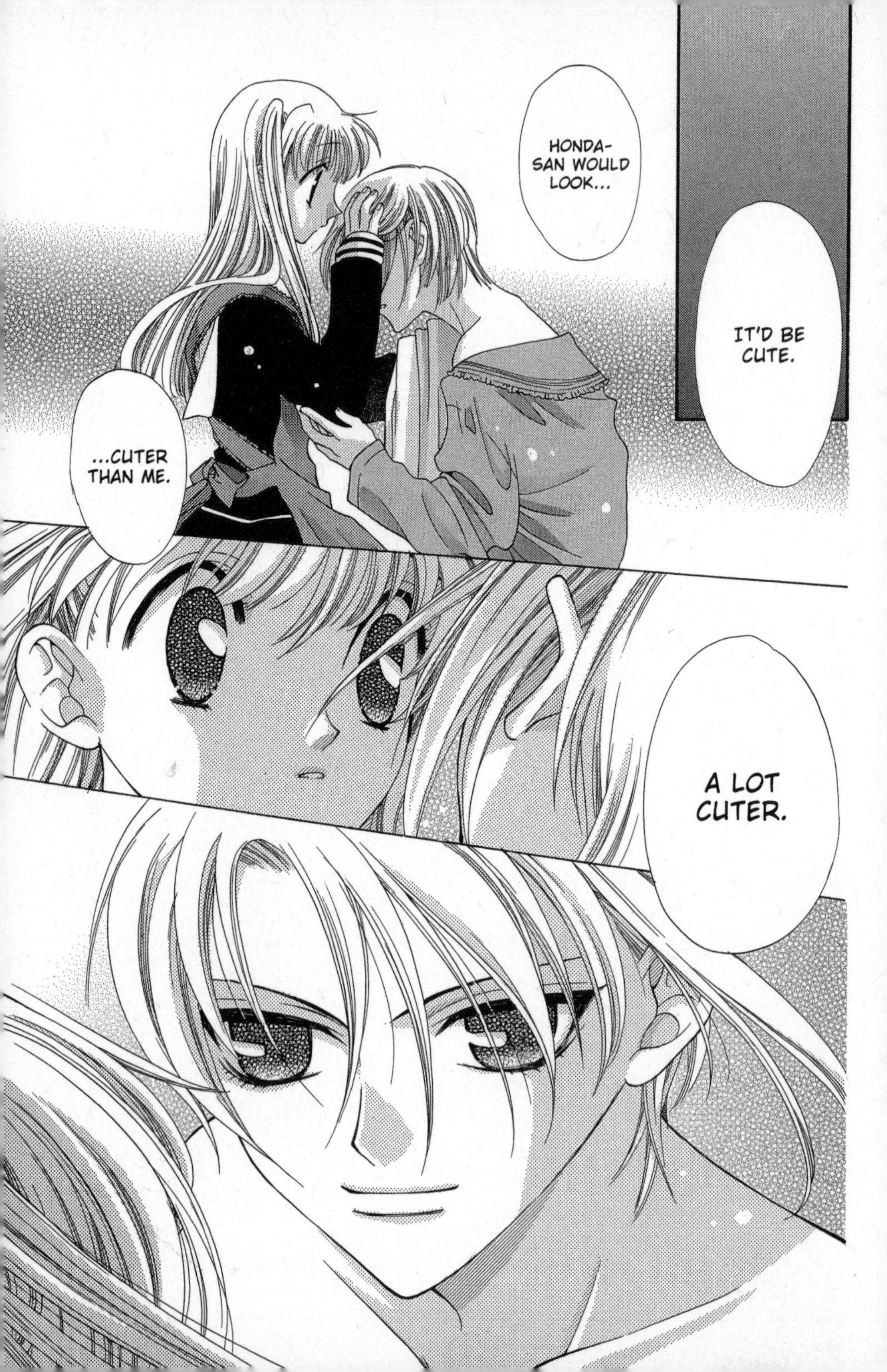
HONDA-SAN WOULD LOOK...
IT'D BE CUTE.
...CUTER THAN ME.
A LOT CUTER.

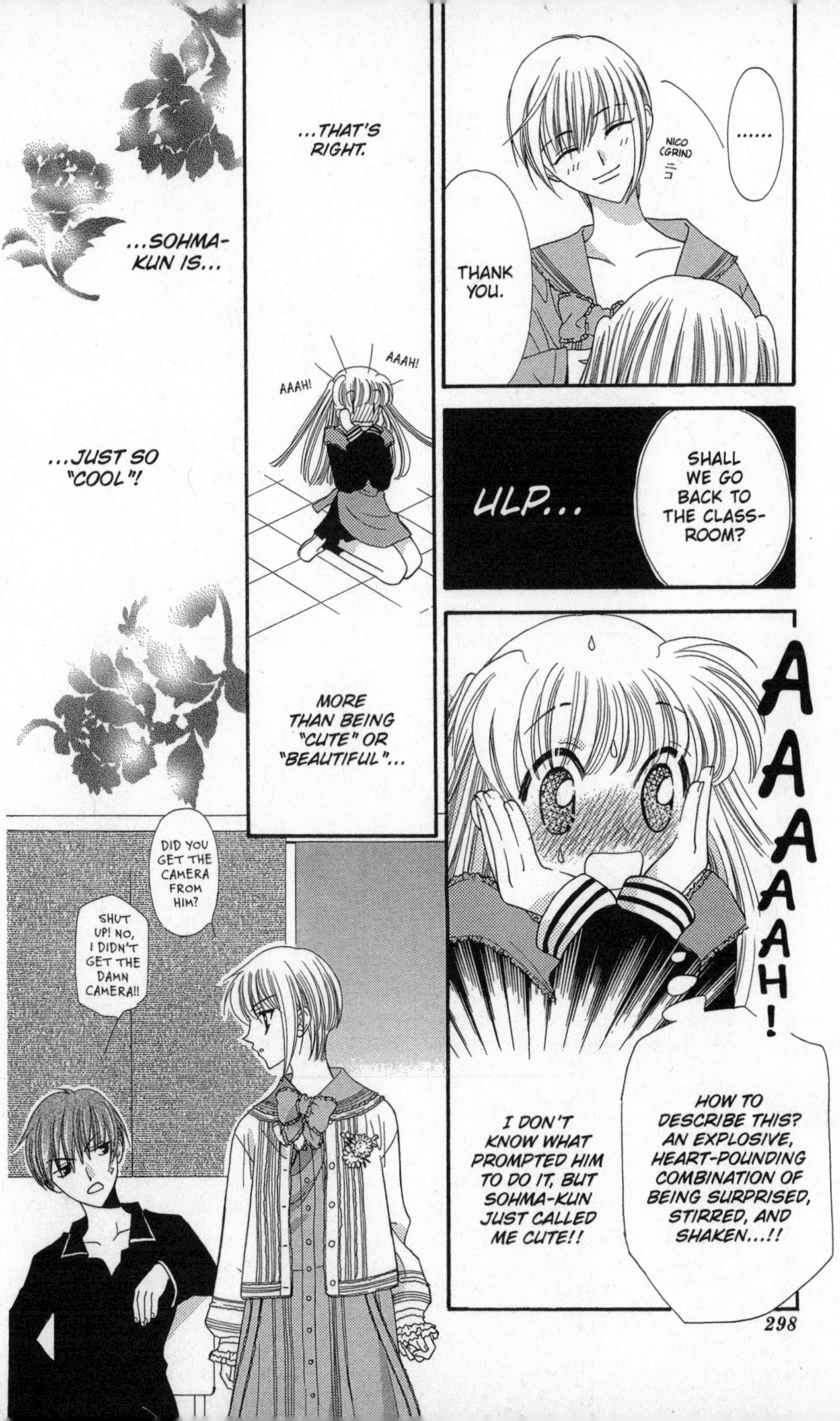
......
NICO (GRIN)
THANK YOU.
SHALL WE GO BACK TO THE CLASS-ROOM?
ULP...
AAAAAH!
HOW TO DESCRIBE THIS? AN EXPLOSIVE, HEART-POUNDING COMBINATION OF BEING SURPRISED, STIRRED, AND SHAKEN...!!
I DON'T KNOW WHAT PROMPTED HIM TO DO IT, BUT SOHMA-KUN JUST CALLED ME CUTE!!
...THAT'S RIGHT.
AAAH!
AAAH!
MORE THAN BEING "CUTE" OR "BEAUTIFUL"...
...SOHMA-KUN IS...
...JUST SO "COOL"!
DID YOU GET THE CAMERA FROM HIM?
SHUT UP! NO, I DIDN'T GET THE DAMN CAMERA!!

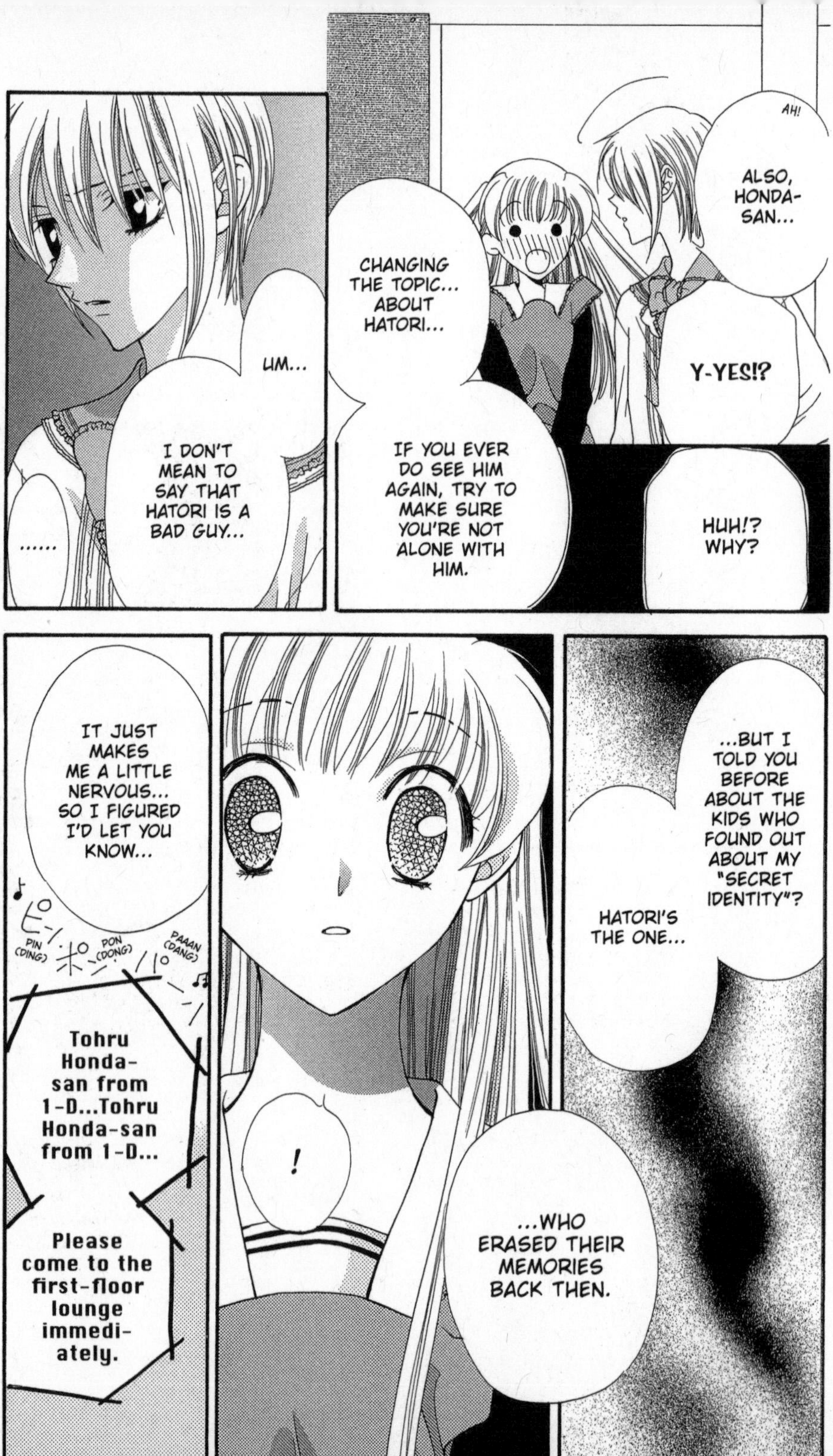
AH!
ALSO, HONDA-SAN...
Y-YES!?
CHANGING THE TOPIC... ABOUT HATORI...
IF YOU EVER DO SEE HIM AGAIN, TRY TO MAKE SURE YOU'RE NOT ALONE WITH HIM.
HUH!? WHY?
UM...
I DON'T MEAN TO SAY THAT HATORI IS A BAD GUY...
......
...BUT I TOLD YOU BEFORE ABOUT THE KIDS WHO FOUND OUT ABOUT MY "SECRET IDENTITY"?
HATORI'S THE ONE...
...WHO ERASED THEIR MEMORIES BACK THEN.
!
IT JUST MAKES ME A LITTLE NERVOUS... SO I FIGURED I'D LET YOU KNOW...
PIN (DING)
PON (DONG)
PAAN (DANG)
Tohru Honda-san from 1-D...Tohru Honda-san from 1-D...
Please come to the first-floor lounge immedi-ately.

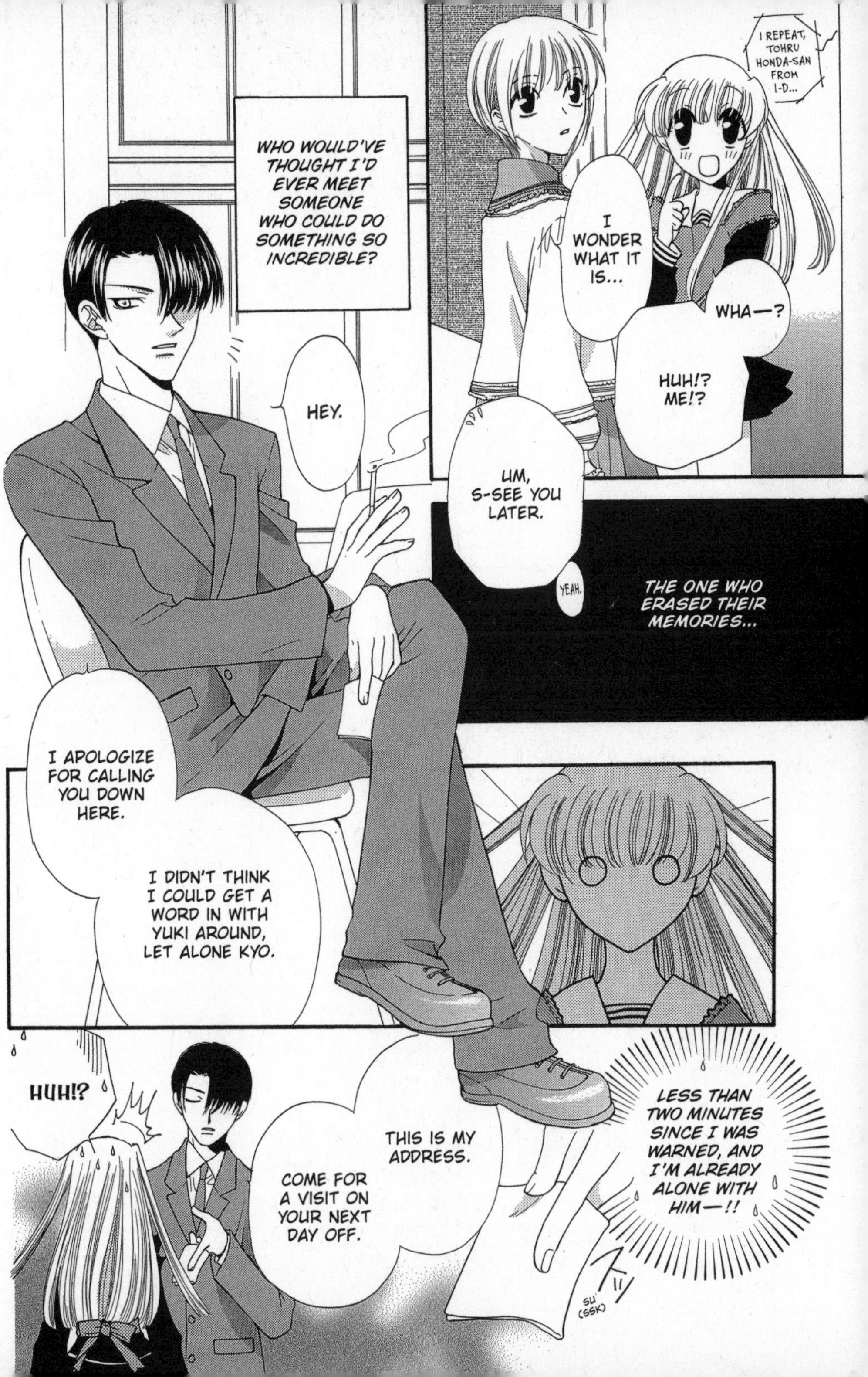
I REPEAT, TOHRU HONDA-SAN FROM 1-D...
I WONDER WHAT IT IS...
WHA—?
HUH!? ME!?
UM, S-SEE YOU LATER.
YEAH.
THE ONE WHO ERASED THEIR MEMORIES...
WHO WOULD'VE THOUGHT I'D EVER MEET SOMEONE WHO COULD DO SOMETHING SO INCREDIBLE?
HEY.
I APOLOGIZE FOR CALLING YOU DOWN HERE.
I DIDN'T THINK I COULD GET A WORD IN WITH YUKI AROUND, LET ALONE KYO.
LESS THAN TWO MINUTES SINCE I WAS WARNED, AND I'M ALREADY ALONE WITH HIM—!!
SU (SSK)
THIS IS MY ADDRESS.
COME FOR A VISIT ON YOUR NEXT DAY OFF.
HUH!?

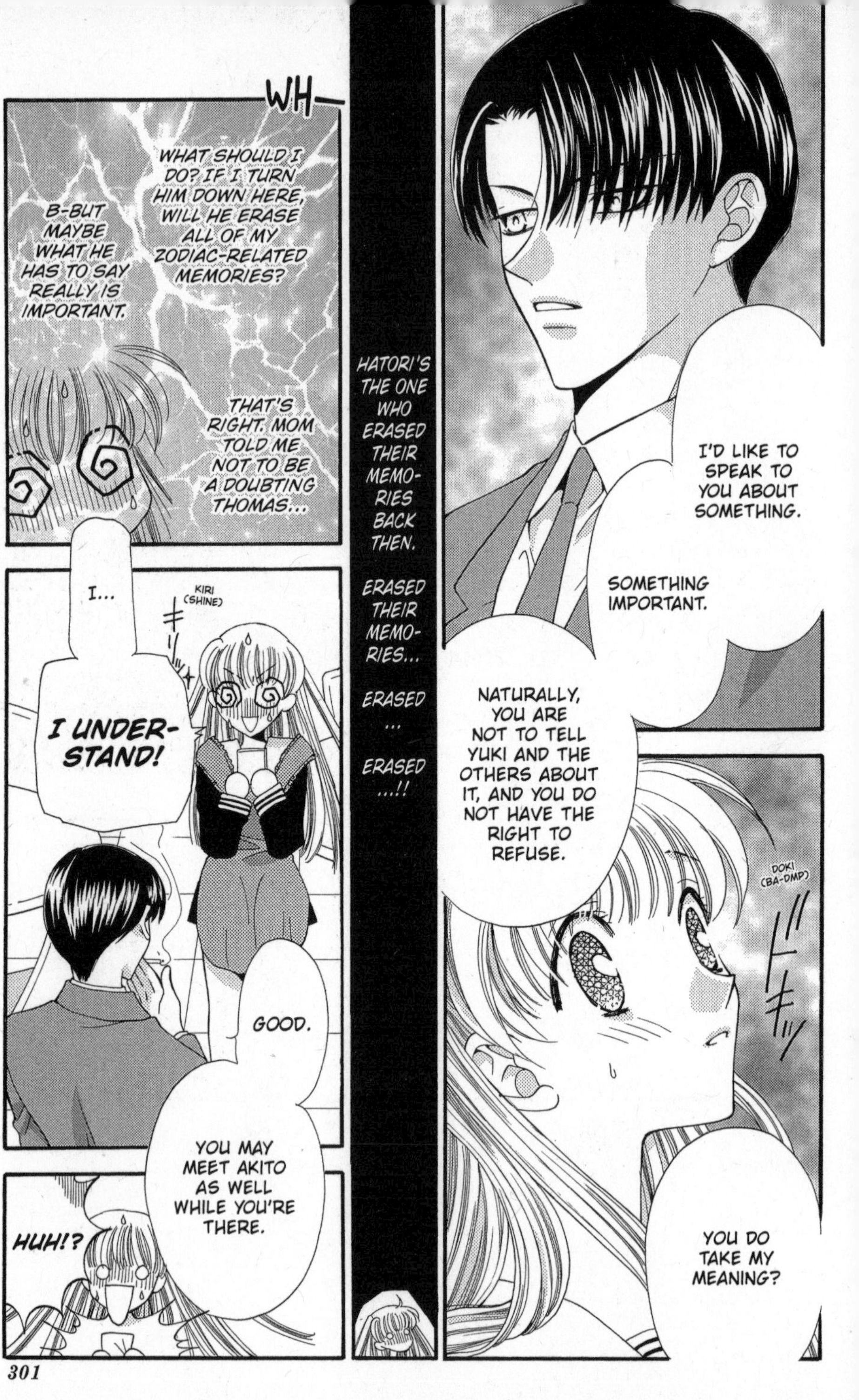
I'D LIKE TO SPEAK TO YOU ABOUT SOMETHING.
SOMETHING IMPORTANT.
NATURALLY, YOU ARE NOT TO TELL YUKI AND THE OTHERS ABOUT IT, AND YOU DO NOT HAVE THE RIGHT TO REFUSE.
DOKI (BA-DMP)
YOU DO TAKE MY MEANING?
HATORI'S THE ONE WHO ERASED THEIR MEMORIES BACK THEN.
ERASED THEIR MEMORIES...
ERASED...
ERASED...!!
WH—
WHAT SHOULD I DO? IF I TURN HIM DOWN HERE, WILL HE ERASE ALL OF MY ZODIAC-RELATED MEMORIES?
B-BUT MAYBE WHAT HE HAS TO SAY REALLY IS IMPORTANT.
THAT'S RIGHT. MOM TOLD ME NOT TO BE A DOUBTING THOMAS...
I...
KIRI (SHINE)
I UNDERSTAND!
GOOD.
YOU MAY MEET AKITO AS WELL WHILE YOU'RE THERE.
HUH!?

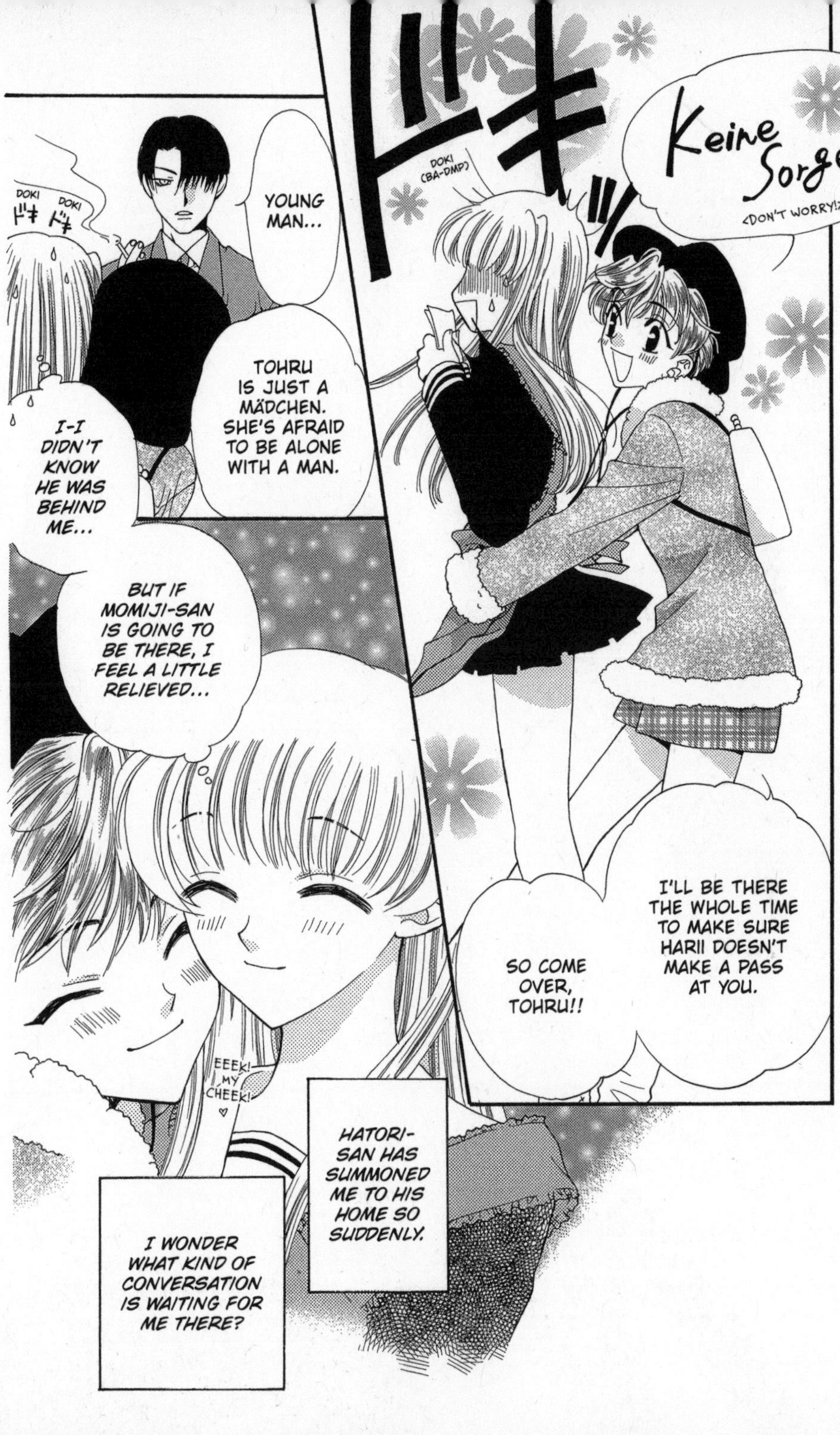
ドキ
DOKI (BA-DMP)
Keine Sorge!
<DON'T WORRY!>
I'LL BE THERE THE WHOLE TIME TO MAKE SURE HARII DOESN'T MAKE A PASS AT YOU.
SO COME OVER, TOHRU!!
YOUNG MAN...
TOHRU IS JUST A MÄDCHEN. SHE'S AFRAID TO BE ALONE WITH A MAN.
DOKI ドキ DOKI ドキ
I-I DIDN'T KNOW HE WAS BEHIND ME...
BUT IF MOMIJI-SAN IS GOING TO BE THERE, I FEEL A LITTLE RELIEVED...
EEEK! MY CHEEK! ♡
HATORI-SAN HAS SUMMONED ME TO HIS HOME SO SUDDENLY.
I WONDER WHAT KIND OF CONVERSATION IS WAITING FOR ME THERE?

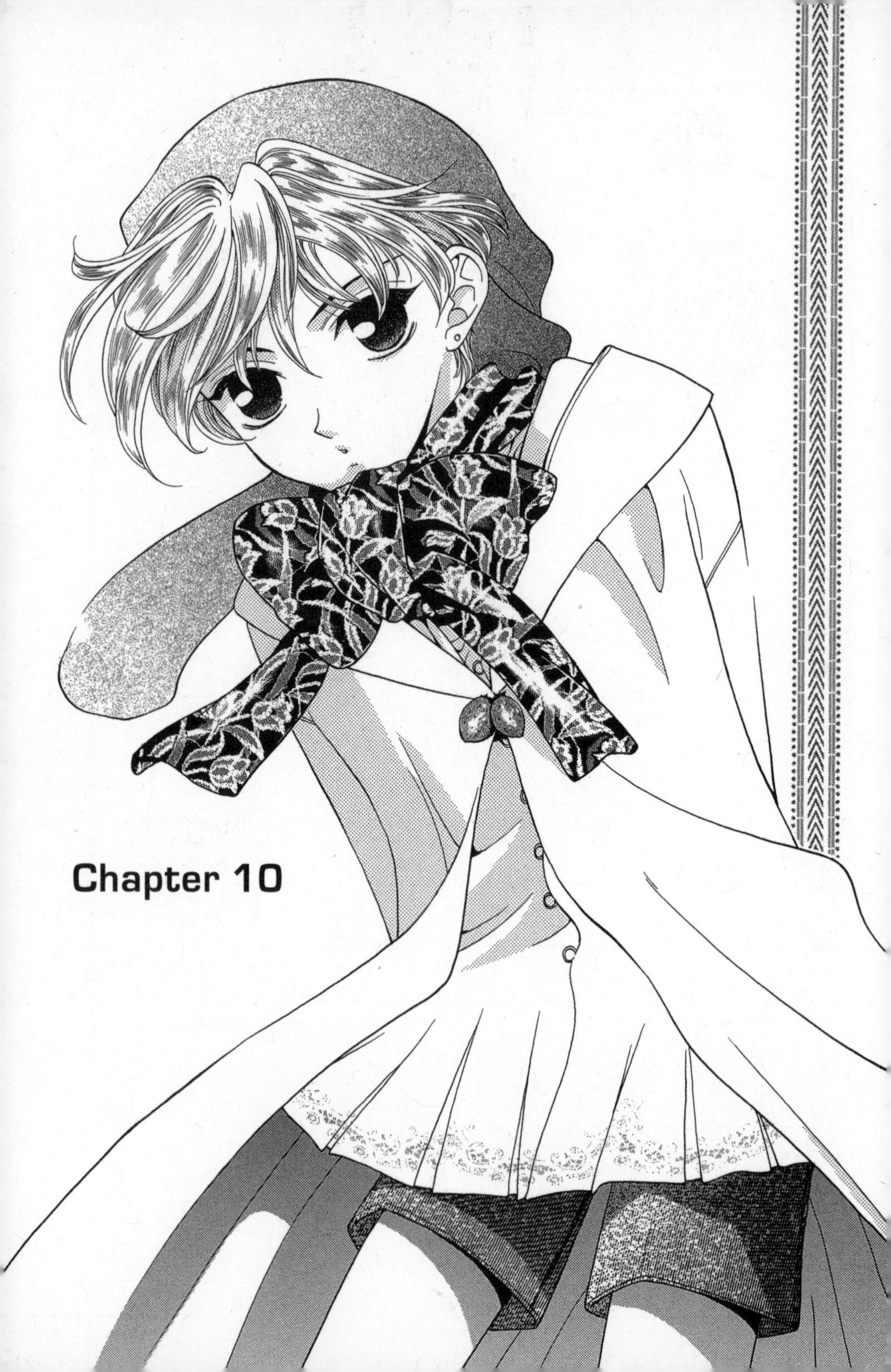

Chapter 10

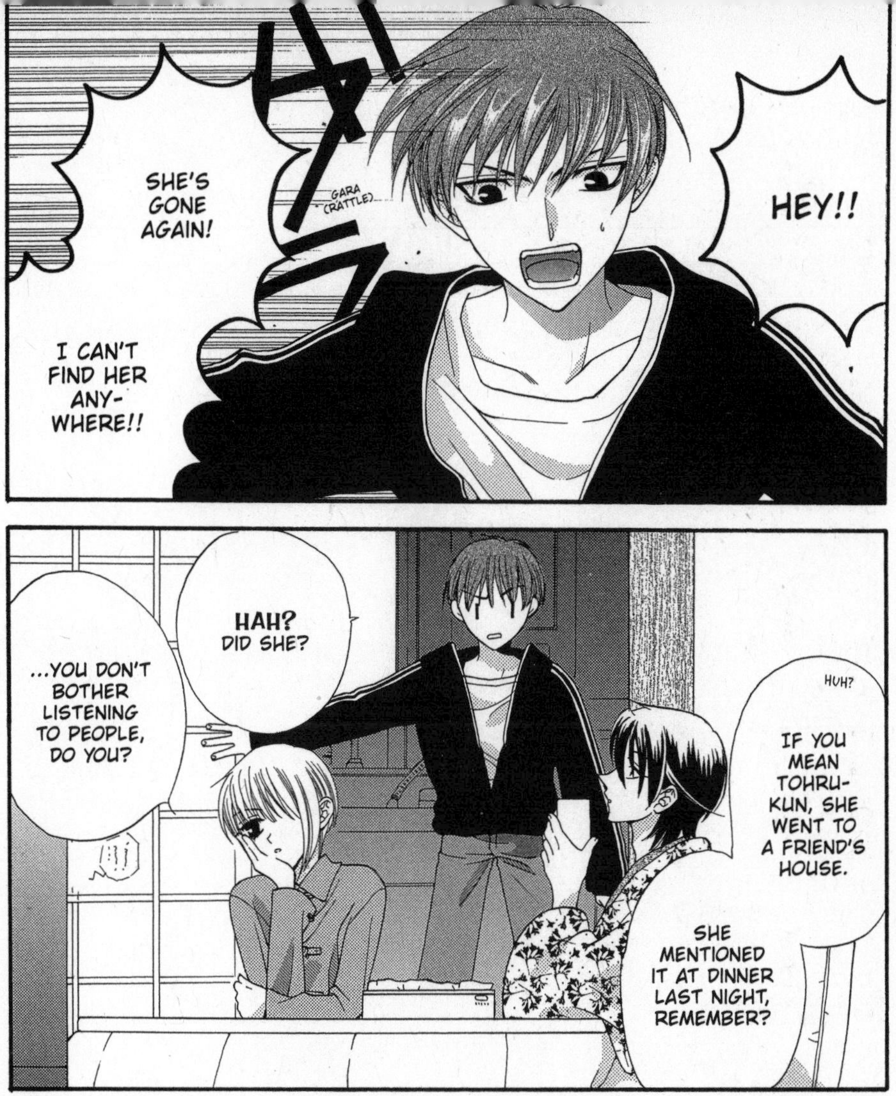
HEY!!
GARA (RATTLE)
SHE'S GONE AGAIN!
I CAN'T FIND HER ANY-WHERE!!
HUH?
IF YOU MEAN TOHRU-KUN, SHE WENT TO A FRIEND'S HOUSE.
SHE MENTIONED IT AT DINNER LAST NIGHT, REMEMBER?
HAH? DID SHE?
...YOU DON'T BOTHER LISTENING TO PEOPLE, DO YOU?

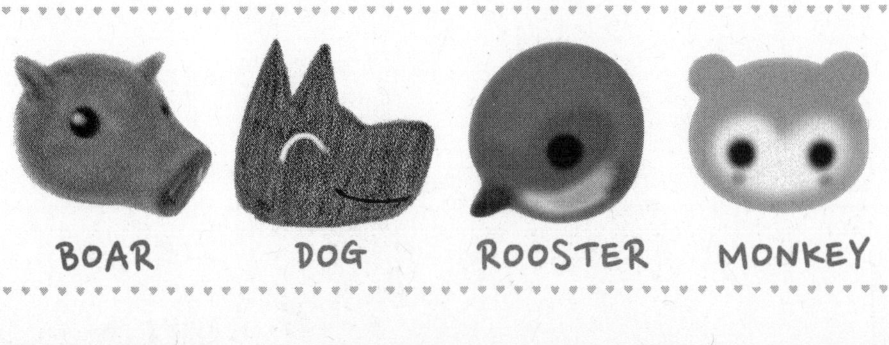
BOAR
DOG
ROOSTER
MONKEY

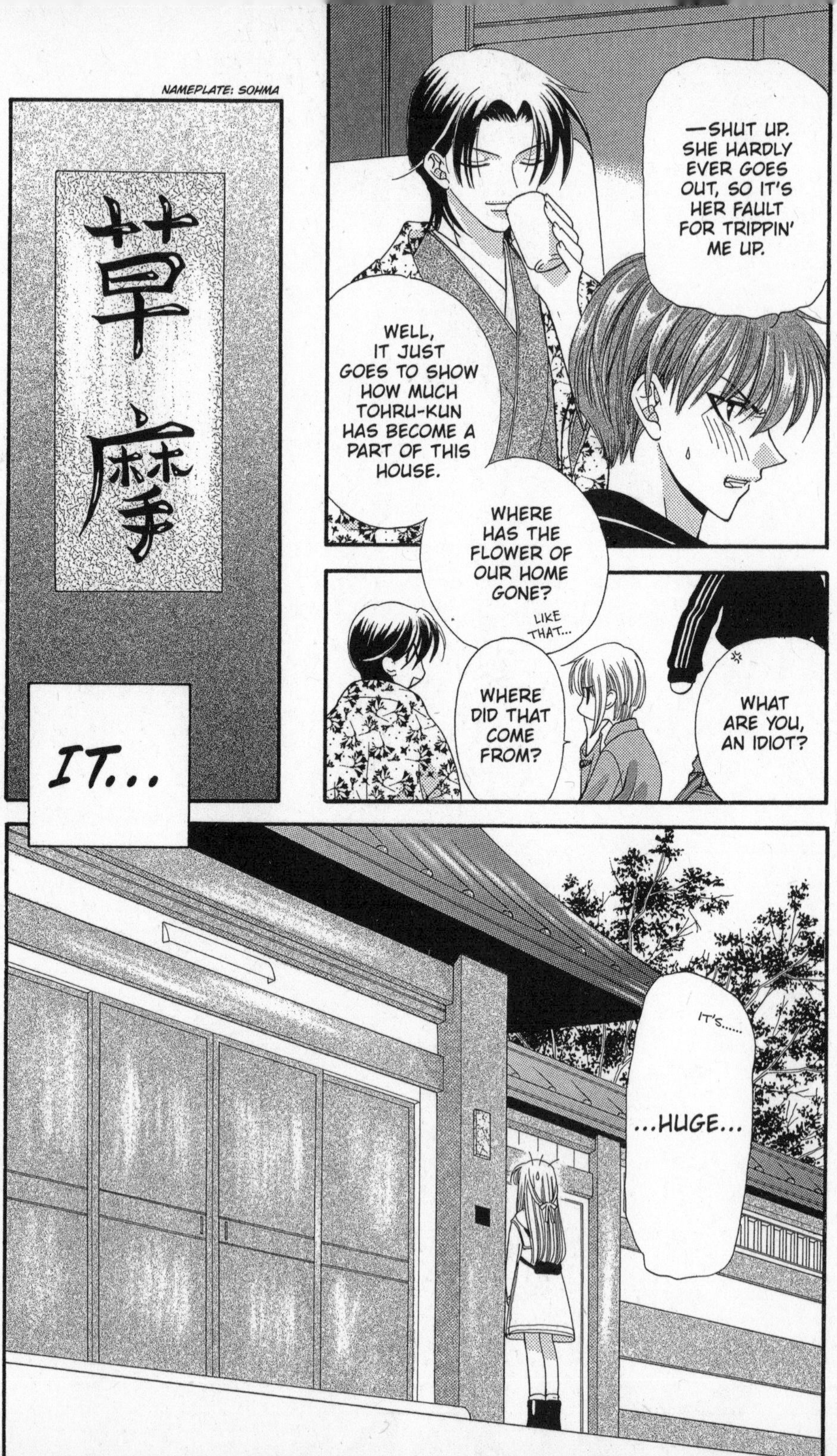
—SHUT UP. SHE HARDLY EVER GOES OUT, SO IT'S HER FAULT FOR TRIPPIN' ME UP.
WELL, IT JUST GOES TO SHOW HOW MUCH TOHRU-KUN HAS BECOME A PART OF THIS HOUSE.
WHERE HAS THE FLOWER OF OUR HOME GONE?
WHAT ARE YOU, AN IDIOT?
LIKE THAT...
WHERE DID THAT COME FROM?
NAMEPLATE: SOHMA
草摩
IT...
IT'S......
...HUGE...

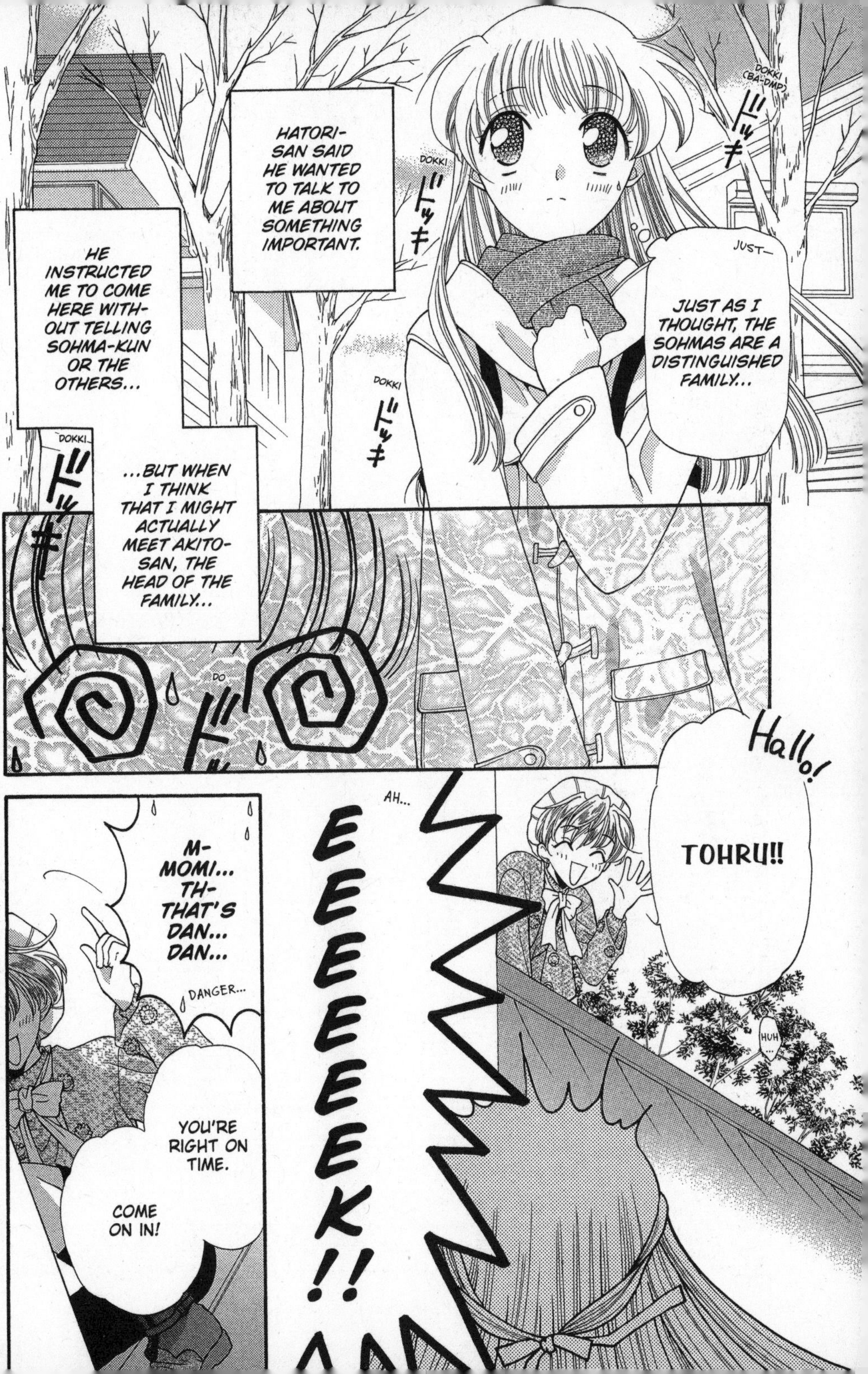
DOKKI (BA-DMP)
HATORI-SAN SAID HE WANTED TO TALK TO ME ABOUT SOMETHING IMPORTANT.
DOKKI
HE INSTRUCTED ME TO COME HERE WITH-OUT TELLING SOHMA-KUN OR THE OTHERS...
DOKKI
DOKKI
...BUT WHEN I THINK THAT I MIGHT ACTUALLY MEET AKITO-SAN, THE HEAD OF THE FAMILY...
JUST—
JUST AS I THOUGHT, THE SOHMAS ARE A DISTINGUISHED FAMILY...
DO
Hallo!
TOHRU!!
HUH...
AH...
EEEEEEEK!!
M-MOMI... TH-THAT'S DAN... DAN...
DANGER...
YOU'RE RIGHT ON TIME.
COME ON IN!

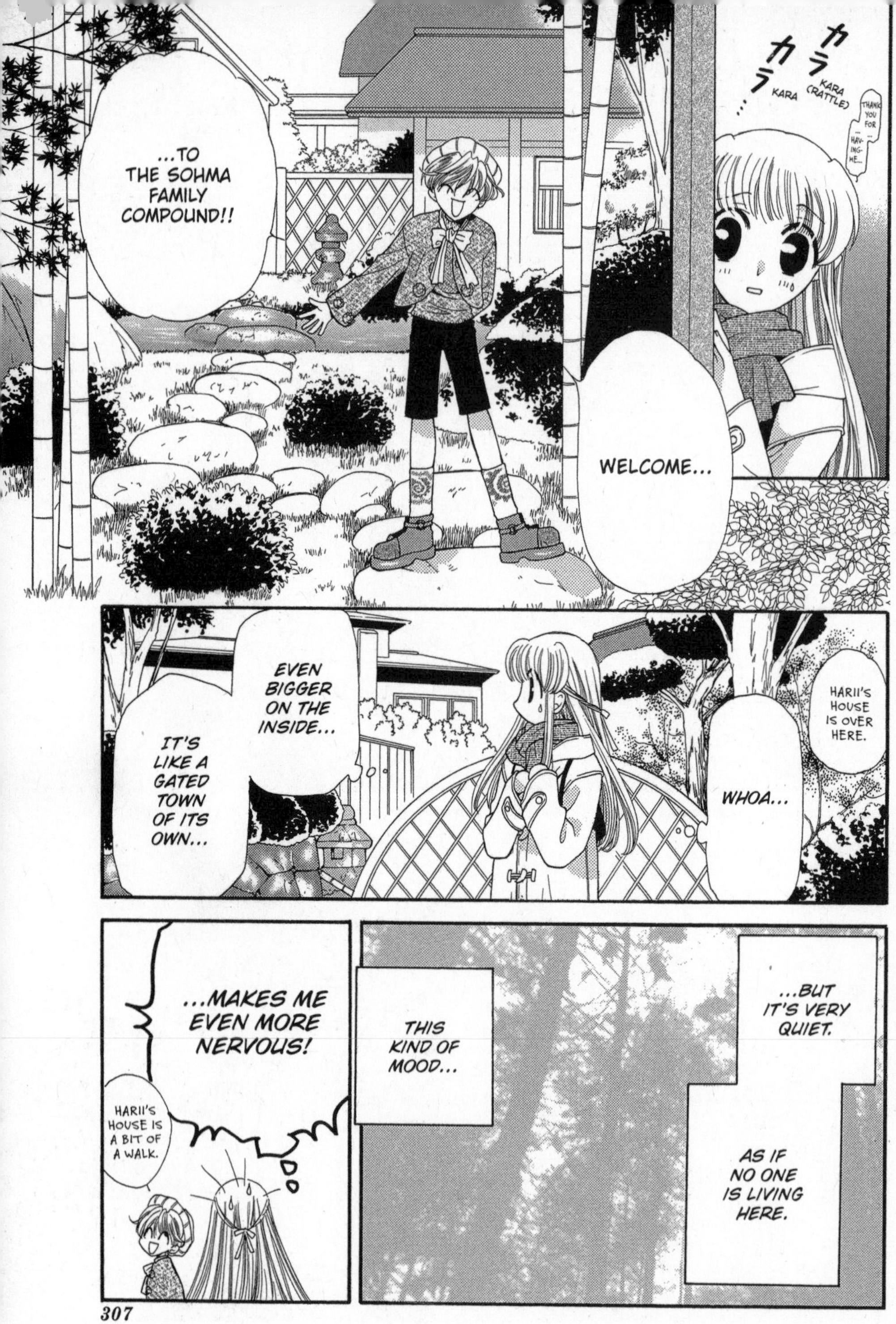
カラ カラ …
KARA (RATTLE) KARA
THANK YOU FOR … HAVING ME…
WELCOME…
…TO THE SOHMA FAMILY COMPOUND!!
HARII'S HOUSE IS OVER HERE.
WHOA…
EVEN BIGGER ON THE INSIDE…
IT'S LIKE A GATED TOWN OF ITS OWN…
…BUT IT'S VERY QUIET.
AS IF NO ONE IS LIVING HERE.
THIS KIND OF MOOD…
…MAKES ME EVEN MORE NERVOUS!
HARII'S HOUSE IS A BIT OF A WALK.

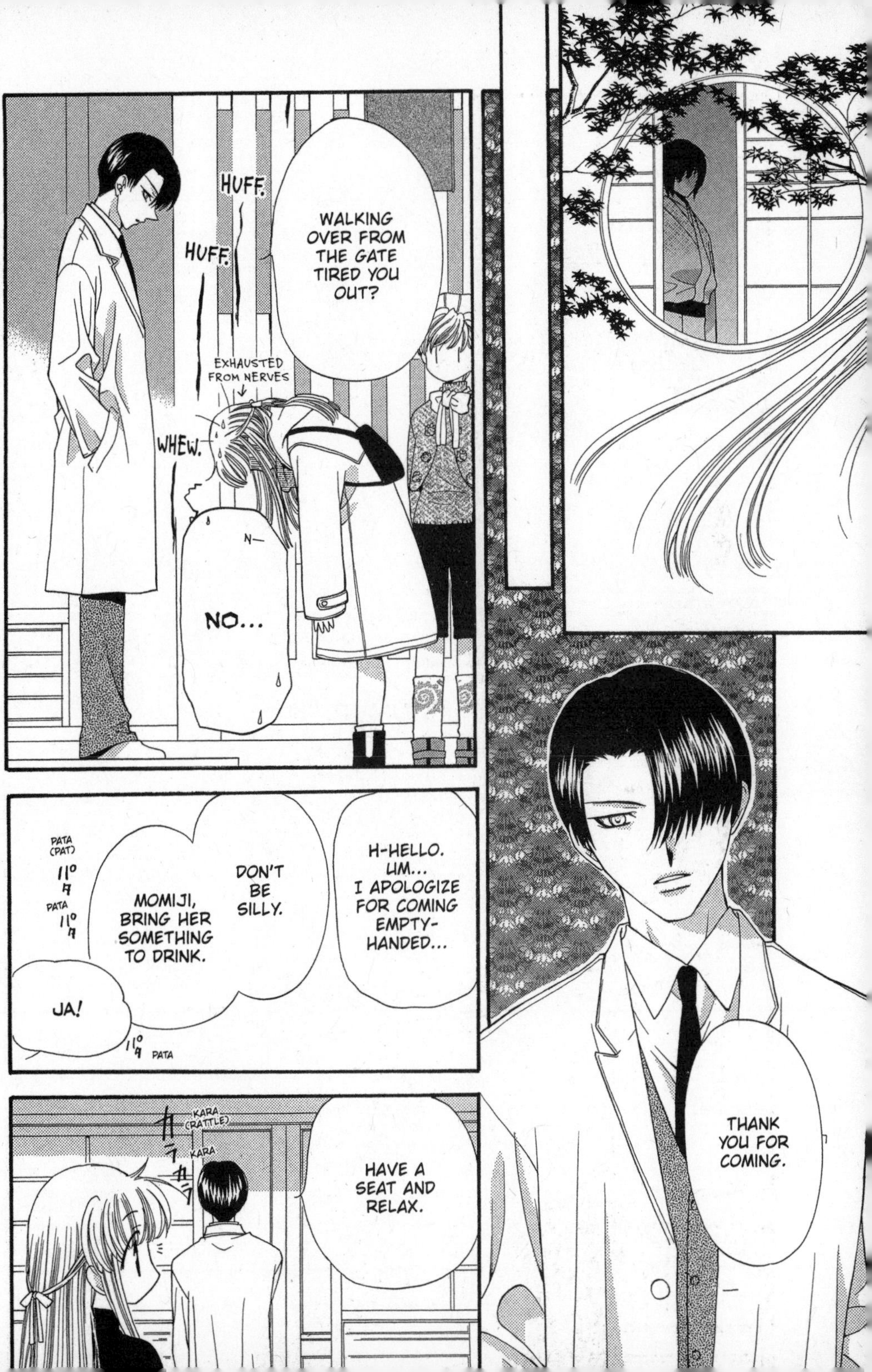
THANK YOU FOR COMING.
WALKING OVER FROM THE GATE TIRED YOU OUT?
HUFF.
HUFF.
EXHAUSTED FROM NERVES
WHEW.
N—
NO...
H-HELLO. UM... I APOLOGIZE FOR COMING EMPTY-HANDED...
DON'T BE SILLY.
MOMIJI, BRING HER SOMETHING TO DRINK.
PATA (PAT)
PATA
JA!
PATA
HAVE A SEAT AND RELAX.
KARA (RATTLE)
KARA

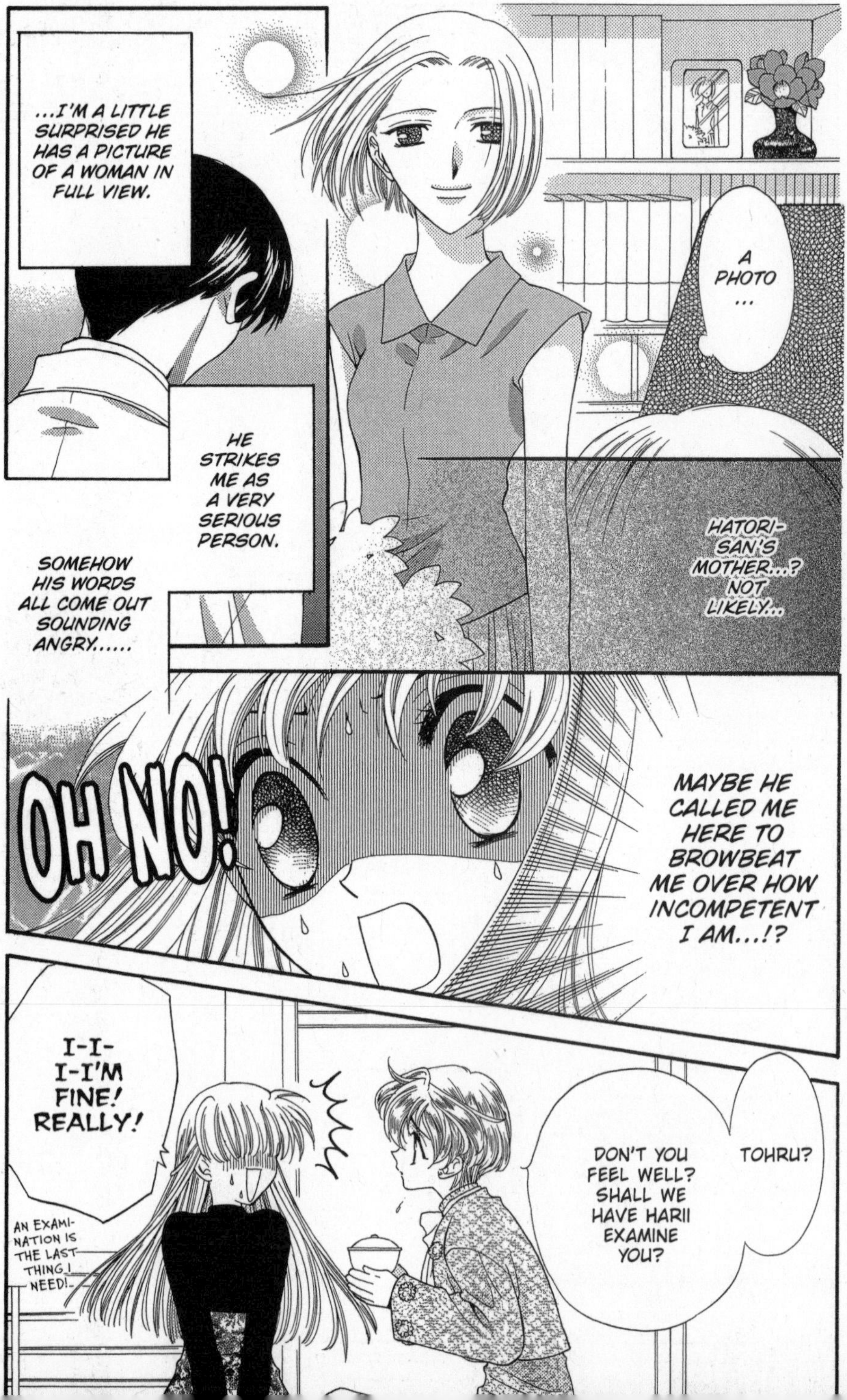

A PHOTO...
HATORI-SAN'S MOTHER...? NOT LIKELY...
...I'M A LITTLE SURPRISED HE HAS A PICTURE OF A WOMAN IN FULL VIEW.
HE STRIKES ME AS A VERY SERIOUS PERSON.
SOMEHOW HIS WORDS ALL COME OUT SOUNDING ANGRY......
MAYBE HE CALLED ME HERE TO BROWBEAT ME OVER HOW INCOMPETENT I AM...!?
OH NO!
TOHRU?
DON'T YOU FEEL WELL? SHALL WE HAVE HARII EXAMINE YOU?
I-I-I-I'M FINE! REALLY!
AN EXAMINATION IS THE LAST THING I NEED!

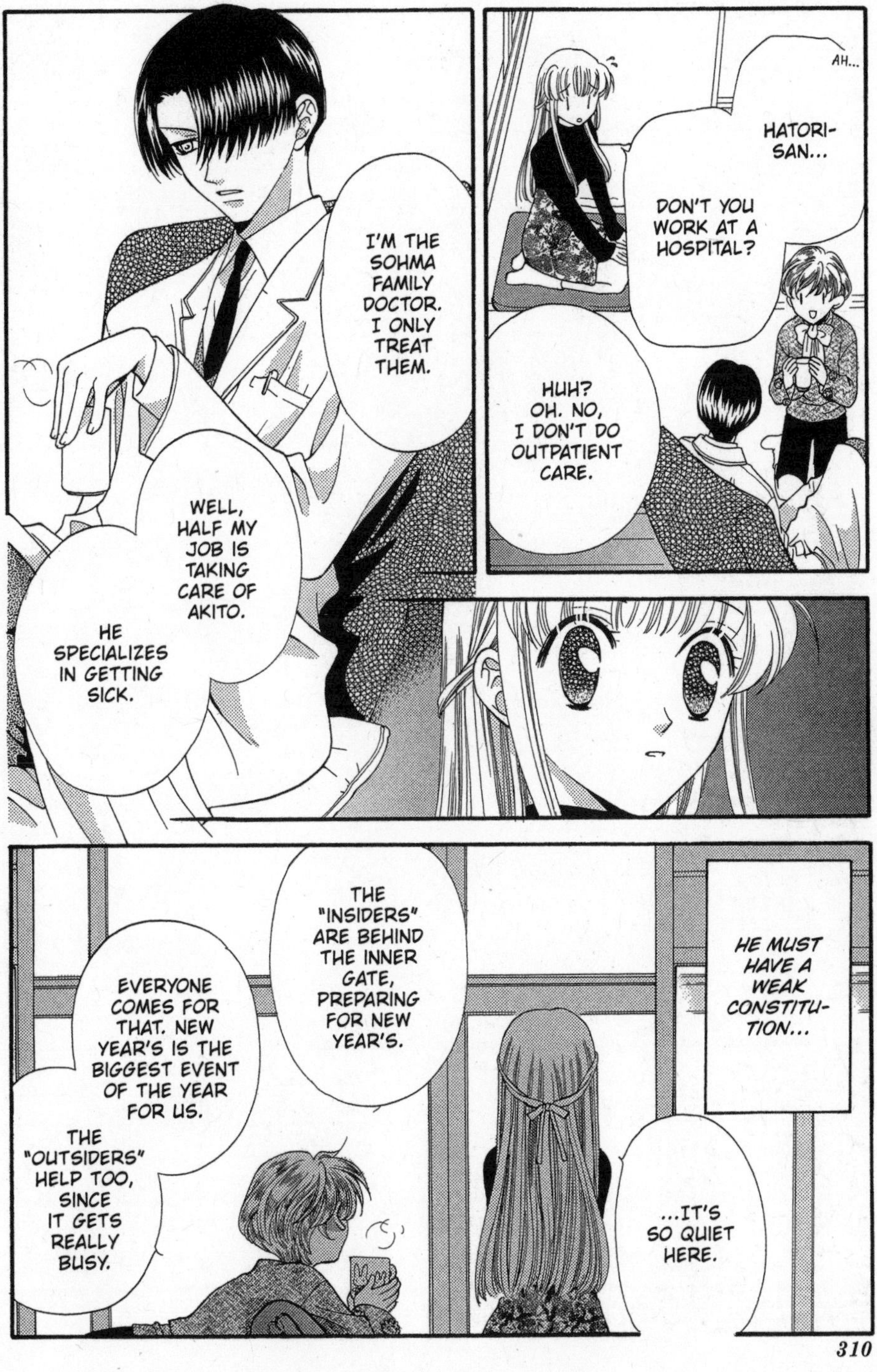
AH...
HATORI-SAN...
DON'T YOU WORK AT A HOSPITAL?
HUH? OH. NO, I DON'T DO OUTPATIENT CARE.
I'M THE SOHMA FAMILY DOCTOR. I ONLY TREAT THEM.
WELL, HALF MY JOB IS TAKING CARE OF AKITO.
HE SPECIALIZES IN GETTING SICK.
HE MUST HAVE A WEAK CONSTITUTION...
...IT'S SO QUIET HERE.
THE "INSIDERS" ARE BEHIND THE INNER GATE, PREPARING FOR NEW YEAR'S.
EVERYONE COMES FOR THAT. NEW YEAR'S IS THE BIGGEST EVENT OF THE YEAR FOR US.
THE "OUTSIDERS" HELP TOO, SINCE IT GETS REALLY BUSY.

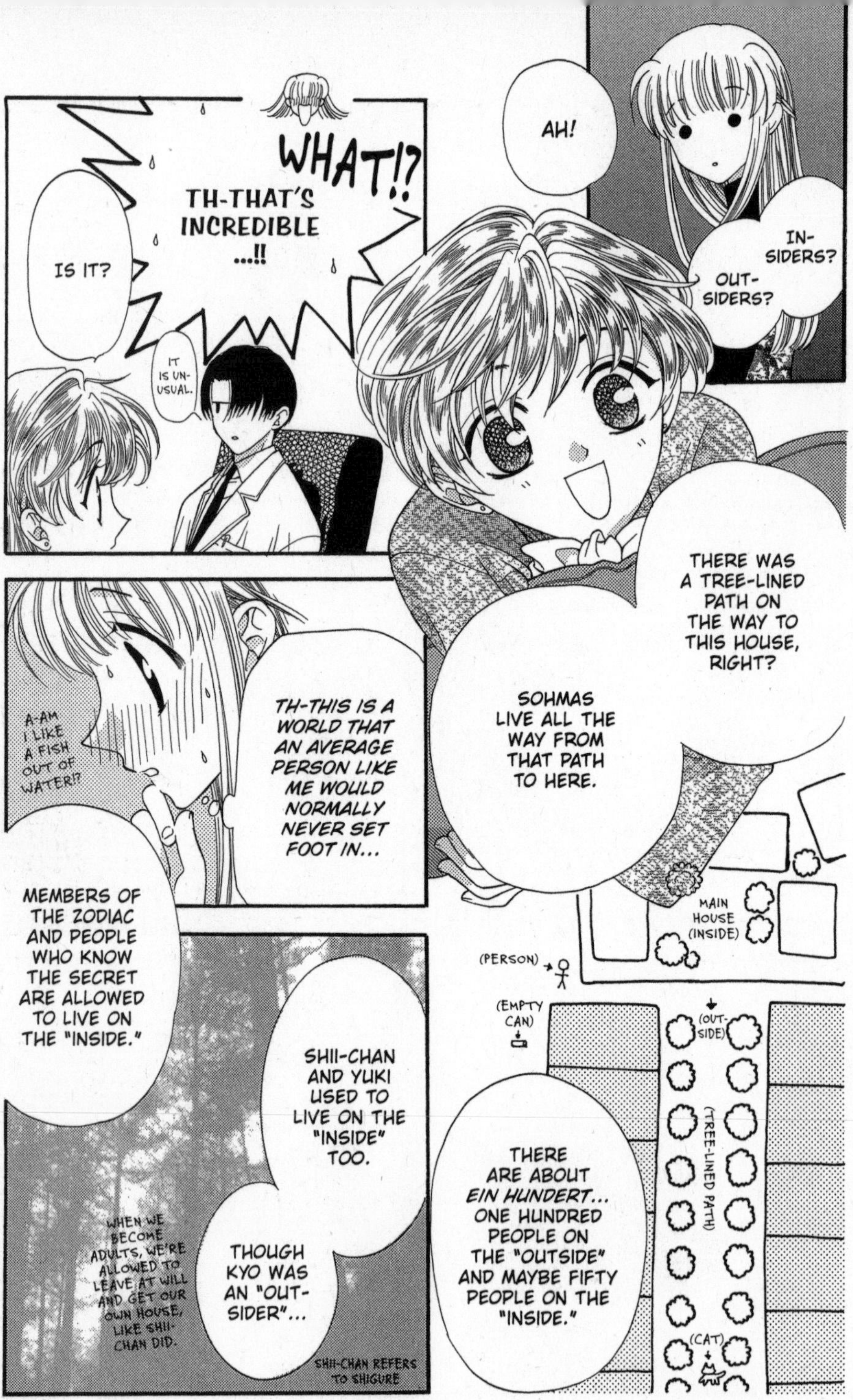
AH!
IN-SIDERS? OUT-SIDERS?
THERE WAS A TREE-LINED PATH ON THE WAY TO THIS HOUSE, RIGHT?
SOHMAS LIVE ALL THE WAY FROM THAT PATH TO HERE.
MAIN HOUSE (INSIDE)
(PERSON)
(EMPTY CAN)
(OUT-SIDE)
(TREE-LINED PATH)
(CAT)
THERE ARE ABOUT *EIN HUNDERT*... ONE HUNDRED PEOPLE ON THE "OUTSIDE" AND MAYBE FIFTY PEOPLE ON THE "INSIDE."
WHAT!?
TH-THAT'S INCREDIBLE ...!!
IS IT?
IT IS UN-USUAL.
TH-THIS IS A WORLD THAT AN AVERAGE PERSON LIKE ME WOULD NORMALLY NEVER SET FOOT IN...
A-AM I LIKE A FISH OUT OF WATER!?
MEMBERS OF THE ZODIAC AND PEOPLE WHO KNOW THE SECRET ARE ALLOWED TO LIVE ON THE "INSIDE."
SHII-CHAN AND YUKI USED TO LIVE ON THE "INSIDE" TOO.
THOUGH KYO WAS AN "OUT-SIDER"...
WHEN WE BECOME ADULTS, WE'RE ALLOWED TO LEAVE AT WILL AND GET OUR OWN HOUSE, LIKE SHII-CHAN DID.
SHII-CHAN REFERS TO SHIGURE

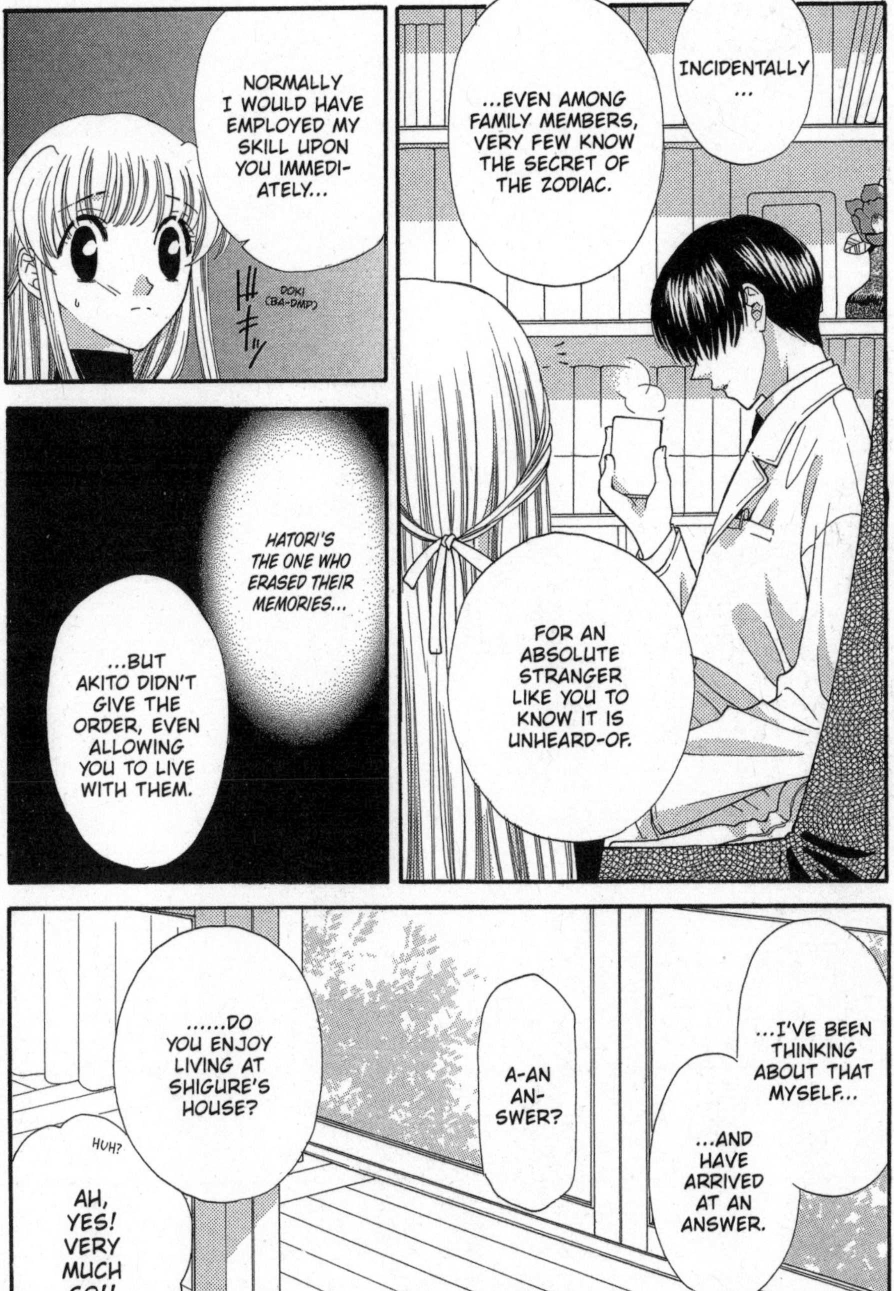
INCIDENTALLY...
...EVEN AMONG FAMILY MEMBERS, VERY FEW KNOW THE SECRET OF THE ZODIAC.
FOR AN ABSOLUTE STRANGER LIKE YOU TO KNOW IT IS UNHEARD-OF.
NORMALLY I WOULD HAVE EMPLOYED MY SKILL UPON YOU IMMEDIATELY...
DOKI (BA-DMP)
HATORI'S THE ONE WHO ERASED THEIR MEMORIES...
...BUT AKITO DIDN'T GIVE THE ORDER, EVEN ALLOWING YOU TO LIVE WITH THEM.
...I'VE BEEN THINKING ABOUT THAT MYSELF...
...AND HAVE ARRIVED AT AN ANSWER.
A-AN AN-SWER?
......DO YOU ENJOY LIVING AT SHIGURE'S HOUSE?
HUH?
AH, YES! VERY MUCH SO!!

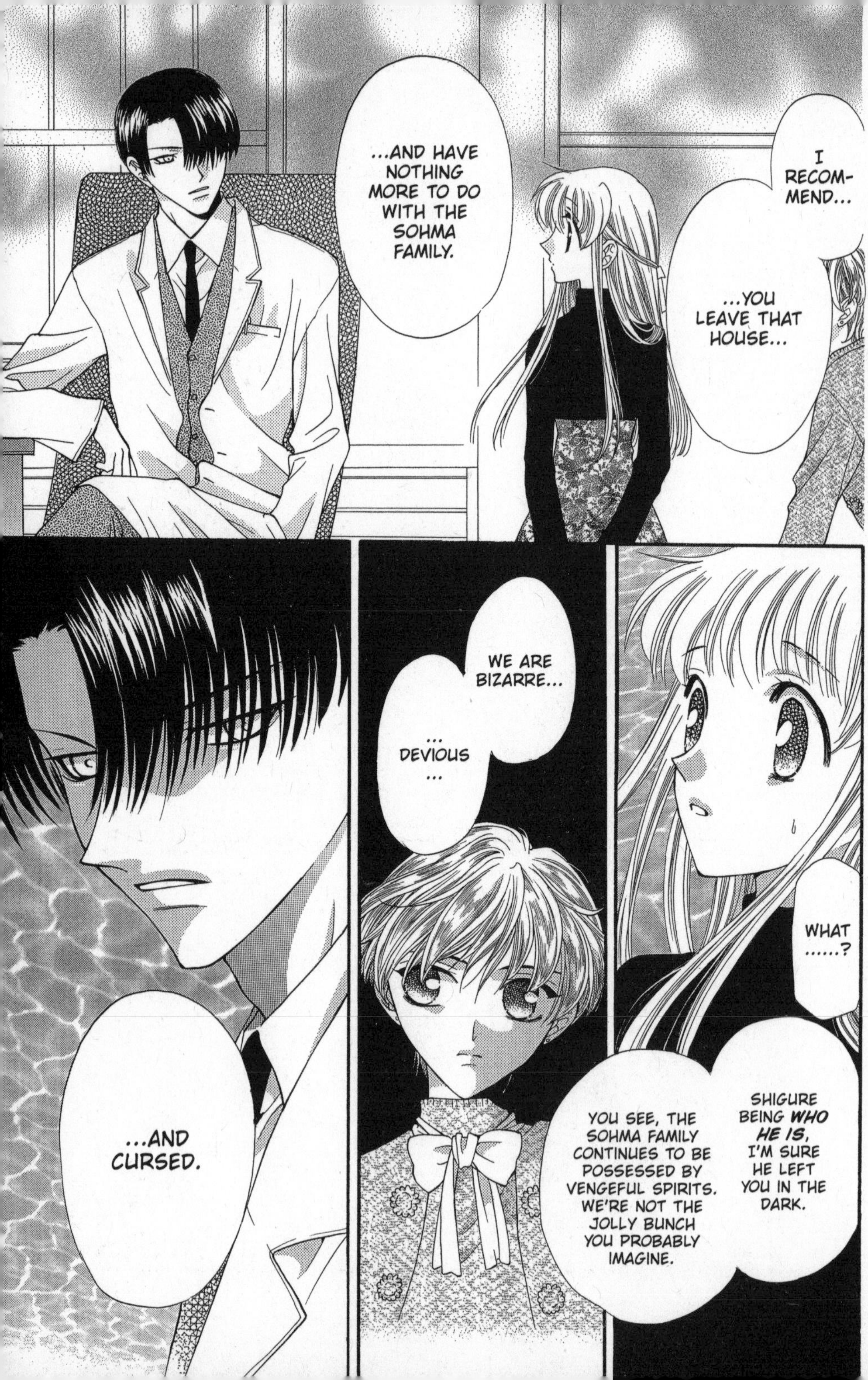
I RECOMMEND...
...YOU LEAVE THAT HOUSE...
...AND HAVE NOTHING MORE TO DO WITH THE SOHMA FAMILY.
WHAT ......?
SHIGURE BEING *WHO HE IS*, I'M SURE HE LEFT YOU IN THE DARK.
YOU SEE, THE SOHMA FAMILY CONTINUES TO BE POSSESSED BY VENGEFUL SPIRITS. WE'RE NOT THE JOLLY BUNCH YOU PROBABLY IMAGINE.
WE ARE BIZARRE...
...DEVIOUS...
...AND CURSED.

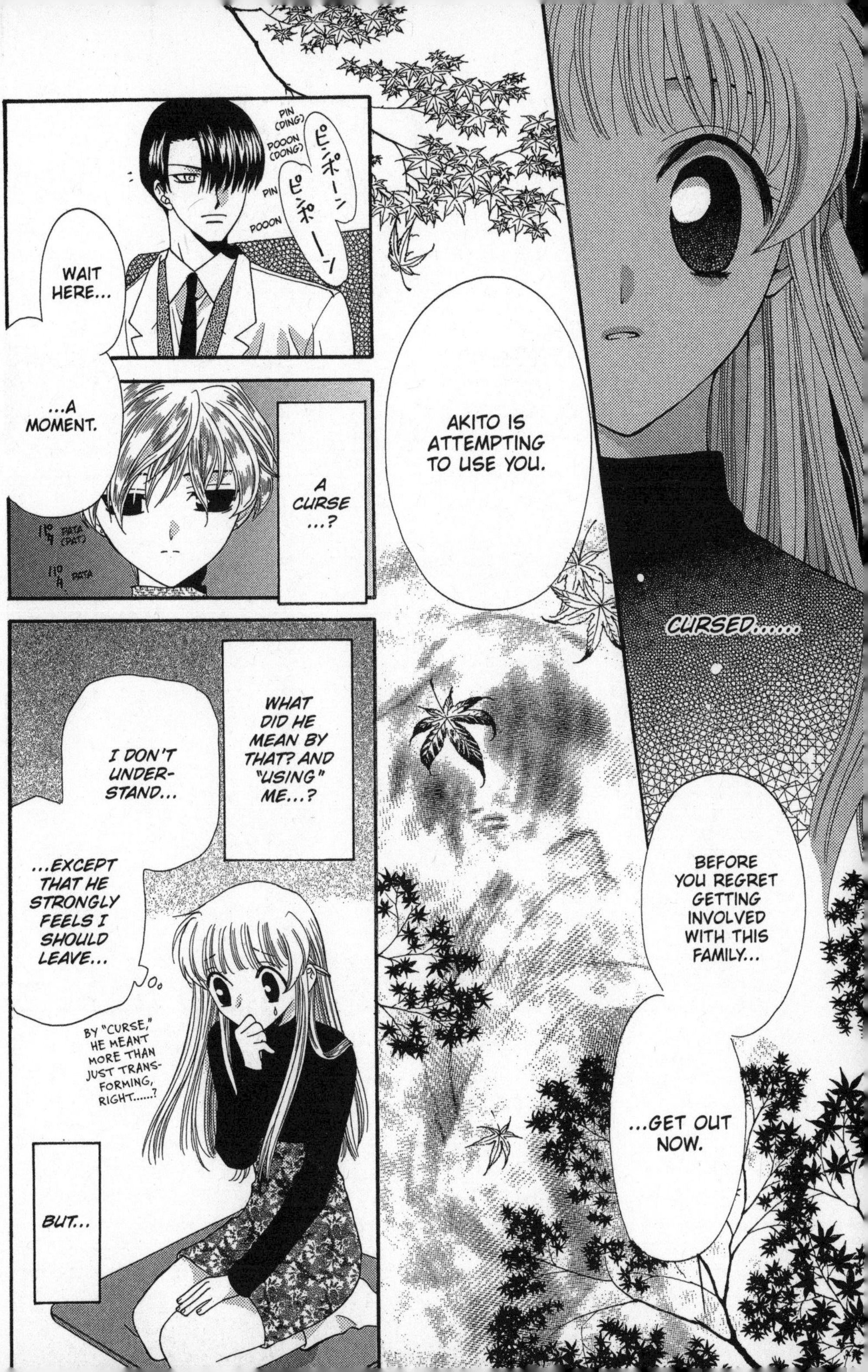
AKITO IS ATTEMPTING TO USE YOU.
CURSED......
BEFORE YOU REGRET GETTING INVOLVED WITH THIS FAMILY...
...GET OUT NOW.
ピンポーン
PIN (DING)
POOON (DONG)
ピンポーン
PIN
POOON
WAIT HERE...
...A MOMENT.
A CURSE...?
パタ PATA (PAT)
パタ PATA
WHAT DID HE MEAN BY THAT? AND "USING" ME...?
I DON'T UNDERSTAND...
...EXCEPT THAT HE STRONGLY FEELS I SHOULD LEAVE...
BY "CURSE," HE MEANT MORE THAN JUST TRANSFORMING, RIGHT......?
BUT...

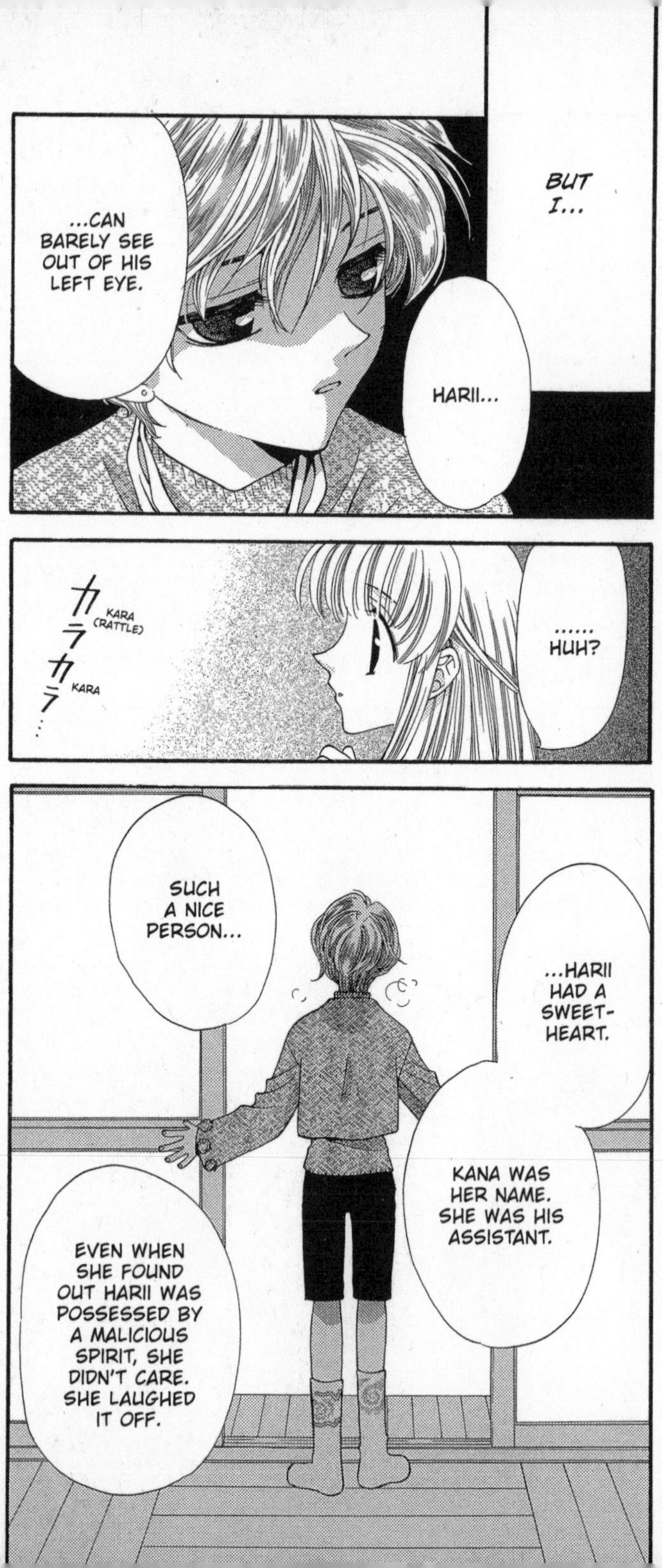
BUT I...
HARII...
...CAN BARELY SEE OUT OF HIS LEFT EYE.
......HUH?
カラカラ…
KARA (RATTLE) KARA
...HARII HAD A SWEET-HEART.
KANA WAS HER NAME. SHE WAS HIS ASSISTANT.
SUCH A NICE PERSON...
EVEN WHEN SHE FOUND OUT HARII WAS POSSESSED BY A MALICIOUS SPIRIT, SHE DIDN'T CARE. SHE LAUGHED IT OFF.

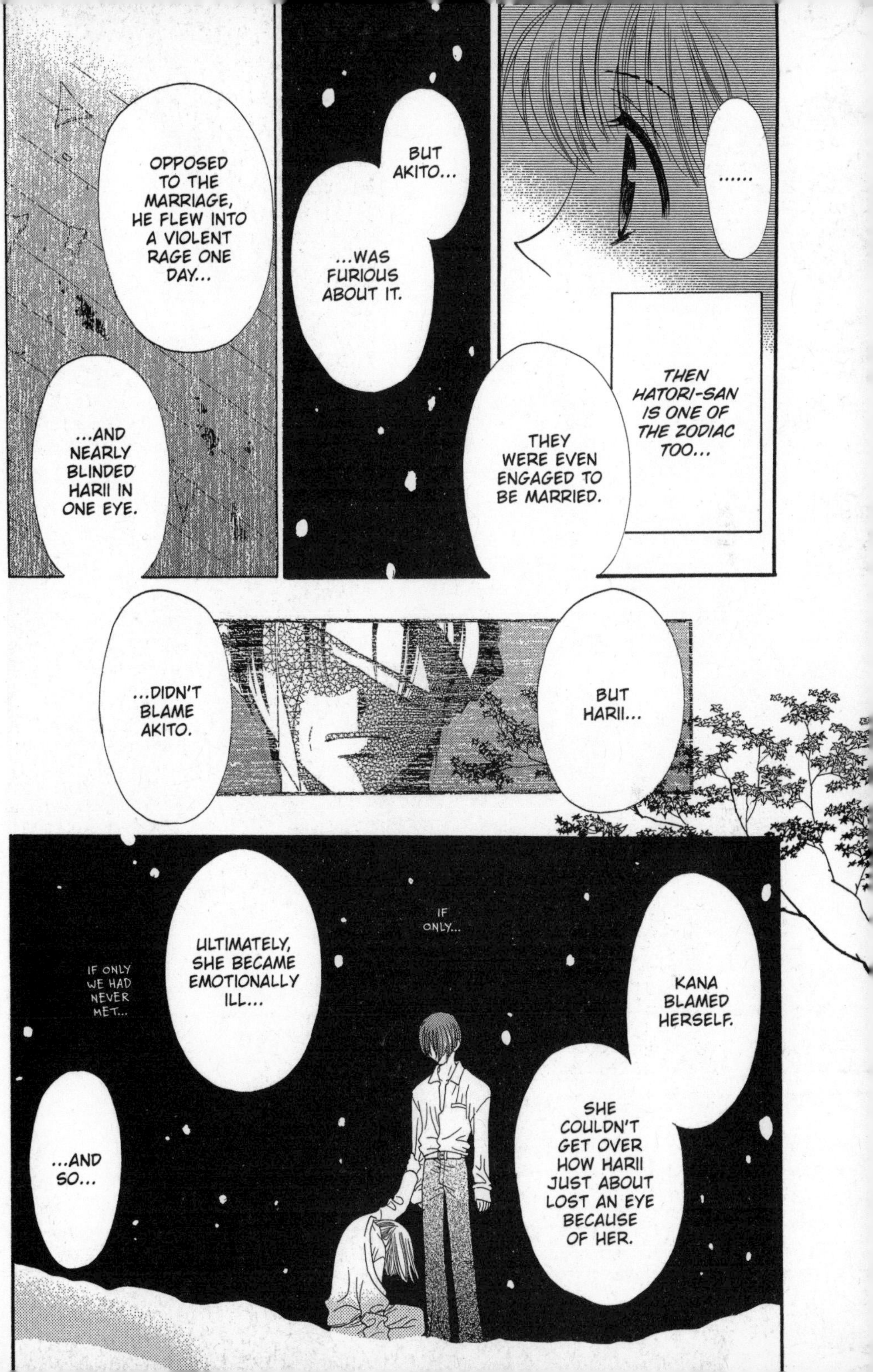
......
THEN HATORI-SAN IS ONE OF THE ZODIAC TOO...
THEY WERE EVEN ENGAGED TO BE MARRIED.
BUT AKITO...
...WAS FURIOUS ABOUT IT.
OPPOSED TO THE MARRIAGE, HE FLEW INTO A VIOLENT RAGE ONE DAY...
...AND NEARLY BLINDED HARII IN ONE EYE.
BUT HARII...
...DIDN'T BLAME AKITO.
KANA BLAMED HERSELF.
SHE COULDN'T GET OVER HOW HARII JUST ABOUT LOST AN EYE BECAUSE OF HER.
IF ONLY...
ULTIMATELY, SHE BECAME EMOTIONALLY ILL...
IF ONLY WE HAD NEVER MET...
...AND SO...

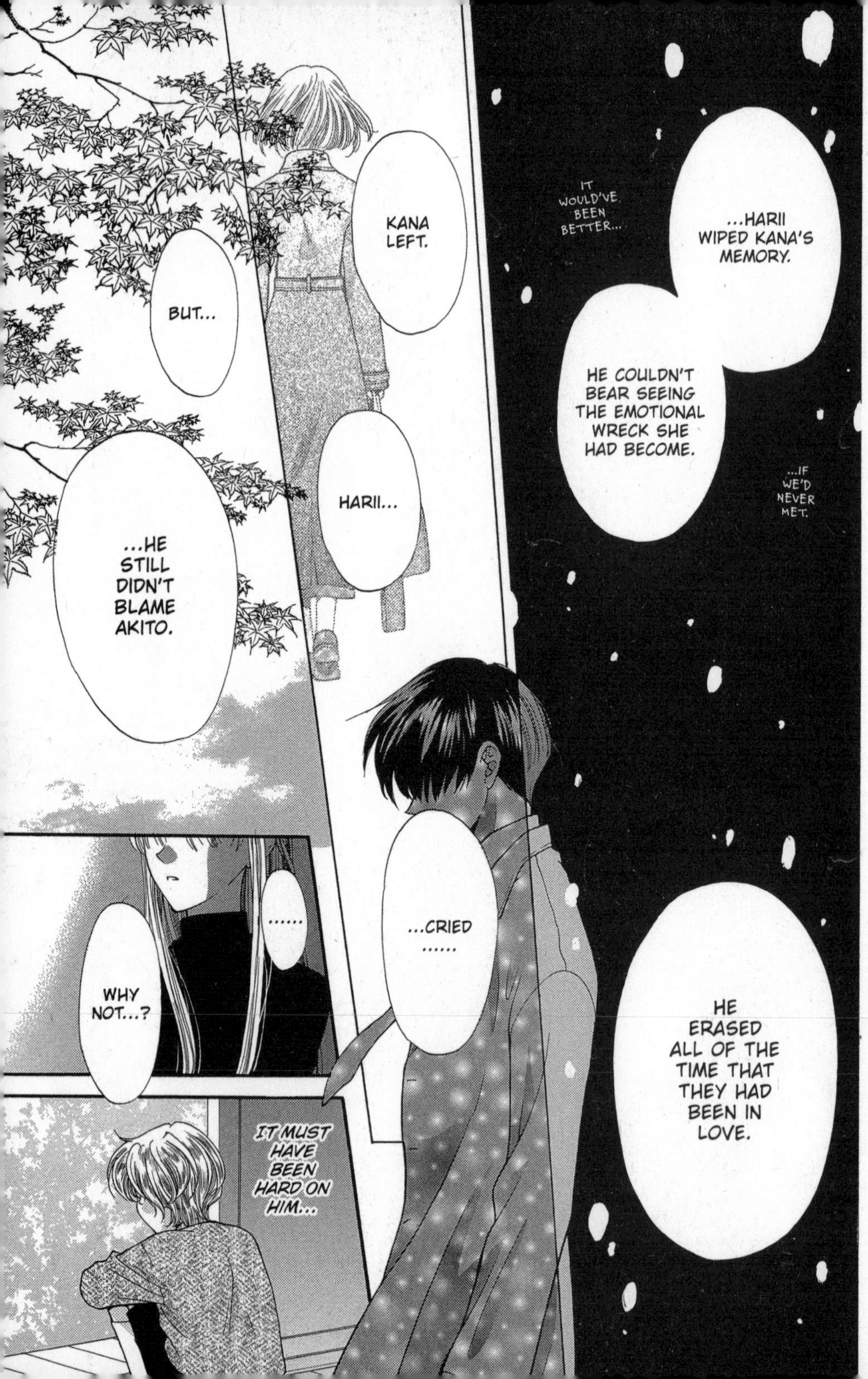
...HARII WIPED KANA'S MEMORY.
IT WOULD'VE BEEN BETTER...
HE COULDN'T BEAR SEEING THE EMOTIONAL WRECK SHE HAD BECOME.
...IF WE'D NEVER MET.
HE ERASED ALL OF THE TIME THAT THEY HAD BEEN IN LOVE.
KANA LEFT.
HARII...
BUT...
...HE STILL DIDN'T BLAME AKITO.
...CRIED ......
......
WHY NOT...?
IT MUST HAVE BEEN HARD ON HIM...

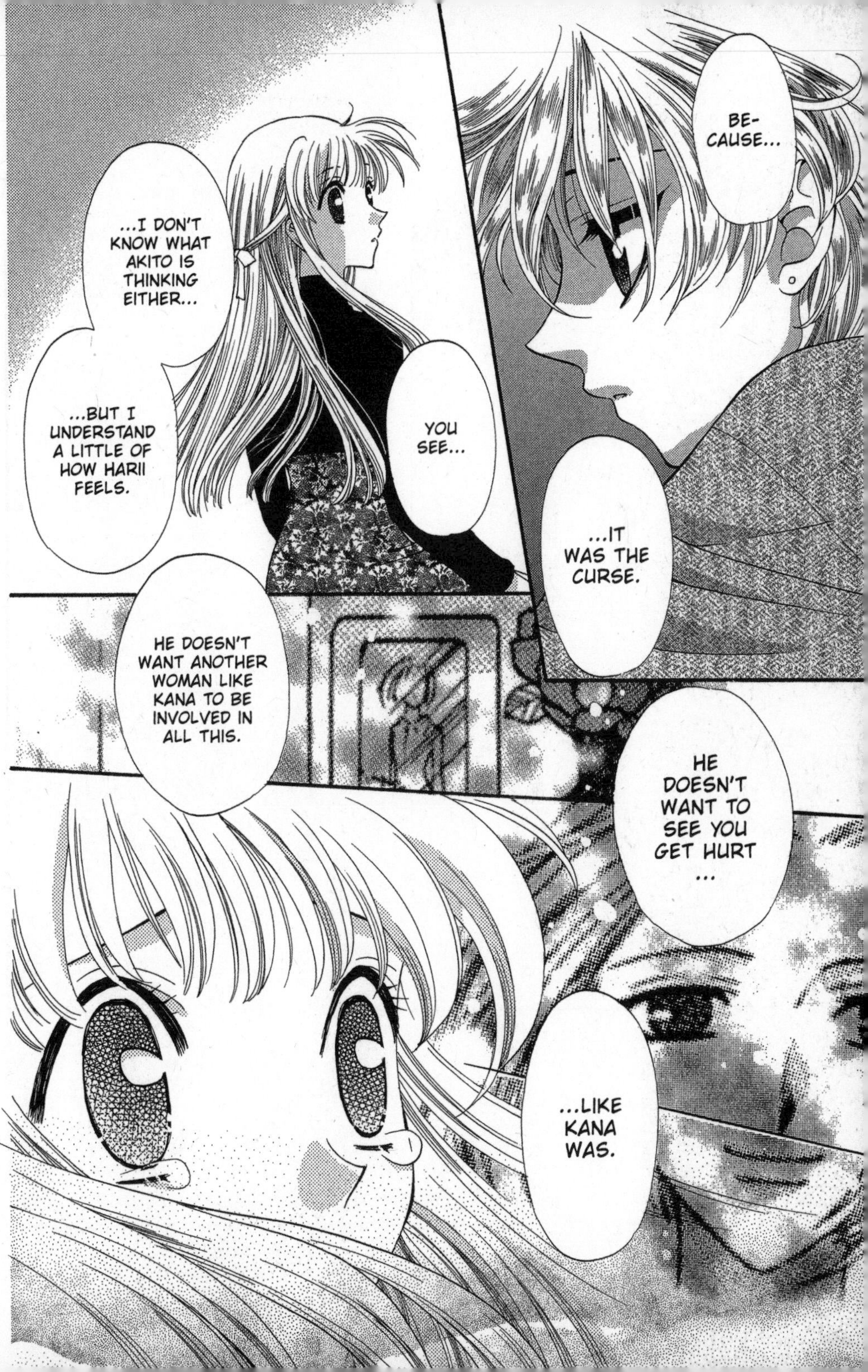
BE-CAUSE...
...IT WAS THE CURSE.
...I DON'T KNOW WHAT AKITO IS THINKING EITHER...
...BUT I UNDERSTAND A LITTLE OF HOW HARII FEELS.
YOU SEE...
HE DOESN'T WANT ANOTHER WOMAN LIKE KANA TO BE INVOLVED IN ALL THIS.
HE DOESN'T WANT TO SEE YOU GET HURT ...
...LIKE KANA WAS.

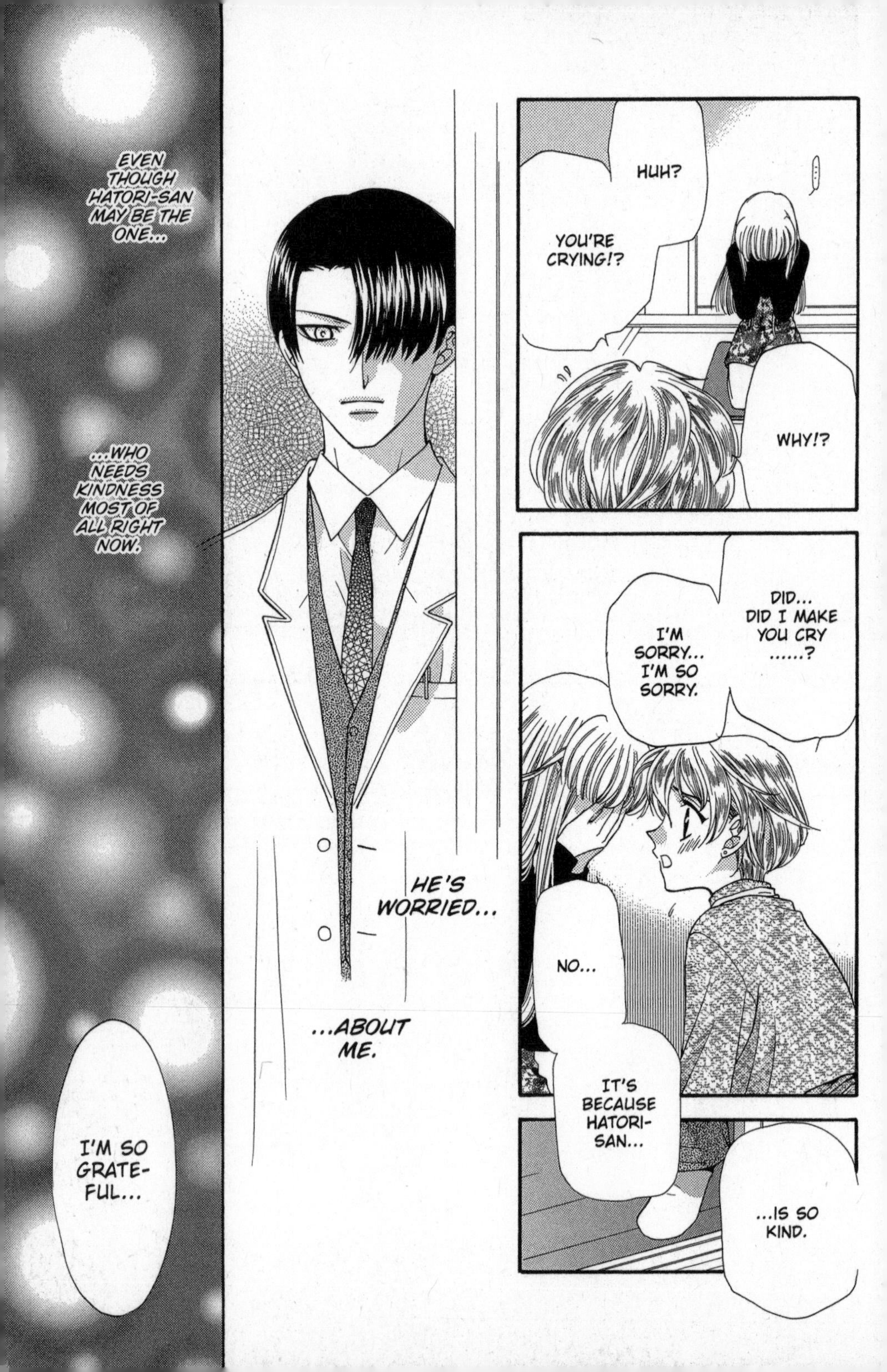
...
HUH?
YOU'RE CRYING!?
WHY!?
DID... DID I MAKE YOU CRY ......?
I'M SORRY... I'M SO SORRY.
NO...
IT'S BECAUSE HATORI-SAN...
...IS SO KIND.
HE'S WORRIED...
...ABOUT ME.
EVEN THOUGH HATORI-SAN MAY BE THE ONE...
...WHO NEEDS KINDNESS MOST OF ALL RIGHT NOW.
I'M SO GRATEFUL...

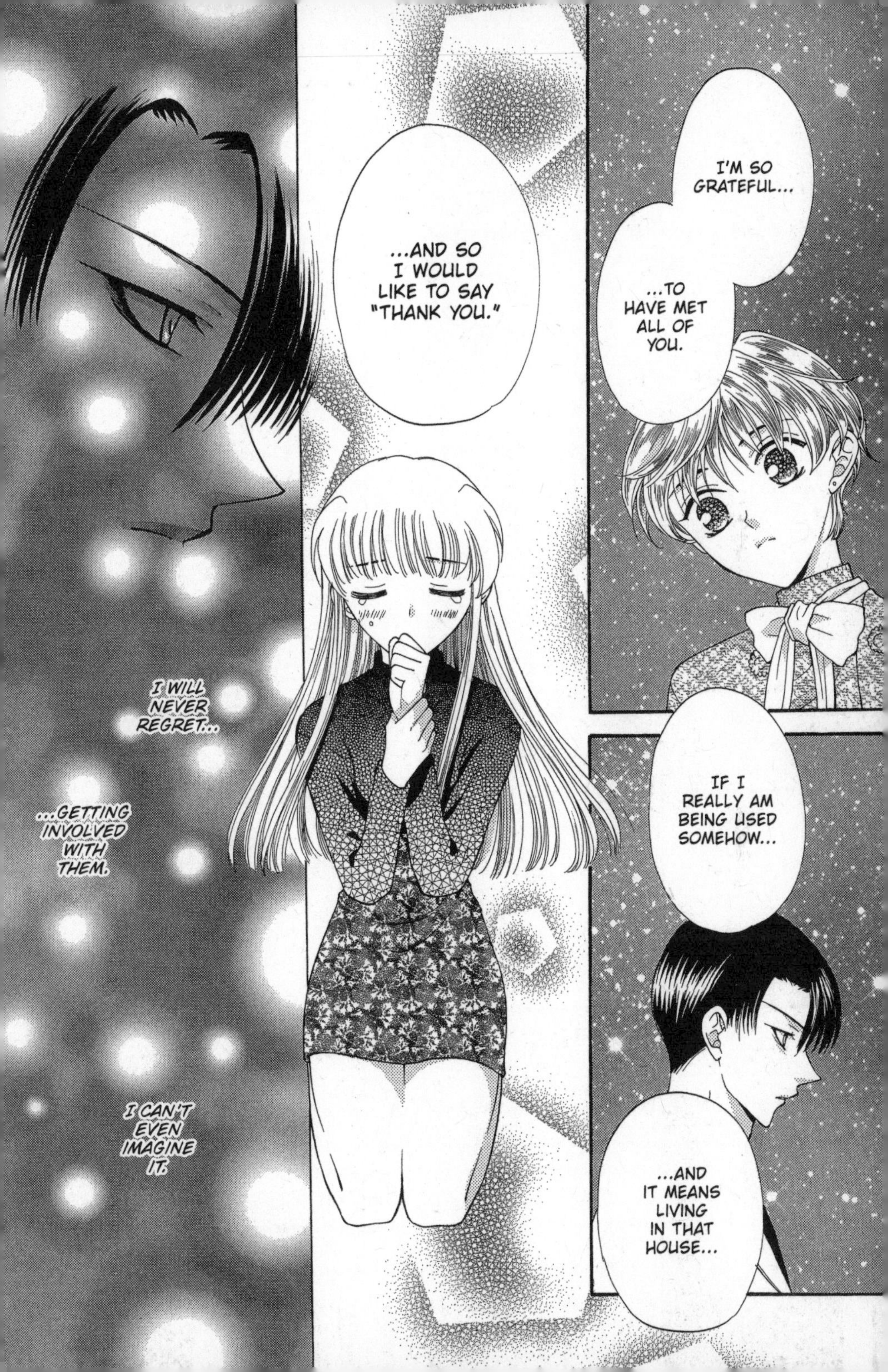
I'M SO GRATEFUL...
...TO HAVE MET ALL OF YOU.
IF I REALLY AM BEING USED SOMEHOW...
...AND IT MEANS LIVING IN THAT HOUSE...
...AND SO I WOULD LIKE TO SAY "THANK YOU."
I WILL NEVER REGRET...
...GETTING INVOLVED WITH THEM.
I CAN'T EVEN IMAGINE IT.

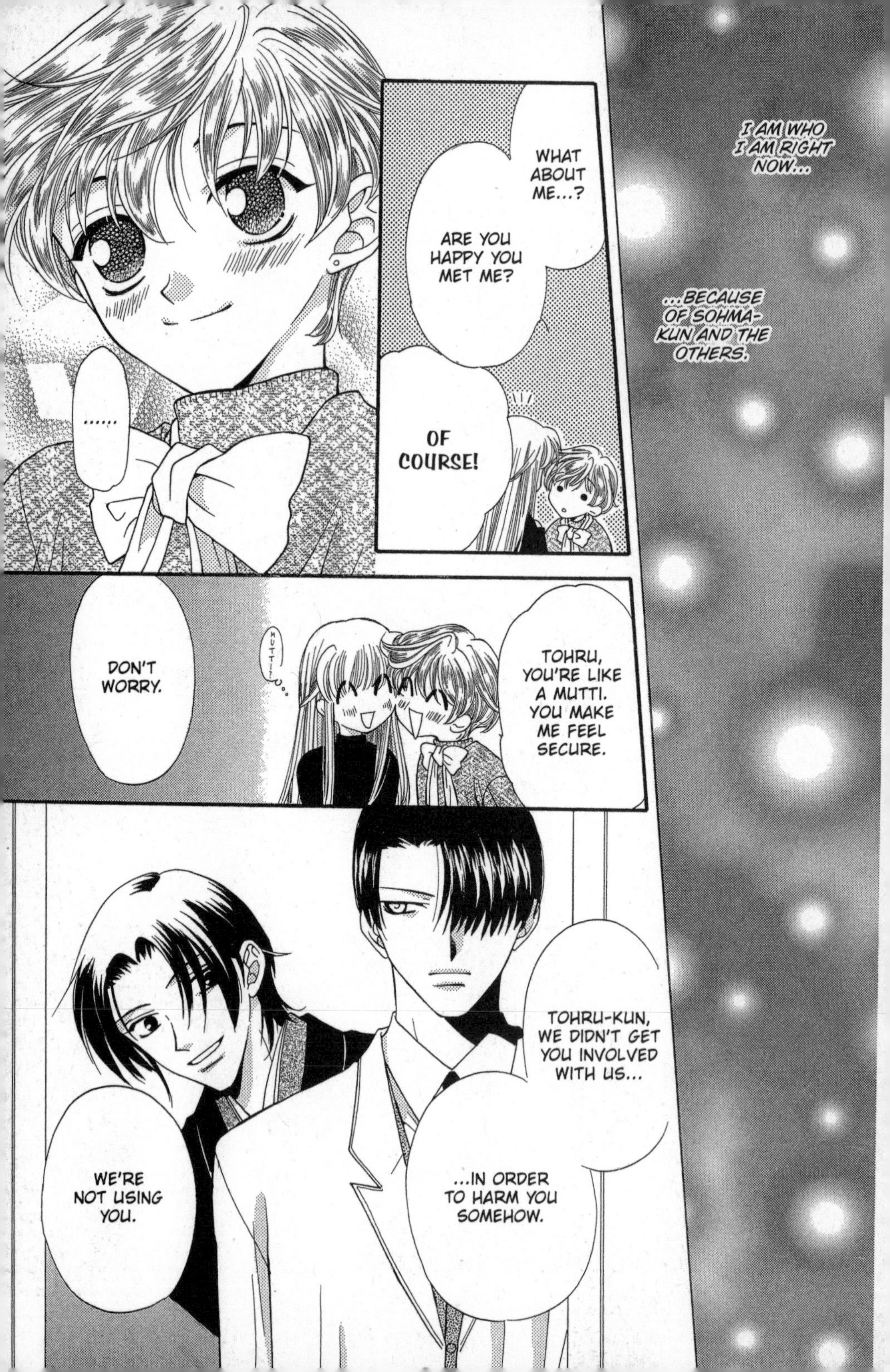
I AM WHO I AM RIGHT NOW...
...BECAUSE OF SOHMA-KUN AND THE OTHERS.
WHAT ABOUT ME...?
ARE YOU HAPPY YOU MET ME?
OF COURSE!
......
TOHRU, YOU'RE LIKE A MUTTI. YOU MAKE ME FEEL SECURE.
MUTTI?
DON'T WORRY.
TOHRU-KUN, WE DIDN'T GET YOU INVOLVED WITH US...
...IN ORDER TO HARM YOU SOMEHOW.
WE'RE NOT USING YOU.

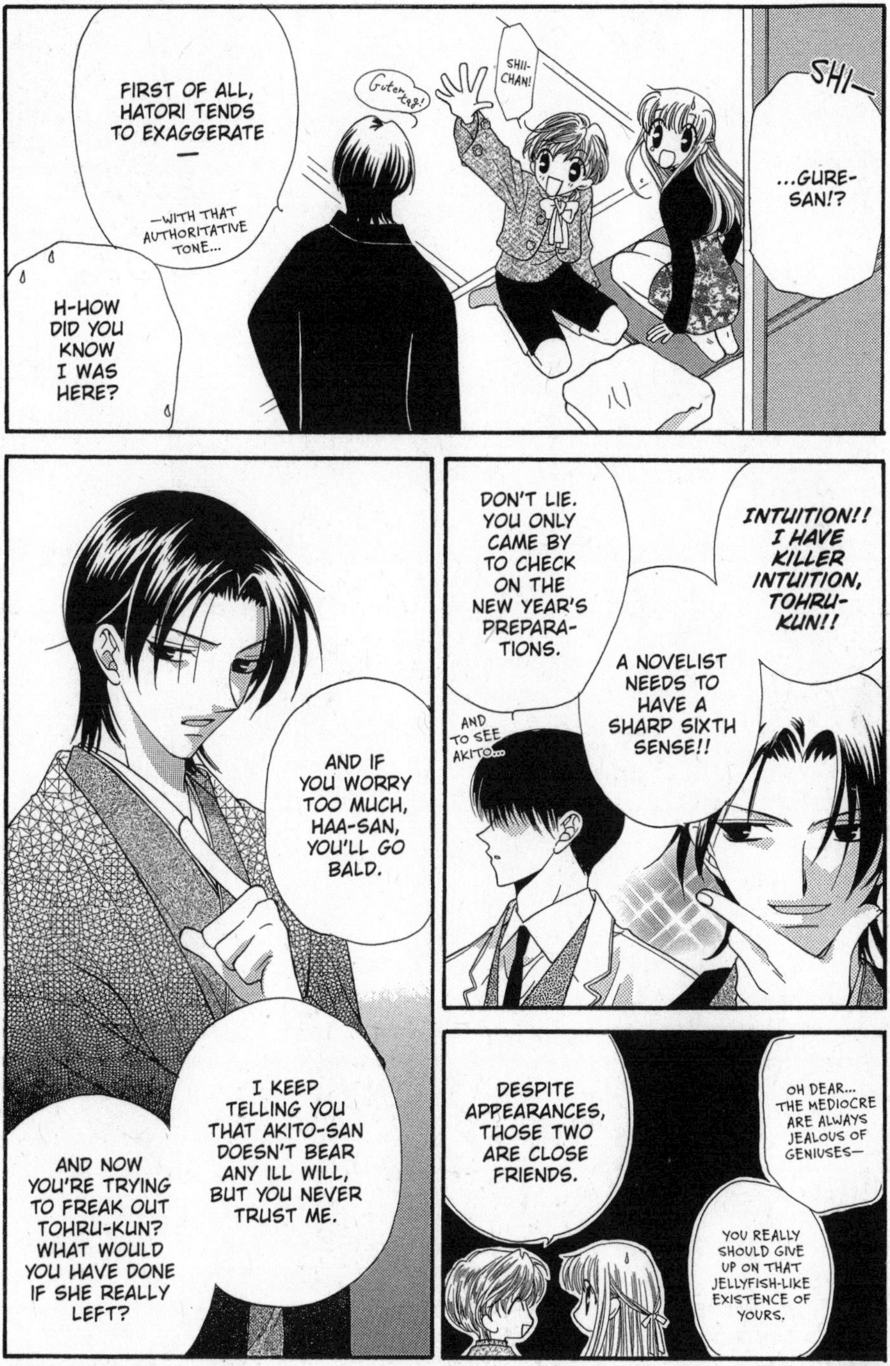
SHI—
...GURE-SAN!?
SHII-CHAN!
Guten tag!
FIRST OF ALL, HATORI TENDS TO EXAGGERATE —
—WITH THAT AUTHORITATIVE TONE...
H-HOW DID YOU KNOW I WAS HERE?
INTUITION!! I HAVE KILLER INTUITION, TOHRU-KUN!!
DON'T LIE. YOU ONLY CAME BY TO CHECK ON THE NEW YEAR'S PREPARATIONS.
A NOVELIST NEEDS TO HAVE A SHARP SIXTH SENSE!!
AND TO SEE AKITO...
OH DEAR... THE MEDIOCRE ARE ALWAYS JEALOUS OF GENIUSES—
DESPITE APPEARANCES, THOSE TWO ARE CLOSE FRIENDS.
YOU REALLY SHOULD GIVE UP ON THAT JELLYFISH-LIKE EXISTENCE OF YOURS.
AND IF YOU WORRY TOO MUCH, HAA-SAN, YOU'LL GO BALD.
I KEEP TELLING YOU THAT AKITO-SAN DOESN'T BEAR ANY ILL WILL, BUT YOU NEVER TRUST ME.
AND NOW YOU'RE TRYING TO FREAK OUT TOHRU-KUN? WHAT WOULD YOU HAVE DONE IF SHE REALLY LEFT?

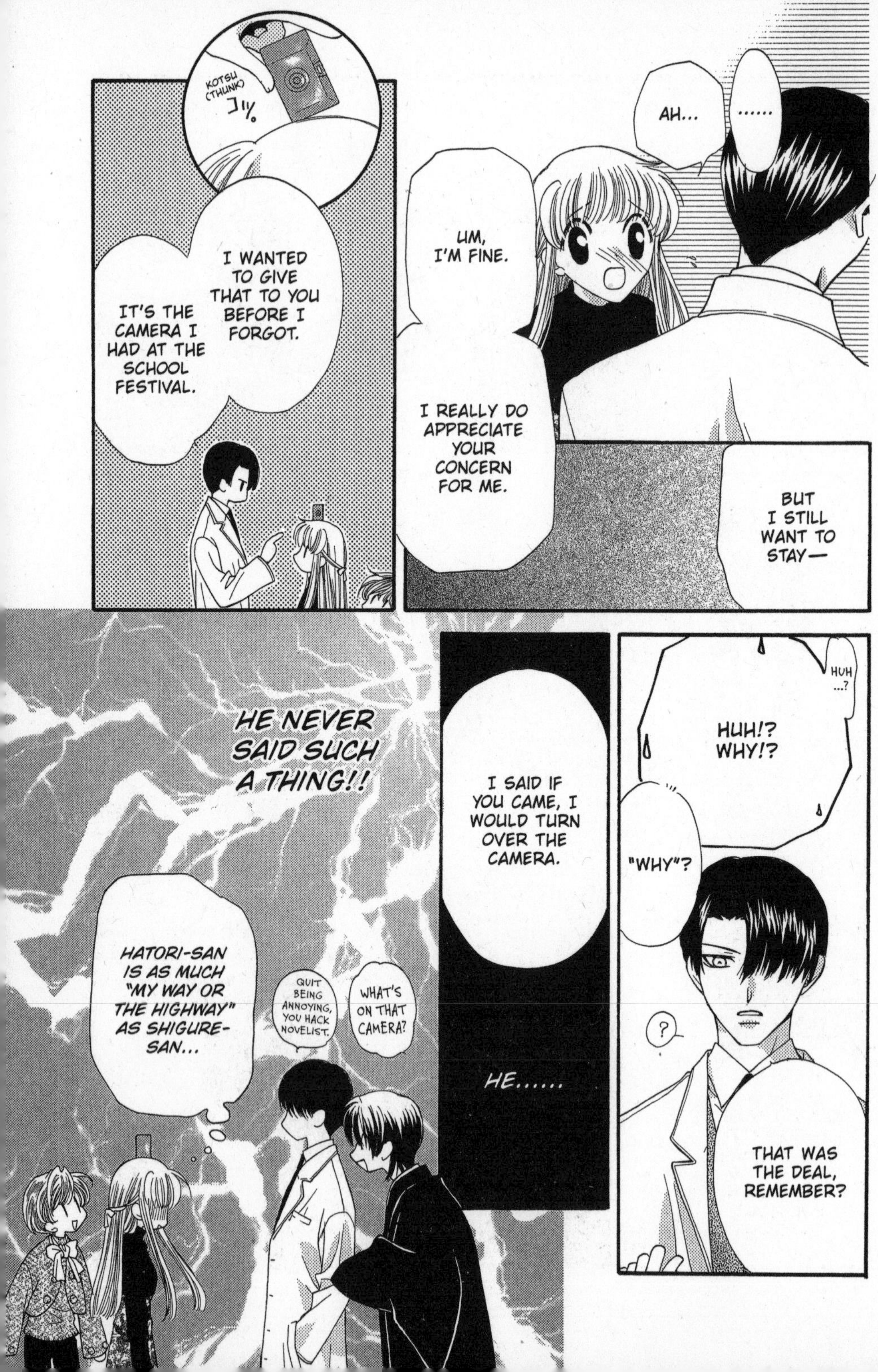
......
AH...
UM, I'M FINE.
I REALLY DO APPRECIATE YOUR CONCERN FOR ME.
BUT I STILL WANT TO STAY—
KOTSU (THUNK)
I WANTED TO GIVE THAT TO YOU BEFORE I FORGOT.
IT'S THE CAMERA I HAD AT THE SCHOOL FESTIVAL.
HUH ...?
HUH!? WHY!?
"WHY"?
?
THAT WAS THE DEAL, REMEMBER?
I SAID IF YOU CAME, I WOULD TURN OVER THE CAMERA.
HE......
HE NEVER SAID SUCH A THING!!
WHAT'S ON THAT CAMERA?
QUIT BEING ANNOYING, YOU HACK NOVELIST.
HATORI-SAN IS AS MUCH "MY WAY OR THE HIGHWAY" AS SHIGURE-SAN...

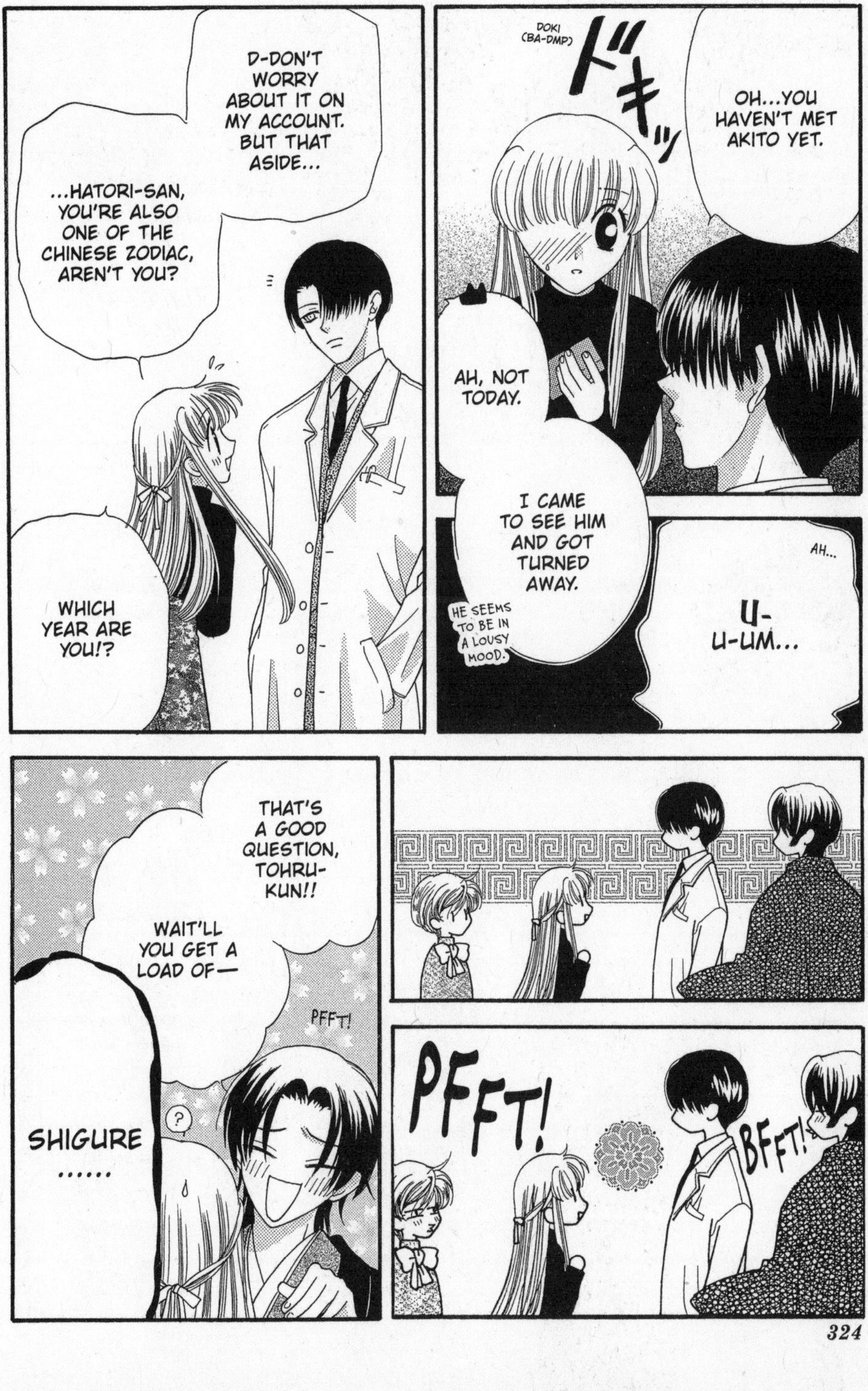
DOKI (BA-DMP)
ドキッ
OH...YOU HAVEN'T MET AKITO YET.
AH, NOT TODAY.
I CAME TO SEE HIM AND GOT TURNED AWAY.
HE SEEMS TO BE IN A LOUSY MOOD.
AH...
U-U-UM...
D-DON'T WORRY ABOUT IT ON MY ACCOUNT. BUT THAT ASIDE...
...HATORI-SAN, YOU'RE ALSO ONE OF THE CHINESE ZODIAC, AREN'T YOU?
WHICH YEAR ARE YOU!?
PFFT!
BFFT!
THAT'S A GOOD QUESTION, TOHRU-KUN!!
WAIT'LL YOU GET A LOAD OF—
PFFT!
?
SHIGURE ......

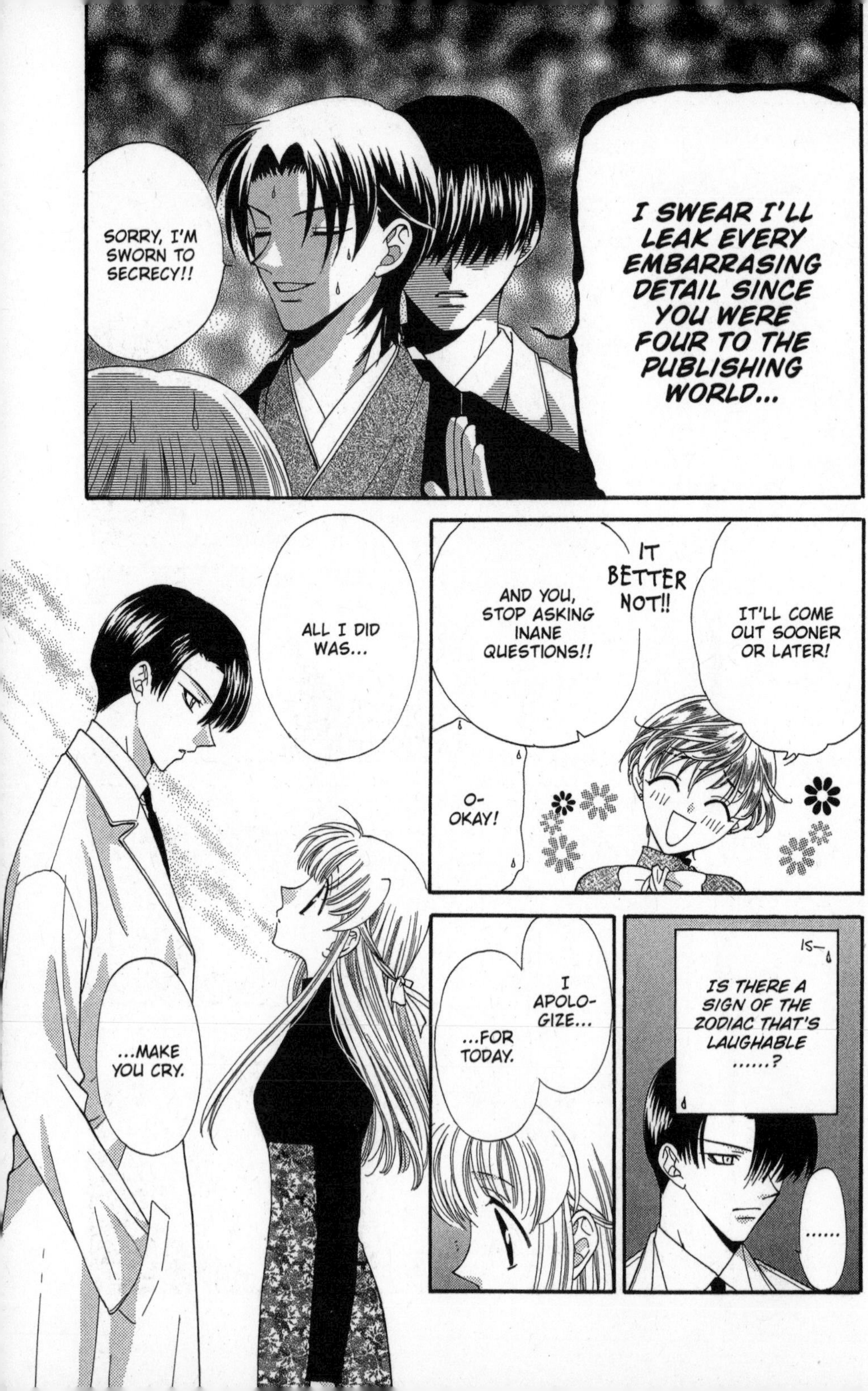
I SWEAR I'LL LEAK EVERY EMBARRASING DETAIL SINCE YOU WERE FOUR TO THE PUBLISHING WORLD...
SORRY, I'M SWORN TO SECRECY!!
IT'LL COME OUT SOONER OR LATER!
IT BETTER NOT!!
AND YOU, STOP ASKING INANE QUESTIONS!!
O-OKAY!
IS—
IS THERE A SIGN OF THE ZODIAC THAT'S LAUGHABLE ......?
......
I APOLOGIZE...
...FOR TODAY.
ALL I DID WAS...
...MAKE YOU CRY.

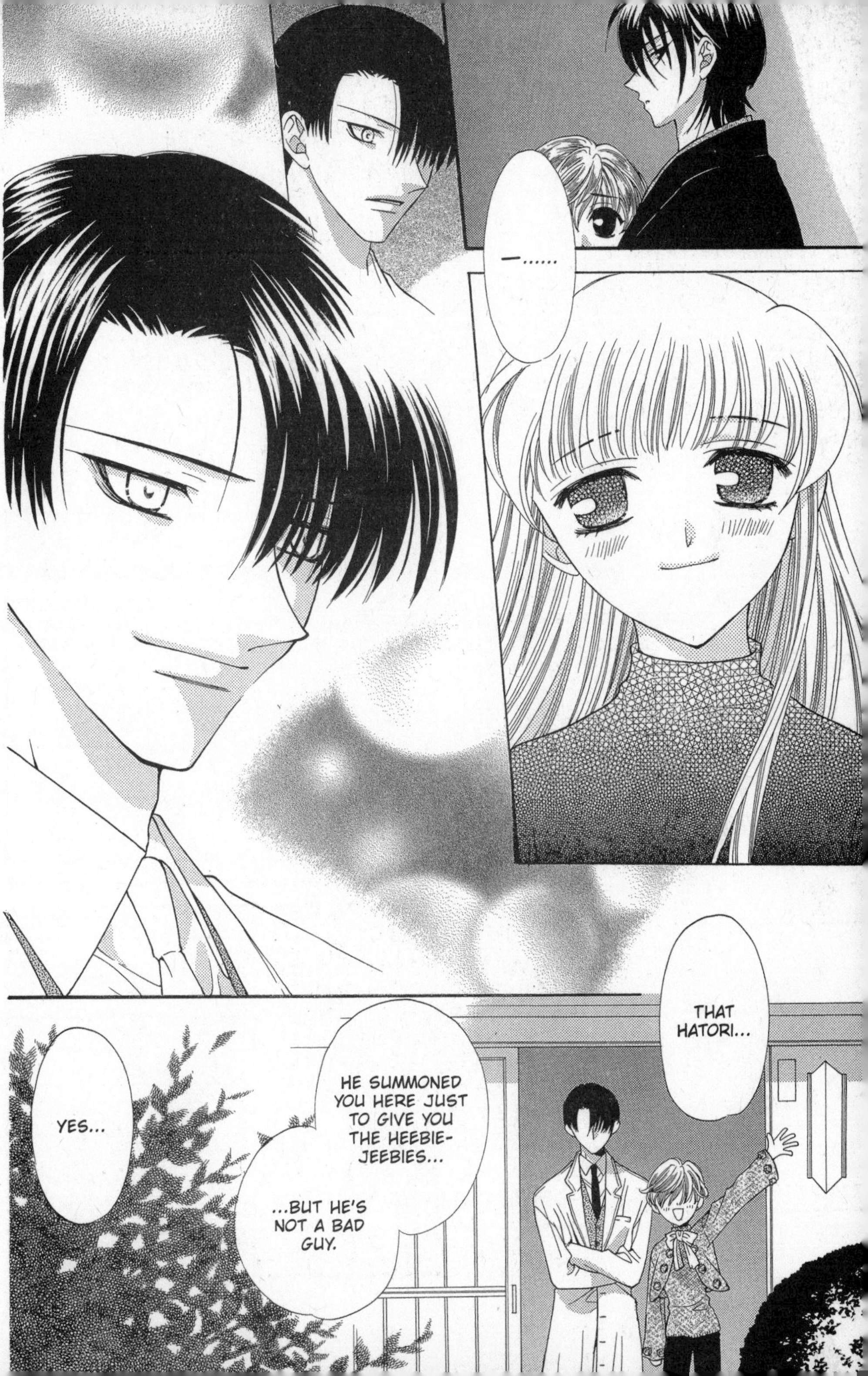
—......
THAT HATORI...
HE SUMMONED YOU HERE JUST TO GIVE YOU THE HEEBIE-JEEBIES...
...BUT HE'S NOT A BAD GUY.
YES...

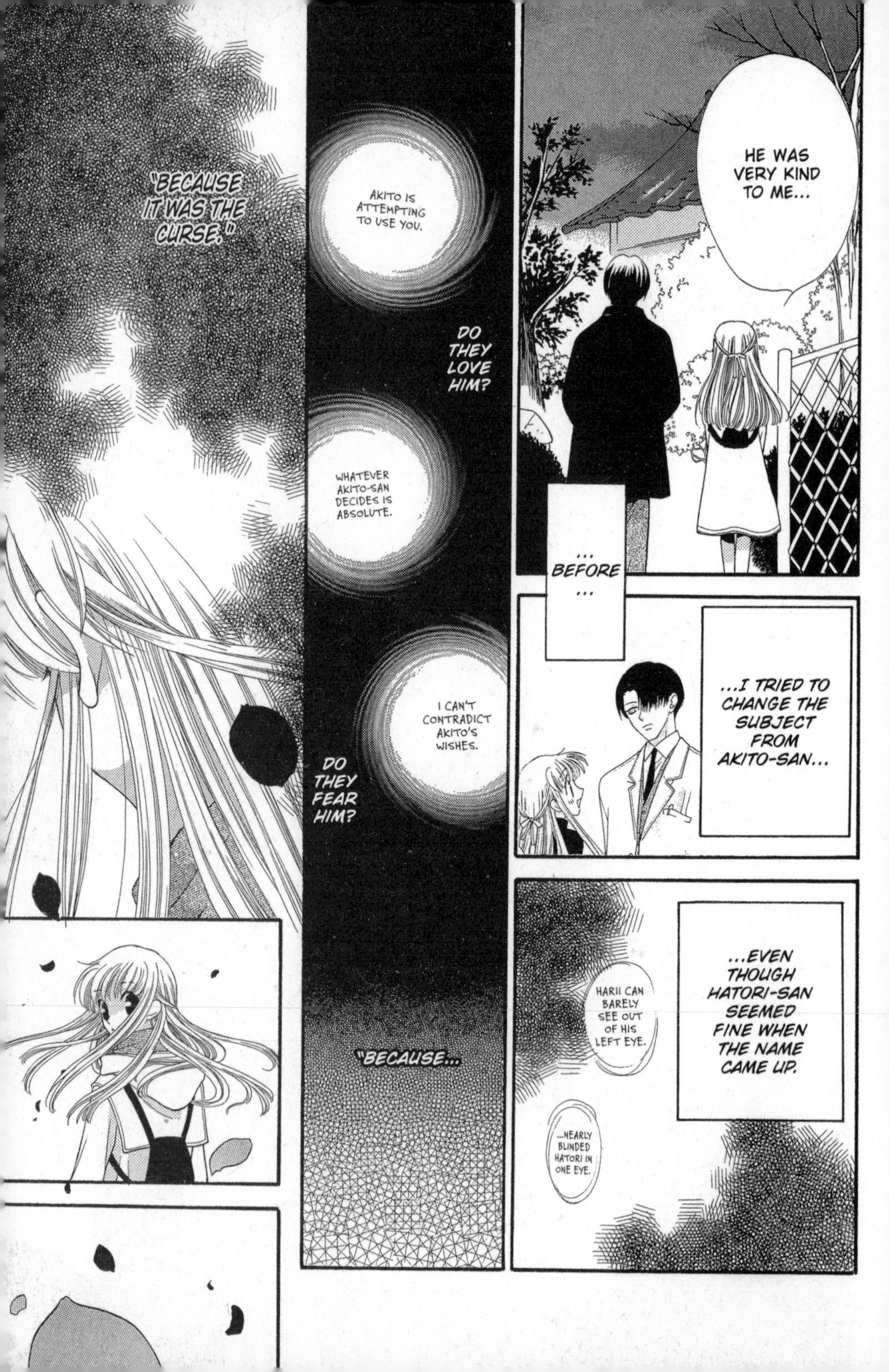
HE WAS VERY KIND TO ME...
...BEFORE...
...I TRIED TO CHANGE THE SUBJECT FROM AKITO-SAN...
...EVEN THOUGH HATORI-SAN SEEMED FINE WHEN THE NAME CAME UP.
HARII CAN BARELY SEE OUT OF HIS LEFT EYE.
...NEARLY BLINDED HATORI IN ONE EYE.
AKITO IS ATTEMPTING TO USE YOU.
DO THEY LOVE HIM?
WHATEVER AKITO-SAN DECIDES IS ABSOLUTE.
I CAN'T CONTRADICT AKITO'S WISHES.
DO THEY FEAR HIM?
"BECAUSE...
"BECAUSE IT WAS THE CURSE."

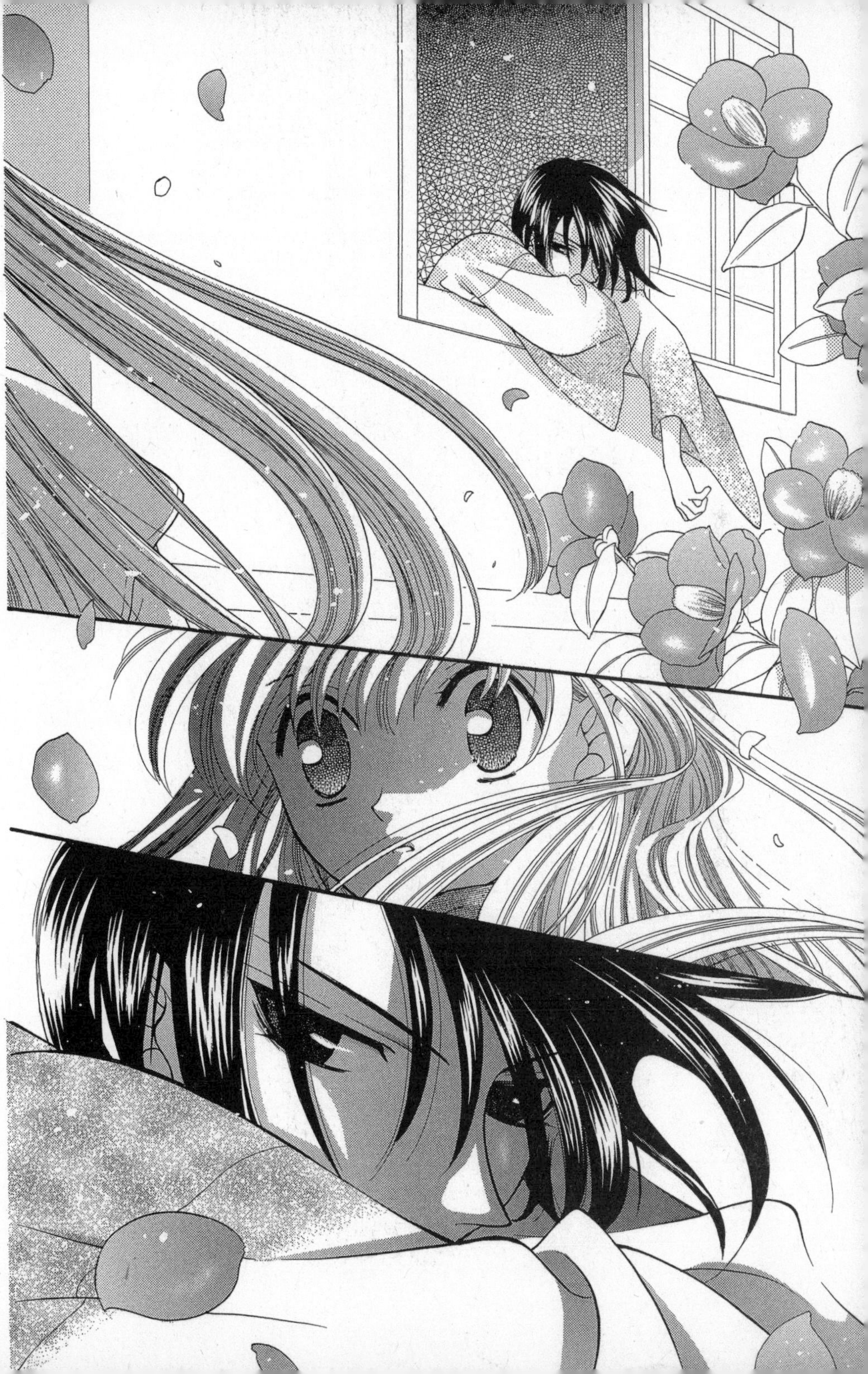

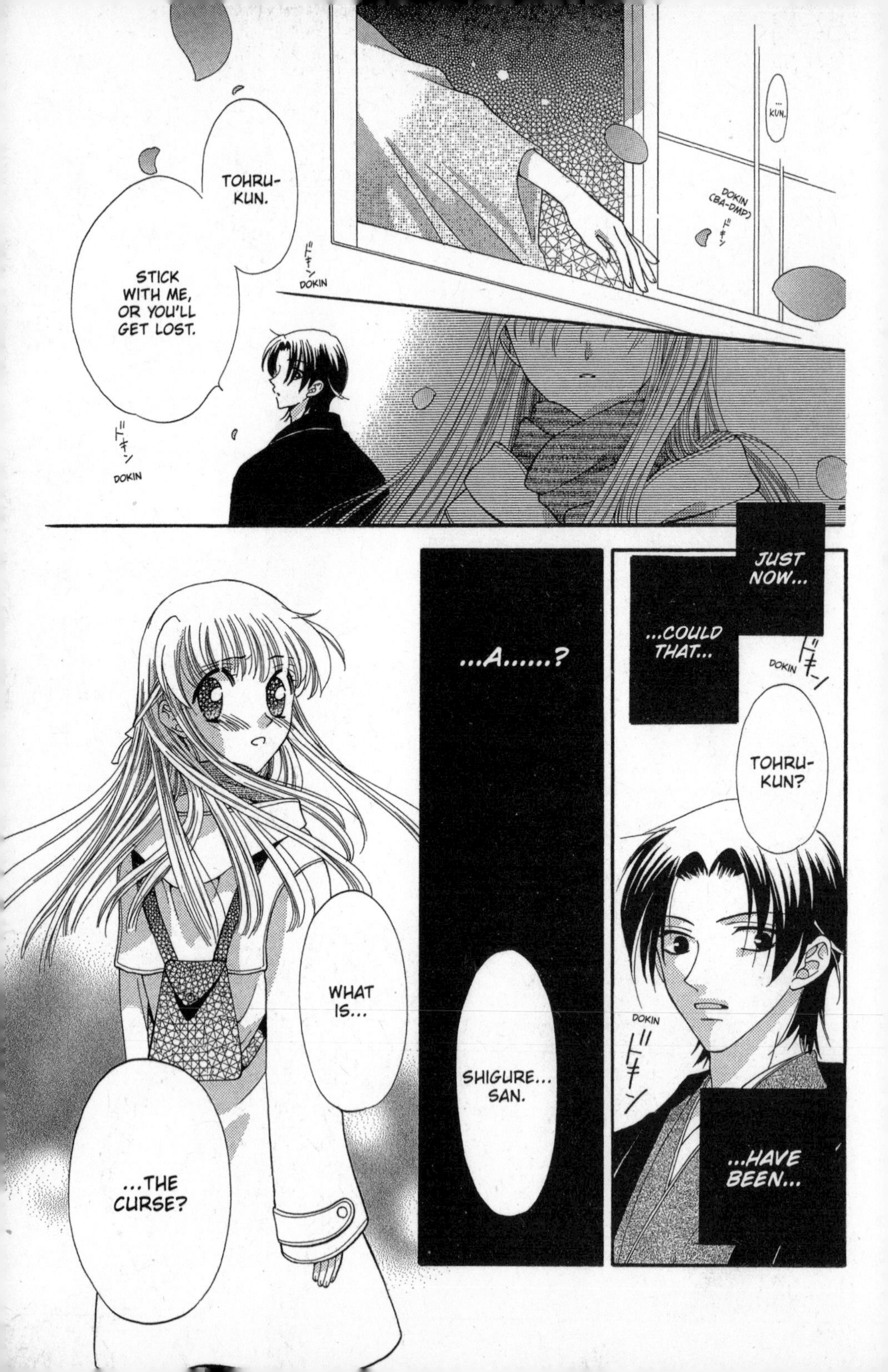
...KUN.
DOKIN (BA-DMP)
ドキン
TOHRU-KUN.
STICK WITH ME, OR YOU'LL GET LOST.
ドキン
DOKIN
ドキン
DOKIN
JUST NOW...
...COULD THAT...
ドキン
DOKIN
TOHRU-KUN?
DOKIN
ドキン
...HAVE BEEN...
...A......?
SHIGURE... SAN.
WHAT IS...
...THE CURSE?

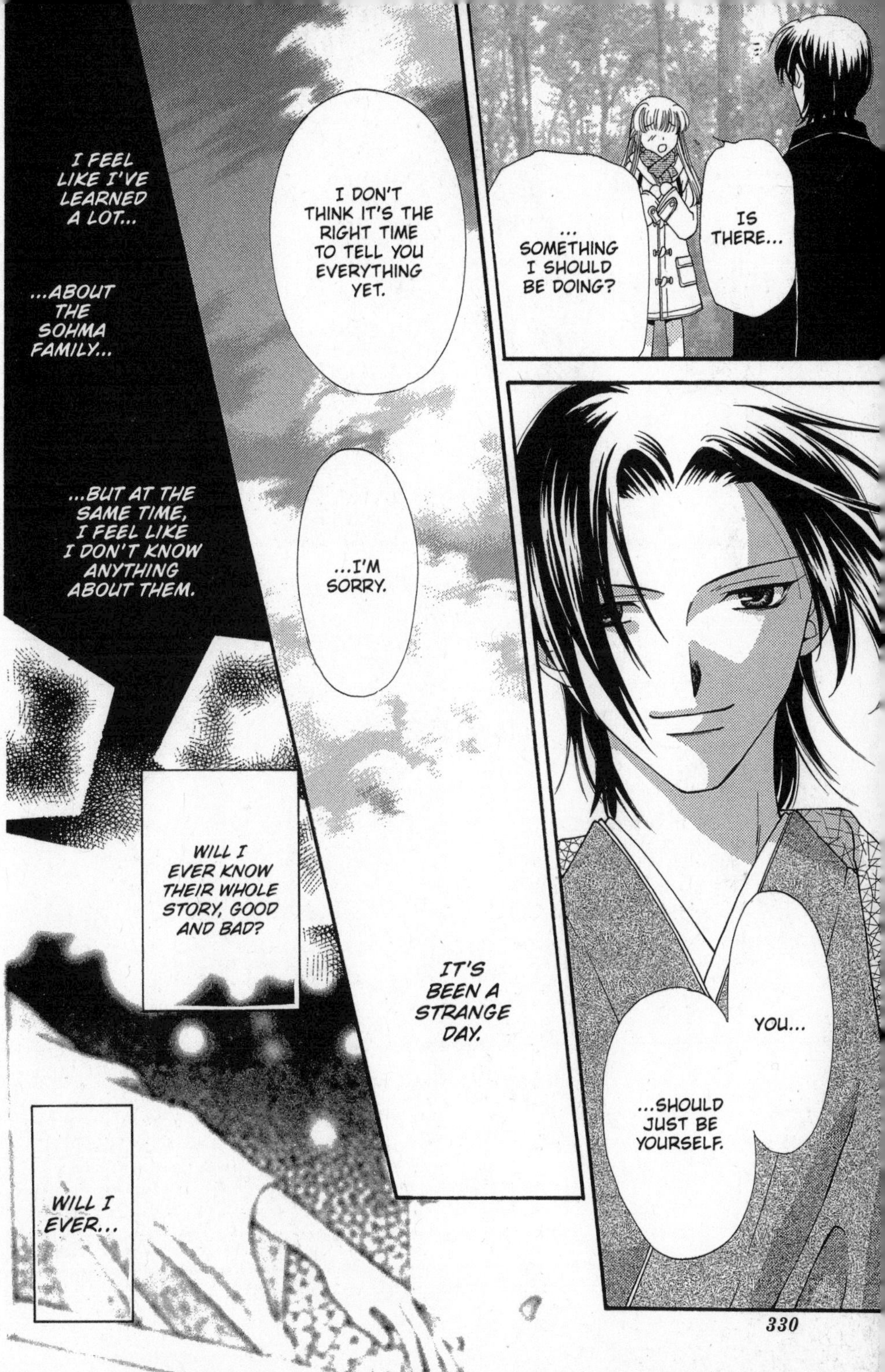
IS THERE...
...SOMETHING I SHOULD BE DOING?
YOU...
...SHOULD JUST BE YOURSELF.
I DON'T THINK IT'S THE RIGHT TIME TO TELL YOU EVERYTHING YET.
...I'M SORRY.
IT'S BEEN A STRANGE DAY.
I FEEL LIKE I'VE LEARNED A LOT...
...ABOUT THE SOHMA FAMILY...
...BUT AT THE SAME TIME, I FEEL LIKE I DON'T KNOW ANYTHING ABOUT THEM.
WILL I EVER KNOW THEIR WHOLE STORY, GOOD AND BAD?
WILL I EVER...

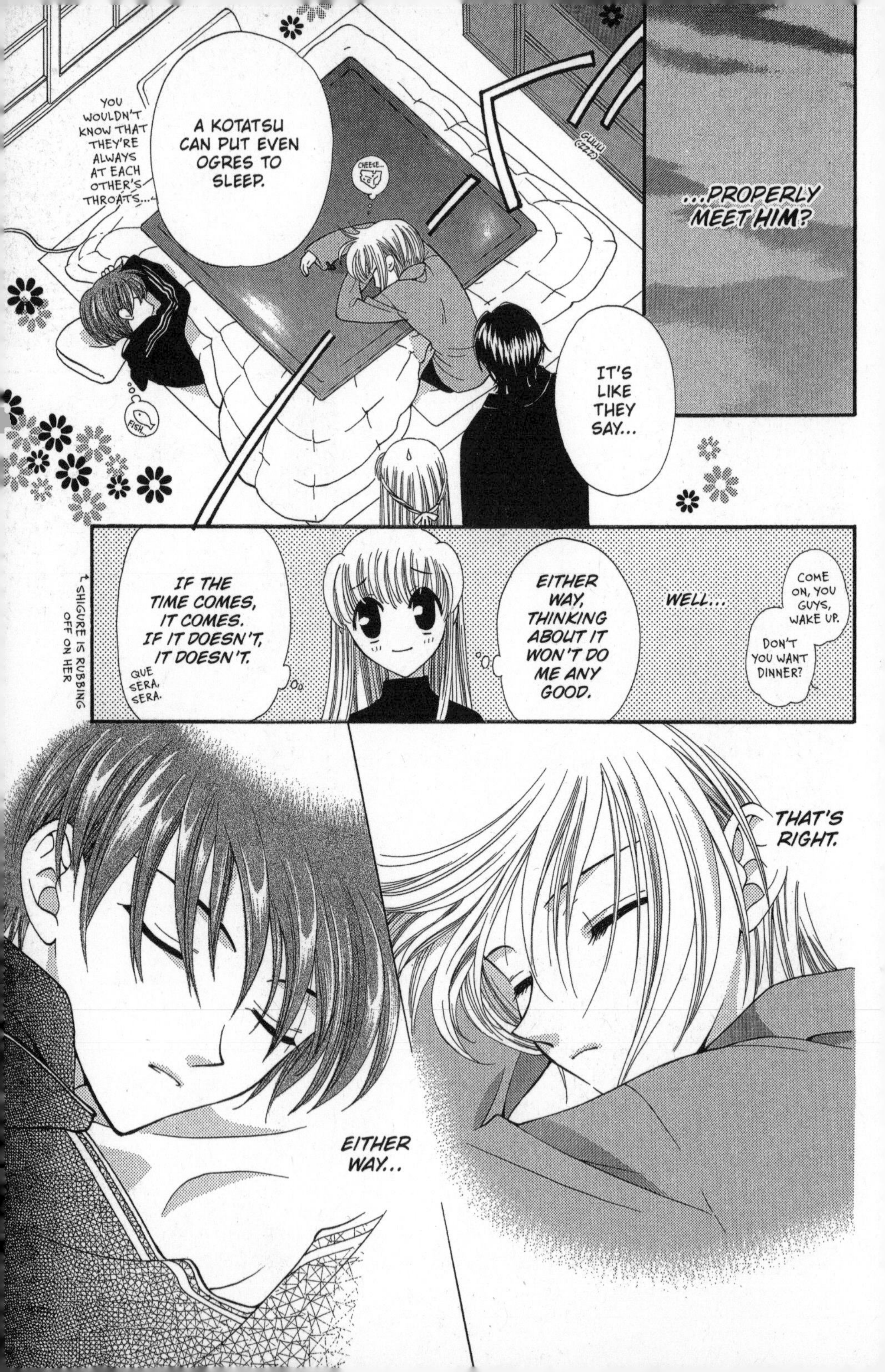
...PROPERLY MEET HIM?
IT'S LIKE THEY SAY...
A KOTATSU CAN PUT EVEN OGRES TO SLEEP.
GUUU (ZZZ)
CHEESE...
YOU WOULDN'T KNOW THAT THEY'RE ALWAYS AT EACH OTHER'S THROATS...
FISH...
COME ON, YOU GUYS, WAKE UP.
DON'T YOU WANT DINNER?
WELL...
EITHER WAY, THINKING ABOUT IT WON'T DO ME ANY GOOD.
IF THE TIME COMES, IT COMES. IF IT DOESN'T, IT DOESN'T.
QUE SERA, SERA.
← SHIGURE IS RUBBING OFF ON HER
THAT'S RIGHT.
EITHER WAY...

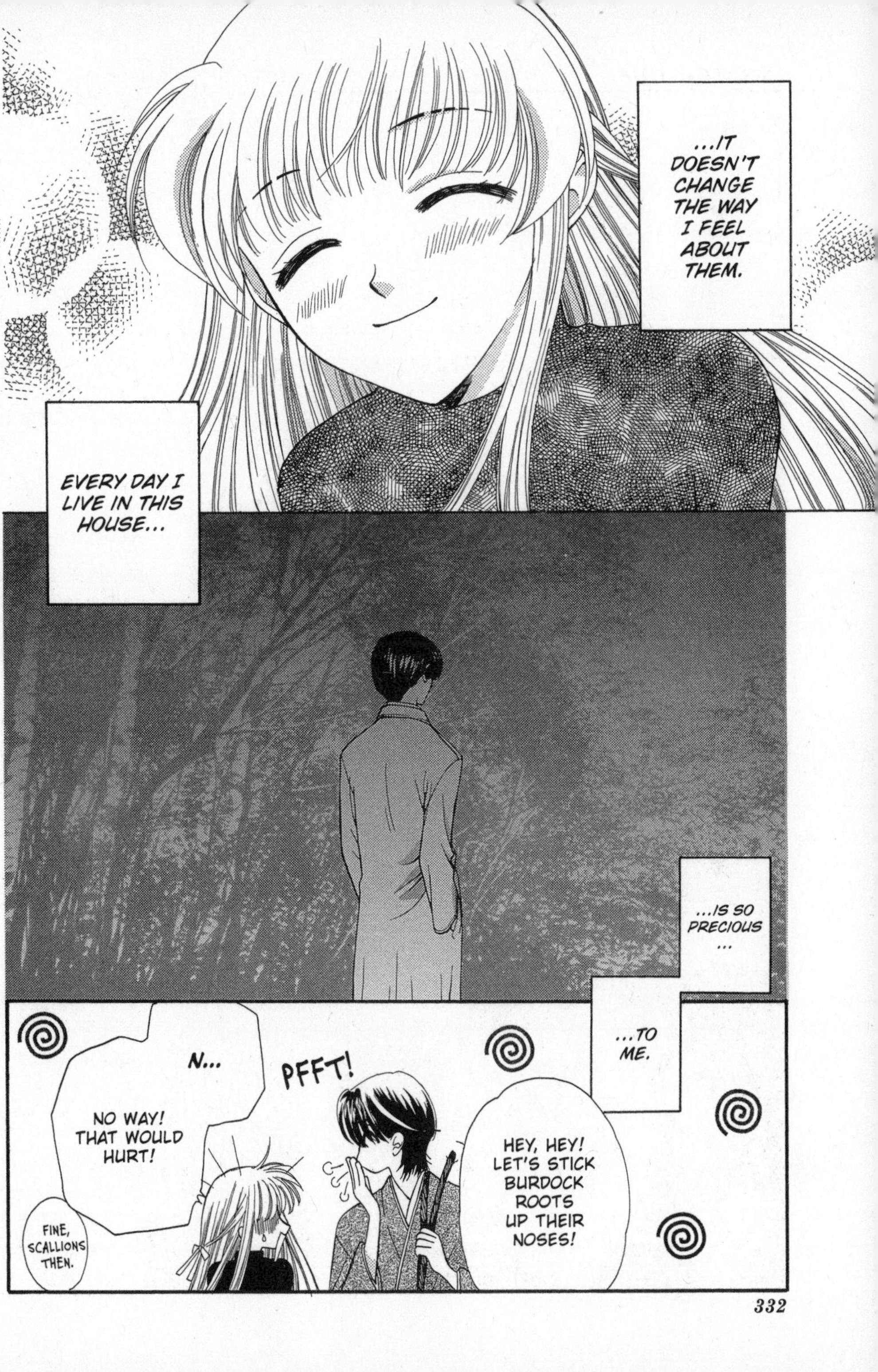
...IT DOESN'T CHANGE THE WAY I FEEL ABOUT THEM.
EVERY DAY I LIVE IN THIS HOUSE...
...IS SO PRECIOUS ...
...TO ME.
HEY, HEY! LET'S STICK BURDOCK ROOTS UP THEIR NOSES!
PFFT!
N...
NO WAY! THAT WOULD HURT!
FINE, SCALLIONS THEN.

THIS HAS NOTHING TO DO WITH ANYTHING, BUT I HAVE A 100-DEGREE FEVER RIGHT NOW...

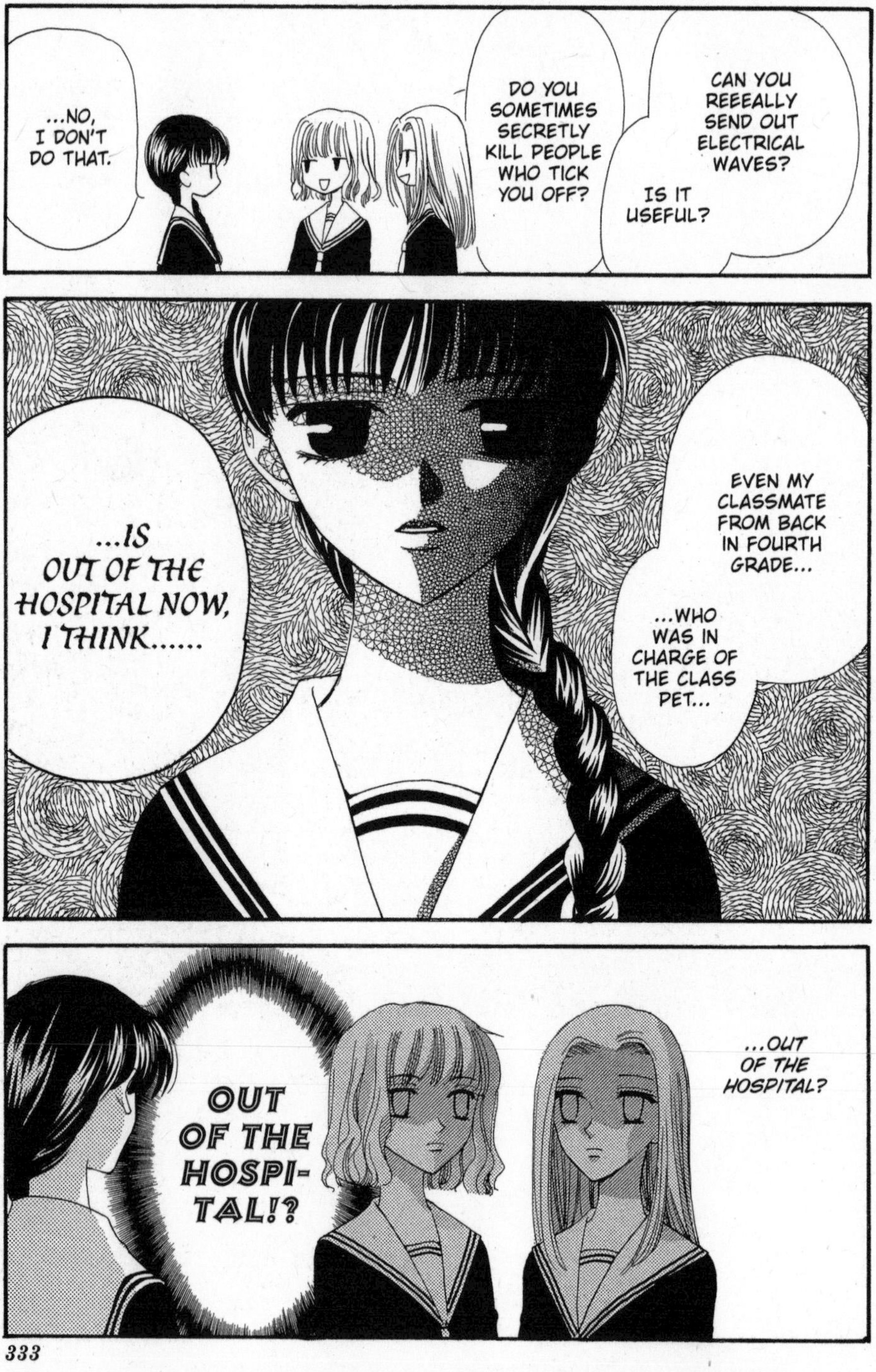
CAN YOU REEEALLY SEND OUT ELECTRICAL WAVES?
IS IT USEFUL?
DO YOU SOMETIMES SECRETLY KILL PEOPLE WHO TICK YOU OFF?
...NO, I DON'T DO THAT.
EVEN MY CLASSMATE FROM BACK IN FOURTH GRADE...
...WHO WAS IN CHARGE OF THE CLASS PET...
...IS OUT OF THE HOSPITAL NOW, I THINK......
...OUT OF THE HOSPITAL?
OUT OF THE HOSPI-TAL!?

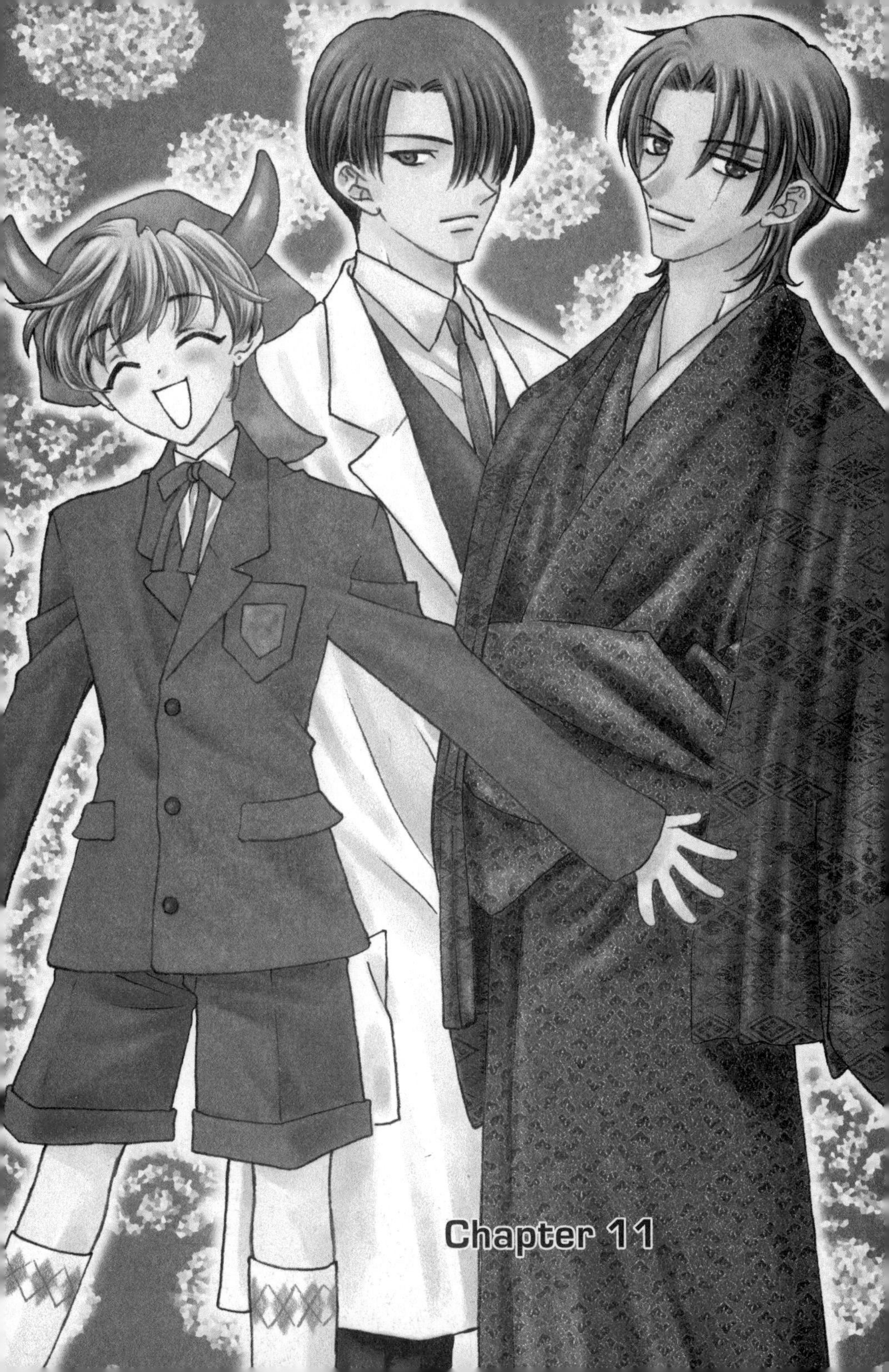
Chapter 11

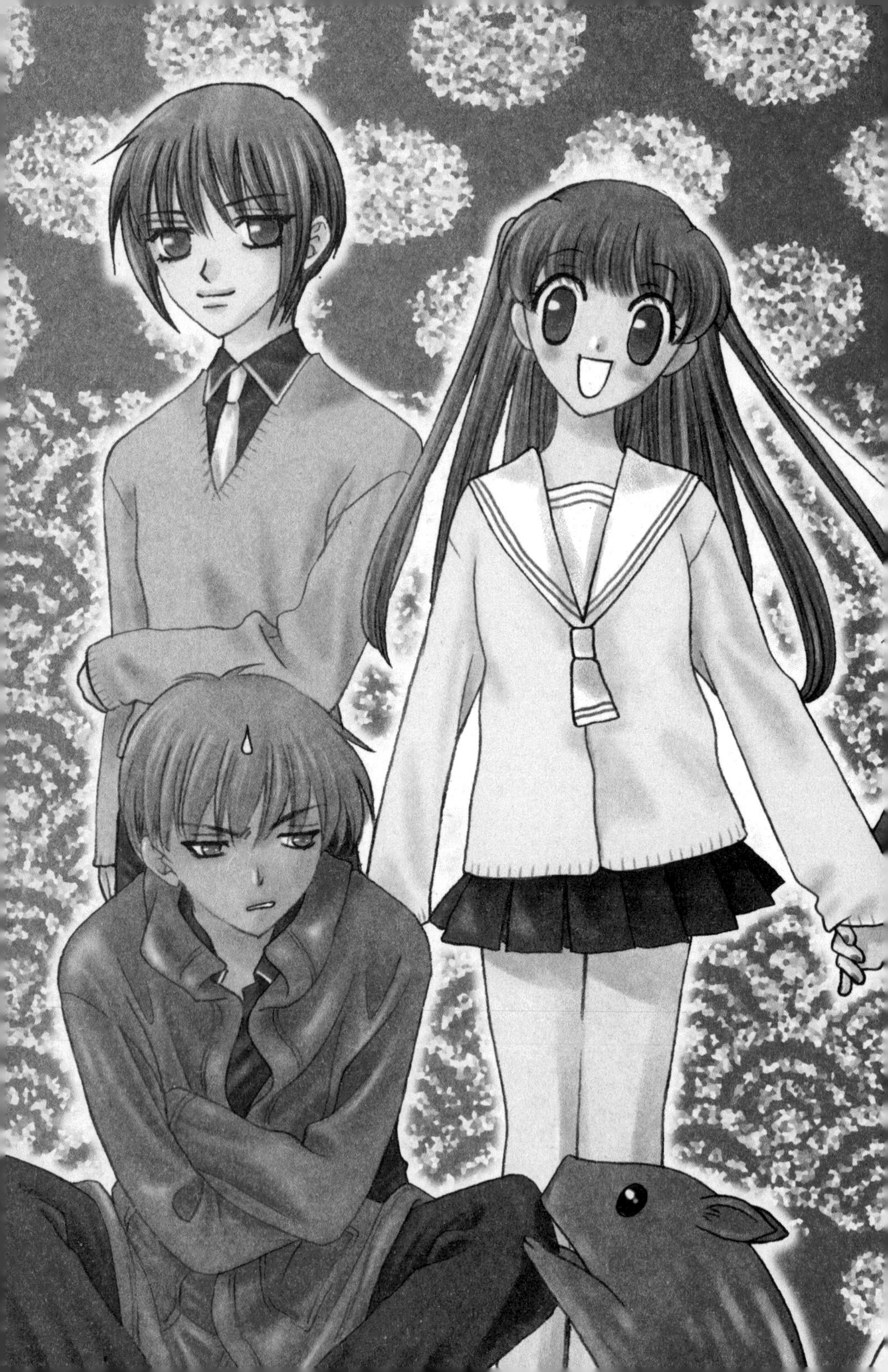

COLLECTOR'S EDITION

Fruits Basket

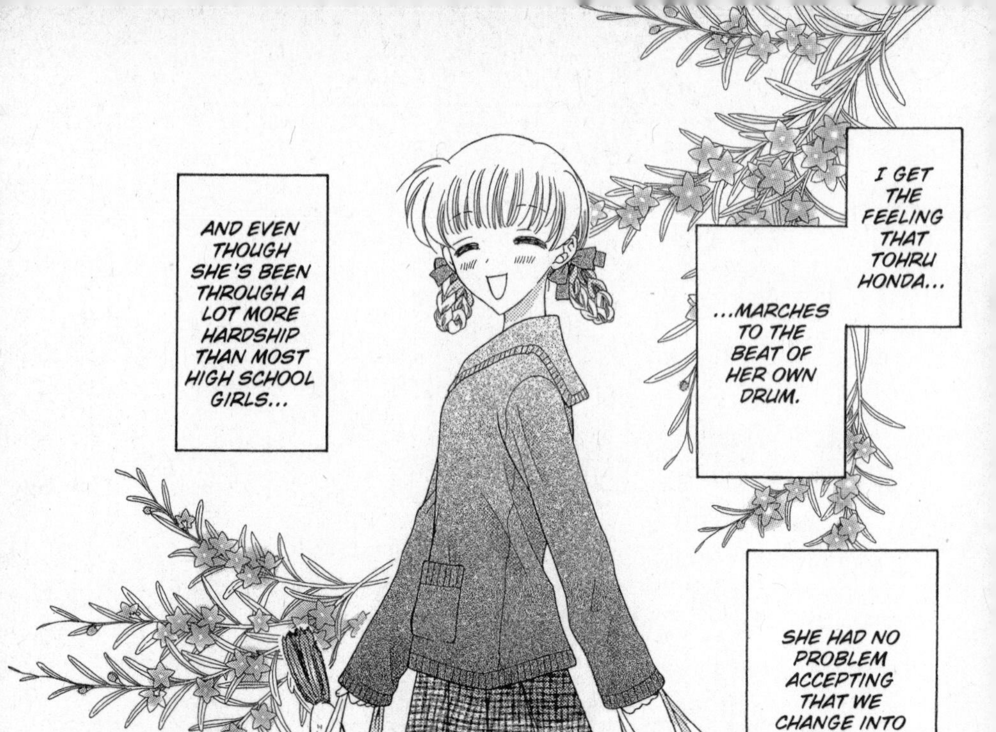
I GET THE FEELING THAT TOHRU HONDA...
...MARCHES TO THE BEAT OF HER OWN DRUM.
SHE HAD NO PROBLEM ACCEPTING THAT WE CHANGE INTO ANIMALS.
AND EVEN THOUGH SHE'S BEEN THROUGH A LOT MORE HARDSHIP THAN MOST HIGH SCHOOL GIRLS...
...SHE'S ALWAYS SMILING, AS IF NONE OF IT WEIGHS HER DOWN.
C'MON OVER

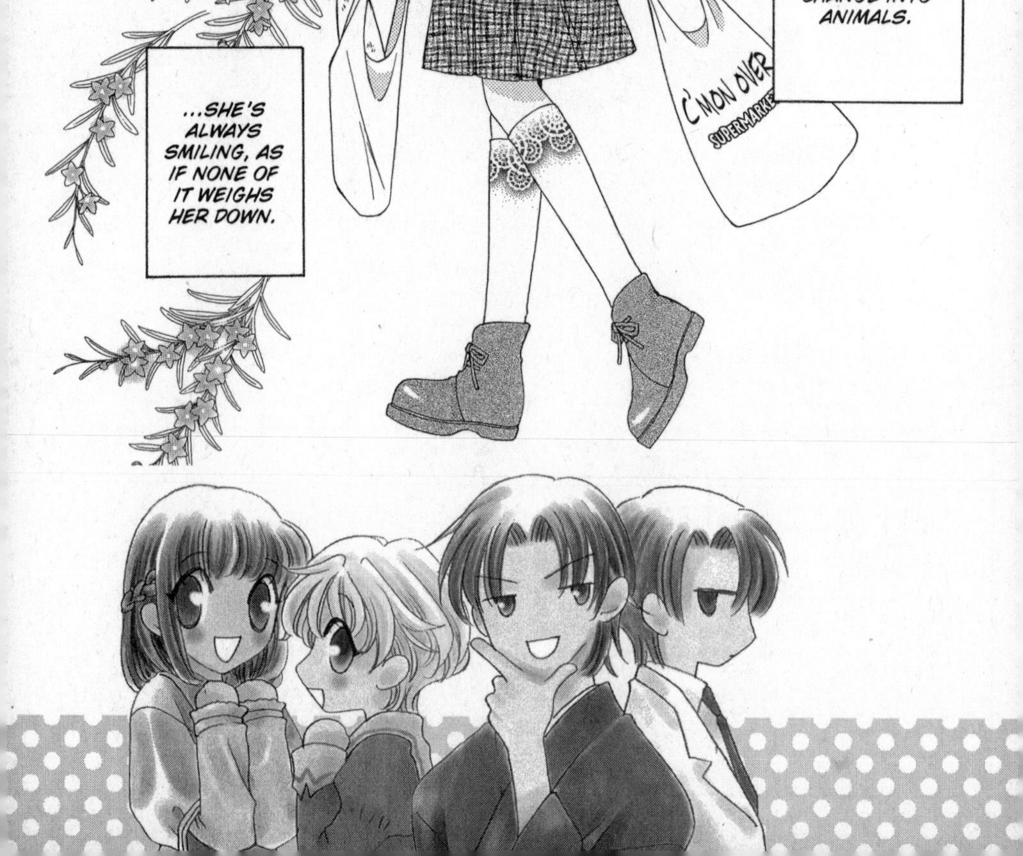

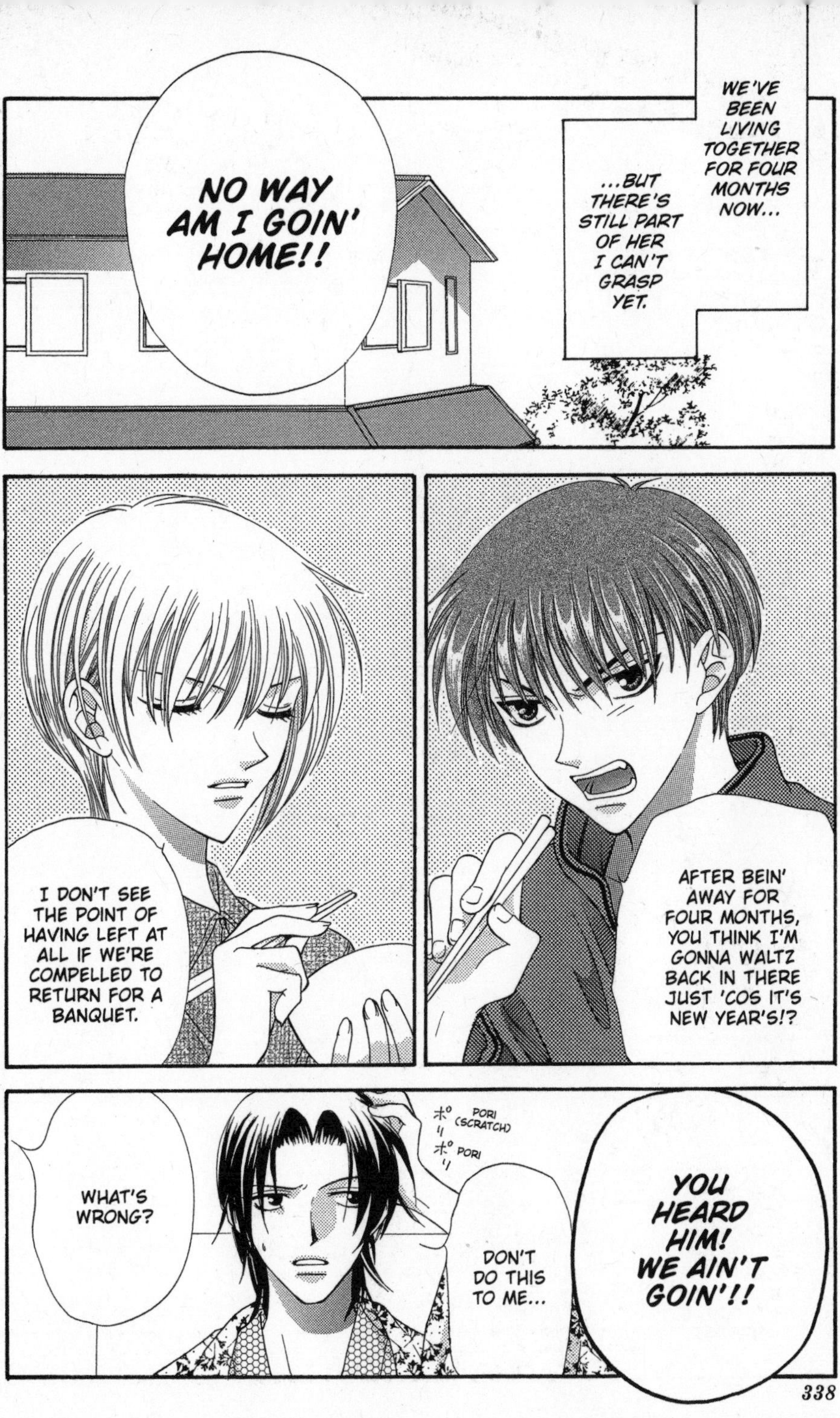
WE'VE BEEN LIVING TOGETHER FOR FOUR MONTHS NOW...
...BUT THERE'S STILL PART OF HER I CAN'T GRASP YET.
NO WAY AM I GOIN' HOME!!
AFTER BEIN' AWAY FOR FOUR MONTHS, YOU THINK I'M GONNA WALTZ BACK IN THERE JUST 'COS IT'S NEW YEAR'S!?
I DON'T SEE THE POINT OF HAVING LEFT AT ALL IF WE'RE COMPELLED TO RETURN FOR A BANQUET.
YOU HEARD HIM! WE AIN'T GOIN'!!
DON'T DO THIS TO ME...
ポリ PORI (SCRATCH)
ポリ PORI
WHAT'S WRONG?

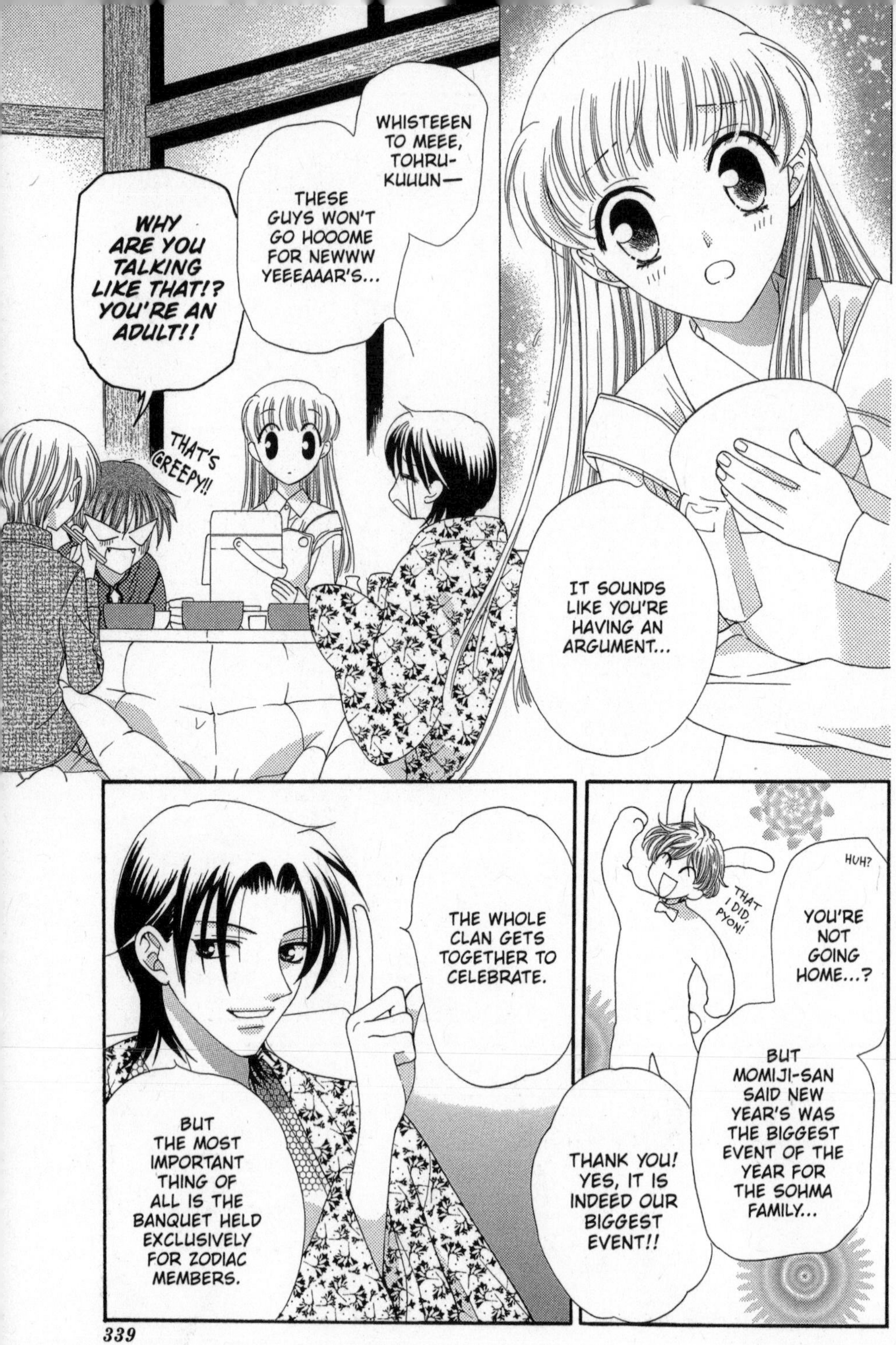
IT SOUNDS LIKE YOU'RE HAVING AN ARGUMENT...
WHISTEEEN TO MEEE, TOHRU-KUUUN—
THESE GUYS WON'T GO HOOOME FOR NEWWW YEEEAAAR'S...
WHY ARE YOU TALKING LIKE THAT!? YOU'RE AN ADULT!!
THAT'S CREEPY!!
HUH?
YOU'RE NOT GOING HOME...?
THAT I DID, PYON!
BUT MOMIJI-SAN SAID NEW YEAR'S WAS THE BIGGEST EVENT OF THE YEAR FOR THE SOHMA FAMILY...
THANK YOU! YES, IT IS INDEED OUR BIGGEST EVENT!!
THE WHOLE CLAN GETS TOGETHER TO CELEBRATE.
BUT THE MOST IMPORTANT THING OF ALL IS THE BANQUET HELD EXCLUSIVELY FOR ZODIAC MEMBERS.

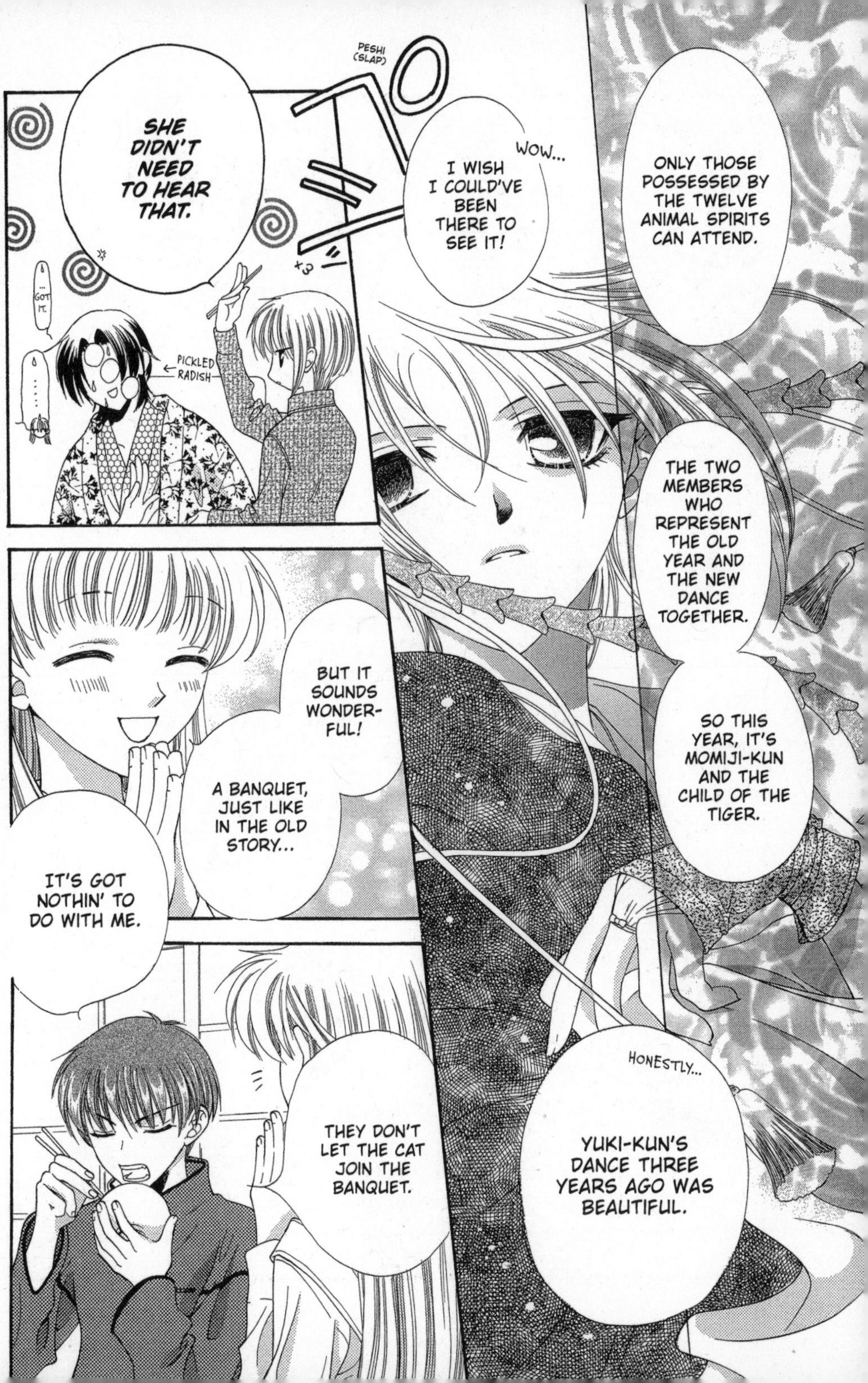
ONLY THOSE POSSESSED BY THE TWELVE ANIMAL SPIRITS CAN ATTEND.
THE TWO MEMBERS WHO REPRESENT THE OLD YEAR AND THE NEW DANCE TOGETHER.
SO THIS YEAR, IT'S MOMIJI-KUN AND THE CHILD OF THE TIGER.
HONESTLY...
YUKI-KUN'S DANCE THREE YEARS AGO WAS BEAUTIFUL.
WOW...
I WISH I COULD'VE BEEN THERE TO SEE IT!
PESHI (SLAP)
×3
SHE DIDN'T NEED TO HEAR THAT.
...GOT IT.
......
PICKLED RADISH
BUT IT SOUNDS WONDERFUL!
A BANQUET, JUST LIKE IN THE OLD STORY...
IT'S GOT NOTHIN' TO DO WITH ME.
THEY DON'T LET THE CAT JOIN THE BANQUET.

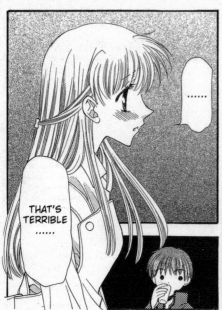

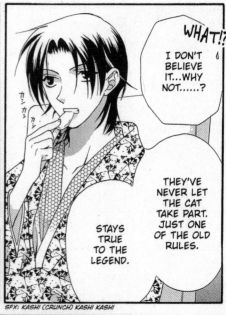

WHAT!?
I DON'T BELIEVE IT...WHY NOT......?
THEY'VE NEVER LET THE CAT TAKE PART. JUST ONE OF THE OLD RULES.
STAYS TRUE TO THE LEGEND.
SFX: KASHI (CRUNCH) KASHI KASHI
......
THAT'S TERRIBLE ......
...YOU DON'T GOTTA LOOK SO HANGDOG ABOUT IT.
IT AIN'T LIKE I REFUSE TO GO BACK BECAUSE THEY WON'T LET ME ATTEND THEIR STUPID BANQUET.
IT'S BECAUSE HE KNOWS KAGURA WOULD BE SO EXCITED THAT SHE'D BEAT HIM HALF TO DEATH.
DON'T SAY IT!!
......
PATA (PAT)
THAT ASIDE...

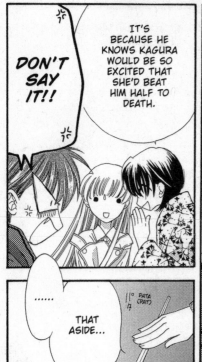

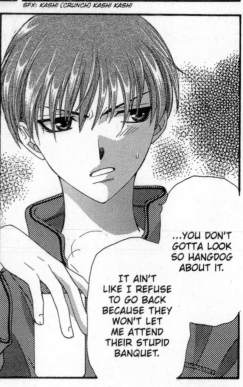

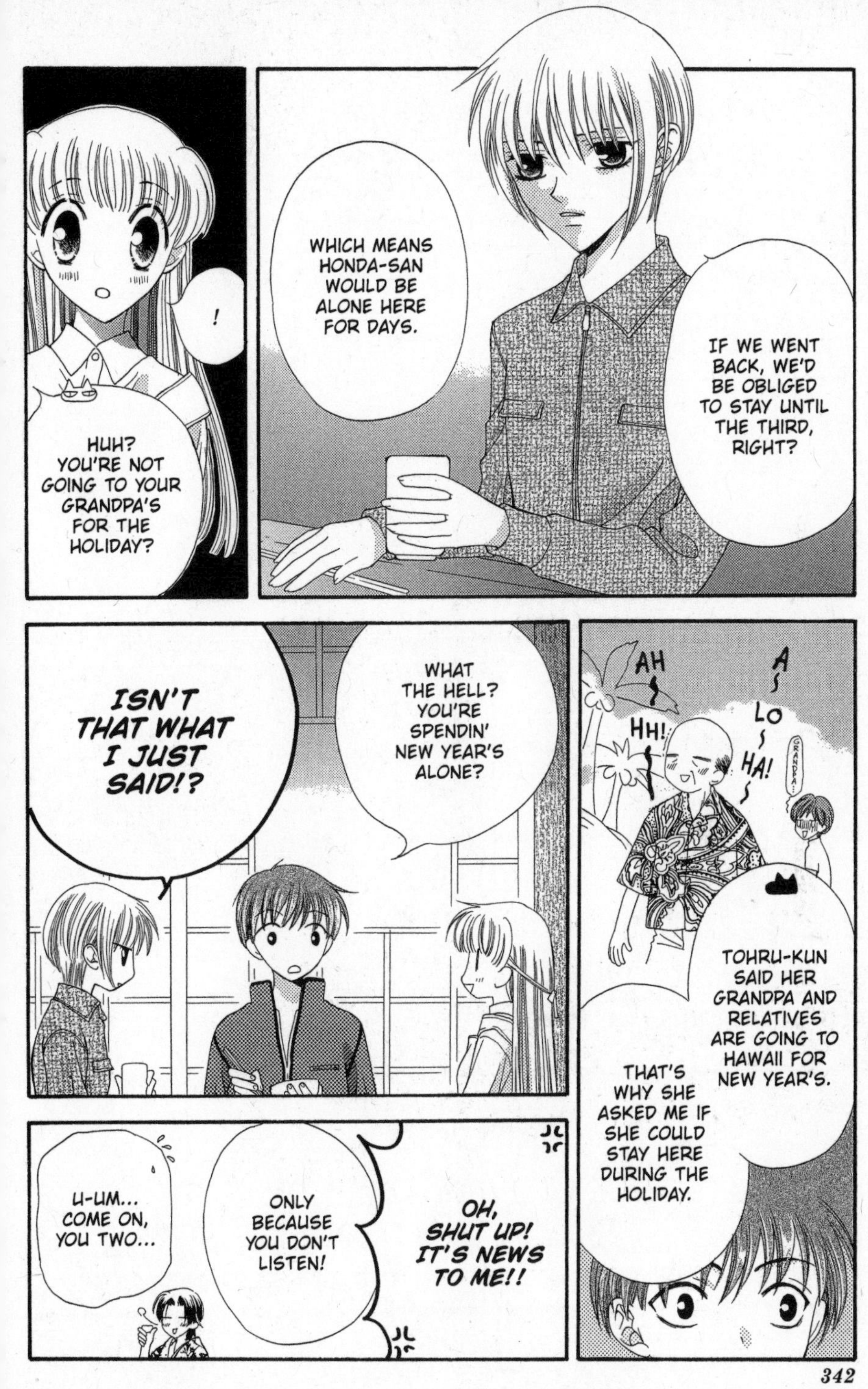
IF WE WENT BACK, WE'D BE OBLIGED TO STAY UNTIL THE THIRD, RIGHT?
WHICH MEANS HONDA-SAN WOULD BE ALONE HERE FOR DAYS.
!
HUH? YOU'RE NOT GOING TO YOUR GRANDPA'S FOR THE HOLIDAY?
A~LO~HA!
AH~HH!
GRANDPA...
TOHRU-KUN SAID HER GRANDPA AND RELATIVES ARE GOING TO HAWAII FOR NEW YEAR'S.
THAT'S WHY SHE ASKED ME IF SHE COULD STAY HERE DURING THE HOLIDAY.
WHAT THE HELL? YOU'RE SPENDIN' NEW YEAR'S ALONE?
ISN'T THAT WHAT I JUST SAID!?
OH, SHUT UP! IT'S NEWS TO ME!!
ONLY BECAUSE YOU DON'T LISTEN!
U-UM... COME ON, YOU TWO...

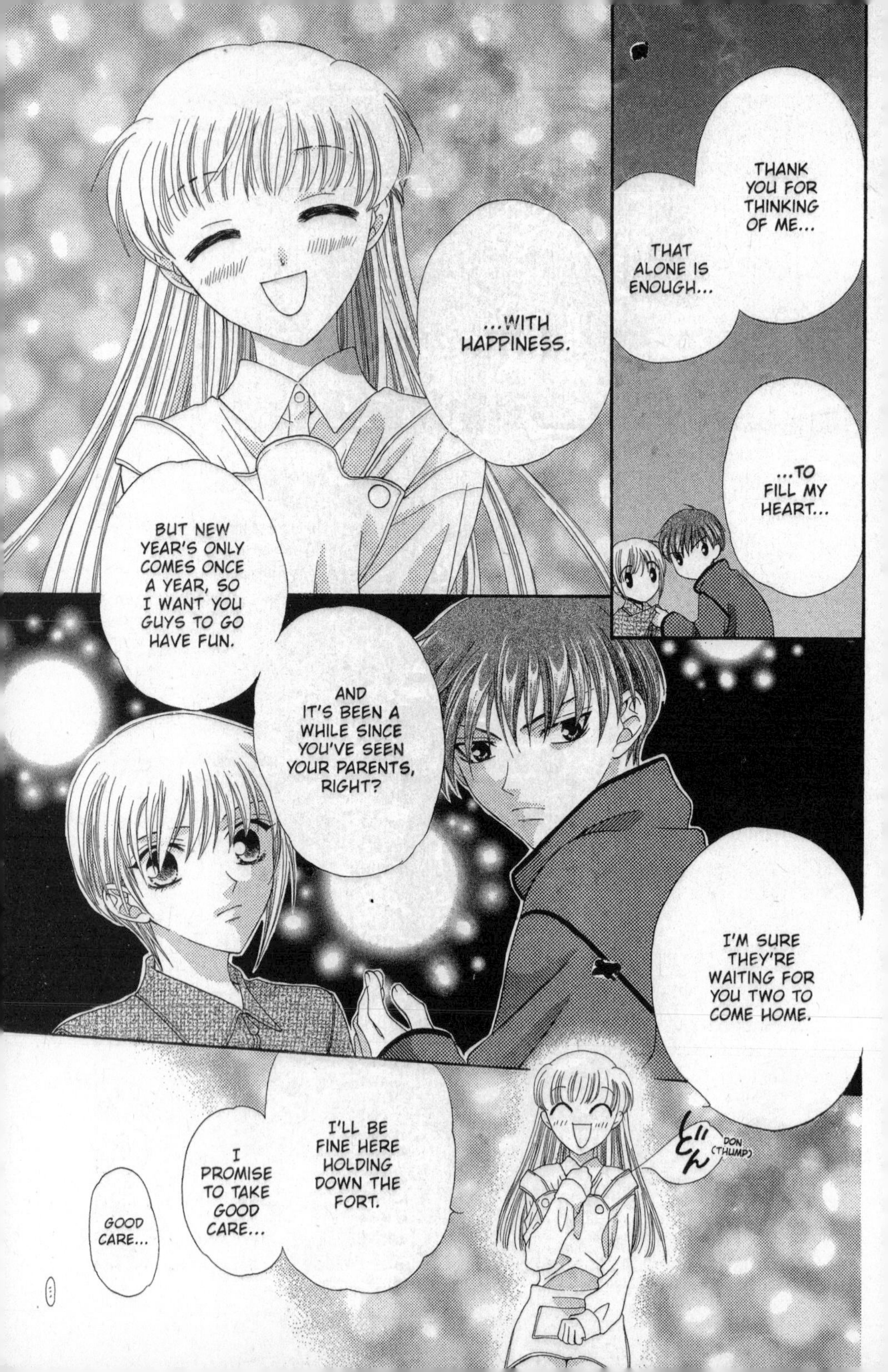
THANK YOU FOR THINKING OF ME...
THAT ALONE IS ENOUGH...
...TO FILL MY HEART...
...WITH HAPPINESS.
BUT NEW YEAR'S ONLY COMES ONCE A YEAR, SO I WANT YOU GUYS TO GO HAVE FUN.
AND IT'S BEEN A WHILE SINCE YOU'VE SEEN YOUR PARENTS, RIGHT?
I'M SURE THEY'RE WAITING FOR YOU TWO TO COME HOME.
どん
DON (THUMP)
I'LL BE FINE HERE HOLDING DOWN THE FORT.
I PROMISE TO TAKE GOOD CARE...
GOOD CARE...
...

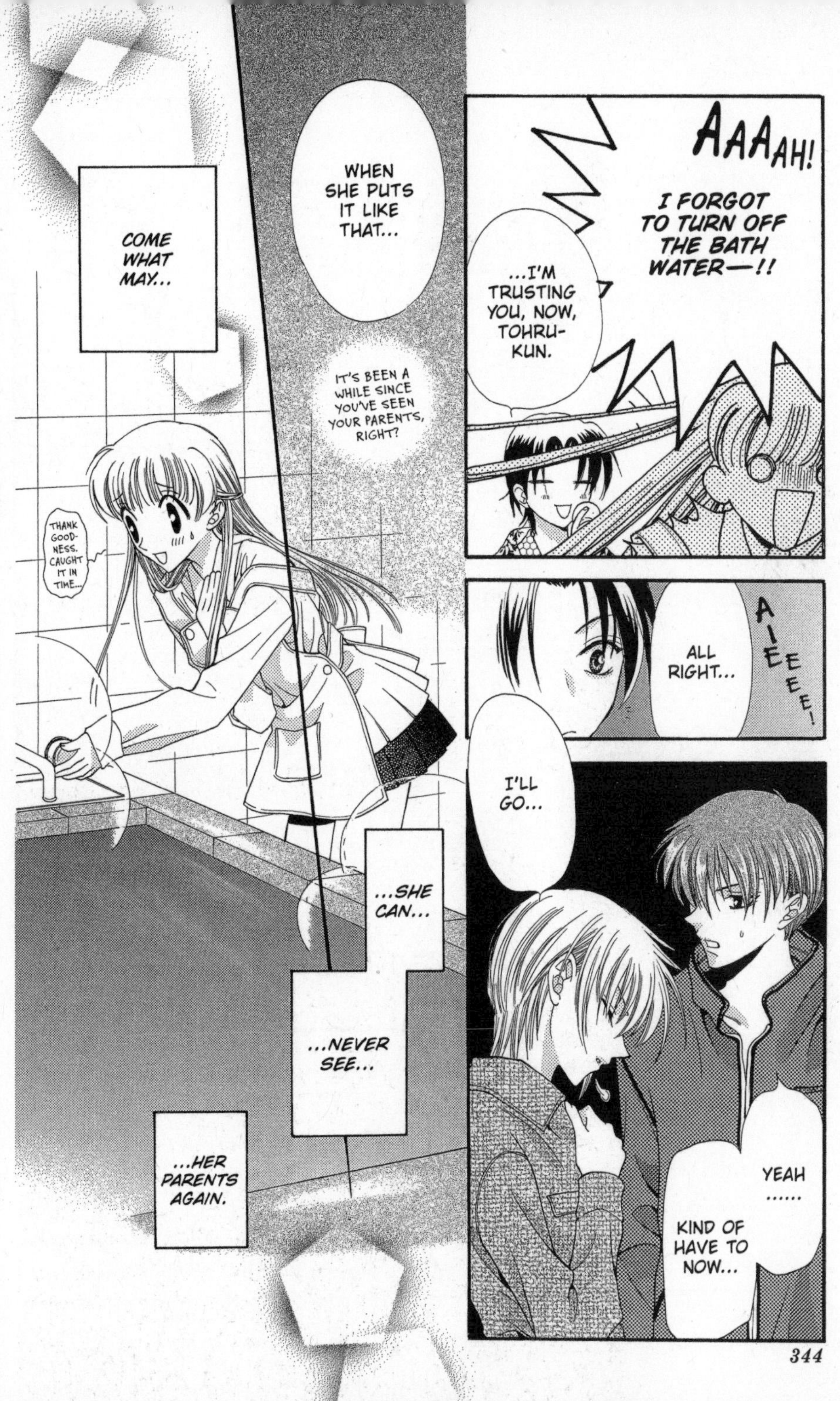
AAAAH!
I FORGOT TO TURN OFF THE BATH WATER—!!
...I'M TRUSTING YOU, NOW, TOHRU-KUN.
AIEEEE!
ALL RIGHT...
I'LL GO...
YEAH ...... KIND OF HAVE TO NOW...
WHEN SHE PUTS IT LIKE THAT...
IT'S BEEN A WHILE SINCE YOU'VE SEEN YOUR PARENTS, RIGHT?
COME WHAT MAY...
THANK GOODNESS. CAUGHT IT IN TIME...
...SHE CAN...
...NEVER SEE...
...HER PARENTS AGAIN.

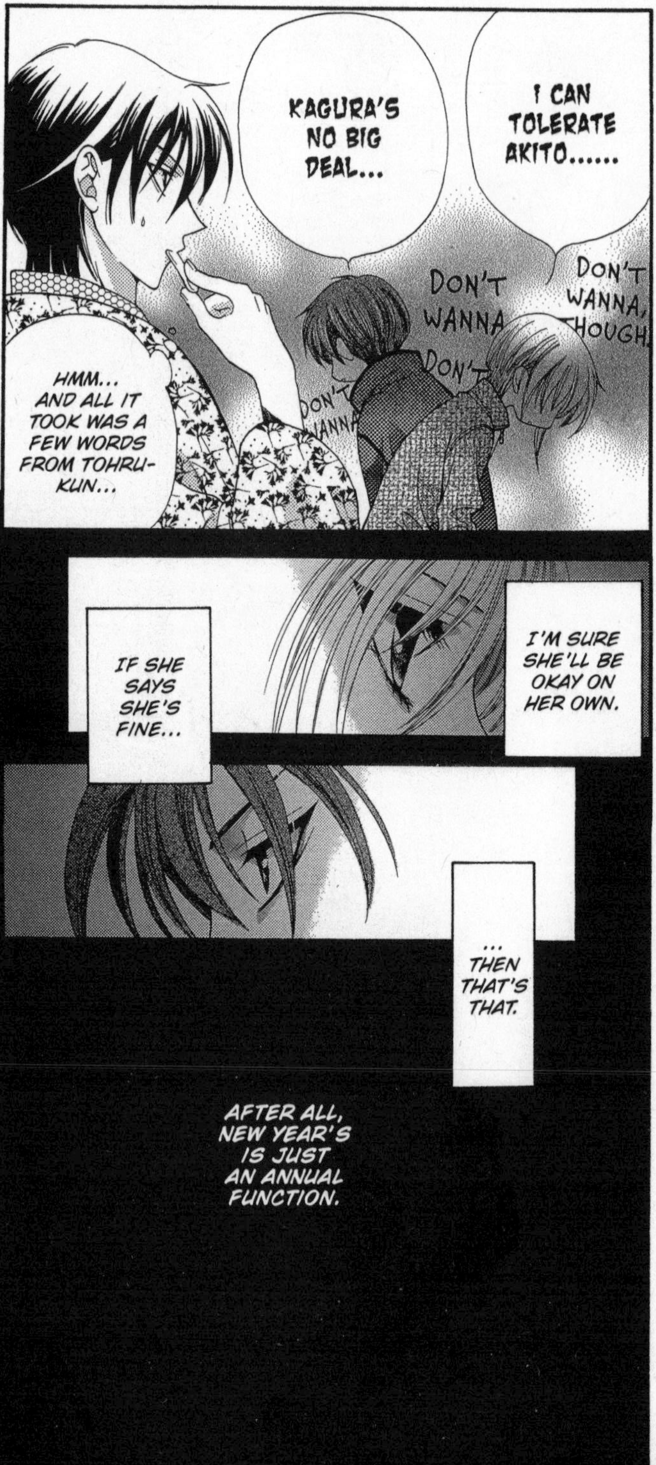
I CAN TOLERATE AKITO......
KAGURA'S NO BIG DEAL...
DON'T WANNA, THOUGH
DON'T WANNA
DON'T
DON'T WANNA
HMM... AND ALL IT TOOK WAS A FEW WORDS FROM TOHRU-KUN...
I'M SURE SHE'LL BE OKAY ON HER OWN.
IF SHE SAYS SHE'S FINE...
...THEN THAT'S THAT.
AFTER ALL, NEW YEAR'S IS JUST AN ANNUAL FUNCTION.
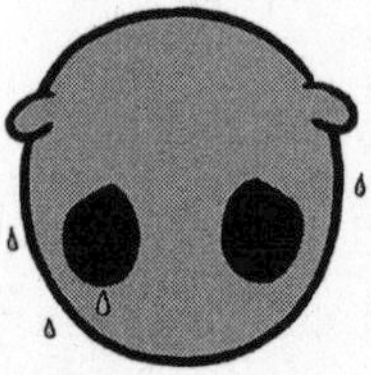

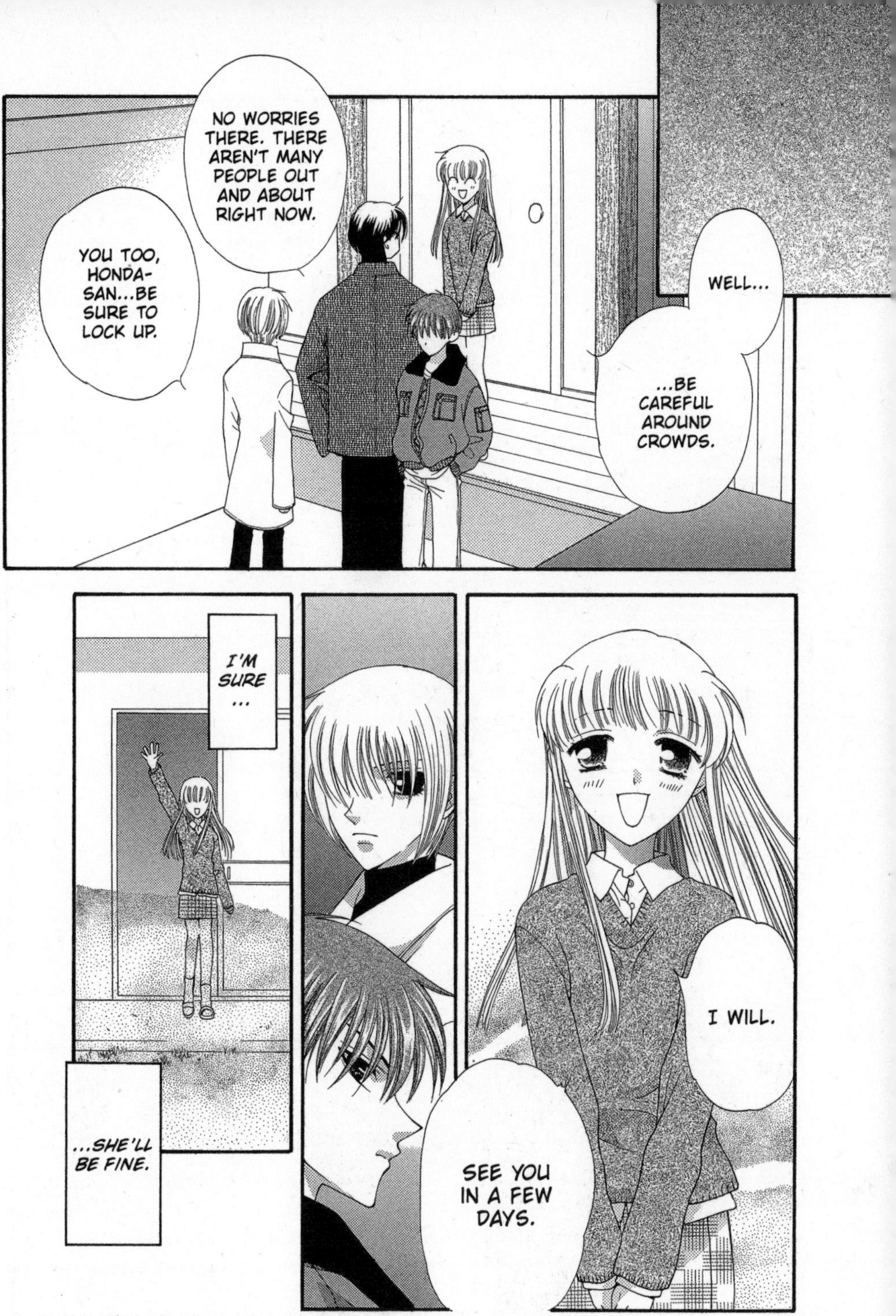
WELL...
...BE CAREFUL AROUND CROWDS.
NO WORRIES THERE. THERE AREN'T MANY PEOPLE OUT AND ABOUT RIGHT NOW.
YOU TOO, HONDA-SAN...BE SURE TO LOCK UP.
I WILL.
SEE YOU IN A FEW DAYS.
I'M SURE ...
...SHE'LL BE FINE.

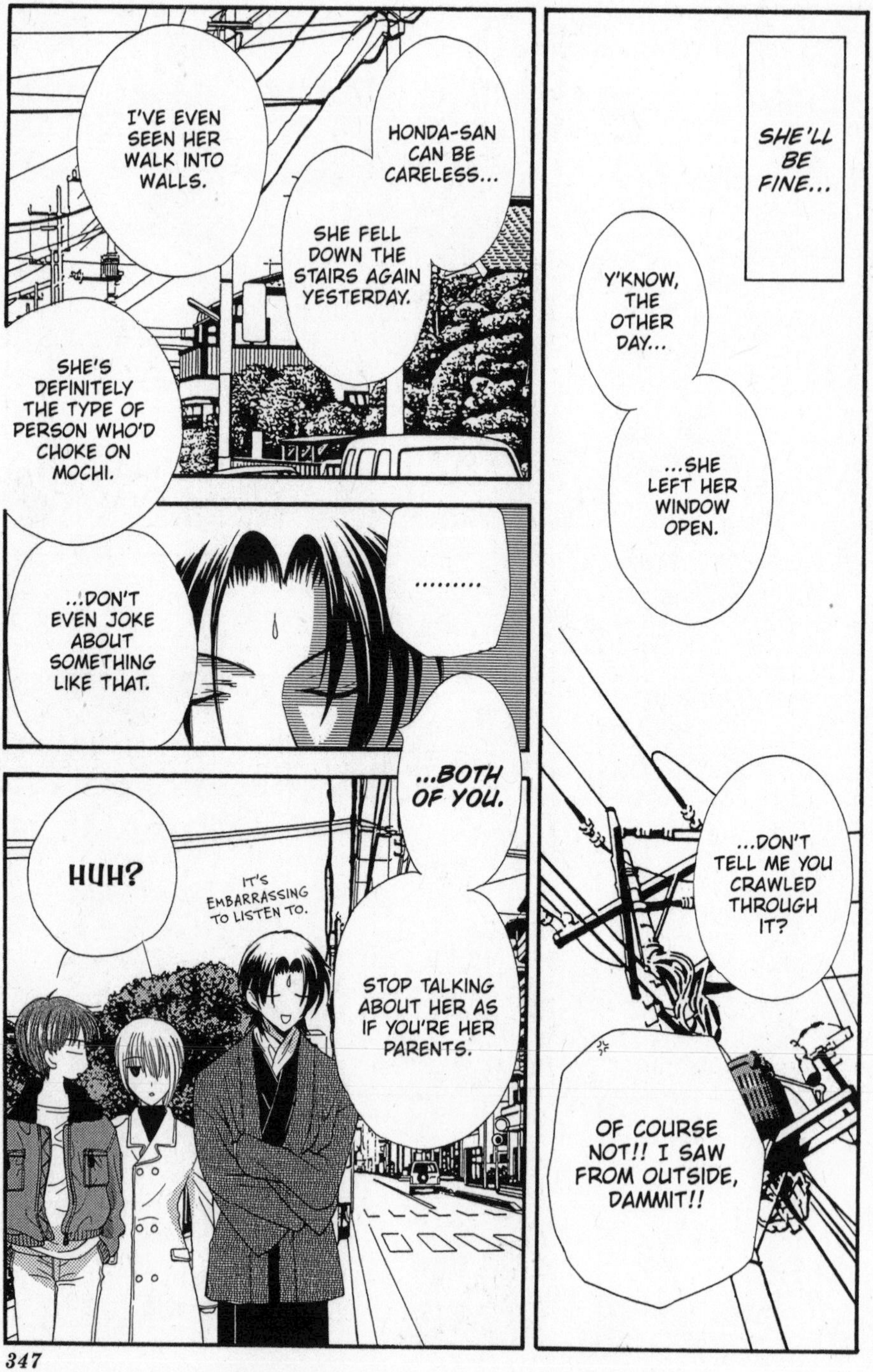
SHE'LL BE FINE...
Y'KNOW, THE OTHER DAY...
...SHE LEFT HER WINDOW OPEN.
...DON'T TELL ME YOU CRAWLED THROUGH IT?
OF COURSE NOT!! I SAW FROM OUTSIDE, DAMMIT!!
HONDA-SAN CAN BE CARELESS...
I'VE EVEN SEEN HER WALK INTO WALLS.
SHE FELL DOWN THE STAIRS AGAIN YESTERDAY.
SHE'S DEFINITELY THE TYPE OF PERSON WHO'D CHOKE ON MOCHI.
....
...DON'T EVEN JOKE ABOUT SOMETHING LIKE THAT.
...BOTH OF YOU.
STOP TALKING ABOUT HER AS IF YOU'RE HER PARENTS.
IT'S EMBARRASSING TO LISTEN TO.
HUH?

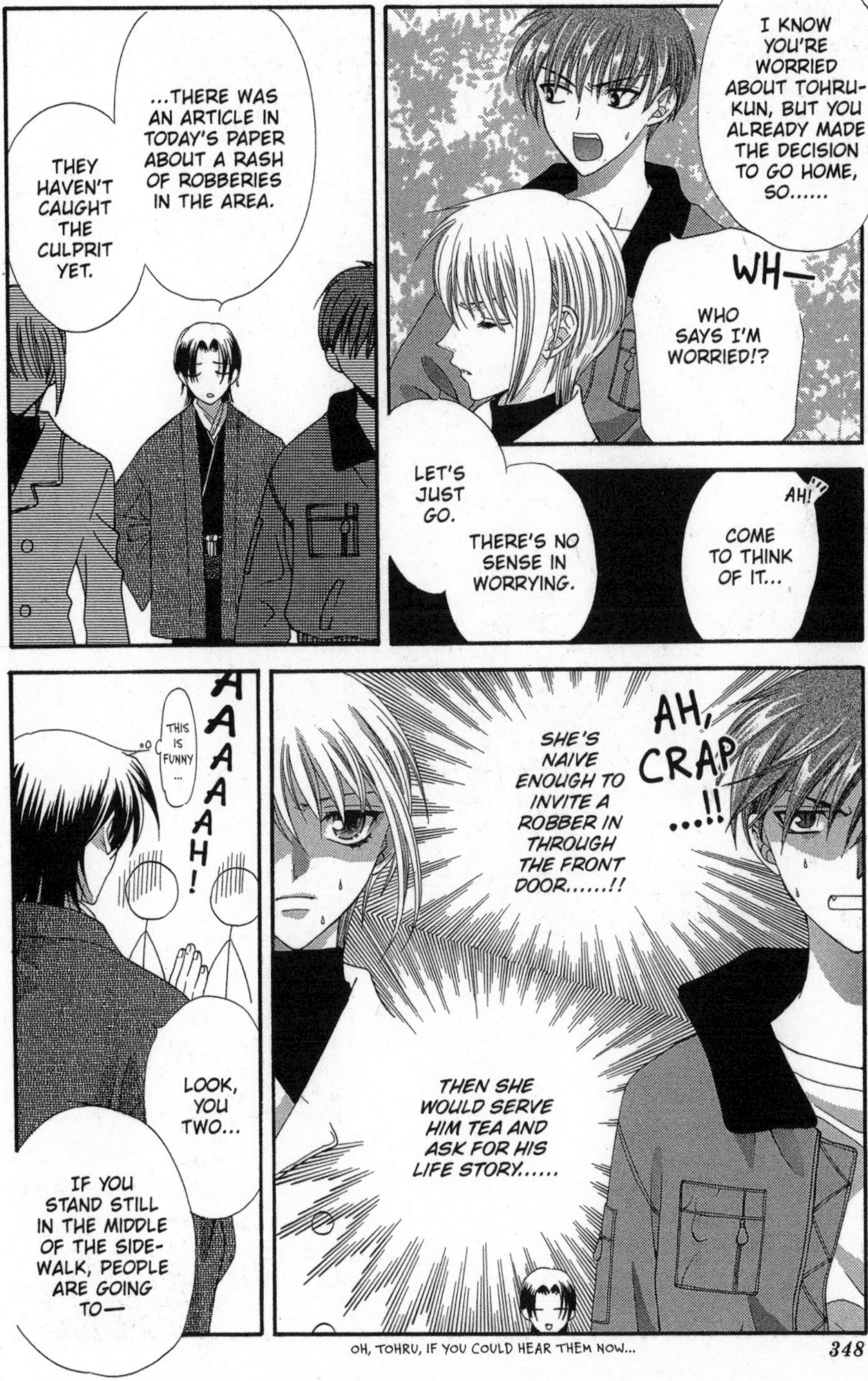
I KNOW YOU'RE WORRIED ABOUT TOHRU-KUN, BUT YOU ALREADY MADE THE DECISION TO GO HOME, SO......
WH—
WHO SAYS I'M WORRIED!?
LET'S JUST GO.
THERE'S NO SENSE IN WORRYING.
AH!
COME TO THINK OF IT...
...THERE WAS AN ARTICLE IN TODAY'S PAPER ABOUT A RASH OF ROBBERIES IN THE AREA.
THEY HAVEN'T CAUGHT THE CULPRIT YET.
AH, CRAP...!!
SHE'S NAIVE ENOUGH TO INVITE A ROBBER IN THROUGH THE FRONT DOOR......!!
THEN SHE WOULD SERVE HIM TEA AND ASK FOR HIS LIFE STORY......
AAAAAAH!
THIS IS FUNNY...
LOOK, YOU TWO...
IF YOU STAND STILL IN THE MIDDLE OF THE SIDE-WALK, PEOPLE ARE GOING TO—

OH, TOHRU, IF YOU COULD HEAR THEM NOW...

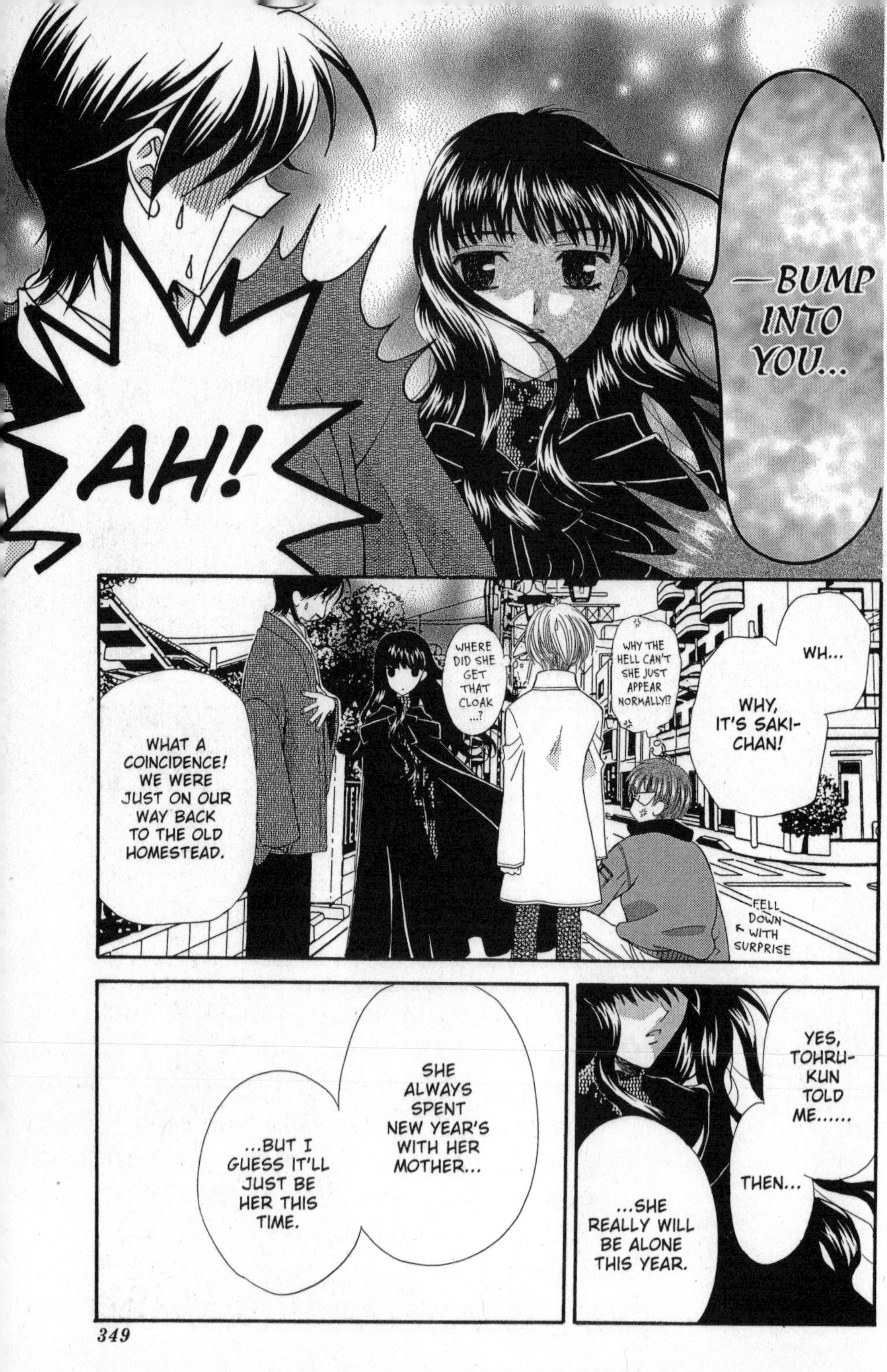
—BUMP INTO YOU...
AH!
WH...
WHY, IT'S SAKI-CHAN!
WHY THE HELL CAN'T SHE JUST APPEAR NORMALLY!?
FELL DOWN WITH SURPRISE
WHERE DID SHE GET THAT CLOAK ...?
WHAT A COINCIDENCE! WE WERE JUST ON OUR WAY BACK TO THE OLD HOMESTEAD.
YES, TOHRU-KUN TOLD ME......
THEN...
...SHE REALLY WILL BE ALONE THIS YEAR.
SHE ALWAYS SPENT NEW YEAR'S WITH HER MOTHER...
...BUT I GUESS IT'LL JUST BE HER THIS TIME.

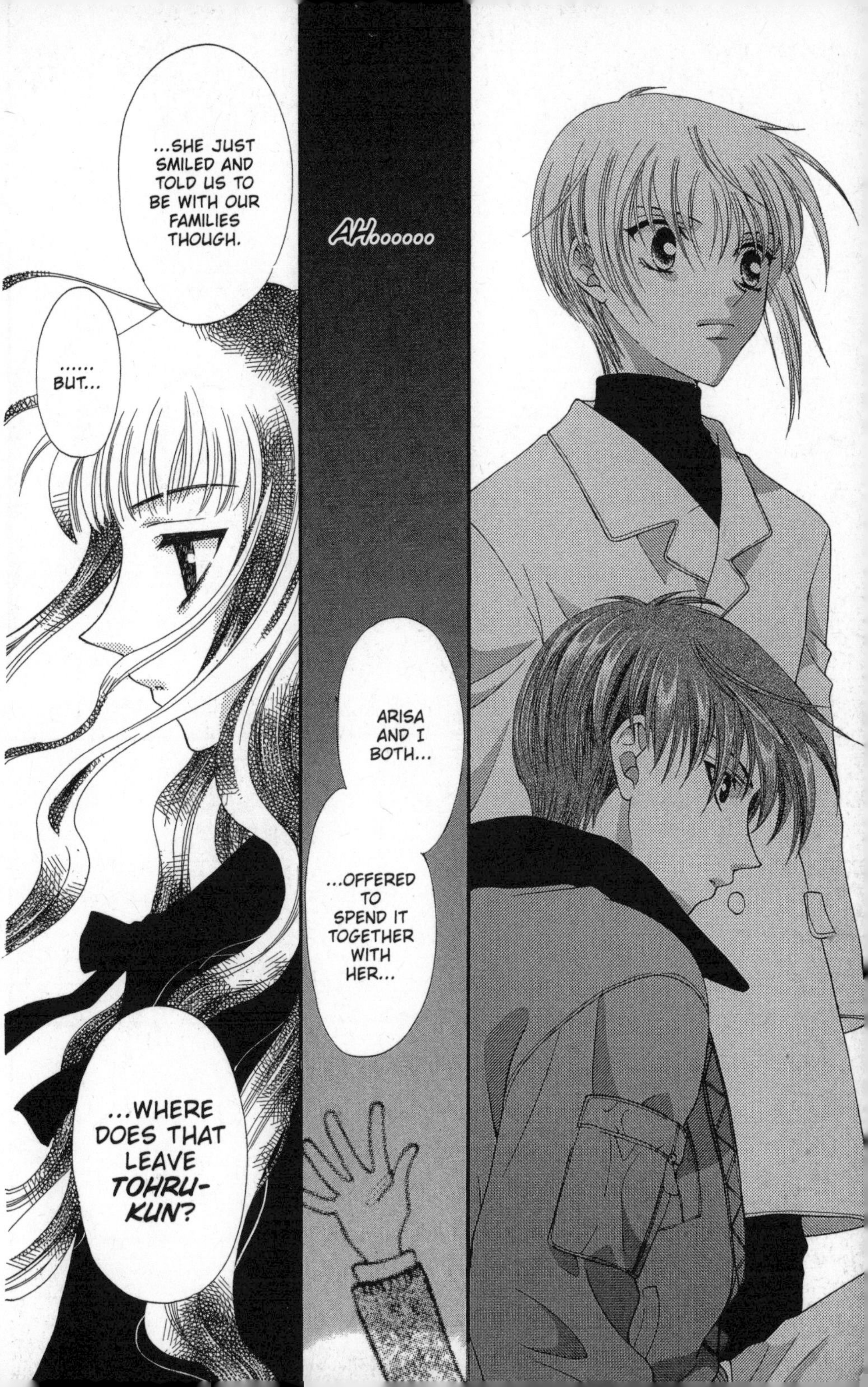
AHoooooo
ARISA AND I BOTH...
...OFFERED TO SPEND IT TOGETHER WITH HER...
...SHE JUST SMILED AND TOLD US TO BE WITH OUR FAMILIES THOUGH.
...... BUT...
...WHERE DOES THAT LEAVE *TOHRU-KUN?*

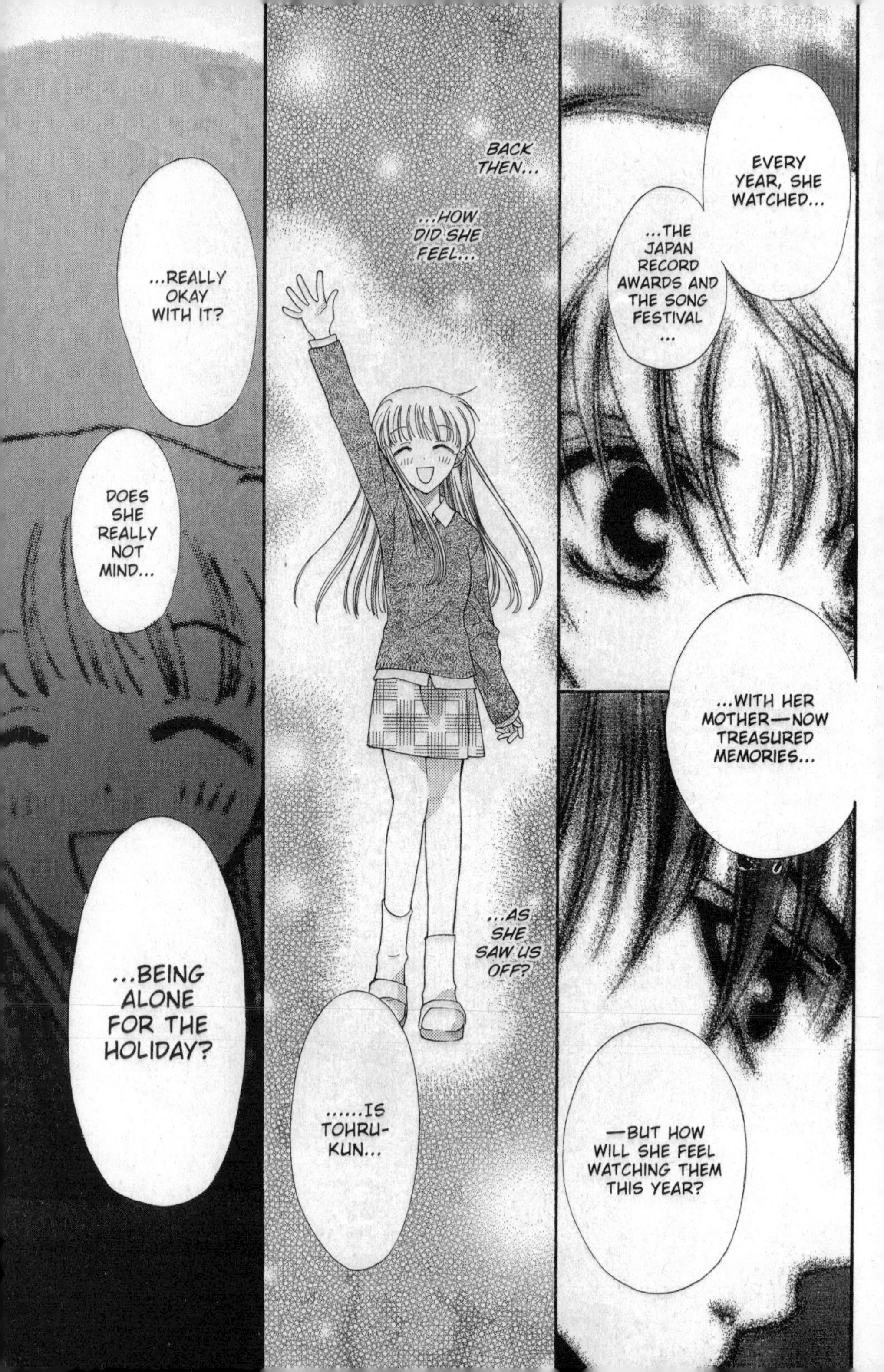
EVERY YEAR, SHE WATCHED...
...THE JAPAN RECORD AWARDS AND THE SONG FESTIVAL ...
...WITH HER MOTHER—NOW TREASURED MEMORIES...
—BUT HOW WILL SHE FEEL WATCHING THEM THIS YEAR?
BACK THEN...
...HOW DID SHE FEEL...
...AS SHE SAW US OFF?
......IS TOHRU-KUN...
...REALLY OKAY WITH IT?
DOES SHE REALLY NOT MIND...
...BEING ALONE FOR THE HOLIDAY?

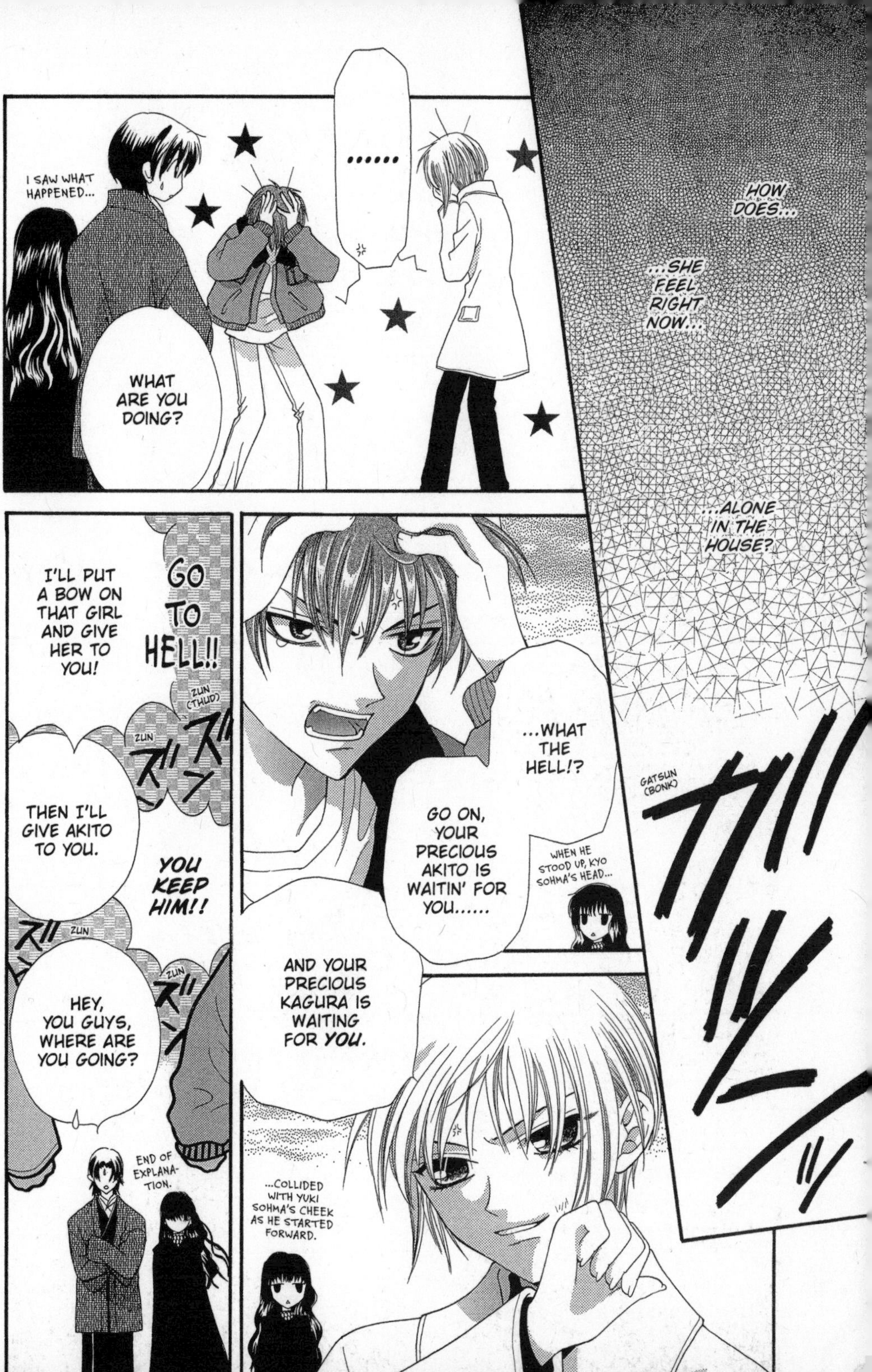
HOW DOES...
...SHE FEEL RIGHT NOW...
...ALONE IN THE HOUSE?
GATSUN (BONK)
......
I SAW WHAT HAPPENED...
WHAT ARE YOU DOING?
...WHAT THE HELL!?
GO ON, YOUR PRECIOUS AKITO IS WAITIN' FOR YOU......
WHEN HE STOOD UP, KYO SOHMA'S HEAD...
AND YOUR PRECIOUS KAGURA IS WAITING FOR YOU.
...COLLIDED WITH YUKI SOHMA'S CHEEK AS HE STARTED FORWARD.
GO TO HELL!!
I'LL PUT A BOW ON THAT GIRL AND GIVE HER TO YOU!
ZUN (THUD)
ZUN
YOU KEEP HIM!!
THEN I'LL GIVE AKITO TO YOU.
ZUN
ZUN
HEY, YOU GUYS, WHERE ARE YOU GOING?
END OF EXPLANATION.

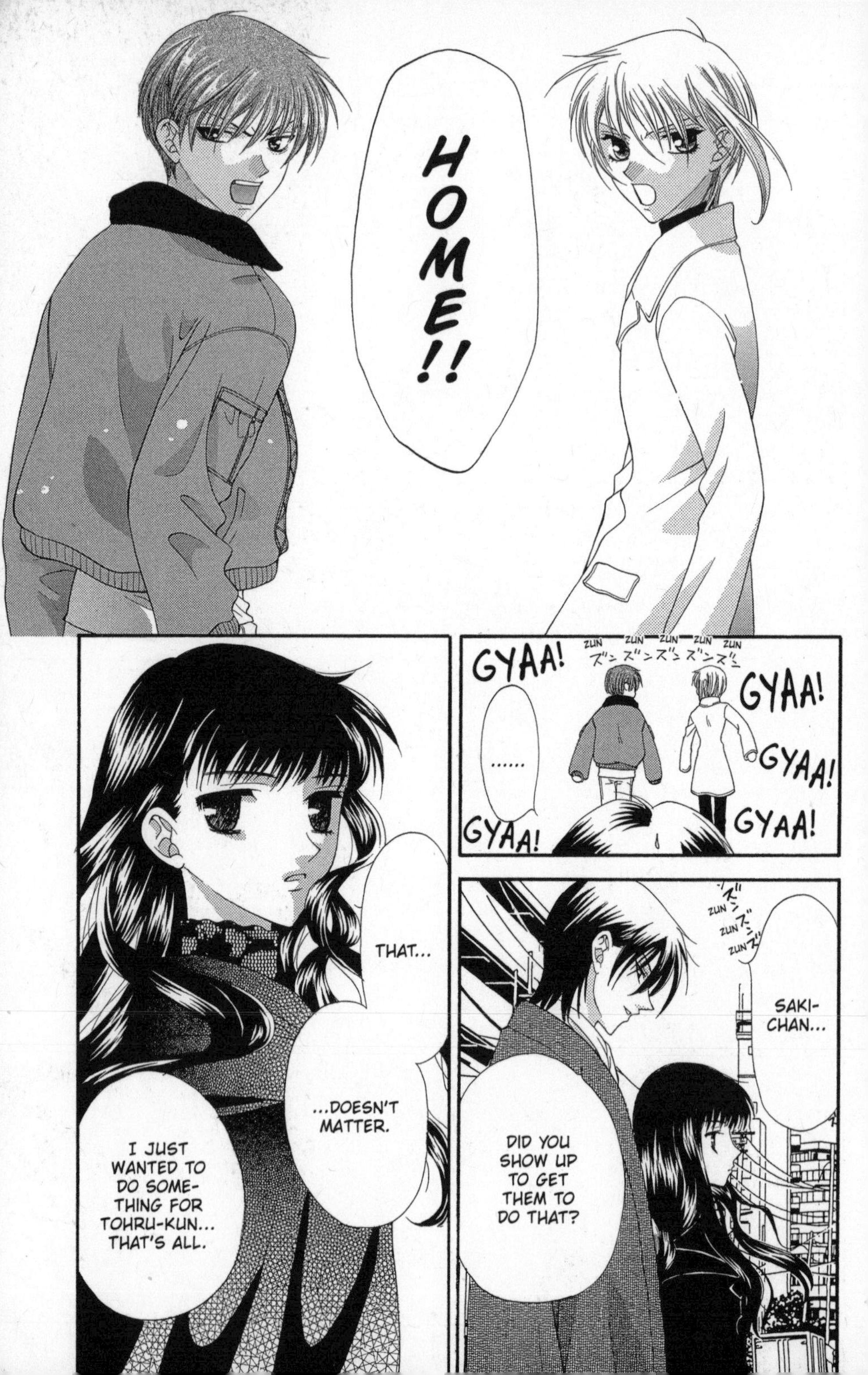
HOME!!
ZUN ZUN ZUN ZUN ZUN
GYAA!
GYAA!
GYAA!
GYAA!
......
GYAA!
ZUN ZUN ZUN
SAKI-CHAN...
DID YOU SHOW UP TO GET THEM TO DO THAT?
THAT...
...DOESN'T MATTER.
I JUST WANTED TO DO SOMETHING FOR TOHRU-KUN... THAT'S ALL.

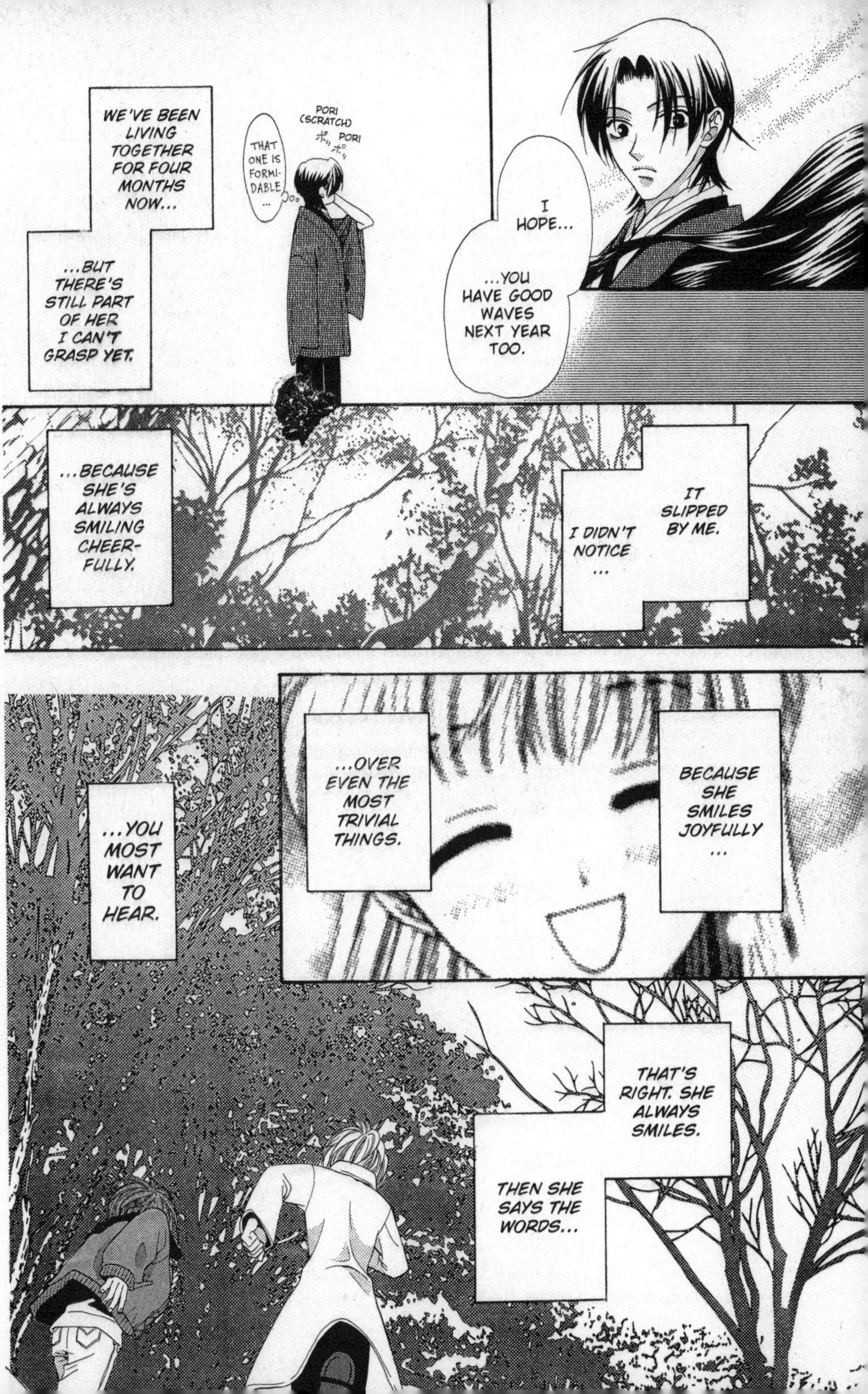
I HOPE...
...YOU HAVE GOOD WAVES NEXT YEAR TOO.
PORI (SCRATCH) PORI
THAT ONE IS FORMIDABLE...
WE'VE BEEN LIVING TOGETHER FOR FOUR MONTHS NOW...
...BUT THERE'S STILL PART OF HER I CAN'T GRASP YET.
IT SLIPPED BY ME.
I DIDN'T NOTICE...
...BECAUSE SHE'S ALWAYS SMILING CHEERFULLY.
BECAUSE SHE SMILES JOYFULLY...
...OVER EVEN THE MOST TRIVIAL THINGS.
THAT'S RIGHT. SHE ALWAYS SMILES.
THEN SHE SAYS THE WORDS...
...YOU MOST WANT TO HEAR.

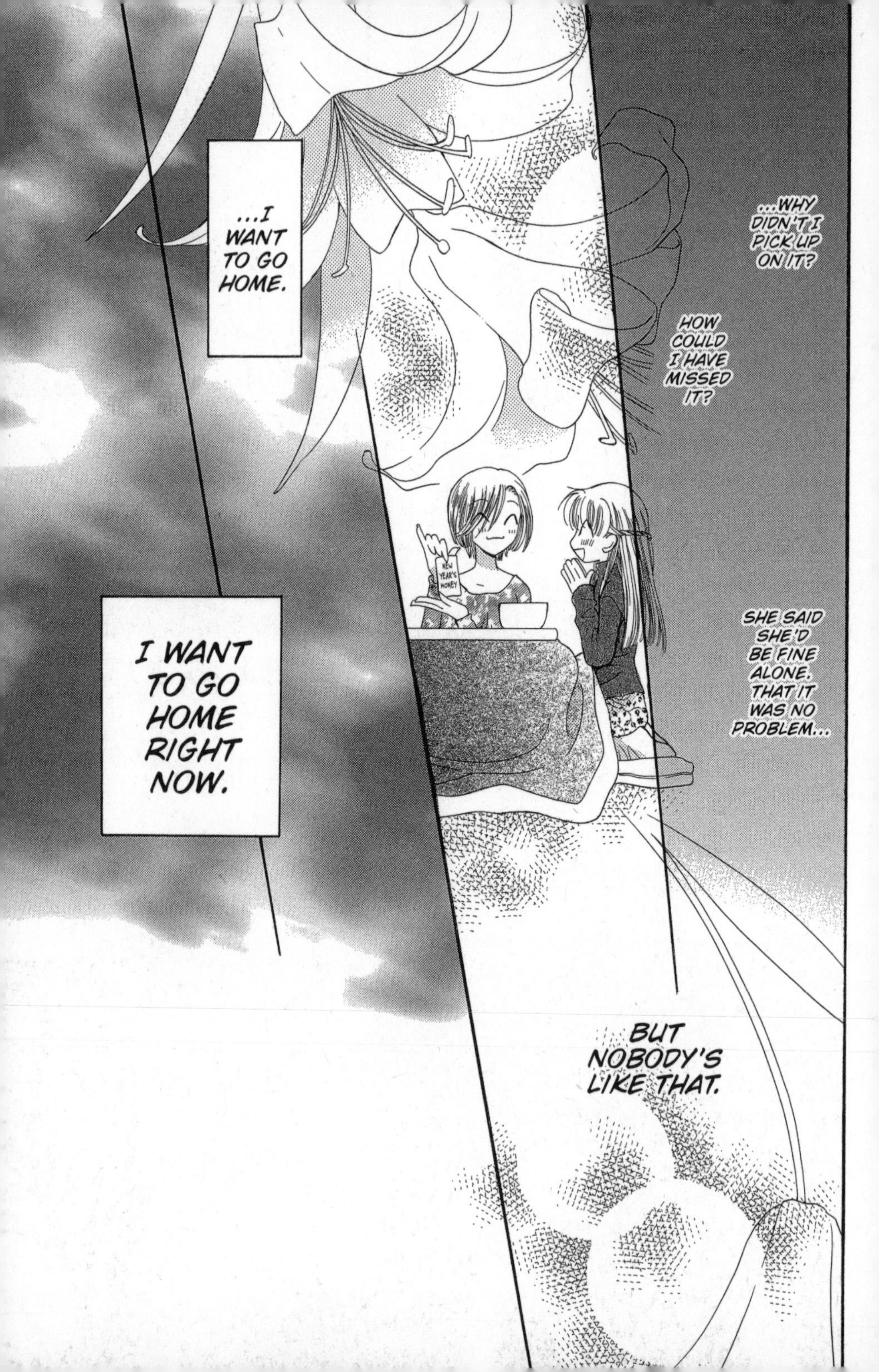
...WHY DIDN'T I PICK UP ON IT?
HOW COULD I HAVE MISSED IT?
SHE SAID SHE'D BE FINE ALONE. THAT IT WAS NO PROBLEM...
BUT NOBODY'S LIKE THAT.
NEW YEAR'S MONEY
...I WANT TO GO HOME.
I WANT TO GO HOME RIGHT NOW.

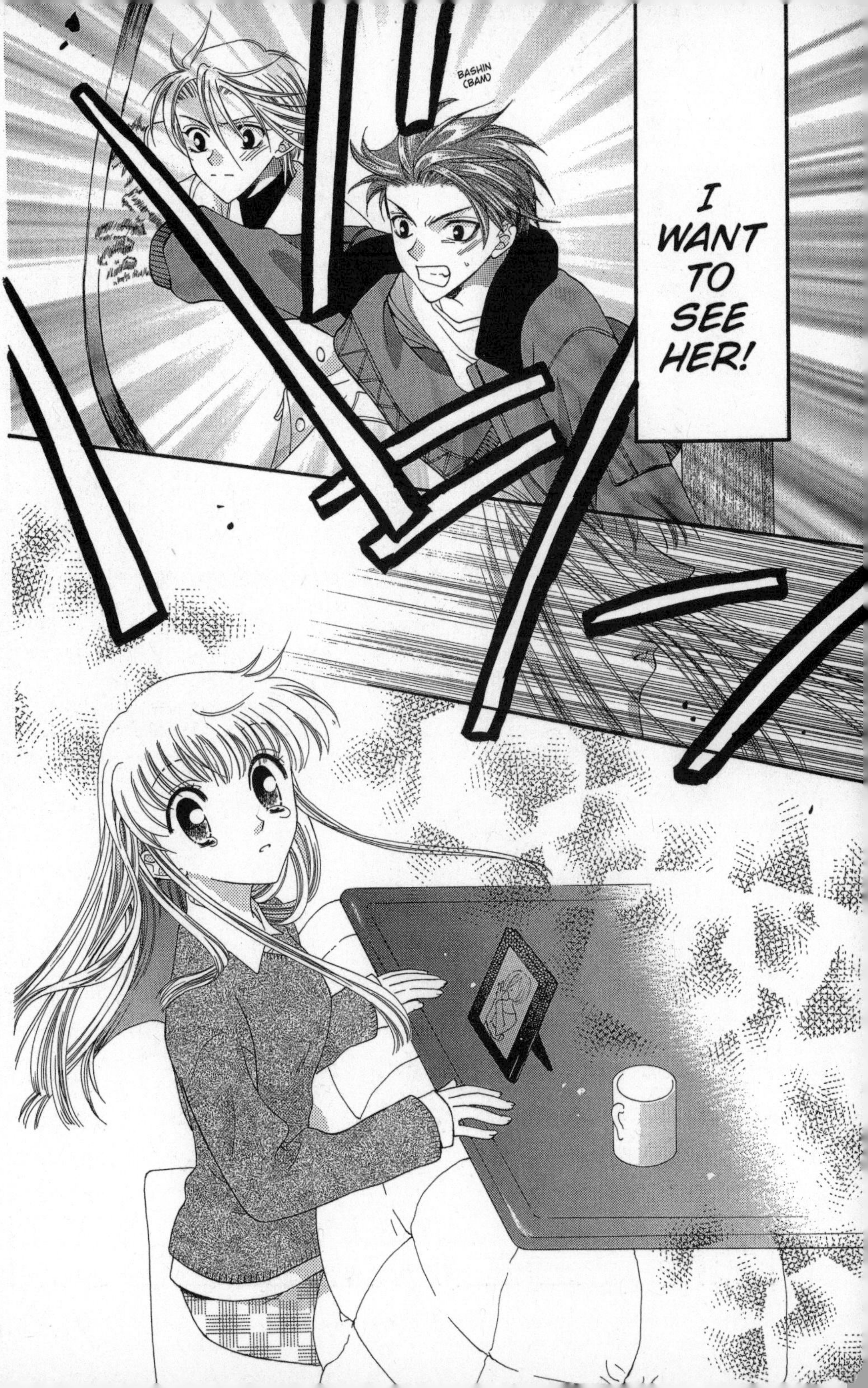
I WANT TO SEE HER!
BASHIN (BAM)

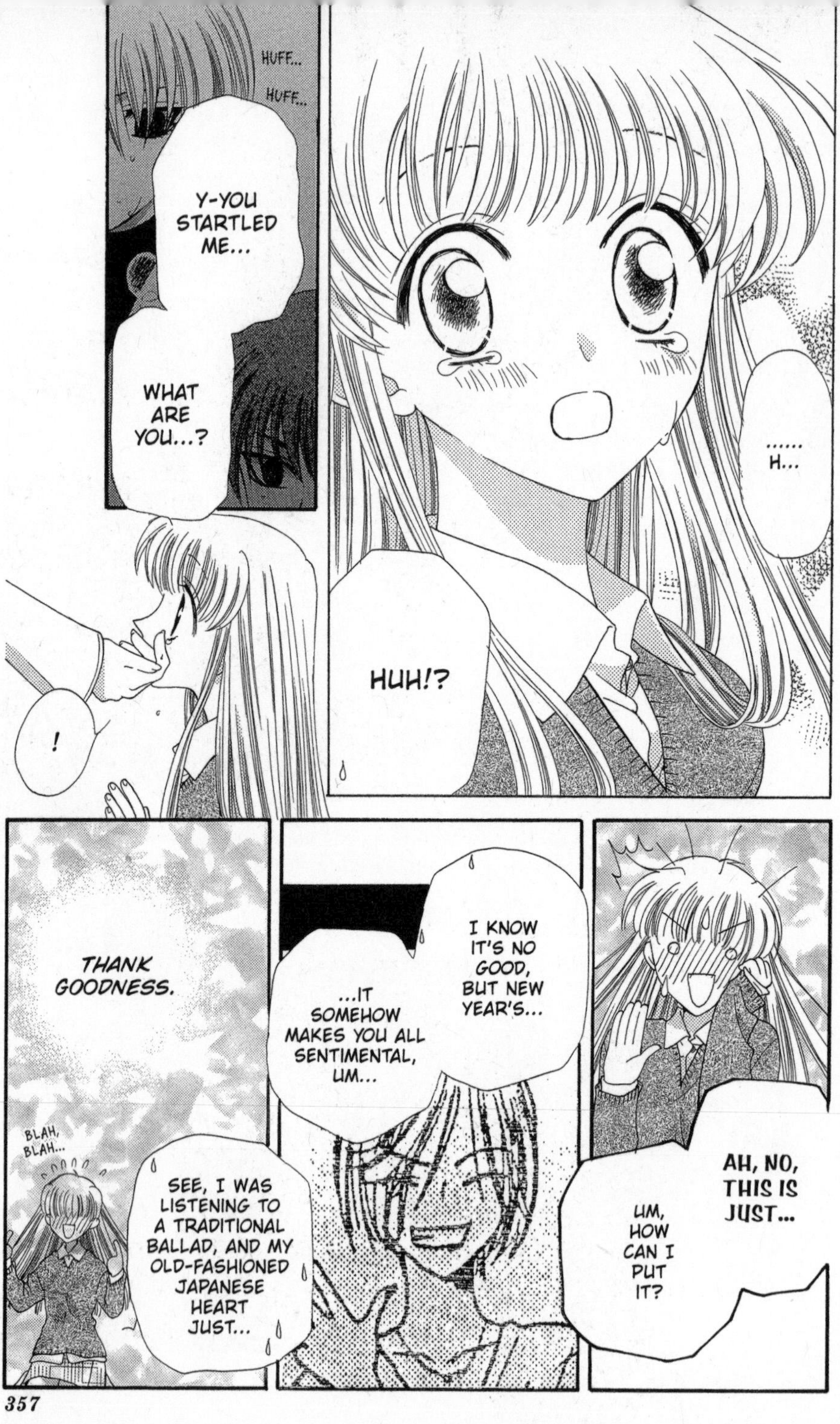
......
H...
HUH!?
HUFF...
HUFF...
Y-YOU STARTLED ME...
WHAT ARE YOU...?
!
AH, NO, THIS IS JUST...
UM, HOW CAN I PUT IT?
I KNOW IT'S NO GOOD, BUT NEW YEAR'S...
...IT SOMEHOW MAKES YOU ALL SENTIMENTAL, UM...
THANK GOODNESS.
BLAH, BLAH...
SEE, I WAS LISTENING TO A TRADITIONAL BALLAD, AND MY OLD-FASHIONED JAPANESE HEART JUST...

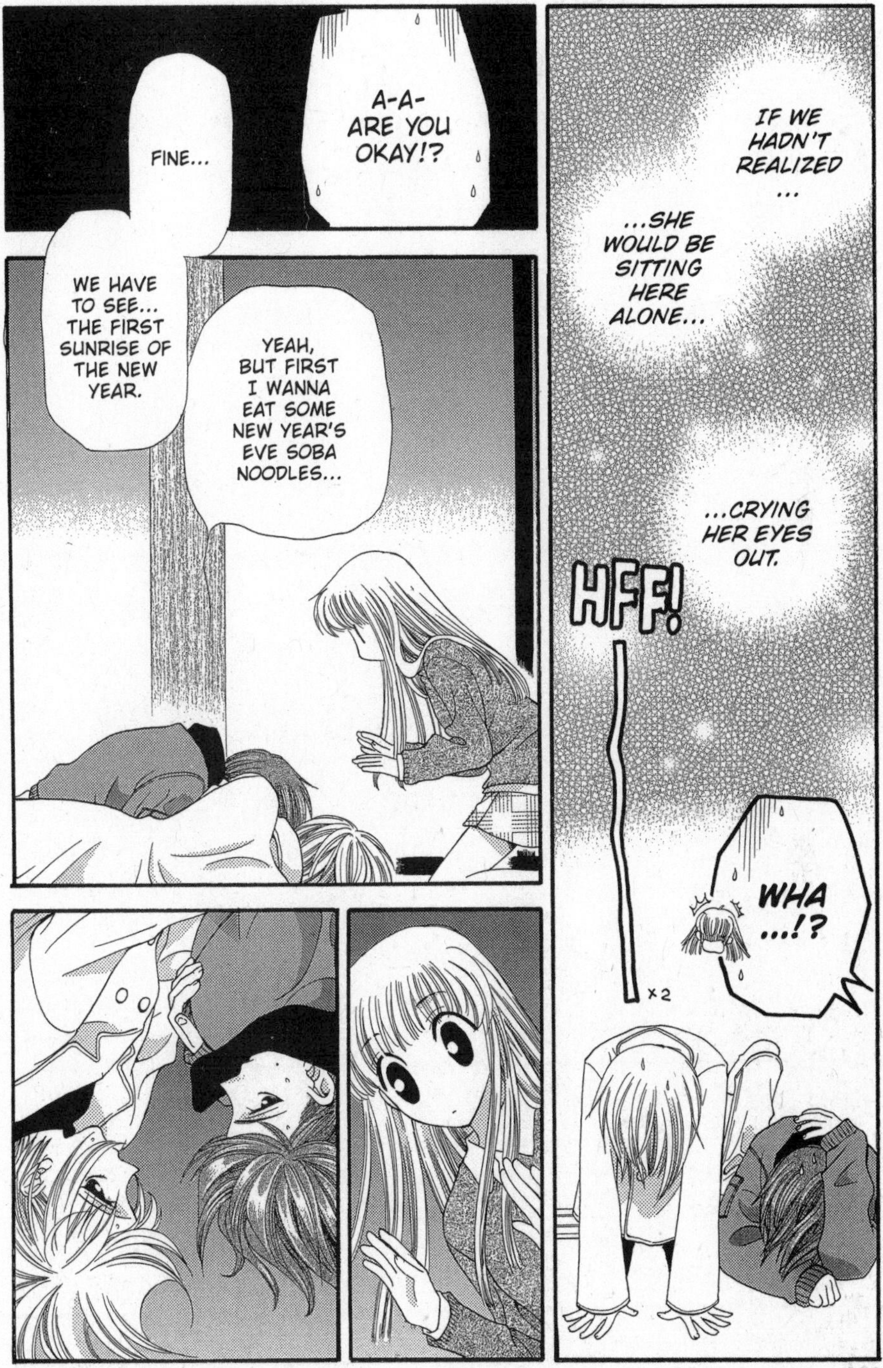
IF WE HADN'T REALIZED ...
...SHE WOULD BE SITTING HERE ALONE...
...CRYING HER EYES OUT.
HFF!
×2
WHA ...!?
A-A-ARE YOU OKAY!?
FINE...
WE HAVE TO SEE... THE FIRST SUNRISE OF THE NEW YEAR.
YEAH, BUT FIRST I WANNA EAT SOME NEW YEAR'S EVE SOBA NOODLES...

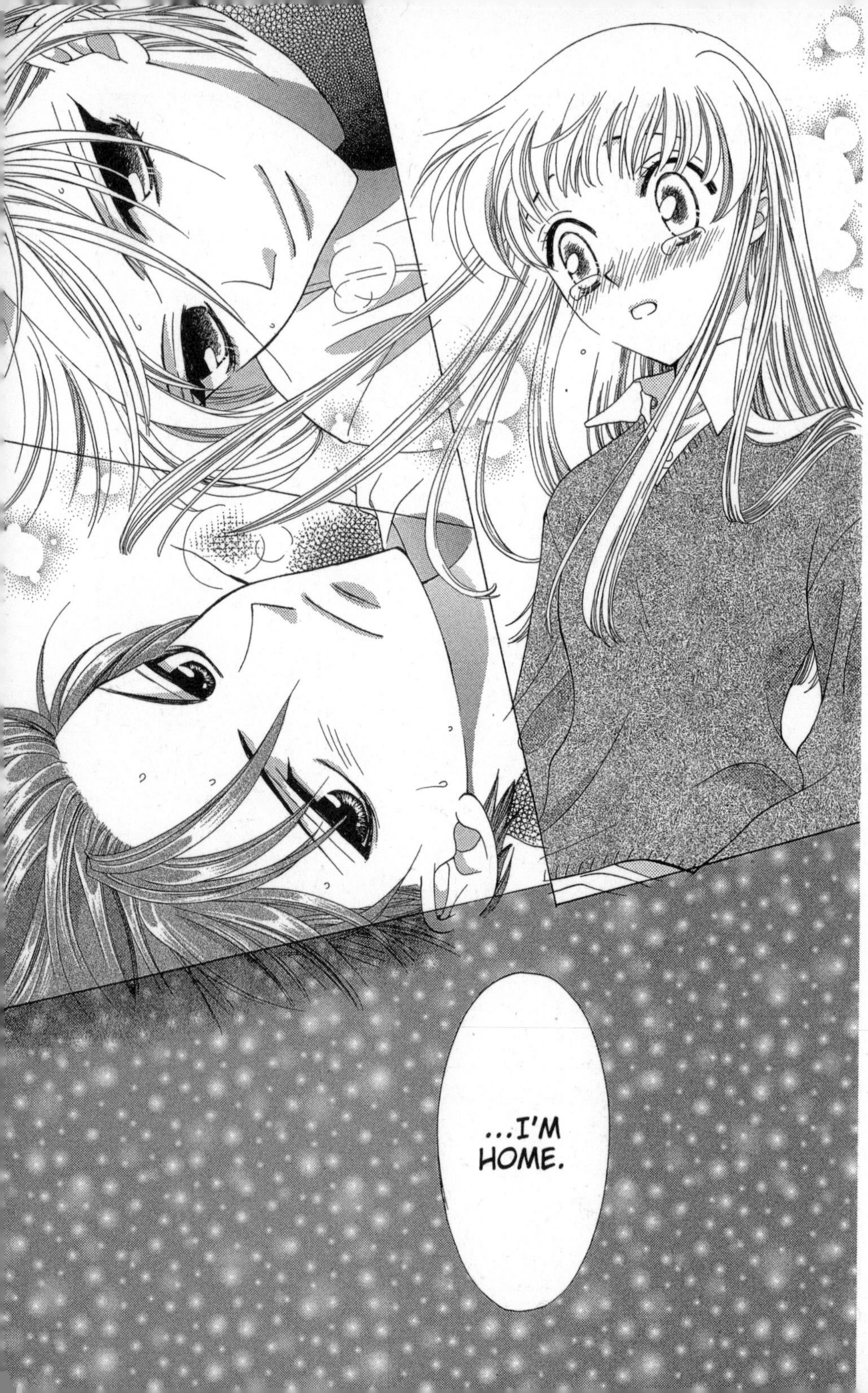
...I'M
HOME.

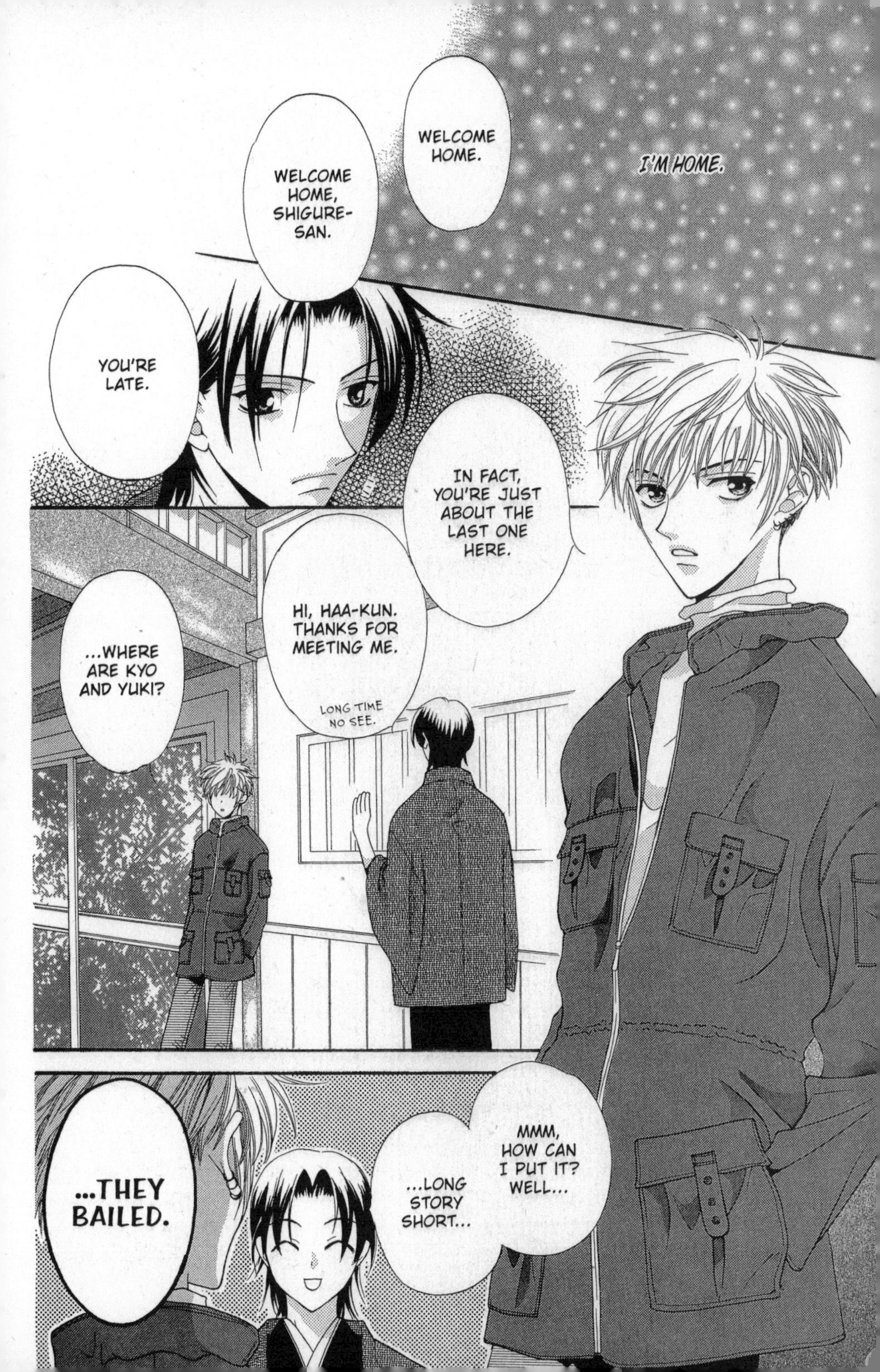
I'M HOME.
WELCOME HOME.
WELCOME HOME, SHIGURE-SAN.
YOU'RE LATE.
IN FACT, YOU'RE JUST ABOUT THE LAST ONE HERE.
HI, HAA-KUN. THANKS FOR MEETING ME.
LONG TIME NO SEE.
...WHERE ARE KYO AND YUKI?
MMM, HOW CAN I PUT IT? WELL...
...LONG STORY SHORT...
...THEY BAILED.

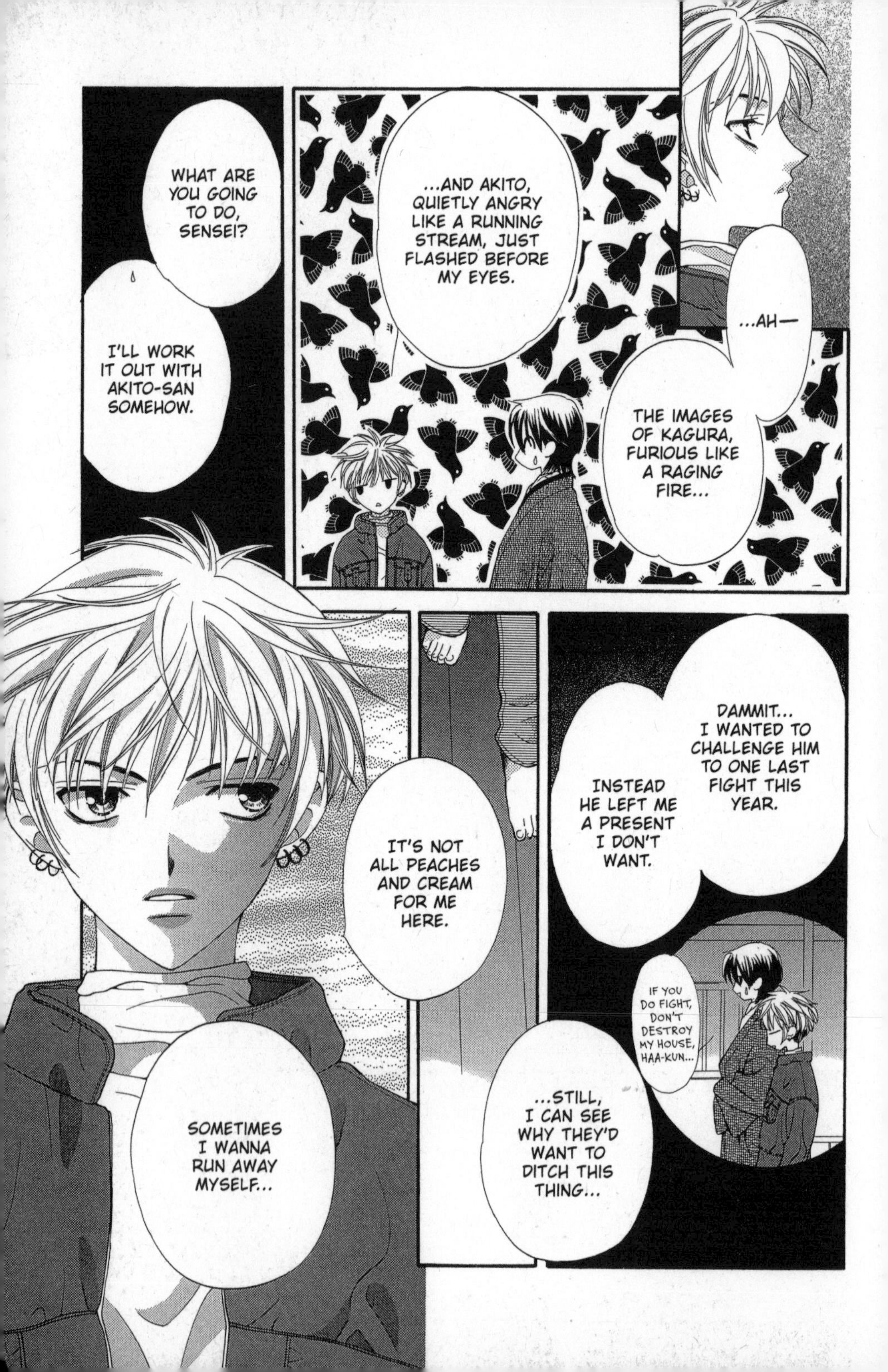
...AH—
THE IMAGES OF KAGURA, FURIOUS LIKE A RAGING FIRE...
...AND AKITO, QUIETLY ANGRY LIKE A RUNNING STREAM, JUST FLASHED BEFORE MY EYES.
WHAT ARE YOU GOING TO DO, SENSEI?
I'LL WORK IT OUT WITH AKITO-SAN SOMEHOW.
DAMMIT... I WANTED TO CHALLENGE HIM TO ONE LAST FIGHT THIS YEAR.
INSTEAD HE LEFT ME A PRESENT I DON'T WANT.
IF YOU DO FIGHT, DON'T DESTROY MY HOUSE, HAA-KUN...
...STILL, I CAN SEE WHY THEY'D WANT TO DITCH THIS THING...
IT'S NOT ALL PEACHES AND CREAM FOR ME HERE.
SOMETIMES I WANNA RUN AWAY MYSELF...

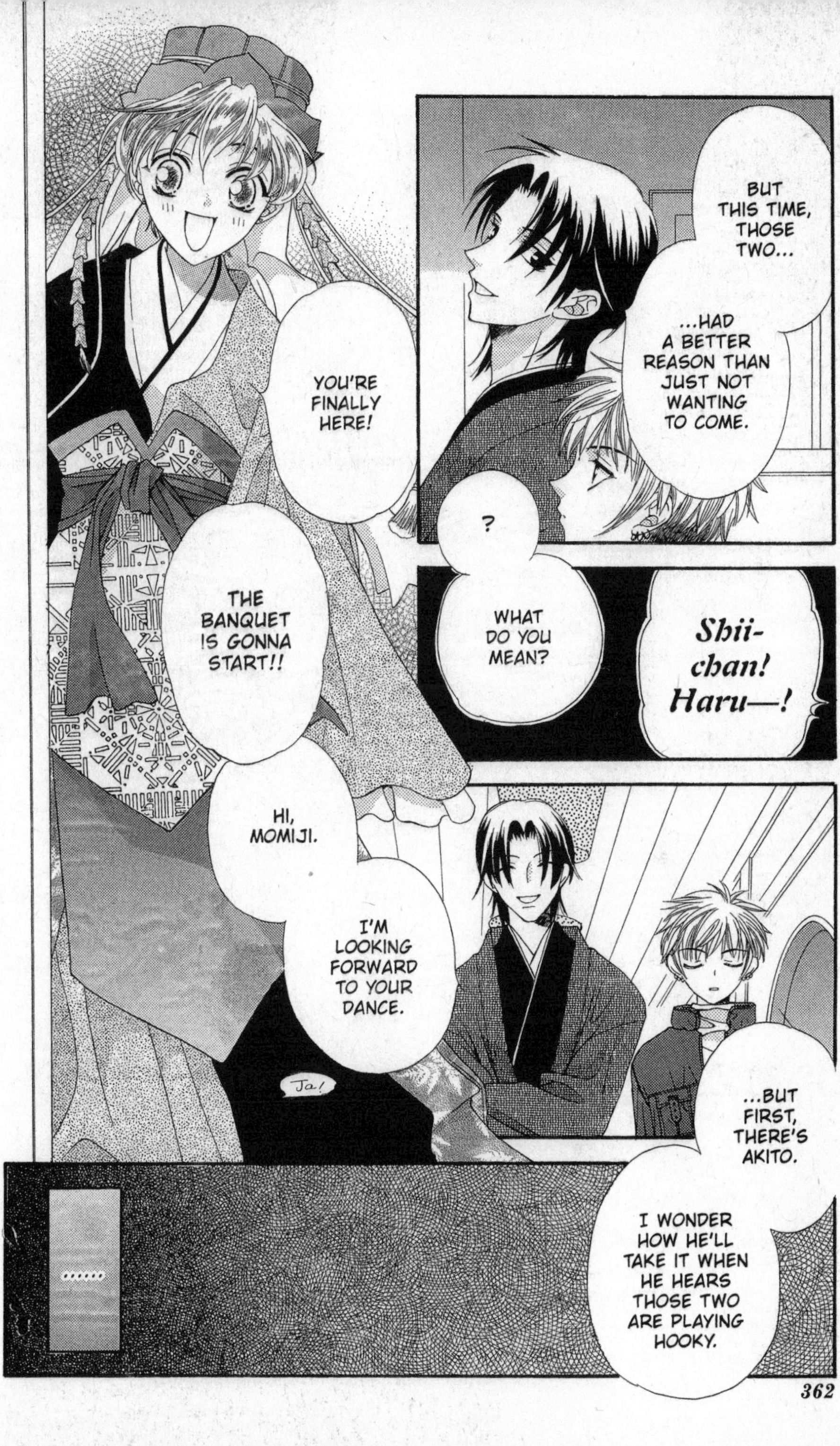

BUT THIS TIME, THOSE TWO...
...HAD A BETTER REASON THAN JUST NOT WANTING TO COME.
?
WHAT DO YOU MEAN?
Shii-chan! Haru—!
YOU'RE FINALLY HERE!
THE BANQUET IS GONNA START!!
HI, MOMIJI.
I'M LOOKING FORWARD TO YOUR DANCE.
Ja!
...BUT FIRST, THERE'S AKITO.
I WONDER HOW HE'LL TAKE IT WHEN HE HEARS THOSE TWO ARE PLAYING HOOKY.
......

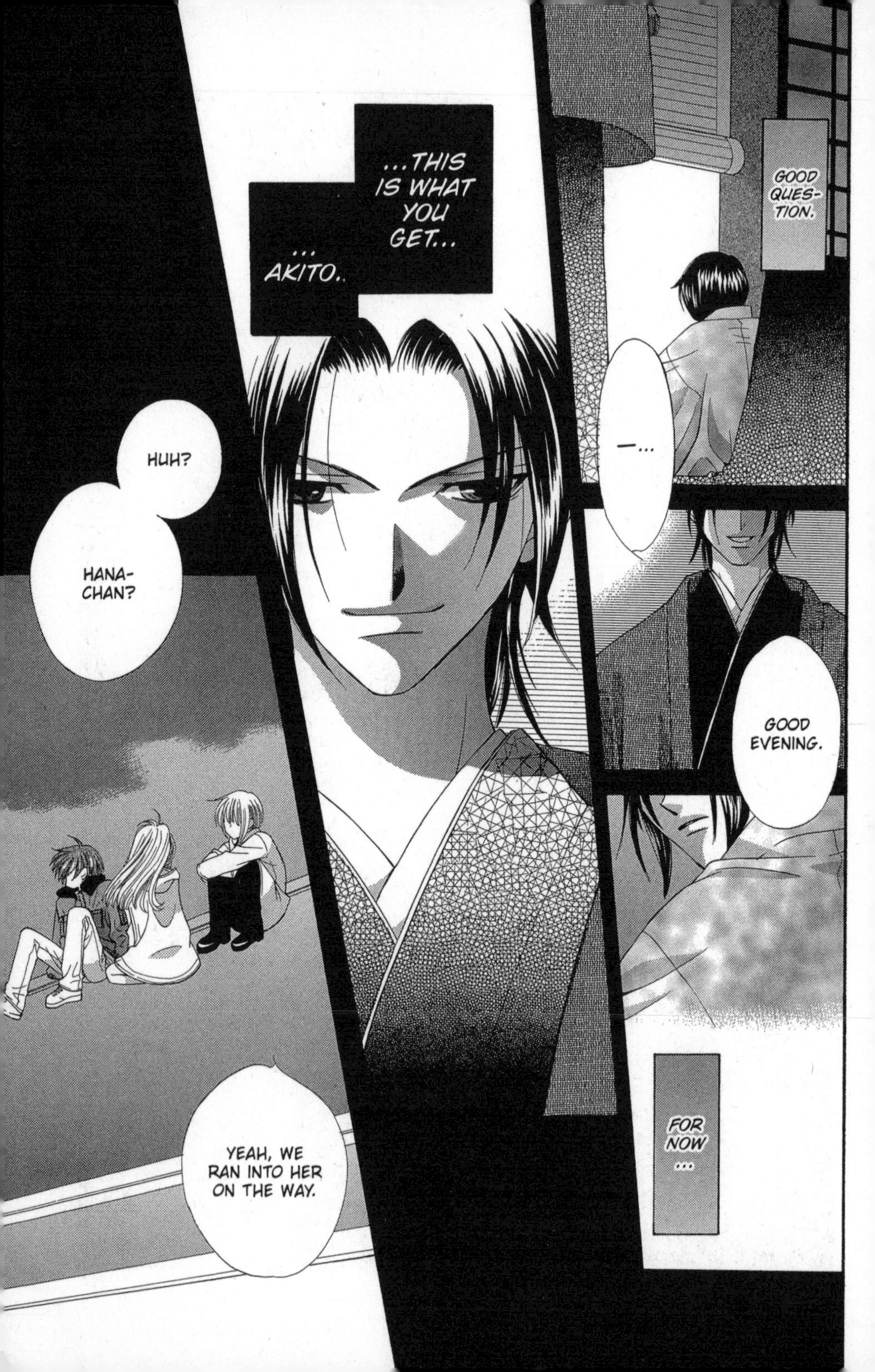
GOOD QUESTION.
—...
GOOD EVENING.
FOR NOW...
...THIS IS WHAT YOU GET...
...AKITO..
HUH?
HANA-CHAN?
YEAH, WE RAN INTO HER ON THE WAY.

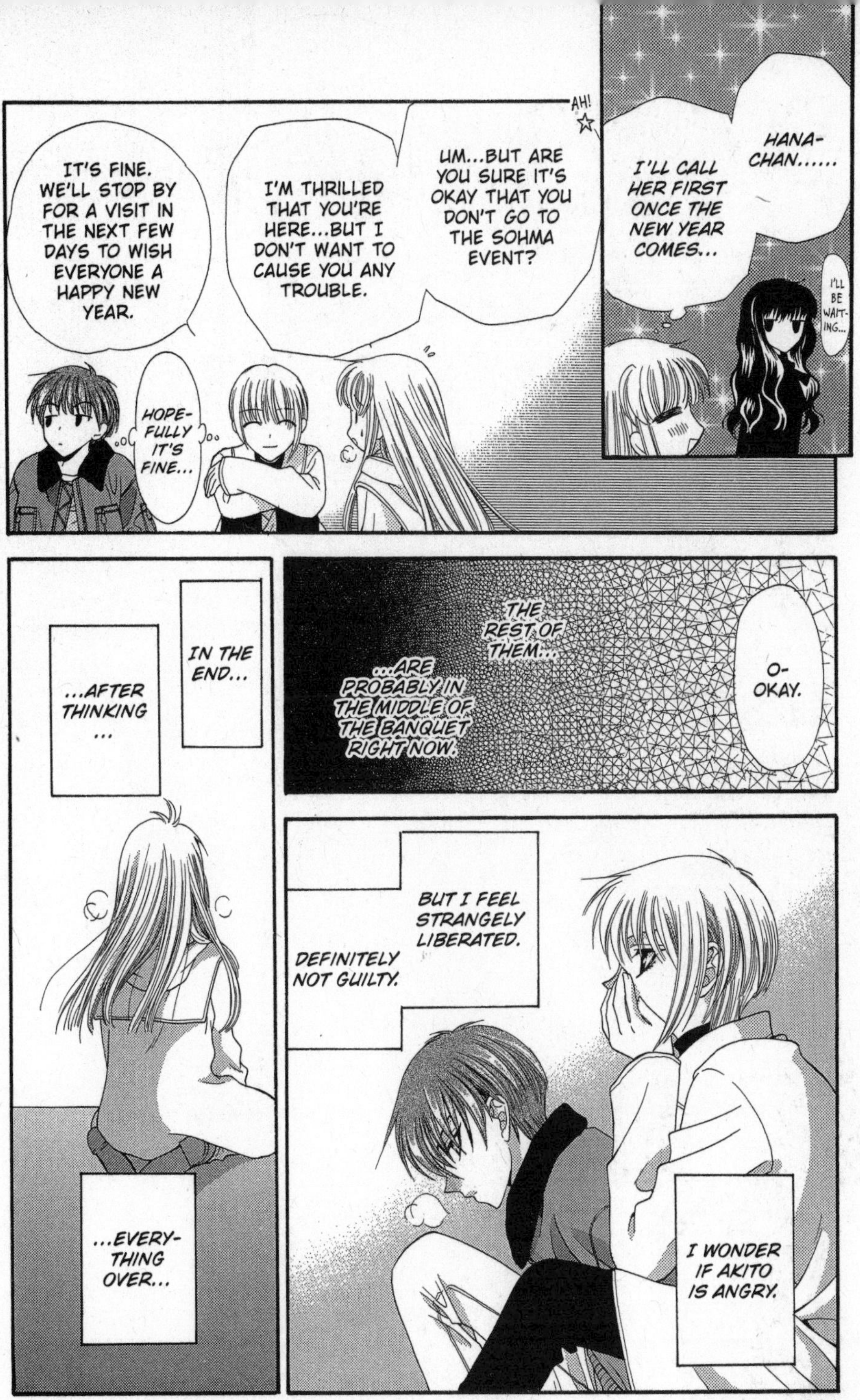
HANA-CHAN......
I'LL CALL HER FIRST ONCE THE NEW YEAR COMES...
I'LL BE WAITING...
AH! ☆
UM...BUT ARE YOU SURE IT'S OKAY THAT YOU DON'T GO TO THE SOHMA EVENT?
I'M THRILLED THAT YOU'RE HERE...BUT I DON'T WANT TO CAUSE YOU ANY TROUBLE.
IT'S FINE. WE'LL STOP BY FOR A VISIT IN THE NEXT FEW DAYS TO WISH EVERYONE A HAPPY NEW YEAR.
HOPEFULLY IT'S FINE...
O-OKAY.
THE REST OF THEM...
...ARE PROBABLY IN THE MIDDLE OF THE BANQUET RIGHT NOW.
BUT I FEEL STRANGELY LIBERATED.
DEFINITELY NOT GUILTY.
I WONDER IF AKITO IS ANGRY.
IN THE END...
...AFTER THINKING...
...EVERYTHING OVER...

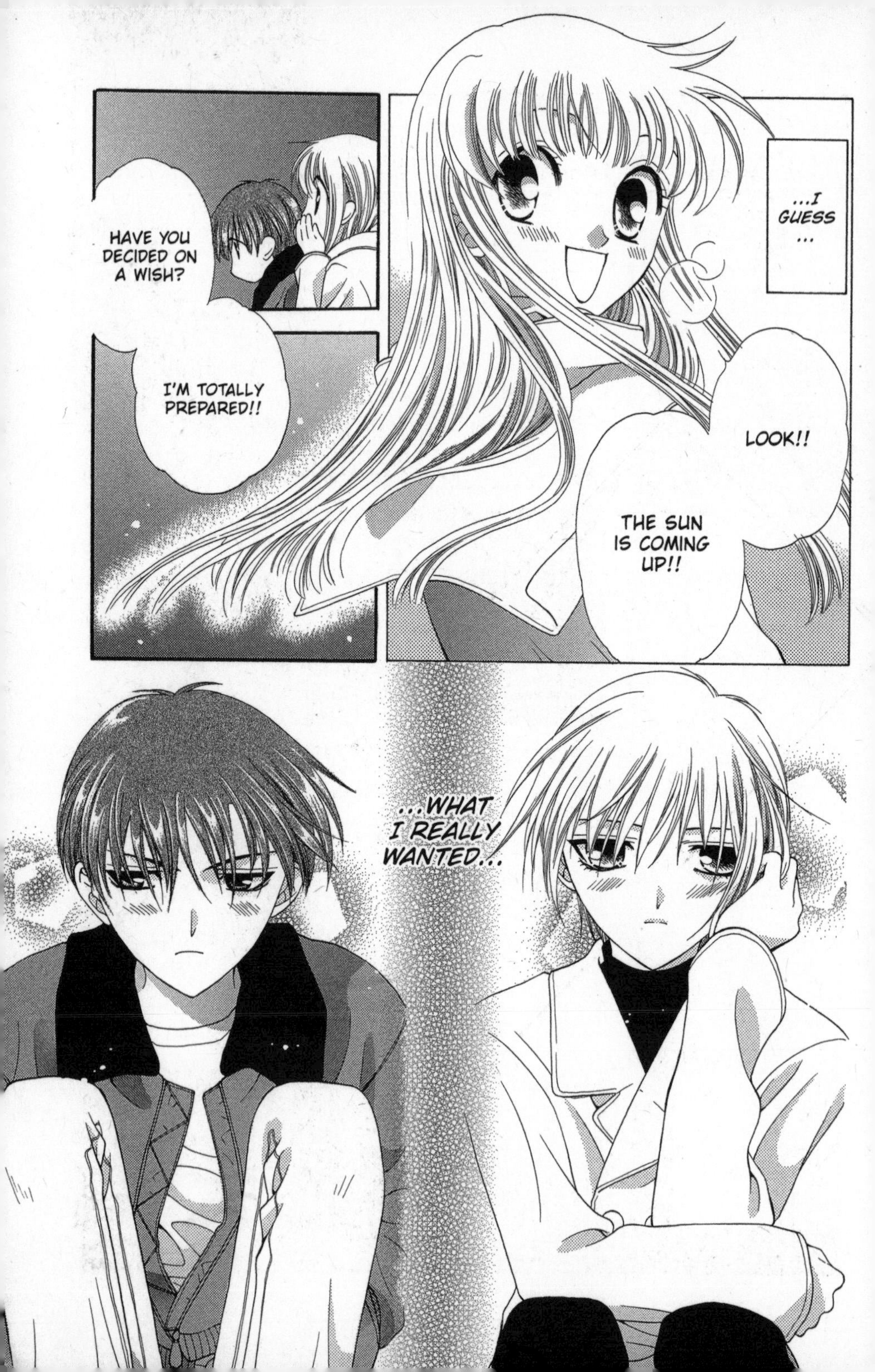
...I GUESS ...
LOOK!!
THE SUN IS COMING UP!!
HAVE YOU DECIDED ON A WISH?
I'M TOTALLY PREPARED!!
...WHAT I REALLY WANTED...

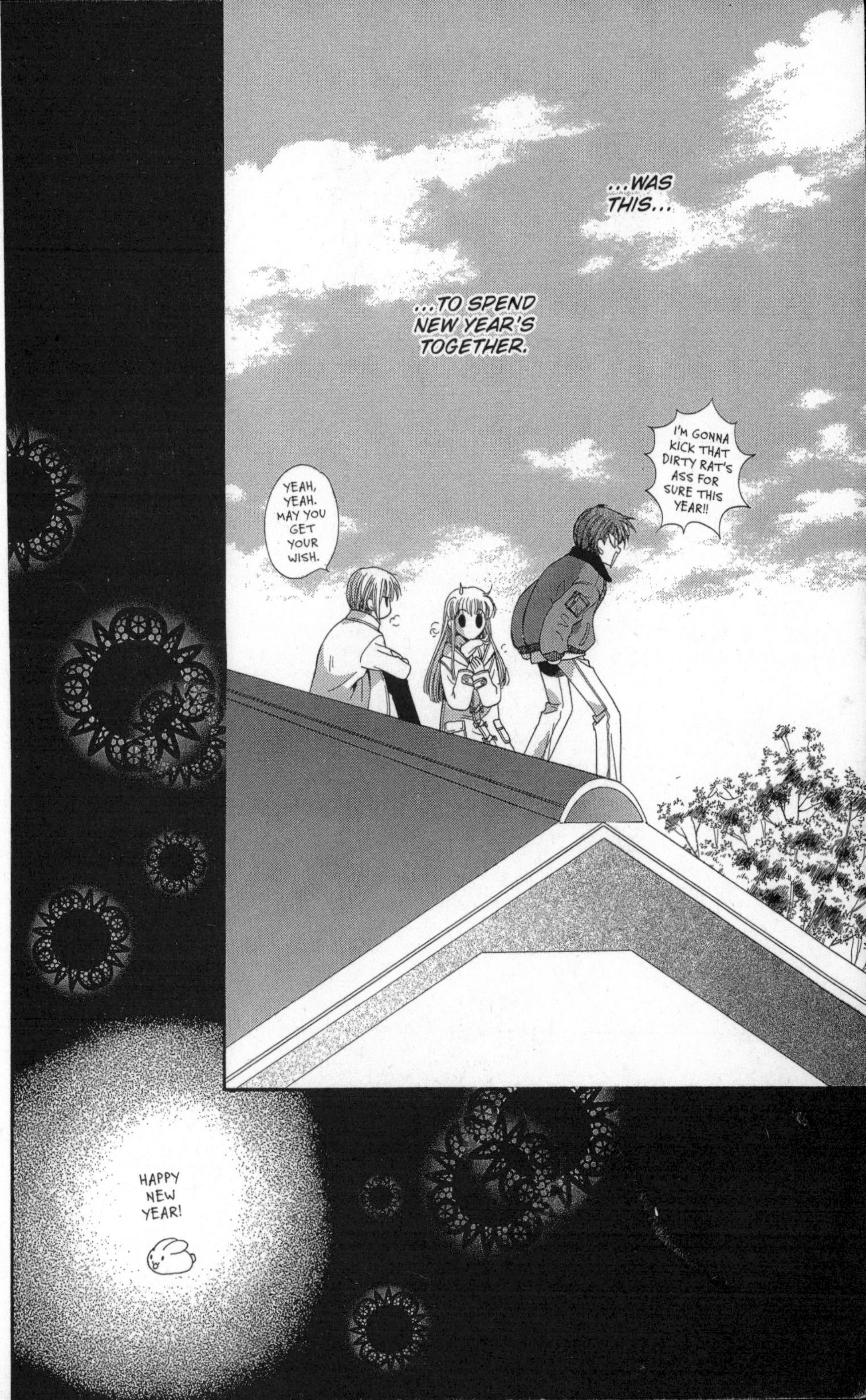
...WAS THIS...
...TO SPEND NEW YEAR'S TOGETHER.
I'M GONNA KICK THAT DIRTY RAT'S ASS FOR SURE THIS YEAR!!
YEAH, YEAH. MAY YOU GET YOUR WISH.
HAPPY NEW YEAR!

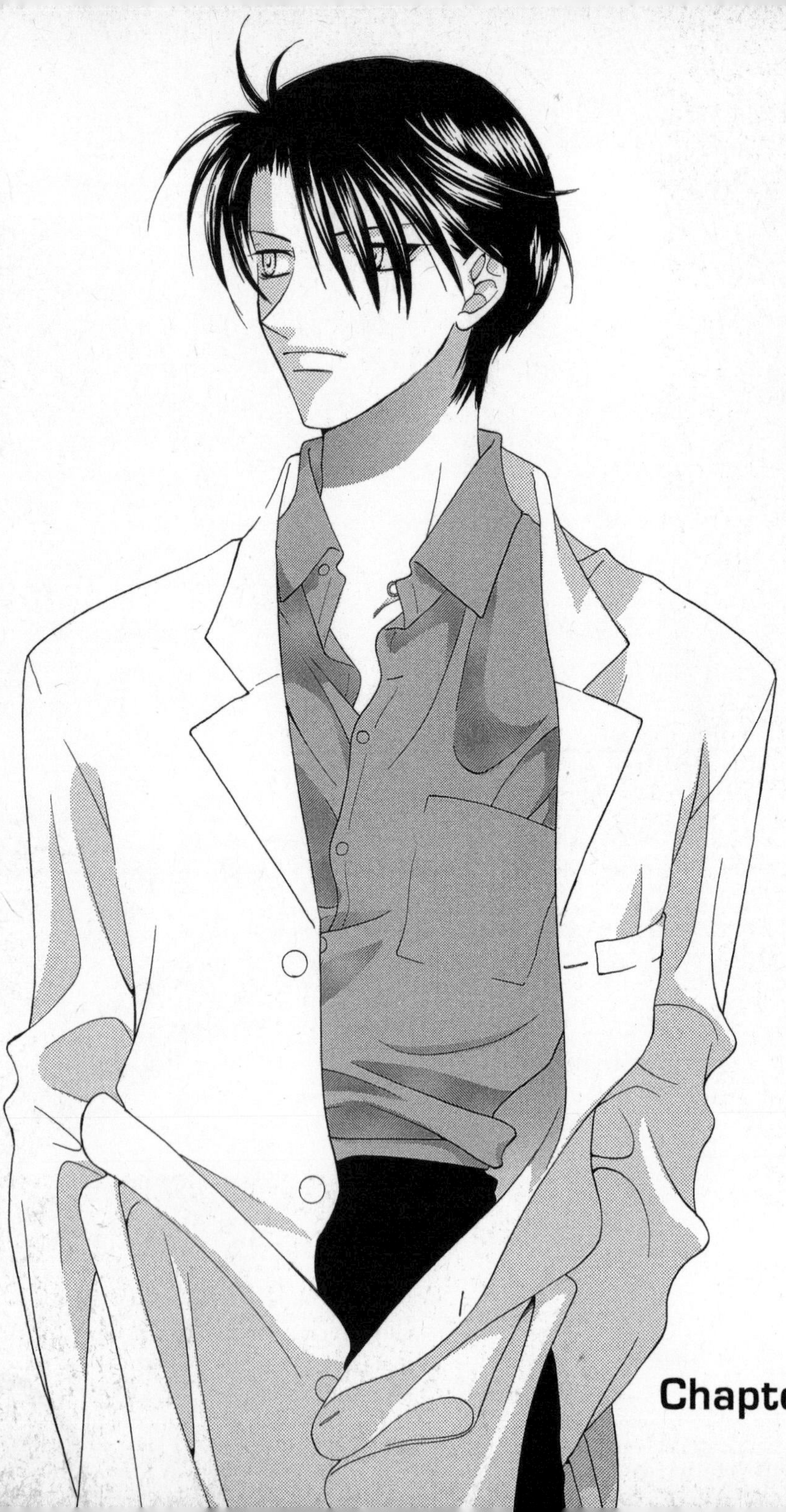

Chapter 12

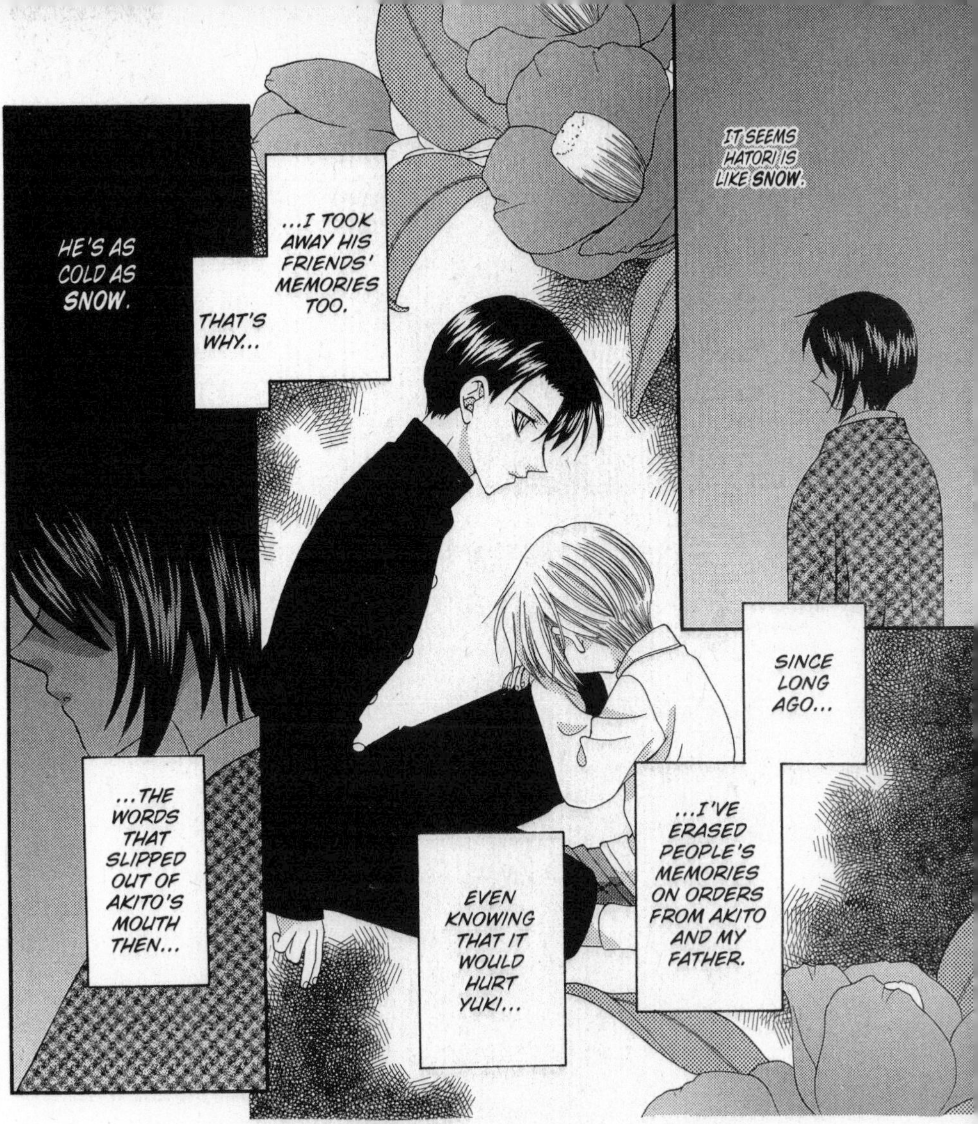
IT SEEMS HATORI IS LIKE SNOW.
SINCE LONG AGO...
...I'VE ERASED PEOPLE'S MEMORIES ON ORDERS FROM AKITO AND MY FATHER.
EVEN KNOWING THAT IT WOULD HURT YUKI...
THAT'S WHY...
...I TOOK AWAY HIS FRIENDS' MEMORIES TOO.
HE'S AS COLD AS SNOW.
...THE WORDS THAT SLIPPED OUT OF AKITO'S MOUTH THEN...

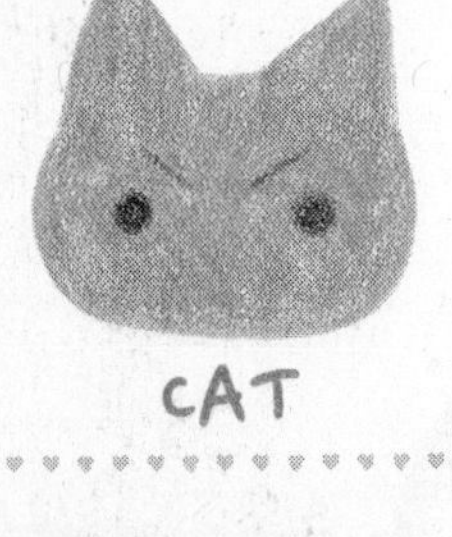
CAT

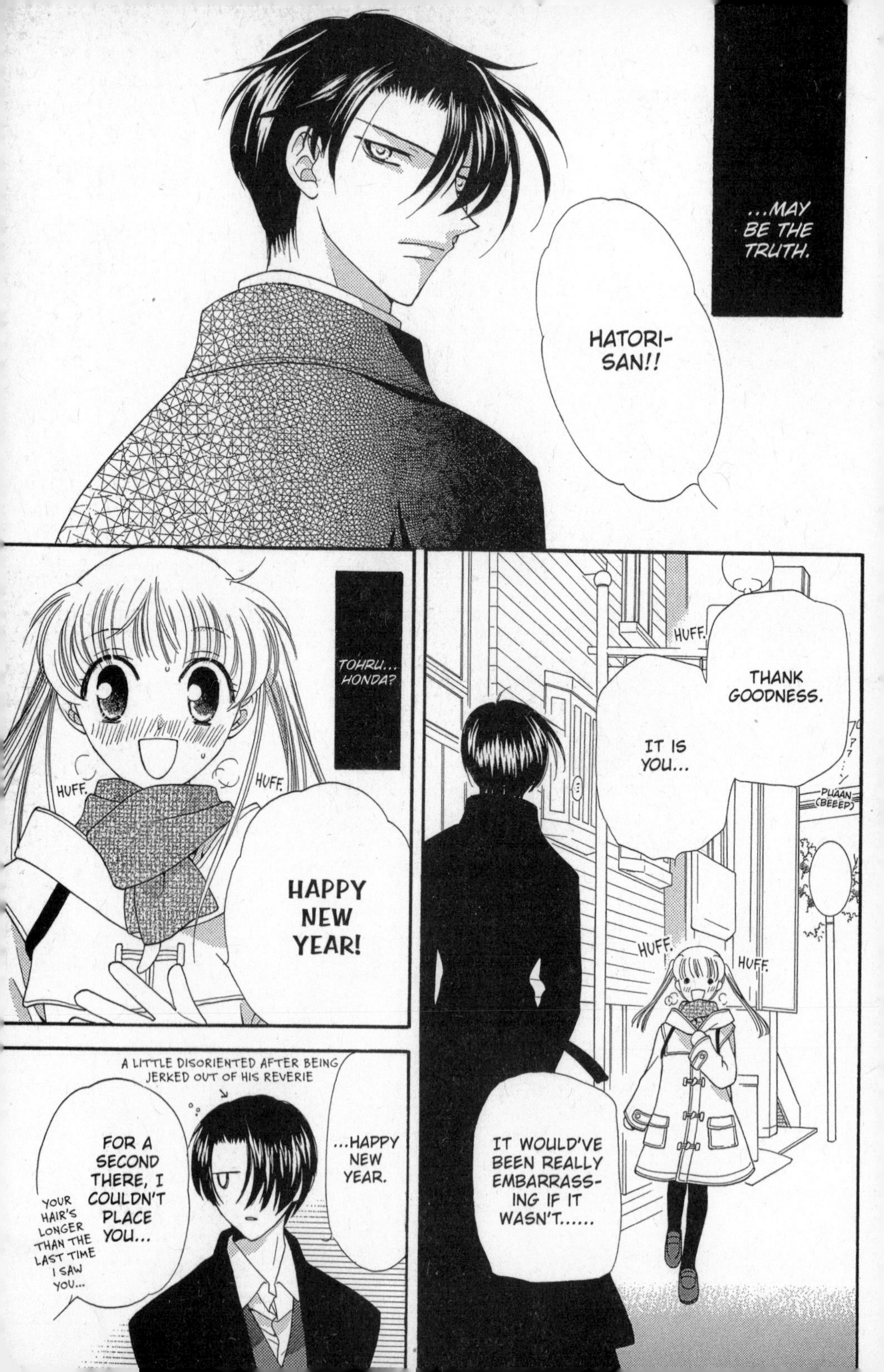
...MAY BE THE TRUTH.
HATORI-SAN!!
HUFF.
THANK GOODNESS.
IT IS YOU...
PUAAN (BEEEP)
HUFF.
HUFF.
IT WOULD'VE BEEN REALLY EMBARRASS-ING IF IT WASN'T......
TOHRU... HONDA?
HUFF.
HUFF.
HAPPY NEW YEAR!
A LITTLE DISORIENTED AFTER BEING JERKED OUT OF HIS REVERIE
...HAPPY NEW YEAR.
FOR A SECOND THERE, I COULDN'T PLACE YOU...
YOUR HAIR'S LONGER THAN THE LAST TIME I SAW YOU...

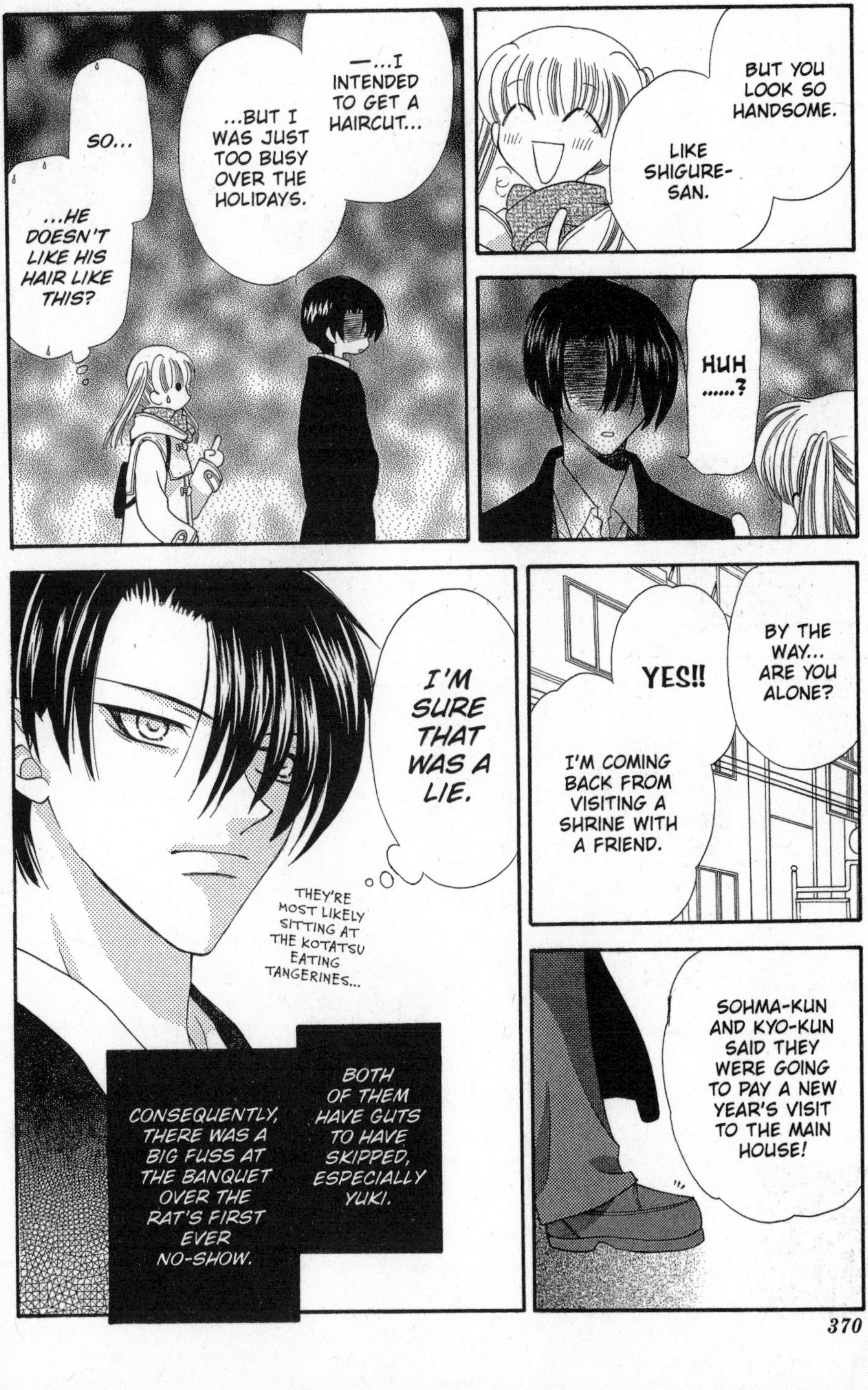
BUT YOU LOOK SO HANDSOME.
LIKE SHIGURE-SAN.
HUH ......?
—...I INTENDED TO GET A HAIRCUT...
...BUT I WAS JUST TOO BUSY OVER THE HOLIDAYS.
SO...
...HE DOESN'T LIKE HIS HAIR LIKE THIS?
BY THE WAY... ARE YOU ALONE?
YES!!
I'M COMING BACK FROM VISITING A SHRINE WITH A FRIEND.
SOHMA-KUN AND KYO-KUN SAID THEY WERE GOING TO PAY A NEW YEAR'S VISIT TO THE MAIN HOUSE!
I'M SURE THAT WAS A LIE.
THEY'RE MOST LIKELY SITTING AT THE KOTATSU EATING TANGERINES...
BOTH OF THEM HAVE GUTS TO HAVE SKIPPED, ESPECIALLY YUKI.
CONSEQUENTLY, THERE WAS A BIG FUSS AT THE BANQUET OVER THE RAT'S FIRST EVER NO-SHOW.

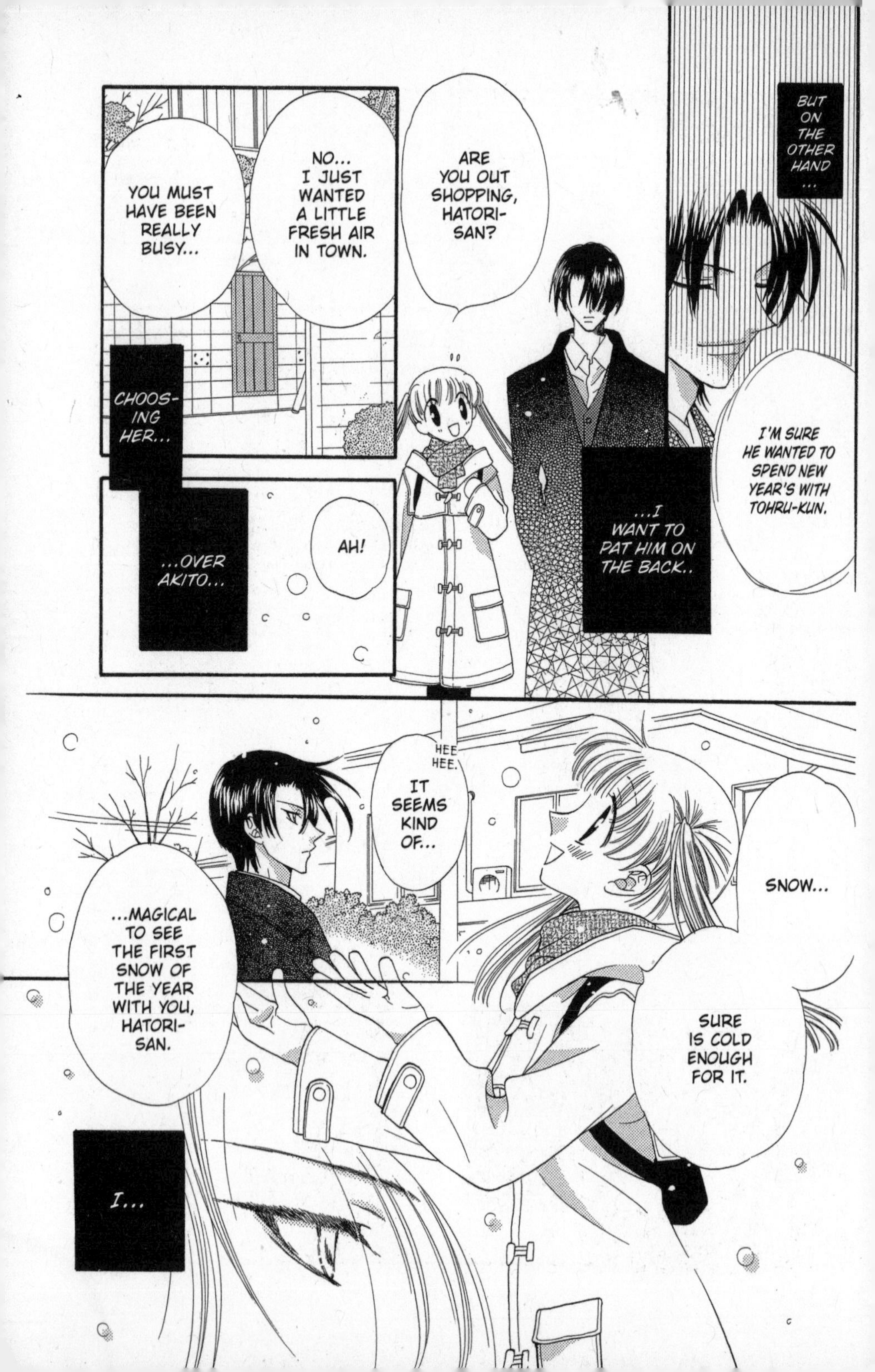
BUT ON THE OTHER HAND...
I'M SURE HE WANTED TO SPEND NEW YEAR'S WITH TOHRU-KUN.
...I WANT TO PAT HIM ON THE BACK..
ARE YOU OUT SHOPPING, HATORI-SAN?
NO... I JUST WANTED A LITTLE FRESH AIR IN TOWN.
YOU MUST HAVE BEEN REALLY BUSY...
CHOOSING HER...
AH!
...OVER AKITO...
SNOW...
SURE IS COLD ENOUGH FOR IT.
HEE HEE.
IT SEEMS KIND OF...
...MAGICAL TO SEE THE FIRST SNOW OF THE YEAR WITH YOU, HATORI-SAN.
I...

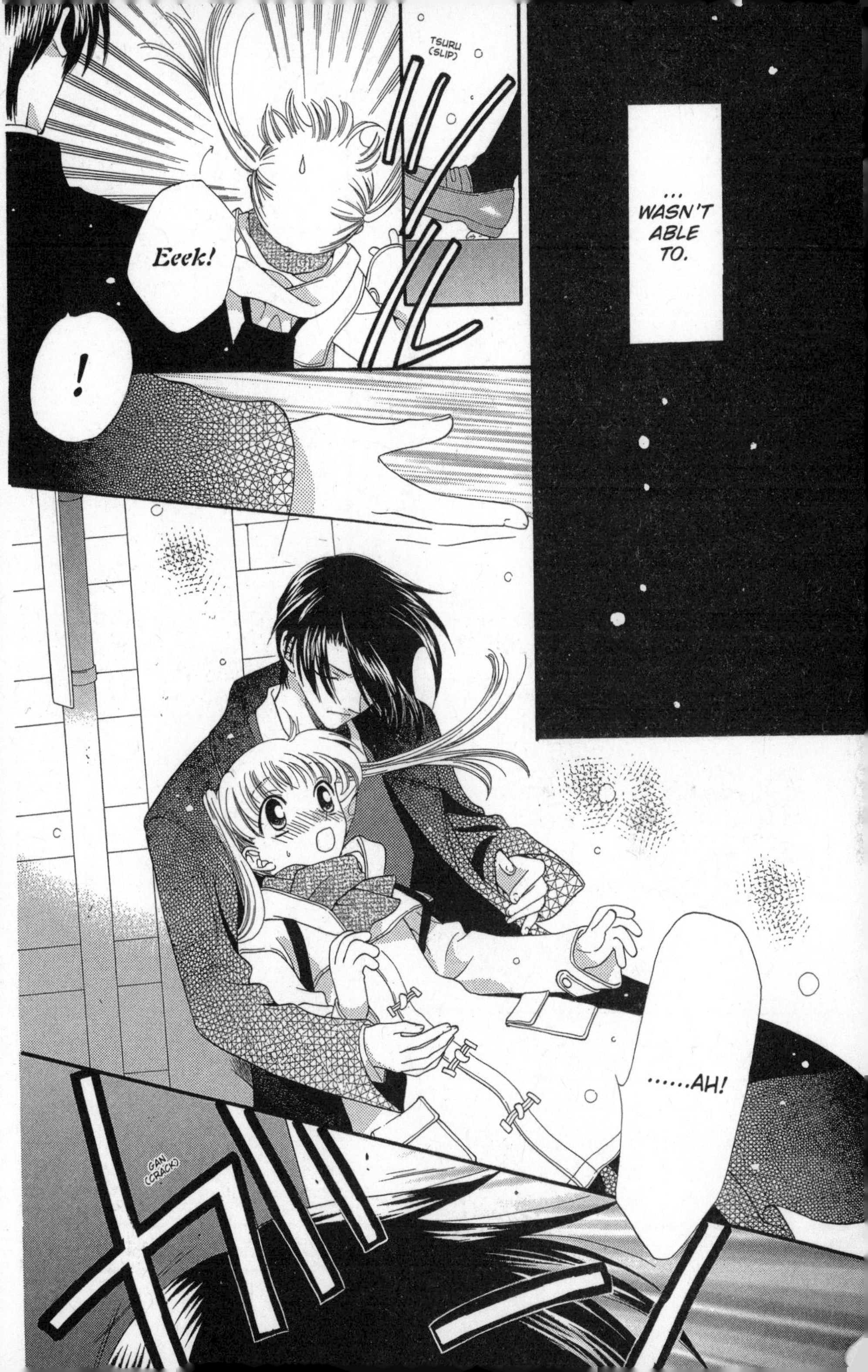
... WASN'T ABLE TO.
TSURU (SLIP)
Eeek!
!
......AH!
GAN (CRACK)

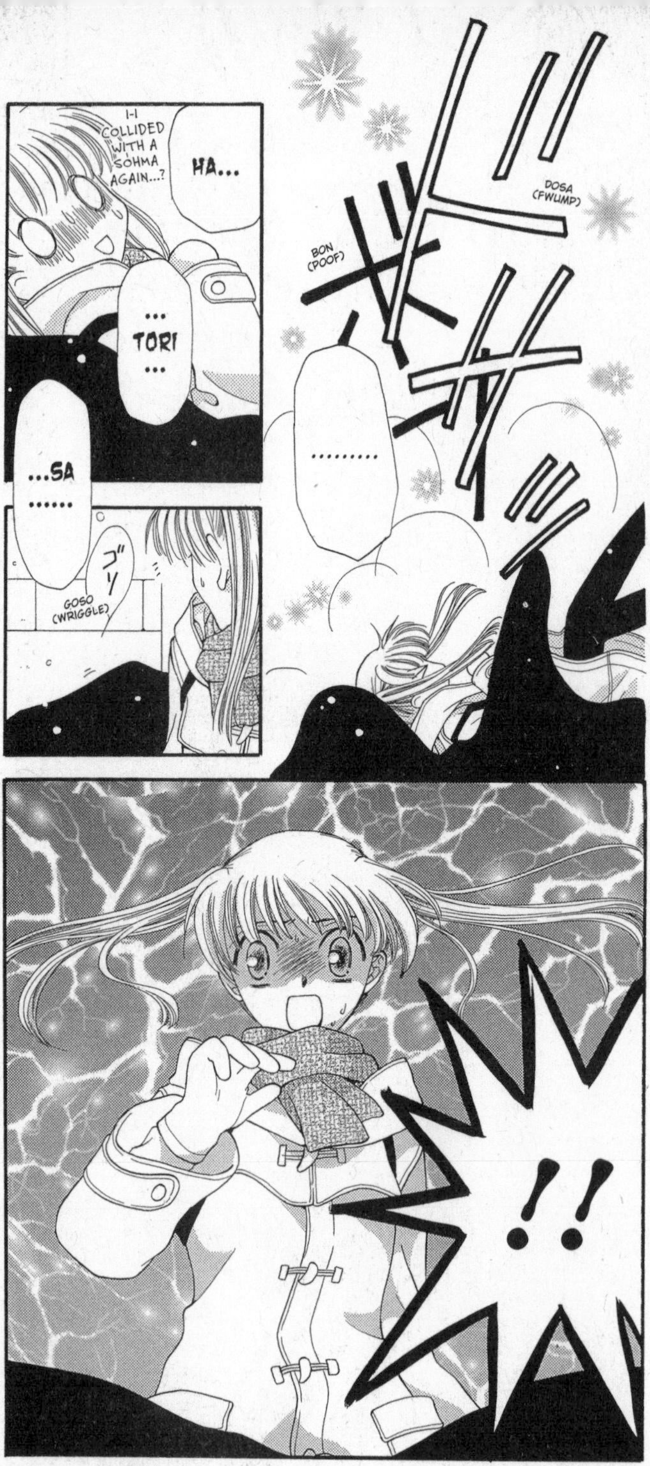
BON (POOF)
DOSA (FWUMP)
....
HA...
I-I COLLIDED WITH A SOHMA AGAIN...?
...TORI...
...SA......
ゴソ
GOSO (WRIGGLE)
!!

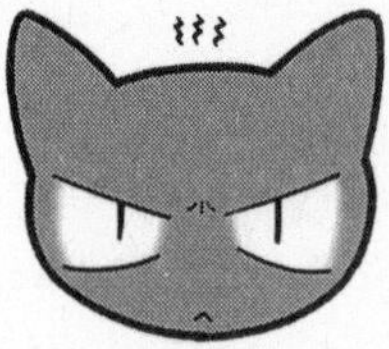

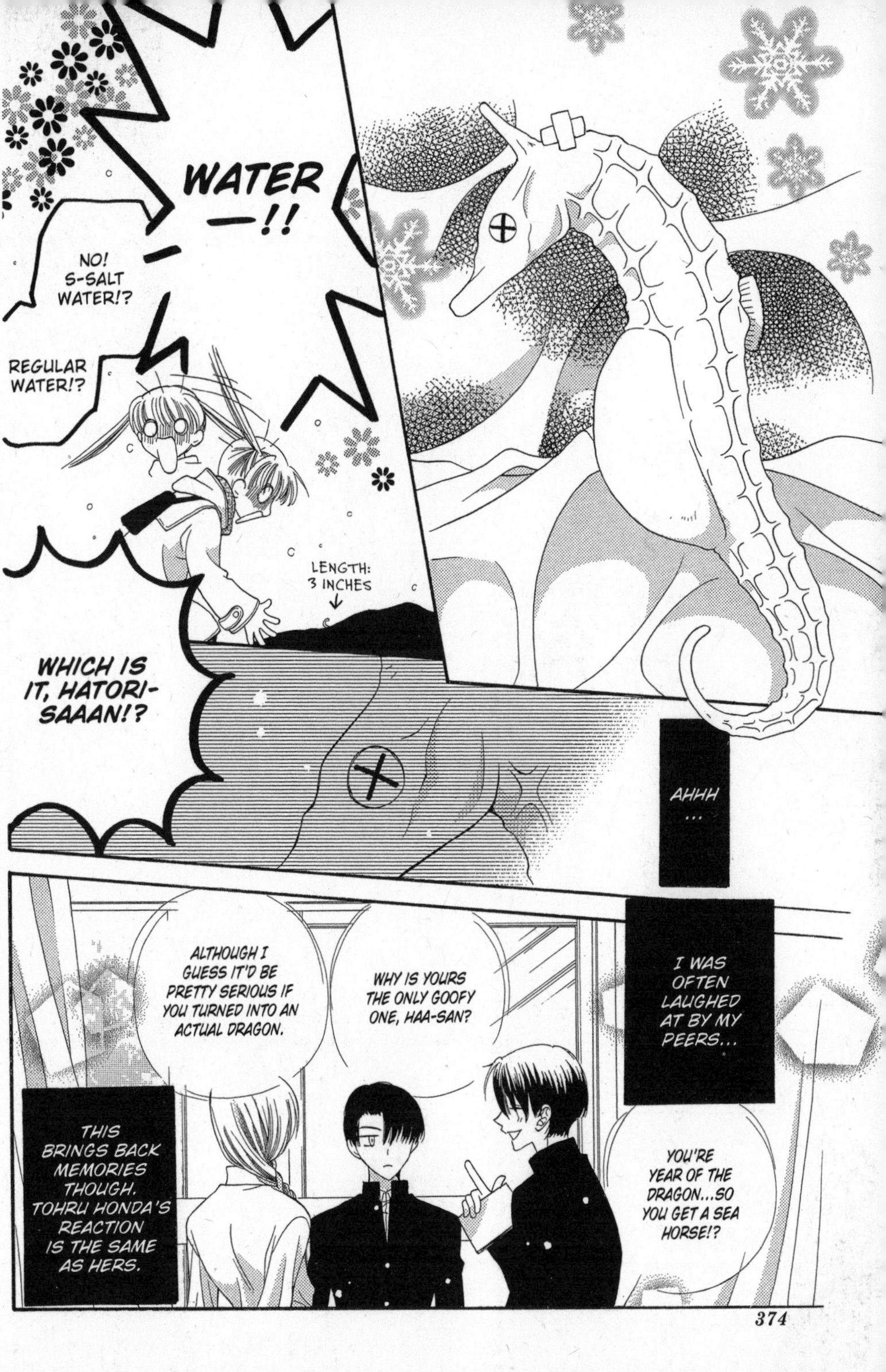
WATER —!!
NO! S-SALT WATER!?
REGULAR WATER!?
LENGTH: 3 INCHES
WHICH IS IT, HATORI-SAAAN!?
AHHH...
I WAS OFTEN LAUGHED AT BY MY PEERS...
YOU'RE YEAR OF THE DRAGON...SO YOU GET A SEA HORSE!?
WHY IS YOURS THE ONLY GOOFY ONE, HAA-SAN?
ALTHOUGH I GUESS IT'D BE PRETTY SERIOUS IF YOU TURNED INTO AN ACTUAL DRAGON.
THIS BRINGS BACK MEMORIES THOUGH. TOHRU HONDA'S REACTION IS THE SAME AS HERS.

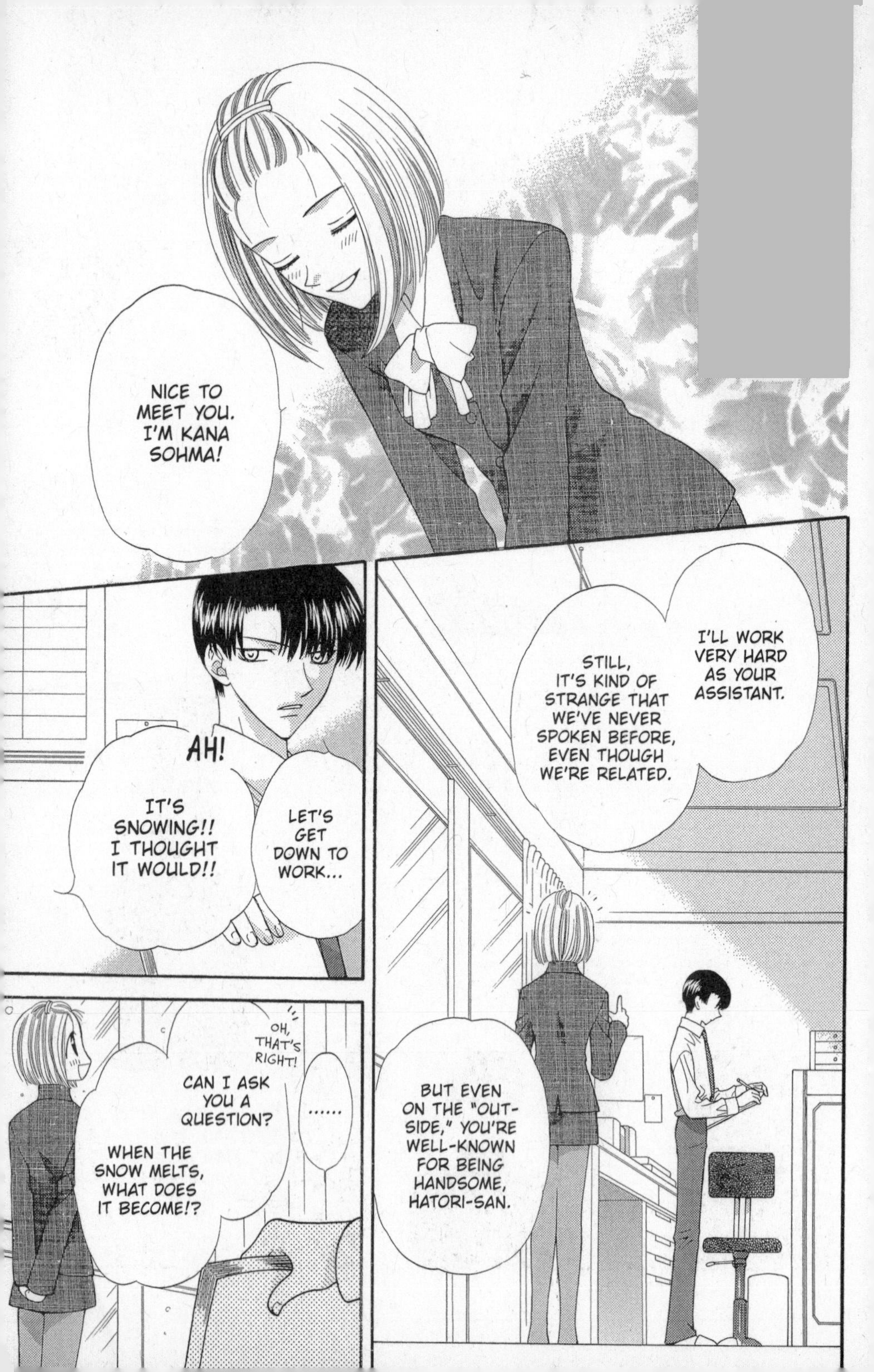
NICE TO MEET YOU. I'M KANA SOHMA!
I'LL WORK VERY HARD AS YOUR ASSISTANT.
STILL, IT'S KIND OF STRANGE THAT WE'VE NEVER SPOKEN BEFORE, EVEN THOUGH WE'RE RELATED.
BUT EVEN ON THE "OUT-SIDE," YOU'RE WELL-KNOWN FOR BEING HANDSOME, HATORI-SAN.
LET'S GET DOWN TO WORK...
AH!
IT'S SNOWING!! I THOUGHT IT WOULD!!
OH, THAT'S RIGHT!
......
CAN I ASK YOU A QUESTION?
WHEN THE SNOW MELTS, WHAT DOES IT BECOME!?

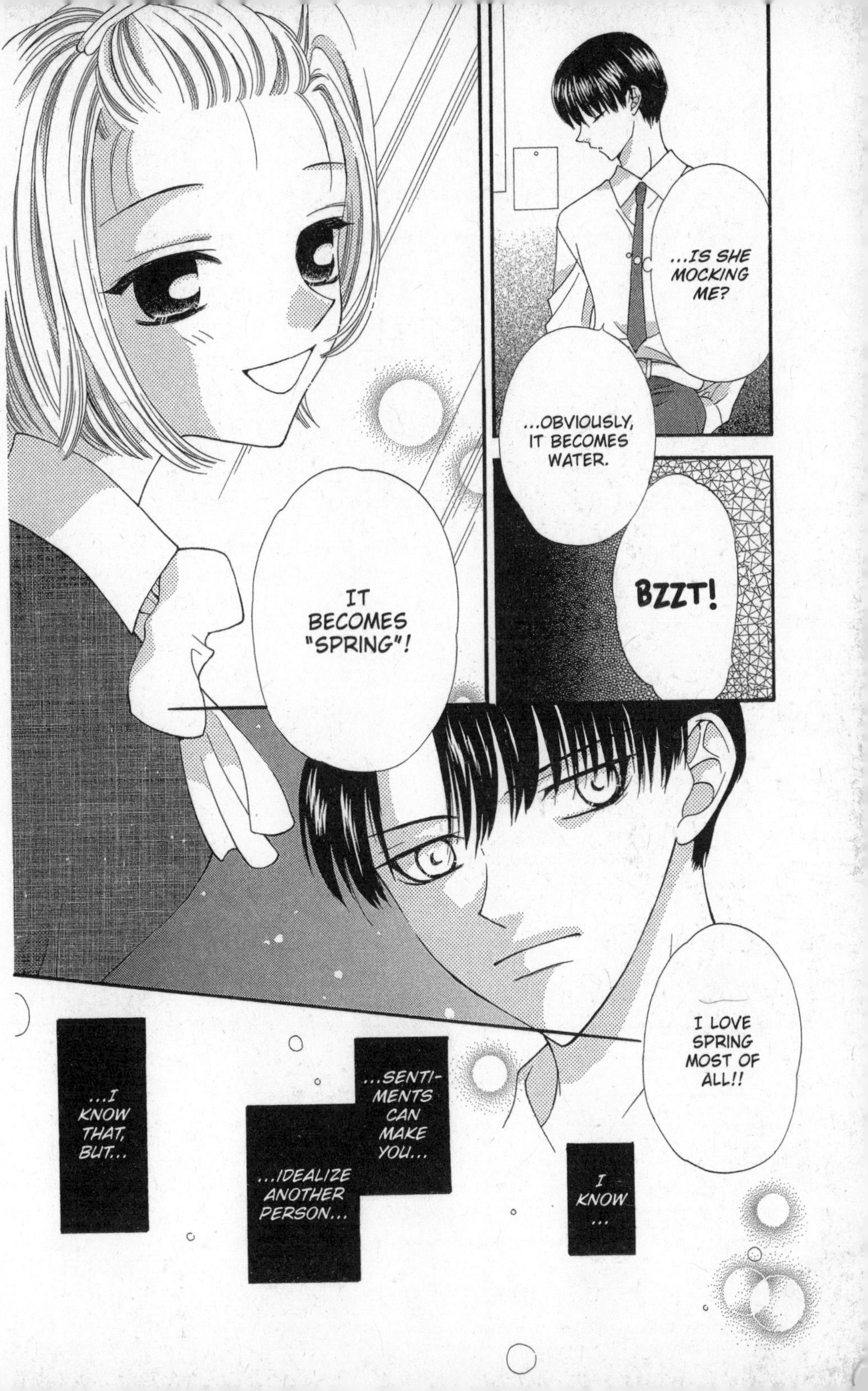
...IS SHE MOCKING ME?
...OBVIOUSLY, IT BECOMES WATER.
BZZT!
IT BECOMES "SPRING"!
I LOVE SPRING MOST OF ALL!!
I KNOW...
...SENTI-MENTS CAN MAKE YOU...
...IDEALIZE ANOTHER PERSON...
...I KNOW THAT, BUT...

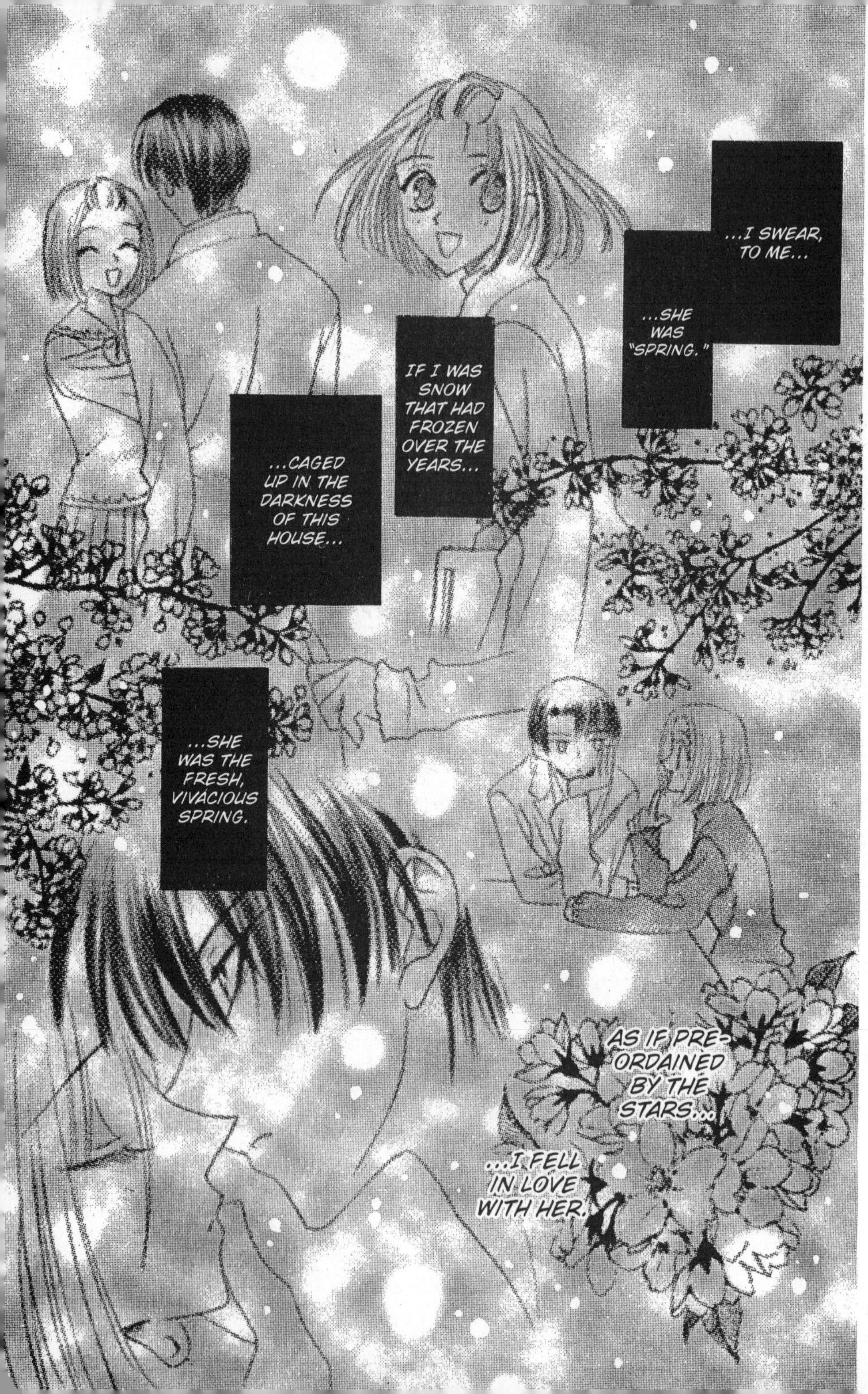
...I SWEAR, TO ME...
...SHE WAS "SPRING."
IF I WAS SNOW THAT HAD FROZEN OVER THE YEARS...
...CAGED UP IN THE DARKNESS OF THIS HOUSE...
...SHE WAS THE FRESH, VIVACIOUS SPRING.
AS IF PRE-ORDAINED BY THE STARS...
...I FELL IN LOVE WITH HER.

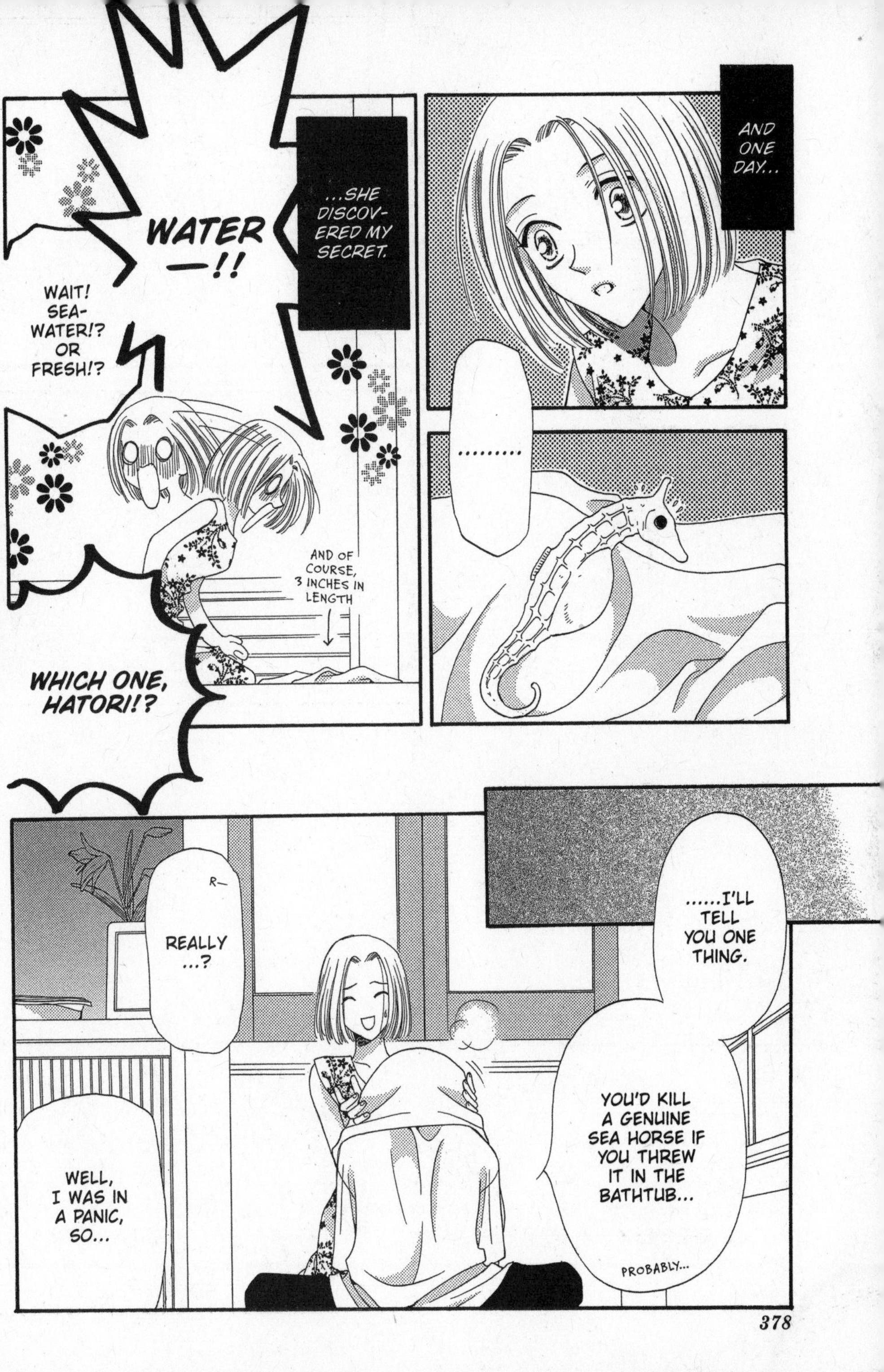

AND ONE DAY...
....
...SHE DISCOVERED MY SECRET.
WATER—!!
WAIT! SEA-WATER!? OR FRESH!?
AND OF COURSE, 3 INCHES IN LENGTH
WHICH ONE, HATORI!?
......I'LL TELL YOU ONE THING.
YOU'D KILL A GENUINE SEA HORSE IF YOU THREW IT IN THE BATHTUB...
PROBABLY...
R— REALLY ...?
WELL, I WAS IN A PANIC, SO...

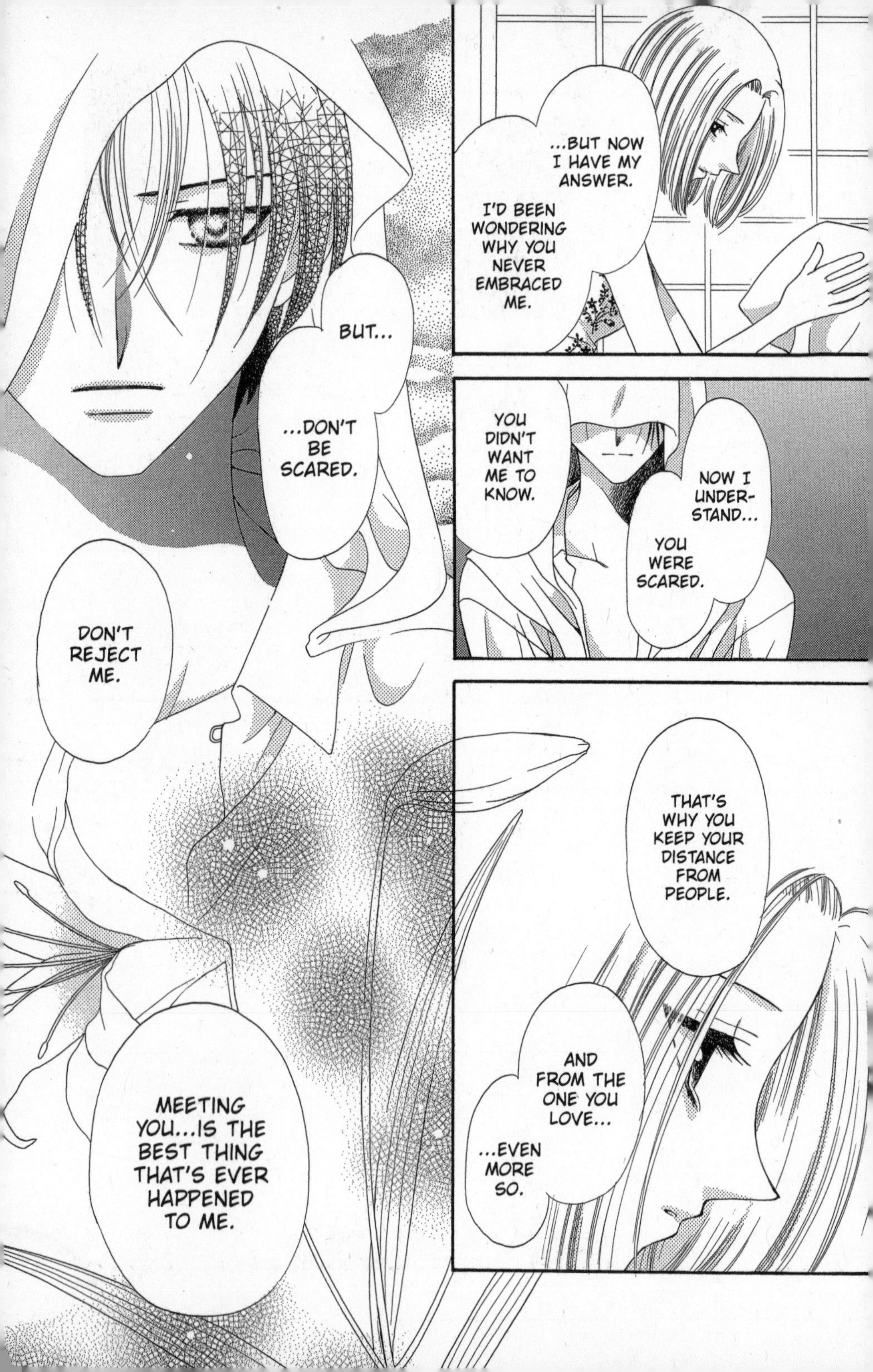
I'D BEEN WONDERING WHY YOU NEVER EMBRACED ME.
...BUT NOW I HAVE MY ANSWER.
NOW I UNDER-STAND...
YOU WERE SCARED.
YOU DIDN'T WANT ME TO KNOW.
THAT'S WHY YOU KEEP YOUR DISTANCE FROM PEOPLE.
AND FROM THE ONE YOU LOVE...
...EVEN MORE SO.
BUT...
...DON'T BE SCARED.
DON'T REJECT ME.
MEETING YOU...IS THE BEST THING THAT'S EVER HAPPENED TO ME.

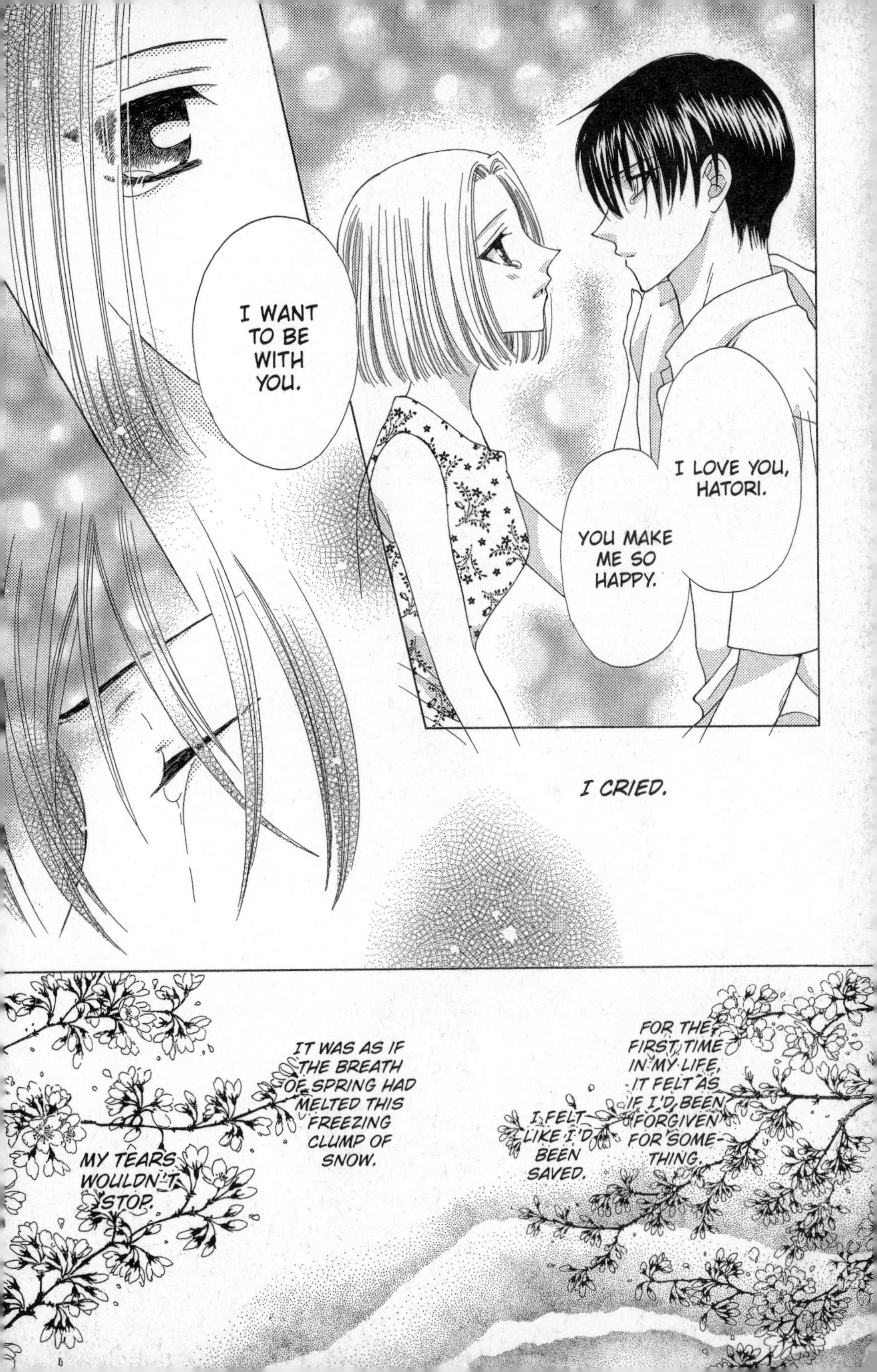
I LOVE YOU, HATORI.
YOU MAKE ME SO HAPPY.
I WANT TO BE WITH YOU.
I CRIED.
FOR THE FIRST TIME IN MY LIFE, IT FELT AS IF I'D BEEN FORGIVEN FOR SOMETHING.
I FELT LIKE I'D BEEN SAVED.
IT WAS AS IF THE BREATH OF SPRING HAD MELTED THIS FREEZING CLUMP OF SNOW.
MY TEARS WOULDN'T STOP.

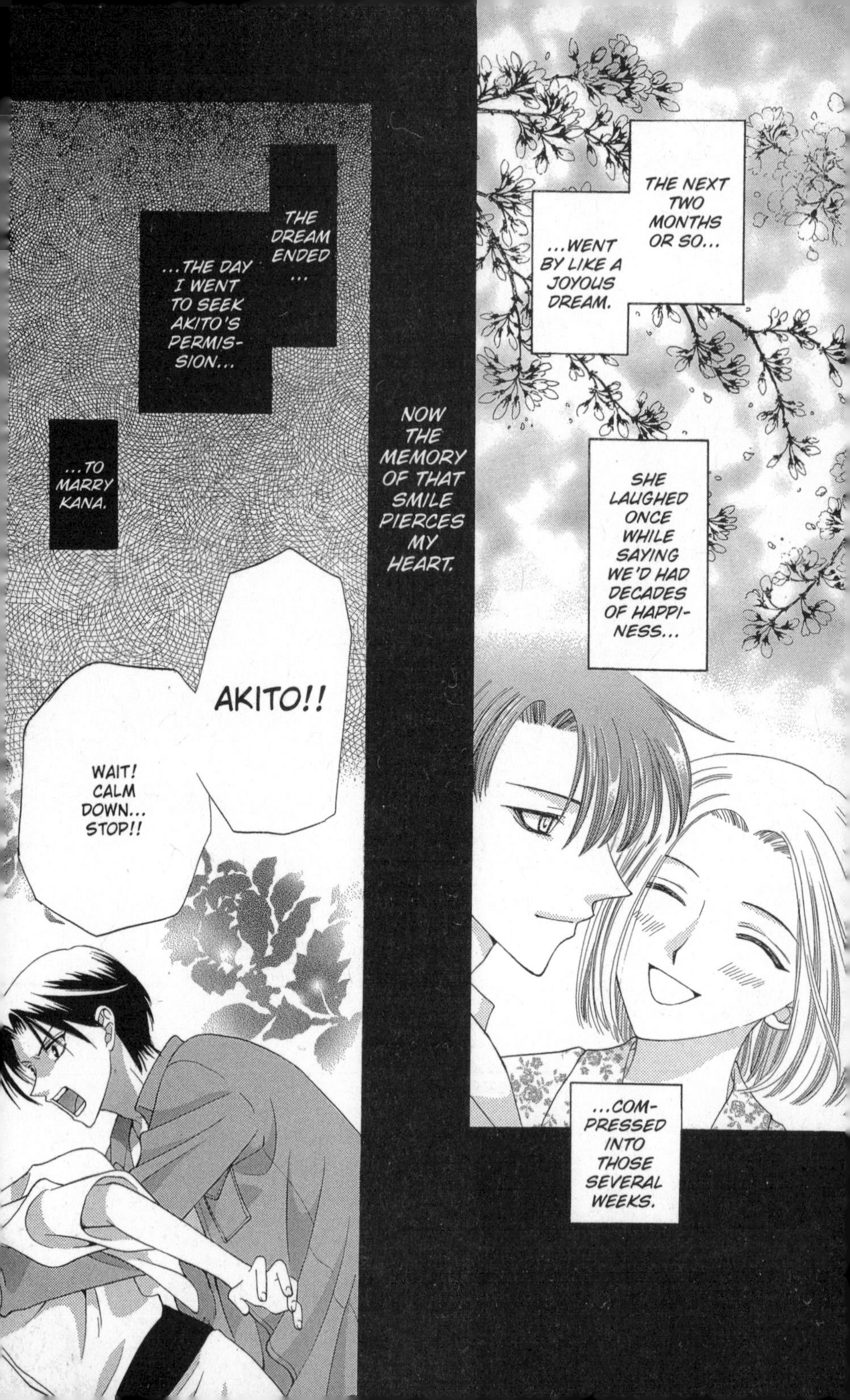
THE NEXT TWO MONTHS OR SO...
...WENT BY LIKE A JOYOUS DREAM.
SHE LAUGHED ONCE WHILE SAYING WE'D HAD DECADES OF HAPPI- NESS...
...COM- PRESSED INTO THOSE SEVERAL WEEKS.
NOW THE MEMORY OF THAT SMILE PIERCES MY HEART.
THE DREAM ENDED ...
...THE DAY I WENT TO SEEK AKITO'S PERMIS- SION...
...TO MARRY KANA.
AKITO!!
WAIT! CALM DOWN... STOP!!

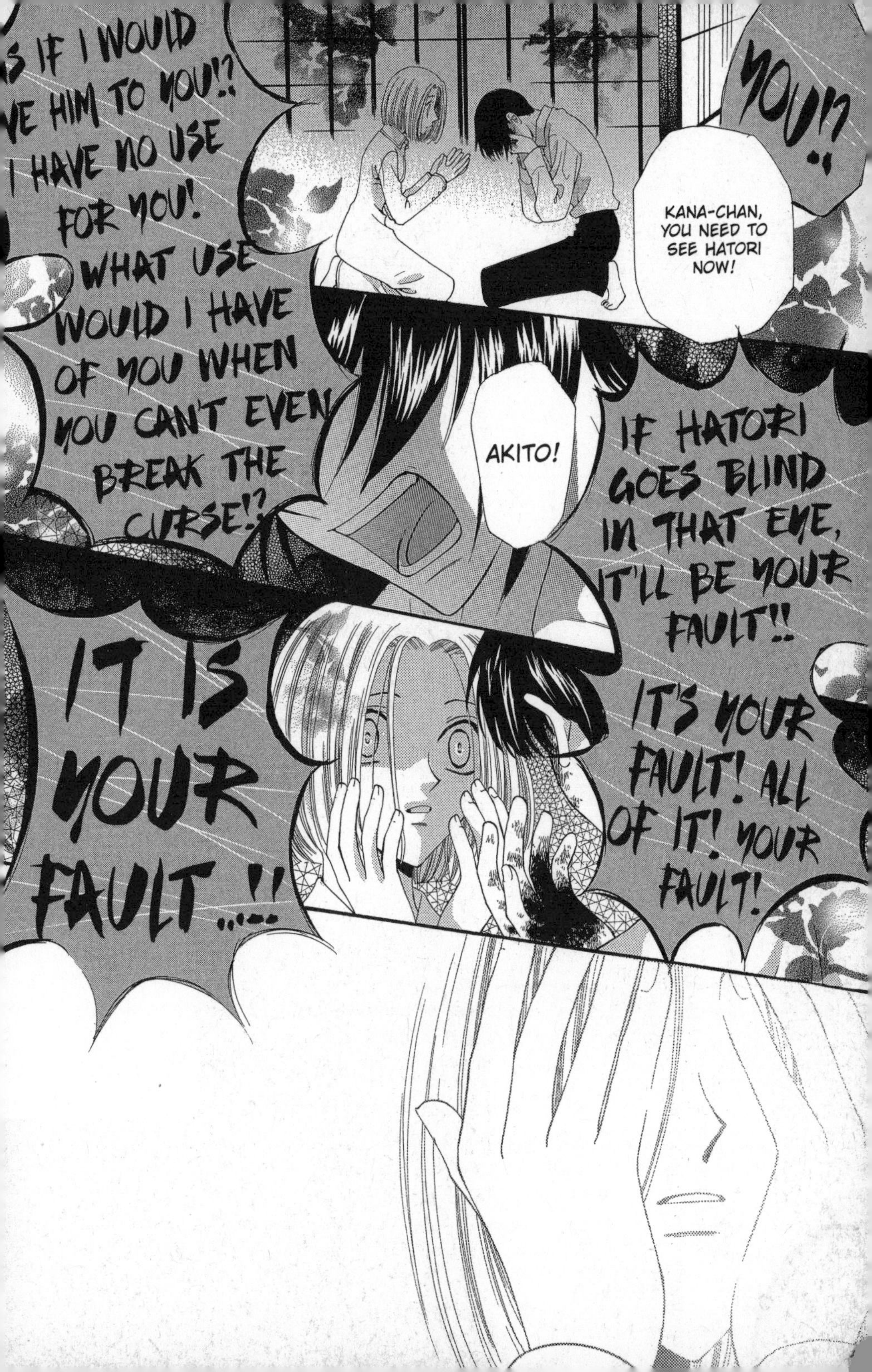
YOU!?..
KANA-CHAN, YOU NEED TO SEE HATORI NOW!
S IF I WOULD VE HIM TO YOU!?.. I HAVE NO USE FOR YOU! WHAT USE WOULD I HAVE OF YOU WHEN YOU CAN'T EVEN BREAK THE CURSE!?
AKITO!
IF HATORI GOES BLIND IN THAT EYE, IT'LL BE YOUR FAULT!!
IT'S YOUR FAULT! ALL OF IT! YOUR FAULT!
IT IS YOUR FAULT..!!

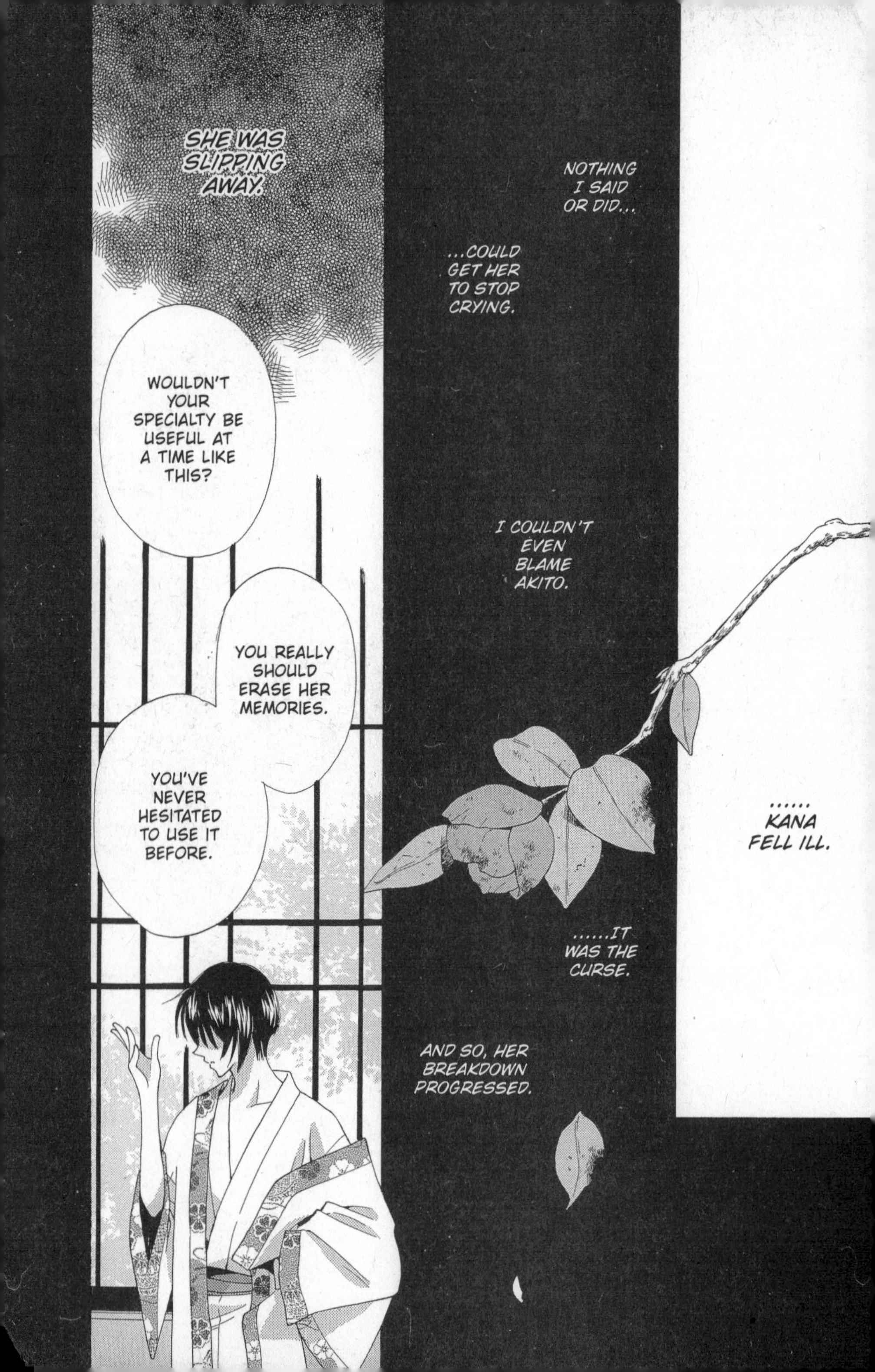
......KANA FELL ILL.
NOTHING I SAID OR DID...
...COULD GET HER TO STOP CRYING.
I COULDN'T EVEN BLAME AKITO.
......IT WAS THE CURSE.
AND SO, HER BREAKDOWN PROGRESSED.
SHE WAS SLIPPING AWAY.
WOULDN'T YOUR SPECIALTY BE USEFUL AT A TIME LIKE THIS?
YOU REALLY SHOULD ERASE HER MEMORIES.
YOU'VE NEVER HESITATED TO USE IT BEFORE.

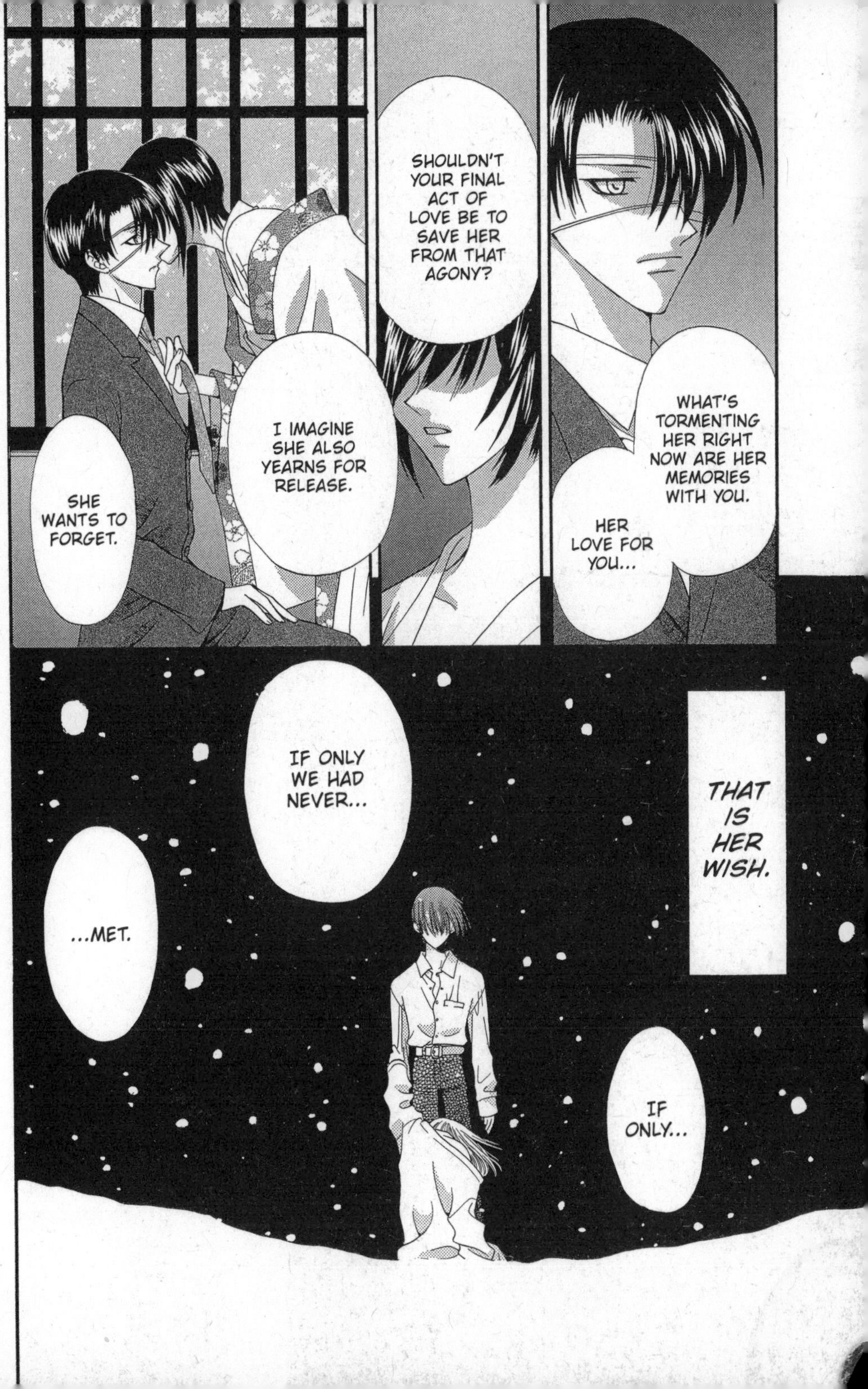
WHAT'S TORMENTING HER RIGHT NOW ARE HER MEMORIES WITH YOU.
HER LOVE FOR YOU...
SHOULDN'T YOUR FINAL ACT OF LOVE BE TO SAVE HER FROM THAT AGONY?
I IMAGINE SHE ALSO YEARNS FOR RELEASE.
SHE WANTS TO FORGET.
THAT IS HER WISH.
IF ONLY WE HAD NEVER...
...MET.
IF ONLY...

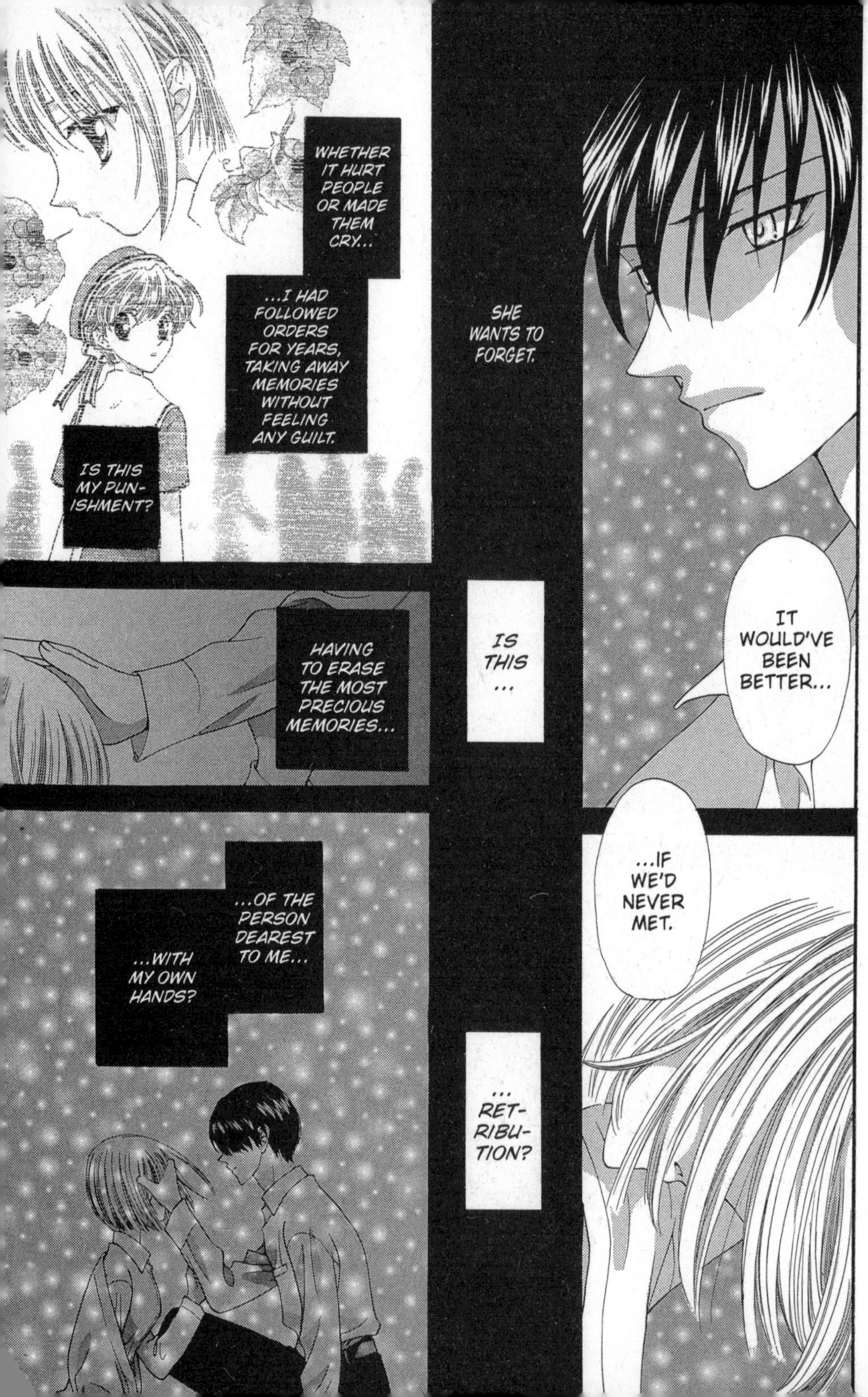
SHE WANTS TO FORGET.
IT WOULD'VE BEEN BETTER...
...IF WE'D NEVER MET.
WHETHER IT HURT PEOPLE OR MADE THEM CRY...
...I HAD FOLLOWED ORDERS FOR YEARS, TAKING AWAY MEMORIES WITHOUT FEELING ANY GUILT.
IS THIS MY PUN-ISHMENT?
HAVING TO ERASE THE MOST PRECIOUS MEMORIES...
...OF THE PERSON DEAREST TO ME...
...WITH MY OWN HANDS?
IS THIS...
...RET-RIBU-TION?

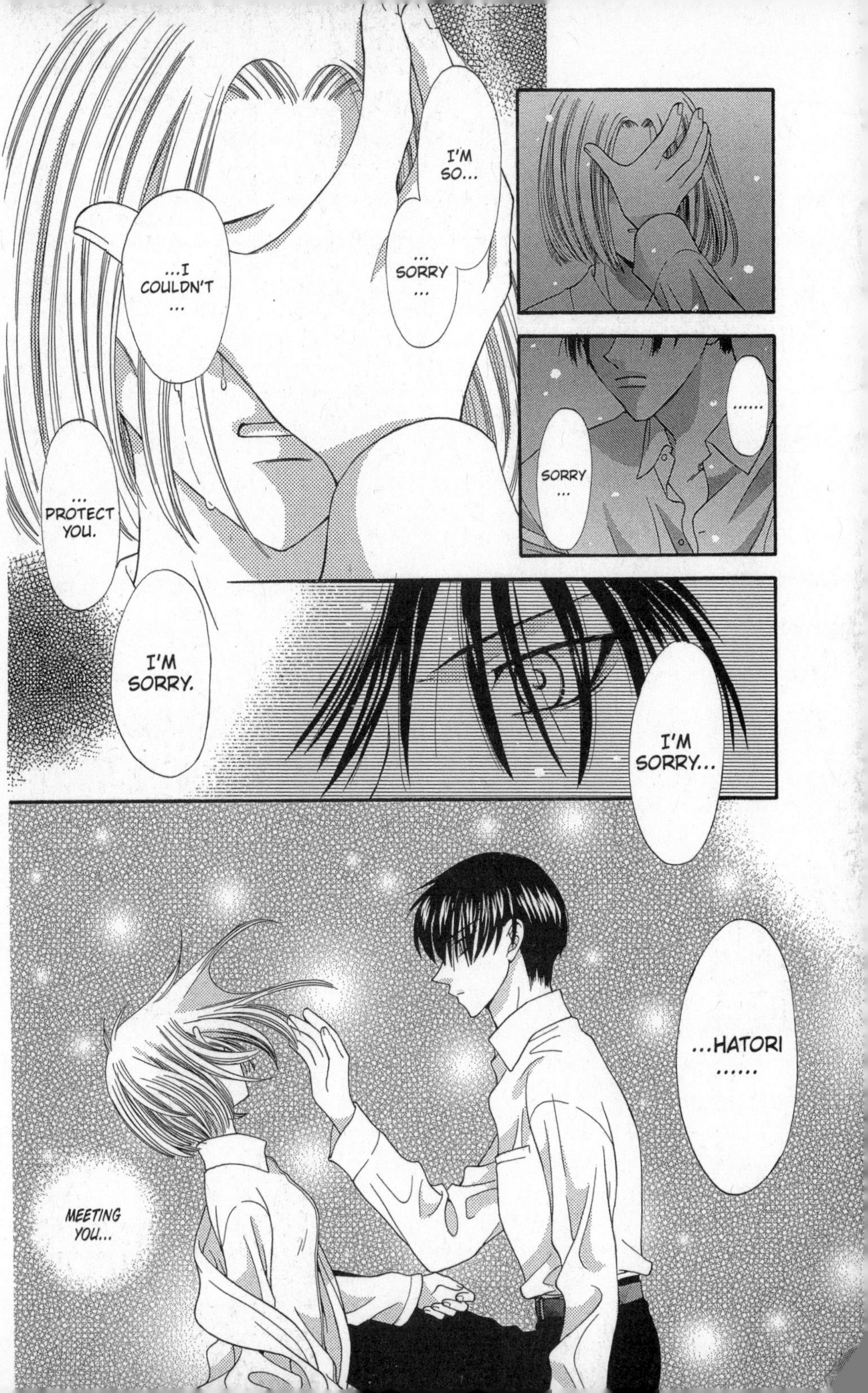

......
SORRY ...
I'M SORRY...
I'M SO...
... SORRY ...
...I COULDN'T ...
... PROTECT YOU.
I'M SORRY.
...HATORI ......
MEETING YOU...

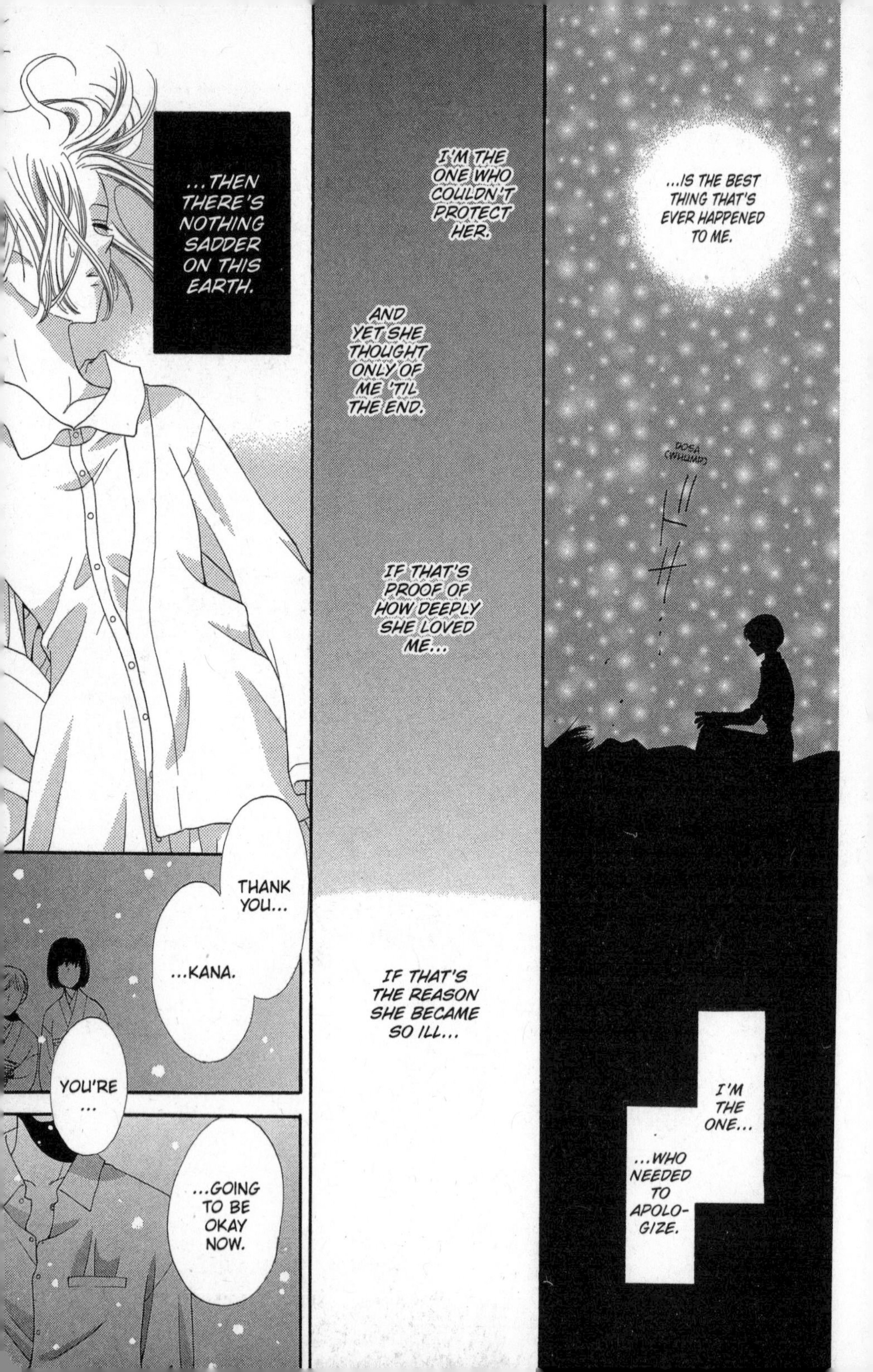
...IS THE BEST THING THAT'S EVER HAPPENED TO ME.
DOSA (WHUMP)
I'M THE ONE...
...WHO NEEDED TO APOLOGIZE.
I'M THE ONE WHO COULDN'T PROTECT HER.
AND YET SHE THOUGHT ONLY OF ME 'TIL THE END.
IF THAT'S PROOF OF HOW DEEPLY SHE LOVED ME...
IF THAT'S THE REASON SHE BECAME SO ILL...
...THEN THERE'S NOTHING SADDER ON THIS EARTH.
THANK YOU...
...KANA.
YOU'RE ...
...GOING TO BE OKAY NOW.

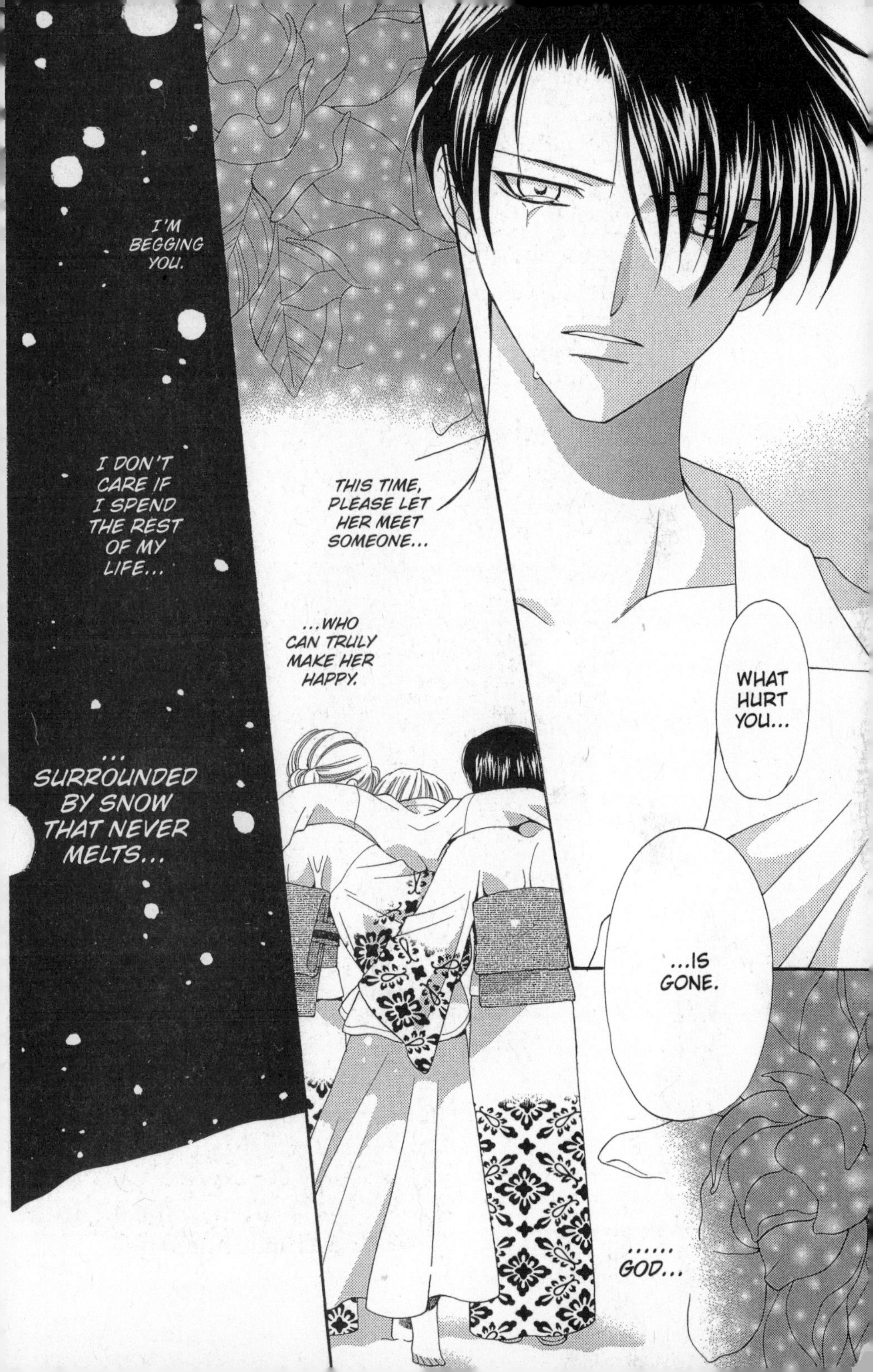
WHAT HURT YOU...
...IS GONE.
......GOD...
THIS TIME, PLEASE LET HER MEET SOMEONE...
...WHO CAN TRULY MAKE HER HAPPY.
I'M BEGGING YOU.
I DON'T CARE IF I SPEND THE REST OF MY LIFE...
...SURROUNDED BY SNOW THAT NEVER MELTS...

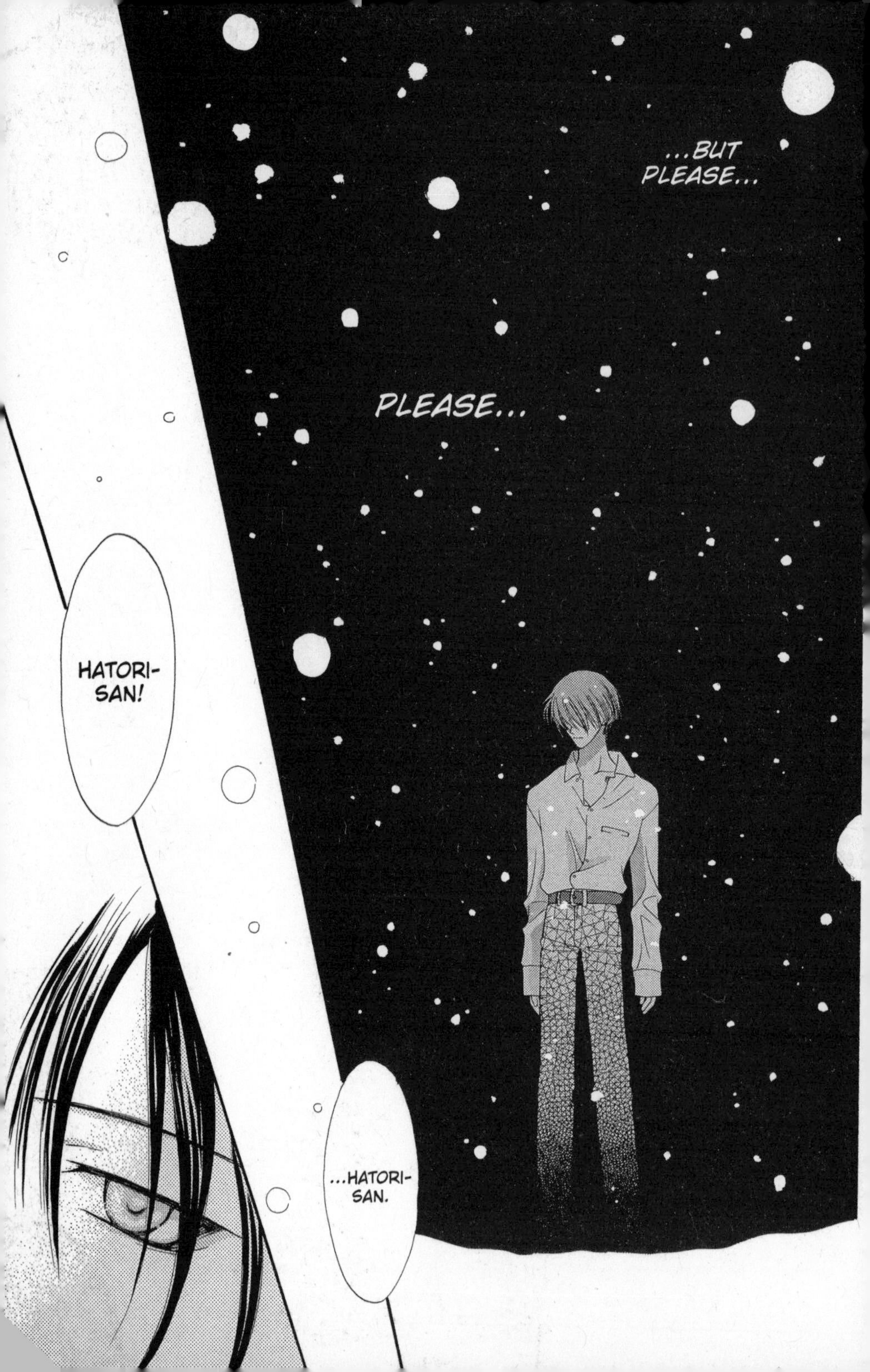
...BUT PLEASE...
PLEASE...
HATORI-SAN!
...HATORI-SAN.

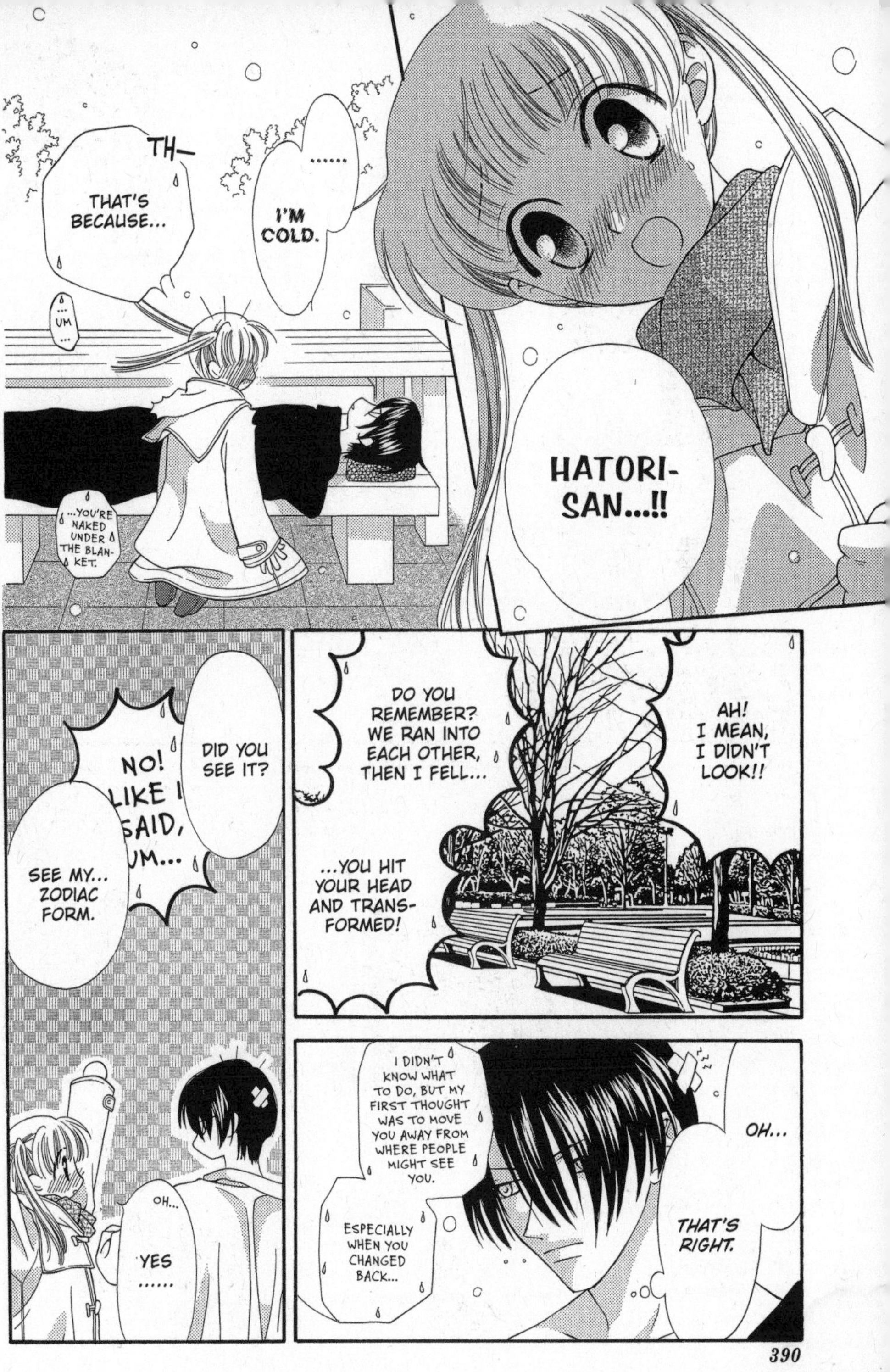
HATORI-SAN...!!
...... I'M COLD.
TH— THAT'S BECAUSE...
...UM...
...YOU'RE NAKED UNDER THE BLAN-KET.
AH! I MEAN, I DIDN'T LOOK!!
DO YOU REMEMBER? WE RAN INTO EACH OTHER, THEN I FELL...
...YOU HIT YOUR HEAD AND TRANS-FORMED!
DID YOU SEE IT?
NO! LIKE I SAID, UM...
SEE MY... ZODIAC FORM.
OH...
THAT'S RIGHT.
I DIDN'T KNOW WHAT TO DO, BUT MY FIRST THOUGHT WAS TO MOVE YOU AWAY FROM WHERE PEOPLE MIGHT SEE YOU.
ESPECIALLY WHEN YOU CHANGED BACK...
OH... YES ......

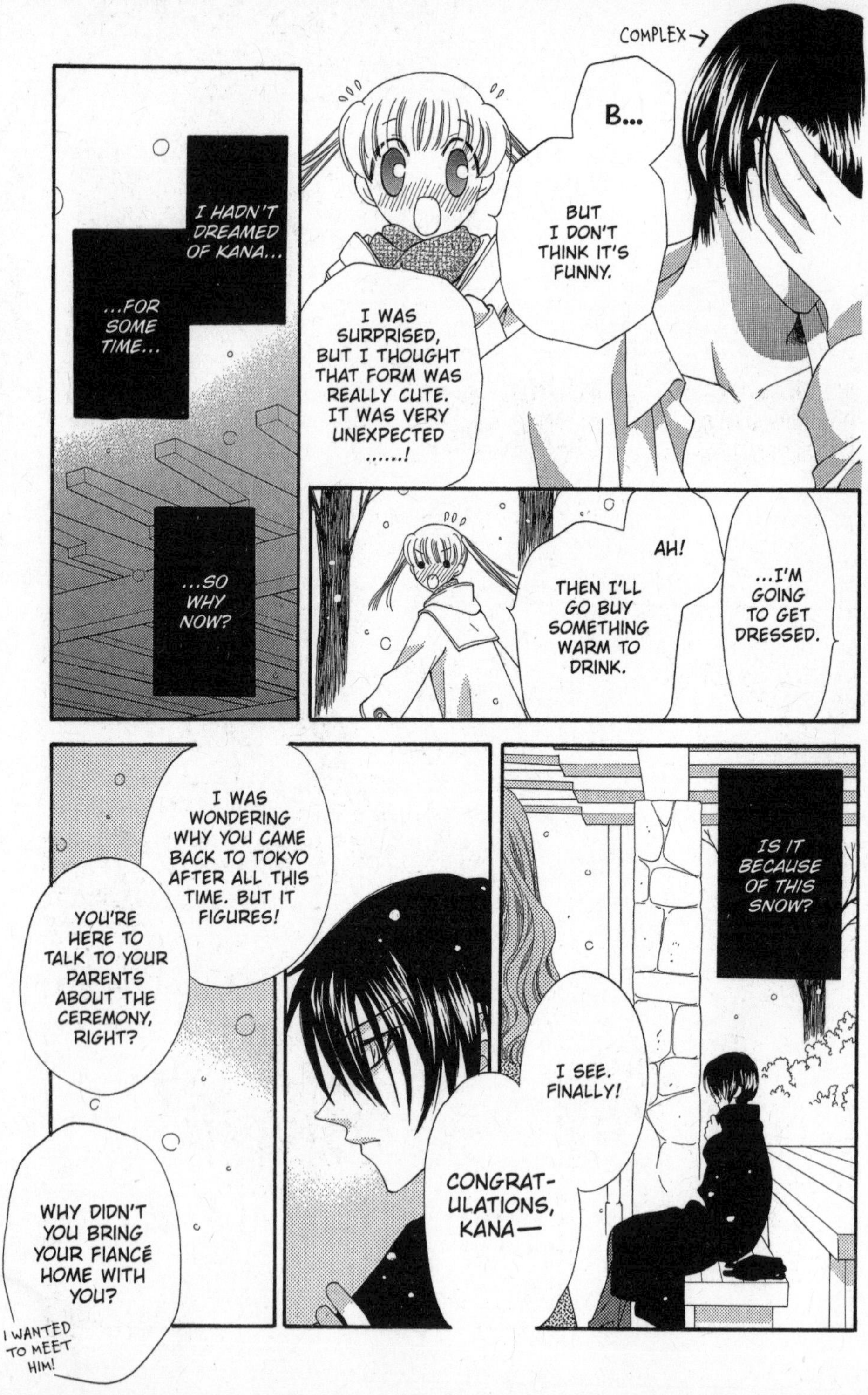
COMPLEX→
B...
BUT I DON'T THINK IT'S FUNNY.
I WAS SURPRISED, BUT I THOUGHT THAT FORM WAS REALLY CUTE. IT WAS VERY UNEXPECTED ......!
...I'M GOING TO GET DRESSED.
AH!
THEN I'LL GO BUY SOMETHING WARM TO DRINK.
I HADN'T DREAMED OF KANA...
...FOR SOME TIME...
...SO WHY NOW?
IS IT BECAUSE OF THIS SNOW?
I SEE. FINALLY!
CONGRAT-ULATIONS, KANA—
I WAS WONDERING WHY YOU CAME BACK TO TOKYO AFTER ALL THIS TIME. BUT IT FIGURES!
YOU'RE HERE TO TALK TO YOUR PARENTS ABOUT THE CEREMONY, RIGHT?
WHY DIDN'T YOU BRING YOUR FIANCÉ HOME WITH YOU?
I WANTED TO MEET HIM!

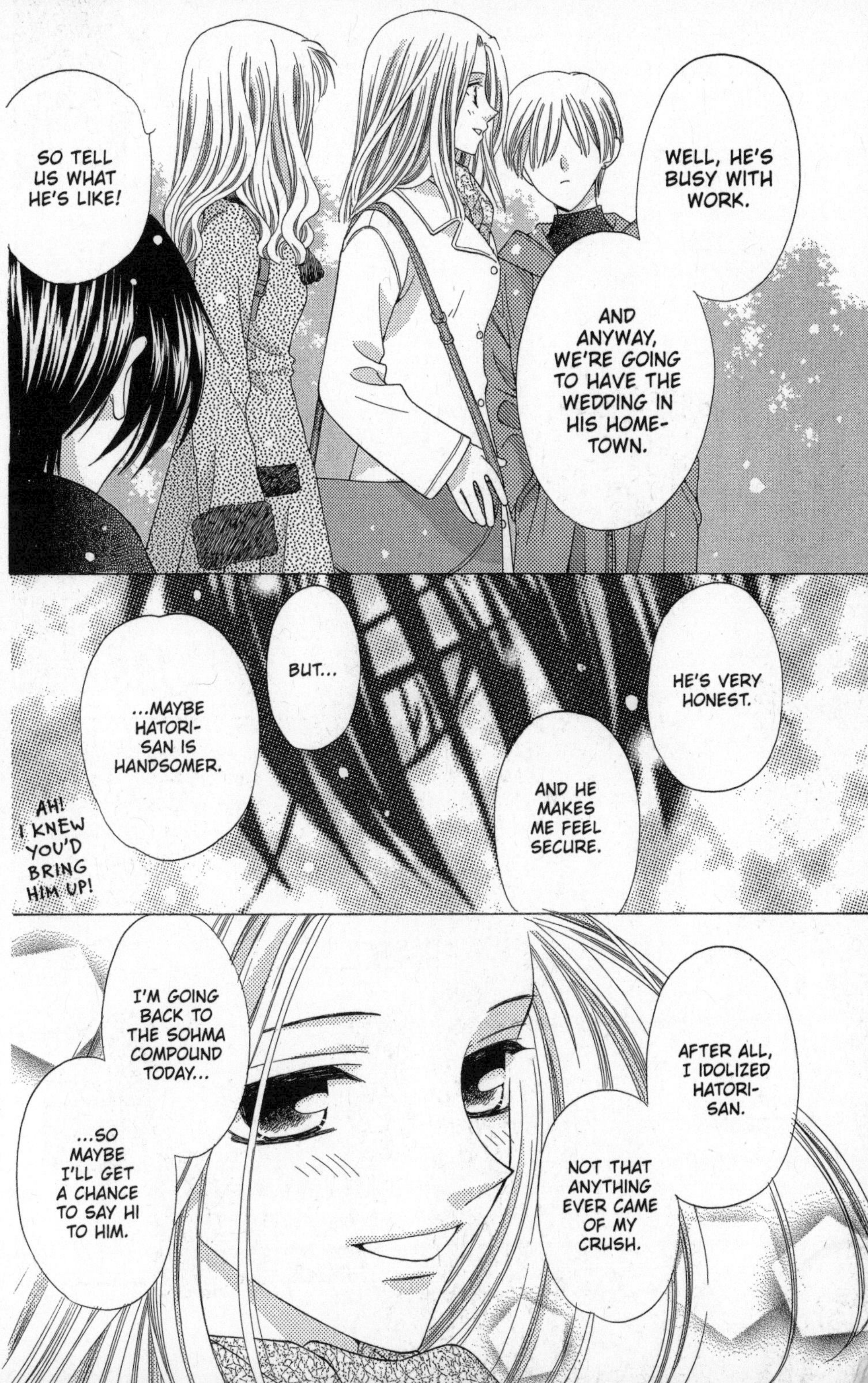
WELL, HE'S BUSY WITH WORK.
AND ANYWAY, WE'RE GOING TO HAVE THE WEDDING IN HIS HOMETOWN.
SO TELL US WHAT HE'S LIKE!
HE'S VERY HONEST.
AND HE MAKES ME FEEL SECURE.
BUT...
...MAYBE HATORI-SAN IS HANDSOMER.
AH! I KNEW YOU'D BRING HIM UP!
AFTER ALL, I IDOLIZED HATORI-SAN.
NOT THAT ANYTHING EVER CAME OF MY CRUSH.
I'M GOING BACK TO THE SOHMA COMPOUND TODAY...
...SO MAYBE I'LL GET A CHANCE TO SAY HI TO HIM.

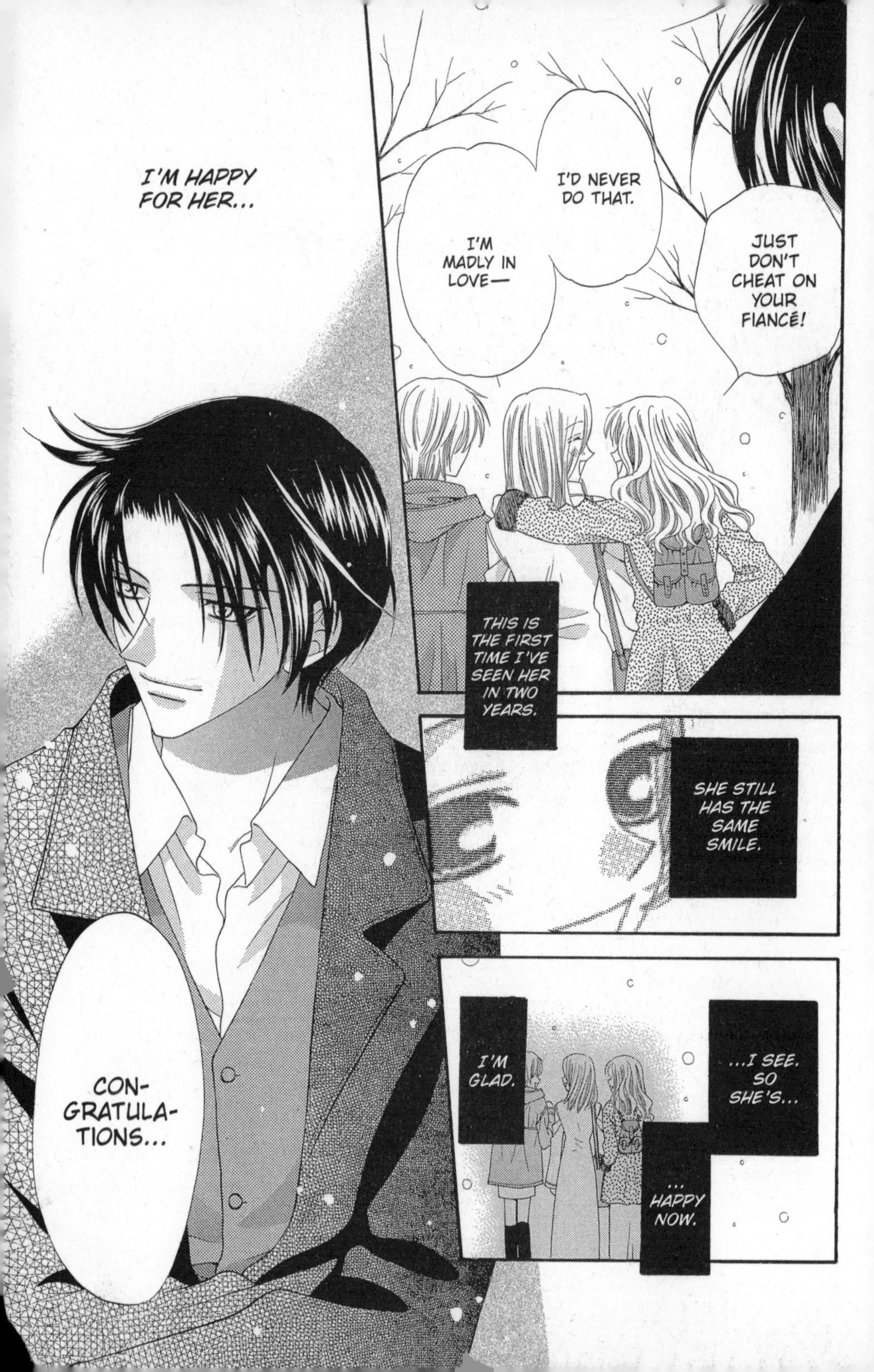
JUST DON'T CHEAT ON YOUR FIANCÉ!
I'D NEVER DO THAT.
I'M MADLY IN LOVE—
THIS IS THE FIRST TIME I'VE SEEN HER IN TWO YEARS.
SHE STILL HAS THE SAME SMILE.
...I SEE. SO SHE'S...
...HAPPY NOW.
I'M GLAD.
I'M HAPPY FOR HER...
CON-GRATULA-TIONS...

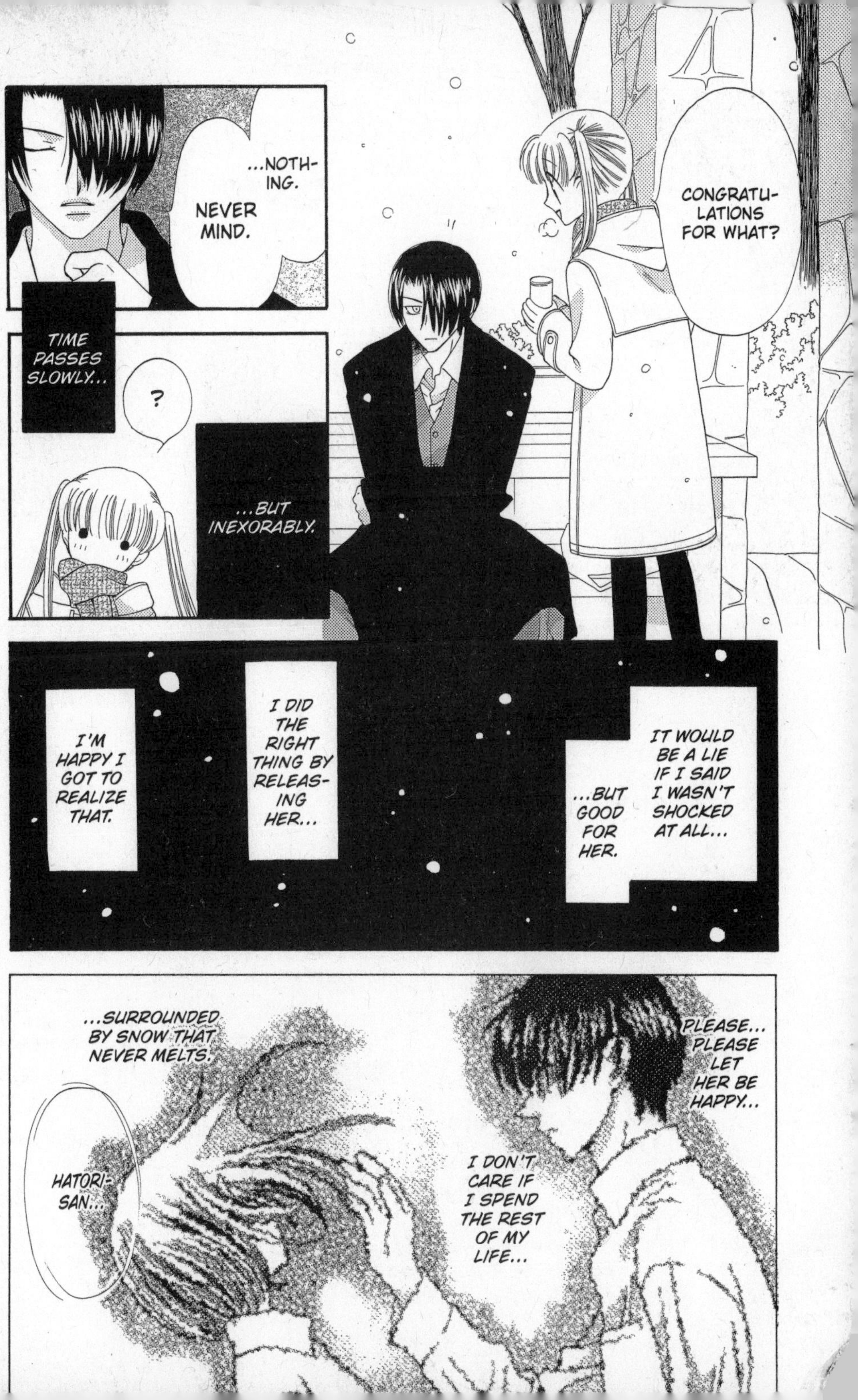
CONGRATULATIONS FOR WHAT?
...NOTHING.
NEVER MIND.
TIME PASSES SLOWLY...
?
...BUT INEXORABLY.
IT WOULD BE A LIE IF I SAID I WASN'T SHOCKED AT ALL...
...BUT GOOD FOR HER.
I DID THE RIGHT THING BY RELEASING HER...
I'M HAPPY I GOT TO REALIZE THAT.
PLEASE... PLEASE LET HER BE HAPPY...
I DON'T CARE IF I SPEND THE REST OF MY LIFE...
...SURROUNDED BY SNOW THAT NEVER MELTS.
HATORI-SAN...

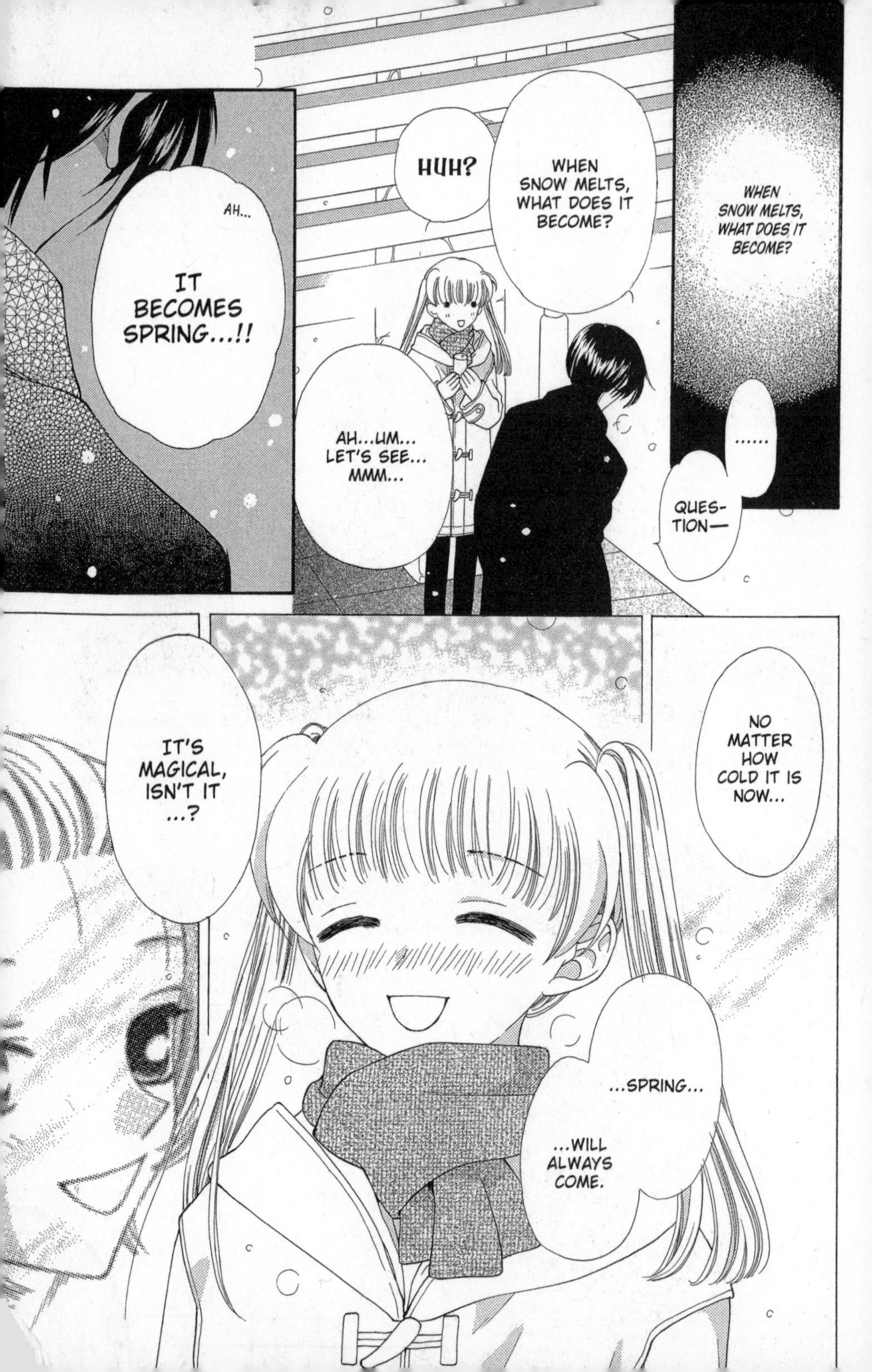
WHEN SNOW MELTS, WHAT DOES IT BECOME?
......
QUES-TION—
WHEN SNOW MELTS, WHAT DOES IT BECOME?
HUH?
AH...UM... LET'S SEE... MMM...
AH...
IT BECOMES SPRING...!!
NO MATTER HOW COLD IT IS NOW...
...SPRING...
...WILL ALWAYS COME.
IT'S MAGICAL, ISN'T IT ...?

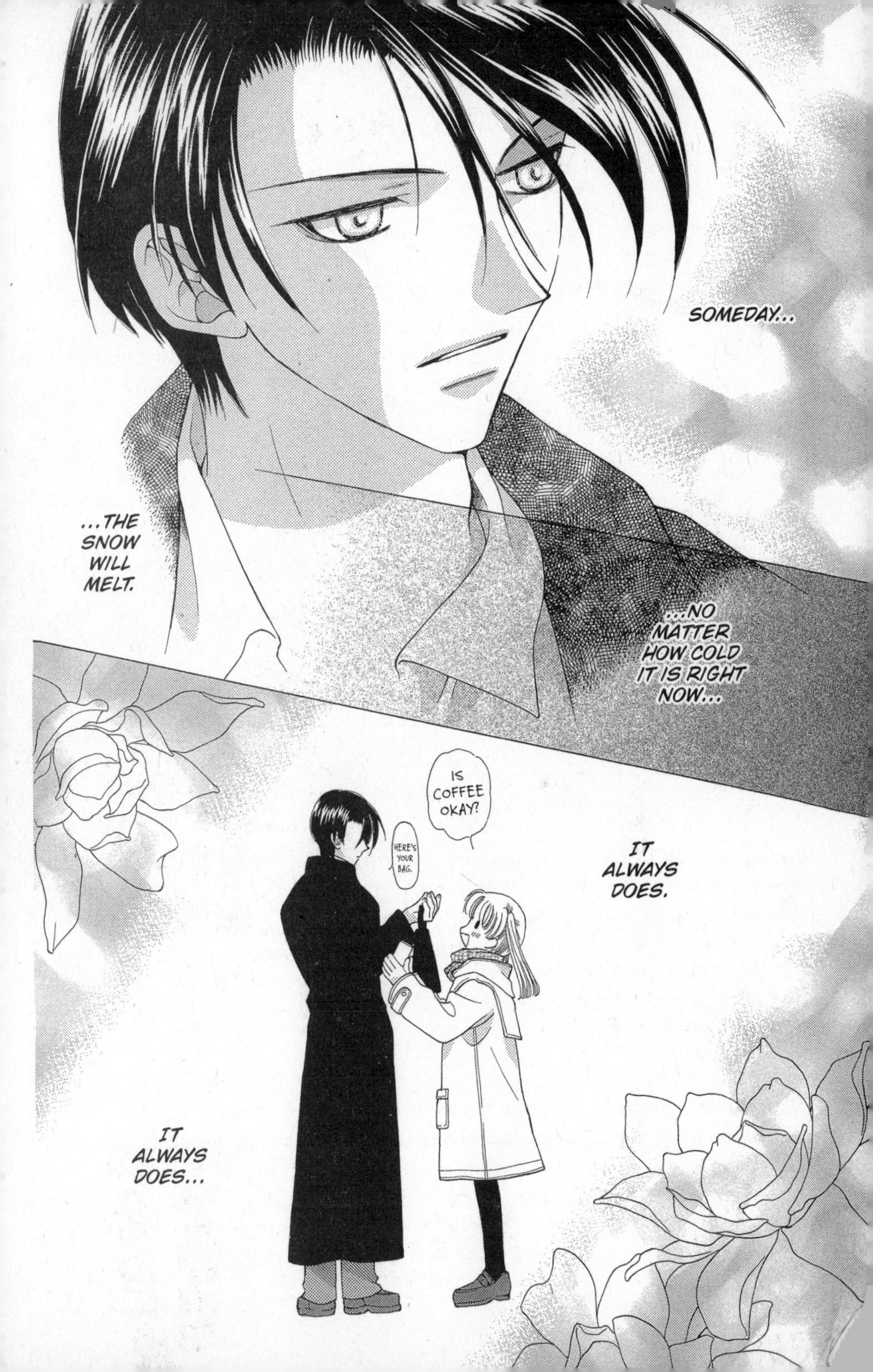
SOMEDAY...
...NO MATTER HOW COLD IT IS RIGHT NOW...
...THE SNOW WILL MELT.
IS COFFEE OKAY?
HERE'S YOUR BAG.
IT ALWAYS DOES.
IT ALWAYS DOES...

Thank you.

Thank you for getting this first volume of the collector's edition of *FRUITS BASKET*. The first volume of the series was originally published in January, 1999...It's now 2015, so sixteen years have passed already...I'm touched from the bottom of my heart that my series from way back then is still appreciated. Thank you so much.

For this edition, I had all of the original sidebar commentaries removed. My comments from over a decade ago have really become outdated, and to be honest, it would have been incredibly difficult for me to come up with something like "what I think now" commentaries. I apologize to the people who enjoy creator commentaries, but I hope you can understand my reasoning.

During the first half of the serialization of *FRUITS BASKET*, I was always under the gun with deadlines. Every day was a desperate one, and I barely had time to wash my face, let alone eat decent meals. But when my weight dropped to under ninety pounds, I had a feeling I was in trouble. (Incidentally, I'm chubby now. In fact, you might say I'm in trouble on the opposite side of the scale, so please don't worry about me.)

Maybe *FRUITS BASKET* is what it is because of the harsh conditions (as I see it) that I went through back then, but I could never repeat that. I apologize, and please forgive me...is how I feel. (LOL)

高屋 奈月。
NATSUKI TAKAYA

TRANSLATION NOTES

COMMON HONORIFICS

no honorific: Indicates familiarity or closeness; if used without permission or reason, addressing someone in this manner would constitute an insult.

-san: The Japanese equivalent of Mr./Mrs./Miss. If a situation calls for politeness, this is the fail-safe honorific.

-sama: Conveys great respect; may also indicate that the social status of the speaker is lower than that of the addressee.

-kun: Used most often when referring to boys, this indicates affection or familiarity. Occasionally used by older men among their peers, but it may also be used by anyone referring to a person of lower standing.

-chan: An affectionate honorific indicating familiarity used mostly in reference to girls; also used in reference to cute persons or animals of either gender.

-senpai: A suffix used to address upperclassmen or more experienced coworkers.

-kouhai: A suffix used to address underclassmen or less experienced coworkers.

-sensei: A respectful term for teachers, artists, or high-level professionals.

Page 12
The Chinese zodiac: The animals of the Chinese zodiac are, in order, as follows: Rat, Ox, Tiger, Rabbit, Dragon, Snake, Horse, Goat, Monkey, Rooster, Dog, and Boar. In this twelve-year cycle, each year is related to an animal and its attributes.

Page 21
Tohru-kun: The *-kun* form is generally used for males (as explained above), but both Saki and Shigure use it with Tohru, which may be in part because Tohru is a masculine name.

Page 190
Kyoko's jacket: The front reads "Southern Alliance," while the sleeve reads "Fifth Daredevil Squad Leader." Kyoko had a number of jackets with various insignia that generally established her as a leader to be reckoned with.

Page 207
"The night has a thousand eyes": In Japanese, the question involves the idiom *okamehachimoku*, an expression that means "onlookers can see more of the game than the players (who are directly involved)." Broken down, the components are *okame* ("looking on from the side") and *hachimoku* ("having many eyes," but literally "having eight eyes.") Tohru takes the idiom at face value and thinks the onlookers have eight eyes, which accounts for her confusion.